ONE CURRENCY, TWO EUROPES

ONE CURRENCY, TWO EUROPES

Bruno Dallago
University of Trento, Italy

World Scientific

NEW JERSEY • LONDON • SINGAPORE • BEIJING • SHANGHAI • HONG KONG • TAIPEI • CHENNAI • TOKYO

Published by

World Scientific Publishing Co. Pte. Ltd.
5 Toh Tuck Link, Singapore 596224
USA office: 27 Warren Street, Suite 401-402, Hackensack, NJ 07601
UK office: 57 Shelton Street, Covent Garden, London WC2H 9HE

British Library Cataloguing-in-Publication Data
A catalogue record for this book is available from the British Library.

ONE CURRENCY, TWO EUROPES
Towards a Dual Eurozone

ISBN 978-981-4759-01-4

Desk Editor: Jiang Yulin

Typeset by Stallion Press
Email: enquiries@stallionpress.com

Contents

Acronyms

2008 SNA	System of National Accounts 2008
ABCP	Asset-Backed Commercial Paper
ABSPP	Asset-Backed Securities Purchase Programme
APEC	Asia-Pacific Economic Cooperation
APP	Asset Purchase Programme
ASEAN	Association of Southeast Asian Nations
ASECs	Anglo-Saxon Eurozone Countries
BEA	Bureau of Economic Analysis
BEPG	Broad Economic Policy Guidelines
BRICS	Brazil, Russia, India, China, South Africa
BRPG	Broad Economic Policy Guidelines
CAB	Cyclically-Adjusted Budget Balance
CAP	Common Agricultural Policy
CBPP	Covered Bond Purchase Programme
CBPP1	First Covered Bond Purchase Programme
CBPP2	Second Covered Bond Purchase Programme
CBPP3	Third Covered Bond Purchase Programme
CCBM	Correspondent Central Banking Model
CDS	Credit Default Swap
CEEC	Central and Eastern European Countries
CES	Comparative Economic Systems
CFSP	Common Foreign and Security Policy
CME	Coordinated Market Economies
DB	The World Bank's Doing Business
DFP	Distance to Frontier Score

EAPG	Economic Adjustment Programme for Greece
EB	Executive Board of the ECB
EBA	European Banking Authority
EC	European Communities
ECA	Europe and Central Asia
ECB	European Central Bank
ECI	Europe 2020 Competitiveness Index
Ecofin	Economic and Financial Affairs Council
ECSC	European Coal and Steel Community
ECU	European Currency Unit
EDP	Excessive Deficit Procedure
EEC	European Economic Community
EFSF	European Financial Stability Facility
EFSI	European Fund for Strategic Investments
EFSM	European Financial Stabilisation Mechanism
EFTA	European Free Trade Association
EIB	European Investment Bank
EIOPA	European Insurance and Occupational Pensions Authority
ELA	Emergency Liquidity Assistance
EMI	European Monetary Institute
EMS	European Monetary System
EMU	Economic and Monetary Union
EOS	Executive Opinion Survey (World Economic Forum)
EPI	Environmental Performance Index
E+P	Euro Plus Pact
EPP	Economic Partnership Programme
EPU	European Payments Union
ERM	European Exchange Rate Mechanism
ERM II	Exchange Rate Mechanism II
ERPT	Exchange Rate Pass-Through
ESA 2010	European System of National and Regional Accounts
ESAs	Joint Committee of the European Supervisory Authorities
ESCB	European System of Central Banks
ESFS	European System of Financial Supervision
ESM	European Stability Mechanism
ESMA	European Securities and Markets Authority

ESRB	European Systemic Risk Board
EU	European Union
EU-15	Pre-2004 15 EU Member Countries
EU-28	28 EU Member Countries
Euratom	European Atomic Energy Community
Eurostat	European Central Statistical Office
EUWIN	European Workplace Innovation Network
EVI	Economic Vulnerability Index
FDI	Foreign Direct Investment
FIRE	Finance, Insurance, and Real Estate
FTA	Free Trade Agreements
FTE S&E	Full-Time Equivalent Science and Engineering
GATT	General Agreement on Tariffs and Trade
GCI	Global Competitiveness Index
GDP	Gross Domestic Product
GeC	General Council of the ECB
GIA	Global Investment Attractiveness
GII	Global Innovation Index
GNI	Gross National Income
GNMA	Government National Mortgage Association
GoC	Governing Council of the ECB
HCI	Harmonised Competitiveness Indicators
HDI	Human Development Index
HICP	Harmonised Index of Consumer Prices
HMDA	Home Mortgage Disclosure Act
ICT	Information and Communications Technology
ILO	International Labour Organization
IMF	International Monetary Fund
IP	Intellectual Property
ITC	International Trade Centre
ITU	International Telecommunication Union
LDC	Least Developed Countries
LME	Liberal Market Economies
LTCM	Long-Term Capital Management
LTRO	Longer-Term Refinancing Operations
M&A	Mergers and Acquisitions

MBS	Mortgage-Backed Securities
MIP	Macroeconomic Imbalances Procedure
MME	Mixed Market Economies
MMF	Money Market Mutual Fund
MoU	Memorandum of Understanding
MRO	Main Refinancing Operations
MTO	Medium-Term Objective for a Country's Budgetary Position
NAFTA	North American Free Trade Agreement
NCB	National Central Bank
NDI	Net Disposable Income
NECs	Northern Eurozone Countries
NEER	Nominal Effective Exchange Rate
NPISHs	Non-Profit Institutions Serving Households
NYSE	New York Stock Exchange
OCA	Optimum Currency Area
OECD	Organisation for Economic Cooperation and Development
OEEC	Organisation for European Economic Cooperation
OMI	ICC Open Markets Index
OMT	Outright Monetary Transactions
PCT	Patent Cooperation Treaty
PI(I)GS	Portugal, Ireland, (Italy), Greece, Spain
PISA	Programme for International Student Assessment
PJCC	Police and Judicial Cooperation in Criminal Matters
PM2.5	Microgrammes of Particulate Matter Per Cubic Metre
PPP	Purchasing Power Parity
PSPP	Public Sector Purchase Programme
QE	Quantitative Easing
R&D	Research and Development
REER	Real Effective Exchange Rate
REPO	Repurchase Agreement
RTA	Regional Trade Agreement
RWC	Revised Washington Consensus
SCT	SEPA Credit Transfer
SDD	SEPA Direct Debit

SEA	Single European Act
SECs	Southern Eurozone Countries
SEPA	Single Euro Payments Area
SGP	Stability and Growth Pact
SIV	Special Investment Vehicle
SME	Small and Medium-Sized Enterprise
SMP	Securities Markets Programme
SNA	System of National Accounts
SPV	Special Purpose Vehicles
SRB	Single Resolution Board
SRF	Single Resolution Fund
SRM	Single Resolution Mechanism
SSM	Single Supervisory Mechanism
SWOT	Strengths, Weaknesses, Opportunities and Threats
T2S	TARGET2-Securities
TARGET	Trans-European Automated Real-Time Gross Settlement Express Transfer System
TARGET2	Second generation of TARGET
TCE	Transaction Costs Economics
TEU	Treaty on European Union (Maastricht Treaty)
TFEU	Treaty on the Functioning of the European Union (Lisbon Treaty)
TFP	Total Factor Productivity
TI	Transparency International
TLTRO	Targeted Longer-Term Refinancing Operation
TNC	Transnational Company
TOR	Traditional Own Resources (of the EU budget)
TSCG	Treaty on Stability, Coordination and Governance ("fiscal compact")
TTIP	Transatlantic Trade and Investment Partnership
ULC	Unit Labour Costs
UN	United Nations
UNDP	United Nations Development Programme
UNESCO	United Nations Organization for Educational, Scientific and Culture

VAT	Value Added Tax
VoC	Varieties of Capitalism
WB	World Bank
WEF	World Economic Forum
WIPO	World Intellectual Property Organization
WTO	World Trade Organization
ZLB	Zero Lower Bound

Preface and Acknowledgments

This book is the outcome of a research that I started upon a challenging suggestion by Steven Rosefielde in 2009. Steven coordinated a research project that ended in a conference in Tokyo in 2010 and resulted in a book that he edited together with Masaaki Kuboniwa and Satoshi Mizobata (*Two Asias: The Emerging Postcrisis Divide*, World Scientific, 2011). In the research that I undertook for preparing the chapter, co-authored with Chiara Guglielmetti ("Eurozone and Global Financial Imbalances"), the evidence of a splitting Eurozone started to become clear.

Since then I had the opportunity to continue to work on the subject and present my ideas in various conferences and publications. In particular, important was the opportunity to work with colleagues at the University of North Carolina, especially John McGowan and, again, Steven Rosefielde, to organise two international conferences on the effects of the crisis in Europe: one in Trento in 2013 and another in Chapel Hill in 2014. These conferences were important for the intense discussion among participants from different continents and countries, and for the two books that I had the chance to co-edit with John McGowan (*Crises in Europe in the Transatlantic Context*, Routledge, 2014, and *A Global Perspective on the European Economic Crisis*, Routledge, 2016). Together, these experiences played an important role in developing my ideas about the crisis in Europe.

The topic appeared increasingly interesting, important and occasionally dramatic. I came to see it as a fundamental aspect of the European Union, an aspect that was growing in intensity under the blow of the international crisis. It was in particular the growing division of the Eurozone into two groups of countries in progressively different conditions that attracted my attention. This division was in a sense hidden for years, but with the crisis the split came to increasingly jeopardise the institutional and economic stability and the effectiveness of policymaking in the monetary union. In this way, the consequences of the division went to negatively affect the economic performance of the European Union, its political and social stability and its international role.

As a European with fair amount of international experience, I came to appreciate the precious achievements of European integration in both my scientific and teaching activities and in my daily life. As a teacher and researcher, I had innumerable opportunities to have European students in my classes, who were there thanks to European programmes. Similarly, many of my students had the opportunity to go to other European universities for periods of study. European integration made these opportunities much more important and numerous than we had when I was a student, with great benefit for students and teachers and hopefully the society at large. Similarly, teachers and researchers, among them myself, had the opportunity to interact strictly with European colleagues and participate in joint teaching programmes and research projects funded by the European Union. Having been involved directly in several of these programmes and projects, I could appreciate their importance and appeal, together with their complex management.

These achievements in the academic domain went in parallel with broader and more important advantages in the economic, political and social life. It appeared to me so evident that European integration has so many and so valuable advantages for everybody, that I found initially difficult to grasp the weak European reaction to the crisis and even more so the evident lack of an integration strategy up to the new challenges. Among the most important challenges, there is the increasingly wide and deep fault between those I call in this book vulnerable and resilient countries. This led me to research the causes for this apparently irrational and certainly weak response and behaviour, in an apparently lose-lose strategy.

As an Italian, the idea of the economic division of a country was not unfamiliar and so I was also motivated by the curiosity for a similar phenomenon in a different context. As a European living quite close to the border between the Northern European and the Mediterranean areas of the EU, which largely coincides with the split between resilient and vulnerable countries, it was not difficult to appreciate the good reasons and the worries of both sides. I am convinced that solutions can be found to the present stalemate, but this requires a new approach to the economic and monetary union, based on the honest understanding of the reasons that led Europe into the present strain. This book is meant as a contribution to this fundamental debate.

When World Scientific proposed that I further developed my original chapter into a book, I was more than glad to do so. The outcome follows in the next pages. This would not have been possible without the support, stimulus and help of many people. Without any pretension of completeness, I limit myself to remind the colleagues who dared to read and comment on an earlier version of the manuscript. Although the responsibility of what follows rests solely with me, the result would have been different and certainly weaker without their effort and criticism. I want to thank in particular Klaus Gretschmann for the particularly precious and detailed notes he made to each chapter, as well as Chiara Guglielmetti, Paul Marer, Giovanni Pegoretti and Steven Rosefielde. Sara Giunti and Joseph Tixet helped me in collecting and elaborating statistics. My department gave me the time and the support to work on the book. My wife Agnes and my children Alice and Michele tolerated or perhaps forgot me during my mental and physical detachment when fighting with the manuscript and when I disappeared for days and nights in my studio. This book is dedicated to their patience and support.

Trento, 22 August 2015

"Of course there is always some gap between theory and practice. It is disastrous for both rulers and ruled when the gap becomes too wide."

— A. J .P Taylor (1961, p. 57)

Introduction: Prolegomena to the International Crisis

For decades, the construction of European integration was considered as the only solution to the problems that led this area of the world to turn into a "dark continent" (Mazower 1998). Although the continent was an area where so much of world civilisation took place, during much of the first part of the 20th century, Europe was both the perpetrator and victim of repeated political and social instability and tragedies that led to its economic and political decline on the world stage.

The economic integration and political coordination of a significant part of the continent was seen as the only effective answer to those dangers and the growing economic and political irrelevance of former world powers. For decades after its start, the construction of the European integration project was a great economic and political success, a success that peaked with the common currency. It was perceived to have provided a stable solution to the German problem that haunted Europe since the 19th century. It also apparently guaranteed that German reunification was supporting European integration. It finally led supposedly to a "European Germany", obliterating previous hegemonic attempts in the direction of a "German Europe".

After 1989, much of the process of transformation going on in the eastern part of the continent converged rapidly to become an important part of European integration. This was perhaps the greatest testimony of the appeal of the European project, even though other factors were also significant. For instance, Central-Eastern European countries strived to enter the integration process for the unilateral economic and political advantages that membership had for them, for instance in the form of a net transfer of resources.

The Crisis and Europe

On another stage, but directly involving European integration, the question of the possible obsolescence of the business cycle became dominant since the late 1960s (Bronfenbrenner 1969). The possibility of a major crisis, like the Great Depression of the 1930s, was considered an extremely unlikely event. This outcome was credited to either improved policies or the efficient working of markets, or to both. The belief was widespread among economists and other social scientists, policymakers, businessmen, the media, and the public at large. For a time, the Washington Consensus on policies (Williamson 1990) seemed to provide the correct approach and recipe to solve even the most difficult cases of countries in great financial and economic difficulty.[1]

The crisis started in 2008 in the United States and came as an economic and political blow that surprised most experts, policymakers and the public. The deep-seated belief of the impossibility or unlikelihood of

[1] John Williamson (1990) coined the term "Washington Consensus" to refer to a set of 10 economic policy prescriptions that the Washington-based institutions (the International Monetary Fund (IMF), World Bank and US Treasury Department) considered as the standard reform package for helping crisis-torn developing countries solve their economic and financial problems. Although these prescriptions shared an orientation towards a market-based approach, they should not be confused with the broader and more popular meaning that the term acquired as the expression of neoliberal or even market-fundamentalist policies. See also Williamson 1999, Williamson 2004a, Stiglitz 1998.

a major crisis progressively and rapidly faded away from the start of the crisis in 2008. The experience of the crisis left a deep and long-lasting impact on the economies and on our way of perceiving the present and the future. Once it became indisputable that crises were still possible with devastating effects, the longheld belief and confidence in ever-growing economies faded away and were replaced by doubts about the forthcoming secular stagnation (IMF 2014a; Summers 2014).[2]

The following events showed that the EU was not immune to contagion and homemade distress. These events raised dramatic questions. Were the crisis and the European distress two unpredictable events, a couple of Black Swan occurrences (Taleb 2007)? Or were they linked together in an unpredictable super-Black Swan? In short, was it a question of objective unpredictability or ignorance? Or were both events the outcome of deeply flawed events and processes that happened previously and of decisions and arrangements that could have been predicted, at least as a possibility, to lead to greater difficulties and serious negative effects? If so, why was that possibility not considered and, more importantly, why were countermeasures not considered and enacted in time?

To be sure, criticism of the mainstream and popular conviction of the impossibility or at least the great implausibility of a major crisis, let alone a double dip, existed. Minsky (1982, 1992), in particular, warned that a major financial crisis was always possible. Shiller (2000) analysed the structural, cultural and psychological factors that cause the alternately soaring and declining of stock markets. Marxist social scholars traditionally maintained that major crises are necessary companions of capitalist economies (Dumenil and Levy 2011; Foster and McChesney 2013; Ticktin 2011).

Others, such as Bernanke (1983, 2004), Galbraith (1954, 1990), and Kindleberger (1978), studied the crises of the past and in particular the Great Depression of the 1930s to learn lessons on how to avoid and devise policies for similar crises in the future. Clearly, they were moved to such an undertaking by their implicit or explicit recognition that major crises

[2] "Secular stagnation and low potential growth in advanced economies remain important medium-term risks, given the modest and uneven growth in those economies despite very low interest rates and the easing of other brakes to the recovery" (IMF 2014a, p. XVI).

were always possible and that it was important to understand and learn from the past to avoid future mistakes. Even some policymakers, such as the former chairman of the US Federal Reserve, Alan Greenspan, who cannot be absolved of the responsibility for creating the conditions for a major crisis through a policy of low interest rates and easy credit, spoke of "irrational exuberance" in 1996 when commenting on the excessiveness and dangerous instability of stock markets.

Although they could not avoid that the crisis broke out, these studies helped to avoid, in the United States and elsewhere, the policy mistakes that transformed the financial crash of 1929 into the Great Depression. Those teachings were not lost and, albeit with some hesitation, the US administration managed to react and avoid the old mistakes and helped the economy to recover.

The events in Europe were quite different. Apparently those teachings were largely unheeded and ignored. Or, for some reason, those teachings were not translated into practice when the crisis hit the European Union (EU) in 2008. In the case of the EU, therefore, it is fundamental to explain why the EU and its member countries did not follow the path that the United States undertook resolutely. In reality, this observation refers only to the Eurozone. In fact, EU member countries which do not share the common currency, e.g. Great Britain, adopted policies much closer to those implemented in the United States. This suggests that the difference may lie in the common currency.

The idea that the EU could be constructed through successive steps that would make the process irreversible, a kind of chain reaction, dates back to the founders of the unification process and its first steps. Progressive steps in the institutional construction of the EU, in particular moving policy functions to the supranational level, would create pressure for further steps, which would make the process irreversible. Jean Monnet,[3] who is regarded among the chief architects and founders of the EU, and other important European personalities (Padoa-Schioppa, Helmut Schmidt, Romano Prodi among others) shared this view (Guiso *et al.* 2014).

[3]Jean Monnet (1888–1979) was the first President of the High Authority of the European Coal and Steel Community (ECSC).

The requirements and the consequences of a common currency were the concern of the European Community as early as the late 1960s. An important step in this perspective was the "Report to the Council and the Commission on the realisation by stages of Economic and Monetary Union in the Community", better known as the Werner Report (1970). The report stated clearly that:

> the advances towards integration will have the result that general economic disequilibrium in the member countries will have direct and rapid repercussions on the global evolution of the Community. The experience of recent years has clearly shown that such disequilibrium is likely to compromise seriously the integration realized in the liberation of the movement goods, services and capital. ... Having regard to the marked differences existing between the member countries in the realization of the objectives of growth and stability, there is a grave danger of disequilibria arising if economic policy cannot be harmonized effectively. The increasing interpenetration of the economies has entailed a weakening of autonomy for national economic policies. The control of economic policy has become all the more difficult because the loss of autonomy at the national level has not been compensated by the inauguration of Community policies. The inadequacies and disequilibrium that have occurred in the process realization of the Common Market are thus thrown into relief. (p. 8)

These words sound quite farsighted of today's problems and analyses. Yet four decades and a half have elapsed since then, without a decisive advancement to the structural and effective solution of those problems. Why is it so? Is it due to unforeseen and unpredictable events? The impossible unification of incompatible economies? Lack of cooperation and national opportunism? Policy mistakes? Biased institutions?

The Strange Fate of Europe

The standard story of the international crisis is that it started in the United States and was due to lax regulation that fostered excess credit, financial and real disequilibria and bubbles. Although the crisis was initially considered a major recession and in spite of massive government support to financial institutions in trouble, the crisis spread soon to the real economy and entered into a "second great contraction" (Reinhart and Rogoff 2009; Rogoff 2011).[4]

The global crisis started in the United States in 2008 and caught Europe unprepared. The EU had no ways of escaping the effects of the US crisis in a context of open and integrated markets and high mobility of resources. However, it was also under the effect of dangerous illusions about itself and its institutions.

Up to that time, the euro was a technical and economic success and supported real processes positively in most of the cases. Growth was dynamic in many latecomer countries, such as Ireland, Spain, and Greece. Popular support to the Union was strong and often enthusiastic, integration looked irreversible and enlargement proceeded briskly and gave the EU an international leadership role. Overall the federalist agenda looked strong and, in the economy, governments and markets appeared to believe in the existence of a common euro umbrella protecting all Eurozone countries, in spite of the severe Economic and Monetary Union (EMU) clauses.

Both internal and external factors explain European illusions at the beginning of the crisis in the US. Externally, the crisis initially appeared to be a domestic problem in the US due to imprudent financial liberalisation and the lack of prudent regulation, both typical of the American financial markets. Internally, the European Union, and particularly the Eurozone, were considered to be safer, thanks to the virtues of integration, the euro, prudent financial regulation and the sturdy features of continental European capitalism (Amable 2003; Hall and Soskice 2001; Hoffmann 2004; Morgan and Whitley 2012). The latter include lower financial depth and integration, conservative financial regulation and the prudent attitude of financial institutions, in particular strong (universal) banks.

Initially, the EU seemed to be effectively in a safe position, with the exception of macroeconomically unbalanced small economies (Greece,

[4] "But the real problem is that the global economy is badly overleveraged, and there is no quick escape without a scheme to transfer wealth from creditors to debtors, either through defaults, financial repression, or inflation. A more accurate, if less reassuring, term for the ongoing crisis is the "Second Great Contraction" (Rogoff 2011).

Hungary, and Ireland). In these economies, the crisis was already apparent in 2008. More than seven years into the crisis, this picture has dramatically changed. The Eurozone is now the problem of the world economy. Its financial situation is shaken, the Eurozone is split into two groups of resilient and vulnerable countries in strikingly different situations, the euro is in distress, and the very future of European integration is at stake. European policymakers are seriously debating and trying to find solutions amidst recurrent crises. Typically, policymaking is concentrated on financial and monetary issues, with institutional implications. The success of financial and monetary stabilisation is seen as a necessary precondition for the revival of the real economy. However, this takes place amidst growing doubts, policy inconsistencies and conflicts, as well as political and social protests. Policy dogmatisms apparently continue to prevail, and in reality, sound pragmatism has been replaced by muddling through issues. However, the real economy has barely moved and in some countries it continues to worsen. A stagnating or falling GDP, widespread unemployment, high inequalities and the danger of deflation are still important aspects of the Eurozone landscape in early 2015.

It is interesting to notice that the European Commission report on the first 10 years of the EMU stressed that disregarding non-fiscal dimensions such as competitiveness, credit booms and current-account deficits was a mistake (EC 2008a). However, since then financial issues have dominated debates and policymaking, and efforts have been focused on the need to strengthen the financial architecture and practice of the Eurozone and its member countries. Critical issues of the Eurozone such as diverging productivity among member countries, the sudden reversal of capital flows between the north and the south, the falling international competitiveness, and decreasing world trade shares are mostly confined to academic debate, barely appearing in governments' concerns.

This book seeks to demonstrate that a fault line is deepening within the Eurozone between vulnerable and resilient countries. Given the present institutional architecture and the priority assigned to financial discipline even to the disruption of real economies, the fault line is bound to dramatically worsen. At the end, this structural Eurozone dualism can jeopardise the sustainability of the common currency. The dramatic reality of the Eurozone is that concentrating on financial discipline is a one-sided approach that, alone, cannot resolve European troubles and is actually one of the main causes of those problems. At the same time, financial discipline cannot be disregarded or infringed in an institutionally incomplete monetary union, one in which trust among member countries is shaken to say the least.

Although it is true that the present financial distress of various EU member countries is a liability on their ability to grow, this is the case only in view of the present incomplete institutional architecture of the Union, and particularly of the Eurozone. However, if one takes a broader, longer and deeper perspective, it appears that the present financial and monetary crisis of the Eurozone is embedded in the real economy and the institutional architecture. In turn, the incompleteness of the latter reflects the strength of national sentiments and aims and the fundamental lack of trust among member countries, which the Eurozone tries to overcome by means of financial discipline. Moreover, concentrating on a fiscal and monetary solution to the crisis by means of restrictive policies is likely to be untenable in the medium–long run because of its depressive effects on the real economy, the heavy social costs, political deterioration and its fundamental conflict with national political sovereignty. The EuroGreek tragedy of the spring and summer of 2015 is full of important teachings in this sense.

Although some of the problems are common to the entire European Union, it is within the Eurozone that they are manifested in their fullest extent. Indeed, the common currency takes monetary policy out of the hands of national governments, which have to finance their activities in a currency that they do not control. Moreover, European treaties and the Stability and Growth Pact (SGP) strongly limit their fiscal policies. These constraints to policymaking exacerbate the effects of shocks, to the disadvantage of economies in vulnerable situations.[5]

[5] These are countries in an unbalanced macroeconomic or financial situation and whose economy is not competitive. They need policies to adjust their situation, but they miss policy sovereignty as members of a monetary union. External shocks may have particularly damaging consequences on these economies. The following countries are considered as vulnerable in this book: Cyprus, Greece, Ireland, Italy, Portugal, Spain. The following countries are considered as resilient: Austria, Belgium, Finland, France, Germany, Luxembourg, and the Netherlands.

The crisis has clarified beyond a doubt that the Eurozone includes economies with different features and in different, apparently divergent situations. Some economies are balanced and resilient, mostly in the north of the Eurozone; others are unbalanced and vulnerable, mostly in the south.

According to the literature on economic vulnerability and resilience (Briguglio *et al.* 2009; Cariolle 2011; Cordina 2004; Guillaumont 1999), economic vulnerability consists of the exposure and proneness of an economy to exogenous shocks and international market fluctuations.[6] More precisely, economic vulnerability results from a country's structural features that influence the size and likelihood of shocks and the exposure to these shocks and from the country's economic policies that determine the resilience to shocks. Therefore, there are both endogenous and exogenous causes of vulnerability. The opposite situation is one of economic resilience, which is the policy-induced ability of an economy to withstand or recover from the effects of such shocks.

Shocks typically arise out of economic openness and export concentration. The typical case is that of small countries, whose economies are, to a large extent, shaped by forces and processes largely outside of their control. Other factors of vulnerability are lack of diversification of production and foreign trade; exports with relatively high income and price elasticity; strong dependence on imports with low price elasticity and limited import substitution possibilities; insularity and remoteness, leading to high transport costs and reduced attractiveness for business and investment; absence of competitive markets; relatively large size of public sector activity in small countries; low absorption capacity for technology, investment and international development initiatives.

[6] Since 2000, the United Nations Committee for Development Policy uses an Economic Vulnerability Index (EVI) as one of the criteria utilised, in addition to GDP per capita and the human capital (measured by the Human Asset Index), in order to identify Least Developed Countries (LDC). The Index is composed of seven indicators. These are grouped into factors of exposure (population size, remoteness from markets, export concentration, share of agriculture, forestry and fisheries in GDP) and factors determining the size and likelihood of shocks (share of homeless population due to natural disasters, instability of exports of goods and services, instability of agricultural production) (Guillaumont 2011 http://www.un.org/en/development/desa/policy/cdp/ldc/ldc_criteria.shtml).

Although not exactly the same as the case identified in this literature, particularly with reference to the causes of vulnerability, the case of vulnerable economies within the Eurozone is similar in terms of the effects. When hit by external shocks, these countries cannot freely use policy instruments to withstand or recover from the effects of such shocks, nor can they rely on the collective Eurozone support. Also in their case, there is typically an exogenous source of vulnerability.

Within the Eurozone, no country can freely dispose of monetary policy, since this is common. Moreover, no country can control the currency in which its budget and debt are denominated. However, asymmetric shocks (such as the appreciation of the common currency or the slump in the world demand) only hit negatively vulnerable economies, but not resilient ones. The difference can be explained in various ways, depending on the kind of shocks. Two factors are particularly important in the case of Eurozone countries. These are: first, macroeconomic, particularly financial disequilibrium, which shakes the confidence of financial markets in the solvency of those countries. A second factor includes microeconomic and systemic inefficiency, which leads to weak competitiveness. In both cases, the fundamental causes of disequilibrium and inefficiency are likely to be endogenous.

These economies are affected by unfavourable market events and conditions until the countries can solve their structural problems, which is quite difficult without policy sovereignty or European support. In principle, the problem of ailing competitiveness can be solved in three ways: currency depreciation, internal deflation ("austerity"), and reforms with investments.[7] In a split Eurozone, the choice is extremely difficult and ridden with intercountry conflicts of interests, along with domestic problems. The fundamental dilemma of the Eurozone lies in this conflict between the national goals of vulnerable countries and the goals of common stability, that largely coincide with the national goals of resilient countries.

---

[7] There is a further way: protectionism. Yet this solution is ruled out in a deeply integrated and open world economy ("globalisation"). And it is anyway contrary to the European principles and rules.

The Book

This book is about the strange case of the Eurozone crisis: a bold process of economic integration and monetary union turning into a cage, possibly into a liability or even a trap. How could it happen? Is it a case of an unforeseen event, a kind of Black Swan (Taleb 2007)? Or is it a foreseeable, and perhaps even foreseen, event that has so far found no solution for some unexplained reason?

The book aims at answering the following questions, each one treated in one or more dedicated chapters:

1. How was the world economy looking like in the decades that preceded the international crisis? Were there any factors and reasons for making the crisis inevitable or at least probable after decades of apparent obsolescence of business cycles and evaporation of major crises? And how did Europe fare in this context? Was it really an economically declining continent that was already weakened and vulnerable when the critical time arrived?
2. Why did a major crisis appear in 2008 and how did it unfold? Was it the effect of the mismanagement of the world's largest economy or was it the consequence of deeper and structural forces, whose destructive power accumulated in previous years and decades? Was it bound to unfold and multiply its effects to other countries in any case or were bad and wrong policies to be blamed? What was the true nature of this crisis? Was it embedded solely in the excessive expansion and lack of control over finance? Or were there (also) deeper and more structural reasons in the real economy?
3. Why did the contagion diffuse from the United States to Europe? Which forces, links, and processes transmitted the crisis to Europe? Were these of a financial or of a real nature? Was Europe a victim only of US economic mismanagement? Or did independent and self-made factors of vulnerability and unsustainability exist within Europe, factors that would have caused a major crisis anyway? If so, where could these factors be found? In the features and management of European economies? Or is the institutional build-up of European integration

and unification to be blamed? And who is responsible for the European crisis: the EU and the Eurozone, Germany and other resilient countries, or vulnerable countries?

4. Is the implementation of the common currency bound to fail because of insurmountable flaws in its very nature? Was it wrong to introduce a common currency in a group of countries which do not share the necessary features? Are the Eurozone difficulties rooted in the lack of correspondence of this group of countries to the qualifications of an optimum currency area? Is therefore the currency structurally ineffective? Or is the lack of proper institutions and actions that made the common currency a liability?
5. Is the common currency really a liability? If the advantages of the common currency were considered to be greater than its disadvantages at the time of monetary unification, is it in the features and mismanagement of the common currency where we should look for the culprit of the European crisis? Were common institutions set up in a way and form that were inappropriate for a sound common currency? Should the introduction of the common currency have been prepared better and more resolutely? Are common institutions excessively incomplete or perhaps unbalanced and ineffective? Or is it in the unsolved balance between the union level and competences and roles of the national states where the fault line lies? Did the EU government commit mistakes or was it irresolute and powerless? Or were the economic situations of the member countries in the economic and monetary union diverging in such a way as to make the common currency and monetary policy a source of growing problems?
6. Once common institutions were settled in a group of countries that did not coincide with the requisites necessary for an optimum currency area, it was the turn of policies. Policies are fundamental for managing the common currency, answering threats to its stability, compensating for the lack of those institutions, and fixing the problematic consequences of the common currency. Are such policies properly and resolutely implemented? Do they have common stability as their goal or are they under the strain of national interests? Are common policymakers sovereign and determined in pursuing the common good?

7. Did the crisis hit the Eurozone when institutions and governance were still incomplete and insufficiently effective? Was then the crisis primarily a question of misfortune? Or did the implicit and hidden strain between common governance and national governments deprive common policies of a master? Were, as a consequence, common policies the outcome of a sub-optimal and unstable compromise between European government and national governments? Was the process of common policymaking excessively cumbersome, lengthy, ridden with uncertainty and consequently ineffective? What was the role of this unbalanced and uncertain setting for policymaking organs? Was it the cause or the perpetrator of ineffective policies and the European inability to effectively manage the crisis in a timely fashion? Did this situation cause the propagation of the crisis coming from outside? Did it trigger a domino effect, causing the crisis to spread within the Eurozone from one country to the next? Did it make the overall policy machinery ineffective or even pro-cyclical?
8. How should the history of the euro up to the crisis be considered? Was it really a success story? Or were the seeds of monetary troubles already germinating in the common currency? Were the European Central Bank's view, mission and management up to the challenge? Or were policies unbalanced and did they disregard fiscal and industrial policies? If so, did this disregard make a difference on the effect of monetary policies? What was the effect of fiscal management of member states under common rules for shared policies and crisis management? Is a currency union viable without a collective government of the economy?
9. Is the European Union in general and the Eurozone in particular really and fully aware of the unsustainability of the present institutional and policy situation? Are the present institutional reforms and policy refinements sufficient to meet the challenges? What is the role of national reforms and policymaking in improving the sustainability and policy effectiveness of the Eurozone? Are there any alternatives? Or is an uneasy and costly muddling through process and long-term stagnation the fate of the Eurozone?
10. What did the European management of the Greek crises show? Is this the victory of consistency to "protect and further solidify the foundation

of the currency union", based on the conviction the "[b]enevolence comes before dissoluteness" (Schäuble 2015)? Is this the end of the European dream and the revival of the German problem for Europe? Is it the appearance of the much dreaded question of a "German Europe prevailing over European Germany" (Fischer 2015)? Or is it a masterpiece of European "constructive hypocrisy" (Kaletsky 2015) showing an unexpected way out of the rigid financial discipline that has prevailed thus far?

Part I

The Facts: The Crisis and the Eurozone

"Countries, therefore, when lawmaking falls exclusively to the lot of the poor cannot hope for much economy in public expenditure; expenses will always be considerable, either because taxes cannot touch those who vote for them or because they are assessed in a way to prevent that."

— Alexis de Tocqueville (1969, p. 210)

1

The World Economy and Europe

The post-war decades were a period of great economic success, particularly in Western countries. Western economies never experienced such sustained growth rates for such a long period of time in their history. This success benefited most citizens and social groups and classes, particularly in the first half of the period. Economic flexibility and social mobility increased in all countries. As a consequence, societies and democratic polities appeared fundamentally strong and stable. There were periods of economic and financial difficulties; however, these never reached systemic levels. The overall performance was such that there was growing confidence in the ability of governments and international organisations to manage instability in ways that kept damages and risks at a controllable level.

There were different reasons to believe that economies were more resilient — and crises in a sense obsolete — as a consequence of a host of important facts and transformations, in both economies and policies. Countries were considered to be less vulnerable, thanks to deep and important transformations, and more resilient due to strengthened and refined policies. Transformations took place in production, trade, finance, international governance, and economic beliefs: production and markets became more open and integrated and trade became distinctively of an infra-sectorial nature; financial activities greatly expanded and their influence on the working of markets and economic outcomes dramatically increased; the activity and role of transnational companies (TNCs) expanded significantly; and the role of international organisations increased.

As a consequence of the deeper integration and international institutional evolution, national economies became increasingly subject to the impersonal rule of world financial and goods markets and the visible power of large countries and powerful international organisations and transnational companies. Policies, although improved in their knowledge and information basis and in their effects, were increasingly considered to be less important and useful. Indeed, the prevailing economic creed created the idea of fundamentally efficient markets, believed to regulate themselves in the best possible way by making use of all the available information, although trials and errors were credited some role (Fama 1970, 1991; Fox 2009). Thus, asset prices would incorporate and reflect all available relevant information and it would be impossible to "beat the market". The business cycle was bound to become obsolete and major systemic crises a memory of the past.

Yet this reading of the changes contributed to misleading of policies. The 1990s was the crucial period when changes and policies proceeded to make a major crisis inevitable. Similarly to the 1920s, the end of the economic cycle and an age of endless growth and prosperity were repeatedly announced. Unfortunately, the very success of these changes and beliefs, together with growing real and financial disequilibria and increasingly uneven distribution of the outcomes of growth, made the appearance of the crisis particularly damaging and difficult to tackle.

1.1 The World Economy and Globalisation

The dynamic growth of the Western economies in the postwar decades was interrupted by various factors starting from the 1970s (Crafts 2003, 2012; Crafts and Toniolo 1996). This period came to be known as "stagflation", a blend of stagnation and inflation comprising low growth rates, considerable price increase and high unemployment. Indeed, and contrary to the policy conviction of the time, inflation and stagnation characterised much of the 1970s and part of the following decade. Traditional policies were based primarily on the Phillips curve, showing an inverse relationship between unemployment and inflation. Under stagflation conditions, traditional policies were ineffective or counterproductive. Policies to combat inflation by means of austerity measures tended to cause stagnation and unemployment.[8] Policies of monetary, fiscal or regulatory stimulation used to combat stagnation and unemployment risked to directly fuel inflation by creating inflationary expectations and decrease markets efficiency through excessive regulation.

Two different explanations of stagflation were identified, depending on the theoretical and policy approach used (Barsky and Kilian 2000; Blinder 1979; Blinder and Rudd 2008). One explanation looked at aggregate supply shocks as the fundamental cause of stagflation. Shocks came from an unexpected and sudden increase in the price of inputs, particularly if these inputs were critically important for the economy. Shocks that increased input prices and made supply more rigid translated into higher costs and lower production. During the 1970s, shocks were important in the raw material markets, and, in particular, in the energy market due to the oil shocks of 1973 and 1979. Shocks were also important in labour markets: since the late 1960s labour became more militant and economically stronger following the economic boom in the postwar decades and wages increased accordingly.

A second explanation found the cause of stagflation to rest in an inappropriate monetary policy that led to an excessive money supply. An excessive money supply in turn caused excessive private and public spending

[8] Blyth (2013) provides an excellent analysis of the history and theoretical foundation of austerity as a policy approach to fiscal stabilisation.

and consequently higher prices and debts. The resulting inflation triggered lower production and higher unemployment. Inflation proved particularly difficult to combat if prices, taxes, profits and wages were indexed: the inflationary spiral that such institutional assets caused led to self-inflating production costs and further contributed to stagnation and unemployment. Changes in the international monetary system and political events fuelled these processes (see next section).

Policy measures implemented to control stagflation were generally based on the rejection of the previously dominant Keynesian consensus. Thus, they opened the way to what was later on defined as "neoliberal" policies. Anti-stagflation policies were mostly based on a "disinflationary scenario", consisting primarily of a sharp increase of interest rates. The latter took place between the end of the 1970s and the first part of the 1980s. Although these policies were successful in stopping inflation, they also pushed Western economies into recession and high unemployment. Expansionary fiscal and monetary policies were used to fight recession and unemployment later in the decade. Also important were measures taken to make economies more efficient and competitive, in particular through deregulation and privatisation.

These policies had success in pushing economies out of stagflation. Yet these policies had a role in changing economic institutions and creating the conditions for the wave of financial crises that characterised the years leading up to the 2008 international crisis. This was a period when the role of finance increased vigorously, at a much higher rate than the real economy. It was also a period when Western economies saw emerging economies overcoming them in the rate of growth of productivity and in the expansion of foreign trade. The West kept absolute advantage in productivity levels through the period, yet this advantage was eroding at a fast pace.

The context that the 1990s provided for the onset and the unfolding of the 2008 crisis included a set of deep and far reaching systemic changes. These on the whole made economies more interdependent than ever before, more financially powerful, governments weaker in their ability and willingness to manage economies through policy instruments, and the production profile of economically advanced countries deeply transformed. When the crisis started, national economies proved to be more vulnerable and their situation less resilient, due to greater interdependence and less effective policies.

Two major forces led to the increase of international economic integration: the decrease of transportation and communication costs, via innovations such as containers and information and communications technology (ICT), and institutional developments (Eichengreen 2006). Compared to the first wave of globalisation prior to 1913, the globalisation of the 1990s was overall more extensive, except for net capital flows and migration. In fact, migration was slowed down and hampered by different kinds of regulations. The second wave of globalisation was also distinguished by greater trade and production integration, higher gross capital mobility, and lower labour mobility. However, the 1990s did not actually bring novelties in the expansion of international transactions. In fact, such expansion was the continuation of trends that had been under way during the preceding half a century, without any significant increase of their pace of growth (Eichengreen 2006).

The most important general developments, particularly during the 1990s, were the growth of emerging economies, the growth of financial activities mainly among Western economies, and the rise of regionalism. These developments accompanied globalisation, in part supported it and in part introduced some mild segmentation in the world economy (Eichengreen 2006). The growth of emerging economies, in particular the so-called BRICS countries (Brazil, India, China and South Africa, while Russia followed later on towards the end of the decade), was perhaps the most important achievement of the 1990s and the following decade and a half. Their rising role became apparent in high growth rates, attraction of foreign direct investments (FDIs) and the expanding share of world exports.

The second important general development was the growth of financial activities, including higher capital mobility. Capital mobility originated in the abundant liquidity of financial markets, growing savings in emerging countries and some Western countries (particularly Germany and Japan), and growing debts in the United States. A distinctive feature of this period, compared to the period preceding World War I, was that capital mobility took place particularly among Western economies and chiefly towards the United States. In mid-1990s, three-quarters of the world's stock FDIs were in the Organisation for Economic Cooperation and Development (OECD) countries, while the latter countries exported more than 90% of the world's stock of FDIs (WTO 1996). In more recent years the BRICS, in particular China, became more active, particularly as destination countries. Yet OECD countries continued to dominate.[9]

The most dynamic component of capital mobility was short-term flows, the most volatile component that contributed to the vulnerability of economies to the crisis. Also important was in this period the internationalisation of production, including FDIs and cross-border mergers and acquisitions (M&A). Before World War I, FDIs were heavily concentrated in developing countries (nearly two-thirds of their global stock) and in extractive industries.

Quite different was the situation in mid-1990s, when more than two-thirds of FDIs were located in developed countries and mostly in manufacturing and services (Eichengreen 2006; OECD 2014a; UNCTAD database; World Bank database; WTO 1996). In nominal terms, the annual outflow of FDIs from OECD countries to all destinations (including other OECD countries) was US$25 billion at the end of the 1970s. This level increased to $60 billion by 1985 and to US$315 billion by 1995, a more than five-fold increase (WTO 1996). In this period, between 1973 and 1995, FDIs increased 1.5 times faster than exports of goods and services, respectively more than 12 times against 8.5 times (WTO 1996). The growth of FDIs accelerated until 2000, and then decreased in 2001–2003. The new upsurge, started in 2004, reached its peak in 2007 on the eve of the great contraction. FDI inflows increased respectively to US$1,500 billion and to around US$2,000 billion (UNCTAD database).

[9] OECD countries were overwhelming in 1990, having 88.4% of overall inflows and 98.2% of overall outflows. By 2013, their shares decreased respectively to 46.3% and 72.9%. By 2013, the shares of developed economies in FDI inflows and outflows were respectively 39.0% and 60.8%. In 2013, the EU and the United States had roughly the same weight in FDI inflows (respectively 17.0% and 17.2%), but their difference was remarkable in FDI outflows (respectively 17.8% and 27.0%). Developing economies accounted for 53.6% of FDI inflows and 32.2% of FDI outflows. Transition economies accounted for the remaining shares (respectively 7.4% and 7.0%). Among developing countries, East and South-East Asia accounted respectively for 23.9% and 20.7% and Latin America and the Caribbean for 20.1% and 8.1% (UNCTAD 2014).

Also noteworthy was the expansion of transnational companies' activities: by 1995 their intra-firm trade accounted for about one third of world trade, while trade among national firms (excluding transnational companies) accounted for another one third. The remaining one third consisted of TNC exports to non-affiliates.

The rise of regionalism in the form of regional trade agreements (RTAs) is a third important feature, particularly since the early 1990s. At the present (7 April 2015), there exist 406 RTAs in force between two or more partners according to the World Trade Organization (WTO) (WTO 2015). However, few of these agreements are truly economically important. Among the most important RTAs, the ones which account for an important share of world trade are the European Union (EU), the European Free Trade Association (EFTA), the Asia-Pacific Economic Cooperation (APEC), the North American Free Trade Agreement (NAFTA), and the Association of Southeast Asian Nations (ASEAN). Some of these agreements also involve a problematic relation between the highly developed and the less developed member countries of each agreement. In spite of this apparent fragmentation of the world economy, regionalism does not appear to have discouraged globalisation: "Regionalism developed quickly but in ways that complemented global markets and institutions rather than undermining their operation" (Eichengreen 2006, p. 66).

The growth of emerging economies, the growth of financial activities, and the rise of regionalism created new opportunities and opened new problems and threats. Economic achievements during the two decades before the crisis notwithstanding, the management of the world economy and of national economies became increasingly difficult and less effective. Also new problems appeared. In particular, the inability of the international economic and financial architecture and of international organisations to keep pace with high short-term capital mobility and financial market volatility became sources of growing concern. Contradictory were also the consequences of deregulation (Bernstein 2006) and, more generally, the shrinking and weakening competence and role of governments. The importance of these developments became apparent during the crisis.

At the microeconomic level, the most important development in the decades preceding the crisis was the new organisation of production and trade. Such development fundamentally changed the structure and working of economies. In industry, the production of components in different parts of the world and their assembly into complex industrial products replaced the production of finished goods. This reorganisation of production generated transnational ("global") value chains, which became a dominant feature of world trade and benefited from productive efficiency (Ash 2015). As a consequence, infra-sectorial international trade replaced the traditional inter-sectorial trade. Global value chains and infra-sectorial trade increased the integration of economies. This gave individual economies greater resilience to external shocks when business cycles were uncoordinated. However, the vulnerability to external economic and financial crises, particularly that of smaller and more open economies, increased when business cycles were coordinated.

The reorganisation of industry and trade became possible thanks to technical progress in production, transportation, and ICT. Open markets increased competition, and that prompted investors to allocate production of individual components to the most efficient and competitive producer, often independently of its location. The growing fragmentation of production across borders that followed obliged countries to have open, predictable, and transparent trade and investment regimes. This was necessary in order to capture international opportunities, pursue domestic employment, and improve the welfare of consumers and efficiency of producers.

1.2 Real Economy and Finance: A Comparative Perspective

Comparative economics (Aoki 2001; Aoki *et al.* 2012; Dallago 2004), the Varieties of Capitalism (VoC) approach (Amable 2003; Hall and Soskice 2001; Morgan and Whitley 2012; Tridico 2011), and various brands of institutional economics (Acemoglu and Robinson 2012; Aggarwal and Goodell 2014; Antonczyk and Salzmann 2014; Charron *et al.* 2012; La Porta *et al.* 2008, North 1981, 1989; Ostrom 1990; Rajan and Zingales 2001a) have highlighted that different countries have different organisations of their economies and that institutions have a fundamental role in influencing outcomes. Unless we understand this influence in deterministic ways, this systemic literature means that "[e]conomic prosperity and stability can be achieved through different combinations of institutional arrangements in labour markets, finance, corporate governance, social welfare, and other areas. Nations are likely to — and indeed are entitled to — make varying choices among these arrangements depending on their needs and values" (Rodrik 2011, p. xviii).

Comparative economics maintains that different institutions bundle in a coherent way around distinct and recognisable patterns or economic systems. Important observations that come from the institutional and comparative literature is that different economic systems are structured in dissimilar ways, their institutions are distinct and work in different ways, and their outcomes descend from distinct combinations of factors. They also move along particular paths of institutional change (Hall and Thelen 2009).

There may be a variety of such economic systems. For the subject considered here, it seems particularly important to follow this literature in identifying two distinct economic systems: the Anglo-Saxon system and the Continental system. The former is typical of the United States and Great Britain, while the latter has Germany as its most representative country. Most countries of continental Europe can be rather easily ascribed to different variants of the Continental system.

In this literature, as much as in economic literature in general, the role of finance appears to be prominent. From systemic literature it appears generally that financial markets are more important — and more difficult to control — in Anglo-Saxon than in Continental countries. Financial markets in the Anglo-Saxon capitalist countries are dominated by risk capital, while in Continental countries it is debt capital that occupies the most prominent role in the economy. Also the role of the state in financial markets, and more generally in the economy, is higher in the latter countries than in the former.

The role of finance in supporting firms in the pursuit and expansion of their activity is the subject of copious literature, both theoretical and applied in nature. In general, it is stressed that financial intermediaries and financial markets are important for firms and consequently for economic growth (Levine 2005; Rousseau and Sylla 2003; Tsuru 2000).

In general, the more financial systems are developed and the deeper financial markets are, the easier it is for firms to overcome their financial constraints. Developed financial markets are important also for making the ownership of firms constestable and consequently for disciplining managers.

Systemic features of finance have important consequences for the subject of our analysis. Financial markets in Anglo-Saxon countries are more liquid and dynamic and financial innovation is more important and faster compared to continental European markets (Dietl 1998). At the same time, governments are smaller and less active in the economy. Risk capital is more important for financing companies in Anglo-Saxon countries than is debt capital, while in Continental economies the opposite occurs.[10] The mobility of resources, including financial resources, is higher than in Continental countries.[11] As a consequence, regulation, although more important for the smooth working of financial markets, is also more complex and difficult. Detailed and reliable public information and effective enforcement are fundamental in Anglo-Saxon countries. This is the case for both the effective control by public authorities and the pursuit of shareholder value. The latter is critically important for companies. Yet these features give this economic system a prevailing short-term perspective which may open the economy to greater instability.

---

[10] According to Bouis *et al.* (2013), the debt-to-equity ratio of non-financial companies was much lower in the United States than in continental Europe during the 1980s. In the early 1980, the ratio was 0.8 in the United States, 1.8 in the United Kingdom, close to 2 in Germany, between 3 and 4 in France, around 1.4 in Italy, and between 2.5 and 3 in Spain. The ratio decreased slightly up to the beginning of the crisis in the United States (to 0.6 in 2007, where it remained also in 2012) and much faster in other countries, which reached the bottom at the end of the 1990s: United Kingdom (0.8 and 0.8, respectively), Germany (0.8 and 0.9), France (0.6 and 0.9), Italy (0.9 and 1.1), and Spain (1.1 and 1.4). In the Eurozone average, the ratio was close to 1.4 in 1995, 0.8 in 2007 and 1.0 in 2012. See also Dietl (1998).

[11] Prior to the crisis labour mobility increased in the European Union and declined in the United States, although in the latter it remained markedly higher than in the former (Dao *et al.* 2013). However, during the crisis inter-state migration again spiked in the United States and remained high among European regions. Labour mobility is important for absorbing shocks, but in Europe it is still short of what is needed for a successful currency union. See also Davis and Haltiwanger (2014), Kahanec (2012).

Along with systemic reasons, the United States presented some important policy and structural reasons for growing financial vulnerability since the late 1960s. These resulted from the international role of the country and the structural nature of some of its internal problems. Among the former, it is worth mentioning the role of wars (both cold and hot wars: Vietnam, Iraq twice, Bosnia, Afghanistan, the "war on terror") and the cost of imperial politics (keeping powerful armed forces worldwide, supporting friendly governments, espionage and antiterrorism networks and operations). Among the latter, the most important and costly undertaking (for public finances) was Lyndon B. Johnson's "war on poverty" and the ailing international competitiveness of the US economy. Investments decreased from around 10% of GDP in the early 1960s to around 6–7% in the early 2000s. Private overspending complemented the overstretching of finances in the form of excess credit and weak family savings. Personal saving as a share of disposable personal income fell from around 10% to the GDP in early 1980s to around 2.5% by the start of the crisis (BEA 2008).

Following the breakdown of the Bretton Woods international monetary system, in the United States current accounts became permanently negative since the early 1980s. The balance of goods and services was permanently in deficit since 1976 (BEA 2014). Federal budget deficits became permanent and have been growing since the end of the 1960s. This led to the "twin deficits", a problem that acquired a serious political and policy role, particularly during the Reagan administration. Many scholars analysed the threats that twin deficits were posing to the economic solidity of the United States, its international role and even its economic sovereignty. Debates of the possibility of "hard" or "soft landing" from the twin deficits highlighted the perceived necessity to recover an economically and financially sound situation. As Frankel (2006) observed, "...one is still left with the reality of an unsustainable path of high budget deficits, low national saving, and high current account deficits" (p. 653). The apparently unsolvable problem of the US twin deficits continues these days and has an important effect on exchange rates, among other things. The only exception was the government budget in the period from mid-1998 to mid-2001, when the balance returned to being slightly positive.

1.3 Booming Finance

Financialisation is a process through which financial flows intensify, financial markets and institutions gain preeminence over economic processes and policies, and financial operators become powerful and influential. Financialisation increases the weight of the financial sector compared to the real sector, enlarges the share of the financial sector in income distribution, and tends to increase distributive inequality. Financialisation thus transforms economic systems and changes the functioning of the economy at both the macro and micro levels (Epstein 2005; Lapavitsas 2009; Palley 2007, 2013; van Treeck 2009a).

Financialisation was the outcome of the accumulation of financial resources, the openness and integration of markets, and important legal and regulatory reforms. Policies of deregulation and liberalisation, in particular of financial markets, also played important roles. Other important sources of financialisation include privatisation of public assets, the prevalence of the shareholder value paradigm in corporate governance, and growing public debts. Technical progress, particularly in ICT, offered increasingly sophisticated, cheap, and fast communication instruments. International agreements decreased transaction costs and increased safety and protection of international financial flows.

Financial flows increased much faster than real flows up to the crisis, particularly since the early 1980s. The drivers included the expansion of TNCs, the emergence of large global banks, the international expansion and activism of institutional investors and private investors such as pension funds and asset managers, and growing foreign investments. According to Manyika *et al.*, between 1980 and 2007, global financial flows increased from US$470 billion to a peak of US$12 trillion, or from 4% of GDP to 21% of GDP (2014, p. 27). According to Piketty, the total amount of financial assets and liabilities increased from four to five years of national income in most countries in the early 1970s to 10 to 15 years of national income by 2010 (2014, pp. 193–194). In Great Britain, the increase was even higher, since it reached 20 years of national income. By adding the value of derivatives that are not included in the previous figures, the overall amount would increase to 20 or perhaps 30 years of national income.

As mentioned above, a well-functioning financial sector performs various critical roles for the success of capitalist economies: allocation of capital, information transmission and risk sharing. It is these considerations that led many policymakers and scholars to defend the vigorous growth of finance in recent decades. Studies have found that there is a positive correlation between a large financial sector and economic growth in a broad cross section of countries.

Such a relationship appears strong in the long run and takes different forms. Rousseau and Sylla (2003) found that between 1850 and the start of World War I, countries with more developed financial systems were advantaged in trade and better integrated with other economies. Moreover, domestic financial development promoted capital inflows from other countries and the country's participation in capital market globalisation. Levine (2005) found from microeconomic-based evidence that better developed financial systems helped firms by easing their external financing constraints. Such effects were found to be so important which lead authors to conclude that "economic growth and increasing globalization of the Atlantic economies might indeed have been finance-led" (Rousseau and Sylla 2003, p. 402), particularly in the period from 1850 up to the Great Depression.

However, not all authors agree with this view. Philippon and Reshef (2013) observe that it is quite difficult to maintain beyond a doubt that the growing financial sector increases the rate of economic growth in high-income economies: "The long-run patterns of the rise of the financial sector since the nineteenth century ... do not have any obvious correlation with trends in growth rates within countries" (p. 92). They also stress the complexity of the relationship between the size of the financial sector and income, and observe that presently the relationship between financial output and income per capita may have changed as compared to in the past. In particular and compared to the post-1980 period, the rise in living standards after 1870 was obtained mostly with less involvement of finance. Indeed, financial output was lower and the share of income spent on finance was smaller.

Analyses and opinions do not agree as to the causal relationship. Although for many economists effective financial intermediation promotes the efficiency of investment and economic growth, for others it is economic development that promotes financial development. Other social scientists are more prudent in evaluating the role of finance in economic development (van der Zwan 2014).

It is important, therefore, to understand whether financial development may have a negative or destabilising effect on economic growth if it exceeds a certain threshold. An International Monetary Fund (IMF) paper, by the revealing title of "Too Much Finance?", finds that in general the relationship between the size of the financial system and economic growth is positive (Arcand *et al.* 2012). In particular, the correlation between financial depth and economic growth is positive and robust in countries with small and intermediate financial sectors. However, finance has a negative effect on output growth when credit to the private sector exceeds 100% of GDP and more finance is associated with less growth.[12] This idea was held by some economists well before the 2008 crisis (Kindleberger 1978; Minsky 1974; Rajan 2005) and became more widespread thereafter.[13] However, the uneasy relation between finance and economic growth may be due more to the composition of finance than to its level. For instance, Beck *et al.* (2008)

---

[12] While up to the end of the 1960s, all countries had a share of domestic credit to the private sector lower than 100% of GDP, by 2006 the share was well above 300 in Iceland (319%), above 200 in Cyprus (223), close to 200 in the United States (198) and Japan (191), and between 200 and 150 in Ireland (181), the United Kingdom (168), the Netherlands and Spain (167), Switzerland (164), Luxembourg (155) and Portugal (152). In other countries, including the main countries of continental Europe sharing the common currency, the share was slightly above or below 100: Austria (116), Malta (115), Sweden (112), China (111), Germany (110), France (98) and Italy (94). In all other Eurozone countries the share was significantly lower than 100: Latvia (88), Greece (85), Estonia (83), Belgium (82), Finland (79), Slovenia (66), Lithuania (50) and Slovakia (39) (World Bank's World Development Indicators). Bélyácz and Szász (2015) investigate the deeper roots of the financial systems' increasing propensity to crisis, which they find to be in the financial bubbles and the accounting scandals that have characterised the US economy since the late 1990s.

[13] In his prescient paper, Rajan (2005) maintains that, although financial sector developments expand the dispersion of risk and greatly enlarge access to finance for firms and households, they also increase risk. This is due to the emergence of new type of financial intermediaries and the change in managerial incentives that the expansion and the transformation of the financial sector have brought about. The collective behavior of these intermediaries accentuate real fluctuations and exposure to risk and may, under certain conditions, expose economies to greater turbulence than in the past.

used data for 45 countries for the period 1994–2005 to show that credit given to enterprises is positively associated with economic growth. However, no correlation was found between growth and household credit.

Other components of financial markets increased more and much faster. The single largest and fastest growing component was the derivatives market: its notional amount outstanding increased by 24% per year between 1995 and 2007 and was estimated at €457 trillion in June 2007 (Deutsche Börse 2008).[14] The derivatives market is more than four times larger than the combined market capitalisation of global equity and bond markets. Its growth was also much faster than that of equities (which increased by 11% per year) and bonds (9%).

The conclusion that there may be "too much" finance is shared also by other scholars. Cecchetti and Kharroubi (2012), based on a sample of developed and emerging economies, find that the size of the financial sector has an inverted U-shaped effect on productivity growth. This means that, after a certain level, further expansion of the financial sector has a negative effect on real growth and financial booms do not enhance growth. They also find that the growth of the financial sector hinders productivity growth. The authors attribute these findings to the competition of the financial sector with the rest of the economy for scarce resources.

The difficulty in interpreting the effect of finance on economic growth led authors to disaggregate the financial sector into its main components and consider the effect of each of them. Greenwood and Scharfstein (2013) show that the growth of finance in the United States since 1980 was due to the increase in active asset management and to an extension of household credit, mostly mortgages. They conclude that the surge of active asset management is an economically beneficial event, although it led to higher management fees. However, the growth of household credit took place at the cost of financial stability.

[14] The term "notional value" refers to the amount of money actually invested in a leveraged position's assets as distinct from the amount of money involved in the whole transaction. In 2010, the notional value of the derivatives market was estimated at US$1.200 trillion, or 20 times the size of the world's annual GDP of US$50–60 trillion (Cohan 2010). The estimated gross market value of all derivatives outstanding is much lower though. According to Deutsche Börse (2008, p. 11), they total €10 trillion, a much lower value than the capitalisation of equity and bond markets (respectively at €43 trillion and €55 trillion).

An important piece of information on the development of finance comes from the financial sector share of GDP. According to Greenwood and Scharfstein (2013), this share increased at a faster rate since 1980 than it did in the 30 years prior. This growth of financial services since 1980, which is associated with asset management and the provision of household credit, explains more than a quarter of the growth of the entire service sector. While asset management facilitated risk diversification and household participation in securities markets, thus decreasing the cost of capital to firms, it also had socially undesirable consequences and likely increased risk.[15]

Credit intermediation was the other major source of growth in the financial sector. It increased as a share of GDP from 1980 to the crisis, particularly in the forms that facilitated the expansion of household credit. Corporate credit grew from 31% of GDP in 1980 to 50% in 2007. Credit intermediation was in the form of residential mortgage in the first place: It grew rapidly, from 48% of GDP in 1980 to 99% in 2007. The growth was particularly rapid since 2000, during the housing boom. It resulted in excessive household leverage and the expansion of shadow banking,[16]

---

[15] According to Greenwood and Scharfstein (2013), there are different reasons why professional asset management had socially undesirable consequences and could have increased risk. The growth of professional asset management may have caused, through the increase in participation and diversification, the large increase in stock market valuation ratios between 1980 and 2007. Professional asset management also introduced agency problems in the market, which led the vast majority of institutions to overpay for active management. This created rents in the sector that lured talented individuals away from potentially more productive sectors. Moreover, active managers tended to cater to the preferences of unsophisticated investors, which decreased the informational contribution of securities prices. There is also evidence that active asset managers tended to herd in their investment decisions.

[16] The Financial Stability Board defines the shadow banking system as "the system of credit intermediation that involves entities and activities outside the regular banking system. Its form is related to the way in which the banking sector and the rest of the financial system are structured and regulated in each jurisdiction" (FSB 2011, p. 3). Former Federal Reserve Chair Ben Bernanke defines shadow banking as comprising "a diverse set of institutions and markets that, collectively, carry out traditional banking functions — but do so outside, or in ways only loosely linked to, the traditional system of regulated depository institutions" (2012, p. 3). Shadow banking includes special purpose entities which perform

which made the financial system more fragile and was a fundamental factor in the subprime mortgage crisis of 2007–2008. In fact, the growth of household credit as a share of GDP was entirely securitised. While banks held approximately 40% of household credit as a share of GDP through the period, incremental loans were packaged into asset-backed securities (Greenwood and Scharfstein 2013).

The booming increase of finance over the real economy in European countries can be illustrated by some simple figures. According to the Austrian Institute of Economic Research WIFO (Schulmeister *et al.*, 2008), the volume of currency transactions was 70 times the world trade of goods and services in 2008, up from 15 times in 1990. During this period, the average trade elasticity to GDP was close to 2. According to the calculations of the Bruegel Institute in Brussels, in 2010 total bank assets amounted to more than 45 times government tax receipts in Ireland, more than 30 times in Cyprus and more than 25 times in Malta. In Spain, the Netherlands and France, this share was around 15 times and slightly less, around 12–13%, in Portugal, Austria and Germany. The corresponding figure was less than 10% in Greece and slightly above 7% in Italy (Pisani-Ferry 2012). When the crisis hit the financial sector, public finances were severely and dangerously strained to rescue the private financial sector, thus reallocating distress from private to public resources, and in the end to the taxpayers. However, the situation was remarkably different among countries, as the data just quoted stress.

---

liquidity and/or maturity transformation (including securitisation vehicles such as asset-backed commercial paper (ABCP), special investment vehicles (SIVs) and other special purpose vehicles (SPVs)), money market mutual funds (MMFs) and other types of investment funds or products with deposit-like characteristics, finance companies and securities entities providing credit or credit guarantees, or performing liquidity and/or maturity transformation without being regulated like a bank, markets for repurchase agreements (repos), investment funds, insurance and reinsurance undertakings which issue or guarantee credit products, and mortgage companies (EC 2012). IMF (2014b) reports that shadow banking constitutes about one-fourth of total financial intermediation worldwide, half the size of bank assets. Assets in the shadow banking system grew rapidly before the crisis, rising from US$27 trillion in 2002 to US$60 trillion in 2007 (FSB 2011, p. 8). See also Adrian and Hyun (2009).

The growing integration and financialisation of the world economy had a double outcome. On the positive side, they have increased demand, output, employment, consumption and welfare, together with financial institutional innovation and market deepening and expansion. It is important to note that finance played a leading role in pulling production by expanding credit and increasing some incomes and through public expenditure. Thus, a substantial part of production responded to finance, creating real bubbles which spread to large part of the Western world through financial, real, political, and psychological linkages. After 2008, the finance sector shrank, with negative effects on real demand. Economies were left with excess production capacity that had to be absorbed. The gloomy economic perspectives made economic actors prudent and, together with budget cuts and expanding unemployment, depressed demand.

On the negative side, growing integration and financialisation have increased the vulnerability of economies, particularly the economies that can be considered as outliers, primarily because of high deficits or debts and ailing competitiveness. However, the stress also affected stronger and more balanced economies through monetary, financial, and real linkages. Moreover, financial deregulation created incentives for financial, particularly credit bubbles and, through these, real bubbles. Along with the size of finance, it is important to look at the quality and role of finance. Finance not only expanded endlessly its lending: it was also increasingly engaged in predatory lending and distorting incentives. State capture by private interests led to bad regulation.[17] Important actors of financial markets, such as rating agencies, sustained fraudulent lending practices and accountancy. As Stiglitz puts it (2012), "The result, as we know now, was not only massive fraud but also bad lending: too much indebtedness, with financial products that could explode with a change in interest rates or in the broader economic conditions, and indeed many did explode" (p. 192).

[17] According to Transparency International, state capture is one of the most pervasive forms of corruption which depicts "a situation where powerful individuals, institutions, companies or groups within or outside a country use corruption to shape a nation's policies, legal environment and economy to benefit their own private interests" (Transparency International 2009). See also Hellman *et al.* (2000); Martini (2014).

Severe effects on the real economy were inevitable. This was due to falling demand caused by unemployment and the reallocation of resources to rescue the financial sector. Negative real effects derived also from the credit crunch that strained financial organisations and pushed them to decrease and secure their market exposure. The financial crisis was transformed into a "great contraction" of the real economy (Rogoff 2011; Stiglitz 2010).

1.4 Boom and Crises in the 1990s and Beyond

The 1990s is considered the most successful decade since the post-war period of economic miracles. However, at the beginning of the 1990s, the United States was in stagnation and Japan was entering the "lost decade", after the stock exchange and the real estate bubble exploded in 1989 and 1990 respectively. Also Europe was losing steam and its catch up to the United States was losing momentum.

The decade started with three historically crucial novelties (Rhode and Toniolo 2006b): the beginning of transformation in Central and Eastern Europe and the break-up of the Soviet Union that brought the end of the Cold War; the deepening of the EU integration process; and the take-off of China and India. The United States started the decade in a critical situation ridden with "industrial decline, Asian competition, rising unemployment, and economic inequality" (Rhode and Toniolo 2006b, p. 3). Yet the 1990s was to become soon the decade of the "new economy", "financialisation", and "globalisation". A remarkable productivity surge was evident by the middle of the decade and a "U-turn in the country's prevailing mood" took over.

The labour productivity surge in the United States started in mid-1990s and was due to technical progress, in particular to ICT (Crafts 2003; Field 2006; Rhode and Toniolo 2006b). ICT contributed in two ways to the productivity increase, namely through capital deepening by investment in hardware and software and communication equipment; and increases in multifactor productivity in the sector producing ICT devices and equipment. However important the productivity surge in the United States was in this period, higher than in the period between 1974 and 1995, it was nevertheless well below the progress achieved in the post-war period up to 1973. It also concentrated in a limited number of industries linked to ICT.

In reality, the decade was contradictory in its economic features and not so successful in its economic outcomes. Indeed, the first years, from 1989 up to 1992 were years of economic stagnation both in the United States and globally. Growth rates in the decade, although higher than in the previous decade at the global level, were lower than the average of the entire post-war period. Although technological innovation was important, total factor productivity (TFP) did not increase for the industrial countries as a whole in general and the United States in particular (Crafts 2006, p. 25).

An important achievement of the decade was a reversal of the world income inequality. Global income inequality increased considerably up to the 1950s, then remained roughly stable until the 1980s, decreased slightly in this decade and more unambiguously in the 1990s (Deininger and Squire 1996; Förster *et al.* 2014; OECD 2014b, 2014c; Piketty 2014). This latter effect was due largely to the acceleration of the growth in emerging economies, particularly China and India. The performance of other economies, particularly in Africa and also Latin America, did not improve or worsened.

The world economy in the 1990s had a revival compared to the previous decade and millions of jobs were created, in spite of the negative performance of many transformation countries, and particularly Russia and Ukraine. International consensus around policy approaches was strong and this formed a solid political basis for a "decade of reform" (WB 2005).

Between 1992 and 2000, yearly growth rates in the United States varied between 2.5% and 4.9%. The performance of the EU economies was lower when compared to both the US economy and to the bonus that Europeans were expecting from deeper integration. While the average GDP annual growth rate of the US was 3.2% during the decade, the European Union average was 2.1%. However, in order to evaluate correctly this difference, unfavourable demographic developments in the European Union, faster decrease of the duration of working time in the EU, and differences in statistical practices and definitions should be considered. Jointly, these factors explain an important part of the difference in growth rates (Faini 2006).

Yet the EU economy fared poorly also under other headings. Its share in world exports declined sharply, while that of the United States improved slightly. A serious reversal hit the EU during the decade, in the case of labour productivity. While in the first half of the decade the growth rate of labour productivity in the EU was twice as high that in the United States, in the second part of the decade labour productivity in the latter was more than twice as high as in the EU.

Thus and although the EU performance can be considered fair in this period and roughly in line with that of the United States, it is clear that the European catching up to the US economy was exhausted. Growth rates of EU economies in the post-war period was higher than US growth rates up to the late 1970s and per capita GDP of EU countries converged to the US level. However, during the 1990s, per capita GDP of the EU moved around 70% of the US level. The relative slowdown of the European performance was partly due to the growing demographic crisis of many European countries, but is also due to the relative slowness of European countries in exploiting the great technological innovations that took place in the decade, particularly in the field of ICT (Balczerowicz *et al.* 2013; Crafts 2003, 2012; Faini 2006).

Although the 1990s was on the whole a successful decade in terms of economic expansion, numerous cases of tensions and disequilibria of differing nature took place in the decade and in the following one. Indeed, the 1990s was a rather complex decade, particularly in the areas of finance and monetary affairs. These years hosted several crises which in a sense was a continuation of the turbulent 1980s. During this latter decade, two major events had particularly severe consequences. The first was the Latin American debt crisis, an event which started in Mexico in 1982. The second and most important event was the stock market crashes that started in Hong Kong on 19 October 1987 and spread rapidly to Europe and the United States. This day is known as Black Monday. In terms of the percentage of capitalisation, it was the largest one-day fall in stock market history. The last major financial event in the decade was the Savings and Loans crisis in the United States, which started in 1986 and reached its peak between 1989 and 1991. This was a dangerous and costly burden to the US economy, and its effects continued until the mid-1990s.

The financial and monetary crises that followed during the 1990s were numerous and had serious and potentially disruptive effects. They consisted of temporary distress, albeit with serious financial and economic consequences in the countries involved. In any event, no crisis caused an international contagion of systemic importance or resulted in a major fall of income or employment at the global level. Each crisis was punctuated in nature and remained an isolated event, albeit one of impressive size and consequences.

The overheating of the Japanese economy during the second part of the 1980s was the first major event, whose effects were felt in the following decade (Ito and Iwaisako 1995; Shiratsuka 2003). The overheating was the outcome of a massive asset price bubble, particularly in real estate and the stock exchange. The burst of the asset price bubble between the end of 1991 and 1992 caused the "lost decade" of the Japanese economy that extended to the following decade. A banking crisis soon followed in Sweden and Finland. This crisis started in the early 1990s and, in spite of the fact that it had a massive impact on those economies, it did not attain systemic dimensions and remained rather isolated.

The mid-1990s was a particularly turbulent period, with various episodes of financial and monetary instability and turmoil in various countries. The most important events include the Mexican monetary and financial crisis at the end of 1994. The effects of this crisis soon spread to various other Latin American countries in a chain-like way. The financial crisis in East Asia followed in 1997. This was a major crisis, since by this time the world was financially deeply integrated and East Asian economies had great economic and financial importance. Indeed, this crisis threatened to contaminate the rest of the world and had heavy financial and economic consequences for the involved countries. In 1998, two other important crises followed: the Russian financial and monetary crisis and the LTCM (Long-Term Capital Management) crisis in the United States. The latter was a hedge fund management firm whose collapse caused perhaps the most serious financial crisis of the decade.

The Argentine crises in 1999–2002 and the Turkish economic crises in 2000–2001 opened the following decade. As in the previous examples mentioned, these represented serious and costly events, but remained isolated episodes. In 2001, the collapse of the dot-com bull market in the

United States had very serious economic implications, and it also had major effects on countries other than the United States, including the EU. In spite of its financial and economic relevance, though, even this crisis remained isolated and concentrated in the internet sector. The remarkable resilience of the world economy to systemic crises continued. Yet, the signs of accumulating tensions appeared, but they went largely unnoticed.

1.5 Conclusions: The World and the EU

Although the catching-up to the United States was discontinued, the 1990s can be considered an economically successful period for the EU. Institutional success was even greater. After years of careful preparation, the common currency, the euro, was introduced at the end of the decade. This move was the fulfilment of a period of considerable financial and monetary convergence efforts and institutional achievements within the European integration process. Imbalances and divergences existed, some of them were significant (e.g. in public debts), but they seemed to be manageable and in any case not worth particularly worrying about.

The European Exchange Rate Mechanism (ERM) was introduced in 1979 in preparation for the Economic and Monetary Union. The Mechanism included the member countries of the European Community which aimed at establishing the common currency. The aim was to reduce exchange rate variability and create monetary stability in the currency area, thus giving a sound and stable basis to the future euro. Member countries set up a semi-pegged monetary system based on a parity grid of bilateral exchange rates among national currencies. National currencies in the ERM were free to oscillate within a band of ±2.25% to the central parity. The latter was expressed in ECU (European Currency Unit). A broader band of ±6% to the central parity was granted to four currencies: the British pound, the Italian lira, the Portuguese escudo, and the Spanish peseta.

Starting from the summer of 1992, the ERM was under severe pressure. The British pound and the Italian lira were under strong speculative attacks. Both currencies had to withdraw from the ERM. Instability and tensions followed also in 1993 and the ERM had to suspend temporarily the narrow band of fluctuations also for the other currencies of the system. As soon as they exited the ERM, the British pound and the Italian lira strongly depreciated. The lira rejoined the Mechanism subsequently, albeit initially with looser rules, while the British government opted to keep the pound out of the system indefinitely.[18]

There were various reasons for the distress of the ERM. These included the rapid increase of interest rates following German policies, adopted to manage the country's unification. Other reasons had to do with divergent national monetary and fiscal policies, which led to sizeable budget deficits and high inflation, particularly in Great Britain and Italy. Other explanations find the deep origin of the crisis in the weak design of the ERM, in particular the elimination of capital controls in a fixed exchange rates regime, before national monetary policies converged. This made the Mechanism vulnerable to disruptive factors. Scholars also linked the above factors in an explanation based on coordination failures within the ERM, whereby national governments failed to coordinate their response to the mounting tensions, thus exacerbating strains (Buiter *et al.* 1998; Higgins 1993).

The ERM crisis seriously jeopardised European monetary unification, exposed its intrinsic weakness and had potentially serious consequences for international monetary and financial stability. However, the ERM recovered rather soon and did not jeopardise the introduction of the common currency. Thus, the crisis remained apparently an isolated episode attributed to unfortunate circumstances.

Policy mistakes apart, this crisis can be seen as a side effect of the European attempt to converge to a fixed exchange rate regime, on the way to monetary unification. Since European economies were divergent for years and to varying degrees used depreciation as a means for recovering competitiveness, the crisis could be seen as a false step along a virtuous path. No serious attention was given to the possibility that the crisis revealed real incompatibilities within the ERM economies that prompted national governments to follow divergent monetary and fiscal policies.

---

[18]The UK secured an opt-out from adopting the euro during the negotiations for the Maastricht Treaty. The British government committed itself to an approval by the Cabinet, the Parliament, and the electorate in a referendum before joining the Eurozone.

This is a problem that we shall meet again with in the discussion of the great contraction in Europe.

The period which includes the 1990s and goes up to the great contraction of the late 2000s was a period characterised by several financial crises. These reached often significant dimensions and had heavy consequences for the involved economies. None of these crises reached systemic significance though, however threatening and costly they were. They remained apparently isolated and separated from one another. What appears remarkable of this period was the ability of the world economy to isolate major financial tensions and smooth their effects, avoiding their degeneration into a general world crisis.

Major financial tensions had their origin outside the Union and only slightly affected the EU. The only crisis that originated in the EU was in a sense unconventional, since it broke out within a process of institutional transformation of the monetary system. Apart from this event, the EU did not even fuel external crises. It may thus appear that the EU experienced an unprecedented financial and economic stability and also enjoyed remarkable resilience to external crises. The initial events of the great contraction apparently validated this conclusion. Yet, the protraction of the crisis proved that such a conclusion would be premature.

"The inability to predict outliers implies the inability to predict the course of history..."

— Nassim Nicholas Taleb (*The Black Swan*, 2007, *p.* xx)

2

The International Crisis and its Origin

The international crisis started in the United States in 2007–2008. It is in that country that the first clear signs of financial distress and the risk coming from unsustainable financial and real bubbles were concentrated. The three decades preceding the crisis were a period of considerable financial innovation and restructuring of industry. The latter took often place through mergers and acquisitions (M&A), often led by financial and fiscal considerations. The US economy became a huge and dynamic financial machine that led to innovation, economic growth and the accumulation of financial and real bubbles.

This flow of events is much in line with the prediction of the Varieties of Capitalism (VoC) literature that maintains that radical innovation and change are typical of the Anglo-Saxon economic system, as much as economic and financial instability is. Financial fervor and greed corresponded to Hyman Minsky's (1974, 1992) explanation of financial crises. Compared to this, the continental European capitalism is a system of incremental innovation and financial and economic prudence.

The world economy continued to expand at the remarkable rate of 3–4% during the last decade. Since 2007, on the contrary, the situation of most developed economies of the West went through a "great contraction" (Rogoff 2011; Stiglitz 2010). The very complexity of the present situation lies in the fact that contraction goes hand in hand with problems and perspectives which are deeply different, although not independent of one another, in diverse countries. In particular, it is necessary to distinguish between the situation of the United States (Reinhart 2012; Reinhart and Rogoff 2011; Rodrik 2011; Stiglitz 2010) and that of a deeply integrated area sharing common institutions, such as the Eurozone.

The deep causes of the crisis go back in time and accumulated gradually. Understanding these causes is important to explain why a crisis which initially did not look particularly dangerous had such serious and lasting economic and social effects. In order to explain the reasons and the ways of the contagion of the US crisis in Europe, it is necessary to understand the underlying factors in the United States, the goals that the different actors pursued and the reasons why policies were either impotent or encouraged the mounting tensions.

The Eurozone was economically and institutionally more prudent and perhaps conservative through the entire period. However, the effects of the crisis were in part similar to those in the United States. However, the Eurozone added endogenous factors whose consequence was to diminish the resilience of national economies to external shocks and to generate asymmetric effects in different countries, even when the external shock was apparently largely symmetric. Common institutions and policies proved to be ineffective in counteracting these factors and events and often contributed to growing vulnerability.

This chapter presents and interprets the main events in the United States and the world economy in order to highlight the consequences for the Eurozone and its member countries, discussed in the following chapters.

2.1 Economies, Policies and the Crisis

The financial crisis was embedded in real problems and in particular in the inability of the dominant economy, the United States, to maintain a safe competitive advantage over emerging economies. Four processes contributed to the onset of the global financial and economic crisis in the United States. First, although the United States continued to be well placed in absolute terms, in relative terms their post-war advantage was greatly eroded. The United States faced increasing difficulties to keep up its competitive advantage vis-à-vis emerging countries: Japan and Western Europe initially, and subsequently, Brazil, Russia, India, China, South Africa (BRICS) and other emerging economies.

Second, deregulation was the solution that Anglo-Saxon countries identified and implemented to counteract the ailing competitive advantage. Together with international institutional innovation and liberalisation, the premises for the largely unregulated unfolding of financial globalisation were laid.

Third are sizeable and growing inequalities of different kinds that resulted from the former processes and policies. Governments tried to revitalise economies by favouring profits and financial rents in income distribution and wealth accumulation, thus supporting investment, financial depth and financial innovation. Inequalities contributed to slow down economic and social dynamism and shrink the domestic market.

Policies and politics constitute the fourth process leading to the crisis. While growing inequalities placed political and social pressure upon governments to find ways to support the traditional standard of living, particularly for the middle class, governments were also under pressure to support business in its fight for competitiveness. Public finances went consequently under pressure. One important consequence was the accumulation of "twin deficits" in the form of sizeable current account and budget deficits.

These four processes started a positive feedback loop that went from slowing productivity through deregulation, growing inequalities, to soft policies and soft budget constraints. Each of these elements in turn reinforced the others. Finances entered this process both because they were part of the relevant context in the form of financialisation of the economy and because they offered policy instruments to ease the above processes and their consequences.

The four processes gave rise to the financial crisis of 2008 and the great recession because of both the features of the US economy and the context of globalisation. The United States had the financially most intense and active economy among large economies, together with Great Britain.

The role of finances in the United States was outstanding in both quantitative terms and concerning the role of financial assets and financial variables in the production of national income and the governance of the economy (Palley 2013). The so-called FIRE sector (finance, insurance, and real estate) contribution to GDP increased from 13.6% in 1973 to 20.4% in 2007. In the same period, payment to capital compared to payment to labour rose from 41.5% to 51.8%. The financial sector share of the private sector corporate profits increased from 20.1% to 44.6% and the ratio of financial profit to non-financial profit increased substantially from early 1980s up to 2003 (Figure 2.1). The financial boom offered new opportunities for inflating the economy in order to maintain the traditional standard of living.

Globalisation provided the context in which finance developed and expanded its activities and took on new roles. Finance played an important role in responding to slowing productivity, contrasting the consequences of growing inequalities, financing economic expansion that deregulation was called to promote, and taking advantage of softening policies and budget constraints. In this way, globalisation contributed to introducing

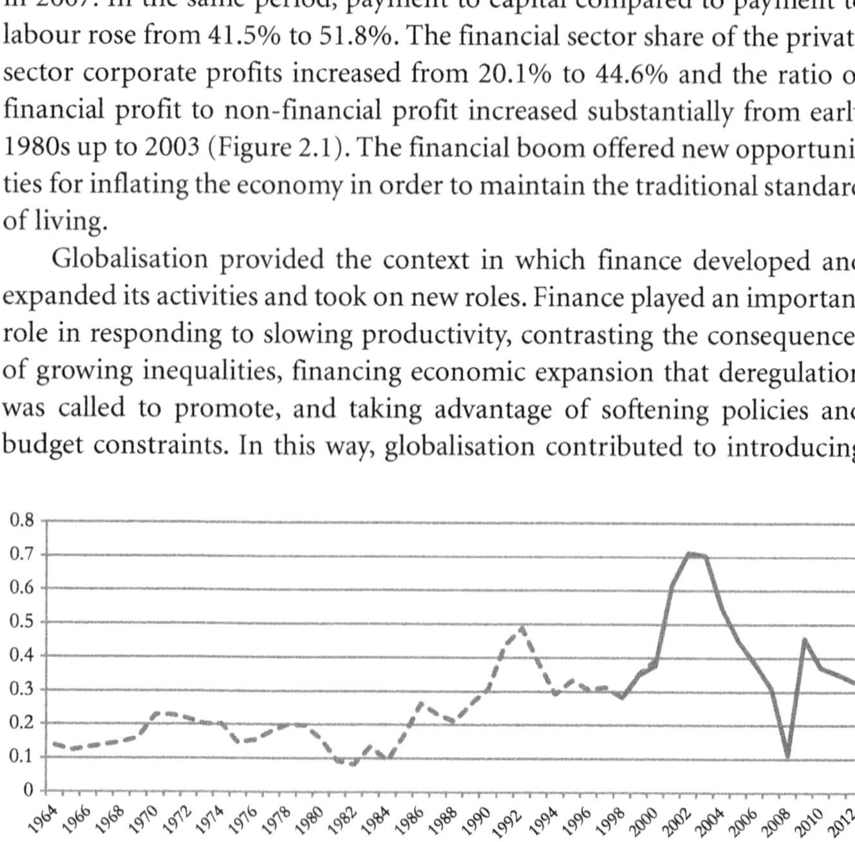

Figure 2.1. Ratio of Financial Profit to Non-Financial Profit in the United States 1964–2012.

Note: Corporate profits with inventory valuation adjustment and without capital consumption adjustment. SIC-based industry data for 1964–2000 (Standard Industrial Classification) use the 1987 SIC for data beginning in 1987 and the 1972 SIC for prior data. NAICS-based industry data for 1999–2012 use 2002 NAICS (North American Industry Classification System).

Source: Author's own figure based on calculations from Table B-91 of *Economic Report of the President* 2013.

an increasing wedge between the real processes and finance that was the basis of the crisis.

The EU economic strength is roughly on pair with that of the United States. The US and EU GDP are very close in absolute terms and each is around 20% of world GDP in Purchasing Power Party (PPP) terms. However, the European Union has just 65% of the GDP per capita of the United States. The EU has a much more open economy: 41% of world exports come from the EU as compared to 12% of the US in 2007, down from 54% and 15% respectively in 1990 (Crafts 2012). However, much of the exports of the EU member countries go to other EU member countries and can therefore be considered as internal exports. According to the European Commission, 37% of the overall EU-28 exports went outside the European Union in 2014 and 63% went to other EU member countries (own calculations based on EC 2015i). Disregarding internal exports, the EU accounts for 15% of the world's exports.

The Eurozone is smaller than the EU: it hosts 64% of the latter's population and 71% of its GDP. In per capita terms, the Eurozone GDP is therefore 10% higher than the EU average and is 71% compared to the United States. At the PPP, the Eurozone GDP corresponds to nearly 15% of the world GDP while in the case of the EU and the United States the corresponding figures are nearly 20% and nearly 21% respectively. The Eurozone also has a more open economy than the EU: the former's exports correspond to nearly 22% of its GDP, while the EU is slightly above 14%. The corresponding figure for the United States is close to 11%. In 2010, the Eurozone exports accounted for about 14% of global exports and imports (Crafts 2012; Trichet 2011).

The sheer dimension of both the EU and the Eurozone guarantee that the globalisation game vis-à-vis the United States is fair, provided that the member countries agree and strictly coordinate their decisions and actions. Since both partners want to uphold globalisation and be active in it, they must compromise on the national determination of economic and trade objectives and conditions. The ongoing, complex and uneasy negotiations over the TTIP (Transatlantic Trade and Investment Partnership) offer a good example of the delicate bargaining surrounding these delicate issues (Hamilton 2014).

2.2 Weakening Competitive Advantages and Market Shares

Among the four processes that contributed to the onset of the global financial and economic crisis in the United States, competitiveness bears probably the greatest economic strategic weight. In fact, competitiveness is fundamental for the international achievements of an economy and the strength of its external position. It is also important because it is directly linked to productivity. In a competitive context, productivity determines the rate of return to investments and therefore the rate of growth of an economy. Thus, competitiveness determines the prosperity of a country through static and dynamic components.

In general, when a country suffers because of weakening competitiveness, an open and integrated economy limits the policy instruments that can be used. Although this goes to the advantage of welfare thanks to the beneficial effect of foreign trade, accommodation to unfavourable competitiveness dynamics becomes more complex and difficult. In fact, the country cannot recover domestic competitiveness by increasing import prices through customs duties, import contingents, and the like.

An alternative for strengthening competitiveness is the manoeuvre of the exchange rate and in particular its depreciation. The positive outcome of depreciation depends on the Marshall-Lerner condition, i.e. upon the elasticity of exports and imports to the changes of the exchange rate. This solution meets two additional problems. First, the effect on exports is typically delayed. Second, the cost of imports increases, which may have a negative effect on domestic prices and real incomes. This effect, which worsens the terms of trade of the country *ceteris paribus*, i.e. the ratio of average export prices to average import prices, may worsen the trade balance depending on the composition of trade.

The higher cost of imports may be particularly harmful for investments. For an economy specialised into transforming imported raw and semi-finished materials and equipment, depreciation makes investment costlier. This effect is high when the imported component of investment goods and equipment is also high. Western European economies and Japan are in this situation, but not the United States.

The third policy instrument for recovering competitiveness consists of decreasing internal prices in order to decrease the cost of production.

A country can follow two roads for decreasing domestic prices. First, it can invest in order to improve productivity or move to more favourable specialisations, typically with higher skill levels and quality content. Or, second, the country can decrease wages, taxes and public expenditure. While the former path requires innovation and long-term strategies, the latter makes sense in the case of export-led strategies or in countries that are part of an incomplete economic and currency union, as we shall see.

However, decreasing wages and public expenditure shrink the domestic market, unless exports increase by a greater magnitude. This effect may be sizeable in a relatively large economy in which the domestic market is more important, often much more important than exports to foreign markets. Moreover, the decrease of taxation would be economically beneficial as tax cuts advantage low income recipients, who typically have a higher consumption propensity and tend to buy local product.

It is difficult to define precisely a composite concept like competitiveness (Durand and Giorno 1987). Competitiveness is generally used in a comparative sense to define and analyse the macroeconomic performance of a country, with particular concern for international trade. Competitiveness depends upon various factors. It depends upon relative prices and natural resources endowment, but in economically developed countries it depends most of all upon qualitative factors. These are in particular technical innovation, the quality of the products in which the country is specialised and other aspects linked to quality, such as customer care and after-sale services. Competitiveness is also directly linked to productivity levels and their growth. Productivity may lead to more exports, but it may also improve the terms of trade of a country via appreciation of the currency. The overall effect on current accounts depends then on the Marshall-Lerner condition, i.e. on the elasticity of exports and imports.

Many of the above factors are difficult to measure. For this reason, competitiveness is often measured by comparing levels and changes of international costs or price differentials. These measures of competitiveness are certainly more precise, but unfortunately disregard factors that are fundamental in explaining the overall competitiveness of an economy. This is particularly important in the long run, when qualitative and institutional factors may change remarkably and thus significantly influence competitiveness.

Different sources agree that innovation is the most strategic factor of competitiveness in an open and integrated world.[19] There is also general agreement that competitiveness derives from investment in research and development (R&D) and innovation. According to Furman *et al.* (2002), there is an important difference between R&D activity and the development and commercialisation of radically new technologies ("new-to-the-world"). While the former takes place in many countries, the latter has been concentrated in a few countries, among which the United States occupies a prominent place.

During the 1970s and the early 1980s, the United States and Switzerland occupied an outstanding position among developed economies in per capita patenting rate. Since then, other countries have converged in measured innovative capacity to the position occupied by the United States and Switzerland. The most notable cases include Japan, Sweden, Denmark, Finland and Germany, but not Great Britain and France. This pattern is the outcome of convergence in the level of resources devoted to R&D activity, the increase in human capital and in particular in FTE S&E (full-time equivalent science and engineering), and improvement in IP (intellectual property) protection and openness. Thus, convergence was due primarily to convergence of fundamental factors of innovation.

Another index that tries to capture the complex and multidimensional nature of innovation is the Global Innovation Index. Different rankings apparently offer a rather consistent picture: the United States is consistently among the top innovators and leads in innovation quality indicators: its competitiveness is consequently high. Yet the country is not at the top and in some critical indicators (e.g. the level of tertiary graduates in science and engineering) its position is weak. Its global competitors, including Germany, China and Russia, all improved their position better than the

[19] In general terms, innovation is the translation of an idea or an invention into a process, a good or a service that creates value for individuals or the society. There are different types of innovation that are important for the economy, including product and process, market, technological, institutional, organisational innovation. There is a growing agreement that innovation depends more and more upon the general context or ecosystem, including a multitude of factors of different nature and their interplay, the governance of innovation processes and social variables. See HLG (2013, 2014).

United States.[20] In the long run, this may jeopardise the United States' leadership in innovation and weaken its competitiveness.

One indicator of weaker competitiveness is the decrease of a country's share in world exports. The US share decreased dramatically since the 1990s, raising concerns over the growth of productivity in the US export sector compared to that of foreign competitors selling similar products.[21] However, and although the decline of relative productivity may have played a role in the early 2000s, there is little evidence of a broad-based decline of competitiveness over the longer term (Mandel 2012). Indeed, industry-level trade data show that the drop in export share was due to the decreased share of US GDP in global output and of the products traded internationally.

---

[20] "The progress of China and the Russian Federation in the rankings is among the most notable of all countries; China's ranking is now comparable to that of many high income economies. ... China ranks 2nd in innovation efficiency in 2014 on a global basis and is improving steadily along many dimensions of the GII. The country enjoys an impressive 2nd position in the Knowledge and technology outputs pillar and shows decent improvements in the Creative outputs pillar, ranking 1st in Creative goods exports. However, there is room for significant improvement in the Institutions pillar" (GII 2014, p. 12). "Since 1995, R&D spending in China has increased at a stunning annual rate of nearly 19% and in 2010 reached a huge US$178 billion PPP13 — the second largest R&D spending rate worldwide and almost double the rate of a basket of comparator countries. The success of this investment supports the arguments of the Beijing Consensus and the notion that innovation and technology has supported 'super-fast change in some sectors'" (GII 2014, p. 119).

[21] According to Husted and Nishioka (2013), who use data from the United Nation's Commodity Trade Statistics Database, the world market export shares of the United States decreased from approximately 25% at the end of the 1940s to 12–13% by the mid-1970s. This share varied little until 2000, but decreased rapidly afterwards, to reach 8% by the beginning of the crisis. According to Mandel (2012), the US share of global exports of goods was fairly stable at a level of roughly 12% between 1984 and 1999. Then, the share dropped by 3.5% between 2000 and 2010. This fall was not limited to merchandise exports. Services fell even more, from about 25% in 2000 to somewhat more than 5% in 2004, after which it slightly recovered. Since the dynamics of the share of services in exports is remarkably similar to that of goods, a supposed shift from manufactured goods exports to services exports does not offer an explanation to the drop in the US export performance.

The changing composition of exports may still be the outcome of the inability to compete with foreign exporters. Virtually every broad sector of US exports registered a decrease of its market share over the period from 1984 to 2008, when the world export share of the United States decreased by 3.5% (Mandel 2012). However, one sector alone accounted for half of the decrease in the US export share over the entire period. This sector is machinery and transportation equipment, a sector that represents almost half of US exports. Within this sector, the drop was particularly striking in the case of office machines and computers, whose exports decreased from about a third of total world sales to just under one-tenth. Although much of the loss of export shares is due to the fall of prices of agricultural materials, an important item in US exports, the loss in the exports of machinery, transportation products, miscellaneous manufactures, and chemicals provides compelling evidence of a fall in US competitiveness in those sectors.

The general picture that the US economy offers is one of a loss of competitiveness up to the end of the 1980s, after which important recovery followed. The recovery appeared rather clearly in labour productivity and somewhat less in total factor productivity (TFP) (Table 2.1).[22] According to ERP (2014, p. 39), TFP increased by an annual average of 1.8% between 1953 and 1973. In the following two decades, between 1974 and 1995 the annual growth rate of TFP was a mere 0.4%. However, TFP

[22] Productivity is usually defined as efficiency in the use of an input in production, i.e. how much output is obtained through the use of a unit of a given input or set of inputs. The most common measure of single-factor productivity is labour productivity, which is generally considered as a reliable measure of productivity. Labour productivity is generally calculated by dividing total output by the number of workers or the number of hours worked. This makes calculation relatively simple. However, labour productivity is an incomplete measure of efficiency, since it depends, among other things, on the endowment of workers with other inputs, such as machines (Syverson 2011). Another measure is total factor productivity (TFP, or multifactor productivity). TFP aims at measuring the efficiency in the use of inputs and is calculated as the percentage increase in output that is not accounted for by changes in the volume of inputs of capital and labour. This makes TFP measurement difficult and submitted to uncertain results. However, in comparisons among countries, TFP has the advantage of not being distorted by national differences in the measurement of real output. See Isaksson (2007) on the determinants of TFP.

Table 2.1. Nonfarm Private Business Productivity Growth in the United States, Average Annual Growth.

	Multifactor Productivity[23]	Labour Productivity
1953–1962	1.5	2.6
1963–1972	1.9	2.8
1973–1982	−0.1	1.1
1983–1992	1.1	2.2
1993–2002	1.1	2.4
2003–2012	0.9	1.9

Source: ERP (2014), p. 184.

started to grow around late 1980s and the average annual growth rate between 1996 and 2012 was 1.1%.

However successful the US recovery of TFP was, other countries did better (Table 2.2). Although these data are not comparable with those just quoted for the US, they show that in particular China, but also India and, for selected periods, Russia, are emerging countries. The Eurozone performed better than the United States only in the first half of the 1990s. Thus the problem of weakening productivity was not limited to the United States, but was shared also by other developed countries to the advantage of emerging countries.

The overall picture is one of general convergence of productivity to the US level until the mid-1990s by emerging countries, Western European countries and Japan (Figure 2.2). After that period, US productivity recovered compared to Western European countries and Japan. However, the catching up of emerging countries and Russia continued.

Comparisons based on productivity per hour worked give a better relative picture of Western Europe compared to the United States. In fact, Western Europe decreased the number of working hours much more rapidly than the United States. This was particularly evident in Germany,

[23] Equivalent to TFP, reflecting technological change and organisational improvements of production.

Table 2.2. Total Factor Productivity Growth by Region, 1990–2013.[24]

	1990–1995	1996–2000	2001–2007	2008–2013
Eurozone	0.8	0.6	0.3	−0.7
EU 27	0.3	0.7	0.5	−0.7
USA	0.3	1.0	0.6	0.3
Japan	0.2	−0.3	0.7	0.1
China	3.8	−1.2	5.3	1.7
India	1.1	1.8	2.1	1.5
Russia, Central Asia and Southeast Europe and other CIS	−1.9	2.2	4.3	−0.5
World	0.6	0.5	1.4	0.2

Source: Author's own calculations based on The Conference Board Total Economy Database, Summary Statistics, 2014.

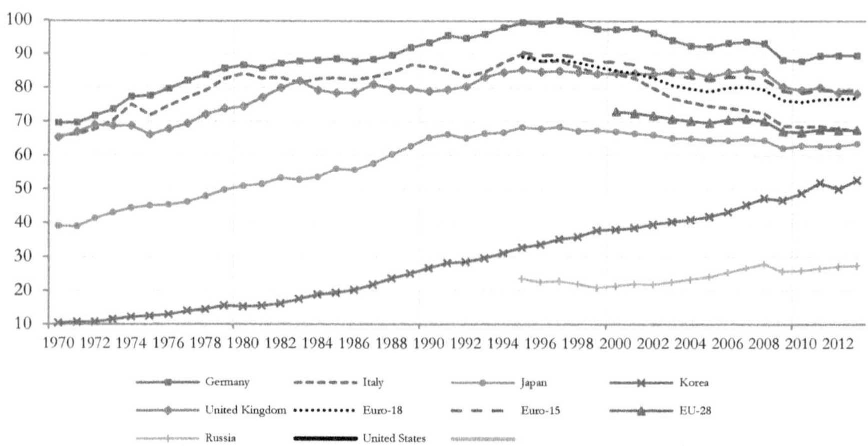

Figure 2.2. GDP Per Hour Worked, in US$ at Constant 2005 PPPs Prices, 1970–2013 (US = 100).
Source: Author's own calculations based on OECD data (http://stats.oecd.org).

France and other Northern European countries. The decrease continued in the 1990s and 2000s, albeit at a reduced speed. Also countries with

[24] This table is based on estimates for 120 countries. Total Factor Productivity Growth measures the growth of GDP over the combined contributions of total hours, workforce

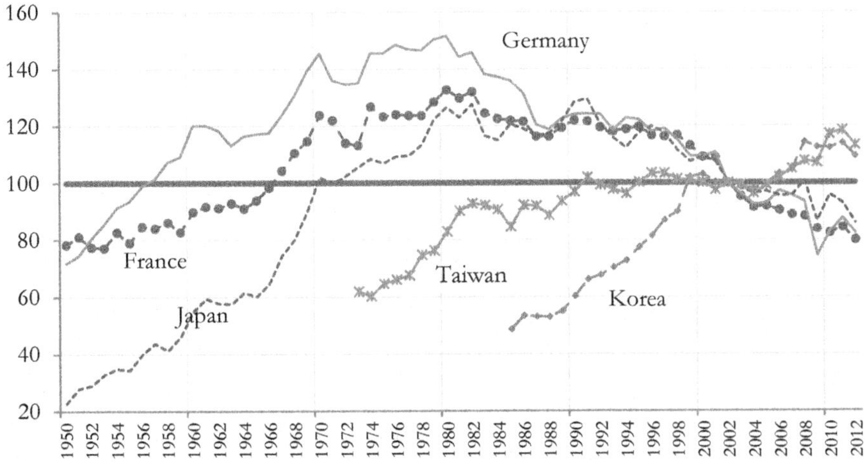

Figure 2.3. Comparison of Growth Rates of Output Per Person Employed in Manufacturing, 1950–2012, 2002 = 100 (US = 100).
Source: Author's own calculations calculation based on CB (2013).

emerging economies decreased the number of worked hours compared to the United States.[25] At the same time Western European countries increased employment better than the United States. As a consequence, comparisons based on the growth of output per person employed give a weaker picture of Western European countries compared to the United States (Figure 2.3). The recovery of US productivity is clear also in this case, although not comparable to that of emerging countries.

In Western economies, average long-term growth of labour productivity slowed down since 2000. At the same time, productivity accelerated in emerging and developing economies, thus reflecting the improving efficiency with which these economies use labour and capital (Chen *et al.* 2010).

The effect of different productivity dynamics, caused by different factors, explains at least in part the different competitiveness of national

---

skills, machinery and structures and IT capital. Growth rates are based on the difference in the log of the level of each variable.

[25] See The Conference Board database.

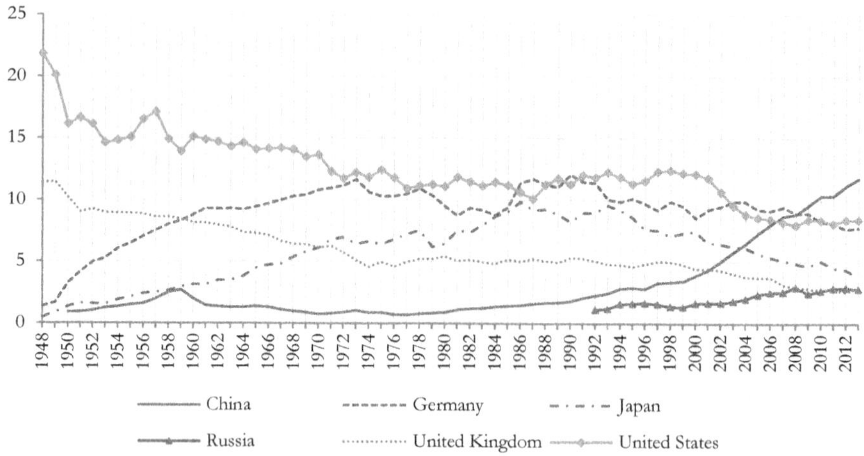

Figure 2.4. World Market Export Shares, 1948–2013.
Source: Author's own graph based on WTO database (http://stat.wto.org). Original data are in US dollars at current prices.

economies.[26] This in turn translates into changes in the exports share to the world market. In general, Western economies lost ground compared to emerging economies (Figure 2.4). The loss was particularly evident in the case of the United States up to the second part of the 1970s, after which the share stabilised. However, after 2000 the share decreased again quite rapidly until 2008. The United Kingdom followed a similar pattern.

Different was the behaviour of Germany and Japan. Germany's share increased rapidly until the first oil crisis in 1973, after which it stagnated,

[26] A shared explanation of what determines productivity, both at the firm and at the country level, is still pending. Productivity identifies in essence the variation of output that is not explained by observable and measurable inputs. Two sets of factors have been identified at the firm level: factors that operate primarily within businesses and thus are potentially under the control of management; and factors external to the firm and belong in the context and which influence production either in a direct or an indirect way (Syverson 2010, 2011). Within-business determinants include managerial practice/talent, higher-quality general labour and capital inputs, information technology and R&D, learning-by-doing, product innovation, firm structure decisions. Contextual determinants include productivity spillovers, competition, deregulation or proper regulation, flexible input markets. Yet many questions remain unanswered, including the role of demand and government policies.

albeit with annual fluctuations. After 1990, the German share started to decrease, except between 1993 and 2004 when it remained overall stable. Japan continued to increase its share until 1986. After having recovered this share in 1993, Japan also started to lose ground and so continues to do presently.

Quite different is the situation of emerging countries and of China in particular. The Chinese share of world exports started to increase around 1978, in coincidence with economic reforms and openness adopted in that country. After that year, the expansion accelerated and reached impressive speed particularly since the late 1990s. China has become the main world exporter since 2008.

2.3 Deregulation

Deregulation is the second process that contributed to the onset of the global financial and economic crisis in the United States. Deregulation was considered a necessary reform to make markets more efficient and to boost competition. It was strongly supported by a great host of academic analysis and publications, conferences and policy support by international organisations, the Organisation for Economic Cooperation and Development (OECD) and the World Bank in particular. Yet the results of the deregulatory movement and polices have been rather problematic.[27]

Deregulation proceeded together with a new set of regulations that led some scholars to theorise the development of "regulatory capitalism" (Levi-Faur 2005; Levi-Faur and Jordana 2005). The main feature of this economic system is a new relation between the market and the state, accompanied by new institutions, technologies, and instruments of regulation. Thus, what is usually labeled as the era of neoliberalism is in reality also the "golden era of regulation" (Levi-Faur and Jordana 2005, p. 6). Neoliberalism and regulation often proceed together, although their mutual relation is often uneasy and even blurred. Thus, although it is true that much deregulation took place, new regulation was also introduced, particularly on the initiative of powerful Western countries.

[27] Crew and Kleindorfer (2002) conclude that "[t]he final lesson that we draw is that the expectations for deregulation should be revised downwards drastically and that further deregulation should be undertaken with caution" (p. 21).

Such regulation, in some cases, introduced new forms of separation of markets (Loayza and Serven 2010).

Privatisation offers an excellent example (Dallago 1994). Privatisation was introduced particularly in the 1980s and 1990s in order to decrease the direct economic role of the state and foster competition, together with rising revenue for the state budget. Privatisation, particularly in non-competitive sectors such as natural monopolies, required the adoption of a great deal of new regulation and the establishment of new regulatory agencies (Parker 2002). Another important case is that of international economic relations. While globalisation was certainly based on deregulation, in the sense that national protective barriers were progressively dismantled, it required an entirely new and wide body of national and international regulation and new regulatory agencies, such as the World Trade Organization.

Studies have tried to assess the economic effect of regulatory policy. An OECD study (Parker and Kirkpatrick 2012) found that poorly designed regulation can have negative effects on economic activities and economic growth, although regulatory governance and the institutional framework may mitigate the damaging effects. However, it is important to highlight that quantitative evaluation of the economic effect is difficult and its results often partial or unclear. It is also important to consider that welfare enhancing effects may be difficult to quantify. Studies have also aimed at assessing the effect of regulation on finance (Kim *et al.* 2013)[28] and have evaluated the effects of considerable re-regulation of banking and financial markets that governments have implemented following the crisis (Smith 2014). Unfortunately, under the pressure of events these regulations have been inadequately prepared and poorly implemented. As a consequence, they may be ineffective in solving future systemic risk and in any case impose high compliance costs on banks, even on those which are too small to represent a systemic risk.

[28] Kim *et al.* (2013) use the financial and macroeconomic dataset of 132 countries to assess the effects of financial regulations and innovations on the global financial crisis. They show that the likelihood of a banking crisis is increased by financial innovation and decreased by restrictions on bank activities and entry requirements. The likelihood of a currency crisis is increased by capital regulation and government ownership of banks and is decreased by financial innovation.

Deregulation and financial innovation were implemented to counteract stagflation and the ailing competitiveness vis-à-vis emerging economies. They were based on the critique of post-Keynesian policies, particularly the critique to the use of the Phillips curve as a basis for policies, and on the idea of efficient markets. This approach clearly disregarded the risks that this could open for economies and overlooked the warning that Hyman Minsky (1992) raised with his financial instability hypothesis.

Financial innovation and deregulation played doubtful roles also in other senses. According to Rodrik (2011), deregulation of markets and activities and financial innovation ended the so-called Bretton Woods compromise between labour and capital. In fact, deregulation and financial innovation made it imperative to find ways to make financial resources continue to finance the economy. Financial resources are highly mobile and, if not restricted by regulation and other forms of institutional constraints, they can only be kept through higher returns to investment. This is not so for less mobile resources, in particular labour.

In this way, the growing difficulties that the United States and other developed Western countries, such as Great Britain, met in keeping pace with Japan and continental European economies first and emerging economies subsequently had important and permanent policy and social consequences. This outcome was in relation to the asymmetric mobility and power of financial vis-à-vis holders of human resources and was under the pressure of the so-called neoliberal economic ideology.

Thus deregulation policies and financial innovation turned out to decrease the strength of labour and support the distribution of income in favour of profit and rents, in order to support investment and foster financial markets and their liquidity. Indeed, this was the explicit aim of different governments, in particular Thatcher's government in Great Britain (1979–1990) and the Reagan administration in the United States (1981–1989). Four components of reforms and policies appear particularly important.

First was the idea that governments were too big and inefficient, since competition was powerless within their activities and governments and politicians were often corrupt. Big inefficient governments not only dramatically increased bureaucratic transaction costs of economic activity and transformed it into what was defined as the rent-seeking economy

(Krueger 1974; Tullock 1967).[29] They also distorted economic calculation and consequently investment decisions through taxation and different types of interference. Governments increased their size following the Great Depression in the inter-war period and in the postwar period through nationalisation, the provision of support to economic activity and employment, and the construction of the welfare system.

The main accusation levelled at this state of affairs was that resource allocation was bound to be inefficient and income would be lower than in a more market-friendly context. A predictable reaction, then, was the privatisation and welfare rationalisation and reduction in order to reduce rent-seeking opportunities and activate market forces. The room for private activity and the role of competition were increased and taxation was decreased. The latter was also an answer to mounting anti-tax movements and the belief that high taxation caused high prices, distorted economic calculation and decision making and led to weaker competitiveness.

Second was the mainstream view that only perfectly flexible prices can adjust distorted economies and stimulate economic actors (enterprises, workers, savers, consumers, financial organisations) to take the decisions and implement the actions that lead to efficiency and competitiveness. The liberalisation of prices included three fundamental steps: flexible exchange rates after the definitive disruption of the gold exchange standard in 1973, free unregulated prices also through anti-monopolistic policies, and wage liberalisation.

---

[29] Gordon Tullock (1967) was the first to develop the concept and Anne Krueger (1974) created the expression of rent-seeking (see also Tullock 1993). By rent-seeking, it is meant the use of resources on political lobbying and the manipulation of regulatory agencies for economic advantages, often in the form of a market monopoly, and to increase one's share of existing wealth. This leads to poor allocation of resources and additional costs and disadvantages imposed upon competitors. Consequences are decreased wealth creation and lost government revenue, weaker incentives to undertaking production, and economic decline. Income inequality is usually increased, since it is typically wealthy agents who engage in rent-seeking as it enables them to protect their wealth from expropriation (Dabla-Norris and Wade 2001). Bertrand *et al.* (2014) provide evidence that lobbyists in the US Federal lobbying process provide primarily special interests access to politicians, although they also provide some issue-specific information to members of Congress.

Third, free prices go together with free and efficient markets. Free markets can only exist if no monopoly power is around, and consequently competition is unchecked and prices are flexible, and if the tax system is non-distortionary. As a matter of fact, anti-monopolistic policies proved to be asymmetric. Anti-labour policies and action were more determinate and effective than anti-monopolistic policies in the business sector. In the United States and Great Britain, policies and government action reached their climax with spectacular conflicts between labour and the government, particularly in the cases of air controllers in the United States in 1981 and miners in Great Britain in 1984–1985. Events less impressive in the form, yet similar in the outcome took place also in other countries, such as Italy in the mid-1980s.

After these events, the strength of organised labour and its ability to influence incomes was severely limited. The decreasing unionisation of workers also played a role. Change of industrial policies was also important, as when previously important and supported sectors, such as mining and ship-building in Great Britain, were abandoned and relentlessly shrank. Anti-monopolistic policies were more episodic, less wide-reaching and less permanent in their outcome.

This is not to say that striking events were absent. Such was, for instance, the use of the Sherman Act by the Reagan administration in 1982 to break up AT&T into one long-distance company and seven regional companies. However, in the following years the pace of M&A accelerated, particularly in the 1990s. In spite of some governmental activism in controlling monopolistic practices, outcomes were overall modest. The well-publicised charge of the US Justice Department against Microsoft in 2000 ended with the government dropping the case and settling with Microsoft, which in turn promised to cease the practices that led the government to accuse the company.

M&A had a boom in the 1980s, and the 1990s simultaneously with a new style of corporate governance (Holmstrom and Kaplan 2001; Lazonick and O'Sullivan 2000; Shleifer and Vishny 1997; Zingales 2008). In the 1980s, M&A led to deep and far-reaching restructuring of companies. Many of these activities were hostile and made use of leverage. Later in the 1980s and the following decade, while leverage and hostility declined, other corporate governance mechanisms became important, such as executive stock options, boards of directors' activism, and shareholder value. Deregulation was the moving force behind these developments, together with the new information and communications technologies.

Capital markets increased in size and power and changed structure. Institutional investors became the most dynamic and mobile component. These changes made capital markets interested in acquiring companies where actual and potential performance diverged via takeovers and leveraged buyouts. This obliged managers to pursue shareholder value through restructuring their enterprise, while they themselves gained from this, thanks to stock options and similar devices. A short-run perspective became dominant in the working of markets. However, under these circumstances, firms with good corporate governance had sizeable advantages in terms of lower cost of equity and lower cost of debt capital, depending on the legal, political and economic features of the country (Zhu 2014).

Tax systems were reformed to make markets more efficient and support the development of financial markets. In general, taxation was transferred from incomes to goods, i.e. from direct to indirect taxation. Moreover, taxation of income became less progressive, thus more favourable to business and highly skilled workers and professionals. In open and integrated economies, cheaper labour and more liquid financial markets were seen as the key devices to make economies more competitive.

In the deregulation perspective, international competition required that inputs, in particular labour, were made cheaper and mobile resources are attracted to and remain with national companies (Alvaredo *et al.* 2013).[30] Taxation on profit was substantially decreased and M&A were made easier and more convenient: taxes were paid on the consolidated budgets, so it was convenient for profitable businesses to merge with or acquire loss-making businesses. These moves supported innovation (Bena and Li 2014) and improved the overall economic situation, but weakened the domestic market and dramatically increased the size and role of

[30] According to the OECD, there are only slight differences between resilient and vulnerable countries in the taxation of incomes (top statutory personal income tax rate and top marginal tax rates for employees). See OECD (2014h).

finance and the financial sector. The accumulation of financial bubbles had now its own instruments.

Fourth, policies relied on faith in effectively self-regulating markets and the existence of trickle-down effects, whereby the success and the wealth of those on top would descend through market processes to those at the bottom. Yet unregulated markets polarised the situation further. Unregulated industrial globalisation made unskilled labour redundant in developed countries through delocalisation (Rodrik 1996), while highly skilled labour became more mobile. Unregulated financial globalisation brought to the forefront the dramatic need to keep financial resources at home and attract new ones. The remuneration of highly skilled workers and profit from investment increased considerably (Piketty 2014). While corporate investment (private nonresidential fixed investment) decreased as a share of GDP, corporate profits after tax increased, particularly since mid-1990s and continued to do so even in the years of the crisis, with the exception of 2008 (Figure 2.5).

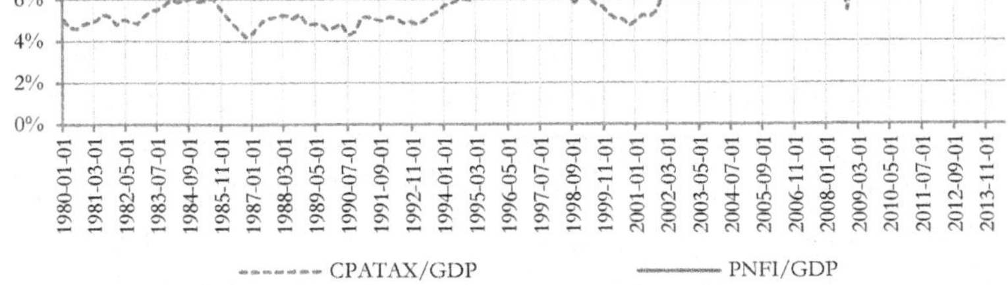

Figure 2.5. Corporate Profit and Investments Share of GDP in the United States, 1980–2014.

Note: CPATAX = Corporate Profits after Tax with Inventory Valuation Adjustment (IVA) and Capital Consumption Adjustment (CCAdj).

PNFI = Private Nonresidential Fixed Investment.

Source: Author's own graph based on US Bureau of Economic Analysis data (FRED database of the Federal Reserve Bank of St. Louis).

These resources were scarce both because they were in high demand and because they were mobile and attracted by the possibility to get higher remuneration elsewhere. Another important reason why highly skilled human resources are scarce is that their production process is lengthy. Firms and anti-monopoly policies had to take account of this transformation (Rajan and Zingales 2001b).

In conditions of high mobility of financial resources and highly skilled workers and professionals, their domestic remuneration had to be in line with their international remuneration, net of the transaction costs on their mobility. This is problematic, particularly for less developed countries. Yet, even in developed and rich countries, globalisation and international competition for scarce and mobile resources led to significant advantages for the owners of these resources in a relatively short period of time. Top managers and financial institutions were among the big winners.

Deregulation extended also to the international arena. Globalisation required that old regulation was replaced by a different, indirect type of regulation under the coordination of international organisations. However, this deregulation was asymmetric and its lack of governance was recognised as one of the main problems of the past decades, particularly in the case of financial globalisation (Stiglitz 2002, 2006). As a consequence of largely unregulated financial globalisation, enormous amounts of short-term financial resources moved rapidly among activities and countries and generated waves of herd behaviour of financial investors and markets.

The high mobility of financial resources required internationally coordinated macroeconomic policies. The freedom and role of national economies weakened as a consequence. Unregulated markets led to the polarisation of opportunities and remunerations, which in turn fostered growing inequalities. Such polarisation created a relatively large class of high-income people, who possessed important financial resources that they wanted to invest in lucrative uses, often short term ones. This further fostered inequalities and created further opportunities for financial bubbles.

2.4 Inequalities

A sizeable increase of inequalities is the third process that contributed to the onset of the global financial and economic crisis in the United States

(Atkinson *et al.* 2011; OECD 2011a; OECD 2015b; Piketty 2014; Rajan 2010; Stiglitz 2012; Tachibanaki 2005).[31] Inequalities increased in the distribution of income, in wealth and in opportunities, particularly in the form of decreasing social and intergenerational mobility.

Two components of inequalities in income distribution appear important. One is that the share of labour in the distribution of income decreased in the United States and in most European countries, with the partial exception of the Scandinavian countries. The other component is that distribution among income recipients polarised.

Wages in the United States lost ground compared to labour productivity since early 1970s (Figure 2.6). However, up to the first oil crisis in 1973, productivity gains translated also into increases in labour compensation. Since then, however, income inequality widened significantly: "productivity growth has not translated into commensurate growth in labour compensation, and income inequality has increased markedly" (ERP 2014, p. 189).[32] As a consequence, the share of labour in the distribution of income decreased consistently.

---

[31] Many types of inequality exist and have important economic, social and political consequences. There are various explanations in economic theories. The most typical types of inequality considered in economics are inequalities of income, wealth, employment, consumption and opportunities. Inequality can be considered and measured in different ways, including interpersonal, interfactorial, intergenerational, intersectoral, international, interregional ways. In the rest of this book that follows, the focus will be on those concepts of inequality that are particularly useful to highlight differences among countries and groups of countries, including inequalities in income, employment and consumption, most typically in international and interfactorial perspectives.

[32] According to ERP (2014, pp. 189–190), real output per hour was 99% higher at the end of 1972 than it was in 1947. In the same period, real average hourly earnings (GDP deflator) increase somewhat less, by 73%. Since the early 1970s and up to the end of September 2013, the divergence between labour productivity and average hourly earnings accelerated: while the former (real output per hour) was 107% higher than at the end of 1972, average hourly earnings increased by a mere 31%. There were some differences in the dynamics of divergence. Real output per hour exceeded the average annual growth rate in hourly earnings for private production and nonsupervisory workers by 0.4%. This difference accelerated up to the years 1983–1992, when it was 1.8%. Then it decreased to 0.5% in the following decade (1993–2002), but increased again to 1.1% in the next years. Overall, from 1973 through 2012, labour productivity grew 1.4% faster than earnings (ERP 2014, p. 191).

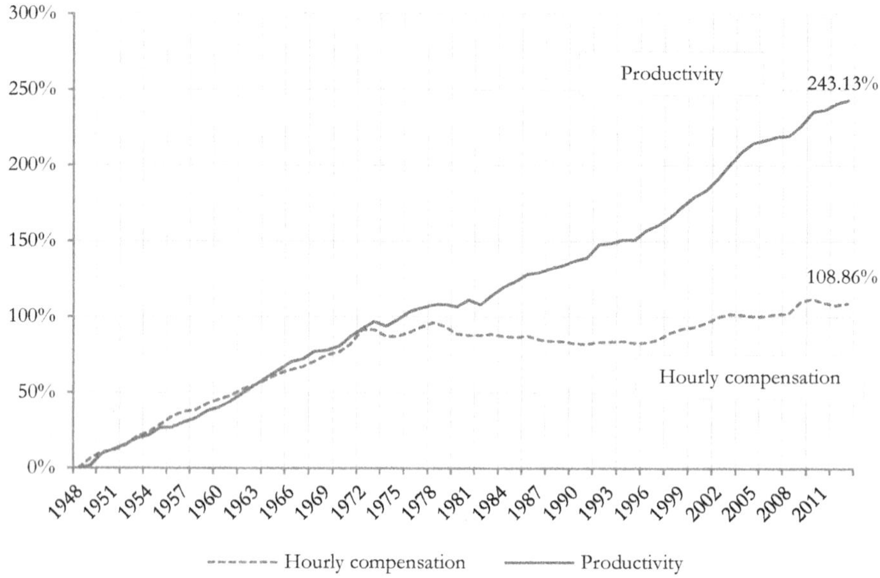

Figure 2.6. Growth in Productivity and Hourly Compensation in the United States, 1948–2013.

Note: Data are for average hourly compensation of production/nonsupervisory workers in the private sector and net productivity of the total economy. "Net productivity" is the growth of output of goods and services minus depreciation per hour worked.

Source: EPI analysis of data from the BEA and BLS (Bivens and Mishel 2015).

Over the period since late 1960s, trends have disadvantaged in relative terms all household quintiles except the top quintile (Figure 2.7) (see also Haskel *et al.* 2012; Lemieux 2008; Piketty 2014; Piketty and Saez 2003). While all quintiles increased their income, the increase in the top quintile was much greater. Between 1979 and 2007, after-tax income (after federal taxes have been deducted and government transfers paid) grew by just 18% for the bottom 20% of households (CBO 2011). In the same period, the growth was 275% for the top 1% and 65% for the remaining 19% of the top quintile. For the remaining 60%, the growth was somewhat less than 40%. As a consequence, the share of after-tax income of the top quintile increased from less than 44% in 1967 to more than 51% in 2013. Most of this increase went to the top 1%. All other income groups decreased their shares by 2–3%.

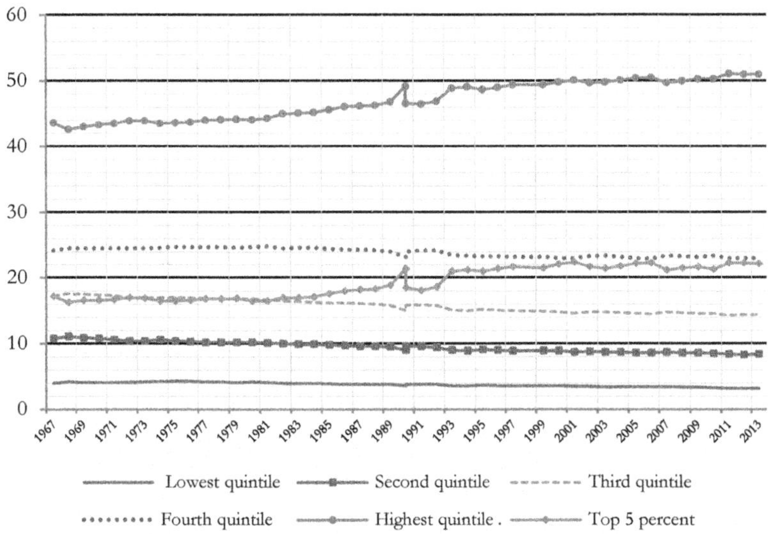

Figure 2.7. Shares of Household Income of Quintiles in the United States, 1967–2013.
Source: Author's own graph based on USCB (2013).

After-tax inequalities were the consequence of greater disparities in market, before-tax incomes and the inability of the tax and transfer systems to compensate for those disparities. Indeed, according to CBO (2011), the equalising effect of federal taxes and transfers was larger in 1979 than in 2007. While overall they reduced the dispersion of income by 20%, the share of transfer payments to the lowest-income households declined and the overall average federal tax rate fell. At the same time, before-tax income distributions became more unequal in two senses. First, business income and capital gains grew faster than labour income. Second, disparities widened also within each source of market income, with top incomes both from capital and labour growing more than incomes at the bottom.

The overall inequality in the distribution of income in the United States became quite strong. The Gini coefficient increased continuously from 0.39 in 1968 to 0.48 in 2003 (Figure 2.8). This was the effect of the substantial increase of top incomes: according to data of the US Census Bureau (USCB 2013), the share of the top household decile over

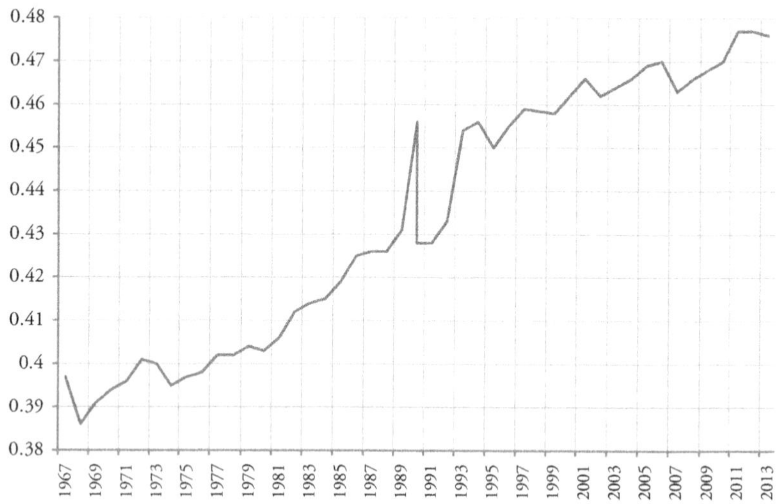

Figure 2.8. Gini Index in the United States, 1967–2013.
Source: Author's own graph based on USCB (2013).

the bottom 10% was 8.5 times in the mid-1970s and increased to 12 times by 2013. Corresponding figures for the ratio between the top quintile to the bottom one were 3.8 in 1968 and more than 5 in 2013. By 2007, on the eve of the crisis, inequalities were substantially higher than two or three decades earlier and impressively similar to the disparities existing in 1928 (Piketty 2014; Piketty and Saez 2006; Reich 2010).

There are many factors at play behind growing income inequalities. Chen *et al.* (2013) find that technological progress is a key driver behind the upward trend of earnings inequality, mainly through raising wage dispersion. Economic globalisation, in terms of both rapidly rising trade and financial integration, appears overall distributionally neutral once other factors, in particular changes in policies and institutions, are controlled for. Regulatory reforms that aimed at promoting growth and productivity appeared to exert contrasting effects: they tended to close the gap between employed and non-employed by increasing job opportunities, yet at the same time, they contributed to greater wage inequality. Finally, the growth in the supply of skilled workers is an important equalising factor contributing not only to reduce wage dispersion among workers but also to higher employment rates.

The situation with wealth is similar to that of incomes. Wealth of top owners increased because top capital and labour incomes increased and because inheritance taxation became more lax. Wealth was traditionally more concentrated in Europe than in the United States. This situation continued until around 1960, when wealth concentration became greater in the United States than in Europe (Piketty 2014). Wealth of top owners increased for the entire 19th century up to the First World War. Then it decreased: in the United States this went on until the Second World War, and then stagnated up to 1970. In Europe, wealth concentration decreased rather dramatically for this entire period. After 1970, wealth inequality (measured by the top decile and percentile in total wealth) started to rise again in both the United States and Europe.

Wealth concentration in the United States during the last century therefore had a U-shape. Saez and Zucman (2014) study the distribution of household wealth since 1913 and find that it fell from 1929 to 1978. It was high in the beginning of the 20th century and continuously increased since the end of the 1970s. The rise in wealth inequality was entirely due to the top 0.1%: it was 7% in 1979 and grew to 22% in 2012, thus reaching a level that was almost as high as it was before the start of the Great Depression in 1929. The situation of the bottom 90% was the reverse: this wealth share increased up to the mid-1980s and then steadily declined. With the crisis, wealth concentration increased further, this time mainly because of the dramatic fall of the wealth of the middle class (Wolff 2014).

The polarisation of opportunities increased further the growth of income and wealth disparities. It is particularly the intergenerational investment in human capital that suffered most. In the United States, higher returns to schooling were associated with lower intergenerational earnings mobility, since the lower part of the middle class found increasingly difficult to finance their children in college.

The inequalities of income and wealth explain in part the inequalities of opportunities. Evidence is growing that greater economic inequality in the present increases the probability that family background will become the determining factor of the economic achievements of young generations in the future. Work and merit are a secondary factor and unable to support intergenerational earnings mobility. However, the relation between these factors is quite complex and it is necessary to go deeply into the subject and refine the analysis of its components before reaching hard conclusions (Hout 2015).

The returns to education were very high in the United States, the highest among Western countries. This feature interacted with the increasing gap in college completion between children from low- and high-income families, which increased significantly during the last two to three decades. Intergenerational earning mobility was thus very low in the United States (Corak 2013). These two occurrences jointly caused inequality of opportunities to become greater and made it more difficult to compete successfully with countries having a larger younger population and high intergenerational mobility, such as China and other emerging economies.

Another important aspect was that growing income inequality had a clear negative effect on social mobility and was inversely related to innovation (Corak 2013; Wilkinson and Pickett 2009). In this way, inequality hampers economic growth and development and weakens the competitiveness of economies, in a self-defeating set of events. Changes and policies intended to foster Western competitiveness led to developments that weakened competitiveness.

Growing inequalities had two serious consequences, particularly important in rich democratic countries. First, the economically and politically most sensitive consequence of growing inequalities was the relative decline of the economic well-being of the middle class.[33] Since it is the median voter who decides the outcome of elections, governments have strong political reasons to be worried that a weakening middle class causes a serious political problem. Since in the United States, governments and

[33] Baird (2014) defines the middle class as including the middle three quintiles and considers how its income distribution changed in the years 1974–2010 in the United States. She finds that the median income has remained roughly stable around US$30,000. However, the combined effect of the decline of the bottom range of the middle class over the first half of the period, and the slow but steady increase of the upper income range of the middle class resulted in a clear widening of the range of income within the middle of the income distribution. The share between the income of those at the top of the middle class and those at the bottom increased from 3 times in 1974 to nearly six times in 2010. The growth in earnings inequality among the middle class outstripped the growth of inequality among the population as a whole: the Gini coefficient grew by 50% (from .16 to .24) among the middle class, while it grew by 30% (from .37 to .48) among the entire population.

most citizens are against using taxation and the welfare system to support the middle class, something different had to be found.

Second and despite some contrary view and scant evidence, much of the empirical work shows that high-income people and households save a larger fraction of their income.[34] Thus, stagnation of incomes and decreasing opportunities of the social groups with higher propensity to consumption limit the size and the expansion of markets. To be sure, consumption inequality rose more slowly and less than income inequality in recent decades. Consumers tend to keep their consumption habits unchanged until they perceive that they have become permanently poorer: when a wealth effect takes over, consequences for consumption tend to become permanent (Jappelli and Pistaferri 2009; Krueger and Perri 2012).

At the same time, policies can convince relatively impoverished middle class people to spend beyond their means in order to expand the market. An alternative to keep demand up would be public expenditure and the accumulation of public debt or increasing exports, both of which are rather difficult in the United States. In the years before the crisis, the propensity to consume increased and the propensity to save decreased in most countries.[35] These trends were particularly strong in the United States.

---

[34] Dynan *et al.* (2004) find a strong positive relationship between saving rates and lifetime income by applying empirical analytical methods to the Panel Study of Income Dynamics, the Survey of Consumer Finances, and the Consumer Expenditure Survey in the United States. They also find a weaker but still positive relationship between the marginal propensity to save and lifetime income. However, Jappelli and Pistaferri (2013) use responses to survey questions in the 2010 Italian Survey of Household Income and Wealth to ask a sample of consumers how much of an unexpected transitory income change they would consume. They find that the average marginal propensity to consume is 48%. However, the marginal propensity decreases rapidly with the affluence of consumers: while it is 65% among the poorest, it is around 30% for the richest households.

[35] This is due to different reasons, happens in different ways and has different consequences through countries. IMF (2008) finds that the influence of house prices on household spending stems mainly from housing's role as collateral. This effect is particularly high in the United States and much lower in Italy and France. Two IMF economists, Bayoumi and Edison (2002) estimate panel regressions of the wealth effect on consumption of both equity and housing wealth. They distinguish countries by type of financial system and examine trends in wealth effects over time. They find that the impact of a $1 increase in housing wealth on consumption is higher than the equivalent increase in equity wealth,

Growing and sizeable disparities contributed to shrink the domestic market and put political and social pressure upon finding ways to support the traditional standard of living, particularly for the middle class (Rajan 2010; Kumhof and Rancière 2010).[36] In a sense, booming inequalities represent the most dramatic structural change that took place in the last three decades in Western countries and created, together with failing competitiveness and deregulation, the premise for the crisis. Jobless recoveries in the 1990s magnified political and policy problems. When reinforced by politics and policies, the crisis became inevitable.

2.5 Politics and Policies

Politics and policies are the fourth process contributing to the global financial and economic crisis in the United States. In fact, the events discussed above would not have been sufficient to increase inequalities, had institutions, policies and politics not provided the ground for that outcome in both the United States (Krugman 2009, Rajan 2010) and elsewhere (Wilkinson and Pickett 2009). They did this through weakening governments and trade unions, changes in taxes and benefits, and implementing policies used to fight stagflation in the 1970s and, more generally, based on the idea of efficient markets. All this led to the end of the post-war capital-labour bargain that was at the basis of the post-war economic expansion (Reich 2007). As a consequence, the remuneration of financial organisations and large industrial organisations and their managers boomed.

---

countries with market-based financial systems have larger effects from changes in equity wealth than those with bank-based financial systems, and that the size of the wealth effects appears to be rising over time. This later effect in their view is probably reflecting financial deregulation.

[36] Brueckner and Lederman (2015) estimate the effect of income inequality on real GDP per capita using a panel of 104 countries during the period 1970–2010. They find that, on average and in more developed countries, income inequality has a significant negative effect on GDP per capita growth and on the long-run level of GDP per capita. To be sure, other authors challenge this view and maintain that there is no evidence of a general relationship between rising inequality and financial crisis through credit boom. See e.g. Bordo and Meissner (2012). For a review, see van Treeck and Sturn 2012.

Deeper and wider globalisation, with overall softer financial discipline of national economies, dramatically changed the relationship between the economy and policies in Western countries. This gave politics and policies a new role. The international coordination of monetary policies opened another problem for the effectiveness of economic governance. Although this is a necessity in a deeply integrated world, nevertheless it decreased the freedom of national monetary policies to manage domestic affairs. The responsibility for macroeconomic adjustment was consequently shifted to fiscal policies and the responsibility for managing and upgrading competitiveness was entrusted to microeconomic policies and reforms. However, fiscal policies were often conservative, because of the level of public debts and the conservative attitude of international organisations under the influence of the Washington Consensus.

Much of the reaction to the shrinking competitive advantage of the West thus had to come from microeconomic policies and from institutional reforms aimed at revitalising the working of markets. Prominent among these were privatisation, liberalisation and anti-monopolistic policies, which — together with macroeconomic stabilisation and other policy instruments — came to be known as the Washington Consensus.

One problem with microeconomic policies is that institutions underlying them — both formal and informal institutions — are generally slow to change. As a consequence, microeconomic policies have effects in the long run and often unforeseen effects. Together with macroeconomic adjustment, microeconomic policies and reforms usually meet social opposition and even more effective opposition by powerful interest groups which feel that they are harmed by such policies and reforms.

Booming inequalities significantly changed the economic and social landscape and created a critical political problem for policymakers. The middle class is the backbone of any democratic government in the West. Its support gives political stability to economic policies. Yet increasing inequalities weakened and split the middle class. Highly skilled workers and professionals in growing economic sectors and owners of capital saw their income increase remarkably. At the same time, employees in stagnating sectors and the public sector lost out on such gains and some of them remained unemployed and impoverished. Due to accelerated technical progress, jobless recoveries since the early 1990s made the split of the middle class stable. The high probability of the crisis was thus embedded in the most dramatic structural changes that took place in the last three decades. Politics and policies in the decade before the crisis transformed what was highly probable into an inevitable occurrence.

Although people at the bottom of the distributive scale lost much ground during the last three decades, it was the middle class which went through the most unfavourable changes. The middle class suffered more through the loss of high salaries and related fringe benefits than through the loss of jobs. Indeed, although it is possible to speak of jobless recoveries in the short-medium run (Schreft *et al.* 2005), perhaps more outstanding in the long run is that new jobs were often less well paid and of lower quality than old jobs (Reich 2010).

Jobless recoveries appeared during the last twenty years, the first one being the recovery that followed the 1990–1991 recession: output grew rapidly, while jobs lagged behind. While generous welfare systems made continental European countries politically and socially more resilient to unemployment, the lack of a strong safety net for the unemployed in the United States created a strong case for policy intervention. A relevant political issue is that the middle class is usually meant to include the large part of the US population, with the exception of the poor and the top decile. When the jobless recovery jeopardised the middle class and its way of life, policymakers felt under political pressure to implement expansionary fiscal and monetary policies, strongly supported by private companies and investors.

The worsening of the middle class position was in some cases absolute, but more important is their loss compared to economic elites. The critical relevance of inequality was recently shown in an important study by Wilkinson and Piketty (2009). People typically compare their situation and well-being to others and are particularly sensitive to the lifestyle of those who are ahead of them in terms of income and wealth.

Although the importance of social influence on consumption decisions — the demonstration effect — was emphasised in the past by different economists (Duesenberry 1949; Frank 1985, 1997; Veblen 1899a, 1909), the relevance of this kind of behaviour was recently proved experimentally by behavioural psychologists, who also proved its significance for economic decision-making (Kahneman *et al.* 1991; Kahneman and

Tversky 2000). Behavioural and cognitive scholars convincingly showed that losses are more painful than gains are pleasurable: consequently, losers are more willing to take risks. It is these psychological and social dynamics that set off "expenditure cascades" by the middle class through increasing indebtedness as a general adaptation to growing inequality and stagnating household income (Frank 2007). Relative losers try their best, even at the cost of extraordinary risk, to keep up with their traditional lifestyle and with that of those who are better off ("keeping up with the Joneses").[37] This is even more understandable in an age of conspicuous consumption and leisure class dominance (Veblen 1899b), the most evident social signs of economic success that dominated the last three decades.

The middle class is politically crucial and the consumption it generates is essential for the health of the economy. When the relative weight in overall income of this social group declined for decades, there is also a serious political problem (Reich 2010). Governments were more than willing to support the consumption attitude of the middle class also in order to support a prolonged economic boom. Governments invested resources and exerted great effort in meeting the demands of the middle class, at least in terms of standards of living. This required soft politics and soft budget constraints, which turned into soft finance, for accommodating the negative effect of increasing disparities. Other social and economic players cooperated in counteracting the unfavourable economic and social effects of increasing inequalities on credit and consumption: middle class families adopting risk-prone attitudes in consumption, financial organisations and industrial enterprises exploiting business and profit opportunities.

Different countries followed diverse routes to this end. Although generalisations in this field risk oversimplifying a complex issue, it is fair to say that in the United States private finance instruments were used primarily, while in most European countries — at least continental ones — the public

[37] The saying is credited to descend from Mark Twain: "The outside influences are always pouring in upon us, and we are always obeying their orders and accepting their verdicts. The Smiths like the new play; the Joneses go to see it, and they copy the Smith verdict." Mark Twain, *Corn-pone Opinions*, written in 1901 but first published in 1923 (Harper & Brothers, ed. by Albert Bigelow Paine).

budget was the main instrument. The consequences were also different: financial and real bubbles in the United States, mounting public debts in various European countries.

In the United States, the easiest and economically most favourable solution was supporting house ownership by means of soft credit. Indeed, the building industry has the policy advantage of being the most nationally and locally based industry and is usually strong in lobbying. The US government used semi-private financial institutions (notably Fannie Mae and Freddy Mac)[38] and exerted growing pressure (with credit guarantee) on the private banking sector for granting easy credit even to risky borrowers (Rajan 2010). The dispersal of risk via mortgage-backed securities opened the booming market of subprime mortgages and the derivative financial instruments (Stiglitz 2010). This mechanism supported the formation of housing bubbles.

The housing sector was perhaps the sector that was the most open to using soft credit and generating excess demand. Formal and informal policies supporting the supply of credit also to subprime borrowers actively sustained and financed this outcome (Rajan 2010). Households came to significantly rely on financial markets both for assets, as pension and insurance, and for liabilities. At the same time, banks started to evolve in the search for profits through intermediation, in the form of commissions and fees and through own trading (Lapavitsas *et al.* 2010).

---

[38] The Federal National Mortgage Association (FNMA, later Fannie Mae) was established in 1938 as part of Roosevelt's New Deal. The aim was to finance home mortgages indirectly with federal money through local banks and create a liquid secondary mortgage market, where banks and other financial institutions could issue more housing loans. In 1968, Fannie Mae was split into two: a Government National Mortgage Association (GNMA or Ginnie Mae) to continue insuring, packaging and securitizing mortgages, and a new, privatised Fannie Mae. The new Fannie Mae was converted into a privately held corporation and removed from the federal budget. Its goal was to finance mortgages by issuing bonds or securitised claims to the public. Freddie Mac (Federal Home Loan Mortgage Corporation) was created in 1970 as a public government-sponsored enterprise. Its goal was to expand the secondary market for mortgages by buying mortgages on the secondary market. It pooled and sold them as mortgage-backed securities on the open market. The crisis made their situation unsustainable and on September 7, 2008 both Fannie Mae and Freddie Mac were put under the control of the Federal Government.

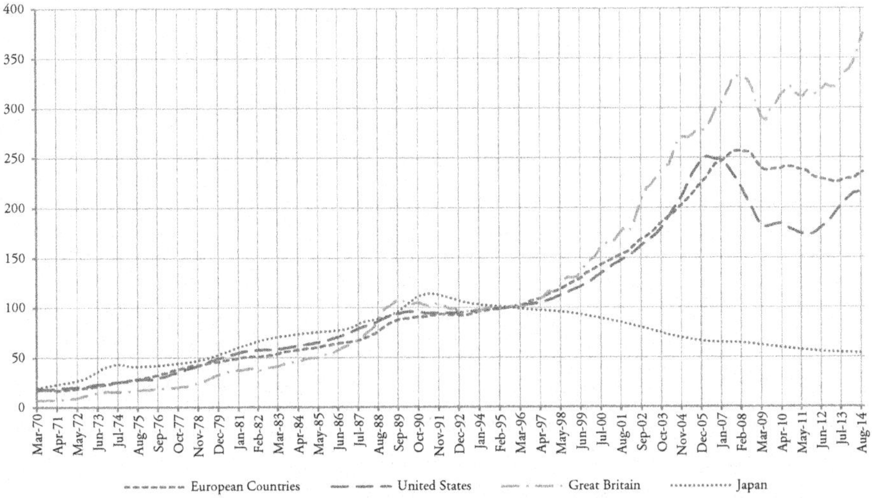

Figure 2.9. House-Price Index (1995 = 100).
Sources: National sources, BIS Residential Property Price database (http://www.bis.org/statistics/pp.htm).

Housing bubbles reflected an uneven situation (Figure 2.9). Price increases led to a true bubble in various countries but not all. Increases were important in the United States, Great Britain, Spain, Ireland, but were absent in Germany (Scatigna *et al.* 2014).[39] Goetzmann *et al.* (2009) argue that one of the factors affecting the rise of the bubble was the effect of econometric analysis of housing price indexes on both the demand and the supply of mortgages. Such analyses supported expectations that could lead to an asset bubble. Before 2006, such analyses generated forecasts of future long-term price growth, while assigned low probabilities to the event of extreme price decreases.

Thus the growing demand for high consumption standards by a relatively impoverished middle class added to the booming consumption by the elites and the public sector and led to growing and riskier credit, largely supported directly and indirectly by the state and by very liquid financial organisations. This effect was made possible thanks to financial

[39] See also the OECD (http://www.oecd.org/eco/outlook/focusonhouseprices.htm) and the Economist (www.economist.com/node/21560599) house price indicator.

innovation, deregulation of financial institutions and markets, soft monitoring and control, and high liquidity from a prolonged boom.

Debt was obviously not the only form of adaptation used by those who remained disadvantaged in the economic race. Among other coping mechanisms were the rapid decrease of saving rates, the use of accumulated savings and the increase in the number of hours worked, together with the general increase of the number of women entering the labour market. The saving rates of families decreased dramatically in nearly all developed countries, while household debt exploded (Reich 2010). But it was particularly the credit lever and the use of accumulated savings that created the force leading to the crisis, namely excess demand through excess credit (Razin and Rosefielde 2011). Indeed, these forces added to the booming speculative demand of financial assets (in particular through the stock exchange) and conspicuous consumption (of luxury real estate and cars) by the financial and economic elites.

While consumption and other kinds of demand by the elite were backed by real purchasing power, demand by the disadvantaged middle class was in substantial part artificial, i.e. not supported by real present or future income and production. Excess demand thus generated bubbles, particularly in the real estate, but also in financial markets and in various consumption markets (e.g. car markets). Bubbles stretched the economy and placed it in an unbearable situation.

2.6 Conclusions: The Crisis and the Great Recession

The financialisation of the economy acted in part as a substitute for the demand that used to come from a prosperous middle class and relatively well-off lower classes of consumers. Yet financialisation was an unstable and weak substitute, since it financed excessive and risky credit and inflated prices and dimly stimulated the production of goods and other services. Financial activity took on and benefited from much financial risk through financial innovation, compensation schemes for financial executives, concentration processes in the banking system, and bailout expectations. This opened a problem for regulators, who had to trade off deregulation to pursue efficiency in the financial sector, with tighter regulation and a more stable supply of credit to foster efficiency in the real economy (Korinek and Kreamer 2014; Stiglitz 2012). These were important events in both leading to the crisis (Crafts 2006; van Treeck 2009b) and, once this started, in making stabilisation more difficult, costly and lengthy.

The four processes, from slowing productivity through deregulation and inequality to lax politics and soft financial discipline, started a causation cycle. While each element reinforced the others, this happened with idiosyncratic features and developments in different countries. Financial distress was thus embedded in real problems: the inability of the financially most developed and active countries, the United States and Great Britain in particular, to maintain the traditional standard of living without inflating the financial economy and running unbearable current account and/or budget deficits.

Along with the factors illustrated above, the extremely high cost of the wars in Afghanistan and Iraq contributed to overheating of the economy (Orszag 2007; Stiglitz and Bilmes 2008). These events led to substantially higher interest rates. The discount rate was increased from 1.25% in November 2002 to 6.25% in August 2007 and interest rates on federal funds grew from 1% in June 2004 to 5.25% in September 2007. These hikes had serious negative consequences for the solvency of many subprime borrowers. The consequence for the solidity of the financial system was staggering: derivatives rapidly lost value and the financial institutions that kept them in their portfolio went into distress.

What made the crisis inevitable were a set of regulatory and policy mistakes on the eve of the crisis (Stiglitz 2010). The crisis was transformed into a great contraction because of three events: the implosion of the financial and real bubble, diffused uncertainty and pessimism, and restrictive regulation and policies. The most evident effect was the dramatic decrease of global financial flows. The great expansion of financial activities of the pre-crisis decades — reflecting the advent of large global banks, institutional investors and international financial activities by transnational companies — was rapidly inverted. By 2012, financial flows had collapsed to 5% of GDP from 21% in 2007, or US$3.9 trillion, down from US$12 trillion. Impressive was the fall in cross-border lending, which fell from US$5.8 trillion in 2007 to US$235 billion in 2012, a mere 4% of the pre-crisis level (Manyika *et al.* 2014).

The implosion of the financial and real bubbles caused a dramatic fall of the demand they had fostered. Financial and real bubbles supported growing prices and business activity and consumption optimism, and led to the massive expansion of credit, demand, investment, employment, and consumption. The implosion of the bubble destroyed an important part of economic activity. Destruction without creation went well beyond what was justified under the aim of leading the economy to a sustainable path characterised by stable prices: demand in line with supply expansion, incomes in line with productivity growth, credit in line with the standing of debtors.

What made the bubble implosion so damaging was its effect in terms of causing uncertainty. The burst made economic calculation for investors and consumers extremely difficult. Economic variables were shaken and their value became uncertain and even doubtful. Prices started to decrease, in some sectors (e.g. housing) rapidly and considerably. The ability of debtors to pay their debt was in doubt. Consequently, the value of investments was uncertain, because the possibility to sell the asset or its product was at risk. All this caused pessimism in economic actors and increased dramatically the uncertainty of business. As a consequence, the time horizon of economic actors was shortened and they became conservative and prudent.

At this point policies intervened, albeit late and with much hesitation and ambiguity. Although the perception of shrinking economic activity was clear, policies chose to give priority to rescuing the financial sector. Massive resources were poured into banks and financial organisations to keep them afloat.

This move was reasonably successful, and policies to fight the crisis were technically successful, yet in political terms they were close to failure (Blinder 2013). They were also extremely costly for public finances, hence for taxpayers. However, they did not solve the problem and further expanded it for two reasons. First, rescued banks and financial organisations became extremely prudent in their business activity. They strongly decreased their lending operations to both businesses, particularly to small and medium-sized enterprises (SMEs), and consumers. Moreover and since their situation continued to be rather shaky, they imposed upon risky borrowers to repay their debt. This move was accelerated by stress tests that governments and international organisations implemented to assess the soundness of financial organisations. Both moves starved the economy of credit and accelerated the recessive effects of the bubble's implosion.

Second, rescuing the financial sector was extremely costly for public finances and put these under stress. In order to avoid public default, governments had to increase taxation and decrease public expenditures. These moves put taxpayers and consumers under further pressure and made them more prudent and conservative in their behaviour. The decrease of many families' disposable incomes led them to decrease consumption, with negative effects for demand, investment, and employment.[40] The level and duration of unemployment increased substantially during the crisis and the recovery was slow in creating jobs (Freeman 2013).

The crisis had sizeable consequences for wealth and income inequalities, in particular due to the high leverage of middle-class families and the high share of homes in their portfolios (Pfeffer *et al.* 2013; Wolff 2014).[41]

---

[40] Various estimates of the cost of the financial crisis exist for the United States. According to a Federal Reserve study by Atkinson *et al.* (2013), the 2007-09 financial crisis implied a huge loss of economic output and financial wealth, increased government expenditures, psychological costs and loss of skills from extended unemployment. Direct costs are estimated at between $6 trillion and $14 trillion, corresponding to $50,000 to $120,000 for every U.S. household and 40 to 90% of one year's output. If lost consumption, national trauma, and other negative consequences are added, the estimate is likely greater than the value of one year's output. The US Government Accountability Office estimated the overall cost at more than $22 trillion (GAO 2013). This sum includes $13 trillion loss of economic output, corresponding to an yearly GDP, and $9.1 trillion paper wealth loss by US homeowners.

[41] Income inequality in the United States rose sharply before and during the crisis, but consumption inequality fell below its 2000 level by 2009 and remained lower afterwards (Meyer and Sullivan 2013). The fact that consumption and income inequality moved in opposite directions during the crisis is due to the fact that, while consumption of the higher income perceivers grew more rapidly than that of the lower income perceivers until the crisis, the opposite was true following the crisis. In the years of crisis, consumers with higher income decreased their consumption more than lower income consumers. This was due mainly to the fall in asset prices (housing and financial assets), that had a disproportionate depressive effect at higher consumption levels.

While all socioeconomic groups experienced declines in wealth and wealthier families had larger absolute declines, in relative terms it was the disadvantaged groups — minorities, the less educated, the young, and pre-recession poorer groups — that suffered greater declines. Ethnic inequality in wealth holdings, that was relatively stable between 1983 and 2007, widened considerably between 2007 and 2010, particularly to the disadvantage of Hispanic households. The consequence was substantial and fast rise in wealth inequality, with little change in the ranking of particular families in the wealth distribution. Overall, median wealth fell by 47% over the years 2007–2010.

The financial crisis was thus rapidly transformed into a real crisis and a great recession. Although the crisis started in the United States, it appeared soon in Europe as an external shock. This put under stress the process of integration and in particular the common currency, the euro. Particularly dangerous was the fact that the external shock revealed the unsustainable institutional architecture of the Eurozone.

2.7 Appendix: Sources of Comparative Data and Information

Competitiveness depends upon productivity levels and their growth and upon qualitative factors, particularly technological innovation and the quality of the products in which the country is specialised. Since many of the factors are difficult to measure, competitiveness is often assessed by comparing levels and changes of international costs or price differentials, export shares in the world market, or improvement of the terms of trade. In spite of these difficulties, some international projects exist that make an attempt at giving a more complete measure of competitiveness by taking a broad approach to it. These include: the calculation of the Global Competitiveness Index (GCI) by the World Economic Forum (WEF); the Europe 2020 Competitiveness Index by the WEF; the Global Innovation Index (GII) by the Cornell University, INSEAD and the World Intellectual Property Organization (WIPO); the World Bank's Doing Business (DB) ranking; the European Competitiveness Report by the European Commission; the Harmonised Competitiveness Indicators (HCI) by Eurostat; the European Commission's publication on price and cost competitiveness.

1. The GCI, by the WEF, aims at calculating an aggregate score that allows assessing the level of productivity of a country. WEF takes a broad approach to competitiveness. Competitiveness is defined as "...the set of institutions, policies, and factors that determine the level of productivity of a country" (WEF, 2014, p. 4). The overall GCI score is the outcome of the weighted average of 12 different but interconnected factors or "pillars" of competitiveness, each one including in turn different components measuring particular aspects of competitiveness. In turn, the 12 pillars are distinct into three different groups of factors or sub-indexes, each one including those pillars that are considered to be more important at any given stage of development:

   a) Basic requirements sub-index, which includes pillars 1 to 4, forming the key for factor-driven economies: 1. Institutions, 2. Infrastructure, 3. Macroeconomic environment, 4. Health and primary education;
   b) Efficiency enhancers sub-index, which includes pillars 5 to 10, forming the key for efficiency-driven economies: 5. Higher education and training, 6. Goods market efficiency, 7. Labour market efficiency, 8. Financial market development, 9. Technological readiness, 10. Market size;
   c) Innovation and sophistication factors sub-index, which includes pillars 11 to 12, forming the key for innovation-driven economies: 11. Business sophistication, 12. Innovation.

   Although each pillar matters for any country, the relative importance of each pillar depends upon the stage of development of that country. The GCI follows the theory of stages of development — following Rostow (1960), further developed by Porter (1990) — in assuming that development goes through three stages and two transition phases (WEF 2014, pp. 3–11). Each stage and transition phase is distinguished by the nature of the drivers of development and per capita GDP. The first stage is when the economy is factor-driven and countries compete based on their factor endowments, in particular unskilled labour and natural resources. The GDP per capita threshold of this stage is at less than US$2,000. The first stage is followed by a transition from Stage 1 to Stage 2 (GDP per capita between US$2,000–2,999). The second stage is the efficiency-driven stage. A country enters this stage when its economy becomes more efficient, productivity increases and wages rise. The drivers of competitiveness are higher education and training, efficient goods markets, well-functioning labour markets, developed financial markets, the ability to exploit the benefits of existing technologies, and a large domestic or foreign market. GDP per capita in this stage is between US$3,000–8,999. Transition from Stage 2 to Stage 3 runs between US$9,000–17,000. Finally, as development progresses further, a country enters the innovation-driven stage. Since wages have increased further, competitiveness depends upon the economy's ability to produce new and unique goods. This can be done by using the most sophisticated production processes and by innovating new ones. An innovation-driven economy is one that has a GDP per capita higher than US$17,000 and a weight for innovation and sophistication factors of 30%, for basic requirements of 20% and for efficiency enhancers of 50%. The weights were obtained by running a maximum likelihood regression of GDP per capita against each sub-index for past years, allowing for different coefficients for each stage of development. The weight of each sub-index changes at different stages of development (WEF 2014, p. 10). More exactly, while the weight of the first sub-index decreases with the increase of per capita GDP (from 60 to 20%), the weight of the second and third sub-index increases (respectively from 35 to 50% and from 5 to 30%).

According to the GCI, the United States, as are all the Eurozone countries, is considered as innovation-driven economies. According to the latest 2014–2015 ranking, the United States is third out of 144 countries and is ahead of any Eurozone and EU member country. Only Switzerland and Singapore in first and second place respectively do better.[42]

---

[42] In the breakdown of the index into its subindexes, the United States is just 33rd in the so-called basic requirements subindex, particularly because of the poor performance in the

2. The Europe 2020 Competitiveness Report is a biannual publication initiated in 2012 under the aegis of the WEF (WEF-EU 2014). The Europe 2020 Competitiveness Report follows the Forum's interest in European competitiveness, which dates back to 1979, when the Report on the Competitiveness of European Industry was first published. This was followed by the Lisbon Review series which, between 2002 and 2010, aimed at evaluating Europe's progress in meeting the goals of its Lisbon strategy. The new Report assesses Europe's progress on its Europe 2020 strategy by means of the Forum's data, analysis and comparisons to non-European economies. The Strategy defines a long-term agenda for a more competitive, inclusive and sustainable society. The approach and method are the same as in the Global Competitiveness Report (WEF 2014). However, the composition of the competitiveness index ("Europe 2020 Competitiveness Index", ECI) is different in order to reflect the Strategy's goals. Indeed, the Forum's standard framework that is used to define its GCI complements many of the measures identified by the Europe 2020 Competitiveness Index. The Report introduces the Europe 2020 Competitiveness Index which focuses on monitoring the implementation of Europe 2020 strategy. Therefore, the index is meant to provide an assessment of the priorities of the European strategy and is not an exhaustive measure of competitiveness.

   The Europe 2020 Competitiveness Index is composed of seven pillars with the same weight (1/7) in the overall Index score (WEF-EU 2014, p. 37). The pillars are organised in three sub-indexes (pillars in parenthesis): Smart growth (including enterprise environment, digital agenda, innovative Europe, and education and training pillars), Inclusive growth (labour market and employment, and social inclusion pillars), and Sustainable growth (environmental sustainability pillar).

   Each pillar, in turn, may or may not include the following sub-pillars (in parenthesis): Enterprise environment (competition, clusters, entrepreneurship, availability of finance); digital agenda (ICT readiness, ICT usage, ICT impact); education and training (education, training); labour

---

macroeconomic environment and health and primary education pillars. However, the country is first in the so-called efficiency enhancers subindex (particularly thanks to the market size) and fifth in the innovation and sophistication factors subindex.

market and employment (labour market efficiency, labour participation); sustainable growth (environmental sustainability).

The data for each pillar are obtained through ad hoc surveys and collected external quantitative data. The survey data are mainly derived from the responses to the World Economic Forum's Executive Opinion Survey (EOS), and range on a scale from 1 to 7. The external quantitative data are collected from various sources, such as the World Bank, United Nations Organization for Educational, Scientific and Culture (UNESCO), the International Telecommunication Union (ITU) and International Labour Organization (ILO). Each of the pillars is calculated as an unweighted average of the individual component variables. For aggregation purposes, survey data and other quantitative indicators are normalised to a 1-to-7 scale using a max-min methodology. Higher values indicate stronger performance.

3. The GII is the simple average of two sub-indices: the Innovation Input Sub-Index and the Innovation Output Sub-Index (GII 2014, pp. 7–8). In turn, each of these sub-indexes is based on different pillars. The index is calculated for 143 economies and uses 81 indicators covering different themes. The Innovation Input Sub-Index includes five pillars that cover the components of the country's economy upon which innovative activity is based. These are: institutions, human capital and research, infrastructure, market sophistication, and business sophistication. The Innovation Output Sub-Index includes two pillars looking at the output side of the innovation process: knowledge and technology outputs, and creative outputs.[43] The ratio between the two sub-indexes, the Output over the Input sub-indexes, is defined as the Innovation Efficiency Ratio and measures the amount of innovation output that a country obtains from its inputs.

---

[43] Each of the five plus two pillars is divided into three sub-pillars as follows (sub-pillars in parentheses): institutions (political environment, regulatory environment, business environment), human capital and research (education, tertiary education, research and development), infrastructure (ICTs, general infrastructure, ecological sustainability), market sophistication (credit, investment, trade and competition), business sophistication (knowledge workers, innovation linkages, knowledge absorption), knowledge and technology outputs (knowledge creation, knowledge impact, knowledge diffusion), creative outputs (intangible assets, creative goods and services, online creativity). Since each sub-pillar is composed of different individual indicators, the total number of indicators is 81.

The GII is revised and updated annually in its components, so it is not easy to have a perfect comparison of changes through time of the performance of individual countries. However, the broad lines are clear. Although there are some variations from one year to the other regarding the precise position of individual countries in the overall ranking, there is relative stability, at least at the top of the ranking. Top positions are filled by high income countries. Switzerland leads also the GII ranking, followed by Great Britain and Sweden. Finland, the first country of the Eurozone, is in fourth place, followed by the Netherlands. The United States is sixth, one place lower than in 2013. In this ranking, Singapore is seventh and Denmark eighth. Luxembourg and Hong Kong follow. BRICS countries are somehow diverging, with China improving at a significantly faster pace than other countries. China is presently (2014) in 29th position.[44]

4. The World Bank's Doing Business (DB) database looks at the microeconomic basis of competitiveness. The World Bank and the International Finance Corporation publish the DB reports since 2004. These reports have descriptive and prescriptive (normative) aims (Hanusch 2012). In fact, they intend to help governments to identify reform areas through a comparison with other countries and to push countries to reform their microeconomic and regulatory framework, when this is not competitive.

   Doing Business is based on the premise that economic activity requires transparent and generally accessible rules to be successful (DB 2012). Thus, regulation should be easy to comply with and accessible to all those who need to use it. It should also effectively balance between safeguarding the stability of the business environment and avoiding distortions that impose unreasonable costs on businesses. Thus, these rules are important for establishing and clarifying property rights and reducing the cost of resolving disputes. In this way, rules enhance the predictability of economic interaction and activity, and

[44] China's achievement is remarkable in various fields, including R&D expenditures and in particular patent filing. China is presently at the top of the ranking of patents filed since 2011. Patent applications worldwide accelerated after 2009 and the 9.2% growth of patent filing in 2012 was the strongest rate in nearly two decades (GII 2014, p. 3).

provide partners to contracts with certainty and protection against abuse.

Doing Business uses various quantitative indicators on business regulation and the protection of property rights to benchmark 183 economies. The aim is to measure and track changes in the regulations applying to domestic companies in 11 areas in their life cycle.[45] This is done by concentrating on the perspective of domestic, primarily smaller companies and with the limited aim of supplying business leaders and policymakers with open information and data, which are considered to be important for policy and decision making.

5. The European Commission publishes the European Competitiveness Report (ECR 2014). This report is different from those mentioned above in that it is neither a database, nor does it attempt to calculate a composite index. It is more properly a thorough analysis of the factors that determine the competitiveness of European economies and an assessment of individual economies along these factors. However, in doing so, it provides a set of data and qualitative information and analysis which is useful for assessing the competitiveness of European economies. It also provides comparative indexes through European economies on particular components of the competitiveness conundrum. Each yearly report is devoted to analyse a critical issue, such as how to help firms to grow, the particular issue of the 2014 report. The growth of firms is taken to measure the effectiveness of industrial policy and the quality of the investment environment in the European Union, along with the success of individual businesses.
6. Eurostat, the statistical office of the EU, publishes regularly a HCI (EBA 2015). The purpose of HCI is to provide consistent and comparable measures of Euro area countries' price and cost competitiveness. HCIs are constructed using the same methodology and data sources that are used for the real effective exchange rates (REERs) of the Euro and are

[45] The 11 areas covered include: starting a business, dealing with construction permits, getting electricity, registering property, getting credit, protecting investors, paying taxes, trading across borders, enforcing contracts, resolving insolvency (formerly closing a business), and employing workers. The employing workers data are not included in the 2012 ranking on the ease of doing business (DB 2012).

consistent with the Euro REERs. While the HCI of a specific country takes into account both intra and extra-Euro area trade and considers the 21 most important trade partners, the Euro REERs are based on extra-Euro area trade only. The HCIs are calculated on the basis of weighted averages of bilateral exchange rates vis-à-vis the currencies of the trading partners of each euro area country and are deflated by appropriate cost or price indices. A positive change points to a decrease in cost competitiveness.

7. Another useful EU publication on price and cost competitiveness is published on a quarterly basis (EC 2014f). The publication includes tables and charts on nominal and REERs of the euro and the other currencies of the EU member countries, as well as other countries, including the United States. Aggregate measures for the entire European Union and for the Eurozone are also presented. Each country (or group of countries) is compared with the Eurozone, the EU, and the other countries considered in the publication. A final set of tables aims at facilitating the comparison of developments in different countries. This group includes cross-national tables of nominal and REERs of the currencies of the EU, the USA and Japan and aggregate measures for the EU and the Eurozone.

"Let us therefore put aside this argument of the old and of the new, because clearly there is nothing new that cannot become old, and nothing old that has not been new, as was well noted by your Aristotle."

— Giordano Bruno, *La cena delle ceneri* — *The Ash Wednesday Supper, First Dialogue, Theophil.*

3

Financial Causes and Real Sources of the European Crisis

The international crisis hit the Eurozone hard. Remarkably distinct patterns among the member countries played an important role in the resilience to the crisis. The Eurozone, and hence the euro, revealed to be highly vulnerable to external shocks, suffering of deep-seated as well as new structural and financial imbalances. At the same time, the Eurozone's ability to cope with its economic vulnerability was weak, revealing rigid and lengthy decision-making procedures and a fundamental lack of trust among governments. Coordinated policy responses were slow. However, the crisis gave an important push to the coordination of economic policies and related instruments. Such coordination was both an important part of the problem and, hopefully, an important component of the solution.

The unfolding of the crisis in the Eurozone was the outcome of the interaction of institutional features and policy failures, and their inability to manage properly their interconnection with real and financial imbalances. The main culprit for the difficulties was identified in different aspects: bad private finance in both the United States and Europe, leading to bubbles and pervasive and risky derivatives; bad public finance based on high sovereign debts and deficits; financial tricks, such as forged data of the real public finance situation; soft and populist governments unable or unwilling to implement the necessary policies; lack of reform at both macro- and microeconomic level and consequently inefficient economies; bad macroeconomic policies, wrong policy priorities, and policy mistakes, such as relying exclusively on austerity measures versus the need to support demand; excessively high labour incomes compared to productivity and excessively generous welfare systems and other labour privileges compared to the strength of the economy; bad regulation, weak competition and diffused rents.

The aim of this chapter is to analyse the pre-existing factors that opened the way to the transmission of the external shock of the US crisis to the Eurozone. The external shock triggered the systemic crisis of the euro in the frame of a wider context of rising inequalities, polarisation of living standards, excess demand and increasing economic and social imbalances, ailing competitiveness. Another aim is to assess whether causes of vulnerability internal to the Eurozone existed and, if so, which role they played in the crisis. The chapter also aims to discuss the structural consequences of these events and analyse the institutional and political reforms facing the Eurozone, in order to enhance its capability to cope with external shocks and to ease and solve its internal vulnerability.

The crisis showed that the internal divergence in the Eurozone is based on important structural components, which are unsustainable in the long run. Indeed, the crisis magnified the pre-existing gap between the vulnerable member countries, mostly Southern European countries, and a more resilient, mostly Northern core. The hidden fault line between these two groups of countries became open and a source of further divergence. There is a need for the convergence of real variables among member countries, which should complement financial convergence.

This perspective is increasingly accepted within the current debt crisis setting, yet it was barely pursued through policies and reforms. This failure exists at the national level, where a short-term national perspective has often outweighed the need for more structural programmes, under the constraints of Eurozone criteria and priorities. The failure also extended to the Eurozone level, where the process stopped whenever there was a strong political obstacle to overcome, regardless of how problematic the consequences were. In this context, severe are the risks of tinkering with existing institutions, barely and partially adjusted.

All these explanations have a role in building up a general picture of the causes of the crisis. Yet each of them is insufficient in itself to account for the present difficulties and policy ineffectiveness at both national and Eurozone level. Moreover, each explanation does not consider how single factors interact with each other and with other factors, which remain outside debates and analyses. Thus policy intervention has typically unilateral and unstable bases. Although the debate is slowly moving forward, perhaps with excessive delay and at an excessively slow speed, it is high time to build up a comprehensive and structural explanation of the Eurozone crisis and reconsider reforms and policymaking from this perspective.

The book aims to work out a comprehensive explanation of the crisis in the Eurozone. It also seeks to provide an explanation of and reason for the mistakes that were committed so far. It also intends to identify which actions — be they reforms or policies or agreements — can be implemented in order to solve the present difficulties and reconvert the integration process, and in particular the common currency, into a powerful factor of development and growth. This is particularly important at the time of writing, in early 2015: the decision by Iceland to stop the ongoing accession process to the European Union (EU) and the common currency and to opt definitely out of both represents a serious blow on the internal and external reputation and appeal of the EU. In the background, the phantoms of "Grexit" and "Brexit", the possible exit of Greece from the Eurozone and Great Britain from the EU, wander.

The Eurozone is the epicentre of the European crisis and the origin of the threats that this is causing to the world economy. Contrary to the illusions that led to the adoption of the euro, the economies of the common currency area are not converging. In fact, they have been dramatically diverging, with some economies getting stronger and others increasingly weak and vulnerable. In part, this outcome is the effect of the common currency. This situation is jeopardising the very survival of the common currency. This situation has serious, perhaps permanent and dangerous economic, social and political consequences, even in the strong Eurozone countries, and is imposing heavy costs to European citizens. There is a serious danger of a permanent fault line within the Eurozone, dividing economically and politically countries according to their degree of resilience in front of an incomplete and asymmetric monetary union.

The recognition of the long-term unsustainability of the present situation is widely held. However, deeply different views dominate the scene on what should be done to exit the danger zone and which steps should get priority. In short, an apparent conflict over policy strategies is obstructing the Eurozone, its institutions and governments, and reveals the lack of trust among member countries.

How did we get to this point? What are the deep causes of this situation? What is to be done to make the situation sustainable and propulsive of development? In this chapter, the main analytic perspective and issues are presented, which will be further elaborated on in the following chapters.

3.1 Europe: Declining Economic Performance?

Western Europe followed many of the developments that have led to the crisis in the United States. However, financial bubbles were more contained in the Eurozone than in the United States and real instability, such as the existence of real bubbles or the growth of inequalities, was relatively moderate overall. This explains why the crisis started in the United States and not in Europe. Those features, however, make difficult to understand why the effects of the US crisis led the Eurozone to such a deep, long, and apparently intractable crisis.

One possible explanation for the Eurozone crisis is that Europe has been declining economically already before the crisis. In this perspective, the effect of the US crisis was to uncover the weakness of the European economy and its declining international competitiveness. Data quoted in the previous chapter show that the European catching-up to the United States in terms of productivity per hour worked had already reversed in the 1990s (Table 2.2). After this period, i.e. well before the international crisis, productivity in the United States recovered compared to Western

European countries and US performance departed again from European performance.

Two explanations for this development were proposed. According to one scholar (Faini 2006), the drawback of Europe is due to negative demographic factors and the decrease in the number of hours worked. A different explanation (Crafts 2003) sees the relative disadvantage of Europe being the consequence of its delay in adopting the advancement of information and communications technology (ICT) in production.

The importance of these questions should be clear. If one finds that the European economy lost strength relative to the US economy, then it is not sufficient to look for the causes of the European crisis in financial events alone. Also real processes should be carefully considered. And when considering the need to complete, balance and reform the institutional architecture of the Eurozone, one should have economic soundness in view together with financial effectiveness. Reform and policy considerations and goals would be quite different in the two cases.

In spite of the expectations concerning the effects of European integration, the economic performance of the Union apparently lagged behind not only compared to that of emerging economies, but also in comparison to its most immediate partner and competitor, the United States. The Union dramatically lagged behind its own agenda, as expressed in the Lisbon Strategy of 2000. When looking at the long-run performance of an economy, it is important to distinguish four main components: a) the existence of different accounting conventions and practices among countries; b) the size, change and measurement of unregistered activities, including the underground and informal economies; c) the role of the exogenous factors such as demography; and d) labour productivity, which reflects employment rate, the number of hours worked, investment and technical progress. By considering separately component d), one can have a fair idea of the efficiency of a certain economic system, while considering this component together with component c) one can have a fair view of the performance of a particular economy.

First, a proper comparison of economic performance at international level requires that all countries have the same accountancy system, which is broadly true at least among Western countries, which all adopt the UN System of National Accounts (SNA). Countries should also adopt the same accountancy conventions and practices. Various studies, particularly by the Organisation of Economic Cooperation and Development (OECD), have stressed the differences existing among OECD countries and attempted to quantify intercountry differences.

An OECD study (Ahmad *et al.* 2003; see also Faini 2006; OECD 2005b) highlighted accounting differences between the United States and other OECD countries. The study found four differences: in the treatment of military equipment, financial intermediation services to households, treatment of software, and the use of hedonic prices. The impact of these differences on the GDP level and its growth rate is important in the case of software and financial intermediation services. Also the treatment of military equipment is fairly important, while the impact of hedonic prices is negligible.[46]

The effect of different accounting conventions and practices, plus the changing importance of the individual components through time, have rather important consequences for the convergence process between the United States and Europe. In fact, the importance of military equipment, use of software and financial intermediation increased in the United States compared to the Eurozone, particularly in the second half of the 1990s. As a consequence, US GDP growth decreases by 0.2–0.3% when accounting differences are taken into consideration, and the impact on per capita GDP growth is also significant. However, it should be reminded that these services contributed in an important way to the revival of competitiveness of the US economy.

Second, there are also significant intercountry differences in the importance of the underground economy, its change through time and the share registered in official statistics (Schneider and Enste 2000; Schneider *et al.* 2010).

Third, the advantage of the US in economic performance over the Eurozone in the second half of the 1990s decreases further if one considers demographic dynamics. The Eurozone went through a demographic decline in the last decades, which is not the case of the United States. This explains an important part of the relative decline of European perfor-

[46] The treatment of various items changed in the 2008 SNA. The issue is considered in Section 12.3.

mance. In fact, one third of the increase of the gap in GDP per capita between the United States and the Eurozone is explained by the faster population growth in the United States. The worsening performance of the European economy accounts for the remaining two thirds. By considering population growth, "Europe's performance was better than that of the United States in the 1980s, worsened markedly during the first half of the 1990s and, in more recent years, has been at par with that of the United States" (Faini 2006, p. 73).

If one considers jointly demographic dynamics and accounting practices, there probably is not much difference in per capita GDP growth between the United States and the Eurozone, at least up to mid-1990s. However, to have a more complete and detailed picture, one has to consider also the fourth component: labour productivity. Statistics show that labour productivity growth accelerated in the United States since the 1980s and in particular during the second half of the 1990s and the first part of the 2000s. Productivity in the Eurozone decelerated in the same period, had a revival in the first part of the 1990s, and a clear slow-down since mid-1990s. According to Crafts (2003), this is the consequence of Western European delay in adopting ICT.

The situation becomes clearer if one decomposes GDP per capita into its components: hourly labour productivity, hours worked per employee, and employment rate. Using PPP-corrected data and disregarding differences in accounting practices, Faini finds that "between 1979 and 1990 per capita GDP rose at a slightly faster rate in the euro area than in the United States, 2.1 percent versus 1.9 percent. Between 1991 and 1996 per capita GDP growth was faster in the United States, while the reverse holds true for the most recent period" (Faini 2006, p. 76). Using OECD data, Faini shows that hourly productivity grew faster in the Eurozone between 1979 and 2001 than in the United States (2.09% compared to 1.54%). However, between 1997 and 2001 the reverse was true (respectively 1.09% and 2.92%), in coincidence with the massive utilisation of ICT in the United States.

The United States compensated slower growth of hourly productivity with the stable number of hours worked per person, which decreased by a mere 0.04% between 1997 and 2001 in the United States compared to a 0.62% decrease in the Eurozone. Also the employment rate increased more in the United States in this period (plus 0.30%) compared to the Eurozone (plus 0.24%). In the years between 1997 and 2001, the situation was remarkably different: the employment rate increased by 2.02% in the Eurozone compared to a decrease of 0.71% in the United States. The number of hours per person continued to decrease in the Eurozone (minus 0.61%) and decreased also, although less, in the United States (minus 0.38%). These data apparently suggest that, even supposing that there is some evidence for the relative economic decline of the European economy compared to the US economy, this decline is less compelling than commonly thought (Faini 2006).

To complete the picture, one has to look at the export performance. Export performance of the Eurozone declined remarkably during the entire decade of the 1990s. With respect to the world exports, the elasticity of the Eurozone exports was well below 1. The decline includes a serious fall of Germany's exports during the 1990s, from more than 12% of world exports in 1990 to 8.5% in 2000. This decline was stabilised afterwards, but resumed as soon as the international crisis started (Figure 2.4). This is in striking contrast with the performance of US exports, which increased by nearly 1% in the decade, from 11.3% of world exports in 1990 to 12.4% in 1998. However, US exports witnessed a dramatic fall to 8% of world exports by 2008, a level that they maintained more or less unchanged afterwards.

There may be different reasons for the decreased performance of European exports. This may be due to decreased price competitiveness of exports, due to relatively increasing production costs. Another important explanation has to do with the European specialisation in slow-growing branches and in goods and services characterised by slow-growing demand. The fact that European exports have decreased also in terms of their volume apparently gives strength to this conclusion. Another important explanation looks at the dollar-euro exchange rate and the price of energy, both of which have overall disadvantaged the Eurozone compared to the United States.

In the end, it is rather difficult to conclude for an economic decline of the Eurozone vis-à-vis the United States. However, various factors point at a systemic weakness of the Eurozone, a weakness having to do particularly with the labour market and technical progress. As to the latter, the Eurozone was unable to absorb new technologies as quickly as the

United States. Considering the labour market and while employment increased substantially in the Eurozone in the second half of the 1990s, its quality was overall weak for both institutional and regulatory reasons, overall poor educational achievements and inadequate research and development (R&D) investment. The substantial increase of inequalities to the disadvantage of labour led to weaker incentives to effort investment in job specific assets and education and to slowly growing domestic markets.

3.2 Performance and Competitiveness: External and Internal Sources

The real economy is an important structural source of the crisis in both its external and internal components. The external component is the falling competitiveness of Europe compared to the rest of the world, as falling world export shares witness. The internal component is the divergent competitiveness among Eurozone economies. The latter is particularly dangerous and should be analysed against the background of the optimum currency area theories, which will be done in Chapter 6.

The term competitiveness is not particularly easy to use, since it is employed in many and sometimes imprecise ways. The debate on competitiveness evolved around three aspects: the market share of a firm or a country, the absolute and relative level and composition of costs, and productivity. The problem is that a firm's or a country's success in each of these three fields can be a sign of genuine competitiveness, but can be due also to other factors, such as unfair policies and distortive subsidies.

Similarly, costs competitiveness, particularly unit labour costs, is often based on the idea that low labour costs would strengthen the position of a firm and a country. This is considered to lead to higher exports, sustainable balance of payments, and in the end superior economic performance and higher employment.[47] This view is controversial for different reasons. If low labour costs are the consequence of low wages, this view is at odds with the pursuit of prosperity and economic performance, since it weakens the domestic market, except the case of export-led growth. It is also important to stress that unit labour costs aligned with external balance can

[47] This is, for example, the position of the European Central Bank (ECB 2008a).

take place at different levels of performance. For instance, external balance can be the outcome of higher exports and performance or lower imports and lower performance. Finally, low labour costs can be obtained in different ways, such as through lower wages or higher investment, with clearly different consequences on performance and its sustainability.

The connection between competitiveness and productivity surged recently to the centre of attention of scholars and international organisations. This relation appears to be strong, in particular if the aim of the analysis is to focus on the relationship between competitiveness and economic performance (Fagerberg *et al.* 2007; Hall and Jones 1999; Porter 1990). Various international organisations based their analysis and the elaboration of broad based international comparative databases on this perspective. Among the others, it is worth mentioning the World Economic Forum (WEF) and its Global Competitiveness Report and the World Bank's Doing Business database and publications. The OECD worked out data sets and published documents based on the importance of productivity for economic performance, competitiveness, sustainability and related policies (OECD 2005a, 2014e). The EU was active for years in supporting this perspective, in particular with the European Commission's Europe 2020 Strategy (EC 2010a) and related publications such as the European Competitiveness Report (ECR 2014).

The second structural root of the crisis, the internal component, has an institutional nature and consists of the incomplete and asymmetric nature of the institutional build-up of the Eurozone, with important consequences for policies. Institutional theories prove that institutions are fundamental for determining incentives and consequently the choice and behaviour of actors. However, the European problem goes beyond this: missing, incomplete, and asymmetric institutions prevent even well-intentioned actors (such as national governments) from doing what would be nationally and collectively advantageous.

One important reason for this situation is that national actors are bounded by their national constituencies; pressure groups; international agreements and relations; intergovernmental dynamics; lack of confidence in and sheer ignorance of alternatives. Many formal common institutions exist in the EU and additional ones in the Eurozone that link governments and citizens to a common action and limit the sovereignty of member countries.

Under these conditions, the inability to implement a fully cooperative strategy among member countries prevents pursuing the actors' and citizens' advantage. As a consequence, everybody may be losing from the common institutions and coordinated action. The split between the national interest and collective advantage entrenches institutional asymmetry, which may create institutional ineffectiveness and protract incompleteness. Policy ineffectiveness may follow.

The Eurozone institutional set-up and, even more so, its workings resemble an ineffectively governed common (Ostrom 1990), whereby ineffectiveness derives from the lack of sufficiently streamlined informal institutions and the absence, asymmetry, or weakness of formal institutions. A further problem derives from the conflict, always potential and sometimes real, between common and national formal institutions. This situation provides an interesting case of lack of cooperation in a reiterated game. A case in point is the management of the euro. Although decisions concerning the currency are formally taken by the European Central Bank (ECB), the ECB presides over the Eurosystem as a matter of fact. The Eurosystem is governed by the Directive Council, which includes the ECB president and the governors of the national central banks (NCB) of the Eurozone. Voting follows a majority system in which each NCB has one vote. Although so far NCB governors had the common interest in mind, during the crisis divisions among governors typically followed the economic and financial situations of their national economy and voting within the Council was sometimes split along these lines. Although so far the overall willingness to compromise apparently prevailed, it is clear that under the pressure of events and difficulties the common interest could fade away.[48]

[48] An important case is the conflict developed between the decisions of the ECB and German national authorities. On 7 February 2014, the German Constitutional Court decided that it considers the ECB's Outright Monetary Transactions (OMT) inconsistent with EU primary law, because it exceeds the limits established by the German act approving the European Stability Mechanism (ESM). The German Court decided to ask for the opinion of the Court of Justice of the EU. On 14 January 2015, the EU Court's Advocate General Cruz Villalón defined that the OMT programme does not infringe the principle of proportionality and may be considered lawful and compatible with the Lisbon Treaty. The Court of Justice of the European Union confirmed this advice and declared that the OMT programme announced by the ECB in September 2012 is compatible with EU law

Axelrod (1984) convincingly proved, by means of a computerised infinitely reiterated game, that cooperation among parties provides a superior outcome. The precondition for this is that the parties can use a tit-for-tat strategy. While initially defections from cooperation are used, parties subsequently start to cooperate consistently and permanently for their own advantage. Why did cooperation apparently weaken within the Eurozone, in spite of stable interaction?[49]

3.3 Eurozone Economic Performance

Data do not appear to definitively support the perspective of a European economic decline. However, such a decline could be the consequence of the crisis or could take forms other than what aggregate statistics and information suggest. It is therefore important to assess whether the Eurozone has inbuilt weaknesses that may generate internal divergence or the economic decline of individual member countries or of the entire Eurozone. Indeed, there are many reasons to maintain that internal divergences are rapidly growing. From these, permanent fault lines may develop, with dangerous consequences for the economic and political sustainability of the Eurozone.

The peculiarity of the Eurozone situation lies essentially in how each economy adapted to the burst of the real and financial bubbles in the United States and other non-Eurozone countries. The most critical aspects

(see Case C-62/14 judgement at http://curia.europa.eu/juris/celex.jsf?celex=62014CJ0062&lang1=en&type=TXT&ancre=). The sentence reads as follows: "Articles 119 TFEU, 123(1) TFEU and 127(1) and (2) TFEU and Articles 17 to 24 of Protocol (No 4) on the Statute of the European System of Central Banks and of the European Central Bank must be interpreted as permitting the European System of Central Banks (ESCB) to adopt a programme for the purchase of government bonds on secondary markets, such as the programme announced in the press release to which reference is made in the minutes of the 340th meeting of the Governing Council of the European Central Bank (ECB) on 5 and 6 September 2012."

[49] There may be a case for maintaining that the internal imbalance between resilient and vulnerable countries and large and small economies, considering the no-exit option, created an internal asymmetry in the possibility to use tit-for-tat tactics. There apparently was an interesting development in late 2014–early 2015 coming from Greece (see Chapter 12).

behind different adaptations are the performance of the economy and that of public finances. In fact, it is the change of these two variables that particularly highlights the main effects of the crisis. In view of the nature of the economic and monetary union, it is important to consider both absolute and relative performance, in relation to the other member countries.

Looking at the effects of the crisis, two groups of countries stand out in the Eurozone for their different situations. These are resilient and vulnerable countries. Vulnerable countries are countries whose economies, due to their structural features and domestic policies, are exposed and inclined to exogenous shocks and subject to international market fluctuations. Following the crisis, these countries are in a difficult economic and financial situation (Table 3.1). They were labeled as PI(I)GS,[50] an acronym formed by the initials of these countries' names: Portugal, Ireland, (Italy), Greece, and Spain. To these, Cyprus should also be added. Italy is in parenthesis because it did not need any bailout. However, the country received an indirect support by the ECB through purchases of its public bonds on the secondary market. Resilient countries are distinguished by their economies' policy-induced ability to withstand or recover from the effects of exogenous shocks. Germany is the epitome of this group and is certainly its economic and financial leader. Other countries included in the group are Austria, Belgium, Finland, France, Luxembourg, and the Netherlands.

The table presents two of the most critical aspects of the Eurozone during the crisis: its disappointing economic performance and inability to recover. It also shows that the economic and the financial situation of individual countries are not the same and not always consistent with their belonging to one of the two groups. For instance, the fall of GDP in 2009 was significant in Germany and Italy, less so in other countries.

One should keep in consideration that the Eurozone shares the common currency, but has no common government of the economy. It is also important to remind that also its fundamental common institutions, such as the European Central Bank, are incomplete. As a consequence, common institutions are less powerful in reacting to and combatting the crisis than the corresponding institutions in non-Eurozone countries. In order to

[50] Sinn (2014) prefers different acronyms: GIIPS and GIPSIC. The latter includes also Cyprus.

Table 3.1. GDP Growth Rate in the Eurozone.

	1996–2000 Average	2001–2006 Average	2007	2008	2009	2010	2011	2012	2013	2014
Belgium	2.9	1.9	3.0	1.0	−2.6	2.5	1.6	0.1	0.3	1.0
Germany	1.9	1.1	3.3	1.1	−5.6	4.1	3.6	0.4	0.1	1.6
The Netherlands	4.1	1.7	4.2	2.1	−3.3	1.1	1.7	−1.6	−0.7	0.9
Finland	5.1	2.9	5.2	0.7	−8.3	3.0	2.6	−1.4	−1.3	−0.1
Austria	3.0	2.0	3.6	1.5	−3.8	1.9	3.1	0.9	0.2	0.3
Luxembourg	0.0	3.4	6.5	0.5	−5.3	5.1	2.6	−0.2	2.0	–
France	2.9	1.8	2.4	0.2	−2.9	2.0	2.1	0.3	0.3	0.4
RESIL	**3.3**	**2.1**	**4.0**	**1.0**	**−4.5**	**2.8**	**2.5**	**−0.2**	**0.1**	**0.7**
Ireland	9.6	5.0	4.9	−2.6	−6.4	−0.3	2.8	−0.3	0.2	4.8
Greece	3.7	4.2	3.5	−0.4	−4.4	−5.4	−8.9	−6.6	−3.9	0.8
Spain	4.1	3.5	3.8	1.1	−3.6	0.0	−0.6	−2.1	−1.2	1.4
Italy	2.0	1.1	1.5	−1.0	−5.5	1.7	0.6	−2.8	−1.7	−0.4
Portugal	4.1	1.0	2.5	0.2	−3.0	1.9	−1.8	−4.0	−1.6	0.9
VULN	**4.7**	**3.0**	**3.2**	**−0.5**	**−4.6**	**−0.4**	**−1.6**	**−3.2**	**−1.6**	**1.5**

Note: — means not available.
Source: Eurostat Database.

appreciate the intricacy of the situation and its complex consequences, particularly in terms of the divergence of features and situations within the Eurozone, three critical aspects should be considered. These are: a) diverging intercountry performances of the real and financial economy; b) inequalities and particularly growing distributive disparities; and c) economic and policy uncertainty leading to short-terminism. The analysis of the first aspect is the topic of the present section. The second aspect is discussed in the next section. Policies are dealt with at length particularly in Chapters 8 and 11.

The process of building up a European common currency area was based on the idea of both real and even more so financial convergence, along with policy convergence. This was clear in the Werner Report of 1970, the 1974 Council Decision on economic convergence, further refined in the Delors Report of 1989. This perspective was finally made operational in the Maastricht criteria, entered into force in 1993, and the Stability and Growth Pact of 1997 and its developments. The founding documents and agreements foresee that convergence would take place through policy and market processes.[51] To this end, member countries have to stick to the behavioural rules stipulated in common agreements.[52]

[51] The Werner Report (1970) stipulates in Section III on "The Final Objective" (p. 10) that "For such a union only the global balance of payments of the Community vis-a-vis the outside world is of any importance. Equilibrium within the Community would be realized at this stage in the same way as within a nation's frontiers, thanks to the mobility of the factors of production and financial transfers by the public and private sectors." In section IV on "The Principles of Realization of the Plan by Stages" (p. 14) the Report states: "In every field the steps to be taken will be interdependent and will reinforce one another; in particular the development of monetary unification must be based on sufficient progress in the field of convergence and then in that of the unification of economic policies. Parallel to the limitation of the autonomy of the Member States in the matter of economic policy it will be necessary to develop corresponding powers at the Community level."

[52] In Section 4.11 of Chapter 1 of the Delors Report (1989, p. 11) it is observed that "Although substantial progress has been made, the process of integration has been uneven. Greater convergence of economic performance is needed. Despite a marked downward trend in the average rate of price and wage inflation, considerable national differences remain. There are also still notable divergences in budgetary positions and external imbalances have become markedly greater in the recent past. The existence of these disequilibria indicates that there are areas where economic performances will have to be made more

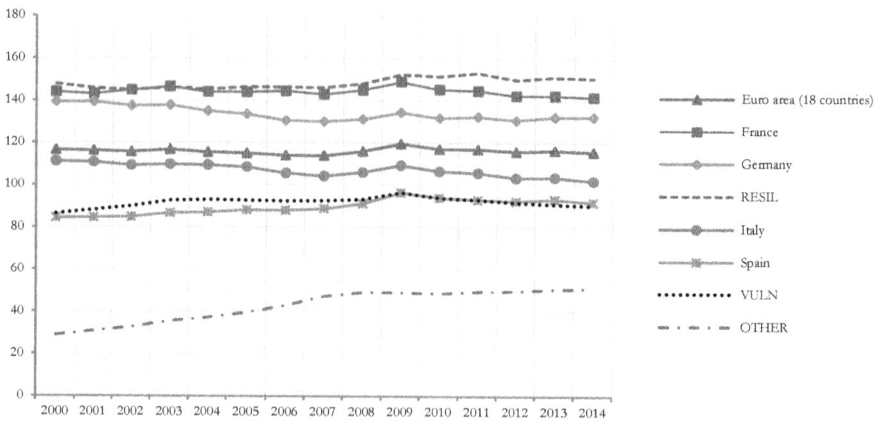

Figure 3.1. Labour Productivity Per Hour Worked (EU-28 = 100).
Source: Author's own graph based on data from the OECD database.

However, the concept of policy convergence remained unclear. What remained unsolved, in particular, was whether and how it is possible to have common or at least compatible policies for member countries in deep real and financial conditions and situations.

Unfortunately, the realisation of those principles and objectives met with difficulties and failures of various kinds and their achievement remained short of what should have been implemented. In general, there was lack of convergence of performance at the aggregate level within the Eurozone, although selected services and manufacturing branches indicate evidence of convergence (Sondermann 2012). With the enfolding of the crisis, divergent national economic performances are manifest within the Eurozone. Labour productivity levels and trends over the last decade have witnessed remarkable differences, to the disadvantage of countries which have been mired in difficult economic and financial situations, although lately there are signs of convergence (Figure 3.1).

convergent." In Section 3.50 on "The principal steps in stage one" (p. 30) it is stated that "Stage one represents the *initiation of the process* of creating an economic and monetary union. It would aim at a greater convergence of economic performance through the strengthening of economic and monetary policy coordination within the existing institutional framework. In the institutional field, by the time of the transition to stage two, it would be necessary to have prepared and ratified the Treaty change."

3.4 On Competitiveness and Productivity

Delgado *et al.* (2012) introduce the new concept of foundational competitiveness that relates directly to performance and prosperity. This concept clarifies the drivers of competitiveness, which are related in particular to labour productivity, and gives due consideration to the role of policies in influencing the drivers. Foundational competitiveness is the expected performance, defined as the level of output per working-age individual, that can be obtained given "the overall quality of a country as a place to do business".[53] The expected performance is thus under the influence of both the productivity of employed workers and the share of the available labour force that a country is able to employ.

Using this approach and framework, the authors define the related concept of global investment attractiveness (GIA), i.e. a country's current factor costs relative to foundational competitiveness. Countries with high

[53] In their study of foundational competitiveness across countries, the authors distinguish between the roles of macroeconomic and microeconomic factors. Macroeconomic factors do not directly establish competitiveness by determining productivity at the firm level or labour mobilisation. However, they are indirectly important, since they define the general conditions for obtaining higher productivity levels. Macroeconomic factors are translated into two composite variables that influence competitiveness. These are social infrastructure and political institutions (SIPI) and monetary and fiscal policy (MFP). The former includes basic health and education, the quality of political institutions, and the rule of law. The latter comprises the management of fiscal sustainability and debt and inflation policies. Microeconomic factors of competitiveness (MICRO) include the sophistication of company operations and strategy (COS) and the quality of the national business environment (NBE). The latter in turn includes factor conditions, context for strategy and rivalry, supporting and related industries (including the state of cluster development), and demand conditions. While these variables are rather sticky, their nature and effect can nevertheless be changed and microeconomic competitiveness can be strengthened through reforms and microeconomic policies. The study also controls for the effect of other factors, which influence competitiveness and which are considered to be inherited and given. These include each country's endowments. Endowments may have a direct influence on prosperity, as in the case of natural resources. Such influence is either positive, e.g. through the sale of natural resources, or negative. In the latter case, the reason may be due, e.g., to the corruption of political institutions and the distortions of policy choices that the abundance of natural resources may foster. Some endowments have or may have an indirect influence on prosperity, e.g. the geographic location of a country or the size of its economy and market.

GIA feature low factor costs compared to potential productivity. This situation is considered be able to positively influence international investment and trade flows and thus lead to higher growth, prosperity of countries and greater sustainability. In their estimate of the relation between countries' GIA and growth, Delgado *et al.* (2012) find that current global investment attractiveness is positively and significantly correlated with subsequent growth.

In order to assess the effect of all these factors on competitiveness, the authors estimate the separate effect of microeconomic competitiveness (MICRO), social infrastructure and political institutions (SIPI), and monetary and fiscal policy (MFP) as the main explanatory variables on output per potential worker in different countries. They also control for endowments and year dummies.

In their study, the authors use multiple data sets including more than 120 indicators of macro- and microeconomic competitiveness and covering more than 130 countries. The period considered spans from 2001 to 2008. The estimate highlights the positive effect of the microeconomic environment on output per potential worker. This effect is strong even after controlling for historical legacies.

An overall competitiveness score for each country and each year is thus computed, using the estimated coefficients of MICRO, SIPI and MFP. The score estimates the comparative competitiveness for each country and allows us to assess the global investment attractiveness for each country through its relationship with labour costs. The findings confirm that countries with high global investment attractiveness have grown rapidly.

The findings of the calculations are important for understanding the complex nature of competitiveness and for assessing the soundness of policies followed in the Eurozone. It is confirmed that both the output per employed person and the ability of a country to mobilise the workforce determine competitiveness. Major findings of the study include a rather skeptical view of the power of cost competitiveness, external balances, and export performance in selected industries to explain satisfactorily the competitiveness of countries.

Although it is true that high labour costs with low productivity are detrimental for economic performance, both countries with better social infrastructure and political institutions and countries with higher levels of performance tend to have higher labour costs. Thus what really matters is to keep labour costs low relative to a country's foundational competitiveness. As to external balances of countries, it appears that they are positively influenced only by monetary and fiscal policies (MFP). The quality of microeconomic competitiveness (MICRO), social infrastructure and political institutions (SIPI), performance levels and output per capita are not important. Export performance reveals mainly the strengths in specific competitiveness dimensions, since it is positively correlated to microeconomic competitiveness and, in manufacturing and high-tech industries, to a country's per capita output. However, it appears rather weak as a comprehensive measure of foundational competitiveness.

At the same time, the important roles of institutional circumstances and of the microeconomic environment are fully confirmed. The role of microeconomic conditions is also likely to become increasingly important at a country's higher level of development. While there is a clear relation between labour productivity of active employees and GDP per capita, both featuring large variation across countries, it also appears that there is large variation in labour mobilisation (Figure 3.2).

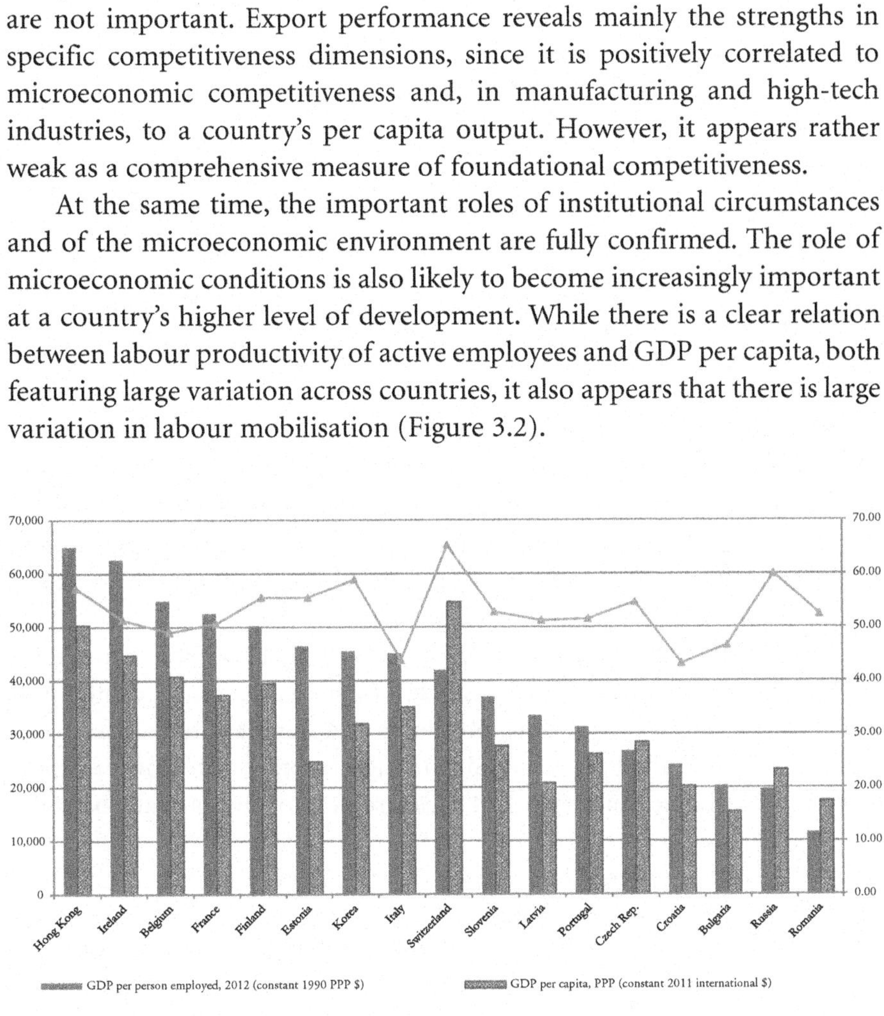

Figure 3.2. Labour Productivity, Employment Mobilisation, and GDP.
Source: International Labour Organization (Key Indicators of the Labour Market database) and World Bank (International Comparison Program database).

The measurement of productivity raises various problems concerning measurement and data quality (Syverson 2011). The most important measurement problems on the output side have to do with the fact that most firms produce more than one output. This opens a problem of aggregation. The standard approach in this case is to use deflated revenues, an acceptable solution when prices fully signal product quality differences. However, when the market power of producers influences price variation, this approach meets serious difficulties and does not properly reflect productivity levels.

Problems also exist on the input side. In the case of labour, different measures exist. These may be both real, such as the number of employees and that of the hours worked per employee. They may also be monetary, in the form of quality-adjusted labour measure, such as the wage bill, considering that wages reflect marginal products of heterogeneous labour units. Marginal productivity is an acceptable approximation in the case of standardised, replicable jobs and functions. However, the concept is doubtful in the case of unique, non-standardised jobs and functions, such as those of managers. Indeed, the measurement of marginal productivity in the case of such jobs is extremely difficult and unreliable. As a consequence, the explanation of the remuneration of these jobs needs also to consider the effect of agency relations, social standards, power and political influence, tournament prizes, and the executive's ability to cater to the needs of the multiple constituents of the firm.

The typical measure used in the case of capital is the establishment or the firm's book value of its capital stock. The measurement of capital productivity meets typically serious problems of different nature. These concern in particular the use of capital stock as a proxy for the flow of capital services, the precise definition and measurement of the capital stock, and the treatment of depreciation.

Along with measurement problems, productivity is influenced by factors other than the measured inputs. Some of these are important at the firm level, which have some degree of control over such factors. Important examples are the quality of labour and capital, managerial talent, learning processes on the job such as learning-by-doing, product and organisational innovation, managerial practice and talent and effectiveness of the decision-making processes, use of ICT and effect of R&D.

Various drivers influencing productivity are external to the production process and therefore are outside the control or influence of the producer. They may also be a subject of policies. These factors act typically in an indirect way on productivity, e.g. by shaping and affecting the incentives that firms have to use the internal factors discussed above. An example of external factors is the presence of spillovers from the external environment to productivity. Other firms or other kinds of organisations may influence other firms' productivity levels through their innovative production practices or through their competitive force and practice. Other examples of external influences are regulatory policies and practices and the institutional features of input markets.

In view of these considerations, labour productivity appears as a reliable measure of productivity. Considering that countries differ remarkably for the number of hours worked, output per potential worker seems to be a reliable measure for assessing productivity differences at international level. This measure has also the advantage to capture workers' productivity and the participation rate of the labour force, both important factors for prosperity.

3.5 Sources of Comparative Data and Information

Competitiveness of vulnerable Eurozone countries is ailing because of different factors. This Eurozone problem should be divided into its two components. First, there is a problem of external competitiveness of the Eurozone vis-à-vis its most important competitors, particularly the United States, Japan, and emerging economies.[54] Second, the problem of the internal competitiveness of the Eurozone member countries is also important.

[54] Since there is no agreed upon definition or measurement of competitiveness, here a broad approach is taken. Competitiveness is defined as the ability of a country to be successful in competing in open international markets and the extent to which this is done. Since this success takes usually place in the long-run, other shorter-term indicators of competitiveness will be considered, mostly referring to price and cost competitiveness. Indirect measures of non-price competitiveness, in particularly those referring to technical progress, such as R&D expenditures and investment in human capital, will also be considered. In fact, these may compensate an appreciation of the domestic currency or increases in domestic prices that would otherwise reduce a country's competitiveness.

This latter is a particularly delicate issue in a group of countries which share a common currency without having a common government of the economy and having incomplete and asymmetric common institutions.

In particular and while external competitiveness can be somehow adjusted through the common exchange rate, internal competitiveness can only be fixed through other means. It should also be reminded that the Eurozone meets additional difficulties in both kinds of adjustments as compared to sovereign countries. As to external competitiveness, the management of the common exchange rate has different consequences for each member country, depending on the latter's economic and financial structure and situation. For instance, a depreciation of the common currency advantages countries with elastic exports more than those with rigid exports. It also disadvantages countries with high external debt in foreign currencies.

In the case of internal competitiveness, the common currency disadvantages those countries whose real (based on quality and technology) and price competitiveness are weaker. In fact, these countries cannot use the depreciation of the national exchange rate to make their production more competitive. While a sovereign country with its own currency can stay afloat through depreciation, a member country of a monetary union cannot. Added to this, the need for an orderly management of the common currency requires that national public finances are kept under control by commonly defined rules, such as those envisaged in the Maastricht Treaty and the Stability and Growth Pact (SGP). This takes away the possibility to support exporting sectors and defend sectors threatened by imports by means of public resources.

Under these conditions, three ways for recovering competitiveness remain: institutional and microeconomic reforms, to make the economic system and firms stronger, more effective and efficient; investment in technical progress; and internal devaluation to decrease production costs. Unfortunately all these actions take time to bring the desired effect, most of them meet strong social opposition, and investment requires resources that may conflict with common financial parameters. Countries with high public deficit or debt particularly suffer under these circumstances. Indeed, the inability to use public resources to implement reforms or investment may leave internal devaluation as the only option available.

Unfortunately, internal devaluation decreases the size of the domestic market and thus worsens their situation, without any guarantee that this may be compensated by greater exports. The discussion of these issues will be resumed in Chapters 10 and 11.

3.6 External Competitiveness

External competitiveness refers to the competitiveness of the Eurozone vis-à-vis its most important competitors, particularly the United States, Japan and China. Although finding comparable measures and data is not easy, various attempts are made at getting a reliable picture of both absolute levels and their changes over time. Sources include the WEF, the OECD, the World Bank and the EU (see Appendix in Section 2.7).

The EU and the Eurozone, which includes the largest economies of the EU with the exception of Great Britain, lost in both production and competitiveness since the 1980s (see Sections 3.1 and 3.2.). As a consequence, the growth of per capita GDP in the EU was slower than in its competitors, with the exception of Japan (Figure 3.3, WEF-EU 2014). Ailing production was the outcome, at least in part, of unfavourable demographics and — particularly in resilient countries — a lower

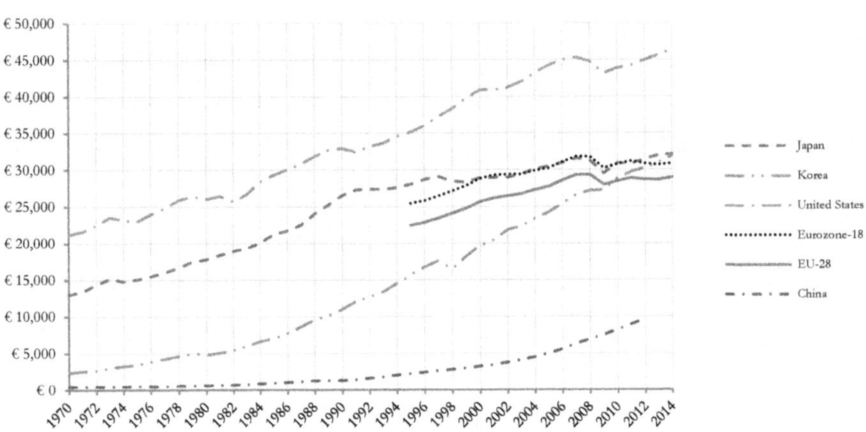

Figure 3.3. GDP Per Capita in US Dollars, Constant Prices, 2005 PPPs.
Source: OECD Database.

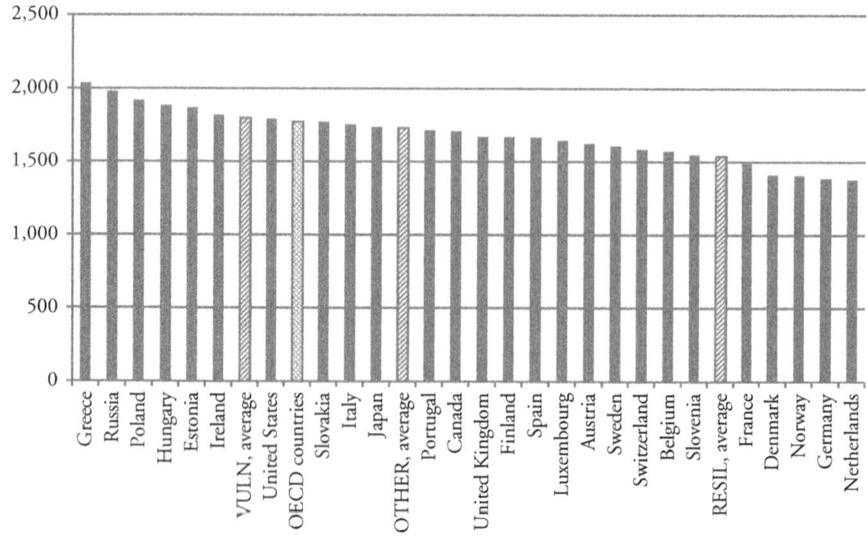

Figure 3.4. Number of Actual Hours Worked Annually Per Worker (2013).
Source: OECD database.

number of hours worked per employee than in the United States and other competitor countries (Figure 3.4).

To better understand the performance of the EU in international comparison, it is useful to look at the main aspects of its competitiveness. Short-term and long-term aspects can be distinguished. The former include unit labour costs (ULC), labour productivity, real prices and real effective exchange rates (REERs). Long-term aspects include institutions, non-price competitiveness and qualitative processes (such as investment in R&D and human capital), and shares in the world market.

Among short-term aspects of competitiveness, ULC in the Eurozone moved rather unfavourably before the crisis (ECORYS 2011),[55] both because wages and taxation increased and the number of worked hours decreased. After the crisis, ULC in the Eurozone countries with current

[55] ECORYS (2011, p. 1) studies the cost competitiveness of European industry based on relative unit labour costs at sectoral level. The study finds that "[w]idening the range of countries considered as competitors results in a higher estimate of the scale of the deterioration in EU competitiveness in the past decade."

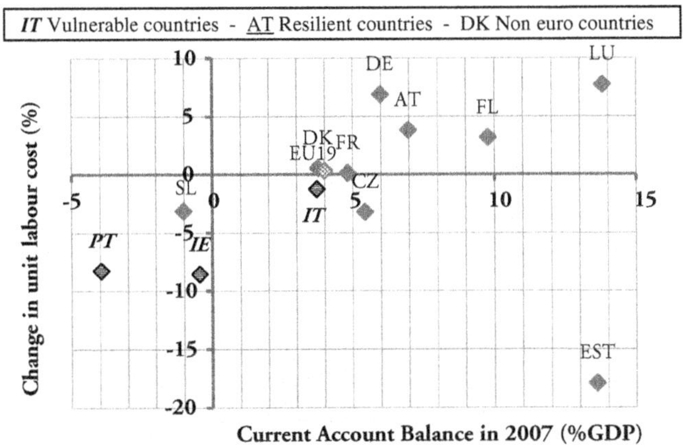

Figure 3.5. Change in Unit Labour Cost between 2010 Q1 and 2014 Q1.
Source: OECD database.

account imbalances decreased considerably, but not in economies with high surpluses (Figure 3.5, OECD 2014f). In principle, this should give an important contribution to the improvement of competitiveness. However, prices adjusted less than wages and this fact reduced the effect of declining unit labour costs on price competitiveness. According to the OECD, slow price adjustment reflected slow product market reforms. Overall ULC moved rather unfavourably in the last 15 years (Figure 3.6).

Labour productivity developed unfavourably in the average of the Eurozone compared to its competitors. The picture appears particularly worrying in the case of productivity per capita (Figures 3.3 and 3.7). The situation looks brighter when considering indicators of productivity per time unit, for the reasons explained in Section 3.1 (Figure 3.8). It is, in particular, the decade before the crisis that looks worrying, since it highlights the declining economic strength of the Eurozone compared to all its main competitors. This situation continued during the crisis, when the performance of all the economies considered worsened.

When using labour productivity data, it is important to take into consideration their actual meaning (ECR 2014, pp. 28–32). ULC is the ratio between labour compensation and labour productivity. The value of this indicator increases if compensation rises faster than productivity, thus denoting falling cost competitiveness. The indicator is sensitive to the

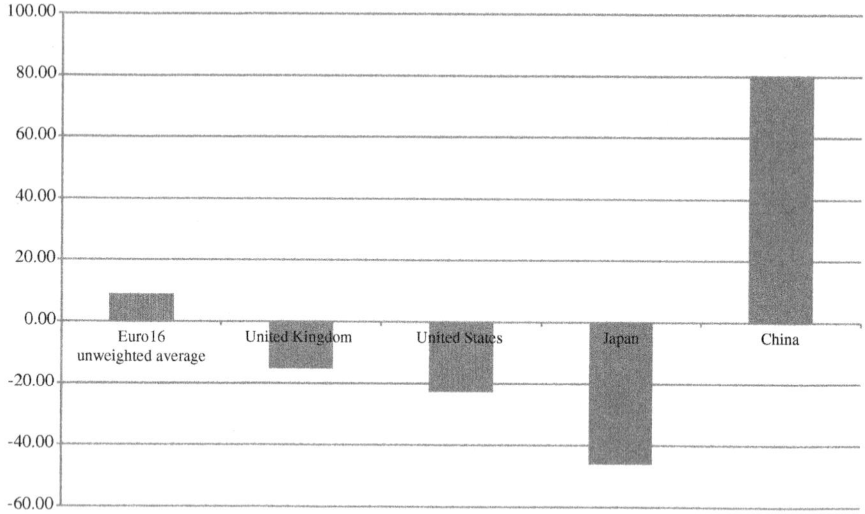

Figure 3.6. Relative Unit Labour Cost % Change, 2000Q1–2014Q3.
Source: Author's own graph based on data from OECD (2014d) (Table A1, p. 70).

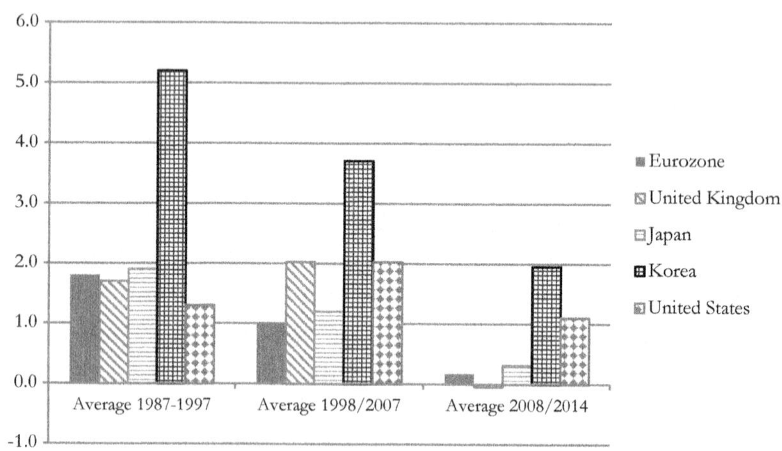

Figure 3.7. GDP Per Person Employed.
Source: OECD (2014d) (Based on author's own analysis of Annex Table 12).

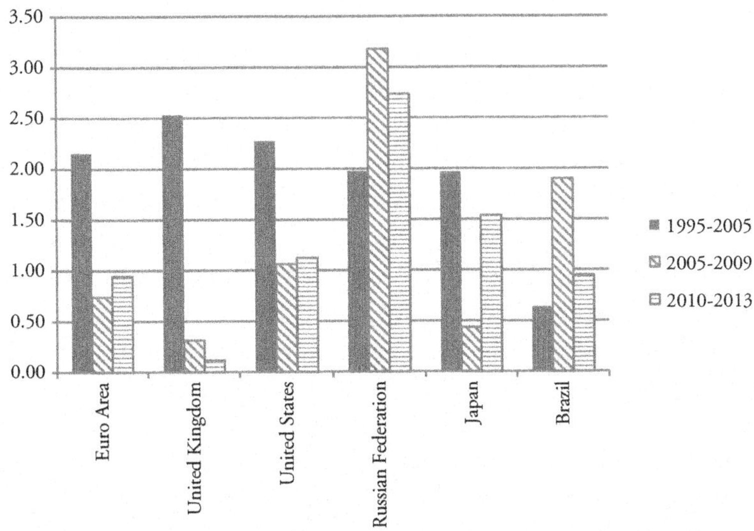

Figure 3.8. GDP Per Hour Worked — Annual Average Growth, %.
Source: The Conference Board (2015), Total Economy Database: Output, Labour and Labour Productivity Country Details 1950–2013.

business cycle and the way in which the labour market is organised. These factors can determine greater fluctuations over the business cycle of production and value added than of the used labour input. This is rather typical in Europe, more than in other countries. It should be considered that other costs enter the determination of cost competitiveness, such as the cost of capital, raw materials and energy, rents, costs that ULC does not consider. Since many of these costs are higher in sectors in which the use of these inputs is more intensive, ULC comparisons are most useful in labour-intensive sectors.

It is also important to notice that the two ways for measuring labour productivity, per person employed or per hour worked, may give considerably different results, particularly during a recession when firms reduce employment and in particular marginal (temporary, part-time) employment. In this case, productivity per person employed increases more (or decreases less) than productivity per hour worked. To have a more precise measure, it would be necessary to calculate labour productivity in full-time equivalent labour, since productivity per person employed does not distinguish between full-time and part-time employment. Finally, productivity is sensitive to the structure of the economy, since different branches have typically different dynamics of productivity, e.g. depending on the role of technical progress and labour intensity. Using a somewhat more refined measure of productivity than the most aggregate one, e.g. productivity in manufacturing, the difference in productivity growth between the European Union and the United States was rather modest up to the crisis (ECR 2014).

For the period considered, ULC growth rates in the United States and the EU were mostly positive and did not diverge in systematic way, except in 2008–2009. In this period, the worst years of the crisis, ULCs in EU manufacturing increased more than in the US. This was so in both economies, because labour compensation adjusted slowly and slightly when labour productivity decreased. The difference in adjustment between the two economies reflects institutional and organisational differences in the labour markets, and perhaps faster technical progress in the United States vs labour hoarding in the EU. In fact, labour productivity in manufacturing grew more in United States than in the EU: by 2.9 and 2.5% respectively (both year-on-year) on average between 2001 and the first quarter of 2014. This was true both before the crisis and since 2012, when productivity in EU manufacturing stagnated. The drop in productivity was quite marked in the EU, both following the 2001 recession and the 2008 crisis, since labour input (hours worked and persons employed) remained more stable than in the United States.

The increase of ULC since 2000 is not sufficient in itself to justify the deterioration of the Eurozone's competitiveness. ULC increased by less than 9% overall between 2000 and 2014 in the Eurozone (OECD 2014d). In the same period, ULC of the Eurozone's main competitors decreased. This refers to the United States, Japan and Great Britain, but not China (Figure 3.9). The Eurozone had the worst performance in both GDP per person employed and unit labour costs. Since the data used here for the Eurozone are unweighted averages, the situation varies for different member countries.

OECD (2012a) offers a useful analysis of Eurozone competitiveness in comparison with at the international level. The study stresses that the

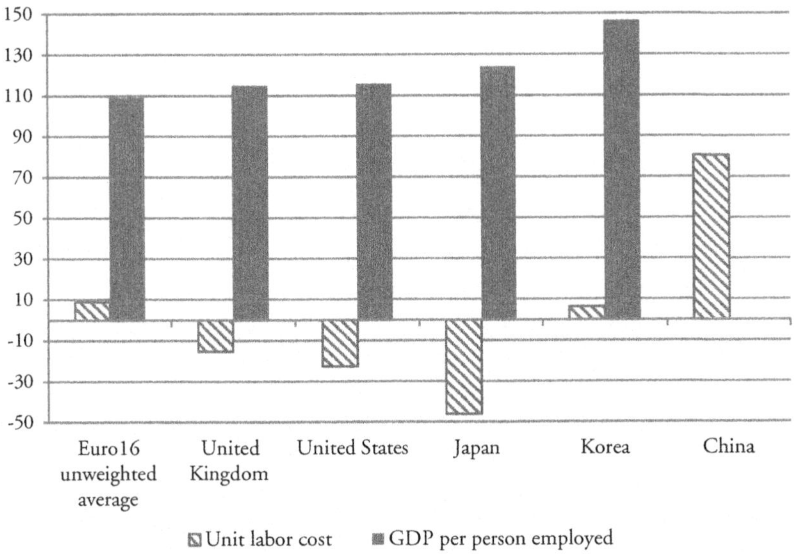

Figure 3.9. Cumulative Growth of GDP Per Person Employed and Unit Labour Cost, 2000–2014 (2000 = 100).
Source: OECD (2014d) (Author's own figure based on on Table A1, p. 70 and Annex Table 12).

Eurozone became less competitive over the past decade. The Eurozone faced a double external challenge, which so far it failed to manage successfully: slowing productivity growth and the loss of market shares in the world exports. Since 2000, productivity in the Eurozone was modest, well below the average of the G7 and the OECD countries. This consequence was due particularly to low growth in multifactor productivity (Figure 3.10). Both the United States and Japan had clearly better productivity growth rates, while the performance of Central-Eastern European countries was much better. Korea and Turkey excel among OECD member countries.

The loss of market shares in the world exports is a long-term feature of the external performance of European countries (Figure 2.4). While the loss characterised most of the advanced OECD countries, the loss was particularly large for the Eurozone countries and quite significant during the crisis (Figure 3.11). Only some Central and East European member countries strengthened significantly their market shares, mostly by improving their international specialisation.

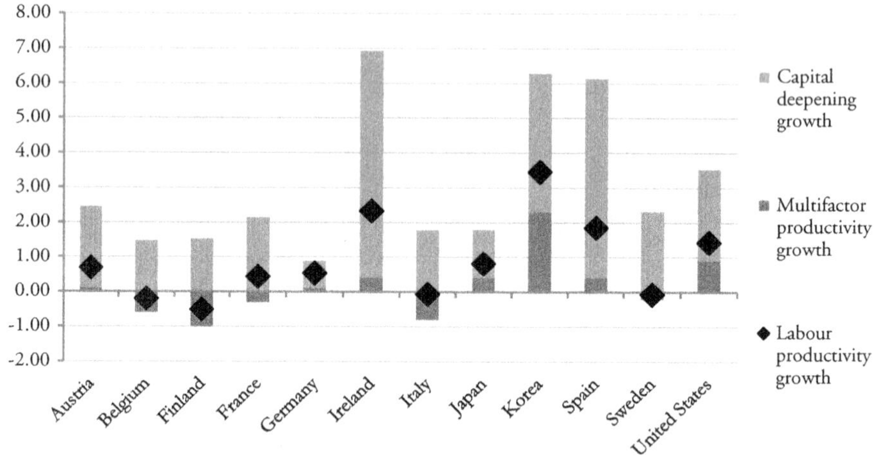

Figure 3.10. Decomposition of Productivity Growth (% Changes 2007–2012).
Source: OECD (2015a).

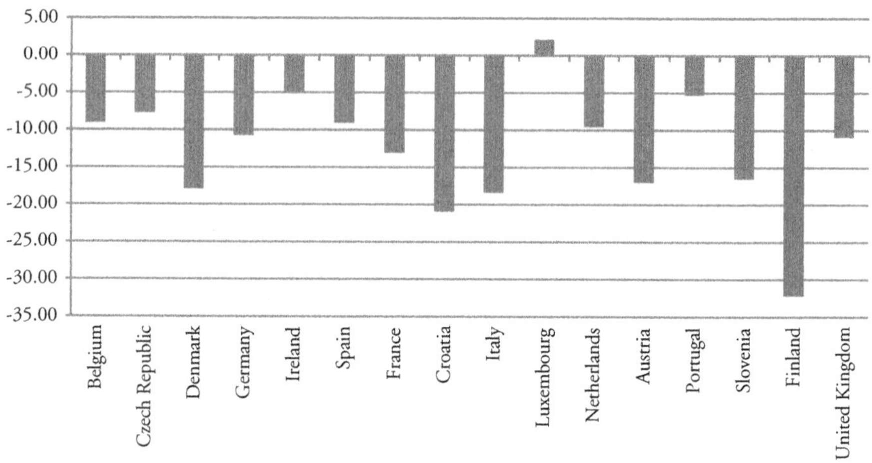

Figure 3.11. Percentage of World Total Market Share, 5-Year Change (2008–2013).
Note: Export performance measures the relative gain and losses of world market share of a given country. If a country's exports are growing faster (slower) that the weighted average demand from its partners, it is gaining (loosing) market share.
Source: Eurostat (2015) (http://appsso.eurostat.ec.europa.eu/nui/submitViewTableAction.do).

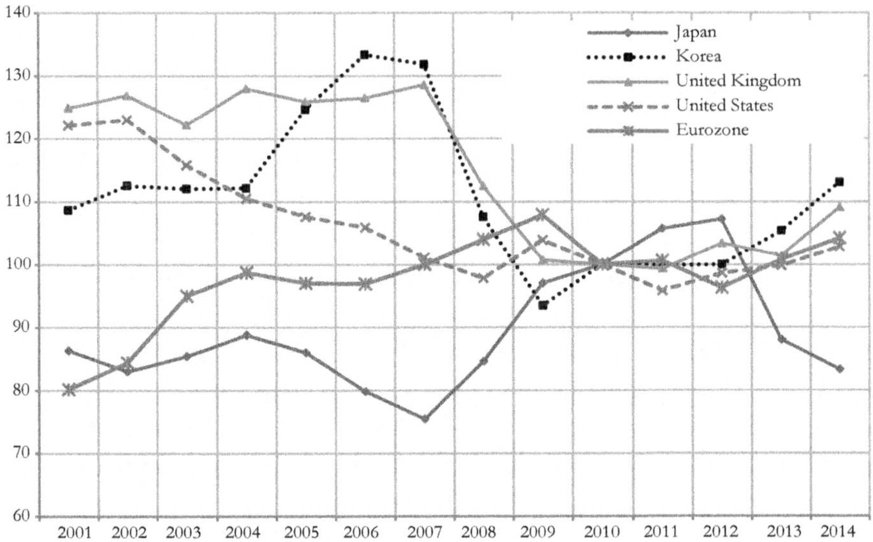

Figure 3.12. Effective Exchange Rates, Indices 2010 = 100, Average of Daily Rates. *Source*: OECD (2014d) (Based on author's own analysis of Annex Table 37, p. 253).

Two further issues should be clarified before reaching a sounder conclusion on the Eurozone competitiveness: prices and REERs. In fact, the Eurozone could recover the aforementioned disadvantage through lower growth of prices and decreasing real exchange rates compared to its competitors.[56] Unfortunately, both prices and real exchange rates moved unfavourably in the Eurozone. The REER of the Eurozone moved in an unfavourable way compared to its competitors until around 2009, after which it moved approximately in line with that of the United States (Figure 3.12).[57]

Prices in the Eurozone (GDP deflator) moved in an unfavourable way relative to the United States and Japan until 2000, after which they varied

---

[56] See also EC (2014f).

[57] It should be noticed that the OECD calculates effective exchange rates in the CPI index and not labour costs. Thus effective exchange rates would reflect the effect of inflation and not the real economy.

roughly in line with the United States, Great Britain and Korea, while deflation in Japan deepened further (Figure 3.13). During the crisis and again apart from Japan, prices increased less in the Eurozone than in its competitors. Consumer price indexes present a rather similar picture. Such moderation helped the Eurozone to recover part of the disadvantage that it suffered in labour costs and productivity.

The developments in prices and costs were thus not particularly unfavourable to the Eurozone in relation to Western competitors. However, productivity had a distinctly unfavourable dynamics in the Eurozone. Dynamics of prices and real exchange rate roughly in line with those of the competitors could not compensate such disadvantage. Clearly the comparison with emerging countries is a different story, to the advantage of the latter. As a consequence, the EU and the Eurozone could not stop the long-run loss of export shares in the world market (Orszaghova *et al.* 2013).

3.7 Long-Term Processes

Any measure of competitiveness based on single factors is problematic and we should take great care in evaluating its meaning. Moreover, competitiveness is largely the outcome of long-term processes. For this reason, various international organisations and individual researchers tried to calculate measurements of productivity that take into consideration many of the factors that may have an influence and do so particularly in the long term. Long-term aspects include institutions, non-price competitiveness and qualitative processes (such as investment in R&D and human capital), and shares in the world market. The latest sources are used here in order to avoid long-term comparability problems that derive from changes in the composition and coverage of indicators so typical of this type of indexes.

In the following the work done at the WEF is considered to assess the long-term aspects of competitiveness (see Appendix in Section 2.7). The WEF works out a comparative analysis in its Global Competitiveness Report, which has been published on an annual basis during the last 35 years, and it presently covers 144 countries and makes use of more than 100 indicators (WEF 2014). The aim of the Report is to highlight the key factors that are at the foundation of past and future economic perfor-

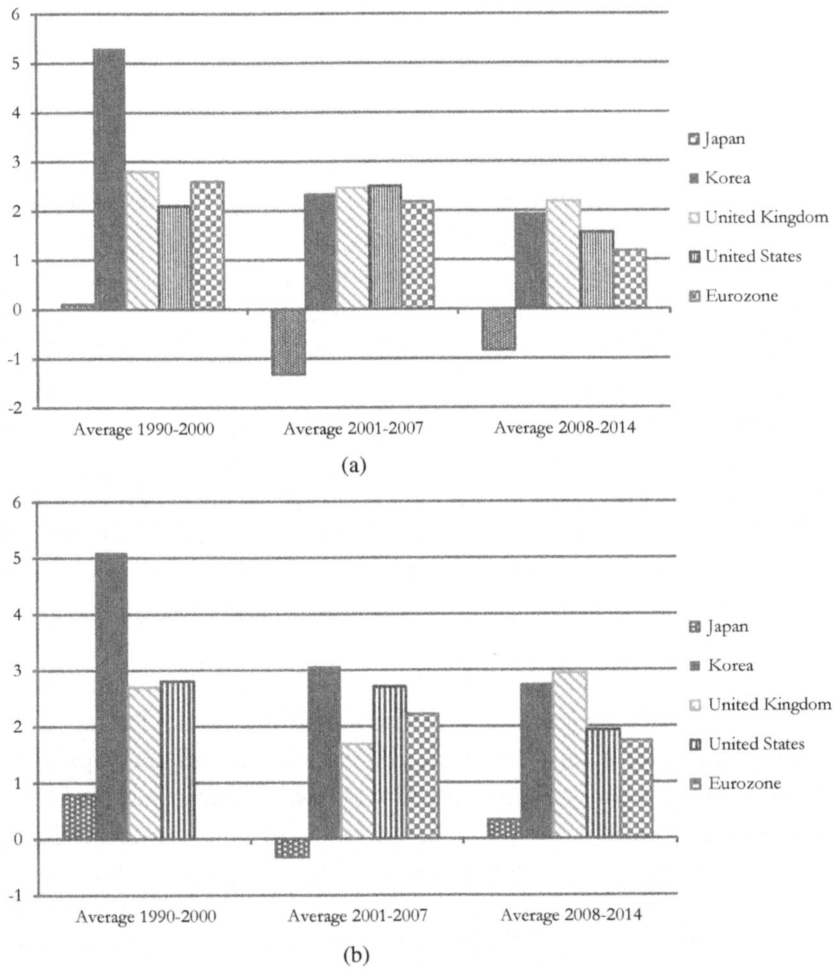

Figure 3.13. GDP Deflators (Figure a) and Consumer Price Indexes (Figure b). Percentage Change from Previous Year.
Source: Figure a — OECD (2014d) (Based on author's own analysis of Annex Table 16, p. 232); Figure b — OECD (2014d) (Based on author's own analysis of on Annex Table 18, p. 234).

mance and growth, and the mechanisms and interrelations that determine them.[58] This approach is aimed at building a shared understanding of the

[58] Similarly to publications by other international organisations, the Report refers to the level of present and future prosperity in a country. Throughout this book, the term

main strengths and weaknesses of each of the economies covered, also for normative purposes.

The core idea of the Report is that "the social and environmental dimensions of an economy need to be fully considered in any growth or development agenda" (WEF 2014, p. xiii). As a consequence, it is important to understand how such dimensions relate to competitiveness and economic performance. To allow for more precise analyses and comparisons in this perspective, the WEF developed its Global Competitiveness Index (GCI) since 2005. The GCI is meant to be "a comprehensive tool that measures the microeconomic and macroeconomic foundations of national competitiveness".

Competitiveness is defined as "the set of institutions, policies, and factors that determine the level of productivity of a country" (WEF 2014, p. 4). In turn, the level of productivity determines the level of performance of an economy, the rates of return to investments, and consequently the growth rates of that economy. The reading thus goes from competitiveness, institutions, endowments and policies through productivity to performance.

The GCI offers some interesting insights into the relative competitiveness of the Eurozone (Figure 3.14).[59] The Eurozone and the EU fare rather weakly, particularly when compared to the United States and Japan.[60] Its only advantage as compared to the United States is in terms of the macroeconomic environment,[61] while it is on par with Japan in technological readiness and health and primary education. The Eurozone and the EU perform weakly compared to Korea and to China in macroeconomic environment and market size, and also for innovation in comparison to Korea.

---

performance is used, since prosperity is identified with high levels of income and economic growth (performance) plus equity. The latter means moderate inequality (lack of excessive income and wealth differences) and the availability of ample opportunities and mobility (chances).

[59] The indicators are converted to a 1 to 7 scale to make the aggregation possible. The Report applies a min-max transformation, thus preserving the order of country scores and their mutual relative distance.

[60] One problem in the GCI is that market size is considered at the national level and no aggregation is calculated for the common EU and Eurozone markets.

[61] The components of the third pillar, macroeconomic environment, are: government budget balance, gross national savings, inflation, government debt, and country credit rating.

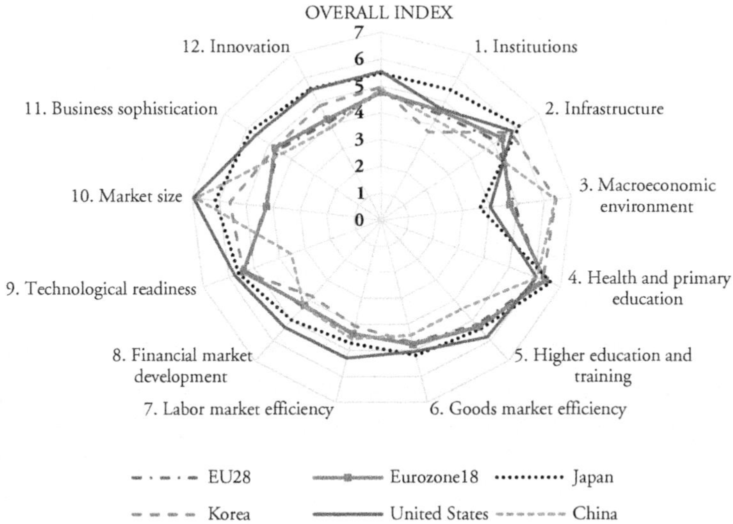

Figure 3.14. Value of the Pillars' Global Competitiveness Index in the EU and Other Countries, 2014.
Source: Authors's own calculations based on data from WEF (2014).

The disadvantage of the Eurozone and the EU is particularly evident in the pillars most important at the highest stage of development: business sophistication and innovation.[62] These pillars include some of the goals of the EU Lisbon Strategy and Europe 2020 Strategy. However, the disadvantage is clear also in the case of labour market efficiency and financial market development.[63] The GCI thus highlights that the Eurozone and the EU have serious problems in fostering competitiveness.

[62] The 11th pillar on business sophistication includes the quantity and quality of local suppliers, the state of cluster development, the nature of competitive advantage, the value chain breadth, the control of international distribution, production process sophistication, extent of marketing, willingness to delegate authority, and in part the reliance on professional management. The 12th pillar on R&D innovation comprises capacity for innovation, the quality of scientific research institutions, company spending on R&D, university-industry collaboration in R&D, government procurement of advanced technology products, availability of scientists and engineers, PCT patent applications, and intellectual property protection.

[63] The seventh pillar, labour market efficiency, includes flexibility factors (cooperation in labour-employer relations, flexibility of wage determination, hiring and firing practices,

The WEF takes the goals of the Europe 2020 Strategy as a benchmark for assessing the competitiveness of the EU (WEF-EU 2014, see Appendix in Section 2.7). The result is the Europe 2020 Competitiveness Index (ECI). The ECI is more a useful instrument to monitor the implementation of the European strategy, than a device for obtaining an exhaustive measure of European competitiveness. The report also calculates the scores for some non-EU countries and thus provides a useful international comparison about the EU performance in pursuing its long-term fundamental goals (Table 3.2 and Figure 3.15).

Although both the EU and the Eurozone fare better than any other country except Switzerland in sustainable growth, both have clear gaps in all other pillar scores compared to Japan and the United States. The only exception is in social inclusion as compared to the latter country. The EU and the Eurozone, though, have better scores compared to China and Russia in all pillars, except the labour market and employment; they also have a very similar score to China in enterprise environment. Overall, as far as the pillars related to growth are concerned, the scores of the EU and the Eurozone are clearly worse than those of Switzerland, Japan and the United States, on par with Korea and significantly higher than China, Russia and the BRIC's average (Table 3.2).

There may be different reasons for this apparently disappointing situation. One reason is that both the Eurozone and the EU include countries at different level of development and with different features. At the same time neither the EU nor the Eurozone have a common government capable of dealing properly with areas of backwardness in particular countries. But these data also point at the difficulties that the EU and the Eurozone have in pursuing the goals of its ambitious agendas for development: the Lisbon strategy previously and Europe 2020 presently. Indeed, both strategies were proposed by the European Commission, which lacks most of the

redundancy costs, effect of taxation on incentives to work) and the efficient use of talent (pay and productivity, in part the reliance on professional management, the country's capacity to retain and to attract talent, and female participation in the labour force). The eighth pillar deals with financial market development and includes efficiency factors (availability and affordability of financial services, financing through local equity market, ease of access to loans, and venture capital availability) and trustworthiness and confidence (soundness of banks, regulation of securities exchanges, and legal rights index).

Table 3.2. A Breakdown of Growth Features in the Europe 2020 Index (2014 Edition, Score 1–7).

	EU28	Euro18	United States	Japan	Korea, Rep.	China	Russia	BRIC	Switzerland
Overall score	4.56	4.66	5.00	5.07	4.63	3.99	3.81	3.87	5.60
Smart growth	4.53	4.64	5.38	5.17	5.13	3.85	3.73	3.71	5.47
1. Enterprise environment	4.05	4.12	4.88	4.54	4.01	4.16	3.46	3.78	4.77
Competition	4.24	4.4	4.57	4.57	4.10	—	—	—	4.89
Clusters	4.32	4.5	5.28	5.60	4.60	—	—	—	5.48
Entrepreneurship	4.60	4.6	5.24	4.29	4.76	—	—	—	4.82
Availability of finance	3.03	3.1	4.42	3.72	2.58	—	—	—	3.87
2. Digital agenda	4.71	4.78	5.72	5.55	6.01	3.43	4.02	3.59	5.42
ICT readiness	4.93	5.0	5.27	4.97	5.31	—	—	—	5.44
ICT usage	5.33	5.4	6.28	5.99	6.39	—	—	—	5.75
ICT impact	3.89	4.0	5.61	5.70	6.35	—	—	—	5.07
3. Innovative Europe	4.34	4.50	5.37	5.28	5.24	3.62	3.04	3.32	5.81
4. Education and training	5.00	5.14	5.55	5.29	5.25	4.21	4.38	4.15	5.88
Education	5.34	5.5	5.73	5.62	6.02	—	—	—	5.72
Training	4.67	4.8	5.37	4.97	4.49	—	—	—	6.05
Inclusive growth	4.57	4.66	4.75	5.13	4.23	4.53	4.03	4.11	5.74
5. Labour market and employment	4.15	4.13	4.83	4.58	4.12	4.76	4.36	4.25	5.60

(*Continued*)

Table 3.2. *(Continued)*

	EU28	Euro18	United States	Japan	Korea, Rep.	China	Russia	BRIC	Switzerland
Labour market efficiency	3.8	3.78	—	—	—	—	—	—	—
Labour participation	4.5	4.47	—	—	—	—	—	—	—
6. Social inclusion	4.99	5.19	4.66	5.67	4.34	4.31	3.69	3.96	5.88
Sustainable growth	4.68	4.77	3.96	4.60	3.41	3.46	3.73	4.03	5.83
7. Sustainable growth	4.68	4.77	3.96	4.60	3.41	3.46	3.73	4.03	5.83

Source: Author's own calculations based on WEF-EU (2014).

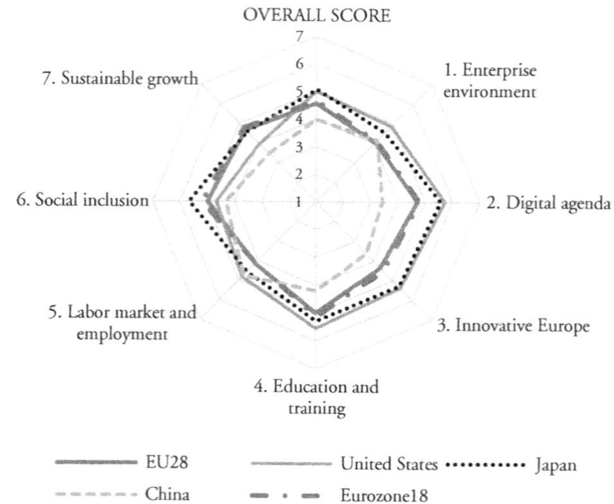

Figure 3.15. Breakdown of Growth Features in the Europe 2020 Index in the European Union and Other Countries (2014).
Source: Author's own figure based on data from WEF-EU (2014).

instruments and competences to implement the goals. Most of instruments and competences belong in national governments. Moreover, the European management of the crisis had negative consequences for many of these indicators, as explained in the following chapters.

Along with institutions, long-term aspects of competitiveness include non-price competitiveness and quality processes, such as investment in R&D and human capital. Although these factors are considered above, a few more hints may be useful to complete the picture. The Eurozone, as much as the EU, scores weaker results on average than its immediate competitors. While keeping an important absolute advantage in most fields in long-term factors, European countries are improving their performance at a slower pace than emerging countries.

The productivity problem of the Eurozone has also to do with other structural features, including the development of human capital and R&D, innovation, the business environment, regulation of labour and products markets, and taxation. The Eurozone on average faces problems in all these areas, compared to its main competitors and emerging economies. These factors are also important because they can activate other drivers of productivity and competitiveness, such as product variety and quality, technological innovation, specialisation and integration in global supply chains.

The EU and the Eurozone are in a relatively disadvantaged position in the international competition for innovation (OECD 2012, pp. 17–18). This conclusion refers also to business R&D intensity. Although some of their member countries, notably Germany and resilient countries more generally, are well placed in gross domestic expenditures in R&D compared to the GDP, most member countries (vulnerable, other Eurozone and non-Eurozone countries) are unable to keep pace with emerging economies and also with the most dynamic of the OECD member countries, such as Korea, Japan and the United States (Figure 3.16). The situation is rather similar in the case of exports with high technology content, with the difference that resilient countries also fare relatively weakly.

The situation concerning investment in human capital is no better (BI 2011a; OECD 2012a, Figure 3.17). Such investment is critical for productivity and competitiveness through the role that a highly skilled workforce has in the economy. The educational system in most of the member

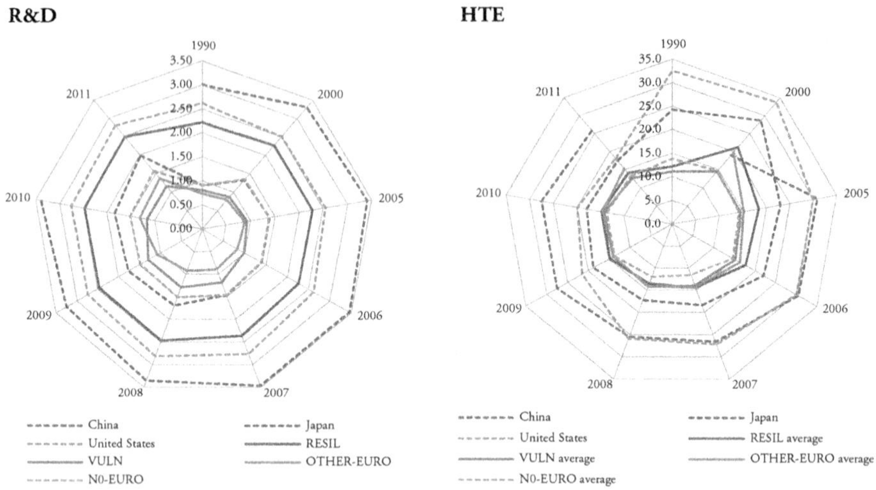

Figure 3.16. R&D Expenditures and High-Technology Exports.
* Research and development expenditures (% of GDP).
** High-technology exports (% of manufactured exports).
Source: Author's own figure based on World Bank's World Development Indicators.

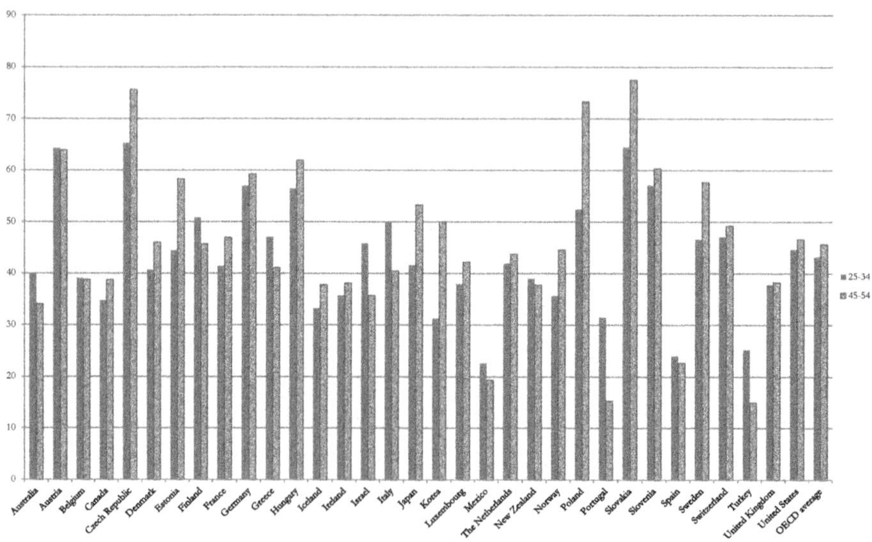

Figure 3.17. Population That Has Attained Tertiary Education (2013, or Latest Year Available). Percentage, by Age Group.
Source: OECD, *Education at a Glance*, 2014 (http://www.oecd.org/edu/education-at-a-glance-2014-indicators-by-chapter.htm).

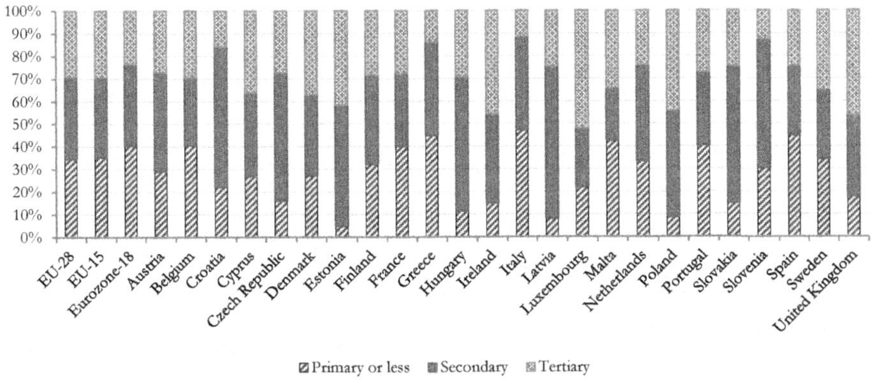

Figure 3.18. Immigrants by Level of Education Share in the Total of Foreign-Born, 2005/06, %.

Note: Bulgaria, Germany, Lithuania and Romania are omitted since data are not available or are incomplete.

Source: Eurostat, 'Population by educational attainment level, sex, age and country of birth (%)' (http://appsso.eurostat.ec.europa.eu/nui/submitViewTableAction.do).

countries of the EU and the Eurozone remains rather problematic, particularly concerning tertiary education, in spite of the good quality of many universities and the good standing in international ranking of knowledge (e.g. the OECD PISA ranking).[64] Although the standing is weak particularly in Southern Europe, even a country like Germany encounters problems in addressing the needs of a rich competitive economy. Problems lie in both the number of people with tertiary education and the content of such education. Low enrolment in fields related to natural sciences and technology is a problem in many EU countries. The problem is intensified by the fact that extra-EU immigrants in most EU countries are predominantly low skilled in comparison with other OECD countries (Dallago 2014, Figure 3.18).

3.8 Conclusions

After a long postwar period of catching up to the United States in production, the countries of Western Europe lost ground and a new process

[64] Programme for International Student Assessment. See http://www.oecd.org/pisa for further information.

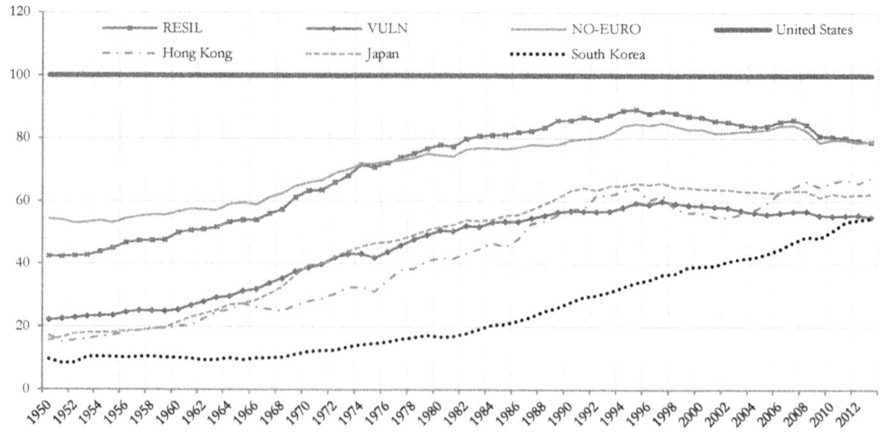

Figure 3.19. Productivity Gap: GDP Per Hours Worked (Geary–Khamis Dollars, US = 100). *Source*: Author's own figure based on The Conference Board Total Economy Database™, *Output, Labor and Labor Productivity Country Details, 1950–2013*, January 2014 (http://www.conference-board.org/data/economydatabase).

of divergence started from mid-1990s. Also productivity and intangible factors, such as the use of ICT in production, showed a pattern of divergence, following the long post-war period when European performance was catching up. As a consequence, the distance between European productivity and that of its competitors, both developed and emerging countries alike, increased and the effectiveness of the European economies decreased in relative terms (Figure 3.19).

Although this pattern concerns the entire EU and Eurozone, it appears that important differences exist among countries and groups of countries. It is thus important to adopt a more disaggregated view and look for the causes of this undesirable situation. The analysis that ensues focuses on the Eurozone. Having one fundamental institution in common, the euro, allows for a more precise comparison. Moreover, the choice is motivated by its economic and political relevance, since divergence among countries in an incomplete monetary union may have important negative consequences that can jeopardise the very viability of the union.

Part II

Institutions and Policies

"A day will come when … all of you, nations of the Continent, will, without losing your distinctive qualities and your glorious individuality, be blended into a superior unity, and constitute a European fraternity…"

— Victor Hugo, the President of the Congress,
Report of the Proceedings of the Second General Peace Congress, Paris, 22–24 August, 1849

4

The Internal Economic Asymmetry of the Eurozone

The Eurozone lost relative economic strength compared to the United States and other countries approximately since the mid-1990s. However, this statement is insufficient to give a correct picture of the Eurozone. The Eurozone is an economic and monetary union, albeit an incomplete one, and not a unified country. In fact, the union lacks a common government capable of transferring resources among its various components. The Eurozone also lacks a true lender of last resort, although a recent interpretation of its mandate under the pressure of worrying economic and financial events transformed the European Central Bank (ECB) into an indirect lender of last resort.

ECB lending cannot take place directly, but only through secondary markets of public debt. Since the ECB can lend directly to commercial banks, this situation goes very close to imitate the existence of a lender of last resort, provided that the different parties (the ECB, commercial bank and national governments) reach mutual, albeit not explicit understanding. The problem is that the ECB is not really sovereign in these decisions. In fact, it must obtain the agreement of the member countries' national central banks.

This situation can work smoothly only if the financial situation of member countries is similar. This was the case until the crisis started in 2008, when no tensions existed in the financial and monetary markets and interest rates converged among countries. The common currency goes to the benefit of all member countries: countries in a resilient economic and financial position may get the advantage of having a currency somewhat weaker than their national currencies would be, because they share the currency with countries that are considered to be economically and financially more vulnerable. At the same time, the latter have the advantage of having to pay a much lower interest rate on their sovereign debt, thanks to the markets' trust in the common currency. In a sense, vulnerable countries can borrow stability and credibility from resilient countries.

The Eurozone was internally asymmetric since its beginning. After serious debates and political skirmishes, countries such as Italy and Belgium were also accepted into the monetary union since the start. This happened in spite of the fact that their public finances were not in line with the criteria that member countries had to meet, in order to give the common currency a sound basis. Greece was initially refused, but could join after two years, in spite of enduring financial problems. These countries were accepted because it was considered that they were converging to the parameters.

In the following years, new asymmetries appeared, e.g. in the form of real estate bubbles in such Eurozone countries as Spain and Ireland. While the financial situation is important for the stability of the monetary union and although monetary decisions can jeopardise financial stability, both public and private finances also respond to the situation of the real economy and to policymaking. For instance, public debts can accumulate as a consequence of social policies or the financing of public investment with accommodating monetary and fiscal policies. If these decisions do not increase output, thus creating the resources to finance their own costs (e.g. there is full employment or resources are spent inefficiently), financial disequilibria may follow. These asymmetries can jeopardise the stability of the common currency.

Thus, it is important to assess whether the goals of the treaties and the basis of Economic and Monetary Union (EMU), as expressed by convergence criteria, were implemented. Since financial and monetary convergence is strongly influenced by the real economy, the topic of this chapter is economic asymmetries among member countries. It considers asymmetries in internal competitiveness, thus following and completing the analysis of the previous chapter, and the distinctive features of European capitalisms as one of the institutional aspects that has to be considered in assessing the Eurozone response to external shocks. The chapter continues by looking at the internal divergence of the Eurozone and shows that two main groups of countries with distinct features and situations exist.

4.1 An Overview

Internal competitiveness, i.e. competitiveness compared to other Eurozone member countries, was diverging well before the common currency was adopted (De Grauwe 2014). Competitiveness measures show that levels of competitiveness and their trends were different in diverse countries. Under these circumstances, having a common currency and missing a common government of the economy expose the disadvantaged countries to serious economic dangers and make their economic situation hard to sustain. The attempt to compensate this disadvantage through accommodating short-term policies is likely to destabilise also their financial situation.

Diverging competitiveness levels are usually attributed to soft wage policies, i.e. to wages that grow more than labour productivity in the vulnerable part of the union. This is nearly obviously so. Yet it is important to understand that higher labour costs may be the outcome of higher net wages, but also of other input costs (e.g. taxation, energy, raw materials) and lower investment and technical progress. Indeed, lower-competitiveness countries in the Eurozone are often countries that have invested less.

This kind of situation is ridden with complicacies in an incomplete monetary union. In principle, fiscal policies are under the control of national governments. However, they can hardly be used, due to the necessary fiscal discipline that the common currency requires. Indeed, the greater real and financial asymmetries are, the more important fiscal discipline is.[65] Although the problem under discussion here is one of national asymmetries, a depreciation of the common currency could be of some help, if countries suffering from recession or depression have price elastic exports. In this case, their external price competitiveness would improve more than that of countries with a more rigid export demand, thus compensating for the unchanged internal competitiveness.

The common central bank's expansionary policies other than depreciation (the so-called unconventional operations, see Section 11.8) may have some effect and gain some time. However, if the union sticks rigidly to its formal respect of the pacts and treaties, expansionary monetary policies would only have mild and temporary effects. If the problem is one of failing competitiveness in one part of the union (vulnerable countries), banks tend to use abundant and cheap money to compensate for bad debts in their portfolio. They also use money outside the productive sector to buy public bonds and lend or invest abroad, perhaps in resilient countries, since domestic productive investments remain low. Thus expansionary monetary policies are good for stabilising sovereign debt, not for reviving economic activity.

If the problems appear intractable in the short run, unless member countries agree to transfer, in one way or another, resources from more competitive to less competitive countries, the situation may be different in the long run.[66] Different competitiveness levels in an incomplete currency

---

[65] The President of the ECB, Mario Draghi, recalled forcefully this reality in his speech at the Italian Parliament on 25 March 2015.

[66] There may be different ways of reaching a more balanced situation, going from a transfer union to fiscal equalisation. A transfer union is used to identify different schemes, including — in its most complete form — permanent direct and horizontal transfers between Eurozone countries, a situation from which the EMU is still far away. Some see this outcome as desirable or inevitable (Hill 2014), others are afraid for the potential complicacies and conflicts it could bring (Heinen 2011a). Fiscal equalisation consists in the transfer of financial resources across countries or regions in order to balance-out the consequences of

union require that unit labour costs (ULC) and/or the cost of other inputs in the vulnerable country decrease compared to the countries in a more resilient position. This may be reached through internal devaluation. However, the same result may result from faster technical progress obtained through higher investments.

Failure to upgrade competitiveness increases real effective exchange rates (REERs) in vulnerable countries compared to resilient countries. This in turn makes vulnerable countries unable to export even to the common currency area and causes the increase of their imports. In the long run, internal reforms and common support to investments is the highway to upgrading the competitiveness of disadvantaged countries in a sustainable way. This requires that financial resources in vulnerable countries are used to improve their real performance and much less current expenditures. However, it may be difficult to keep wages and consumption levels in vulnerable countries much lower than in resilient countries without running into economic recession and political and social problems. Some kind of external transfer is necessary to guarantee economic success. These issues will be discussed in Chapters 11 and 12.

4.2 Internal Competitiveness

Relative ULC continued to diverge until 2009 (Table 4.1). The case of labour productivity in Italy is the most remarkable one within the Eurozone. It was substantially higher than the EU average in 2000, but decreased to the EU average by 2010 (Aiello *et al.* 2010; Aquino *et al.* 2012; Bugamelli *et al.* 2012). Other vulnerable countries fared better. In Spain, labour productivity decreased to the EU average by 2000, but it returned to the original relative level, well above the EU average, by the end of the decade. Productivity in Greece was constantly about 20% below the EU average and worsened only with the unfolding of the economic crisis. Productivity in Germany and France was significantly

---

disparities in incomes and revenue raising capacity and provide all citizens with similar levels of public services at a similar tax burden (Blöchliger 2013; Blöchliger and Charbit 2008). The EU budget may be seen as a rather rudimentary and modest form of fiscal equalisation.

Table 4.1. Unit Labour Costs, Index, Seasonally Adjusted (2010 = 100).

	1995	1996	1997	1998	1999	2000	2001	2002	2003	2004	2005	2006	2007	2008	2009	2010	2011	2012	2013	2014
RESISL	79.8	80.8	80.6	81.0	81.8	82.6	84.9	86.8	88.0	88.3	89.2	90.1	91.3	95.2	100.6	100.0	101.5	105.0	107.2	108.0
VULN	64.5	67.5	70.2	72.4	74.1	75.8	78.6	81.8	84.7	86.6	90.4	92.0	94.8	99.6	102.1	100.0	98.8	97.3	97.2	95.8
OTHER EURO	46.9	52.0	56.1	58.9	61.4	65.6	69.0	72.2	75.4	78.3	80.5	83.4	88.4	96.5	102.0	100.0	99.8	101.5	104.3	106.8
NO EURO	61.2	64.1	67.8	70.3	72.3	77.4	81.8	84.2	85.4	86.5	87.4	88.5	92.0	96.4	100.1	100.0	101.0	103.7	104.7	106.6
Eurozone-19	79.6	80.7	81.1	81.5	82.4	83.3	84.9	87.0	88.9	89.5	90.8	91.5	92.9	96.4	100.7	100.0	100.6	102.4	103.8	104.8
France	79.1	79.8	79.8	79.6	80.4	81.2	83.1	85.5	87.3	88.1	90	91.5	93	95.8	99	100	100.9	102.7	103.7	105.1
Germany	93.7	94	92.8	93.2	94	94.4	94.2	94.9	96	95.9	95.2	93.3	92.6	95.1	101	100	100.6	103.7	106	107.9
Greece	53.9	57	61.7	65.9	68.8	69.1	70.8	77.6	78.5	80	87	85.9	88.4	92.8	99.3	100	99.7	96.3	89.6	87.9
Ireland				74	75.1	77.2	81.6	82.5	86.8	90.2	94.5	97.9	103.1	110.9	108	100	96.7	97.2	101.2	
Italy	69.1	72.9	74.9	73.6	74.8	75.3	77.8	80.8	84.3	86.3	88.2	90.1	91.9	95.8	100.1	100	100.7	102.1	102.7	104
Portugal	67.9	70.8	73.6	76.4	78.5	81.9	85.2	87.9	91.1	91.3	94.4	95	95.9	98.6	101.3	100	98	94.9	97.3	96.4
Spain	67	69.1	70.7	72	73.5	75.3	77.7	80.2	82.6	85	88	90.9	94.6	100	101.6	100	98.9	96	95.4	95
United Kingdom	65.5	66.6	68.8	71.8	74	76.2	79.1	80	81.2	83.7	85.4	88.5	91.7	93.8	98.3	100	99.9	102.3	103.7	104.6
Japan	133.0	130.3	130.8	131.4	128.5	125.1	122.8	118.4	113.8	109.9	108.9	106.7	103.6	104.8	105.1	100.0	100.7	99.0	98.0	99.6
Korea	79.7	84.6	87.3	86.7	87.7	89.6	92.1	97.2	101.4	103.3	106.6	107.3	107.6	100.4	100.1	100.0	98.3	103.4	104.6	105.5
United States	77.9	78.9	80.4	82.6	83.8	87.1	89.0	88.7	89.6	91.4	92.9	95.8	98.8	101.2	100.4	100.0	102.0	103.7	104.1	105.8

Source: OECD database (stats.oecd.org).

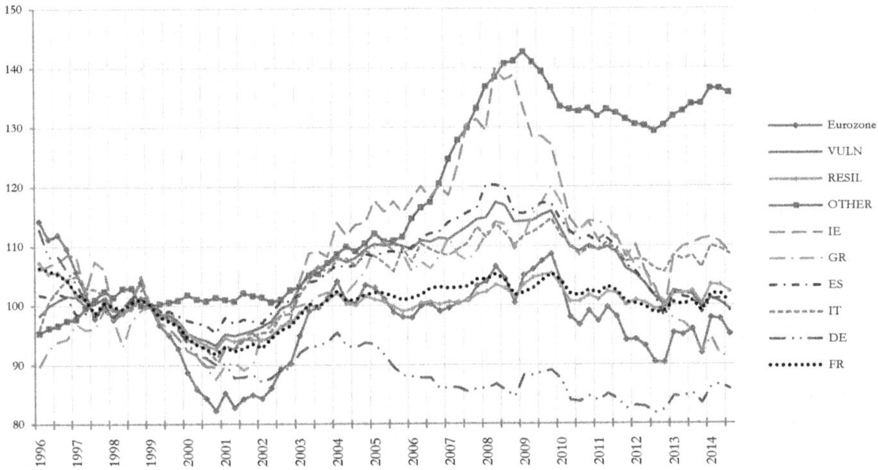

Figure 4.1. Harmonised Competitiveness Indicators (HCI) Based on Unit Labour Costs Indices for the Total Economy (Period Averages; Index 1999 Q1 = 100).
Source: European Central Bank.

higher than in vulnerable countries, although decreasing compared to the EU average. Therefore, in the second half of the past decade Spain's productivity converged to Germany's and France's, while Italy's diverged.

The ECB calculates the Harmonised Competitiveness Indicators (HCIs) to provide consistent and comparable measures of the price and cost competitiveness of the Eurozone countries. These measures are also consistent with the REERs of the euro (Figure 4.1).[67]

Stagnating productivity in a member country of a monetary union where productivity is growing causes price inflation in that country

[67] The HCIs are constructed using the same methodology and data sources that are used for the euro REER. While the HCI of a specific country takes into account both intra and extra-euro area trade, however, the euro EERs are based on extra-euro area trade only. Therefore, the HCIs and euro EERs reflect different phenomena and are not directly comparable. The HCIs complement other competitiveness indicators published by some national central banks (NCBs) which may follow different methodologies and, in some cases, use different price and cost measures in order to account for the specific circumstances in the respective country.

Table 4.2. Inflation Rates Spread in the Euro Compared to Germany (German Inflation Rate = 0; Annual Average Rate of Change, All-Items HICP).

	1997–2001	2002–2007	2008–2012	2013–2014
Ireland	1.8	1.4	−1.2	−0.8
Greece	2.5	1.7	1.1	−2.4
Spain	1.2	1.6	0.5	−0.6
France	0.0	0.3	0.1	−0.4
Italy	0.9	0.7	0.7	−0.5
Cyprus	1.5	0.8	1.0	−1.2
Portugal	1.5	1.1	0.2	−1.1

Source: Author's own calculations based on Eurostat data.

compared to the others. This is exactly what happened, to the disadvantage of vulnerable countries (Table 4.2). This effect corresponds to real exchange rate appreciation in the vulnerable country.[68] The appreciation remains implicit because the exchange rate cannot change, yet the consequences are similar and include loss of competitiveness which worsens the country position in international trade, and lower inflow of foreign direct investment (FDI).

The need to finance high debts may increase interest rates (Figure 4.2), in particular if it is clear that no common umbrella exists to guarantee sovereign debt. To make things worse, the existence of infra-union demonstration effect may push nominal earnings in vulnerable countries to converge to the level of the more resilient countries (Table 4.3), while this effect does not work in the case of productivity, unless investment increases.

Resilient countries take advantage of the weakening effect that vulnerable countries have on the exchange rate of the common currency.

[68] Real exchange rates are also measured based on ULC. In manufacturing, the latter increased quite substantially in both Italy and Spain since the beginning of the last decade according to the OECD (respectively 135.1 and 128.8 in 2010, where 2001 = 100). At the same time, the leading countries of the Eurozone, particularly Germany, enjoyed decreasing real exchange rates (91.1), while in France it was slightly increasing (109.7). The average real exchange rate for the Eurozone has been 121.0.

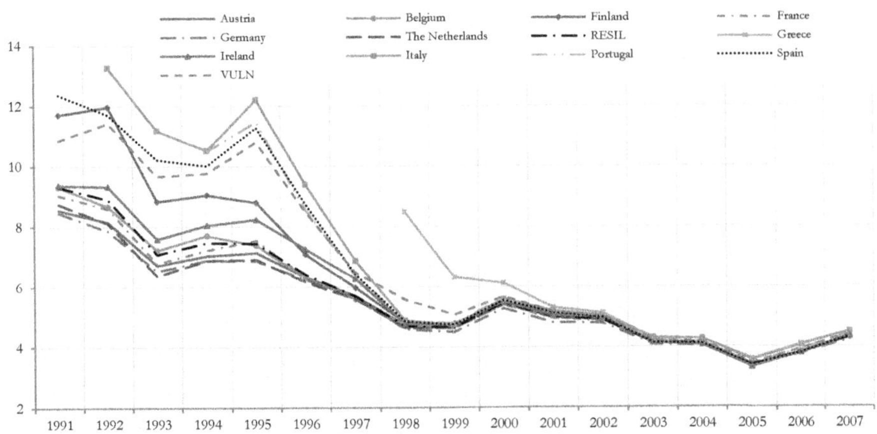

Figure 4.2. Harmonised Long-Term Interest Rates in the Euro Area (1991–2007).
Note: Long-term interest rate for convergence purposes, monthly data on debt security issued, 10 years' maturity.
Source: Statistical Data Warehouse.

They may also obtain additional capital inflow from the riskier vulnerable countries thanks to their stronger reputation in the international financial market. Their market interest rates remain lower, thus easing the financing of enterprises and public finances alike (Mallaby, 2011).[69] The resilient economies' competitiveness is consequently fostered further. These effects may give a powerful incentive to implement reforms in vulnerable countries, but may also transform the monetary union into an unbearable trap to their disadvantage. This issue is reconsidered in Chapter 12.

Vulnerable countries had difficulties in supporting investments, although this is not true for the entire period since 1997, when the final decision to adopt the Euro was taken. Indeed, gross fixed capital formation in Germany was particularly weak up to 2005. During this period, Italy's

[69] According to the calculations of Nathan Sheets and Robert Sockin (2012) of Citigroup, the implicit real exchange rate for Eurozone Germany has depreciated by 15–20% compared to a hypothetical freely floating national currency. This weaker real exchange rate is providing a significant windfall for Germany's export sector both outside the Eurozone and within it, since some 40% of German exports go to Eurozone countries. For a criticism of this view see Steinherr 2015.

Table 4.3. Hourly Earnings in Manufacturing (2010 = 100).

	1996	1997	1998	1999	2000	2001	2002	2003	2004	2005	2006	2007	2008	2009	2010	2011	2012	2013	2014
Austria	71.7	73.0	75.0	76.8	78.7	81.2	83.0	85.0	87.0	89.5	92.3	95.0	97.9	97.3	100.0	103.6	106.9	109.9	113.0
Finland	60.7	62.4	64.7	66.7	69.7	73.1	75.9	79.1	82.4	85.6	87.8	90.9	95.2	98.4	100.0	102.1	105.1	107.8	109.4
France	66.9	68.7	70.1	71.9	75.4	78.7	81.3	83.5	85.7	88.2	90.7	93.2	96.2	98.2	100.0	102.4	105.0	107.1	108.8
Germany	77.1	78.3	79.7	81.9	84.0	85.3	86.8	88.9	90.7	91.6	92.4	93.6	96.2	97.9	100.0	102.5	105.5	108.1	111.1
Luxembourg	74.2	75.7	77.9	79.6	83.7	88.2	89.5	91.1	92.7	94.2	97.1	99.6	101.1	97.2	100.0	103.1	97.3	98.3	99.1
The Netherlands	69.7	71.6	73.9	76.2	78.9	82.0	85.0	87.2	88.6	89.4	91.0	92.5	96.0	98.7	100.0	101.3	103.2	104.9	106.6
Ireland	52.5	54.4	57.2	60.3	63.6	69.1	73.2	76.8	80.4	83.9	86.5	90.7	95.2	99.5	100.0	99.0	101.0	100.9	103.5
Italy	68.0	70.6	72.5	74.1	75.6	77.1	79.2	81.2	83.6	85.8	88.7	91.2	94.3	97.3	100.0	102.4	104.9	107.1	109.7
Portugal					98.3	102.9	103.3	101.0	100.7	100.0	101.0	103.2	105.6	100.0	100.0	99.9	96.8	95.0	96.3
Spain	58.5	61.1	63.1	64.8	66.7	69.4	72.9	76.6	79.2	82.5	85.9	89.7	94.0	98.6	100.0	102.7	104.6	106.1	106.8
VULN average	59.7	62.0	64.3	66.4	76.1	79.6	82.2	83.9	86.0	88.1	90.5	93.7	97.3	98.9	100.0	101.0	101.8	102.3	104.1
RESIL average	70.1	71.6	73.6	75.5	78.4	81.4	83.6	85.8	87.9	89.8	91.9	94.1	97.1	98.0	100.0	102.5	103.8	106.0	108.0
United Kingdom	59.4	61.8	64.6	67.3	70.4	73.0	75.6	78.5	82.2	85.2	88.5	92.1	94.8	95.9	100.0	101.5	103.2	105.6	107.7
Eurozone_19	68.3	70.1	71.6	73.7	76.1	78.8	81.3	83.6	85.5	87.6	89.9	92.7	95.9	98.5	100.0	102.6	105.0	106.5	107.9
EU-28	63.1	65.6	67.6	70.1	72.7	75.9	78.6	81.0	83.6	86.0	88.8	92.2	96.1	98.3	100.0	102.6	104.9	106.4	108.1
United States	68.5	70.6	72.3	74.4	77.0	79.3	82.2	84.6	86.8	89.0	90.3	92.8	95.4	98.0	100.0	101.7	102.5	103.7	105.1

Source: Author's own calculations based on OECD data.

unimpressive performance was not inferior to Germany's, while the performance of Spain and even Greece's was better than Germany's, France's, and Italy's (Table 4.4). The situation changed dramatically since 2006, when Germany's investment performance recovered, while France's continued to be remarkable.

With the international crisis, gross fixed capital formation in vulnerable countries decreased dramatically and stabilised only in 2014 (Figure 4.3). Gross fixed capital formation in vulnerable countries in 2014 was at 65% of the highest level reached in 2007. The situation was much worse in some countries, though. Thus in Greece, gross fixed capital formation in 2013 (the year of worst performance) was slightly more than 34% the 2007 level (the year of highest performance). Also in Cyprus, gross capital formation in 2014 was less than 40% the 2008 level. In other vulnerable countries, the performance was better, although quite severe: the share of investments in the worst year compared to the best pre-crisis year was less than 58% in Ireland (2013), more than 62% in Portugal (2013), 63% in Spain (2013) and more than 70% in Italy (2014).

The situation was quite different in resilient countries. Nearly all of them had the worst performance in 2009 or 2010, with the exception of Finland and the Netherlands, which had the worst performance respectively in 2014 and 2013. While in these two latter countries, gross fixed capital formation was respectively at 82% and 80% of the 2008 level, in the other resilient countries the worst performance was around 90% of the 2008 level. Particularly good was the situation of Germany, a country whose performance was constantly above the 2008 level since 2011. These data give a clear idea that vulnerable countries are going through a very serious and prolonged depression. Conversely, most resilient countries experienced a serious but limited crisis, after which Germany resumed expansion, while the others are still in stagnation.

An effect of increasing real exchange rates that is seldom considered is the inability of vulnerable countries to invest in frontier technical progress. Indeed, the difficulty of vulnerable countries to support investment push them to specialise in labour intensive branches (Memedovic and Iapadre 2009; Yilmaz 2008). To be competitive in these branches it is necessary to keep wages down to keep labour cost low and use lower qualification human capital. At the same time, investment in research and

Table 4.4. Gross Fixed Capital Formation (Chain Linked Volumes, Percentage Change over Previous Period).

	1996	1997	1998	1999	2000	2001	2002	2003	2004	2005	2006	2007	2008	2009	2010	2011	2012	2013	2014
EU-28	2.6	2.5	6.2	5.3	4.6	0.6	−0.6	1.7	3.0	2.9	5.6	5.9	−0.5	−11.9	0.2	2.0	−2.8	−1.5	2.3
Eurozone*	1.5	2.5	5.6	6.1	4.8	1.0	−1.2	1.2	2.5	2.5	5.2	4.9	−0.5	−11.0	−0.4	1.6	−3.7	−2.5	1.0
RESIL average	3.9	4.4	5.9	5.2	4.7	1.5	−3.4	1.2	3.5	1.8	3.7	6.5	3.1	−9.6	0.0	6.3	−0.8	−2.7	1.0
VULN average	5.2	8.5	7.4	9.7	4.5	2.7	3.8	3.6	4.6	2.9	8.7	6.2	−2.3	−13.7	−8.4	−8.3	−13.0	−7.6	−0.4
OTHER average	21.7	8.2	19.6	0.8	5.2	11.8	5.2	7.7	11.1	14.0	15.4	15.2	−3.6	−29.9	−5.5	16.9	1.1	0.7	3.4
United Kingdom	4.7	−1.6	6.8	2.5	3.4	−1.3	2.5	3.1	3.2	1.6	3.3	5.3	−4.7	−14.4	5.9	2.3	0.7	3.4	7.8
United States					6.3	−0.5	−1.6	3.9	5.7	5.5	2.2	−1.2	−4.8	−13.0	1.1	3.7	5.4	2.8	3.9
Germany	−0.6	0.8	4.0	4.7	2.4	−2.4	−5.7	−1.4	0.0	0.3	7.0	4.4	1.2	−9.9	5.1	7.3	−0.7	−0.6	3.4
France	0.8	0.8	6.4	7.8	6.6	2.3	−0.9	1.9	3.5	2.9	3.6	5.5	0.9	−9.1	2.1	2.1	0.3	−1.0	−1.5
Ireland	15.6	23.3	13.5	14.0	5.4	5.4	5.4	5.1	10.4	14.4	4.0	2.7	−9.6	−20.6	−18.1	−2.6	5.2	−2.8	11.3
Greece	9.7	2.4	21.0	8.1	2.7	1.4	−1.1	15.7	5.5	−12.9	17.4	17.8	−6.6	−13.2	−20.9	−16.8	−28.7	−9.5	2.7
Spain	2.5	5.3	10.7	10.0	7.4	4.9	4.6	7.0	5.1	7.5	7.4	4.4	−3.9	−16.9	−4.9	−6.3	−8.1	−3.8	3.4
Italy	2.1	1.8	3.9	4.1	6.7	2.9	4.2	−0.3	2.1	1.7	3.2	1.6	−3.1	−9.9	−0.5	−1.9	−9.3	−5.8	−3.3
Cyprus	−4.0	3.9	−16.6	15.9	0.5	0.4	13.1	1.3	4.2	6.8	21.1	7.8	9.0	−13.9	−5.1	−9.4	−20.7	−17.1	−18.8
Portugal	5.1	14.3	11.7	6.1	4.1	1.0	−3.4	−7.3	0.1	0.1	−0.8	3.1	0.4	−7.6	−0.9	−12.5	−16.6	−6.7	2.5

Note: * Variable composition.

Source: Author's own calculations based on OECD data.

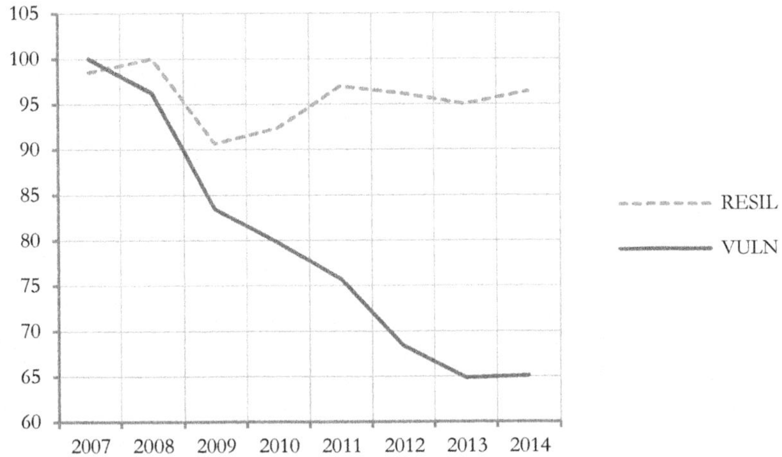

Figure 4.3. Gross Fixed Capital Formation, Chain Linked Volumes, Index: 2010 = 100 (2005–2014).
Note: Calculated on chain linked volumes[70] (2010), million euros compared to the year of highest performance (2007 or 2008). Data refer to unweighted averages.
Source: Author's own calculations based on Eurostat data.

development (R&D) is of little use and costly (Figures 3.17 and 3.18; see also OECD 2011a, country notes; Eurostat 2011).

The consequence for vulnerable countries is that, being unable to keep wages down and technically update their production, exports suffer and countries lose export quotas (Figure 4.4). According to the OECD data base and compared to 1999, when Italy's market share of goods and services in international trade was still 4.07%, in 2008 such share decreased to 3.35%. In the same years, Spain's share decreased slightly from 2.28% to 2.14% compared to the world share of GDP. Quite different was the performance of Germany, specialised in the sector of research-intensive goods (Eurostat 2011): its market share remained virtually unchanged (8.73 and 8.72% respectively).

[70] Eurostat chain-linked level series are obtained by successively applying price growth rates of the previous year to the current price figure of a specific reference year (2010).

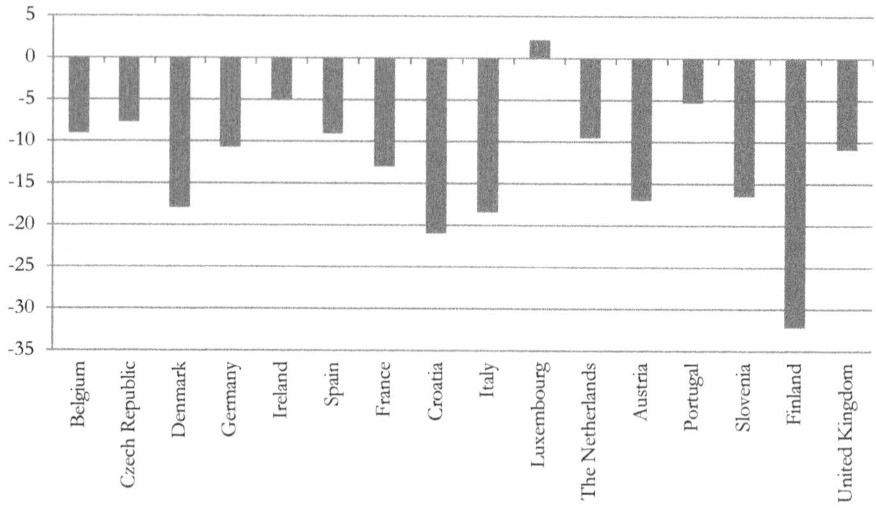

Figure 4.4. Export Performance: Cumulated Gains or Losses in Market Share, Percentage Change (Percentage of World Total, 5 Year Change, 2008–2013).
Source: Eurostat (2015) (http://appsso.eurostat.ec.europa.eu/nui/submitViewTableAction.do).

As a consequence of this unfavourable evolution, vulnerable countries increased current account imbalances at the global level (Table 4.5). This contributed to the mounting foreign debt, which in any case also characterised resilient countries (Table 4.6, Gros and Alcidi 2011).[71] Strong countries and in particular Germany registered current account surpluses in intra-EU trade (Table 4.7).

The private insurance mechanism, that was expected to function through capital and labour mobility, worked at least on the capital side. This was considered to be sufficient to make an incomplete monetary union work smoothly, provided that markets were fully open and integrated and

[71] Cingolani *et al.* (2015) find that trade imbalances registered within the European Union are in part explained by the expansion of international fragmentation of production and the creation of production linkages among European countries. In particular, the current account in EU countries worsens if the offshoring to low-income partners is high, while it improves when offshoring is to high-income partners. In the latter case, the gains in competitiveness thus obtained may overcome the potentially negative effect of importing intermediate inputs.

Table 4.5. Current Account Balances (as Percentage of GDP).

	1995	1996	1997	1998	1999	2000	2001	2002	2003	2004	2005	2006	2007	2008	2009	2010	2011	2012	2013
RESIL average	3.0	1.9	2.7	2.2	2.3	3.6	3.3	4.4	3.7	5.1	4.4	4.7	4.6	2.8	2.8	3.7	2.7	2.6	3.1
VULN average	0.5	−0.4	−0.9	−1.7	−2.8	−4.5	−4.3	−3.9	−3.5	−4.0	−5.9	−7.2	−8.2	−8.8	−6.0	−5.2	−4.4	−0.4	1.9
OTHER average	1.1	−4.4	−4.1	−4.7	−4.3	−3.9	−4.4	−5.8	−6.0	−7.1	−6.6	−8.2	−8.3	−6.7	−0.1	−0.3	−0.5	1.1	2.3
NO–EURO av.	−0.5	−1.3	−1.5	−1.5	−1.1	−1.9	−0.9	−1.5	−1.2	−2.0	0.0	−0.4	−1.4	−0.9	0.6	0.7	0.8	1.4	2.8
France	0.7	1.3	2.5	2.6	3.1	1.4	1.7	1.2	0.8	0.5	−0.5	−0.6	−1	−1.7	−1.3	−1.3	−1.7	−2.1	−1.3
Germany	−1.1	−0.6	−0.4	−0.8	−1.3	−1.8	0	1.9	1.8	4.4	4.8	6	7.2	6	5.7	6	6.6	7.3	7.4
Greece	−2.3	−3.5	−3.8	−2.6	−3.4	−7.3	−6.8	−6.7	−6.5	−5.4	−7.3	−10.9	−14	−14.4	−10.8	−9.4	−10	−2.6	1.2
Ireland	2.6	2.7	2.3	0.8	0.3	−0.3	−0.6	−1	0	−0.6	−3.4	−3.5	−5.2	−5.4	−2.2	1.1	1.2	4.2	6.2
Italy	2	3.1	2.7	1.6	0.7	−0.5	−0.1	−0.7	−1.2	−0.9	−1.6	−2.5	−2.3	−2.8	−1.8	−3.3	−2.9	−0.2	1
Portugal		−4	−5.8	−7	−8.6	−10.3	−10.2	−8.1	−6.3	−8.1	−10	−10.4	−9.7	−12.2	−10.5	−10.2	−6.8	−2	0.5
Spain	−0.3	−0.2	−0.1	−1.1	−2.8	−3.9	−3.9	−3.2	−3.4	−5.1	−7.2	−8.8	−9.7	−9.4	−4.7	−4.3	−3.6	−1.2	0.8
Japan	2.1	1.4	2.2	3	2.6	2.5	2.1	2.8	3.2	3.7	3.7	3.9	4.8	3.3	2.9	3.7	2	1.1	0.7
United Kingdom	−0.7	−0.5	−0.1	−0.4	−2.6	−2.8	−2.2	−2	−1.6	−1.9	−1.8	−2.7	−2.1	−0.9	−1.4	−2.6	−1.4	−3.6	−4.2
United States	−1.5	−1.5	−1.6	−2.4	−3.1	−4	−3.7	−4.2	−4.5	−5.1	−5.6	−5.8	−4.9	−4.6	−2.6	−3	−3	−2.7	−2.3
China				3.1	1.9	1.7	1.3	2.4	2.6	3.6	5.9	8.5	10.1	9.3	4.9	4	1.9	2.3	

Source: OECD database.

Table 4.6. Total (Public Plus Private) Gross External Debt to GDP Ratio.

	France	Germany	Greece	Italy	Spain
1995	58.7	52.4	39.0	50.4	40.5
1996	56.3	56.1	38.5	52.4	40.7
1997	62.4	59.4	45.1	58.6	46.0
1998	67.1	75.8	49.6	69.6	55.6
1999	69.8	79.1	52.3	73.0	59.4
2000	83.5	95.4	66.3	82.8	74.9
2001	94.0	115.2	74.8	80.8	77.2
2002	118.0	135.9	99.3	91.3	93.4
2003	127.5	136.0	104.9	96.2	110.7
2004	138.4	137.4	109.6	95.3	118.1
2005	142.1	128.1	108.0	94.1	119.3
2006	168.2	144.9	124.8	113.0	146.0
2007	186.4	153.7	146.3	120.3	159.5
2008	169.6	140.4	143.4	103.8	145.2
2009	194.5	153.2	178.0	120.4	173.9
2010	192.0	149.1	171.5	115.8	—

Source: Elaboration from Data Set of Reinhart and Rugoff (2011) (https://www.aeaweb.org/articles.php?doi=10.1257/aer.101.5.1676).

the mobility of factors was very high. Unfortunately, there were one obstacle and one problematic effect to the smooth working of such adjustment. The obstacle was the relatively low mobility of labour, lower than what would be desirable in a monetary union. We discuss this issue in the next chapter.

The problematic effect was the inflow of private capital, in significant part from resilient countries and into vulnerable countries.[72] Although

[72] Gross and net capital flows grew rapidly during the 2003–2007 period in the Eurozone. This growth was simultaneous with the similar process that took place in the advanced countries. However, its scale was larger in the Eurozone due to the introduction of the common currency (Lane 2013). The Eurozone, which previously had a roughly balanced net financial account, experienced sizeable capital outflows since 2011, while increasing the overall current account surpluses (Darvas *et al.* 2014).

Table 4.7. Intra-EU 27 Trade Balance by Member States (Intra- and Extra-EU-27, in million euro).

	2005		2007		2009		2011		2013	
	Intra EU-27	**Extra EU-27**	**Intra EU-27**	**Extra EU-27**	**Intra EU-27**	**Extra EU-27**	**Intra EU-27**	**Extra EU-27**	**Intra EU-27**	**Extra EU-27**
Austria	−10,092	7,696	−7,709	7,316	−9,504	4,557	−15,885	5,373	−13,407	7,279
Belgium	21,539	−9,110	27,345	−13,392	22,173	−10,694	18,890	−12,760	22,464	−8,498
Germany	98,946	55,260	126,577	65,668	71,799	65,411	55,998	99,937	43,419	154,014
Ireland	19,479	13,531	13,479	14,010	21,403	16,726	18,900	23,552	14,215	22,523
Greece	−18,627	−12,875	−22,682	−18,151	−19,846	−14,566	−12,356	−11,725	−9,257	−9,947
Spain	−36,898	−40,535	−48,212	−51,265	−17,251	−30,123	−7,249	−43,235	9,205	−26,212
France	−37,210	4,174	−52,381	75	−63,325	7,067	−87,277	−1,600	−88,849	12,341
Italy	−186	−10,200	6,721	−16,726	−2,804	−3,964	−5,062	−21,214	9,622	19,997
The Netherlands	116,108	−82,259	133,624	−91,646	120,389	−81,588	169,833	−121,356	176,678	−115,215
Portugal	−14,858	−5,387	−16,362	−5,281	−16,484	−3,203	−11,738	−4,669	−7,608	−1,647
Finland	−1,600	6,994	−855	6,893	−3,340	4,712	−5,563	1,830	−7,585	5,346
VULN	**−10,218**	**−11,093**	**−13,411**	**−15,483**	**−6,996**	**−7,026**	**−3,501**	**−11,458**	**3,235**	**943**
RESIL	**31,282**	**−2,874**	**37,767**	**−4,181**	**23,032**	**−1,756**	**22,666**	**−4,763**	**22,120**	**9,211**

Source: Eurostat (2015) (http://ec.europa.eu/eurostat/web/international-trade/data/database).

capital inflow drove Irish and Spanish sustained growth rates, it was invested mainly into non-tradable activities, such as construction. This contributed to create real estate bubbles (Dallago and Guglielmetti 2012; see also Collignon and Esposito 2013). The benefit for vulnerable countries was thus transitory, if not illusory (Wolf 2010). When vulnerable countries came under the attack of international financial markets, the direction of capital flows was inverted. Vulnerable countries started to export sizeable amounts of capital to resilient countries, in particular to Germany.[73] At the same time, resilient countries were prudent in supporting vulnerable countries through imports and preferred to also accumulate current account surpluses (Table 4.6). The outflow of capital from vulnerable countries was consequently counterbalanced by public means.[74]

4.3 National Institutions and European Features

The factors discussed in the previous section need to be understood in the frame of the peculiarities of the Eurozone. These peculiarities led to the differential impact of the crisis in the member countries, as well as to an

[73] Private capital flows to vulnerable countries, in particular to Southern European countries (Greece, Italy, Ireland, Portugal, and Spain) increased significantly as a share of their GDP from 2002 to 2007–2009. The share of cumulative inflow of private capital was as high as 90% of 2007 GDP in Portugal, 80% in Greece and 70% in Spain. In Ireland and Italy, it was slightly above 25% (Merler and Pisani-Ferry 2012b). This remarkable inflow was followed by a significant "sudden stop" (a common feature of balance-of-payments crises in emerging countries — see Calvo *et al.* (2004) between 2008 and 2011. Sudden stop episodes hit countries in three distinct periods, in function of country-specific risk factors (Schmidt and Zwick 2013): Greece in early 2008 and Ireland from October 2008, concomitant with the international financial crisis; Greece again in spring 2010, causing a contagion that hit Portugal and Ireland; Italy and Spain at the end of 2011 following the pressure by their sovereign bond market during the summer, and again Portugal (Merler and Pisani-Ferry 2012b; Pisani-Ferry and Merler 2012).

[74] Three different instruments were used to counterbalance the outflow of private capital: EU/IMF assistance programmes, Eurosystem intervention in the form of liquidity provision to the banking sector (the most important type of intervention, except for Greece), and ECB support in the form of purchases of sovereign bonds under the Securities Market program. The five countries accounted for a very significant share of liquidity allocation by the Eurosystem since 2008 and between September 2010 and September 2011, they accounted for 70–80% of the Eurosystem Main and Long-Term Refinancing Operations (IMF 2012a; Merler and Pisani-Ferry 2012a, 2012b; Pisani-Ferry and Merler 2012).

uneven economic recovery. It is these peculiarities which constitute the basis upon which a systemic crisis developed.

The following three aspects are critical in shaping the Eurozone vulnerability and response to external shocks: a) the distinctive features of European capitalisms; b) the divergent economic situation of individual countries, in particular the condition of public and private finance and the structure of the economy; and c) the institutional architecture of the Eurozone, which — given the previous two aspects — leads to different shocks in different countries. The first issue is discussed briefly in this section. The second issue was treated in the previous section and is further considered in the next one. The third issue is the main topic of Chapter 7.

The distinct features of European capitalisms were only marginally affected by the European integration. European integration, together with globalisation, made the different systems mutually compatible through a set of shared rules, standards and behaviour, without generating clearly converging institutions and, for years, policies. Indeed, the basic features of the Eurozone can be summarised as follows:

- common currency (euro);
- common fiscal parameters (convergence criteria);
- common procedures (procedures for excessive budget deficit);
- economic and commercial openness and integration (economic freedoms and integrated markets);
- nationally separated, open financial markets and flow of financial resources (under different national rules and taxation and different levels of reputation);
- banks organised along national lines;
- unintegrated labour markets. Rules in the labour market remain national, in spite of the efforts by European institutional architects. This is due to political and cultural factors, social interests, institutional and real constraints, such as the different recognition of degrees and the rigidity of the housing market in many countries. The main EU role is to ensure the freedom of migration and equal rights of migrants.

The main differences between European forms of capitalism concern financial systems and labour markets. Different approaches to the variety of capitalisms have highlighted various distinctive structural features and idiosyncrasies (Amable 2003; Baumol *et al.* 2007; Hall and Soskice 2001; Morgan and Whitley 2012). Most of these features and idiosyncrasies are important within the present European Union (EU).

As far as the financial system is concerned, the capitalisation and liquidity of stock markets and the ratio between risk and debt capital are much higher in the USA and UK than in continental European markets such as Germany, France and Italy. In the latter and in spite of significant changes in the last two decades, banks are relatively more important in financing firms than in the former countries, have a more universal nature, and their monitoring of and control over firms is stronger (Dietl 1998; Rajan 2010). In such a way, they are often able to detect early risky situations in firms and support their rescue, thus avoiding default. Although capital re-allocation is slowed down, rapid contagion in financial crises can also be hindered.

In this economic system, though, the risk of private gain from control, entrenched management, side dealings between banks and firms, and prudent bank attitude may slow down post-crisis recovery.[75] European progress towards truly unified financial markets and taxation was bumpy and controversial. The most important "European" instrument so far is periodical cross-controls of so-called fiscal paradises within the Union by national authorities with some support by the EU and the control over taxpayers paying taxes in the country where they reside. The recently implemented Single Supervisory Mechanism (SSM) under the ECB may bring some stronger European coordination in the banking sector (ECB 2014a). However, it is too early to assess whether this change will be sufficient to really bring convergence.

As to the labour markets, entry and exit flexibility are usually greater in the US, UK, and Ireland, and seniority relations and firm specific investment are more important in continental Europe. Due to these features,

[75]According to Joseph Lutton at JP Morgan (quoted in Rajan 2010, p. 238), "the U.S. Federal Reserve started raising rates 20 months after peak unemployment in the 1990–91 recession and 12 months after peak unemployment in the 2001 recession. By contrast, the euro area not only cut rates less but also was quicker to rise rates, doing so 7 months after peak unemployment on average in the 1991 recession and 9 months after peak unemployment in the 2001 recession."

European labour markets are usually less reactive to financial shocks, thus hindering the contagion of the real economy. In countries like Germany, alternative instruments of flexibility exist, such as reduced working hours. In countries where these instruments do not exist or are ineffective, labour re-allocation is slow and youth and long-term structural unemployment are high.

The institutional architecture of the Eurozone is intended to create opportunities for European countries and increase systemic resilience through an enlarged market and greater financial discipline. However, it also introduced new elements of vulnerability, in particular through the decoupling between fiscal and monetary policies and asymmetric mobility and flexibility of financial and labour markets. The common currency exacerbated both.

In an interesting paper, Hassel (2014) uses the Varieties of Capitalism approach, as developed in Hall and Soskice (2001), to show how the interaction between the institutional setup of different kinds of capitalism and the consequences of monetary unification can explain both the evolution of and the adaptation to the crisis. In this perspective and considering in particular four Southern European member countries of the Eurozone (Greece, Italy, Portugal, Spain), the paper explains the sovereign debt crisis in the Eurozone as the combined effect of the architecture of the common currency area and the specific institutional features of two different economic systems, coordinated market economies (CMEs) and mixed market economies (MMEs), included in the Eurozone. While there is a common interest rate in the common currency area, irrespective of the wide heterogeneity of national economies, the different systemic features of Eurozone countries explain why the Southern European countries were particularly vulnerable to the rapid growth of their public debts. This interrelation also explains why policymakers persistently preferred austerity as a cure for the crisis over alternative policies, in particular the mutualisation of public debt.

The fundamental reason for this asymmetry is centred in the role of the state in MME of Southern Europe. Here the state plays an important role in supporting and managing economic activity, along with the market. At the same time, the state is under the pressure of and is conditioned by firms and trade unions (Molina and Rhodes 2007). There is a profound difference with CME, which include the resilient core of the Eurozone. Germany, the Netherlands, Austria, Belgium and Finland belong to this group of economies. Their distinctive feature is that non-market coordination governs such key areas of market support functions as training, wage setting, research and development (R&D) and corporate finance (Hall and Soskice, 2001).[76]

Given the central role of the state in MMEs, it is clear that austerity policies, which weaken the state and curb its action, undermined the effectiveness that financial bailouts could have for economic growth in MME. The inevitable consequence was that Southern European countries saw their economic situation worsen.

An idea of institutional differences may be obtained from the data published by the World Economic Forum (WEF) (Figure 4.5). I grouped the 18 countries of the Eurozone (I exclude Lithuania, which entered only on 1 January 2015) into three groups: vulnerable countries (VULN, which includes Cyprus, Greece, Ireland, Italy, Portugal and Spain), resilient countries (RESIL, which includes Austria, Belgium, Finland, France, Germany, Luxembourg and the Netherlands) and other euro countries (OTHER, which includes Estonia, Latvia, Malta, Slovakia and Slovenia). The first group includes those countries which encountered the most serious problems during the crisis and continue to be in a vulnerable position. The second group includes the countries which have so far been in a relatively safe economic and financial situation. The third group includes mostly the former transition countries which adopted the euro, plus Malta.

Figures 4.5 and 4.6 show clearly that differences between vulnerable and resilient countries are not significant in terms of infrastructure and are moderate with regard to social achievements (health and primary education), higher education and training, goods market efficiency, and technological readiness. Differences are moderate in macroeconomic environment, financial market development, and business sophistication.

---

[76] Other groupings of countries would be possible and would bring even more striking results. It would be so, for instance, if one were to identify a distinct Northern European group that includes Finland, Sweden and Denmark (WEF-EU 2014, p. 20). However, this group includes only one Eurozone member country. At the same time, when it comes to policies, the important separation is the one between resilient and vulnerable countries.

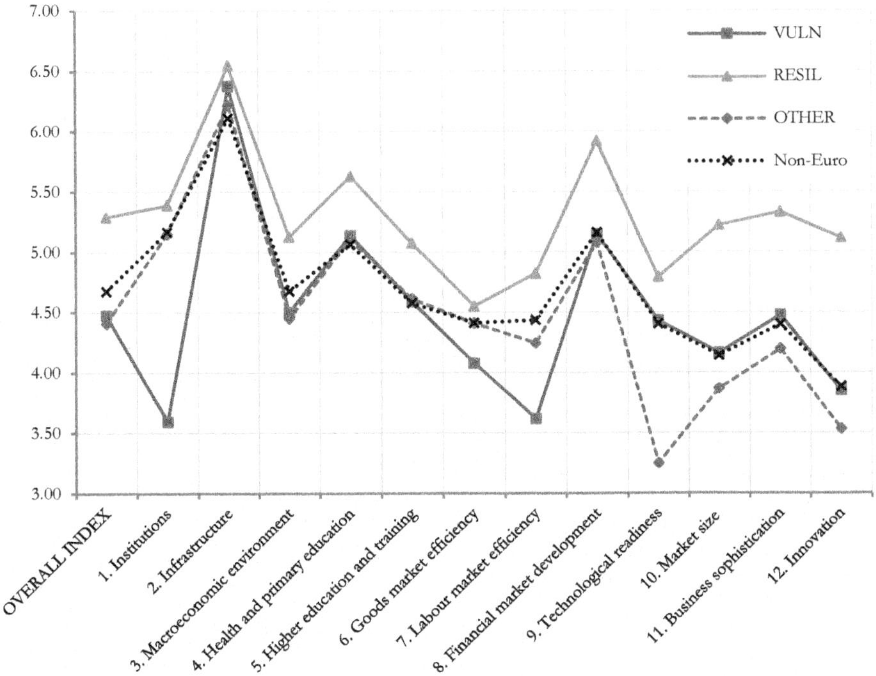

Figure 4.5. Average Values of Global Competitiveness Index Pillars of Each Group of Countries in 2014.
Source: Author's own calculations based on data from WEF (2014).

Differences are large in labour market efficiency, market size, and innovation. These features are important for competitiveness and development of economies and are also significant determinants of an optimum currency area. Differences are particularly wide in the case of institutions. This is an important conclusion for reforms and policies, to be discussed in Chapters 8 through 12.

Other countries which adopted the euro have a remarkably similar profile to that of the EU member countries which kept their national currencies. The most remarkable difference is in technological readiness, where the former group performs much worse than the latter group. More contained differences exist for market size, business sophistication and innovation. Minor differences also remain in macroeconomic environment

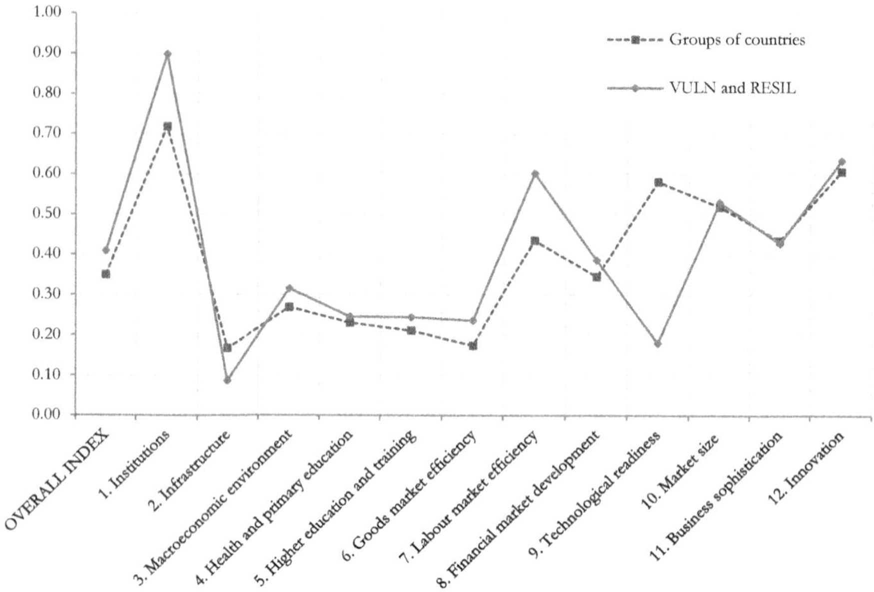

Figure 4.6. Standard Deviation among Groups of Countries and between Vulnerable and Resilient Countries in 2014.
Source: Authors's own calculations based on data from WEF (2014).

and labour market efficiency, all to the disadvantage of other euro countries. It is interesting to notice that non-euro countries have a sounder profile than vulnerable countries in all the cases, except for infrastructure, health and primary education, higher education and training, and financial market development, all cases in which the performance of the two groups of countries is remarkably similar.[77]

4.4 National Features and European Convergence

The institutional asymmetry among countries has to be seen in conjunction with the inherited and new structural imbalances, i.e. the imbalances which derive from the economic history of the member countries

[77] In the figures, unweighted averages are used to highlight the conditions of countries and reflect the importance of countries' sovereignty.

and from the consequences of significant events, in particular monetary unification. These are, in particular, productivity differentials and the relation between public and private finance. It has also to be seen in conjunction with the conjunctural situation of national economies. Given the institutional architecture, these imbalances set the scene for idiosyncratic and asymmetric adaptation to the global crisis and for asymmetric and divergent outcomes.

Structural features are important, because they determine not only the ability of national economies to adapt and react to the crisis, but also their ability to attract external and internal resources for investments. Section 3.1 shows that Eurozone countries differ along various measures of competitiveness. Delgado *et al.* (2012, pp. 2–3) define investment attractiveness as the gap between a country's foundational competitiveness and its current factor costs. Foundational competitiveness is the expected level of output per working-age individual supported by the overall quality of a country as a place to do business. This means that the performance of a country depends upon the achievement of high productivity per employed worker and the ability to involve a high share of the available workforce in the production process. It should be considered that the latter depends upon various factors under the full or partial control of governments, such as policies and the retirement system, but also upon the demographic structure of a country, and in particular its age structure (Mamolo and Scherbov 2009).

A location with higher attractiveness should grow more rapidly than locations with lower attractiveness. A location is more attractive than another location when, given similar potential productivity, the former has lower factor costs. Attractiveness influences international investment and trade flows and thus supports growth. When countries have low investment attractiveness, they find hard to support economic growth and are unable to sustain the degree of prosperity they have attained.

This is the case of such countries as Italy, Greece, Spain and Ireland. Before the crisis, these countries had unfavourable foundational competitiveness and endowments and low global investment attractiveness. The growth of their actual output per potential worker in the worst crisis years (2008–2010) was higher (Spain) or significantly higher (Greece and Italy) than the output predicted by their foundational competitiveness.

This mismatch may be due to different causes, such as credit-fuelled consumption driving growth, excessive investment in real estate, and wage growth above the growth of productivity.

Chapter 3 highlights that Eurozone growth was rather unfavourable in international comparison. Yet this is a general statement that has to be verified in the case of the individual member countries. Indeed, there are many and deep differences among member countries. It is important to appreciate these differences in order to understand the difficult sustainability of the Eurozone situation.

4.5 Eurozone Segmentation

The WEF assessment of the performance of EU member countries related to the Europe 2020 strategy is a good starting point (WEF-EU 2014). In fact, this perspective highlights how individual member countries fared relative to the objectives that European countries choose to pursue with priority in the long run. It is important to remind that these are objectives on which the European Commission has only very partial jurisdictional competence. Thus, the countries' performance in these objectives reflects primarily national features and implementation. Convergence criteria are the main short-term set of objectives to be considered in assessing the performance of member countries.

Eurozone member countries diverged substantially from each other both in the case of long-term and short-term objectives. It is useful to group countries according to their degree of vulnerability or strength, to see whether the dualism within the Eurozone holds also in these cases. The first important observation obtained from the data of the WEF, in the case of compliance with the objectives of Europe 2020, is that both vulnerable and resilient countries form two relatively homogeneous groups of countries. In fact, the standard deviation within each of these two groups is clearly lower than in the case of the other groups of countries: other euro and particularly non-euro countries (Figure 4.7).

This conclusion is important, because if there are clearly different situations among groups of countries, then such groups are structurally separate. Thus, the Eurozone could be considered as an economically heterogeneous and segmented integration of internally homogeneous groups of member countries. Clearly, this would have important policy

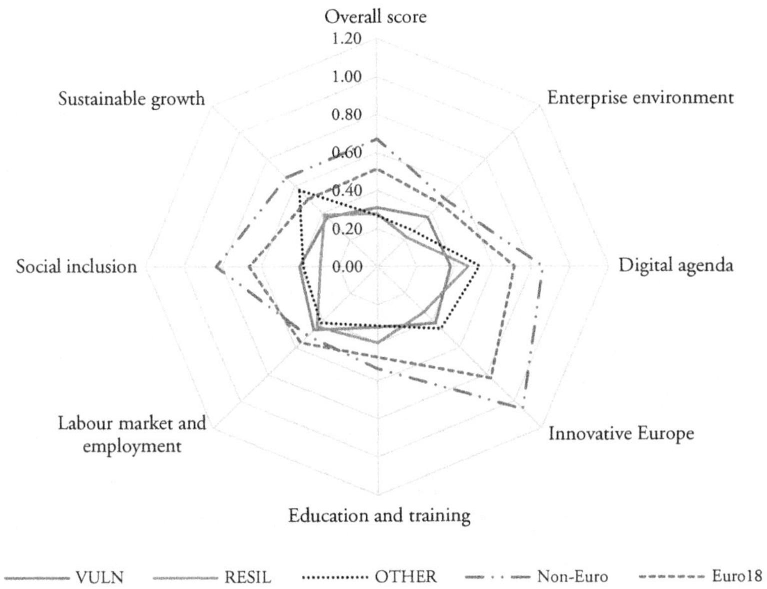

Figure 4.7. Standard Deviation within Each Group of Countries.
Source: Author's own figure based on data from WEF-EU (2014).

consequences. Figures 4.8 and 4.9 give an answer to these questions. Both consider the seven pillars of the Europe 2020 strategy.

Strong countries have clearly better performance than any other group of countries in all the seven pillars (Figure 4.9). Vulnerable countries have lower performance than the Eurozone (Euro18) average in all cases. This group of countries has the distinctly worst performance in the case of labour market and employment. Their performance is also slightly weaker than any other group in the areas of enterprise environment, digital agenda and sustainable growth, so that their overall score is the weakest of all. They perform slightly better than other euro and non-euro countries only in the Innovative Europe pillar.

Clearly, vulnerable and resilient countries form the two distinct and separate groups within the Eurozone.[78] The differences between these two

[78] Other grouping of countries would be possible and would bring even most striking results. It would be so, for instance, if one were to separate a distinct Northern European group including Finland, Sweden and Denmark (WEF-EU 2014, p. 20). However, this

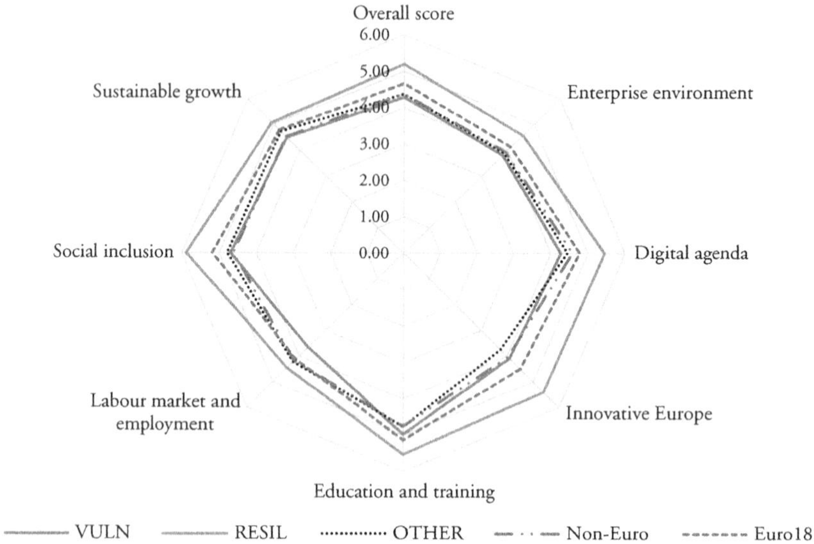

Figure 4.8. Average Score of Pillars of Different Groups of Countries.
Source: Author's own figure based on data from WEF-EU (2014).

groups are clearly larger than those existing among all group of countries (vulnerable, resilient, other euro, non-euro and Euro18), except in the pillar of education and training (Figure 4.9). While resilient countries have the highest score for each pillar, the difference (standard deviation) among vulnerable and resilient countries is the highest for most of the pillars. Different is the situation in the pillar of innovative Europe (highest standard deviation between resilient/other euro), education and training (resilient/other euro and resilient/non-euro), and social inclusion (resilient/non-euro) (data are not in the figures).

Thus, the separation between vulnerable and resilient countries represents a significant and consistent break within the Eurozone. Differences exist consistently when we go to a more detailed level of sub-pillars (Figure 4.10). For instance, in the case of the sub-pillars included under the heading of "Smart and Inclusive Growth" (see Appendix 2.7), resilient countries score clearly and consistently better than vulnerable countries in all cases.

---

group includes only one Eurozone member country. At the same time, when it comes to policies, the important separation is the one between resilient and vulnerable countries.

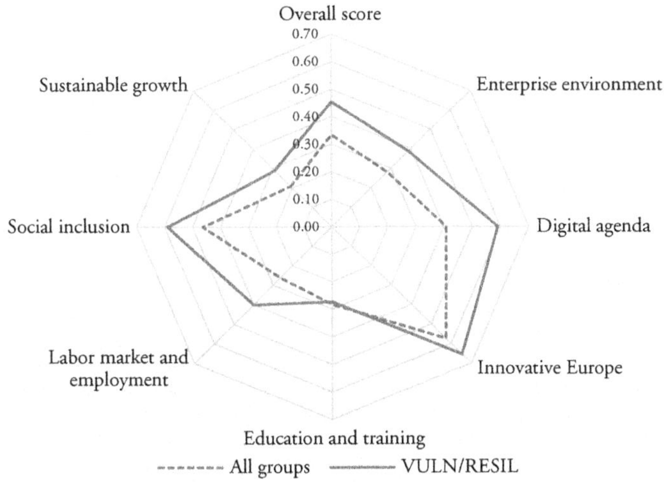

Figure 4.9. Standard Deviation of Pillars Scores among Groups of Countries.
Source: Author's own figure based on data from WEF-EU (2014).

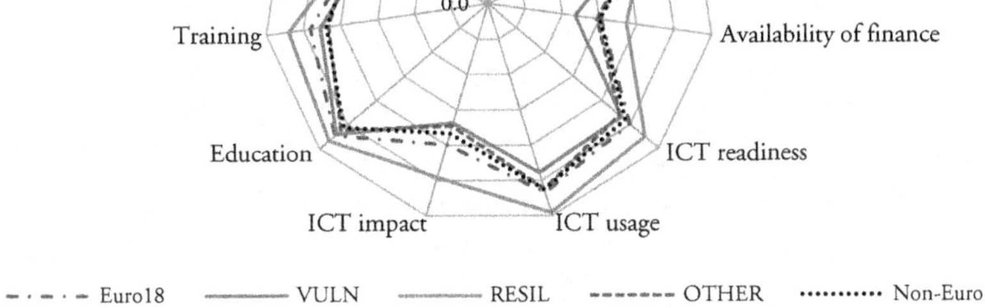

Figure 4.10. Average Score of Smart and Inclusive Growth Sub-Pillars.
Source: Author's own figure based on data from WEF-EU (2014).

According to WEF-EU (2014) data, the greatest difference between vulnerable and resilient countries exists in the pillars of innovative Europe, digital agenda and social inclusion. Intermediate differences exist in labour market and employment and in enterprise environment. Smaller differences are in sustainable growth and education and training. It is therefore important to go deeper into these pillars to better understand where the greatest differences, i.e. the most serious problems exist.

The largest differences concern the pillar of innovative Europe, where resilient countries have scores that are on average 32% better than vulnerable countries. The pillar includes 14 items concerning such issues as patents, scientific publications, number of researchers, and R&D expenditures. The greatest difference between resilient and vulnerable countries is in the number of applications for patents filed under the Patent Cooperation Treaty (PCT) per million population. On average, resilient countries have 5.2 times more patents than vulnerable countries. The difference is also remarkable (3.5 times) for the total industrial design counts in applications by residents at domestic and foreign offices, related to the population. Also R&D expenditures as a percentage of GDP show a sizeable difference (2.1 times) between the two groups of countries.

It is interesting to notice that government procurement of advanced technology products for fostering innovation are twice as important in vulnerable countries than in resilient countries. This suggests a greater role of governments in promoting technical progress. The availability of scientists and engineers is very similar in the two groups of countries. Resilient countries fare better in all the other items as well. For instance, the number of researchers in R&D relative to the population is nearly 1.6 times higher, while the capacity of companies to innovate is 1.4 times greater. It is also interesting to notice that resilient countries are considered to have competitive advantages that are more based on unique products and processes and less on low-cost labour or natural resources as compared to vulnerable countries. Similar is the situation for the delegation of authority to subordinates and collaboration between university and industry, both estimated to be nearly 30% greater in resilient countries.[79]

Differences are more limited in other fields: the number of highly cited scientific articles (scientific publications within the 10% most cited scientific publications worldwide, as a percentage of total scientific publications of the country) is 25% higher in resilient countries. Moreover, companies are credited to make greater use of sophisticated marketing

[79] Data refer to the ratio between average scores for each group of countries.

tools and techniques (21% more), firm-level absorption of new technology is considered to be 15% higher, while the availability of the latest technologies is estimated to be 13% higher. Resilient countries are thus clearly more innovative than vulnerable countries, they are more efficient in the use of highly skilled human resources, and rely much less on the state to promote innovation.

The next pillar in which differences are the greatest (average scores of resilient countries are 28% better and they have better scores in all items) is the digital agenda. Differences are the largest in international internet bandwidth per internet user (measured in kb/s: resilient countries have an average score that is 7.1 times higher than vulnerable countries).[80] Next come the number of applications for ICT-related patents filed under the PCT, per million population (5.4 times higher) and the E-participation Index (2.0 times higher). This last index measures the quality, relevance, usefulness and willingness of government websites in providing online information and participatory tools and services to their citizens. For other items differences are less important, although often not negligible.

Social inclusion is the third pillar where differences between the two groups of countries are sizeable. Also in the case of this pillar, all differences are to the advantage of resilient countries. Gini coefficients show significantly greater equality in resilient countries, which have on average a coefficient of 27.5, than in vulnerable countries, with a coefficient of 32.8. There is great difference in the government's effectiveness in reducing poverty and inequality, which is considered to be 45% higher in resilient countries. Next comes the formal social safety net protection, which in resilient countries is considered to offer 35% more protection from economic insecurity, in the event of job loss or disability. The average score for social mobility (the extent to which individuals can improve their economic situation through their personal efforts, regardless of the socio-economic status of their parents) is 1.3 times higher in resilient countries.

More contained differences between the two groups of countries exist also in the remaining pillars. Within the pillar on labour market and

---

[80] Most of this difference is due to the extremely high score of Luxembourg. Without this country, resilient countries would have a score one-third higher than that of vulnerable countries.

employment the greatest difference is in youth unemployment, as a share of total labour force aged 15–24. While in resilient countries the share is 17.9%, it is 41.6% in vulnerable countries, which is 2.3 times higher. While youth unemployment may have different causes in different countries, other differences in labour issues between the two groups of countries give a clear picture of the institutionally and socially disadvantaged and ineffective situation of vulnerable countries compared to resilient countries. However, differences are not particularly striking and in some cases they are close to negligible.

The most important differences are in taxation and in industrial relations. Taxation is considered to reduce to a lesser degree the incentives to work in resilient countries (the difference is estimated at 21%). Labour-employer relations are more cooperative (16%) and pay is better related to worker productivity (15%) in the latter group of countries. In resilient countries, businesses do better in terms of providing women with the same opportunities as men to rise to positions of leadership (12%), hiring and firing of workers is more flexible (10%), female participation in the labour force compared to male participation is higher (8%) and labour participation activity rate (the ratio of the population aged 15 and older to the working-age population aged 15 and older) is also higher (4%).

Enterprise environment is consistently sounder in resilient countries. The greatest difference is in the availability of finance. Companies meet friendlier and more efficient approaches in their need for financing. Differences with vulnerable countries are sizeable: in resilient countries it is much easier (79% easier in the survey results) to obtain a bank loan with only a good business plan and no collateral. Also other forms of raising capital are easier and more effective: for companies it is much easier (by 52%) to raise money by issuing shares in the stock market and for entrepreneurs with innovative but risky projects to find venture capital (by 50%).

Also conditions of compliance are consistently better in resilient countries. This refers particularly to the difficulty and cost for businesses to comply with governmental administrative requirements (considered to be 20% more burdensome in vulnerable countries). The effectiveness of antitrust policy in promoting competition and the more limited extent of market dominance are other fields of important advantages for resilient countries (respectively 20 and 19% higher in the Executive Opinion Survey (EOS)).[81] Agricultural policy is considered to balance better the interests of taxpayers, consumers and producers, while government subsidies and/or tax breaks are considered to distort less competition (in both cases the difference compared to vulnerable countries resulting from EOS is 18%). EOS reveals a somewhat lower advantage in terms of the extent to which rules and regulations encourage FDI (15%), while differences of opinion in how intense is competition in the local markets are more contained (9%).

The EOS shows a significant advantage of resilient countries also in clustering of firms. Companies in resilient countries have a broader presence in value chains (24% advantage) and better developed clusters (14%). However, in this latter case, the lack of homogeneity of vulnerable countries is great, with Italy having the highest score among all countries in the two groups and also Ireland standing favourably out among vulnerable countries.

Entrepreneurship indicators show an advantage for resilient countries, but they also show a lack of consistency of the overall picture and a certain lack of homogeneity within each group. The clearest advantage of resilient countries concerns taxation, which is more favourable to incentives to invest than in vulnerable countries (by 25% according to an EOS finding). However, in the latter group, Ireland and Cyprus present a rather favourable situation, while France and in part Belgium in the former group have an unfavourable standing. Highly uneven picture is obtained concerning the number of days required to start a business. While the data (from the World Bank Doing Business database) show that resilient countries perform worse overall (12.6 days compared to 10.7 in vulnerable countries), both groups are extremely uneven.[82] Worst performers

---

[81] The WEF's Executive Opinion Survey is carried out on an annual basis among chief executive officers and top executives in each of the countries under analysis. The results obtained can therefore be interpreted as reflecting the business community's evaluation of the relative performance of European countries in meeting the Europe 2020 goals (WEF-EU 2014, p. 8).

[82] According to WB (2014), the average score for the Ease of Doing Business Rank was 38 for vulnerable countries and 29 for resilient countries. However, the standard deviation was high, 18 and 16 respectively.

are Austria (25 days) and Spain (23 days); best performers are Portugal (3 days) and Belgium and the Netherlands (4 days).

The lack of internal homogeneity within the groups can also be seen in terms of the number of procedures required to start a business. The Doing Business data show that, while in this case resilient countries have a slight advantage (5.4 procedures against 5.7), Spain and Germany have the highest number of procedures of all countries (respectively 10 and 9), while Belgium, Finland and Portugal have the lowest number (3 procedures each). Apparently, regulations of entry do not explain the overall difference between the two groups of countries, although it may be an important factor behind the performance of individual countries. It is interesting also to notice that in both groups attitudes towards the failure of entrepreneurial projects are the same (roughly neutral) and also intercountry differences are limited. This may point to roughly similar cultural attitudes towards business within the Eurozone.

Indexes of environmental sustainability show overall better performance of resilient countries, with some limits. The difference is striking in the case of terrestrial biome protection (40% higher in resilient countries), although intercountry differences are considerable.[83] Resilient countries stand out also in terms of the enforcement of environmental regulations (36% better, measured through EOS, although with sizeable intercountry differences) and in particulate matter (PM2.5) concentration (32%, measured by EPI). These countries are also more efficient in managing CO_2 intensity compared to vulnerable countries, since they use only 76% of kilogrammes of CO_2 per kilogramme of oil-equivalent energy. Resilient countries have a less important, although clear advantage in the share of renewable energy production and in the quality of the natural environment. They have 13% higher share of electricity produced from renewable sources,[84] while EOS estimates that the quality of the natural environment

[83] A biome, or ecosystem, is a major regional or global biotic community with similar climatic and geographic conditions and similar dominant forms of plant and animal life (e.g. grassland or desert). The main data source is the Environmental Performance Index (EPI) worked out by Yale University and Columbia University.

[84] However, without Cyprus, vulnerable countries would be slightly better than resilient countries, while the latter position without Austria would be definitely worse. Even without these countries, there would remain a substantial intergroup heterogeneity of situations.

is some 12% better than in vulnerable countries. However, the total number of ratified environmental treaties is similar in all countries.

In the fourth pillar on education and training, the main differences among the two groups of countries are in the area of training. Differences among countries are evident and each group is relatively internally homogeneous. All data are collected through EOS and thus reflect executive opinions. Executives in resilient countries give better evaluation of the extent to which companies invest in training and employee development than vulnerable countries' executives (30% difference). Similar is the situation of the availability of high-quality, specialised training services (24% difference). Their assessment of the quality of management schools is also better (14% difference). They also give a better evaluation of the quality of the educational system, which better meets the needs of a competitive economy (19% difference). All these data show that resilient countries have a system of training and education that better and more effectively serves the needs of enterprises than in vulnerable countries.

On more basic issues concerning the educational system, the situation is apparently similar, with lower differences between the two groups of countries. The greatest difference exists in the gross enrolment rate to tertiary education, which is some 9% higher in vulnerable countries. However, it is not easy to assess the effective meaning of this figure, since students from small countries like Luxembourg tend to enroll in universities of other countries. At the same time, the figure for countries where students may spend longer years at the university has an overestimated score than countries where the university studies are better managed. Resilient countries have an advantage also in the PISA scores for combined reading, mathematics and scientific literacy performance (average score is respectively 509 and 490), with greater differences among vulnerable countries. Differences in gross enrolment rate to secondary education are negligible, although there are differences among countries within each group.

Pasimeni (2016) works out a comprehensive index to quantify, measure and monitor the progress towards the objectives of the Europe 2020 strategy. On this basis, Pasimeni performs a quantitative evaluation of

---

However, these data could reflect different sensibility to environmental issues in the two groups of countries.

countries' performance and assesses the factors that are at the basis of the manifest differences among countries and across time. He uses to this end a model that includes potential explanatory variables, such as level of wealth, growth, sustainability of public finances and institutions. The findings of the exercise confirm that the most important explanatory variables, both in absolute and in relative terms, are formal and informal institutions, such as good governance and social capital. Institutions have the strongest estimated effects on countries' performance among all the variables considered.

4.6 A Forgotten Dimension

While international databases do not consider explicitly the underground and illegal economies, these activities are often included in official statistics. The recent revision of the system of national accounts pushed this process further (see Section 11.3). Available estimates of the underground economy, although problematic in their reliability (Tanzi 1999), highlight its quantitative importance, particularly concentrated in certain activities, and the importance of intercountry differences (Schneider 2005; Schneider and Enste 2000, 2002). Clearly, higher importance of underground and illegal activities — even if partially registered in official statistics — means narrower tax basis and consequently lower tax revenue. However, the income thus fraudulently obtained is mostly spent in the regular market and pays indirect taxes.

In spite of variation through time, if countries in vulnerable and resilient groups are assembled in the same way done above, the differences between the two groups are consistent and significant (Table 4.8). Differences also remain nearly unchanged through time. When outliers from each group (Ireland from vulnerable countries because of its consistently and evidently lower size of the underground economy and Belgium from the resilient countries group for the opposite reason) are removed, each group becomes more homogeneous. However, the difference between the average value of each group increases. Thus, the consideration of the underground economy confirms the consistent separation of the two groups of countries within the Eurozone.

Table 4.8. Size of the Underground Economy as a Percentage of GDP: Averages of Country Groups and Standard Deviation among the Countries of Each Group.

		Average						
		1989/1990	**1994/1995**	**1997/1998**	**1999/2000**	**2001/2002**	**2002/2003**	**2013**
VULN	Average	17.7	22.9	23.7	23.4	23.2	22.9	20.0
	Stand. Dev.	4.5	4.5	4.4	4.4	4.5	4.4	4.2
RESIL	Average	12.1	15.0	15.6	15.7	15.8	15.7	11.0
	Stand. Dev.	3.9	4.0	4.2	3.9	3.6	3.5	3.0

Source: Author's own table based on data from Table 3.8 in Schneider (2005) and Schneider (2013) for 2013 data.

4.7 Conclusions

In this chapter and the following ones, the distinction between resilient and vulnerable countries in the Eurozone has great importance. As explained in Section 3.3, the distinction between the two groups of countries relies on structural economic and financial features and, as a consequence, on policy effectiveness. However, both structural features and policy effectiveness may vary through time and indeed they do vary. This may be the consequence of external events (e.g. changes in the price of raw materials or in the export markets) or, more often, of domestic decisions and actions (most typically, effective institutional and structural reforms).

The most often quoted example is that of Germany. An article in an issue of *The Economist* published on 3 June 1999 was titled "The sick man of the euro". It went on to explain that "The biggest economy in the euro area, Germany's, is in a bad way. And its ills are a main cause of the euro's own weakness". The same magazine, on 17 November 2004 still referred to the country as to "the sick man of Europe". In fact, the country's performance was gloomy until about 2005: economic growth was about 1.2% per year from 1998 to 2005, including a recession in 2003. Unemployment rate, which was 9.2% in 1998, increased to 11.1% in 2005. Apparently Germany was a vulnerable country.

The reforms under the Schröder government — Agenda 2010 and the so-called Hartz IV, the labour-market reform implemented since January 2005 — are credited for having changed the situation and converted Germany into the prototype of resilient countries. Yet, and without denying the importance of these changes, Germany was less vulnerable than other countries even before the reforms: "Since 1995, Germany's competitive position has persistently improved, while the competitiveness of some of its main European trading partners has deteriorated (Spain and Italy) or remained close to the 1995 position (France)" (Dustmann *et al.* 2014).

Thus, there is something structural and more permanent in the distinction between vulnerable and resilient countries, something that has to do with deeply engrained institutions, economic and social structures, political systems, and levels of development. Change is possible through reforms and proper policies, but to be effective it needs a sound institutional, economic, social and political basis. The great merit of reforms in Germany was apparently more one of having revived those fundamental features and freed them from transitory difficulties, than of having completely reshuffled the German economy. Reforms and policies transformed it from a potentially resilient economy into a vibrant resilient economy.

Thus, resilience is a potential based on a strong and effective economic and social system that can be blocked by different economic, social and political events. If not reformed, the potential can deteriorate, but when proper reforms are implemented, the effect can be surprisingly fast. Conversely, vulnerability is the feature of a less effective economic and social system. This can be changed through reforms and policies, but these are definitely costlier and less effective than in the former case. Perhaps more important, they take much more time and require much more determination and consistency to convert a vulnerable country into a resilient one.

Given these differences, certainly known to national governments and the EU governance organs, it is important to understand why the Eurozone agreed on the definition and implementation of a set of common criteria that in the end was to the disadvantage of the countries in the weaker position, namely the vulnerable countries. The following chapter aims at assessing how the two groups of countries behaved in relation to the convergence criteria.

"Prince I know all things
I know the rosy-cheeked and the pale
I know death who devours all
I know everything but myself."

— François Villon (*Ballade*, 1458)

5

Convergence and Divergence in the Eurozone

To work properly, the Eurozone buildup and functioning should comply with a number of requirements. Among the most important are the following. First, European integration and globalisation should be compatible in order to assure the smooth working of markets. While regional economic integration is known for creating trade within the integrated area and diverting trade from outside the area to its inside, in an open and integrated world economy this process should advantage the member countries of the area without reducing its trade with the rest of the world. This aim was largely implemented and also trade of the European Union (EU) with the rest of the world increased.

Second, common monetary policy should accompany monetary integration. This goal was implemented successfully. In fact, since the adoption of the euro, yearly inflation was around 2% until recently. In spite of this success, the question of the common monetary policy is not fully solved, since the Eurozone missed so far a complete central bank which could act as a lender of last resort, while its role in the supervision of the banking system has evolved only lately. Also monetary decisions are taken within the Eurosystem, a solution that showed to weaken the ECB decision making power and prolong the time necessary for taking decisions. These aspects weakened the common monetary policy in confronting the crisis.

Third, common criteria for fiscal policies were identified and imposed upon member countries. There is a major problem here concerning the very essence of the monetary union. The basic original idea was to have a common currency and monetary policy for dealing with symmetric shocks, while leaving financial policies in the hands of national governments for dealing with asymmetric shocks (Buti and Shapir 1998). This was a wise solution, in principle. However, since national economies were in different economic and financial situations and followed different and often incompatible fiscal policies, it was clear that the fiscal freedom of the national governments had to be checked and perhaps curbed in order to preserve the stability of the common currency. As a consequence, common stability criteria were identified that all member countries in the monetary union had to observe. These criteria became part of European treaties and pacts and constituted what is still today perhaps the most intractable problem of the Eurozone.

Fourth, while the attention of the Eurozone was mainly concentrated on macroeconomic issues, there were serious microeconomic questions that did not receive proper treatment, let alone solutions. It was initially believed that markets would have taken charge of the problems and fostered the convergence of the national economies. It was thought that resources would flow from countries with strong financial situations to countries in more vulnerable conditions. This was labelled as the private insurance mechanism. The integration of financial markets, the stability that the common currency assured, and the dramatic decrease of transaction costs and risk were expected to result in resources flowing to where they were more needed, thus supporting the process of financial and real convergence.

This process worked fairly well up to the international crisis. Yet the resources that vulnerable economies obtained this way were invested in large part in activities that did not support fiscal and microeconomic convergence and contributed to create financial and real bubbles (e.g. in real estate). This effect was due to the fact that investors were looking for the most remunerative uses and real estate in booming economies offered high returns. Moreover, host governments relied on the boon of imported resources and relaxed convergence policies. Finally, both the private sectors and governments refrained from investment in strategic sectors, which disadvantaged competitiveness in open markets. Therefore, microeconomic convergence was a major failure of the integration process.

Overall, and in spite of important successes, the integration process was to the disadvantage of the microeconomic and the financial aspects, as compared to the macroeconomic and monetary ones. The outcome was asymmetric, unbalanced integration that strengthened the effect of its institutional and organisational incompleteness. This asymmetry is the most critical element of the Eurozone weakness, particularly in the long run and in a time of international economic turmoil.

In order to appreciate these problems, it is useful to consider the convergence criteria and the compliance of the Eurozone countries with them. The convergence criteria are also known as the Maastricht criteria and were introduced with Article 121(1) of the Treaty on European Union (TEU or Maastricht Treaty). The treaty was signed on 7 February 1992 and entered into force on 1 November 1993. The Maastricht Treaty was subsequently amended by the treaties of Amsterdam (1997), Nice (2001) and Lisbon (2009) (See Section 7.1).

The latter treaty is presently the fundamental document defining the criteria that EU member countries are required to meet when adopting the euro as their currency. To do so, a country must be ready for entering the third stage of the Economic and Monetary Union (EMU) (see in particular Section 7.8). The third stage started on 1 January 1999, when the euro became the official currency of the Eurozone member countries and the European Central Bank (ECB) became the sole authority for the common monetary policy. The euro was initially an accounting currency for cashless payments and accounting purposes. National currencies were used for cash payments. Banknotes and coins with a euro denomination started to circulate on 1 January 2002 and soon became the only legal tender in the Eurozone.

5.1 Convergence Criteria and the Missing Requirements: A Preliminary Balance

The original purpose of convergence criteria was to ensure price and financial stability within the Eurozone, also in case of accession of new countries. There are four fundamental convergence criteria: price stability, government finances, exchange rates and long-term interest rates. Price stability in a member country is defined by the Harmonised Index of Consumer Prices (HICP): the inflation rate in a country should be no more than 1.5% higher than in the three best-performing member countries in terms of price stability during the year preceding the assessment. As to government finances, the assessment is over two variables. First, member countries should have a ratio of the annual government deficit to GDP at market prices that does not exceed 3% at the end of the preceding financial year. Second, the ratio of gross government debt to GDP at market prices must not exceed 60% at the end of the preceding financial year.

The third criterion concerns exchange rates, which must remain stable compared to the currency of any other member country during the two years preceding the examination of accession and free of severe tensions. Finally, the nominal long-term interest rate (the average yields for 10 year government bonds in the past year) must not exceed by more than 2% that of the three best-performing member countries in terms of price stability during the year preceding the examination.

On the basis of the four criteria, the Commission and the ECB prepare a "convergence report" to the Council at least once every two years (EC 2014c). The reports assess the progress made by the member countries in complying with the criteria and other obligations. Convergence criteria provided the basis for European, and in particular Eurozone policies. It is therefore important to have a first look at the effect of these policies and the compliance of the Eurozone member countries with the convergence criteria.[85] For a more detailed discussion, refer to Chapters 8 and 11.

[85] For analyses on the effect of convergence criteria before the crisis see Castro (2011), Giuliodori and Beetsma (2008), Kočenda *et al.* (2008), Polasek and Amplatz (2003) and Kolasa (2010).

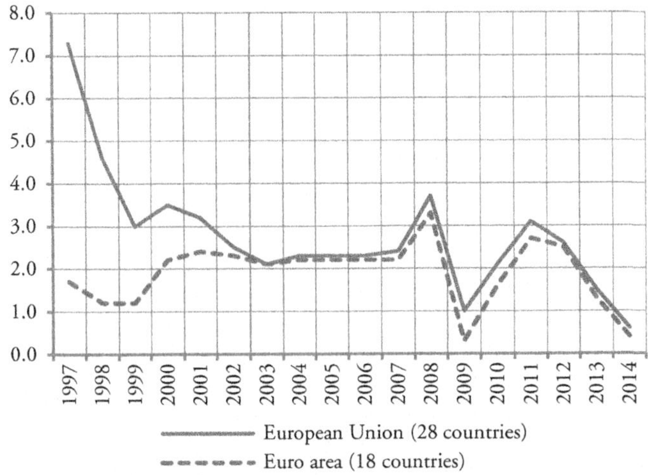

Figure 5.1. All-items HICP, Annual Average Rate of Change in the Eurozone and the European Union.
Source: Author's own figure based on data from Eurostat.

Price stability was overall a remarkable success (Figures 5.1 and 5.2). The average HICP inflation rate in the Eurozone was on average moving around the ECB objective of 2% with remarkable consistence. Also intercountry differences were modest and decreasing.[86] The situation changed with the crisis. The behaviour of vulnerable countries contributed to this achievement: while their HICP inflation rate was around 1% higher than that of resilient countries until 2003, afterwards it decreased consistently and became lower since 2009. In 2014, the rate for vulnerable countries became negative. Thus the price convergence was fully implemented. However, clear signs of deflation appeared in vulnerable countries in 2014.

[86] Reiff and Rumler (2014) analyse within- and cross-country price dispersion in European countries and find that cross-sectional price dispersion by far dominates price dispersion over time. The authors also find that cross-country price dispersion is by an order of magnitude larger than within-country price dispersion, even after controlling for product heterogeneity and although price dispersion has declined in the Eurozone since the beginning of the Monetary Union. Different tax rates, income levels and consumption intensities explain large part of such cross-country price differences.

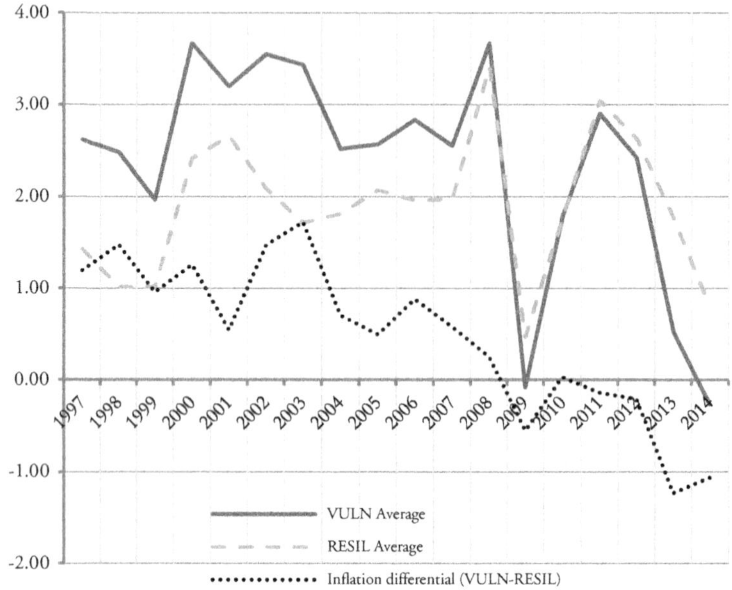

Figure 5.2. All-items HICP Annual Average Rate of Change in Resilient and Vulnerable Countries.
Source: Author's own figure based on data from Eurostat.

Convergence in government finances was more complex and less successful (Figure 5.3). However, it is important to distinguish between the successful time when the introduction of the euro was prepared, the uncertain period before the crisis, and the problematic post-crisis years. The first period was characterised by remarkable discipline of both groups of countries. By 2000, all vulnerable countries, with the partial exception of Portugal, had significantly decreased their budget deficit well within the requirement of the convergence criteria. Ireland reached a remarkable surplus of +4.8 of GDP. Italy and Spain decreased their current deficit from 7.3% and 7.0% respectively to 1.3% and 1.0%. Among resilient countries, all of them safely within the convergence requirement by 2000, Luxembourg further increased its surplus to 5.7% and Finland went from a deficit of 5.9% in 1995 to a 6.9% surplus in 2000. The most noticeable performances were implemented by Germany and the Netherlands, which went from a deep deficit of 9.3% and 8.6% respectively to a surplus of 1.0% and 1.9% over the same period.

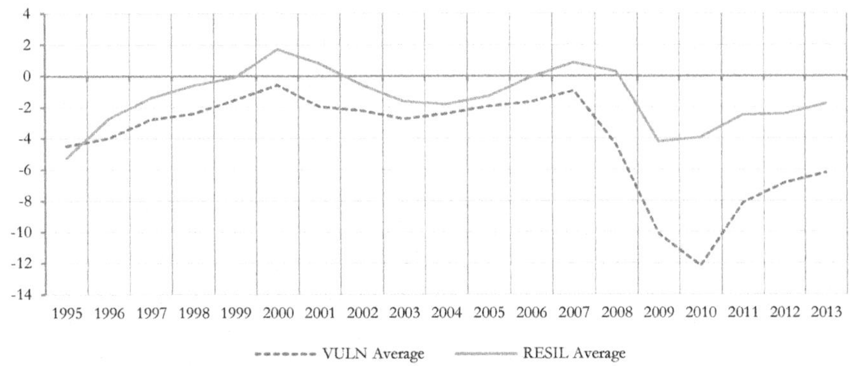

Figure 5.3. General Government Net Lending (+)/Net Borrowing (−) (Percentage of GDP).
Source: Author's own figure based on data from Eurostat.

In the following years up to the crisis, the behaviour of vulnerable countries started to change and they became less respectful of the convergence criteria. While the revised data for Greece are not available yet, for most of this period, only Spain maintained a remarkable budget discipline and remained continuously well below the 3% deficit. The other countries went well beyond the convergence limit in the middle of the period and then returned to below the limit by 2007, with a mild exception in Cyprus. Ireland's budget was balanced at the end of the period. Among resilient countries, France and Germany behaved like most vulnerable countries and surpassed the admitted deficit between 2002 and 2005. However, by 2007 all countries were safely within the limit; Finland and Luxembourg reached a significant budget surplus of 5.1% and 4.2% respectively.

The crisis dramatically changed the situation. All countries went into deficit, with the exceptions of Germany and Luxembourg, which reached a modest surplus respectively in 2012 and 2011. Among vulnerable countries, only Italy returned below the 3% deficit in 2012. All other countries were clearly above that limit. Ireland had a deficit of 32.4% of GDP and Greece's deficit was 12.2% of GDP in 2013. In this period, the average deficit of vulnerable countries was above 6% of GDP in 2013, although this was half the level reached in 2010. Resilient countries' deficits were on average less than 2% of GDP in 2013, which was less than half the level reached in 2009 and 2010. It is interesting to note that while resilient

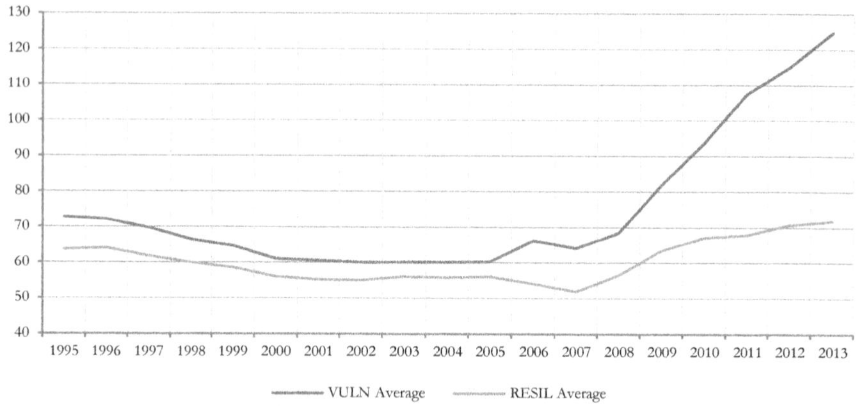

Figure 5.4. General Government Consolidated Gross Debt (Percentage of GDP).
Source: Author's own figure based on data from Eurostat.

countries moved in a synchronised way, the divergence among vulnerable countries increased.

The dramatic increase of budget deficits had inevitably negative consequences for public debts (Figure 5.4). Public debts decreased rather consistently in the period up to the beginning of the crisis and were at 60% of GDP between 2002 and 2005 in the average of vulnerable countries, with the major exception of Italy, and below that level in resilient countries. However, since 2008 debts have increased dramatically as a share of GDP in vulnerable countries: the average national debt surpassed 100% of GDP in 2011 and reached 125% in 2013. However, the heterogeneity among countries further increased until 2011, but decreased afterwards. This was due to previously low debt countries, Ireland and Spain, that saw their debts accelerate dramatically: from 24% and 35% in 2007 to 123% and 92% in 2013.

The burden of payable interests on public debt was on rapid decrease, particularly so in vulnerable countries. With the crisis, the burden increased above 4% of GDP since 2011 in the average of vulnerable countries, up from 2.6% in 2005 (Figure 5.5). The level was at 5.7% in 1995 and its dramatic decrease was one of the most significant achievements of the common currency. At the same time, resilient countries saw their burden decrease continuously from 4.1% in 1995 to 1.9% in 2013.

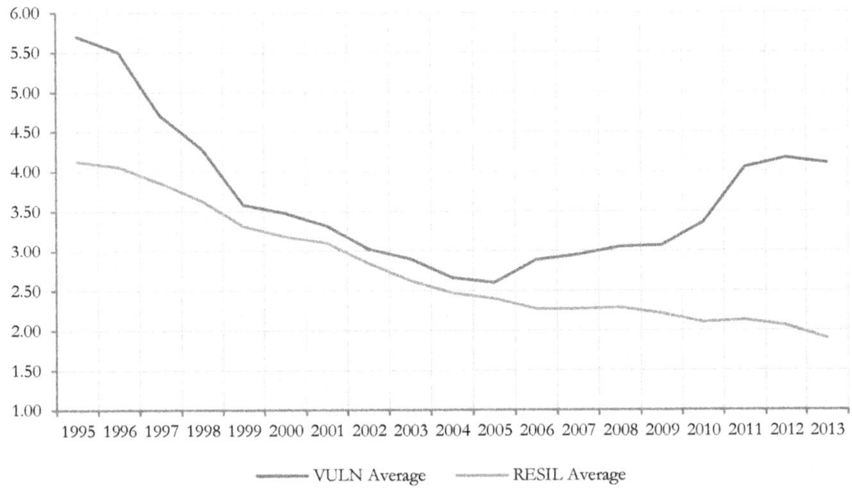

Figure 5.5. General Government Interest, Payable, Percentage of GDP.
Source: Author's own figure based on data from Eurostat.

The effect of the monetary union on exchange rates was twofold. First, the success in keeping nominal exchange rates before the adoption of the euro was remarkable and effective. Thanks to this, the euro became a reality. Second, real effective exchange rates (REERs) in vulnerable and resilient countries, measured both against unit labour costs and against consumer prices, diverged seriously and continuously (Figure 5.6). The effect of prices was slightly stronger than that of costs throughout the period in resilient countries. In vulnerable countries, this was true until 2004, after which the effect of costs dominated, particularly in 2008 and 2009. With a strong common currency, it was easy to predict that vulnerable countries would lose competitiveness and therefore would see an appreciation of their real effective exchange rate, unless these countries were able to significantly reform their economies and invest in technical progress on a large scale.

This was true up to the crisis, when internal devaluation was successful in making vulnerable countries regain competitiveness and depreciate their REERs, while the situation of resilient countries improved less and later. However, the situation was uneven. Among resilient countries, Germany was on the whole successful in depreciating its REER against costs. Against prices, the rate remained stable in general. The other successful

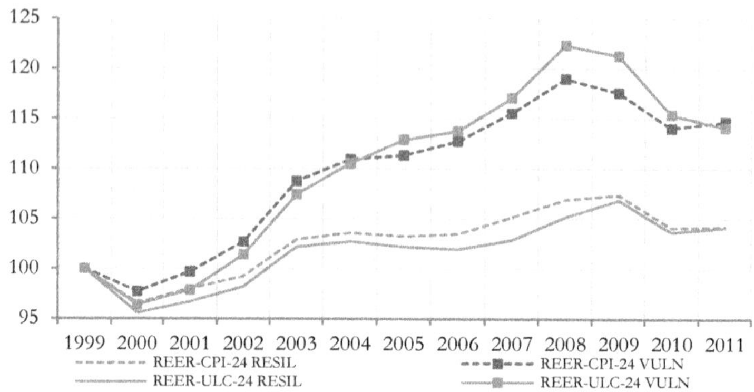

Figure 5.6. Real Effective Exchange Rate (Deflator: Unit Labour Costs in the Total Economy and Consumer Price Indices — 24 Trading Partners) — 18 Trading Partners — Euro Area) — 1999 = 100.

Note: A rise in the index means a loss of competitiveness.

Source: Author's own figure based on data from Eurostat.

country was Austria, whose rate against costs overall stagnated, while slightly appreciated against prices. In the other resilient countries, rates against both costs and prices appreciated. Among vulnerable countries, Ireland had the fastest and strongest appreciation particularly against costs, but also against prices, until 2008. Since 2009, a strong depreciation followed in both cases. Appreciation until 2008 and depreciation since 2009, were significant in all vulnerable countries, although less than in Ireland, with the partial exception of Greece, where depreciation was delayed by one year.

The fourth criterion, convergence of long-term interest rates, was perhaps the one that initially obtained the most impressive results (Figure 5.7). With the announcement of the euro, interest rates started to decrease rapidly. The effect was much stronger in vulnerable countries than in resilient countries, although it was also important in this latter case. However, the crisis abruptly interrupted this win-win situation. While there was a modest overall increase in interest rates in resilient countries, with remarkably contained intercountry disparity, this increase was dramatic in vulnerable countries.

Among vulnerable countries, Greece is clearly an outlier. For years, the country enjoyed a dramatic decrease of interest rates, which converged

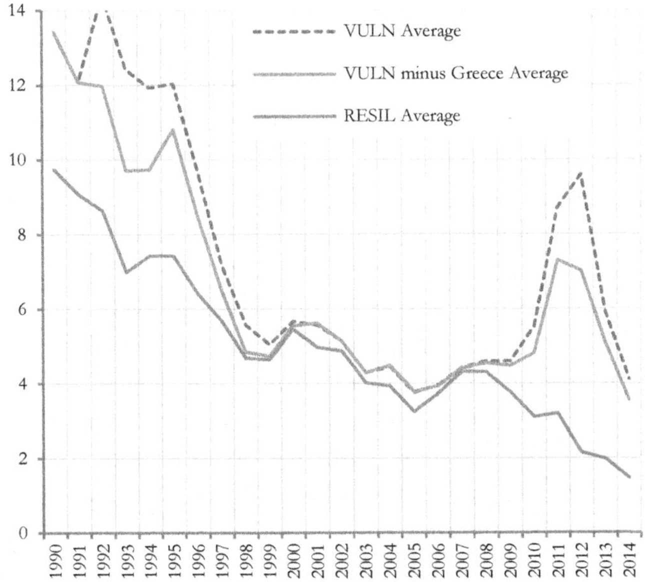

Figure 5.7. EMU Convergence Criterion Bond Yields: Group Average.
Source: Author's own figure based on data from Eurostat.

with those of the other countries in the group by 2000. However, in 2009 there was a dramatic and abrupt increase of Greek interest rates. These reached 22.5% in 2012, after which they decreased to 7% in 2014. The other countries in the group moved in a synchronised way and most of them, with the partial exception of Cyprus, enjoyed virtually the same interest rate between 1998 and 2008. Then, with the crisis, interest rates in Ireland and Portugal in 2009 increased rapidly to around 10% in 2011. The descent was rapid and fully successful in Ireland, while it was delayed by one year in Portugal. However, the spread of interest rates in resilient and vulnerable countries remained significant, above 2.5% on average in 2014.

5.2 Convergence and Divergence

Eurozone countries diverged in many fields. The previous sections provide evidence to show that there are two distinct groups within the Eurozone which had distinct economic and financial features before the crisis. Yet convergence worked in some other areas, often to the disadvantage of its sustainability. The following analysis assesses the convergence in real variables: investments, incomes and consumption levels. The aim is to see whether the situation in these areas occurred in parallel with other forms of successful convergence, namely interest rates and inflation rates convergence, or jeopardised them.

The member countries of the EU had divergent development of gross capital formation for many years, particularly in the 1990s. In the 1980s, total gross fixed capital formation grew particularly fast in Spain, while Germany registered a sluggish performance in both total gross fixed capital formation and investment in machinery and equipment. During the following decade, the growth of total fixed capital formation was lower than in the preceding decade, with few exceptions in total investment (Denmark and the Netherlands) and in select components (investment in machinery and equipment in Italy and the United Kingdom). In this decade, it was Finland and Germany that registered the lowest growth rates of fixed capital formation.

Investment is the most volatile component of GDP and depends on many factors. The divergent development witnessed that these factors were somehow different in different countries. The most important determinants of investment that various theories and empirical analyses have highlighted include aggregate demand. Other determinants of investment are interest rates, prices, depreciation and taxation. Weyerstraß (2003) estimates an investment function for a panel of 10 EU countries (Belgium, Denmark, Finland, France, Germany, Italy, the Netherlands, Spain, Sweden, and the United Kingdom) and analyses the determinants of investment in these countries. The analysis considers total demand, the real interest rate, the inflation rate of capital goods, and the relative price of capital goods.

The result of the analysis is straightforward: the most important determinant of investments is the growth of final demand. This was particularly evident in the 1990s. The effect of the convergence of nominal interest rates was negligible. It was the divergent development of demand in different countries that better explained the deviating paths of investment. Total demand was more homogeneous during the 1980s than in the 1990s. The increased differences of demand among countries determined the greater heterogeneity of intercountry investment performance through the accelerator effects.

The real interest rate, the growth rate of capital goods prices, and the relative price of capital goods constitute the different components of the user cost of capital. Nominal interest rates decreased and converged in the EU during the 1980s and up to the crisis and reached a low level in all countries. Since the monetary union became effective in 1999, short-term nominal interest rates were the same in all Eurozone countries, although they remained higher in the other EU member countries.

However, real interest rates behaved differently and influenced investment decisions. During the 1980s, real rates had an uneven pattern and increased significantly in some countries (Italy, France, Spain, Finland, the UK, and Denmark). Rates reached a peak in 1991–1992, after which they declined in all countries, albeit to various extents. They were contained between the slightly negative level in the Netherlands in 2001 and 2.5% in France and 3% in the United Kingdom. However, investments stagnated or moved in a way that was out of line with real interest rates developments.

Relative prices for capital goods, measured by the deflators of gross fixed capital formation normalised by GDP deflators, also showed divergent paths in the considered countries and a rather weak relation to investments. In a group of countries (Finland, Germany and the Netherlands), the relative price of investment goods stagnated during the 1980s. The price declined by 6% in Belgium, Denmark, Sweden and the United Kingdom between 1980 and 1990 and by 10% in the remaining countries (France, Italy, Spain). In the following decade, the decline accelerated in Denmark and the United Kingdom (15%) and in France, Germany, Italy and Sweden (10%). The relative price stagnated in Belgium, Finland, the Netherlands and Spain.

Within the Eurozone, the growth of gross capital formation was faster in vulnerable countries over the period 1960–2014 than in resilient countries (Figure 5.8). Capital formation in the former group of countries was particularly dynamic up to 1973.[87] Afterwards, capital formation in

[87] With the partial exception of Italy, a country in which capital formation grew roughly in line with resilient countries.

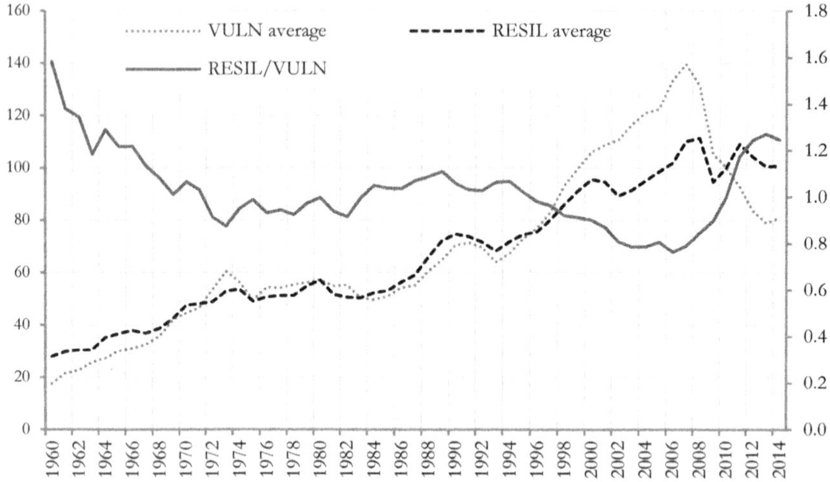

Figure 5.8. Gross Capital Formation at 2010 Prices: Total Economy 1960–2014 (2010 = 100).

Note: Country groups averages (left scale) and inter-group share (right scale).

Source: Author's own figure based on AMECO data.

vulnerable countries moved roughly in line with the performance of resilient countries until mid-1990s. Between mid-1990s and 2007 capital formation in vulnerable countries was again more dynamic than in resilient countries.

The situation changed dramatically since 2008 as a consequence of the crisis and stabilisation policies. While in resilient countries gross capital formation decreased slightly (its level in 2013 was at 91% the 2007 level), albeit with considerable yearly fluctuation, investments in vulnerable countries fell impressively. Their amount in 2013 was roughly 64% the pre-crisis level in 2007, at 2005 fixed prices. This observation apparently confirms Weyerstraß's (2003) conclusion that investment activity depends primarily upon demand.

As a percentage of GDP, gross fixed capital formation in vulnerable countries overcame investment in resilient countries between the end of the 1980s and the crisis (Figure 5.9). This remarkable performance was the outcome of the outstanding investment share of Ireland and also Greece, Portugal, Spain and Cyprus. This was due primarily to investment in

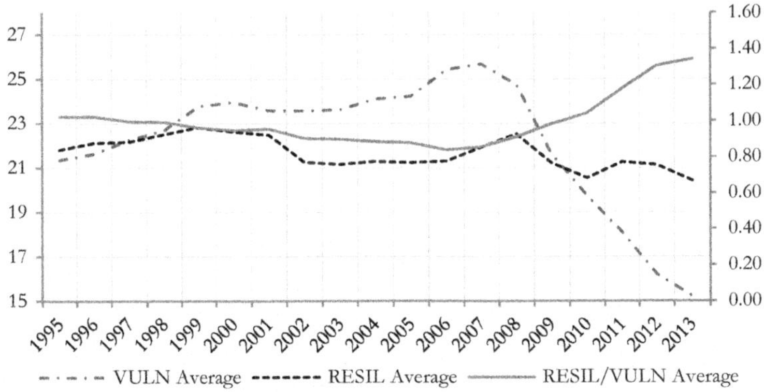

Figure 5.9. Gross Fixed Capital Formation as a Percentage of GDP (RESIL/VULN Average on Right Scale).
Source: Author's own figure based on Eurostat data.

dwellings and constructions, followed by transport equipment. Italy was the only country where investment moved roughly in line with the performance of resilient countries, although their fall in this country during the crisis was stronger. The dramatic fall of investment in dwellings and constructions during the crisis was stronger than total investment, as much as their increase was before the crisis. This led to the overall fall of vulnerable countries' investment, both as a share of GDP and relative to investment in resilient countries.

The weakness of investment in industry contributed to the ailing competitiveness of vulnerable countries. It is difficult to imagine, under these conditions, that labour cost could decrease in vulnerable countries. In fact, total labour cost measured in euro in vulnerable countries increased more rapidly than in resilient countries until the effect of the crisis and stabilisation policies stopped the growth (Figure 5.10). Afterwards, average labour cost in vulnerable countries stagnated at around €20, while labour cost in resilient countries continued to grow, albeit at a pace lower than before the crisis. As a consequence, and while the scissors between labour cost in the two groups of countries decreased before the crisis from more than 1.8 times in 2000 to below 1.5 times in 2008, the share between average labour cost in resilient and vulnerable countries increased again to nearly 1.7 in 2013.

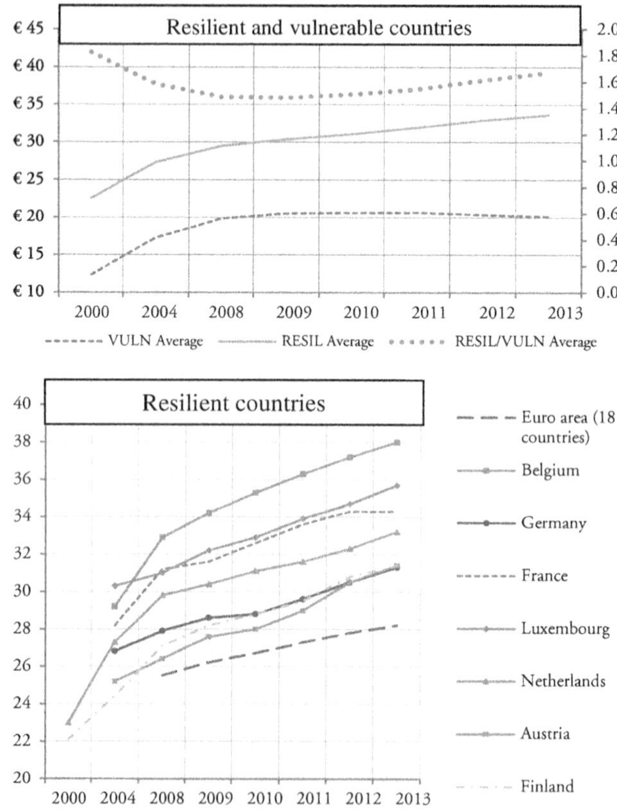

Figure 5.10. Total Labour Cost, in Euros.[88]

Note: Industry, construction and services (except public administration, defence, compulsory social security). Ratio between resilient and vulnerable countries' averages on right scale.
Source: Author's own figures based on Eurostat data.

[88] Eurostat defines the aggregate in the following way. In the context of the Labour Cost Index, labour costs are defined as the core expenditure borne by employers for the purpose of employing staff. They include employee compensation, with wages and salaries in cash and in kind, employers' social security contributions and employment taxes regarded as labour costs minus any subsidies received, but not vocational training costs or other expenditure such as recruitment costs and spending on working clothes (in contrast with multiannual and annual labour cost data). See Eurostat (2015b).

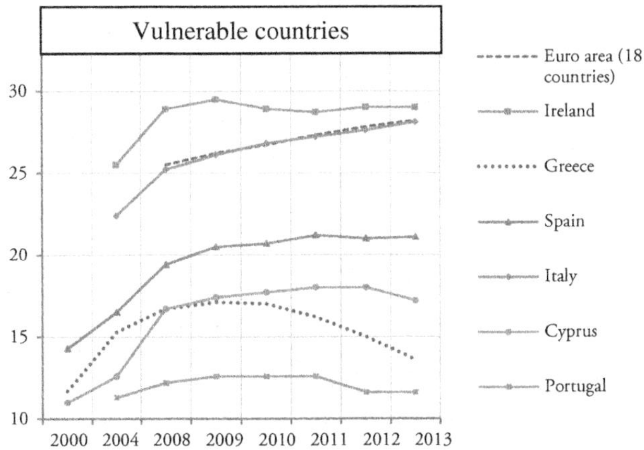

Figure 5.10. (*Continued*)

However, the situation is very different in individual countries (Figure 5.10). It is interesting to notice that labour cost in all resilient countries was higher than the Eurozone average since the crisis started. The Eurozone average also continued to increase during the crisis in all resilient countries. Among vulnerable countries, only Ireland kept labour cost higher than the Eurozone average, while Italy's was roughly the same as the average. However, within this group of countries, the rise continued even after the crisis only in Italy, albeit at a slower pace. It also continued to a lesser extent in Spain until 2011. In Greece, labour cost decreased considerably since 2009, a sign of significant dismissals.

If investments did not support higher productivity, as shown in Section 4.1, then the stagnation of labour cost must have resulted from lower wages. Indeed, wages and salaries in vulnerable countries increased up to the crises, then stagnated, but in 2012 they started to decrease (Figure 5.11). This development was in striking contrast with what happened in resilient countries, where wages and salaries continued to increase, albeit at a slower pace. Indeed, the line of the average for the Eurozone continues to have a positive inclination, albeit with a lower slope.

The pattern of wages and salaries is apparently similar to that of labour costs. All resilient countries have higher earnings than the Eurozone

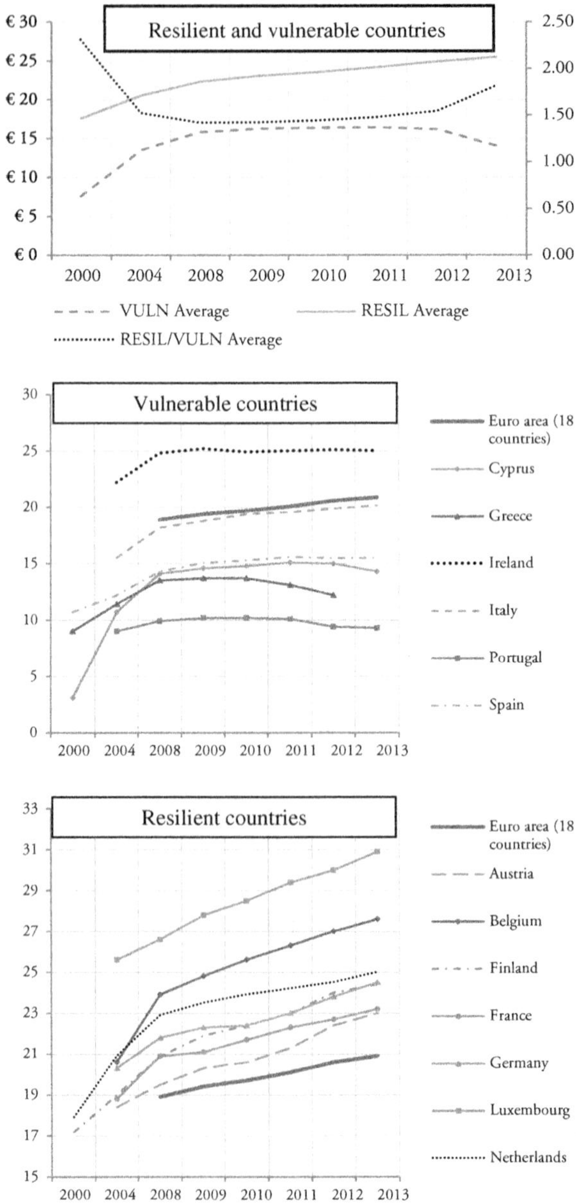

Figure 5.11. Wages and Salaries, in Euros.

Note: Total average hourly wages and salaries in industry, construction and services (except public administration, defence, compulsory social security). Ratio between resilient and vulnerable countries' averages on the right scale in the the top figure.

Source: Author's own figures based on Eurostat data.

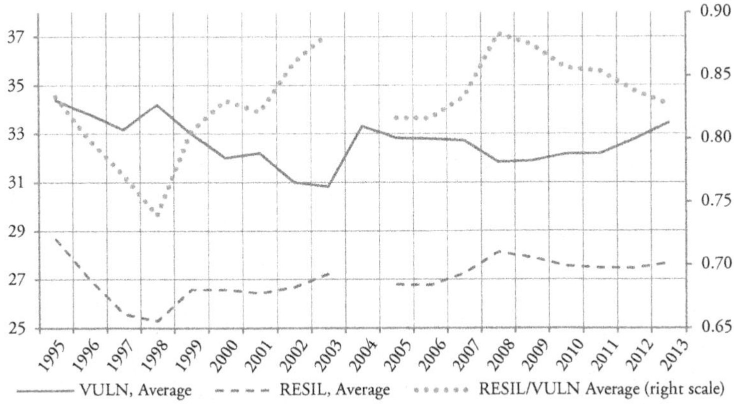

Figure 5.12. Gini Coefficient of Equivalised Disposable Income.
Source: Author's own figure based on Eurostat data.

average, while among vulnerable countries only Ireland is above the average. However, wages and salaries in this country have stagnated since the crisis. Earnings in Greece decreased, but less than labour cost, a sign of labour dismissals.[89] Earnings also slightly decreased in Portugal and Cyprus. In Italy and Spain earnings continued to increase at a much lower speed than before the crisis.

Overall, developments in labour cost and wages and salaries confirm the clear distinction within the Eurozone of two groups of countries in strikingly dissimilar economic situation. Investments also confirm this pattern. The development of wages and salaries suggests that inequalities were likely to move in different ways in the two groups of countries. Indeed, Gini coefficients confirm this (Figure 5.12).

[89]Alfred Marshall (1890) (2013 ed., p. 191) noted that "any change in the distribution of wealth which gives more to the wage receivers and less to the capitalists is likely, other things being equal, to hasten the increase of material production, and that it will not perceptibly retard the storing-up of material wealth." This point was recently strengthened in Jarand (2015) and Wolfers and Zilinsky (2015), who enumerate a host of reasons that can be found in theoretical and applied literature for concluding that higher wages benefit enterprises and the economy, along with workers. In this light, the evolution of vulnerable countries sheds a grim light on economic and social perspectives of these countries.

The average Gini coefficient for all vulnerable countries is constantly above the average for resilient countries. The difference between the two groups of countries moved around 5–6 points, a considerable difference. At the same time, all resilient countries have Gini coefficients that are constantly below the average for vulnerable countries. The difference is not only quantitatively significant. It also depicts two groups which seem worlds apart, in spite of the common currency and a long-run and deep integration.

The misery index may be a good way to summarise the negative differences among countries. The index was first introduced by Arthur Okun as the Economic Discomfort Index. Okun defined it as the sum of the inflation and unemployment rates. Subsequently, Robert Barro amended this original misery index by including two further variables: real GDP growth rate and long-term interest rate. He also used changes in values instead of their levels.

Asher *et al.* (1993) criticise the index for its technical shortcomings and particularly for disregarding the fundamental issue of distribution. They present a different index, the PAIN index, which adds together the poverty rate and the degree of income inequality. More recently, Steve Hanke (2014) presents another version of the index, that calculates the misery index score as the sum of the unemployment rate, the lending rate, and the inflation rate (consumer prices, end of period), minus the percentage change in real GDP per capita. Cohen *et al.* (2014) elaborate an index that measures the level of economic discomfort as a function of three key factors: (1) the misery index in the previous period; (2) the output gap in growth rate terms; and (3) cyclical unemployment.

In a study on the misery index in Europe, Lechman (2009) distinguishes among four different misery indexes (Figure 5.13).[90] The study only considers the countries for which there are complete data for the period 2001–2007: Belgium, Bulgaria, Czech Republic, Denmark, Germany, Estonia, Ireland, Greece, Spain, France, Italy, Cyprus, Latvia, Lithuania,

[90] Lechman (2009) specifies Okun's version of the Misery Index (OMI_1) as follows: $OMI_1 = \pi + u$, where: π is the annual inflation rate and u the total unemployment rate. Barro's Misery Index (BMI) is calculated as follows: $BMI = \Delta\pi + \Delta u - \Delta Y + \Delta I$, where: $\Delta\pi = \pi_t - \pi_{t-1}$, etc., Y is the annual GDP growth rate.

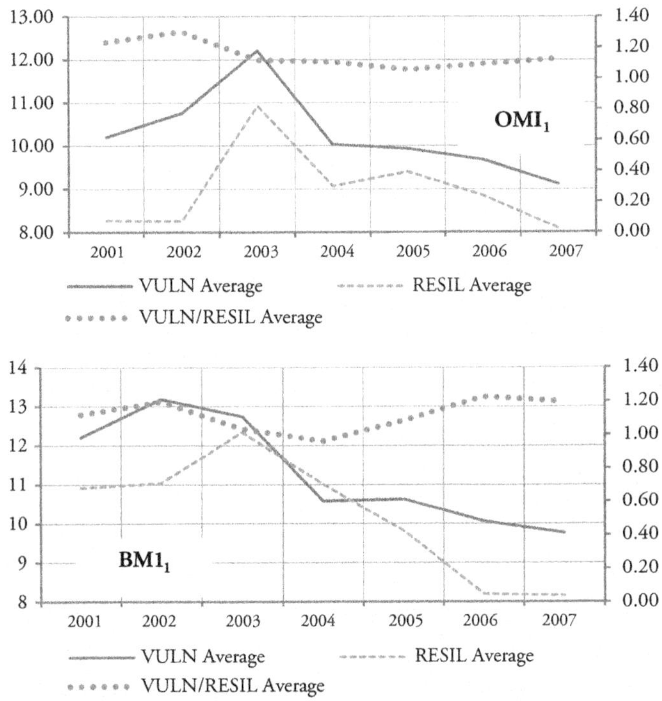

Figure 5.13. Okun's Misery Index (OMI_1) and Barro's Misery Index (BMI_1), European Union Countries, 2001–2007 (RESIL/VULN Average on Right Scale).
Source: Author's own figures based on data by Lechman (2009).

Luxembourg, Hungary, Malta, the Netherlands, Austria, Poland, Portugal, Romania, Slovenia, Slovakia, Finland, Sweden and the United Kingdom. The author considers the index to be rather rudimentary and based on an assumption about the marginal substitution rate among different economic outcomes and indicators. However, it is useful as a proxy of economic and social welfare and to reflect changes in economic performance.

Given its limitation, the index is better used to get information on the potential "misery" or "unhappiness" of individuals in a country, and not to get answers on the people's preferences. In this sense, the index also has a normative value, in that its change through time is useful to make sure that economies are developing in right direction. If taken in this meaning, Lechman's (2009) exercise is useful to shed light on a further consistent

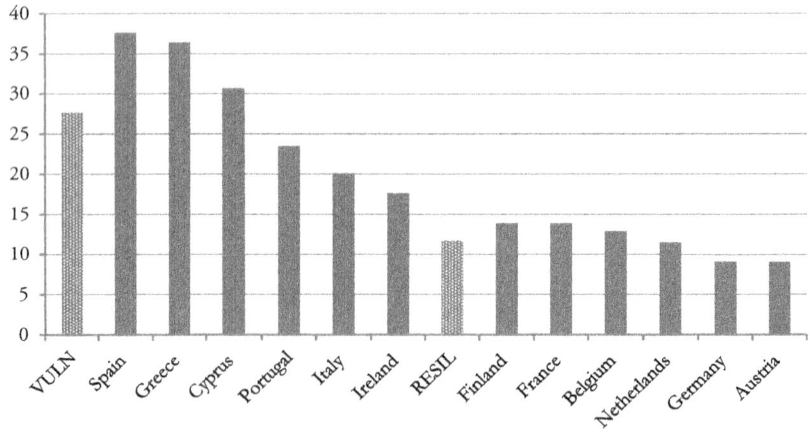

Figure 5.14. Hanke's Misery Index.
Source: Author's own figure based on data by Hanke (2014).

difference between the two groups of countries. As Figure 5.13 clearly shows, throughout the period considered vulnerable countries have a higher score, i.e. a higher "misery" than resilient countries. This is particularly evident in Okun's version of the index. In Barro's version, the difference is in part blurred, due to the overlapping of the two lines in 2004. However, for most of the years the pattern is clear also in this case.

The Misery Index Score for 2013 calculated by Hanke (2014) reaches similar conclusions through a different way (Figure 5.14). The author calculates his misery index score for 90 countries. The exercise gives an incontrovertible result: vulnerable countries have definitely higher scores than resilient countries, i.e. they have higher degrees of "misery", nearly 2.4 times higher.

5.3 An Overall Picture

The preceding analysis of a set of indicators on the situation of individual Eurozone economies demonstrates that, in most cases, Eurozone countries pool consistently around two distinct positions. These are the positions of vulnerable countries, usually in weaker economic and financial situations and with lower performance, and resilient countries, which usually have opposite features. This distinction is important for common and national policies, as the following chapters explain.

In addition to the structural factors considered in the previous sections, vulnerable economies suffered before the crisis from low or negative savings, low productivity and activity rates (mostly to the disadvantage of women), high disparities and unemployment (with remarkably elevated youth unemployment), rapidly rising ratios of debt to gross domestic product, high fiscal and current account deficits, and high interest rates.

There are specific differences among Greece, which possessed all the aforementioned features, and the other countries. Portugal had low public and high private debt; Spain had low savings and low public debt; Ireland experienced a bank and financial system crisis hampering financial stability; and Italy had elevated private savings, but suffered from high public debt. All of these countries were unable to comply with structural and microeconomic reforms and to implement and sustain financial constraints; they suffered consequently from weak competitiveness, both externally and internally.

When the euro was introduced in 1999 (2001 in Greece), member countries differed remarkably in fundamentals as well as in the structure and the dynamism of the economy. The working of the Eurozone has generally reinforced previously existing patterns, amplifying divergences rather than easing structural convergence. The common currency and monetary policy prevented imbalances from being resolved through currency depreciation. At the same time, common fiscal parameters significantly limited the members' freedom to set fiscal policies. Indeed, in an integrated area with a common currency and with the union's institutional incompleteness, only microeconomic reforms are possible and effective in improving the performance and competitiveness of individual economies.

In this context, the idea behind the free circulation of capital is that capital should flow from resilient countries to vulnerable countries, where interest rates are higher. The flow of capital to vulnerable countries should re-establish equilibrium and even out interest rates' net-of-risk. To this end, the EU established hard rules in the treaties (no-bailout and no-monetisation) and convergence criteria. It also established related procedures and third party enforcement for excessive deficit, to avoid governments' free-riding in public finance.[91] These criteria include a set of controls and also the possibility of penalty for non-complying countries.

As mentioned previously, however, the equilibrating mechanisms foreseen in the EU build-up did not work properly. In particular, this was due to the lack of effective control over fiscal policies, the implicit EU guarantee over national finances and the failure of microeconomic reforms in vulnerable countries.

Due to their inefficient microeconomy, vulnerable countries suffered higher price increases than resilient countries. Higher prices had effects similar to exchange rate appreciation and led to export discouragement. Had labour market reforms worked as expected, lower wages could have counterbalanced this negative effect. However, this kind of reform encounters two serious problems, which highlight that it is easier to pursue them successfully in resilient economies such as Germany than in vulnerable countries. These problems are related to the structure of the economy and of welfare state provisions.

First, the scope of these reforms was narrower in the vulnerable countries, where real wages were lower and social services worst. Compression of wages exacerbated the negative consequences of increasing inequalities, jeopardised labour incentives and shrank the domestic market. Second, the negative consequences of focusing on downward wage flexibility rather than on investment in infrastructure, research, innovation and human capital in stagnating economies with low technological level were serious for long-term competitiveness. The effect was to push these countries to choose more labour intensive and lower productivity technologies.

Relative costs in vulnerable countries rose for a decade, leading to their loss of competitiveness also within the Eurozone. This effect was particularly unfavourable for vulnerable countries, which had to move faster to restructure their export markets from the Eurozone to third

[91] Compared to a fixed exchange rate system, the common currency area has to solve the critical and potentially dangerous problem of avoiding free-riding among member countries to the disadvantage of virtuous ones.

Table 5.1. Intra EU-28 Export (in Percent of Total Export).

	2000	2005	2010	2014	2014–2000	2014–2005	2014–2010
Austria	75.7	73.1	72.3	69.9	−5.8	−3.2	−2.4
Belgium	76.8	76.8	73.0	70.7	−6.1	−6.1	−2.3
Finland	63.1	56.9	54.4	57.3	−5.8	0.4	2.9
France	64.9	63.6	61.0	60.3	−4.6	−3.3	−0.7
Germany	64.9	64.6	60.3	57.9	−7.0	−6.7	−2.4
Luxembourg	86.8	89.5	83.9	82.7	−4.1	−6.8	−1.2
The Netherlands	81.4	79.9	77.3	75.9	−5.5	−4.0	−1.4
RESIL	**73.4**	**72.1**	**68.9**	**67.8**	**−5.6**	**−4.2**	**−1.1**
Cyprus	60.0	73.3	66.3	56.3	−3.7	−17.0	−10.0
Greece	62.1	64.2	54.9	47.9	−14.2	−16.3	−7.0
Ireland	64.8	63.8	58.1	54.7	−10.1	−9.1	−3.4
Italy	62.1	62.0	57.9	54.7	−7.4	−7.3	−3.2
Portugal	81.6	80.3	75.4	70.9	−10.7	−9.4	−4.5
Spain	73.1	72.5	68.8	63.8	−9.3	−8.7	−5.0
VULN	**67.3**	**69.4**	**63.6**	**58.1**	**−9.2**	**−11.3**	**−5.5**

Source: Author's own table based on Eurostat database.

countries.[92] The Eurozone, as much as the EU, is in fact rather closed, since the — albeit decreasing — bulk of trade takes place among member countries (Table 5.1, Eurostat 2011). This situation favoured resilient countries, also thanks to their traditional competitors being unable to recover by depreciating their currency. Moreover, the euro was more conducive to additional Eurozone exports from resilient countries than a stronger national currency would have been.

For these reasons and for their own efficiency, resilient countries accumulated increasing current account surpluses (Figure 5.15). Resilient countries kept balance of payments equilibrium by exporting capital to vulnerable countries, where returns were higher. The inflow of capital

[92] By 2014, Greece is the only EU country — together with Great Britain and Malta — which exports more to third countries than to the EU.

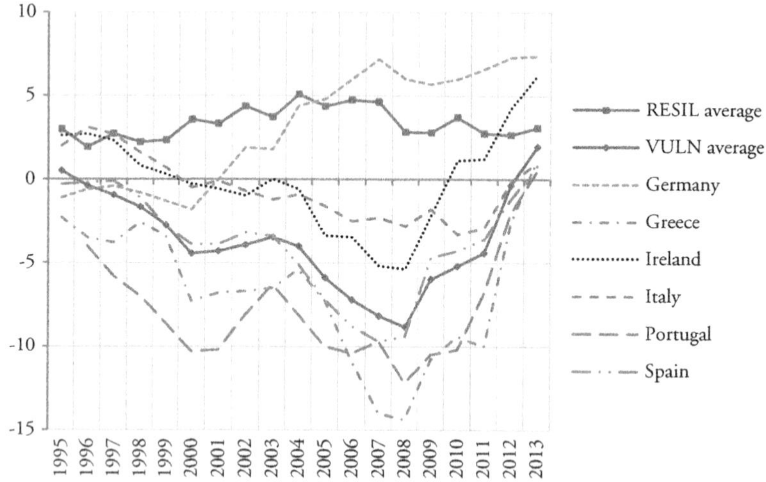

Figure 5.15. Current Account Balance (% GDP).
Source: Author's own figure based on data from the OECD database.

fueled the high growth rate in Ireland and Spain. Capital, however, went mainly into non-tradable activities like construction, granting vulnerable countries with transitory, if not illusory gains (Wolf, 2010). Resilient countries' advantage came at the cost of the vulnerable countries' inability to comply with common fiscal rules. This increased systemic risk that, in turn, hit the credibility of resilient countries. If the Eurozone economy proved to be stable in the short run, it nevertheless progressively accumulated tensions. Clearly the Eurozone lacked any forward-looking coordinated fiscal and trade policy.

The second critical aspect of Eurozone fragility was deregulation of markets and policies favouring capital and highly specialised professionals, disfavouring labour and causing growing infra-county distributive disparities. According to the OECD (2011a), the substantial increase of inequality in OECD countries was largely driven by the shift from earnings to self-employment income as well as from labour income to capital income. The rise of capital share was particularly significant in France, where it doubled since the mid-1980s (OECD 2011b), and Germany, where the contribution of capital income to total income inequality increased from 8% to 15.5% in the past decade (OECD 2011c; Piketty

2014; Piketty and Zucman 2013). In vulnerable countries, increasing distributive disparities derived more from the decrease of wages than the increase of profits (OECD 2011d, 2011e), at least recently (Balducci and Staffolani 2002; Tronti 2008). With increasing interest rates, the true winner could only be rents.

Long-term effects of these processes are decreasing returns to human capital in the vulnerable countries, which discourage investment in human capital (BI 2011b), lower social mobility, and higher migration to resilient countries, in particular of young qualified people (Arslan *et al.* 2014; Dallago 2014). These processes contributed to the shrinking of the middle class and created mounting social and political problems. These, in turn, put the public budget under strain for softening the negative consequences. As a matter of fact, according to Eurostat (2012), the risk of poverty rates before and after social transfers in EU 27 increased respectively to 25.7% and 16.4% in 2010, while 8% of Europeans were severely materially deprived. According to the definition adopted for the Europe 2020 strategy, around 23% of Europeans were considered to be at risk of poverty or social exclusion in 2009 and 2010 (Eurostat 2012). In the following years, their number increased further.[93]

The decline of real incomes, in particular those of social groups with high propensity to domestic consumption, depressed the domestic market. In Greece, disposable income started to decrease in 2008 and private consumption in 2009. Savings decreased dramatically between 2006 and 2009, decreasing slightly until 2011, after which it started to increase (Eurostat databases). In Spain and Portugal, the sharp decrease experienced in 2009 was followed by a moderate increase in 2010, which in any case did not restore consumption to the pre-crisis level. In Italy, net disposable income decreased slightly after 2008 and consumption stagnated. Net savings was negative between 2010 and 2013 and returned positive in 2014.

As noticed in Chapter 2, consumption is usually more resilient to economic downturns than income and increases in consumption inequality occur at much slower rates than increase of income inequality. In fact, income shocks can be compensated through the use of savings

[93] See Eurostat (2015c).

and borrowing. However, if shocks translate into wealth effects and are considered to be permanent, consequences for consumption tend to become permanent (Jappelli and Pistaferri 2010; Krueger and Perri 2012).

Families can attenuate the fall of private consumption by decreasing savings (Table 5.2). In Italy, a traditionally high savings country, household net savings rate decreased since 1997 and decreased further during the crisis. By 2010, it was remarkably lower than in Germany and France, although households' wealth compared to disposable income remained high and indebtedness low, even compared to Germany. However, after reaching an unusually low level in 2012, savings in Italy started to increase since 2013 and continues till the present, a clear sign of precautionary savings. The dramatically negative case of Greece aside, this pattern is approximately similar in other vulnerable countries, although these were at lower levels of saving. Vulnerable countries feature a dramatic trough in 2007, a peak in 2009 followed by a decrease and a new surge since 2013.

Among resilient countries, Germany and in part also France have a particularly smooth behaviour, with net savings virtually unchanged around 11–12% respectively since the mid-1990s. On average, savings in resilient countries decreased until 2000, then stabilised around 10%, increased slightly in 2009 and then decreased to around 8% by 2013. The level, though, remained distinctly higher than in vulnerable countries.

Before the crisis, vulnerable countries were catching up to resilient countries in consumption expenditures. Ireland had a higher level than Germany until 2009. Also Italy and Cyprus surpassed Germany in 2007 and 2008. Consumption in 2008 and 2009 decreased slightly in all countries, although in vulnerable countries the decrease was more evident, particularly in Greece and Ireland (Figure 5.16). Subsequently, it continued to decrease in vulnerable countries, but returned to increase in resilient countries. Initially, consumption decreased less than incomes and in 2010 and 2011 it slightly increased. In 2012, the situation turned around. Falling consumption, the fundamental component of demand, drove falling investments. This process was particularly severe in a time of fiscal crisis and rigid fiscal rules, when governments reduced public demand or slowed down its growth.

Table 5.2. Household and Non-Profit Institutions Serving Households Net Saving Ratio (in Percent).

	1995	**1996**	**1997**	**1998**	**1999**	**2000**	**2001**	**2002**	**2003**	**2004**	**2005**	**2006**	**2007**	**2008**	**2009**	**2010**	**2011**	**2012**	**2013**
Eurozone-15	12.0	11.4	10.7	9.5	8.7	8.1	8.8	8.9	8.9	8.6	8.2	7.8	7.9	8.2	9.3	7.6	7.0	6.6	6.7
Austria	14.65	11.92	10.43	10.36	11.73	10.47	8.82	8.95	9.17	9.21	10.74	11.30	12.09	11.95	11.26	9.44	7.83	9.03	7.27
Belgium	15.83	13.91	13.12	12.56	12.49	11.73	13.01	12.21	11.66	10.27	9.93	10.59	10.84	11.24	12.76	10.09	8.53	7.51	6.89
France	10.81	10.02	11.11	10.58	10.17	10.04	10.66	11.63	10.86	10.95	9.41	9.38	9.77	9.46	10.82	10.35	10.04	9.62	9.49
Germany	10.95	10.48	10.07	9.90	9.42	8.94	9.55	9.57	10.27	10.04	10.04	10.01	10.20	10.46	9.96	9.93	9.56	9.39	9.08
The Netherlands	13.69	12.76	12.69	10.59	8.61	6.94	9.25	8.98	8.34	7.73	6.75	5.00	5.17	5.38	8.70	5.14	6.02	6.51	7.84
RESIL	**13.19**	**11.82**	**11.48**	**10.80**	**10.48**	**9.63**	**10.26**	**10.27**	**10.06**	**9.64**	**9.38**	**9.26**	**9.61**	**9.70**	**10.70**	**8.99**	**8.40**	**8.41**	**8.11**
Greece												−3.37	−3.50	−5.56	−4.45	−9.04	−8.21	−8.26	−16.36
Ireland					1.17	−3.52	1.20	0.02	0.39	1.20	1.93	−0.59	−0.69	6.30	12.20	9.56	7.25	8.47	8.13
Italy	15.98	16.45	13.63	9.91	8.70	7.34	8.82	9.50	9.00	9.45	8.93	8.32	7.87	7.62	6.85	3.99	3.53	1.96	3.76
Portugal	5.47	4.33	3.72	5.07	4.54	3.47	4.05	3.86	2.70	2.71	1.79	0.36	−0.78	−1.13	2.73	1.34	−0.91	−0.45	0.67
Spain					5.91	6.45	6.17	5.97	7.44	5.76	4.06	2.26	0.02	2.59	9.53	4.63	5.99	3.51	4.89
VULN					**5.08**	**3.44**	**5.06**	**4.84**	**4.88**	**4.78**	**4.18**	**2.59**	**1.61**	**3.85**	**7.83**	**4.88**	**3.97**	**3.37**	**4.36**
United Kingdom					3.75	5.29	5.90	4.47	3.56	1.29	0.57	−0.62	−0.18	−0.76	3.52	5.48	2.94	2.26	0.27
United States	6.61	6.15	5.96	6.42	4.58	4.33	4.50	5.20	5.00	4.73	2.63	3.42	3.08	5.14	6.39	5.80	6.24	7.48	5.03

Source: OECD database.

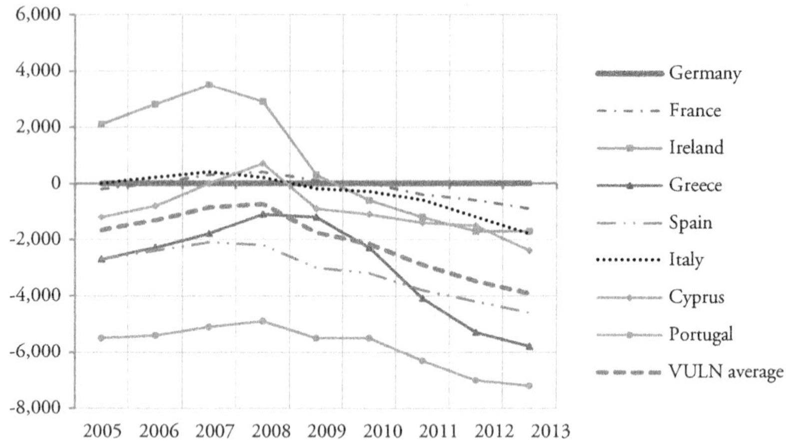

Figure 5.16. Per Capita Final Consumption Expenditure of Households (Differences from the Level of Germany, Current Prices, Euro Per Capita).
Source: Eurostat.

5.4 Conclusions: Beyond the Economy and Alternative Scenarios

Two groups of countries became increasingly distinct within the Eurozone. They were different before adopting the common currency under various economically and socially fundamental aspects. These differences made the situation of the weaker part, the vulnerable countries, hardly sustainable in the monetary union. These countries often failed to implement important reforms and to better manage macro-policies, and saw their economic and financial situation deteriorate over time. Yet some of them reached important performances in different fields, including economic growth and financial stabilisation.

Their situation became more difficult within a differentiated economic space with one currency, incomplete common institutions and ineffective national sovereignty over macroeconomic policies. Once they adopted the euro, their financial and economic situation was apparently eased thanks to decreasing interest rates. However, it became untenable as soon as the crisis started. Their situation and their fate became increasingly separated from those of the economically stronger and more resilient part of the Eurozone, namely the resilient countries.

One important aspect of these developments was that the compliance of vulnerable countries with the convergence criteria failed. They also threatened to be a liability for the monetary union, one that could potentially impose costs on resilient countries through unbalanced finances and depressed economies. The implementation of the common fiscal rules was sometimes rather loose or even openly circumvented. The union muddled through for years, relying on the apparently inexhaustible strength and overall stability of the international economy and its drive to growth.

However, the crisis convinced European authorities and national governments, and in part also international economic organisations, to push governments to adopt austerity measures. In the Eurozone, this was justified with the need to defend the value and the very existence of the common currency. Vulnerable countries had to adapt to and implement internal devaluation, a policy that was in the interest of resilient countries and, admittedly, the strength of the common currency. The latter, to be sure, was in the interest of the latter group of countries, but not the former.

It is by now clear even to European authorities and the governments of resilient countries that the two groups of countries need different policies and better coordination of the economic positions of the two groups of countries to manage the crisis. The Eurozone and its constituent parts are apparently moving towards a new consensus, this time less centred on short-run finances and more attentive to long-run goals (growth) and social and political sustainability. Yet it is a long way from recognising the problems and identifying the goals, let alone finding the pragmatic path and the instruments needed to move from here to there.

When the crisis moved from the United States to the EU, the latter discovered its economic and institutional unsustainability. In fact, financial and economic events placed governments under pressure for putting their accounts in order. The pressure had different roots, but two of them were particularly relevant and can be best understood looking at theories of optimal currency areas. First, doubts appeared — or, better, were renewed — that the Eurozone may not be an optimum currency area. In fact, it was stressed that labour mobility was insufficient, national economic systems were sometimes significantly different and could introduce further obstacles to the mobility of resources, and intercountry fiscal transfers met apparently insurmountable political obstacles. Second, during the crisis, the perception of the commonality of destiny also came under question and mutual trust among countries was weakened, particularly with regard to policymaking.

This situation thus posed two fundamental questions:

1. Is the aforementioned situation the outcome of mistakes in the European integration and its management? In particular, is the Eurozone an ill-conceived area for a monetary union? This problem is assessed and answered in the next chapter on optimum currency areas.
2. Given the fact that monetary unification took place, what is to be done now? Is there a way to solve the present untenable situation by means of reforms and policies or through institutional development? These issues are discussed in the following chapters in order to arrive at a coherent answer in Chapter 12.

One market, one money.

— European Commission, One Market, One Money: An Evaluation of the Potential Benefits and Costs of Forming an Economic and Monetary Union, *European Economy*, Economic Papers, 44, 1990.

Ein Volk! Ein Reich! Ein Euro!

— Slogan seen on a sign carried by a protester in Greece in early November 2011.

6

The Eurozone as a Quasi-Optimum Currency Area

The previous chapters assessed the external economic context of the Eurozone and its internal consistency in the years before the crisis. The overall conclusion was that the Eurozone economic performance and competitiveness were decreasing. Moreover, the process of catching-up to the United States had slowed down, lost momentum and gone in reverse. Yet the situation was far from being hopeless. Some of the main reasons for the diminished relative performance of the Eurozone (such as the decreased number of hours worked compared to other countries and the ageing of the population) were traded off for better welfare and quality of life. Consequently, they should be ascribed to the preferences of Europeans compared to those of other countries.

The decreased dynamism of the economy worried European policymakers for years. One of the important goals behind the adoption of the euro was the belief that the common currency would have enlarged markets and fostered economies of scale and scope, boosted growth by decreasing transaction costs and solving the uncertainty of exchange rates, fostering competition and the size of enterprises. All these factors were expected to help production and trade.

Yet the common currency is a delicate, economically and financially critical undertaking and is not easily comparable to previous attempts to implement monetary unions (O'Rourke and Taylor 2013). Indeed, it could turn out to cause a dramatic fall of economic performance and standard of living, the deindustrialisation of the relatively less efficient countries, and permanent large scale unemployment. This may happen in spite of resource mobility, unless a common government or an intergovernmental agreement implements a massive transfer of resources to the weakening countries, as the case of the German unification clearly demonstrates (Sinn 2000). The situation is more delicate in the case in which a political unification does not accompany the monetary union, as is the case of the Eurozone. In this case, intercountry transfers of resources are feeble in the best case, grossly insufficient to compensate for the inbalances that an improper monetary union may cause (Pasimeni 2014).

In order to be sustainable — that is, avoid excessive adjustment costs or intercountry distribution of resources and income — the monetary unification should take place among countries which share certain features that make them compatible with each other. The theory of the optimum currency area (OCA) highlights the most important such conditions. A true monetary union is also a political and social undertaking that may draw energy and support from different directions and adjust progressively through time. Although OCA offers a somewhat static approach, at least in its original formulations and is thus unable to capture those effects, the approach has the benefit of calling attention to the most important technical aspects and conditions for a properly functioning monetary union. Thus, it also highlights potential compensations for countervailing actions or the missing elements.

It has long been known that the Eurozone presents problems as an OCA (Eichengreen 1991; Eichengreen *et al.* 1990; Feldstein 1991; Friedman 1997; Obstfeld 1997; Sala-i-Martin and Sachs 1991). However, it was considered that consistent integration of markets, the activation of the private insurance mechanism, reforms, and strong political will and commitment would either create or complement the missing factors. *Ex post*, it is fair to say that this adaptation worked up to the crisis. In fact, the external effects of an expanding international economy and careful policy management created incentives to economic activity and avoided asymmetric shocks. However, the international crisis changed the situation and put the euro at risk. Unfortunately, the quality of an institutional setup, like a monetary system, corresponds to its value and resilience in a stressful situation. One additional factor to be considered is that, in spite of its vicissitudes, the euro continued to be strong compared to the most important currencies, in particular the US dollar. This appreciation increased the problems of some of the Eurozone member countries. The euro threatened to become a liability for those countries.

This chapter is devoted on reviewing the main features, advantages and costs of an OCA and to discuss whether the Eurozone could be considered an OCA. It then proceeds to examine the adoption of the euro and what follows from the perspective of the OCA theory. The aim is to see whether the Eurozone has become closer to the theoretical prescription or whether the distance between the two may be considered as a major cause for the ongoing internal distress of the Eurozone. Finally, it is considered whether the strength of the euro and the post-crisis management of the currency can be considered as causes of the present difficulties within the Eurozone.

6.1 Optimum Currency Area Defined

An OCA is usually defined as a region that presents such economic and institutional features that make the use of one common currency as advantageous and economically superior (efficient) to having two or more currencies. A region in this case can be a group of countries or a set of sub-national units within a country. An example of the latter is the United States. Some economists consider that even within the United States some states do not fit into an OCA together with other states (Kouparitsas 2001). In the case of the euro, the theory was used to assess whether the Eurozone presents the features that make the replacement of the national currencies with one common currency economically efficient and sustainable.

Since a common currency area has one unique central bank, monetary policy is also unique. This means that monetary policy cannot deal with the effects of asymmetric shocks in the different parts of the monetary union. Fiscal policies and reforms are needed to this end. A monetary union includes regions and countries which inevitably present differences and the larger the union, the greater those differences are likely to be. Therefore, chances are that the probability of having asymmetric shocks in a large union is greater.

The internally asymmetric effect of the currency union and the common monetary policy derives from two fundamental features. First, economic, social, and institutional features of regions or countries within a monetary union may differ substantially. For instance, their labour markets may be structured and work differently, the price elasticity of their exports can be different, their imported energy intensity may vary, the industrial structure and the size of enterprises could be dissimilar, the role of the state and the size of the public debt may be very different. Second, financial structures may differ from one region or country of a monetary union to another. The nature and size of asymmetric shocks and the transmission mechanism of the monetary policy may differ consequently. For instance, the features and structure of financial markets (financial depth) and the ability of enterprises to get credit and conditions attached to credit may vary.

Thus, in a large and internally dissimilar monetary union, the unique currency and monetary policy have asymmetric effects. These effects may be negligible if the external economic situation is booming and the private insurance mechanism works. However, such a situation can impose a set of important asymmetric costs to the member states. It can also result in common costs for the complex management of the common currency area. These include the costs of managing the currency in a more complex situation, the costs necessary to balance the asymmetric effects by means of other policies or mechanisms, and the costs of the consequences for the inability to deal directly and precisely with local problems by means of independent policies and protect the regional and national economy. The cost of conflicts among countries and the cost to national economies can complement common costs.

The problem of asymmetric situations and effects in a monetary union among different countries can be pervasive. In a currency union, the unique monetary policy tends to enlarge the problems of the vulnerable part (regions or countries) of the union. Since the common currency reputation depends typically upon the strongest regions or countries of the union, the common monetary policy is likely to give priority to the situation in the economically, financially and politically strongest partners and disfavour the weak and vulnerable ones. However, the latter may take advantage of the strength of the former through capital import and expanded exports. The interlink among countries may have different outcomes in vulnerable countries, depending on the use of the additional resources: growth and additional employment, or financial and real bubbles may follow.

The monetary policy in a currency union is at the same time more limited in its management (if monetary authorities aim at avoiding risks for the economic and political sustainability of the monetary union) and more problematic in its effects, an important part of which are felt internally to the union. In particular, a symmetric shock, such as the appreciation of the common currency, is likely to create expansion in countries with rigid export demand and recession and possibly inflation in member countries with elastic export demands. These consequences may create political and social tensions within the monetary union which are not easy to manage, given the incomplete institutional and policy setting.

It is therefore of the utmost importance that the common currency and monetary policy are accompanied by compensating factors, that counteract the asymmetric effects of the common monetary policy. A common budget and transfer of common resources to the advantage of regions in need is the strongest solution, although it may be difficult to implement in the absence of a common government. Other factors include fiscal equalisation, independent (regional or national) budget policies and related policies, the transfer of resources among the different regions or countries by means of bilateral or multilateral government actions or through private insurance mechanisms. Additional devices include a bank union and supervision that can implement and interregional or inter-country transfer of financial resources and guarantees. A common central bank that acts as a lender of last resort can ease asymmetries and tensions. Political will and social preferences supporting the common currency are also important components of success.

Given price and wage rigidity, an asymmetric shock in a monetarily independent country can be adjusted through a variation of the nominal exchange rate. However, this is not possible within a common currency area, where partner regions or countries usually trade intensively. If the transfer of resources from other regions or countries is not possible, economic difficulties can be solved only by diminishing in some way prices and wages in the less competitive country or region (internal devaluation). This can be done in different ways: through enacting reforms that cut costs (e.g. by cutting taxation or rents, or more efficient and effective public administration), decreasing the cost of production (e.g. through investments that make infrastructure more efficient or decrease the cost of energy), or increasing competition. Alternatively, adjustment may take place through the decrease of wages, or by weakening the rights of workers (e.g. by decreasing welfare or pension rights). However, the latter is likely to increase income disparities and may easily weaken aggregate demand and incentives to work. The consequence may be smaller internal market and lower investment, with long-term negative consequences.

6.2 OCA Theories

The existence of costs, difficulties and threats is not a sufficient reason to refuse a monetary union. In fact, a monetary union also has advantages and offers opportunities. It is therefore important to assess whether the advantages of a currency and monetary union surpass disadvantages (Baldwin and Wyplosz 2012). OCA theories identify a set of features that are important to assess whether a group of regions or countries share the conditions for building a currency union that guarantees superior advantages. Various economists contributed to the development of OCA theories. Their conclusions were used to assess whether the Eurozone is actually an OCA or whether the adoption of the euro imposed upon the area costs and tensions bound to lead to the failure of the experiment. The debate was intense on the eve of the adoption of the euro and it was once again revived with the start of the financial and monetary crisis that hit the Eurozone, particularly in 2011 and again with the more recent Greek crisis in 2015.

Robert Mundell's seminal article (Mundell 1961) is usually credited to have introduced the concept of OCA. In a world where asymmetric shocks are pervasive, a floating exchange rate regime can adjust economies to such shocks without causing unemployment, provided that prices and wages are flexible. In a currency union, in which regions and countries trade intensively, the exchange rate is unique and it is only the mobility of resources among regions or countries of the union that can avoid their massive unemployment. Yet labour is generally slow to move and may need to be retrained. Also capital mobility faces obstacles. Even if financial capital can move quickly in a monetary union, physical capital is transformed slowly; this prevents adjustment mechanisms from being sufficiently fast and effective. According to Mundell, it is particularly important that labour mobility in a common currency area is high in order for a monetary union to be beneficial.[94] Thus the question is eminently empirical and can be reduced to "...whether or not Western Europe can be considered a single region."

Therefore, a monetary union is not without costs. These include the transmission of depression through the foreign trade multiplier, and interregional balance of payments problems.[95] Thus, a monetary union may

---

[94] "If the world can be divided into regions within each of which there is factor mobility and between which there is factor immobility, then each of these regions should have a separate currency which fluctuates relative to all other currencies" (Mundell 1961, p. 663).

[95] "...under a common currency, depression in one region would be transmitted to other regions... If the gold standard imposed a harsh discipline on the national economy and induced the transmission of economic fluctuations, then a common currency would be guilty of the same charges; interregional balance-of-payments problems are invisible, so to speak, precisely because there is no escape from the self-adjusting effects of interregional

lead to periodic balance of payments crises, when price and wage rigidity prevents automatic adjustments.[96]

In a later article, Mundell (1973) considers that asymmetric shocks do not undermine the common currency, which acts as a shock absorber. Indeed, the currency union spreads the shocks by allowing the negatively hit region or country to rely on the resources of the rest of the union, thus spreading the effect of the shock over a much larger area.

These problems nurtured the skepticism of earlier writings. According to Meade (1957), the conditions for a common currency in Western Europe do not exist, in particular because of the lack of labour mobility. In spite of being in favour of a common currency, that in his view would induce a greater degree of capital mobility, Tibor Scitovsky (1958) warned that policies should promote labour mobility also by means of supranational employment policies. Unlike these authors and while restating his 1961 article conclusions, Mundell maintains that "[b]oth the U.S. and Europe possess enough of the characteristics of an optimum currency area to move toward narrower, rather than wider fluctuations in exchange rates. In matters of finance it is better for Europe to move toward the US pattern of high capital and labour mobility than to break up, by the crawling peg system, the degree of integration already achieved" (Mundell 1969, p. 5).

Peter Kenen (1969) identifies a second important feature. Kenen stresses the role of product diversification among countries as a necessary condition of an OCA. Countries with highly specialised production profile that form a currency union are liable to the asymmetric consequences of an external shock that concerns the goods or services in which they are specialised, without having the possibility to adapt to the shock through the variation of the exchange rate. Such a shock can derive, for instance, from a change in the production conditions and hence the price of a good or a fundamental input in the production of that good, the change in

---

money flows. (It is true, of course, that interregional liquidity can always be supplied by the national central bank....)" (Mundell 1961, p. 660).

[96] "It is patently obvious that periodic balance-of-payments crises will remain an integral feature of the international economic system as long as fixed exchange rates and rigid wage and price levels prevent the terms of trade from fulfilling a natural role in the adjustment process" (Mundell 1961, p. 657).

consumers' preferences, and other conditions of demand. Wide product differentiation in each member country of the monetary union and similarity of the production profile of the member countries is a guarantee that the effects of shocks, concerning particular goods, are not asymmetric to start with and are dispersed through a wide array of goods and services that each country produces.

Ronald McKinnon (1963) highlights a third feature that a currency union should have: openness of markets. In open markets, goods are intensely traded and their price tends to be the same in each country by the force of international competition. As a consequence, if the nominal exchange rate varies, also the internal price of the goods changes, so that their external price is equal to the world price. Market openness also guarantees that business cycles in member countries are synchronised, thus supporting coordinated, non-competitive stabilisation policies. In these conditions the exchange rate loses much of its importance for supporting the competitiveness of national goods and for adjusting the economy to the effect of external shocks.

The classical analysis thus stresses that, in order to have a sustainable OCA, member economies must be open, their production profile should be wide and production diversified, resources should be mobile and prices and . Under those conditions, the common currency assures its benefits without major costs or threats. A common currency is after all a political undertaking. Countries may decide to proceed with a currency union for the sake of its political benefits even if the above criteria are not fully respected. In these conditions, the currency union has additional instruments to its benefit.

External shocks tend to randomly hit activities and countries. It is in the interest of the countries that form a currency union to activate a sort of mutual insurance mechanism by transferring resources to the advantage of the members of the union that are hit negatively. Intercountry fiscal transfers have the advantage of alleviating the recession in the country hit by the shock and mitigating the expansion in others. Such a solution can be implemented through the common fiscal capacity (a common budget) that acts as a mechanism of shock absorption and risk-sharing.[97]

---

[97] On the features and advantages of a common budget, see Caudal *et al.* (2013).

The question remains open whether such transfer mechanism should be based in common institutions, such as the common government of the economy, or rely on intergovernmental agreements or other solutions. A common central bank acting as lender of last resort could also effectively intervene to alleviate the consequences of the shock. Intergovernmental agreements may also be effective, although cumbersome.

The role of the common economic government and the central bank is a critical one in an OCA and, to be effective, needs that policy preferences are homogeneous among member countries. This is technically and politically important, since policy responses to shocks typically have distributive consequences that may create winners and losers. Since this is inevitable and since policy preferences in different countries are different, the union is viable if the members trust that the advantages of being members of a currency union are greater than the costs and if losers are compensated at least in the long run. These sentiments help the union to foster mutual solidarity that can temper tensions and prolong the time horizon of all the involved actors.

6.3 A Comparison with the United States: Labour Mobility

Some scholars challenged the idea that the United States is an OCA and supported the view that it would be economically rational if different US regions use different currencies (Kouparitsas 2001). However, there is no doubt that the United States respects the criteria of an OCA much better than the Eurozone. And in fact, various authors have derived insights and teachings for the European monetary unification from the United States' experience. The exercise consists of assessing whether member countries activate risk sharing through both market and fiscal means, in order to smooth intercountry differences to a level compatible with a sustainable common currency.

The United States is usually found to fare better than the Eurozone under any of the OCA criteria. Therefore, a comparison of the Eurozone with the United States is useful to shed light on the sustainability of the European monetary union and for understanding whether the Eurozone is evolving in a favourable direction. The United States proves that, even while admitting that it is not a perfect OCA, political will and social support can nevertheless effectively compensate for the economic drawbacks.

Labour market (im)mobility is the OCA criterion which is credited for being the most problematic (Dallago 2014; Zimmermann 2009). Various studies, referring to different periods of time, have found that labour market shocks led to weaker migration in Europe than in the United States (Bonin *et al.* 2008; Decressin and Fatás 1995; Bentivogli and Pagano 1999).[98] In a paper comparing labour mobility between states in the US and between regions of the European Union (EU) at the NUTS-2 level in 2008, Gáková and Dijkstra (2010) find that labour mobility to another EU country or to another region of the same country was much lower than in the United States.[99] In the EU, 1.21% of the working age population moved the residence to another region. This average was the outcome of very different situations in the "old" 15 member countries, where the share was 1.46%, and the "new" member countries of Central and Eastern Europe (CEEC), where it was 0.38%. A further difference was the spatial concentration of mobility of the working age migrants, which was definitely higher in the EU than in the US. In the EU, few (22) regions had a very high share of arrivals and many of them (211) had very low shares.

While in the US, the share of working age residents who moved from a different state was 2.80%, in the EU (27 member countries) only 0.18% of working age residents moved to another member country. This is slightly lower than the share of working age residents who moved from

---

[98] Molloy *et al.* (2011) find that there has been a long-term decline in internal migration in the United States during the past thirty years, while regional mobility in the European Union at NUTS-2 level was on the rise in the second half of the 2000s. However, European internal mobility continued to be lower than in the United States.

[99] In a previous paper, which studied changes of working age residents in 2006, Gáková and Dijkstra (2008) introduce the use of two indicators to replace for the lack of EU-wide data sources. These were the share of the working age population who changed their region of residence within the previous year, and net migration. The latter is the difference between the number of people who arrived and left during one year and was used in order to show which regions attracted more people. The data did not take into account intercountry or interregional movement of people due to movement of workplace without a change in permanent residence, seasonal work and education/training (unless they implied a change of residence), or daily commuting. This study generated slightly different data compared to the following one, yet the overall picture is similar.

outside the EU (0.19%).[100] The EU had a clear disadvantage also in this case of immigration from other countries, since in the US the share was four times higher (0.74% of working age residents). Foreign immigrants to the EU were still much more concentrated than in the case of foreign immigrants to the US. In both cases, they chose destinations different from those selected by internal migrants from other regions of the same EU member country or another US state.

Labour mobility lower than in the US is a typical feature of the entire EU and is irrespective of the time of joining the EU, the level of development of the country or region, and the degree of openness of labour markets. There are many reasons that can explain this difference. Cultural and linguistic factors apart, there are differences in labour legislation between the EU and the US, while there are still some obstacles to the free movement of labour in some parts of the EU.[101] Moreover, the latter is not a state like the United States and has a much more recent history of internal mobility. Comparisons of labour mobility between the EU and the US are consequently difficult and their outcome somehow uncertain.

The role of labour mobility in reducing the differences in economic development between the states is important in the United States, thanks to a rather high share of the US working age population who moves every year to another state of residence. In the EU, however, this effect is much lower and labour mobility is not an important factor in reducing the disparities between EU member countries.

Moreover, in the EU there are important cross-country differences in labour mobility. In particular, there is a clear distinction between the new and the old member countries. In the latter, the share of the working age population who changed their region of residence is nearly four times higher than in the Central and Eastern European member countries.

The general situation of substantially lower labour mobility in the EU than in the United States changes somewhat when interregional mobility

---

[100] Again, this share was much higher (0.23%) in the EU-15 than in CEEC (0.03%) (Gáková and Dijkstra 2010).

[101] With the exception of Great Britain, Ireland and Sweden, "old" EU-15 member countries introduced limits on labour mobility, when eight CEEC joined the EU in 2004. Finland, Greece, Italy, Portugal and Spain removed restrictions in 2006.

within EU member states is taken into consideration. This measure is perhaps more significant, since the EU is far from being a unified country and linguistic, cultural, administrative and institutional differences also matter in explaining labour mobility (Heinz and Ward-Warmedinger 2006), together with poorly functioning rental markets (Caroleo and Pastore 2010). Although differences with the US decrease in this case, these still remain important: interregional mobility in the EU (1.03% of working age population per year) is lower than interstate mobility in the US (2.8%). Also in this case the EU average is the outcome of a much higher mobility in EU-15 (1.26%) than in CEEC (0.24%).

Gáková and Dijkstra (2010) estimate that 85% of overall labour mobility in the EU was within regions of the same country. However, even in this case, mobility was very unequal through regions: also interregional mobility presented much higher dispersion in the EU than interstate mobility did in the US. In fact, the difference of mobility between top and bottom regions was 45.9 times in the EU, against only 3.1 in the US.

The comparison with the US shows that labour mobility in the EU is not negligible, particularly in the EU-15. However, it is significantly lower than in the US even in the more favourable sense of interregional mobility. Thus, taking the US situation as a benchmark for requirements for an OCA, labour mobility is insufficient as an adjustment mechanism in a monetary union featuring important inter-regional differences of performance.

Given this background, it is important to see whether and how the crisis influenced the EU disadvantage, also considering that the crisis in the EU is much longer than it was in the US. An OECD study (Jauer *et al.* 2014) compares interregional migration in the EU and the United States before and after the crisis, and their association with asymmetric labour market shocks. The study estimates the relationship between migration (rounded up by population changes) and one-year lagged regional unemployment and non-employment differentials.

The findings modify the overall picture of labour mobility. It is confirmed that labour mobility in response to labour market shocks before the crisis was stronger in the United States than in the EU. However, the situation changed with the crisis, with migration in the EU having reacted more strongly to changes in labour market conditions than in the

United States.[102] In fact, while in the EU labour mobility increased, in the US internal mobility seems to have declined (Dao *et al.* 2014; Jauer *et al.* 2014). Tentative evidence shows that the migration response to the crisis was considerable in Europe (Beine *et al.* 2013).[103] Vice versa, in the United States labour market shocks did not prompt greater interstate labour mobility.

There were two sources of labour migration, both of which strongly influenced recent migration flows in the EU. The two sources were the two successive EU enlargements to CEEC in 2004 and 2007, and the proper crisis. Based on increased regional disparities during transformation in CEEC (Huber 2007) and a great variety of situations both between old and new member countries and within individual countries (Huber 2009), enlargement greatly increased labour mobility within the EU and the Eurozone (Von Weizsäcker 2008). In addition to this, the crisis increased disparities among countries and regions more significantly in Europe than in the United States, particularly with regard to unemployment rates. Divergent situations among EU immigration countries changed the attractiveness of destinations to the advantage of Germany and other resilient countries and the disadvantage of vulnerable countries (Bertoli *et al.* 2013). These differences were larger in the EU, with unemployment at the regional level more than twice higher in Europe than in the United States. However, despite positive developments, a host of problems and obstacles still hamper intra-EU labour mobility (BS 2014).

Important and growing differences also exist among EU-15. Yet so far these differences did not push migration from vulnerable countries to resilient countries on a significant scale. Within the Eurozone, it was

[102] According to Jauer *et al.* (2014), who use slightly different definitions than Gáková and Dijkstra (2010), interstate migration relative to the total population was considerably larger in the United States than in the EU: almost 3% in the United States in 2005/2006 (decreasing slightly with the crisis), but only one-tenth of that level in the EU (intercountry mobility increased from 2005/2006 to 2011/2012).

[103] The upper limit estimate is that about a quarter of asymmetric labour market shocks would be absorbed by migration within a year, supposing that all measured population changes in Europe were due to migration for employment purposes (Jauer *et al.* 2014). However, other authors are more skeptical on the effect of labour mobility in the countries of origin (Bräuninger and Majowski 2011; Elsner and Zimmermann 2013).

mainly labour migration from CEEC that fed labour market adjustment, in particular thanks to citizens of CEEC who have taken on the nationality of a Eurozone country.

6.4 Openness of Markets and Integration

Along with labour mobility, there are various other important criteria for assessing the correspondence of the Eurozone to an OCA. Under some of these criteria, the Eurozone shows no important differences with the United States. Openness of markets of Eurozone countries is high and, if infra-Eurozone exchanges are included, is higher than the United States.

Openness of markets includes various aspects of an economy, such as foreign trade, foreign direct investments, external debt, and participation in global value chains. ICC (2013) calculates the ICC Open Markets Index (OMI), a composite index made of four components and calculated for 75 countries. OMI focuses on the ease of market access and includes: (a) openness to trade; (b) trade policy; (c) foreign direct investment (FDI) openness;[104] and (d) infrastructure for trade. The four components are constructed on the basis of 28 time series relating to the years 2010 and 2011 and taken from publicly available data by international organisations, World Bank surveys, and direct communication from the International Trade Centre (ITC). In calculating the score, the maximum and the minimum values are attributed respectively to the highest and lowest scores obtained by individual countries, along a scale going from 1 (minimum openness) to 6 (maximum openness).

OMI provides information for some interesting reflections (Table 6.1). The average rank and score of Eurozone member countries (unweighted average of the values of individual member countries) show that the Eurozone economy is more open than the US economy. Resilient countries have a clear advantage over the United States: according to the ICC (2013), the former group of countries has above average openness, while the

---

[104] Jansen and Stokman (2014) investigate the relationship between FDI and business cycle synchronisation in the period 1982 to 2011 for eight industrialised countries. They find that more synchronised business cycles were associated with stronger FDI relations in the period 1995 to 2011, but not before 1995.

Table 6.1. The ICC Open Markets Index in Different Groups of Countries.

	Rank	Score
Eurozone	22	4.2
VULN	35	3.8
RESIL	15	4.4
United States	38	3.7

Source: Author's own analysis of data by ICC (2013).

United States is in the group of average openness. The US score is remarkably similar to that of vulnerable countries.

Average scores of the four components of OMI provide more interesting information (Table 6.2). Resilient countries not only have higher scores on average under any of the components than all the vulnerable countries, but also have higher scores than the United States, except for trade policy. Resilient countries have above average scores for all components. In trade-enabling infrastructure, they are the best performers. Vulnerable countries have below average trade openness, average FDI openness, and above average scores in trade policy and trade-enabling infrastructure. Vulnerable countries have the same or higher scores than the United States, except than in trade-enabling infrastructure.

In the case of economic openness, the Eurozone is on average better off than the United States. This is an excellent support for OCA scores. However important, economic openness is not sufficient, since greater openness could produce more and greater asymmetric shocks if demand shifts from the products of one country to the products of another country. There can be two alternative effects. The first is that greater openness does not create asymmetric shocks, because greater integration smoothes away shocks, thanks to greater product diversification (EC 1990). Much of the trade involving European countries is intra-industry trade, i.e. EU and Eurozone member countries trade mainly components of complex products. Their high product differentiation takes place within the same industries and in the production of components of similar goods or variants of the same product (e.g. cars). Under these conditions,

Table 6.2. Average Scores of ICC Open Markets Index in Different Groups of Countries.

	Trade Openness	Trade Policy	FDI Openness	Trade-Enabling Infrastructure	Total Trade
Eurozone	3.6	4.6	4.0	4.5	4.2
VULN	2.8	4.6	3.7	4.1	3.8
RESIL	4.0	4.7	4.1	5.3	4.4
United States	2.2	4.7	3.4	5.1	3.7

Source: Author's own analysis of ICC data (2013).

a demand shock affects all countries and consequently does not have important asymmetric effects.

The alternative view is based on the concept of localisation of economic activity. Economic forces, such as economies of scale and localisation, lead to the concentration of specific economic activities in particular regions (Krugman 1991). Barriers to trade may hamper this regional concentration. However, when greater trade integration dismantles such barriers, production differences increase not only among countries, but also among regions. This creates further opportunities for asymmetric shocks, since even symmetric shocks may have asymmetric effects as a consequence of regional concentration of economic activity.

Clearly, consequences for the common currency are very different in the two cases. While the former case would strengthen the Eurozone as an OCA, the latter would increase the cost of the common currency and weaken its sustainability. There are three reasons for thinking that the EU view may be more convincing (EC 1990). First, as integration proceeds and leads to greater regional concentration of production, this concentration may be inattentive to the countries' borders (De Grauwe 2014). In fact, border regions attract a disproportionate share of the relocation of high technology and increasing-returns industries (Tsiapa 2013). If so, productive activities may localise where it is more convenient and involve more countries. This would smooth asymmetric shocks.

The second reason is that regional concentration of production may be based in intra-industry trade. If so, the effect of regional concentration would be dispersed over more regions and countries, which would in turn smooth the effect of asymmetric shocks.[105] To these two reasons, one should add the effect of the growing importance of services. Since many services are not subject to scale and localisation economies, they tend to be regionally more dispersed even if economic integration proceeds. As a consequence, the increase of their importance diminishes the likelihood of asymmetric shocks.

Third, the evolution of the export mix is strongly path-dependent (Boschma and Capone 2014). This is so because the current productive structure is important for defining the comparative advantages of countries and diversification of production is often in contiguous products. EU countries are likely to keep their specialisation and participation in intra-industry trade. The production specialisation of countries may change this picture.[106]

There is some evidence that the possibility of asymmetric shocks from greater integration is not compelling and the opposite may well be true. The latter would be the case if business cycles in a monetary union are coordinated, as shown later in this section. Moreover, although there is evidence that integration increases in a monetary union, the degree of this increase is uncertain (De Grauwe 2014). It is also important to take into consideration that the EU and Eurozone include countries featuring remarkable differences. In studying the development of the productive structures of the EU and its member countries, Reinstaller *et al.* (2012) find a considerable dispersion in economic complexity and international trade patterns across member countries. While some countries (such as Germany and Finland) are among the most complex economies worldwide, other countries (such as Greece and Portugal) have a more traditional and slowly changing development of their productive structures. Also, opportunities and potentials for upgrading the production structure of countries, which is a highly cumulative process and deeply rooted in

[105] However, Saiki and Kim (2014) find that intra-industry trade, and in particular vertical intra-industry trade did not increase in the Eurozone.

[106] Varela (2013) studied export performance and export diversification in Europe and Central Asia (ECA) region. ECA region includes Armenia, Azerbaijan, Belarus, Georgia, Kazakhstan, Kyrgyz Republic, Moldova, Russia, Tajikistan, Turkmenistan, Ukraine and Uzbekistan. It was found that countries that were poor in natural resources increased their export product scope.

current capabilities and industrial specialisation, are distributed very unevenly across countries and sectors. Such disparities further increase at the regional level.

The progressive expansion of services in the structure of production, to the disadvantage of manufacturing, is an important cause of decreasing probability of region specific shocks (Hallet 2000). In this sense, specialisation of regions moves in the same direction, with specialisation being influenced also by regional size, market access and geographical location (Ezcurra *et al.* 2006).

Sectors differ as to their degree of concentration (Hallet 2000). While agricultural activities and the food industry are highly dispersed due to their link to the terrain, manufacturing industries and traded goods in general (including credit, insurance and other market services) are concentrated in fewer locations, in particular when scale economies are high. At the same time, non-traded goods follow the spatial pattern of GDP. These include building and construction, trade and tourism, transport and communication services, and non-market services. These features of activities, together with the high costs and time that relocation requires, give a fundamental stability to the countries' and regions' industrial structures. Together with the general trend of structural change from manufacturing to services making regions' specialisations more similar, these factors explain the relatively mild spatial effects of European integration.

Aiginger and Leitner (2002) consider 10 manufacturing sectors in a comparable number of US and EU regions in the period 1987–1995/98. They find that the United States had a higher level of regional concentration, but the difference was not large and was declining over time. Thus, the United States converged to the lower European level. The decline is significant, particularly in the case of value added, although the pattern differs through industries. Concentration in Europe has been declining since the implementation of the Single Market Programme.

A different process was apparently under way in the distribution of economic sectors. In Western European regions over the 1975–2000 period, manufacturing became gradually more concentrated (Brülhart and Traeger 2003). However, Tsiapa (2013) finds that industrial activities moved towards the most dynamic countries, but this move was towards regions that are different from the traditional ones. Thus, the effect was somehow contradictory: while in the case of manufacturing the locational bias towards central regions became weaker, market services relocated towards centrally located regions. Overall, the countries' internal concentration trends strengthened with EU integration.

6.5 Fiscal Transfers, Flexibility and Coordination

Fiscal transfers within the Eurozone in comparison with the United States are usually considered as one of the most problematic aspects of the Eurozone as an OCA (Baldwin and Wyplosz 2012). In fact, the Eurozone lacks a fiscal pillar complementing the monetary pillar. The main explanation is that the common EU budget moved around a bare 1% of the EU GDP. Its expansion above that dimension is not even foreseen. This compares to an average share of public budget to GDP of 50% in the member countries of the EU and 27% in the United States (to this, the states' public budgets should be added).

In a sovereign country, the central budget is available to counteract unfavourable shocks hitting particular regions or other territorial and social components of the country. The budget has cyclical revenue, such as income tax, and is used to finance countercyclical spending. The latter takes place through both automatic stabilisers, such as unemployment benefits, and discretionary spending. Within the Eurozone, the common currency coexists with formal national sovereignty over fiscal matters. However, common fiscal rules severely curb national sovereignty, particularly in those vulnerable countries which most need active fiscal policies. In recent years, some greater flexibility was allowed in national fiscal matters, particularly through the 2005 reform of the Stability and Growth Pact (SGP), and additional flexibility was introduced since the end of 2014 (see Chapter 11). However, it is clear that the very dual institutional and governance architecture of the Eurozone, which splits monetary and fiscal matters and competences, prevents the possibility of having effective and efficient macroeconomic and financial stabilisation.

Following the Eurozone construction, part of the stabilising effect is in the hands of national governments. Macroeconomic stabilisation depends largely upon national finances, but these are constrained by restrictive common rules and there is no effective common umbrella that protects vulnerable countries. This situation has two negative consequences. First, markets charge a high risk premium on the vulnerable countries' borrowing and may ration credit. This exposes vulnerable countries, and consequently the Eurozone, to the risk of instability and default in the sovereign debt market. Governments of vulnerable countries may consequently be under pressure to adopt pro-cyclical fiscal policies in the form of austerity.

Second, the SGP hampers the role of national governments particularly in the most vulnerable countries, i.e. those countries which are in a weak and problematic economic and fiscal situation that need most fiscal support. Moreover, in a currency union, monetary policy reacts more intensely and rapidly to the situation in the largest economies and is obviously less sensitive to the situation of the smallest economies. Since countries in a monetary union lack the option to adjust to shocks via the exchange rate and discretionary monetary policy, fiscal policy plays a particularly important role.

One of the IMF Technical Background Notes maintains that, since it lacks fiscal schemes for sharing income risk across member countries, the Eurozone is vulnerable to large country-level shocks (Bornhorst *et al.* 2013). These national shocks can become systemic for the area as a whole. Cross-country risk sharing in the Eurozone amounts to only half the sharing existing in other federal states and is similar to that in the EU. Moreover, risk sharing also decreases sharply in severe downturns. All these features lead to an increased vulnerability of the Eurozone compared to any other arrangement existing in modern economies.

One way of adjusting differences of macroeconomic conditions in a monetary union is to have different interest rates in various parts of the union. The Taylor rule is a "rule of thumb" that can be used for identifying optimal interest rates (Taylor 1993) as a function of inflation and unemployment gaps in different countries. Interest rates identified through the rule in both the Eurozone and the United States fit quite well in the past and corresponded well to the ECB interest rate policy. However, following the crisis, the Taylor rule identifies large differences in interest rates for the Eurozone resilient and vulnerable countries, thus stressing the remarkable differences that exist in economic conditions between the two regions (Nechio 2011, Wynne and Koech 2012). Malkin and Nechio (2012) have found that divergences from Taylor-rule based optimal interest rates are wider in the Eurozone than in the United States, which the authors attribute to lower labour mobility and lesser use of fiscal transfers. During the crisis, the gap between European Central Bank (ECB) and country-specific Taylor rates widened (Wynne and Koech 2012). In 2011, the average range of Taylor rule policy rate prescriptions ranged from –7.8% to 3.8%. The Taylor rule policy rate prescribed for the eight Bureau of Economic Analysis (BEA) regions in the US 1999–2012 was 5.2% compared to 10.6% for the Eurozone in 1999–2011. It is useful to remind that, in spite of the common target rate established by the ECB, market interest rates diverge among Eurozone countries.

A further source of flexibility concerns wages relative to economic conditions. In particular during slumps, downward flexibility of wages may translate into downward flexibility of prices, which helps economies to adjust. However, this also depends upon the conditions of competition in markets and the institutional setting of the economy. It is also worth stressing that this kind of adjustment to shocks via wage and price reduction is a double-edged sword, particularly so for heavily indebted countries. In fact, the decrease of wages and prices shrinks the domestic market and increases the real value of the debt.

Downward wage rigidities were particularly pronounced before the crisis in many OECD countries, but they decreased due to labour market reforms that various countries have implemented since then. Holden and Wulfsberg (2008) find that downward nominal wage rigidity is stronger when unemployment is low, union density is high and strict employment protection legislation is effective. The authors use data for hourly nominal wages at industry level in 19 OECD countries over the period 1973–1999. Similarly to the findings of recent microeconomic studies, the authors note that downward wage rigidity is important and the number of industries affected increased. However, the fraction of wages protected by downward rigidity decreased over time, from 61% in the 1970s to 16% in the late 1990s.[107]

These effects are not uniform. Holden and Wulfsberg (2008) find stronger downward nominal wage rigidity in Southern European countries (Italy, Greece, Portugal and Spain) and in Northern European

[107] The fraction of wages protected has increased in Northern European countries, which constitute therefore an exception.

countries (Denmark, Finland, Norway and Sweden). In these two groups of countries, employment protection legislation is stricter and/or unions are stronger. In resilient countries (Austria, Belgium, France, Germany, Luxembourg, and the Netherlands) and Anglo-Saxon countries (Canada, Ireland, New Zealand, the UK, and the US), downward nominal wage rigidity is weaker. In resilient countries, union density is lower than in Northern countries and employment protection legislation is softer than in Southern countries. In Anglo-Saxon countries, both features are weaker than in any other group of countries.

With the crisis, downward rigidity of wages weakened further, particularly in vulnerable countries. According to OECD (2014g), during the years 2010–2013 real wage growth was essentially flat for the OECD as a whole. However, in all vulnerable countries, real wages decreased by between 2% and 5% a year on average in the period 2009–2013. Real hourly wages decreased by between 0.2% and 3.8% (Table 6.3). Conversely, in all resilient countries, with a minor exception for the Netherlands, real

Table 6.3 Growth in Real Hourly Wages (Annual Average Growth Rates, 2008–2013).

		2008–2013
VULN	Greece	−3.8
	Ireland	−0.3
	Italy	−0.3
	Portugal	−0.5
	Spain	−0.2
	VULN, average	**−1.0**
RESIL	Austria	0.9
	Belgium	0.4
	Finland	1.0
	France	0.9
	Germany	0.7
	The Netherlands	0.1
	RESIL, average	**0.7**

Source: Author's own analysis of data from OECD (2014g).

wages increased in the same period. Real hourly wages increased also in the Netherlands, the difference being due to the decrease in the number of hours worked. In the same period, real hourly wages increased on average by 0.5% in the Eurozone (18 countries) and 0.2% in the United States.

In the Eurozone, producer prices tend to change slightly more often than consumer prices, which proves to be more rigid probably because of lesser competition in the retail sector. The monthly frequency of price changes is respectively 15% and 21% (Dhyne *et al.* 2009). This frequency is lower than in the United States, where it is over 25% per month. In the United States, the situation is reversed compared to the Eurozone, with higher frequency in the retail sector than in the case of producer prices. The difference in the frequency of price changes across product categories is more important than across countries. However, price changes are generally not synchronised within or across countries.

Business cycle coordination is another factor that decreases the possibility of asymmetric shocks in a monetary union. Frankel and Rose (1998) show empirically that countries with closer trade links tend to have more tightly correlated business cycles. Saiki and Kim (2014) compare the Eurozone and East Asia. They find that business cycle correlation increased over time in both regions. However, synchronisation progressed much faster in East Asia. Intra-industry trade, and in particular vertical intra-industry trade, unambiguously increased business cycle correlation. Both increased in East Asia, but not in the Eurozone, a finding consistent with the rapid increase in business cycle correlation in East Asia.

Business cycle coordination or lack thereof may be due to various causes. Smets and Wouters (2005) consider three characteristics: the type of shocks that affected the US and the Eurozone economies over a common sample period (1974–2002), differences in the propagation mechanism of those shocks, and differences in the way the central bank responded to those economic developments. They find that each of the three characteristics considered is remarkably similar across both currency areas.

A certain synchronisation of business cycles exists within the Economic and Monetary Union (EMU). However, frequent and sometimes wide and uncoordinated national cycles exist. Konstantakopoulou and Tsionas

(2011) find that synchronisation is stronger among subgroups of Eurozone countries. In particular, there is a core of resilient countries (Germany, France, Belgium, the Netherlands and Austria) showing the strongest synchronisation. Other vulnerable countries (such as Greece and Portugal), but also Luxembourg and Finland, present no synchronisation with the rest. However, Furceri and Karras (2008) find that there was an increase of synchronisation after the establishment of the EMU. This increase was present in all components of aggregate demand, as well as two supply-side variables, although it was more pronounced in the trade components. Afonso and Sequeira (2010) obtain a similar result for aggregate output in the EU27 countries for the period 1970–2009. They also show that external demand is a particularly important determinant of business cycle synchronisation, a result that Pentecôte *et al.* (2015) confirm in the case of the 11 founding members of the EMU over the period 1995–2007.

Differences in synchronisation are in part the outcome of national specialisation and productive structure, which explain why different national economies are hit in different ways by external shocks and react asymmetrically. The different state of public finances also generates cyclical asymmetries. This is the case particularly because public finances in dissimilar conditions may require uncoordinated fiscal policies. Since these policies are under common fiscal discipline, the national capacity for countercyclical action may be constrained, which generates uncoordinated business cycles. The latter is a problem in a union with common monetary policy. There is also the danger of pro-cyclical policies, due to the long bargaining and coordination time that negotiations at a common level usually require.

However, the Eurozone has divergent national finances. The Eurozone as a whole is better balanced than the United States, Japan, or Great Britain. This refers to private debt, current account, and public deficit and debt. In a recession, this situation prevents the possibility to have a balanced aggregate position and balanced national positions at the same time. In fact, the aggregate policy causes divergent national outcomes: while aggregate policies may require fiscal stimulus to combat the recession, common fiscal rules prevent countries in vulnerable positions — the ones needing most the fiscal stimulus — from doing so (De Grauwe and

Ji 2012).[108] As Caudal *et al.* (2013) observe, the Eurozone macroeconomic stabilisation should be seen as a public good and should be financed centrally. Fundamental steps in this direction would be a combination of significant common budget, full central bank acting as lender of last resort and the creation of full banking union.

6.6 Social Perceptions and Support

The overall picture of the EU and the Eurozone in terms of OCA requirements is somehow blurred. The EU and the Eurozone are disadvantaged compared to the United States, even if the distance is not unbridgeable. The improvement of the most sensible OCA criteria, including labour mobility and fiscal transfers, is fundamental. Policies and reforms are consequently essential, but require time and political and social support. After a particularly long and severe crisis, it is important to assess whether such support is still strong and credible.

Years of austerity policies imposed serious strains upon the citizens of most countries, in particular in vulnerable countries. It is remarkable indeed that there apparently is a majority of European citizens that continue to support the common currency, even in the countries which were most heavily hit by austerity policies. It seems fair to conclude that the commonality of destiny is rather sound in the Eurozone. Or in any case, citizens generally do not want to lose the economic and political advantages of the common currency and afford the costs, disadvantages and uncertainty that the return to a national currency would imply. This provides the common currency with an important, apparently resilient support.

In fact, only one-third of the respondents living in the Eurozone consider the euro as being negative for their own country in 2014, while 57% consider it a good thing (Eurobarometer 2014a; see also Stokes 2015). It is worth nothing that no change is registered compared to one year before. The share of Eurozone citizens who consider the euro as good for the EU

---

[108] De Grauwe and Ji (2012) show that, compared to countries that issue debt in their own currencies, government bond markets in the Eurozone are more fragile and more susceptible to self-fulfilling liquidity crises. These features cannot be explained by underlying increases in the debt-to-GDP ratios or fiscal risks.

is even higher (69%). However, there are striking differences among countries. Although in 16 out of 18 Eurozone member countries, the majority of respondents think that the euro is good for their own country, this share is below 50% in Italy and Cyprus. In the former, the share is rapidly decreasing, by minus 9% between 2013 and 2014. It is also noteworthy that three of the four most populous countries of the Eurozone (Spain, France and Italy) are at the bottom, with a support share of 56% or below. The only exception is Germany. A positive opinion is overwhelming in smaller member countries, including one of the vulnerable countries, Ireland, and is rather high (59%) even in Greece.[109]

More in general, the absolute majority (56%) of EU citizens supports "an economic and monetary union with a single currency, the euro" (Eurobarometer 2014b; Stokes 2015). This share is higher than three citizens out of four in nine countries, which include resilient countries like Luxembourg, the Netherlands, Belgium and Finland, but also Ireland. The support has been growing by 4% per year since spring 2013. However, and although it is higher within the Eurozone than in the average of the EU (respectively 67% and 35%), the support within the Eurozone is stable, while growing in the EU member countries that have kept their national currencies. Aggregate stability is the outcome of increasing support in some countries and decreasing support in other countries. There are seven countries where opposition to the euro has been growing, with Greece standing out with +6% per year.

The average position of the two main groups of countries forming the Eurozone is distinct (Table 6.4). The most noteworthy aspect is that in both groups the majority of the interviewees are in favour of the euro, both considering the interviewees' country and the EU, with significant differences. In the case of the own country, the share of those who think that the euro is advantageous in vulnerable countries is 1.6 times more than those who think that it is negative. In the case of the EU, this share increases to 2.3 times. The support for the euro is definitely stronger in resilient countries, where the shares are respectively 3.4 and 3.7 times. However, the correspondent difference between respondents from the two groups of countries is just 10%.

---

[109] In Greece, the outcome of referendum on 5 July 2015 can also be taken as a manifestation of support for the common currency, although it was against austerity policies.

Table 6.4. The Degree of Support to the Euro (Average Share of Respondents, in Percent.[110]

	Average	A Good Thing	A Bad Thing	Can't Decide	Don't Know
VULN	Country	54.3	35.0	8.2	2.5
	EU	68.0	20.2	6.7	5.2
RESIL	Country	63.4	27.1	7.6	1.9
	EU	83.7	22.5	7.0	3.5

Source: Author's own table based on data by Eurobarometer (2014a).

The difference between national and European perceptions may explain an important aspect of the strange behaviour of Europeans, in particular the citizens of vulnerable countries. When considering the particular situation of their own country and the effect of national politics and events, Europeans take a shorter time perspective and are more pessimistic than when considering common affairs. In this latter case, probably over a longer period of time, a cooler perspective prevails. If so, this opens an important reason for the resilience of the common currency, one that policies should nurture and support, because it may provide an important support for completing the European OCA.

The support is stronger for European policies and reforms. Overall, nearly seven Europeans out of ten (69%) support the perspective of having more coordination in Eurozone policies, including budgetary policies (Eurobarometer 2014a). However, this share was 3% higher one year earlier; it decreased in most countries and most of all in Germany (by 8%). Interestingly, the support for greater coordination is higher among the citizens of vulnerable countries, while the position that there is enough coordination is higher in resilient countries (Figure 6.1). Particularly high is the support in Spain (85% of respondents support the idea), Italy (82%) and Greece and Portugal (80%). At the same time, this share is below 50% in Estonia (41%), Finland (42%) and Ireland (47%).

Eurobarometer surveys show that there is strong support for reforms in all Eurozone countries. Nearly four Eurozone citizens out of five (79%)

[110]The question posed was the following: "Having the euro is a good thing or a bad thing for your country/EU?"

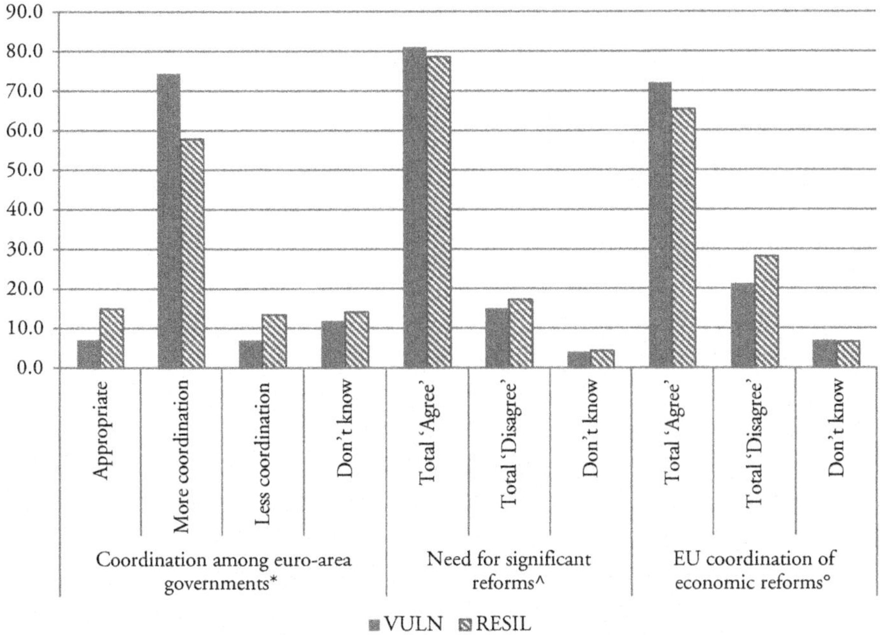

Figure 6.1. The Opinion of Eurozone Citizens on Policy Coordination and Reforms.
Notes: * Do you think that the degree to which economic policy, including budgetary policies, is coordinated in the euro-area is appropriate? Should there be more or less coordination among euro-area governments?
^ Governments in all euro-area countries are implementing various economic reforms, such as labour market reforms, pension, social security or health care reforms, reforms of education systems or market reforms to open sectors to competition. Would you agree or disagree with the following statements related to such reforms? "There is a need for significant reforms to improve the performance of our economy."
° Governments in all euro-area countries are implementing various economic reforms, such as labour market reforms, pension, social security or health care reforms, reforms of education systems or market reforms to open sectors to competition. Would you agree or disagree with the following statements related to such reforms? "Economic reforms would be more effective if they are carried out in a coordinated way at EU level."
Source: Author's own expansion of data from Eurobarometer (2014a).

recognise that there is a need for significant reforms in order to improve the performance of the economy. A large majority of respondents (70%) also agree that reforms would be more effective if they were implemented in a coordinated way at EU level. The support is particularly high in the case of reforms of the labour market (91%), the education systems (90%),

Table 6.5. Level of Trust of EU Citizens in the European Union (% of Respondents).

	Tend to Trust	Tend not to Trust	Don't Know	Trust/Non Trust
EU28	32	59	9	0.5
VULN	23.8	69.0	7.2	0.3
RESIL	40.1	52.4	7.4	0.8
RESIL/VULN	1.7	0.8	1.0	

Source: Author's own analysis of data from Eurobarometer (2014d).

and the health system (90%). However, this support is somehow contradictory. In fact, only 41% of respondents agree that successful reforms in other Eurozone countries facilitated reforms in their own countries. Moreover, a rather strong minority thinks that particular reforms had a negative effect on the economy of their country. In the case of labour market reforms, this share amounts to 25% of respondents.

The good news is that the majority of European citizens are in favour of European integration and the common currency. Although the support for a European economic and monetary union with one single currency, the euro, has moved slightly over time, it keeps an overall remarkable stability. In the Eurozone, it was 70% of respondents in fall 2004, decreased to 62% in spring 2013 and increased to 67% in fall 2014 (Eurobarometer 2014b). This was constantly stronger than the support in the entire EU, 7% as compared to 13% depending on the period.

While support is strong, trust is shaky. Only 32% of respondents tend to have trust in the EU, against 59% who tend not to trust (Table 6.5). Trust is stronger in resilient countries (more than 40%) and lack of trust is lower (slightly more than 52%). The situation in vulnerable countries is quite different, where the share of those who have trust in the EU (nearly 29% of respondents) are only one-third of those who do not have trust (69%).

The difference between the two groups of countries is understandable, yet striking. Individual vulnerable countries are at the bottom in the level of trust in the EU. Only Ireland is right above Germany and France, which occupy the 22nd and 23rd position in the list, followed by all other vulnerable countries. Italy and Greece close the list, being preceded by the UK. It is noteworthy that most of the old EU member countries are in the second half of the ranking and that the three large founding members (Germany, France and Italy) are at the bottom. Among the founding members, only Belgium is at the top (6th position) and the Netherlands is in the middle. It is also worth nothing that trust in the European institutions (European Parliament, European Commission, ECB) decreased from 55% on average in September 2007 to 32% in March 2014 (Eurobarometer 2014c, 2014d).

A possible interpretation of these data is that Europeans are strongly in favour of European integration and the common currency. Yet they are not satisfied with the current situation, which they consider too bureaucratic, costly, ineffective and a cause of the high cost and lengthy duration of the crisis. They would like to have a better EU. Their preferences are clear, yet when they are confronted with the reality they become disappointed. Overall they seem critical and impatient when dealing with the euro, yet prudent. It is evident that the support for the institutions of the European integration is lower in the member countries which are in economic and social distress. But it is perhaps fair to attribute even this disappointment to dissatisfaction with what the EU actually implemented, not with what it could potentially implement. Even this disappointment can be interpreted as a keen demand for better European institutions.

In this perspective, European preferences for the common currency can be considered as supportive, albeit they are heterogeneous when considering the real situation. The prevailing attitude seems one of wait and see, and hope in the case of vulnerable countries. The overall situation of the Eurozone as an OCA compared to the United States is summarised in Table 6.6.

Table 6.6. The Eurozone and the United States as OCAs.

OCA criterion	Eurozone	United States
Labour mobility (Mundell)	Low, but growing	Yes
Trade openness (McKinnon)	Yes	Yes
Product diversification (Kenen)	Yes	Yes
Fiscal transfers	Low, but growing	Yes
Homogeneity of preferences	Partial	Yes
Commonality of destiny	Partial (support to euro)	Yes

6.7 The Benefits of an OCA

There are sizeable benefits in going from a set of national currencies to a common currency.[111] Most of these benefits are microeconomic nature, in that they lead markets and economic actors to pursue efficiency. However, efficiency gains of a monetary union are diminished by the costs of the latter. These mostly have to do with macroeconomic management and institutional reform. For a currency union to be economically convenient and politically sustainable, gains and other benefits must exceed costs and other drawbacks. OCA theory provides important clues to appreciate the viability and sustainability of a monetary union.

Some gains and benefits have a general nature, although the exact nature and size of others depend upon the features of the economies that participate in the monetary union. The elimination of foreign exchange markets within the currency area removes the costs of exchanging currencies. The resulting reduction of transaction costs in economic interaction among the member countries is considered to be among the most important general benefits of a common currency. These benefits go mainly to the advantage of enterprises, consumers and tourists. Reduced transaction costs are also likely to attract more foreign investment to the common currency area. According to the European Commission, benefits from decreased transaction costs were expected to amount to 0.25 to 0.50% of GDP. The full advantage of the reduction of transaction costs is gained when a fully integrated payment system is implemented within the common currency area.

A second important benefit is the disappearance of currency risk and exchange rate uncertainty. With flexible exchange rates, economic tensions can cause abrupt and sizeable swings in the relative value of the domestic currency, which may cause excessive and unjustified fluctuations of economic activity and large adjustment costs. This reduces the efficacy of prices as signals for resource allocation and impairs the possibility of economic calculation for operators, including in investment, foreign trade and international financial operations. This creates uncertainty among

---

[111] Both the European Commission and the ECB have published many studies on the benefits of a common currency. See also De Grauwe 2014; Marer 2016.

businessmen, which can impair investment and other economic undertaking. By eliminating currency risk and exchange rate uncertainty, a common currency should promote trade and investment and consequently growth.

Greater transparency of prices is a third important potential benefit of a common currency. This is important for both enterprises and consumers, who can access cheaper inputs and consumers goods respectively. Thus price transparency should reduce price differentials among the member countries of a currency union and this should make prices converge to the cheapest level under the pressure of competition. This in turn should promote further competition and growth to the advantage of consumers, although at the cost of possible bankruptcy and failure of less efficient producers. The disappearance of the transaction costs and the risk and uncertainty typical of a multi-currency setting should make markets more efficient and lead to greater competition because prices can be compared directly.

This fourth benefit is to the advantage of consumers and of exports (depending on the value of the exchange rate of the common currency with other currencies) and should foster growth. The effects of a currency union on growth are uncertain and have been apparently overestimated. Empirical studies have reached dissimilar conclusions. First generation empirical studies found little evidence of a positive relation between exchange rate volatility and economic performance. Following studies have found greater positive impact of monetary unions on trade.[112]

A fifth benefit lies in the greater macroeconomic stability of the common currency area. Such an area is larger than individual countries, its economy is more deeply integrated than the corresponding set of individual economies, and it shares a set of common macroeconomic policies. As a consequence, the common currency area should have greater economic stability and should be more resilient and better able to absorb external shocks and avoid major destabilisation. It is not only the size of the common currency area that brings the benefit of greater

[112] Rose (2000), using cross-section evidence, finds that a monetary union doubles trade among the union members; Frankel and Rose (1998) find that the positive relation between monetary union and trade has positive effects on per capita income.

stability and resilience. Indeed, such an area requires clear and properly enforced common rules and sound management of its economy. These should be based on stricter discipline of its national parts in order to avoid potential political conflicts, which would result from uncoordinated behaviour of individual countries. This arrangement should remain in force at least until there is full and stable political unification, an undertaking that may require a long time in the case of previously sovereign national states.

Sixth, the international role of a common currency creates seigniorage gains for the currency union. Estimates of yearly seigniorage gains in the case of the United States are at less than 0.5% of GDP.

Other benefits that a common currency potentially generates include improved economic stability, economising on foreign currency reserves and policy autonomy. The latter depends on the economic size of the common currency area and its monetary and financial stability. However, it should be noted that policy benefits and drawbacks are asymmetrically related to monetary and fiscal policies. Benefits derive from the monetary effect of the currency unification, in that the common currency and unique monetary policy decrease the variability of output that derives from monetary aggregates. However, the fiscal effects in the monetary union tend to increase the variability of output, due to the asymmetric impact of the common currency.

Benefits should advantage member countries and the financial sector via more integrated financial markets. Together with the effect of reduced transaction costs, it should be easier and more advantageous to conduct banking and insurance activities with a common currency. A common currency is also expected to have beneficial effects in terms of low inflation rate, a benefit that should come from more attentive monetary and financial policies addressed to avoid inflation. In fact, inflation would activate undesired distributive processes among the member countries. Finally, a common currency also has political and social benefits, in that it endorses political stability and unity and common identity. By simplifying and giving greater stability to political and economic relations, the common currency should also breed a longer time horizon in economic actors, including governments.

In reality, benefits depend in part upon such features of individual countries as the industrial structure of the economy, the size of enterprises, the openness of the economy to trade and capital flows, the elasticity of the world demand for the exported products, and the state of public and private finance. In general, the more open an economy is to foreign trade with the currency partner countries and the deeper and integrated its financial system is, the greater are the advantages from the common currency. As a consequence, the benefits of a monetary union should be larger for small open economies and for their firms.

6.8 The Drawbacks of an OCA

There are two main drawbacks of an OCA: loss of policy instruments and loss of flexibility in the use of policy instruments. A country joining a monetary union loses monetary policy instruments, in particular the control over the exchange rate. Within a currency union, there can be only a unique monetary policy. While external shocks can have asymmetric consequences within the currency area due to economic and structural differences, adjustment could be left to flexible fiscal policies. However, these are viable only if a common government of the economy exists or if all member countries are in a balanced or, better, surplus position. The individual components of the currency area — be they regions within a country or countries within a supranational currency area — cannot have fiscal freedom, which would jeopardise the monetary sustainability of the area.

The situation of a country which is member of a monetary union is similar to that of countries in the gold standard monetary system and corresponds to the case of the impossible trinity or trilemma (Baldwin and Wyplosz 2012; Obstfeld *et al.* 2004). The trilemma illustrates the impossibility for an open economy to pursue at the same time the three fundamental policy objectives. These are: a fixed exchange rate, free capital movement, and an independent monetary policy. The trilemma is based on the condition of interest rate parity[113] and is supported by empirical

[113] A more stringent and appropriate condition is that of uncovered interest rate parity, with capital mobility and perfect substitutability among domestic and foreign assets. An

studies, providing substantial evidence of failures when governments tried to pursue the three objectives at the same time.

Given the impossible trinity, policy authorities can only pursue two of the three objectives simultaneously. They use consequently only two of the related policies. A country can: (a) keep a fixed exchange rate and free capital movements; (b) have an independent monetary policy and allow for free capital movements; and (c) have a fixed exchange rate and independent monetary policy. While the Eurozone is in the situation identified under (b), member countries in the Eurozone are in situation (a). The latter is indeed a fundamental condition for Eurozone membership. From this, it follows that the central bank of member countries cannot have an independent monetary policy. At the same time, the ECB has an independent monetary policy, which includes the ability to set interest rates independently, with free capital movements. However, the ECB cannot fix exchange rates and the euro is part of an international floating exchange rate system.

An OCA has other drawbacks along with the constraints that the impossible trinity highlights. In particular, Keynesian economists criticised the OCA's analysis of money and stressed that, in being part of a monetary union, a government has to give up deficit spending (Goodhart 1988; Toporowski 2013; Wray 2000).[114] The loss of countercyclical public expenditure has important consequences, depending upon the nature of shocks. In particular, in liquidity trap situations countercyclical public expenditure is the only effective policy instrument. This argument became prominent during the international crisis.

---

uncovered parity makes no use of forward contracts to hedge against exposure to exchange rate risk. The parity assures that risk-neutral investors are indifferent between investing in two countries with different currencies. Such a condition requires that the expected return on investment in domestic assets is equal to the expected return on foreign assets, after adjusting for the exchange rate and its expected variation. This situation eliminates the possibility of obtaining interest arbitrage gains.

[114] Toporowski (2013) highlights two important limitations. First, OCA theory disregards the import intensity of exports and the complementarity between wages and exchange rates that descend from it. Downward wage adjustments are needed to reinforce exchange rate adjustments when a country leaves a currency area to decrease trade deficits. Second, OCA is a commodity money theory, while in a credit economy banking systems absorb trade imbalances into their balance sheets.

Austrian economists offer a very different argument in opposing OCAs (Glăvan 2004; Hayek 1990). Their criticism is based on the nature of a common currency, which is the outcome of an intergovernmental agreement. According to the Austrians, such an agreement creates a common currency through a centrally planned process, while only free market processes can separate or denationalise any currency from politics. Only currencies that are created through free market processes, i.e. through the voluntary action of the currency users, can limit deficit spending and increase the accountability of monetary authorities to currency users. Thus, the Austrian argument is not against any kind of OCA, but criticises OCAs that are constituted through political processes.[115]

A country outside a monetary union can adjust its economy, when hit unfavourably by an asymmetric shock, by depreciating the exchange rate. This is a rapid adjustment that decreases all prices and wages impersonally. The economy thus regains its competitiveness. The risk is that an institutionally incomplete currency area is left with internal devaluation as the only adaptation mechanism to an external shock. In this case, the adjustment takes longer and is typically costlier and more painful, because the downward adjustment of prices and wages must take place directly and nominally through explicit decisions and actions concerning individual prices and wages, only in the disadvantaged country. However, prices and wages are typically sticky, firms and employees resist the unfavourable adjustment and labour reallocation is slow. This process may be cumbersome, since it requires the renegotiation of individual contracts and may meet strong social opposition. Perhaps more importantly, internal devaluation runs the risk of starting a race to the bottom, with negative social and long-term economic consequences. It shrinks the domestic market and causes substantial unemployment, unless increased exports and the inflow of investments smooth out the negative effect.

[115]"... [O]nly on a free monetary market would it be possible to discover what is the 'optimum' circulation of a certain currency. Since political action is not a substitute for voluntary cooperation, a discretionary intervention on money cannot bring any benefits to the community of money users. OCA theory fails to acknowledge this, precisely because it conflates the proper nature of money, focusing exclusively on a single type of money, namely fiat government-produced money" (Glăvan 2004, pp. 38–39).

6.9 The Institutional and Policy Aspects of a Monetary Union

The conclusion obtained by balancing benefits and drawbacks of a monetary union is that this confers member countries greater resilience to external shocks, although with costlier adjustment. Negative effects from shocks are less likely but, when their effects appear within the union, the consequences tend to be deeper and lengthier.

In a monetary union, an asymmetric shock (such as the fall of the world demand for some of the exported goods) disadvantages one country or group of countries relative to others. The disadvantaged country cannot use monetary policy to stimulate demand. As a consequence, the real exchange rate of the country appreciates and the balance of payments accumulates deficits. To regain competitiveness, the real exchange rate of the disadvantaged country should depreciate. Since nominal depreciation is impossible within a monetary union, alternative mechanisms have to be activated.

Fiscal policies could be used in a monetary union as mechanisms against asymmetric shocks. The mechanism works differently depending on the institutional features of budgets. If there is a centralised budget under a common government of the economy, this can work as a public insurance system by allowing for automatic transfers between countries within the monetary union. This mechanism can offset asymmetric shocks as in an independent country with automatic stabilisers. However, this is not the situation of the EU or the Eurozone, also due to the tiny size of the common budget (around 1% of the EU GDP).

An alternative is the existence of flexible national budgets. Centralised budgets with automatic stabilisers and discretionary intervention exist in each individual member country. In this case, the vulnerable country can allow deficits to accumulate in order to support demand. If capital markets are integrated, as is typically the case of a monetary union, capital markets can redistribute income in order to finance the deficit. However, this mechanism causes transfers between generations within the same country. It may also create problems of debt accumulation and fiscal sustainability. Moreover, if national budgets can intervene, either automatically or discretionarily, without any constraint, this can create problems of moral hazard within the monetary union. In turn, this jeopardises stability.

The EU has agreed on the Maastricht criteria and the SGP to avoid such consequences.

Integrated capital markets offer an alternative mechanism that can be compared to a private insurance system. With integrated capital markets, the mobility of capital allows for automatic insurance against shocks if capital flows where there is more need, i.e. to deficit countries. However, there are three problems with this private mechanism. First, the insurance works at the cost of higher returns in the deficit country. This takes the form of a positive spread over benchmark return rates in balanced countries. Second, there is no guarantee that capital accrues to finance activities useful to bridge the financial gap and may create financial or real bubbles. Third, if capital markets perceive the deficit country as particularly risky, capital may abstain from flowing to the deficit country. Even worse, when risk is perceived as high, domestic capital can leave the deficit country. Therefore, differential risk may hamper the working of integrated capital markets as insurance systems. This typically happens during a crisis.

These problems proved to be nearly intractable in the Eurozone for a while during the crisis. The private insurance mechanism worked rather smoothly before the crisis, but contributed to the creating of bubbles. Capital of surplus countries, particularly Germany, financed deficits in Greece, Ireland and Spain. However, when the crisis hit vulnerable countries, German capital left in spite of higher returns. Domestic capital of vulnerable countries expatriated to strong surplus countries, primarily because of the perc eived excess risk.

6.10 Sources of Asymmetric Effects

Even in the case of an external symmetric shock, the effects within the monetary union can be asymmetric. There are two groups of different reasons for this outcome. A first group includes the country idiosyncratic institutional, economic and social features. A country reacts differently to a symmetric external shock due to its economic structure and the relative importance of economic sectors and industrial branches. Other reasons include the depth of financial markets and their liquidity; the ratio between debt and risk capital and the roles of credit and banks and the stock exchange; external debt and public and private domestic debt; the size structure and the legal nature of enterprises; and the economic role of the government; the nature of trade unions and business associations, their function and interaction; and the role of the government in industrial relations and agreements.

The institutions of the labour market and the features of enterprises play a particularly important role in the determination and behaviour of wages and prices. The features of labour markets establish the degree of rigidity of wages, the nature of competition and of enterprises, their control over markets, and their ability to establish monopoly prices and define price rigidity. Price and wage rigidity makes adjustment processes difficult, lengthy, and costly.

Eurozone countries have different labour markets and other types of institutions. The features of trade unions existing in a country and the degree of centralisation of wage bargaining are particularly important. Another important difference lies in legal systems. Different legal systems lead to varying transmission of symmetric shocks. Indeed, different legal systems and other formal institutions define the constraints of economic activity and the incentives for economic actors. The way in which economic actors react to shocks defines the effects that shocks have for the economy.

Economic structures are also important aspects to be considered when dealing with the effects of external shocks. For instance, when the world price of a good increases, the domestic effect depends upon the intensity of the use of that good, which is a function of the industrial structure of an economy together with local production of that good. The classical case is that of oil: the domestic effects of an increase of oil price are different for oil producers and oil importer countries and, within these, are worse for energy intensive economies. Depreciation (appreciation) of the common currency advantages (disadvantages) countries featuring high demand elasticity of their exports, compared to countries with rigid exports.

A second group of reasons for the asymmetric effect of an external symmetric shock in a monetary union has to do more specifically with the functioning of monetary policy. The effects of a particular monetary intervention — such as an increase of interest rates — following an external symmetric shock, which is the same all over the monetary union, depend on the financial features of the member economies. The national features and liquidity of capital and financial markets are among the most important reasons for these differences. Other features include the size and ownership structure of enterprises that can determine the enterprises' ability to borrow and invest; and the efficiency of public administration, which influences the borrowing needs of the public budget and the economic effect of public administration activities. These and other features establish how different economies react to changes of interest rates.

To summarise, when shocks are asymmetric, a monetary union is the origin of costs compared to monetary independence. The common central bank cannot deal with these asymmetries. In these cases, it is wise to leave fiscal policies in the domain of national governments, as the EU did for years. Independent fiscal policies could be used to adjust national situations to asymmetric shocks. Unfortunately, unless countries follow the same fiscal rules and behave in the same way (in particular, by keeping the same public and private budget constraint), it will be necessary sooner or later to restrict the national use of financial policies. This is exactly what happened with the Maastrich criteria and the SGP, particularly with such clauses as the no-bailout clause of the Lisbon Treaty.

Different is the case of symmetric shocks. In this case, a monetary union is advantageous compared to monetary independence. The common central bank can deal effectively with these shocks and avoid policy competition among countries. Conversely, independent monetary policies can easily generate "beggar-my-neighbour" measures, such as competitive depreciation of national currencies. Unfortunately, a monetary union that includes only countries which are institutionally and structurally so similar, that no asymmetric effects can be felt internally is very rare indeed. The outcome depends upon how the union manages these asymmetric effects.

6.11 Conclusions

When looking at the effects of a monetary union, it is necessary to consider the institutional and structural features of the countries, knowing that these differences lead to asymmetric effects. Under these conditions, the classical solution in a monetary union is to have a common government of the economy that can transfer resources from the regions or countries benefiting from the common monetary policy to the disadvantaged member regions or countries. A further solution is to have the common central bank that acts as a lender of last resort.

If such a government does not exist, as in the Eurozone, and the central bank is limited in its action as a lender of last resort, the only sustainable condition is when all economies have similar economic and financial situations. In this case, the internal effect of external shocks is symmetric. Under these conditions, the private insurance mechanism is effective. Shocks are easily smoothed out among the countries and the sectors. Economic similarity causes economies to react in the same way to shocks and policies. Similar financial situations prevent the propagation and amplification of shocks.

When important differences exist among countries, a monetary union leads to the appreciation of the real exchange rate for the vulnerable economies if prices and incomes converge and productivity does not. Such appreciation has to be adjusted by decreasing prices and incomes in vulnerable countries or increasing them in resilient countries, a step that is likely to be opposed since this would decrease their international competitiveness. However, this adaptation has negative long-run consequences for the vulnerable countries and may lead to further problems. In the short run, the depressive effect of wage cuts is usually faster and stronger than price decrease. This is due to both the employees' psychology impinging upon consumption expenditures, and the control that enterprises and their associations have on prices. These effects create negative consequences in consumption, welfare, and investment of vulnerable countries. In the long run, price and wage reduction can push the country to a low-skill specialisation and slow down technical progress. Under these conditions, much depends upon the strength of the common currency compared to other currencies. If the former reflects the position of resilient member countries, vulnerable countries may find difficult to export.

An incomplete OCA requires exogenous supportive devices to work properly and smooth out asymmetric shocks. Sociopolitical support is necessary, yet it cannot avoid the cost and disadvantage that derive from the implementation of a common currency. Sociopolitical support, in fact, can only make the system socially and politically more resilient to the asymmetric effects that hit an incomplete OCA. Supportive devices that can help to attenuate the effect of shocks and help the monetary union to move towards a complete OCA are institutions, governance, and policies. Given the gap between the Eurozone and an OCA, it is important to see whether institutions, governance and policies are effective in filling the gap. This is done in Chapters 7 and 9 for institutions and governance and in Chapters 8 and 11 for policies.

"... travelers who, when they have lost their way in a forest, ought not to wander from side to side, far less remain in one place, but proceed constantly towards the same side in as straight a line as possible, without changing their direction for slight reasons, although perhaps it might be chance alone which at first determined the selection; for in this way, if they do not exactly reach the point they desire, they will come at least in the end to some place that will probably be preferable to the middle of a forest."

— *Rene Descartes, Discourse on The Method of Rightly Conducting the Reason, and Seeking Truth in the Sciences.*

7

A Detour on the Working of the EU: The Asymmetric and Incomplete Build-Up of the Union

Compared to ideal blueprints, reality always presents idiosyncratic features, and elements and processes of change are ridden with unforeseen events and unintended consequences. In spite of a shared ideal blueprint backed by strong political will and ideal and institutional commitment, the European move to economic and monetary unification was bumpy, sometimes ineffective and inefficient. So far, the outcome was both impressive and problematic, both forward looking and ridden with asymmetries and incompleteness. These contradictions may jeopardise the sustainability of the present setting and future developments, particularly if external tensions are strong and the situation of individual member countries is progressively polarised, thus creating important internal tensions. It is therefore necessary to take a detour and look at how the European integration evolved in different fields — from macro-institutional to micro-industrial — in order to understand how this could happen and why. This is important in order to assess consequences and problems and look for ways out.

The debate and the clash among the federalist aims and agenda and those of intergovernmental agreements have accompanied European integration since the beginning. In spite of the significant tensions and dangers that divided European countries, federalist ideas were strong, both among intellectuals and politicians, already in the interwar period, (Delanty 1995; Mazower 1998; Pagden 2002; Parsons 2003). Ideas and proposals of a European federation were flourishing in the 19th century. Proposal of a (Central) European federation under the German leadership was advanced during the two World Wars. However, it was at the end of World War II that the ideal and political bases for the process of European unification were advanced.

Prominent among the proposals were those worked out by Altiero Spinelli and Ernesto Rossi in the 1941 "Ventotene Manifesto", whose title was "Towards a Free and United Europe" (Spinelli and Rossi 1941). The Manifesto became the political basis for the European Federalist Movement that Spinelli, Rossi and others established in Milan in August 1943. A second, important intellectual and political basis for the new post-war Europe was advanced by Jean Monnet, a member of the Committee of National Liberation, the French government in exile during the war. During a meeting of the Committee, in August 1943, Monet declared that "The European states must constitute themselves into a federation".

The process of European integration, thus, started from the federalist agenda. The Agenda aimed at finding stable solutions that would rid the continent of the conflicts and threats that led to two destructive world wars. Yet the first moves had the nature of intergovernmental agreements for very practical purposes. In fact, a true federalist agenda required well-defined and effective common institutions, and a long time to implement and test them. Intergovernmental agreements represented a ready-made shortcut to an objective that was largely shared among countries and their politicians. The shortcut required no particular institutional transformations. Its outcome could be effectively used to devise and foster the first formal common institutions and organisations.

Political feasibility apart, federalism in general and fiscal federalism in particular both have sound economic rationale, based in some of the fundamental trade-offs of economic activity. The trade-offs require that an economically efficient and effective governance takes advantage of both centralisation and decentralisation, by finding the cases and circumstances under which one of the two approaches has a relative advantage over the other. These trade-offs include the diversity existing among local economies and require that (certain aspects of) governance and policies are tailored to and take advantage of diversities and the localisation of information and knowledge (Rodrik 2009). Also scale and scope economies have important local aspects, as much as spillovers; they also may take advantage of a federalist approach. Finally, there are political considerations that require a federalist approach in cases of political and social variety. These include reasons of democratic control and jurisdictional competition.

7.1 The Problematic Nature of the Common Currency

Since the start, European integration has moved between the idealism of the federalist agenda and the realism of intergovernmental agreements. This uneasy process could only give birth to incomplete institutions, ill-defined and repeatedly re-interpreted common treaties and organs (such as the European Commission, the Parliament, the European Central Bank), and continuous dialectics and conflicts between the common goal of integration and national goals and between the aspiration to unity and inter-governmental distrusts. This fundamental dialectics found its utmost achievement in the euro. The euro, the most typical achievement of the federalist agenda, ended up for being governed largely through intergovernmental agreements. Predictably, the euro was fragile in the case of external shocks and required adjustment policies that could not be differentiated by the country. As a consequence, policies were bound to impose undue costs on the member countries and in the end on citizens, in particular on those of vulnerable countries. This situation was at the root of the poor performance of the Eurozone during the crisis and its uneasy perspectives.

The problematic nature and role of the euro result from its ill-defined nature as a common currency, with particular reference to institutional incompleteness, and the multiple aims the euro was called to serve. These include the traditional efficiency gains of a common currency, including lower transaction costs, price transparency and more competition, removal of foreign exchange uncertainty and risk, and stronger resilience to external symmetric shocks. To these the benefits of an international currency should be added, given the international importance of the euro. A second set of aims of the euro, which derives in part from efficiency gains and the decrease of interest rates, includes support to economic growth and convergence of member economies.

The trickiest aim is however a third one: the euro was intended to foster European integration. It is usually considered that a common currency represents the final crowning of the process of political integration of a group of regions or countries. In the case of Europe, political integration met with serious, perhaps insurmountable obstacles in terms of national sentiments and national governments. Moreover, the efficiency gains that the common currency was expected to deliver were seen as fundamental to accelerate the process of catching up internally and once again give Europe a central economic role in the world. Federalists thought that political opposition could be overcome by instituting the common currency before political unification. The common currency would demand such extensive and deep coordination among national governments that political unification would be eased.

The Eurozone was innovative in the way it was planned and implemented. It could be considered as an incomplete optimum currency area (OCA) forced by common political will. Institutional theories highlight that informal institutions are usually sticky in the sense that they change slowly. They may also be quite powerful and may obstruct the working and effect of formal institutions when the two are not streamlined. The vicissitudes of the euro show that sticky national informal institutions were stronger than envisaged, particularly for countries under the stress of implementing the policies that the common currency requires. This effect was even stronger during the international financial and economic crisis. In a sense, the implementation of the common currency and its management up to the crisis were a prelude to the true market test to follow.

An important question in economic transformations is to assess how institutions were set up, why they were left incomplete, and in whose interest were European institutions set up. This question becomes tricky when sticky national institutions, particularly informal ones, and preferences may fail to converge and incentives are ineffective. Predictably, institutions were called to serve the common interest. However and since the latter was ill defined, national interests played an important role in defining institutions, in a double sense. First was the request that common institutions avoid jeopardising national interests. Unfortunately, each country had its own goals and priorities. These were not always in harmony, and sometimes were in conflict with those of the other countries. Moreover, the common currency created further reasons for non-converging or diverging national interests. Public finances were a very important case of international divergence of interests.

Second was the goal of pursuing national gains from common institutions, as part of gains from cooperation. If the whole had a value superior to the sum of the parts — which was the economic and political rationale of European integration and the euro adoption — then any member country could obtain a net benefit, e.g. in terms of lower interest rates. Institutions were important in defining the national distribution of the benefits from cooperation. Yet, if national priorities and goals and the economic situation of the member countries were different, the understanding, nature and definition of the common interest and benefits were different. The outcome could be unstable, particularly if some countries were asked to pay a price in the present in order to make the common benefit materialise, while other countries gained a share of that benefit in the present.

Countries have to follow the many requests of the *Acquis Communautaire*[116] and be in line with the convergence criteria before

[116] The EU website offers detailed information on the process of accession. On joining the EU see http://europa.eu/about-eu/countries/joining-eu/index_en.htm; on the conditions for membership see http://ec.europa.eu/enlargement/policy/conditions-membership/

entering the Eurozone (See Section 7.5).[117] Yet these requirements are mostly formal and concern the real economy and its workings only indirectly. *Ex post* real adaptation is necessary, while collective action becomes costly and unstable. The Eurozone looks like an incomplete OCA forced by inconsistent political will and action amidst sticky informal national institutions and incomplete formal common institutions. The latter have formal power, but lack fundamental credibility, are exposed to national opportunism and weakened by the lack of fundamental mutual and common trust. This opens the critical issues of completing institutions.

It is therefore necessary to clarify why monetary integration was built in an apparently ineffective way, how it happened that it remained asymmetric and incomplete, how it failed to solve fundamental problems in the allocation of decision making power between national and common organs, and how it discriminated against individual countries. These issues are considered in this chapter in order to clear the ground for the analysis of policies and elucidating the critical issue of completing and making symmetric institutions, which is the focus of the following chapters.

European integration found its origin and foundation in its economic advantages as much as in its political and ideal motivations. It is clear that, in order to lead to sustainable integration, any of these motivations require trust and properly defined and enforced institutions. Only in this way the danger of moral hazard in intercountry dealings is placed under control and can be effectively curbed. However, trust alone is not sufficient. Mutual trust is sustainable only if each participant in the integration feels that no member country is permanently advantaged or disadvantaged. At least in the long run, the rules upon which interaction are based must guarantee that integration is to the advantage of all participants in roughly the same way and measure. Thus, institutions and their enforcement must

---

index_en.htm; on the chapters of the acquis see http://ec.europa.eu/enlargement/policy/conditions-membership/chapters-of-the-acquis/index_en.htm; on accession criteria see http://ec.europa.eu/enlargement/policy/glossary/terms/accession-criteria_en.htm.

[117] On preparing for the euro and related documents see http://ec.europa.eu/economy_finance/euro/adoption/preparing/index_en.htm; on convergence criteria before adopting the euro see http://ec.europa.eu/economy_finance/euro/adoption/who_can_join/index_en.htm.

be transparent, fair and impartial, long-lasting, and not subject to bargaining or opaque pressures and dealings. However, even this is insufficient.

Institutions, both formal and informal, strongly influence economic and social activity. They define incentives and determine costs, in particular transaction costs. Since there is mutual adaptation between formal and informal institutions, economic activity, social and political relations, the choice of institutions has a fundamental influence on economic and social relations and activities. Clearly the choice of the institutions governing the common currency is among the most powerful ones in molding economic and social relations and activities. Since countries enter economic integration in different conditions and with different institutions and economic and social features, the choice of common institutions (in particular the ones governing the common currency) has deep and long lasting consequences for the different countries. Predictably, some countries whose institutions are more in line with the common ones will be advantaged, while the others will be at a disadvantage. The existence of some kind of compensating mechanisms is fundamental to guarantee the sustainability of the common currency. Unfortunately, the Eurozone is dramatically short of such mechanisms. Some hints on the build-up of the Union and the Eurozone may highlight the reasons for this dangerous development.

7.2 From the Single Market to the Eurozone: A Historic Institutional Digression

A necessary precondition for a common currency is the establishment of a single market. A single market is a standardised system of institutions and related organisations, which applies in all member countries of the single market area. Although in principle institutions and organisations can be under the aegis of national governments, provided that there is a credible intergovernmental agreement to streamline them, the single market gains if institutions and organisations were supranational. In fact, in this case transaction costs net of the cost of supranational organisations are decreased and the behaviour of actors is better coordinated. Both events favour the decrease of costs of economic interaction and favour the expansion of market activity. A single market does not require necessarily a common currency and also mutually convertible currencies are sufficient in principle. However, it is evident that a common currency greatly enhances the development of the common market by eliminating the uncertainty and risk that go with exchange rates and making economic calculation easier and the outcome more reliable. The European Union (EU) moved rather consistently in the direction of a supranational set of institutions and organisations.

The EU took form through a set of acts and treaties that involved national governments (Baldwin and Wyplosz 2012).[118] These agreed not only to standardise and coordinate institutions, organisations, and policies. They also agreed to transfer a set of former national competences to newly set up common organs, in particular the European Commission. National governments thus gave up parts of their sovereignty.

The basis of any policy activity in the EU is the variety of European treaties, which have accompanied the evolution of the European integration process. Signed in 1951, the first treaty was the Treaty establishing the European Coal and Steel Community (ECSC). This treaty brought six countries together as equal partners, creating interdependence in coal and steel industries on the basis of shared institutions. The Treaty of Rome, signed in 1957, set up the European Economic Community (EEC) and the European Atomic Energy Community (Euratom). The Brussels Treaty of 1965 created a single Commission and a single Council and merged the EEC, Euratom, and ECSC into the European Communities (EC).

The Single European Act (SEA) was a milestone in the integration of Europe. Signed in February 1986 and entered into force on 1 July 1987, it was the first major revision of the founding 1957 Treaty of Rome. SEA foresaw the establishment of a single market by the end of 1992. The Act also provided for speeding up decision-making in preparation for the single market. In particular, the Act introduced an extension of qualified majority voting in the European Council, thus making harder for a single country to veto the proposed legislation. The Act also foresaw the creation of the cooperation and assent procedures, giving the European Parliament more influence.

---

[118] On the construction and evolution of European integration see Dinan (2004), Kaiser *et al.* (2008), McAllister (2009), Moravcsik (1998), Pinder (2001).

A milestone in the creation of the single market and the introduction of the common currency was the Treaty on European Union (TEU), also known as the Maastricht Treaty. The Treaty was signed on 7 February 1992 and entered into force on 1 November 1993. Its purpose was to prepare the European Monetary Union and introduce some elements of a political union, including European citizenship, and the common foreign and internal affairs policy. The Maastricht Treaty introduced various important changes in the European architecture. These included the establishment of the EU and the introduction of the co-decision procedure, thus giving the European Parliament more say in decision-making. It also introduced new forms of cooperation among EU governments, such as those on defence and justice and home affairs.

An important achievement of the Maastricht Treaty was the introduction of a new institutional structure based on three pillars. The first pillar was the European Community, which came to constitute the most important instance of supranational integration, before the introduction of the euro. The remaining two pillars were in line with intergovernmental agreements: the Common Foreign and Security Policy (CFSP), and the Police and Judicial Cooperation in Criminal Matters (PJCC).

The Treaty of Amsterdam was signed on 2 October 1997 and entered into force on 1 May 1999. The treaty's purpose was to reform the EU institutions in preparation for the arrival of future member countries, in particular various former Eastern European countries. The main changes that the Treaty introduced were the amendment, renumbering and consolidation of EU and EEC treaties. The Treaty also introduced more transparent decision-making, in particular through the increased use of the co-decision voting procedure. This procedure substantially extended the role and power of the European Parliament.

The Treaty of Nice, signed on 26 February 2001 and entered into force on 1 February 2003, had the purpose of reforming European institutions, so that the EU could function efficiently after including 25 member countries. It changed the composition of the European Commission and redefined the voting system in the European Council. There was also a Treaty establishing a constitution for Europe, which was signed in 2004 but was never ratified. Some of its fundamental aims were resumed by the Treaty of Lisbon.

The Treaty of Lisbon was signed on 13 December 2007 and entered into force on 1 December 2009. Its overall purpose was to make the EU more democratic, more efficient and better able to address global problems, such as climate change, with one voice. The Treaty of Lisbon represents a milestone in the integration of Europe and created the present EU. The Treaty abolished the pillar structure and created the EU. Moreover, the Treaty clarified which powers belong to the EU, which ones belong to EU member countries, and which ones are shared between the EU and the member countries. Along with important achievements, it is worth emphasising that the Treaty also suffered major failures. In particular, the intergovernmental method continues to apply to the CFSP, although some questions relating to justice and internal affairs have been placed under the common umbrella. Also questions relating to police and judicial cooperation in criminal matters continue to be intergovernmental.

The Treaties also defined the governance structure of the EU, based on both representative organs and common governance organs. The latter are organs responsible for functions and activities that national governments delegated to the Union and work as true governments in their own field. The former function on the basis of the egalitarian representation of the member countries and are generally the most important organs of the Union in operational issues. However, their role and operations are somehow ill-defined. In fact, while the individual members of these organs represent their own countries and constituencies, as a whole they are responsible for the effective and orderly working of the Union. In a sense they constitute a peer body that set standards and goals that everybody in the Union should keep and follow. While the representation is egalitarian, it is inevitable that the largest and more resilient countries play a leadership role, albeit informally. Since the collective action of smaller member countries has proven to be difficult and ineffective, except in a few cases to the advantage of some specific national interest, collective decisions tend to be biased in favour of the resilient countries' interest and view of the common good.

The new institutional architecture of the EU took shape with the Maastricht Treaty. There are seven principal decision-making bodies: the European Parliament, the European Council, the Council of the European Union, the European Commission, the Court of Justice of the European Union, the European Central Bank (ECB) and the Court of Auditors. The working of the institutional architecture was further developed with the Treaty of Lisbon of 2007, or Treaty on the Functioning of the European Union (TFEU). The Treaty introduced some important changes in the European architecture, including: more power for the European Parliament, change of voting procedures in the European Council, citizens' initiative, a permanent president of the European Council, a new High Representative for Foreign Affairs, a new EU diplomatic service.

The European treaties created the framework and the basis for the integration of European economies. A standardised system of laws was introduced in all member countries for the creation of the single market. To make the single market viable, EU institutions and policies guarantee the free movement of people, goods, services, and capital, and have a role in justice and home affairs. Common policies also deal with trade, agriculture, fisheries, and regional development.

Representative organs include the Council of the European Union, the European Council, and the European Parliament. The Council of the European Union is composed of one representative per member country, usually a national minister. The Council is the fundamental decision- and law-making organ of the Union. Decisions are taken in most cases by qualified majority voting. However, unanimity is required in the case of fundamental issues.

The European Council is composed of the national prime ministers and is chaired by the president of the European Commission. Although the European Council has no decision- or law-making role, it is nevertheless the most influential European institution. Its main role is to define strategic issues, including changes in the Treaty, enlargement, the three-year budget, or other reforms of the Union. The European_Parliament has 754 members who are directly elected by European citizens every five years according to a "degressive proportionality". According to this principle, large countries have more representatives, but smaller countries need a lower number of citizens to elect a representative.[119] The European Parliament has competences in the law-making process, including the

[119] Presently, Germany has 99 representatives; France, Italy and the UK have 72; Poland and Spain have 50. The smallest countries (Cyprus, Estonia, Luxembourg, and Malta) have 6 representatives each.

budget, and controls all EU institutions, particularly the European Commission.

The common governance organs are the European Commission and the Court of Justice of the European Union. The European Commission is the fundamental operational organ and plays various roles. These include proposing norms to the European Council and the Parliament; and representing the Union in those international negotiations where the Union participates. These are in particular trade negotiations and negotiations with non-member countries. The Commission also cooperates with the Court of Justice of the European Union, particularly in the implementation and fulfilment of the Treaties. The most important role of the Commission consists of the management and implementation of EU policies, in particular those policies for which the Union has the sole competence. These include, among others, competition in the internal market and the common commercial policy. The Court of Justice of the European Union has supranational jurisdiction over legal affairs. It intervenes particularly in the disputes between member countries, between the EU and member states, between EU institutions, and between individual citizens and the EU.

Other important European organs include the ECB, which is responsible for European monetary policy. The European Investment Bank (EIB) finances EU investment projects and supports small businesses through the European Investment Fund.

7.3 Enlargement and the Allocation of Competences[120]

The EC went through three enlargements: the six original members who set up the ECSC and signed the Treaty of Rome (Belgium, Germany, France, Italy, Luxembourg and the Netherlands) were joined in 1973 by Denmark, Ireland and the United Kingdom and in 1981 by Greece. The Single European Act of 1986 reformed the institutions in preparation for Portugal's and Spain's membership, which happened in 1986.

The next enlargement in 1995 brought Austria, Finland and Sweden into the Union. This enlargement was to be followed by a much larger and

[120] The EU website offers detailed and updated information on the treaties and the institutional architecture of the EU. See also EC (2014d).

problematic enlargement in 2004. Ten new member countries were accepted: Cyprus, Czech Republic, Estonia, Hungary, Latvia, Lithuania, Malta, Poland, Slovenia, and Slovakia. For the first time, eight of these were former centrally planned economies. This line of enlargement was furthered in 2007, when Bulgaria and Romania joined the Union, and finally in 2013, when was the turn of Croatia. In 2014, the Commission announced that no further enlargements would be considered for the next five years.

These enlargements expanded the number of member countries from 15 to 28. The population increased by 19.6% or 74.7 million in 2004 and by 6.5% or 30.1 million in 2007. GDP increased by nearly 9% in 2004 and by another 2% in 2007, since the new member countries were on average poorer than old member countries. Enlargements opened a new delicate chapter that was bound to deeply transform the nature of the Union: the reform of the decision-making process, which until then was based on unanimity. Important steps in the reform include the Treaty of Amsterdam, signed in 1997 and the Treaty of Nice of 2001. The main purpose of these treaties was to make European institutions viable and effective in a Union with a significantly higher number of member countries and with a much greater variety of economic, political and social situations. Reforms included new methods for changing the composition of the Commission and redefining the voting system in the Council.

7.4 The Integration of Markets and of Enterprises

Along with fundamental political and social goals, the Union has as an essential economic goal: the integration of markets. A fundamental prerequisite of the integration of markets is the possibility for capital and labour to freely move across the borders. Capital movements which are carried out across borders include foreign direct investments (FDIs); real estate investments or purchases; portfolio investments in equity and debt securities (in equity, bonds, bills, unit trusts); granting of loans and credits; and other operations with financial institutions (e.g. inheritances, endowments).

The liberalisation of capital movements in Europe took place through various steps. Although the Treaty of Rome of 1957 provided for the free movement of capital, the abolition of capital restrictions was to take place "to the extent necessary to ensure the proper functioning of the common market" (ToR 1957, p. 26). During the first decades of European integration, and in spite of some initial progress in the 1960s, capital movements were under the control of national governments. In fact, many member states had safeguarding measures in place and various financial operations with other member states were subject to prior authorisation requirements.

This situation persisted until the late 1980s and was changed when the European Council adopted a capital liberalisation directive in 1988 (EC 1988). The directive provided for the removal of all remaining exchange controls by the mid-1990s, with transition periods for some member countries (Spain, Ireland, Portugal and Greece). In the process towards achieving the Economic and Monetary Union (EMU), the freedom of capital movements became a fundamental precondition, as did other internal market freedoms. This happened in particular with the entry into force of the Maastricht Treaty. As a consequence and starting from 1 January 1994, all restrictions on capital movements and payments between EU Member States were cancelled and prohibited. The same happened with restrictions between EU Member States and third countries. This change concerned also future EU member countries, which had to eliminate controls on capital movement in the period before EU membership. An exception was introduced for the new member countries of Central and Eastern Europe, which were granted transitional periods for capital operations involving the purchase of real estate, in particular agricultural land.

The liberalisation and integration of capital markets had a set of positive consequences for the European economy, particularly when the introduction of the common currency is considered (Baldwin and Wyplosz 2012). Following the liberalisation and integration of capital markets, the cost of capital decreased and the profit rate adjusted to risk increased. However, the integration of labour markets proceeded slowly and labour markets remain largely national, in spite of the free circulation of workers at EU level. Even the banks' cross border activity remained below expectations (Buch 2000). By eliminating exchange rate risks, the euro was expected to enhance the incentives that banks have in expanding cross-border within the Eurozone. However, a strong home bias remained and was encouraged by national governments.

Capital, trade and industry integration enlarges markets, increases competition, and improves the flow of technical progress. These effects bolster productivity gains. While the latter should decrease the demand for labour by enterprises, the enlargement of markets and enhanced productivity of enterprises should result in higher demand for labour and higher employment. The effect of integration is consequently not clear in terms of employment. However, it should be positive in qualitative terms: it should support technical progress and the move towards higher demand of skilled and highly educated workers. As mentioned in Chapter 5, this happened only in part and the effect was important only in resilient countries and was strictly linked to national policies.

One problem with the liberalisation and integration of labour markets lies in the existence within the EU of countries with different economic and social systems. These differences are particularly important and sticky in the case of the institutions of the labour market. As a consequence, labour markets tend to remain largely national. Along with the prevalence of distinct national formal institutions, there are many, less structured and informal factors that slow down the integration of labour markets, including the existence of social and cultural traditions and language barriers.

The buildup of the single market and the liberalisation and integration of markets were expected to have positive consequences for the European economy. It was foreseen that liberalisation and integration of markets create much larger markets than national markets and foster competition. This in turn leads to defragmentation of the enterprise sector through mergers and acquisitions (M&A), thus creating European enterprises strong enough to compete successfully in the international market. Since competition encourages industrial restructuring, more efficient enterprises and the re-allocation of resources to more dynamic branches were expected. Deep restructuring looked inevitable in the bank sector. The increased efficiency of the European economy resulting from these processes was expected to lower prices and increase production, which would result in increased welfare and stronger competitiveness.

The number of (M&A) increased significantly in the EU, both within the Eurozone and outside it. Their yearly number reached the highest level in 2000, after which they decreased. What is interesting to observe is that the share of M&A that involved only Eurozone firms remained roughly a constant share of overall M&A involving EU firms (Table 7.1). Their share decreased in the mid-1990s from close to 47% to slightly more than one-third. However, by 2000 they returned to and slightly surpassed the share they had in early 1990s.

According to TF (2015), M&A in Western Europe reached the highest number of approximately 17,000 cases in 2000. In value terms, the peak was one year before, with slightly more than 1.8 trillion euros in value. A trough followed in 2002–2003 and another peak of similar magnitude in 2007. After this year, M&A decreased to the 2002–2003 level with approximately 10,000 cases, with a revival in 2004. This behaviour was very much in line with what happened worldwide. The main difference was that the 2007 peak worldwide was higher in both numbers and value than the 1999–2000 peak, while in Western Europe the two peaks were roughly on par. While M&A in Western Europe formed the bulk of European M&A in

Table 7.1. Mergers and Acquisitions between Different Groups of Countries (as a Share of All Countries).

	Number of M&A within Eurozone	Eurozone Countries	EU Countries	Non-euro EU Members	Non-EU Countries
1991	867	46.7	68.0	21.3	32.0
1992	801	45.4	66.0	20.6	34.0
1993	696	40.4	59.5	19.1	40.5
1994	793	40.7	60.3	19.6	39.7
1995	864	38.8	59.6	20.8	40.4
1996	752	34.7	54.3	19.6	45.7
1997	851	34.2	54.7	20.5	45.3
1998	995	34.5	54.2	19.7	45.8
1999	1330	41.6	63.0	21.4	37.0
2000	1778	47.5	68.1	20.6	31.9
2001	1288	47.0	68.9	21.9	31.1

Source: Author's own analysis of data by Manchin (2004).

both peaks, their share decreased significantly in the second peak compared to the first one in both number and value (Table 7.2).

The distinction between resilient and vulnerable countries turns out also at microeconomic level. In fact, the performance of vulnerable countries was distinct from that of resilient countries also in the restructuring of the banking sector. Resilient countries proceeded to restructure consistently their credit sector (Table 7.3): number of credit institutions, number of branches (from 15,587 to 12,531) and number of branches related to inhabitants all decreased rapidly by between one-fourth and one-fifth between 1997 and 2003 (from 57 to 44 per credit institution on average). This means that the number of branches per credit institution slightly

Table 7.2. Mergers and Acquisitions in Europe as a Share of Worldwide M&A (in Percent).

	Western Europe		Europe		Of which: RESIL*	
	2000	2007	2000	2007	2000	2007
Number	43	35	48	40	43	38
Value	45	36	45	36	46	40

Note:* Austria, Belgium, France, Germany and the Netherlands as a share of Europe.
Source: Author's own analysis of data by TF (2015).

Table 7.3. The Restructuring of the Credit Sector in the Eurozone.

		1997	1998	1999	2000	2001	2002	2003
Number of credit institutions	RESIL	100.0	96.1	90.9	85.4	81.3	77.4	73.5
	VULN	100.0	100.8	97.0	93.8	93.0	90.3	88.1
Number of local units (branches)	RESIL	100.0	96.6	94.8	92.8	89.3	85.4	80.4
	VULN	100.0	103.8	105.4	107.2	108.5	109.3	111.3
Number of local units (branches) of CIs per 100000 inhabitants	RESIL	100.0	97.5	96.2	93.4	86.6	82.8	77.8
	VULN	100.0	104.2	105.5	106.3	107.6	106.7	106.7
Number of employees of CIs per 100000 inhabitants	RESIL	100.0	101.1	104.0	108.1	110.4	107.5	103.8
	VULN	100.0	99.0	112.3	108.6	112.2	107.6	105.5

Source: Author's own analysis of data by ECB (2004).

increased, from 15.7 in 1997 to 17.2 in 2003 on average, or by 9.4%. Only the number of employees related to inhabitants kept growing until 2001, but then also this indicator started to decrease.

Quite different was the evolution in vulnerable countries. With the exception of the number of credit institutions, which by 2003 decreased to the 88% the number they had in 1997, the number of branches kept growing (from 14,368 to 15,986), while the number of branches related to inhabitants increased from 48 in 1997 to 51 by 2000, after which the number stagnated. The number of branches per credit institution increased much more than in resilient countries, by more than 26% between 1997 and 2003, from 42.5 to 53.7 on average. The number of employees related to inhabitants had a change similar to that of resilient countries, though: it kept growing until 2001, after which it decreased.

It is interesting to note that in vulnerable countries the number of employees per 100,000 inhabitants remained much lower than in resilient countries: relatively constant around 46% of the resilient countries' level. Thus vulnerable countries, in a period of strong consolidation of the strategically important credit sector and compared to resilient countries, continued to have a lower number of credit institutions compared to the inhabitants, higher number of branches per credit institutions,[121] rather similar number of branches related to inhabitants, and lower number of credit sector employees related to inhabitants. These are signals of greater fragmentation and lower specialisation of the credit sector in vulnerable countries.

7.5 Sharing Competences and Decision-Making

The EU is in many senses a supranational body that acquired competences that used to belong to the national states. Therefore, the EU has sovereignty in various fields following the voluntary and concerted transfer of those competences by national states and governments. Yet in other fields, competences are shared with national governments or the Union

[121] The number of branches per credit institutions in vulnerable countries increased from 2.7 times the number in resilient countries in 1997 to 3.1 times in 2003 (calculations on ECB 2004 data).

and national governments have parallel competences. In the remaining fields, sovereignty belongs in national governments and states and the Union only has coordination and supportive roles.

Such a structure and distribution of competences between the Union and the member states was defined in the Treaty of Lisbon and is based in the principle of conferral (Article 5 of the Maastricht Treaty). The principle provides that the Union acts only within the limits of the competences conferred upon it by the member states in specified areas. Another important piece of the distribution of competences and decision-making is the principle of subsidiarity. The principle is defined in Article 5 of the Maastricht Treaty, which stipulates that decisions are taken as closely as possible to the citizens. Except in the areas that fall within its exclusive competence, the Union proceeds only in those cases where its action is more effective than action taken at national, regional or local level.

Even in these cases, the Union is bound by the principle of proportionality. This principle stipulates that any action by the Union should stay within the limits of what is necessary to achieve the objectives of the Treaties. However, the Union's competences may be extended through the application of the flexibility clause. This clause is defined in Article 352 of the Lisbon Treaty and may be activated when the Treaties do not foresee the means necessary for achieving one of the Union's objectives. These principles give a clear mandate to supranational competences and activities and put them under clear and strict limits, yet they also have an important degree of flexibility built in.

The EU has exclusive competence in a number of important fields. These include: customs union; competition in the internal market, including establishing the relevant rules, their enforcement and the control over potential anti-competitive situations and practices; within the Eurozone, design and implementation of monetary policy; the common commercial policy; and the common fisheries policy, including the conservation of marine biological resources. In addition to these competences, the EU is also solely responsible for those international agreements whose conclusion is foreseen in a law of the Union or is necessary for the exercise of the Union's internal competence, or in cases when the international agreements affect common rules.

In many important areas, the Union shares competences with national governments. These cases include the internal market; social policy, for the aspects that are defined in the Treaty; issues of economic, social and territorial cohesion; agriculture and fisheries matters;[122] the environment; consumer protection; transport; trans-European networks; energy; issues of freedom, security and justice; and common safety concerns in public health matters.

There are also few areas in which the Union competences are parallel to those of the national governments and states. These cases include research, technological development and space; and development cooperation and humanitarian aid. When competences are parallel, the Union carries out activities and conducts common policies that coexist with the exercise of similar competences by the member countries.

In the instance of some of the most important issues for the European economy, the Union has only a role of coordination of national competences. Yet the coordination role is based on such stringent rules (primarily the Maastricht criteria and the Stability and Growth Pact (SGP)) that the role of the Union organs is overwhelming, at least for those member countries that do not comply with the common rules. Coordination of competences exists in the case of economic policies, when the European Council adopts guidelines for these policies and other measures. Other cases include employment policies and social policies of the member states. In all these cases, the guidelines that member countries are required to follow are defined at the Union level.

Finally, some of the Union's competences are supportive of those of the member countries, in the sense that the Union carries out actions for supporting, coordinating or supplementing the action of the member countries. These include competences in the protection and improvement of human health; industry, culture, and tourism; education, vocational training, youth and sport; civil protection; and administrative cooperation.

Although the institutional architecture of the EU was carefully planned and long-term tested, the complex allocation of competences may open the risk of conflicts, dilutes responsibility and may foster some

---

[122] This would exclude the conservation of marine biological resources, the sole competence of which rests in the Union.

opportunism in member states. The success of this architecture is keenly dependent upon the member countries' goodwill and propensity to cooperation and the effectiveness of the peers' pressure. However, the Union disposes of instruments and sanctions to force member countries to comply with the rules and the decisions, an outcome that is a fundamental precondition for a sustainable monetary union.[123]

7.6 Convergence and Stability

The monetary union requires that all its member countries implement compatible and possibly coordinated policies. However, the EU does not have sovereignty in fiscal policies, which continue to belong to the national governments. In order to attenuate the potentially dangerous consequences of such institutional incompleteness, the European Council defines and adopts the Broad Economic Policy Guidelines (BEPG). The guidelines consist of non-legally binding recommendations to the member countries. In spite of their non-binding nature, such recommendations come to form a true surveillance mechanism through information and peer pressure, a mechanism that plays a fundamental role in coordinating national economic policies. The Commission has the critical role of providing regularly the Council with detailed information on policies and economic and fiscal developments in each member country. The Commission may also issue a warning in case a particular country does not comply with the guidelines and thus risks jeopardising the stability of the EMU. In this case, the Council can address private or public recommendations to the concerned member country.

The guidelines clearly need a benchmark against which policies and achievements of member countries may be assessed. The fundamental benchmark is the convergence criteria. Their rationale is to make the economic and monetary union sustainable and to avoid the threat that divergent fiscal policies by member countries represent for other countries sharing the same currency. The convergence or Maastricth criteria were originally defined in Article 121.1 of the Maastricht Treaty and further

[123] For a description of the basic EU instruments and procedures, see http://europa.eu/legislation_summaries/glossary/.

reaffirmed in Article 140 of the Lisbon Treaty (TFEU).[124] All those countries which want to enter the third stage of the EMU and adopt the common currency must meet the criteria. Obviously, the same refers to those countries which are already members of the Eurozone.

There are four sets of convergence criteria (see Section 5.1) (Table 7.4). The criteria are the following: (a) the ratio of the government deficit to GDP and the government debt to GDP ratio must not exceed respectively 3% and 60%; (b) a country must pursue price stability, defined as an average inflation rate which does not exceed, in the year before the examination, by more than 1.5% that of the three best performing member countries in terms of price stability; (c) the long-term nominal interest rate should not exceed by more than 2% that of the three best performing member countries in terms of price stability; and (d) during the last two years before the examination the exchange rate mechanism must be stable and not submitted to severe tensions.

After the introduction of the euro, exchange rates between the Eurozone countries disappeared and price stability became the main competence of the ECB. As a consequence, the surveillance concentrated on the government deficit and debt, since these are in the competence of national governments. To this end, the Amsterdam European Council adopted the Stability and Growth Pact (SGP) in June 1997 and amended in June 2005, in order to assure that member countries coordinate their fiscal policies and avoid excessive government budget deficits.[125] Member

---

[124] The Lisbon Treaty (TFEU) set a number of convergence criteria that EU member countries have to meet before adopting the euro. These are: a) not be subject to a procedure for excessive budgetary deficit; b) price stability and low average inflation rate; c) low long-term nominal interest rates, not exceeding by more than 2% that of the three best performing member countries in terms of price stability; d) stable exchange rates with the other Eurozone countries for at least the last two years; d) national legislation compatible with EU norms and treaties. Convergence criteria are meant to avoid tensions within the EMU. They complete the Maastricht criteria that served the preparation of the euro and strengthened the SGP. The SGP was adopted at the Amsterdam European Council in June 1997. It has the role of assuring the compliance with the criteria after the euro is adopted, in particular regarding government deficit and government debt.

[125] Along with the SGP, a number of institutional arrangements were introduced with the Lisbon Treaty. These were intended for pursuing sound fiscal policies and price stability and include: the prohibition of monetary financing (Article 123), the prohibition of

Table 7.4. The Convergence Criteria.

	Price Stability	**Sound and Sustainable Public Finances**		**Interest Rates Convergence**	**Exchange Rate Stability**
Indicator	Consumer price inflation rate	Government deficit	Government debt	Long-term interest rate	Deviation from a central rate
Benchmark	Not more than 1.5% above the rate of the three best performing member countries	Not more than 3% of GDP	Not more than 60% of GDP	Not more than 2% above the rate of the three best performing member countries in terms of price stability	Participation in ERM II for at least 2 years without severe tensions

countries must also strive to keep balanced budgets and to work out and submit to the Council and the Commission a yearly stability programme.

One aspect that traditionally softened the harshness of formal rules is the fact that the no-bailout clause, foreseen in article 125 of the Lisbon Treaty, remained unused for many years. This clause means that fiscal transfers are not allowed among member countries, not even in the form of higher national budget deficits for the countries in economic difficulty or financial distress. During the 2010–2011 Eurozone crisis, the no-bailout clause remained *de facto* unused and was apparently abandoned in April 2010. However, the fiscal compact signed in 2012 foresees a more rigid application, although postponed in time, of the no-bailout clause. In fact, it includes the request to countries to make the principle of balanced budgets mandatory in their national budgets (ECo (2012)).[126] The full implementation of the fiscal compact was postponed to 2016, in the hope that by that time the EU would be out of the crisis. Events suggest

---

privileged access to financial institutions (Article 124), the no-bailout clause (Article 125), and the fiscal provisions to avoid excessive government deficits (Article 126).

[126]The Fiscal Stability Treaty, or simply fiscal compact (formally, the Treaty on Stability, Coordination and Governance in the Economic and Monetary Union or TSCG), is a stricter version of the SGP. All member countries of the European Union signed it on 2 March 2012, with the exception of the Czech Republic and the United Kingdom. The treaty entered into force on 1 January 2013 for 16 countries; the remaining nine countries joined by 1 April 2014. The Treaty builds on the budgetary rules outlined in the Stability and Growth Pact. Signatories to the Treaty agreed to implement a balanced budget rule in their national legislation through permanent, binding provisions, preferably of a constitutional character. The Treaty includes a provision for limiting deficits (annual structural government deficit must not exceed 0.5% of GDP; the deficit must be in line with the country-specific minimum benchmark figure for long-term sustainability; this figure is set by the preventive arm of the SGP); automatic correction mechanism (countries must implement a correction mechanism, i.e. design measures to reduce the budget deficit. These measures are triggered automatically in the event of a significant deviation from the agreed benchmark figure for long-term sustainability); reinforced coordination (Treaty signatories also agreed to inform each other, the Council of the EU and the European Commission in advance when they plan to issue new debt; they also discuss all plans for major economic policy reforms); Euro Summit meetings (the signatories agreed to hold Euro Summit meetings, which bring together heads of state or government of the Eurozone, at least twice a year). The Eurogroup is responsible for the preparation and follow up of these meetings.

that this optimistic view is probably wrong. Thus the fiscal compact risks placing an unbearable blow upon the most vulnerable economies of the Union. Apparently, the pursued solution is to pay formal respect while softening its implications through ad hoc concessions to national governments and their policies.

The SGP is an intercountry agreement taken through a European Council resolution and complemented with two Council Regulations. With this, the undersigning countries assume the obligation of delegating the European Commission with the role of monitoring their budgetary positions and the coordination of economic policies. They also accept to be under the excessive deficit procedure in case of non-compliance. The surveillance system, then, works through the political pressure that publicity to non-compliance activates, and through the political pressure of the peers, whose financial position may be jeopardised by the non-complying country.

Monitoring has the form of a multilateral surveillance procedure. In case of non-compliance, the Commission may address an "early warning" to the member country in question and start the "excessive deficit procedure". The procedure is governed by Article 126 of the Lisbon Treaty. The Commission, when preparing its report, has to take into account such events as cyclical conditions and reforms under implementation, which may have important consequences for fiscal stability. Based on the recommendation prepared by the Commission, the Council may deliver recommendations to the member country to correct the situation within a given period of time. In case the country fails to end the excessive deficit or to take the appropriate measures, the Council may instruct the country on the appropriate measures to take. In case of failure, the Council may impose penalties or fines and may invite the European Investment Bank (EIB) to reconsider its lending policy towards the member country.

7.7 The Common Budget

In order to function and pursue policymaking, the EU has an independent budget (Matthijs 2010). An independent budget is a fundamental instrument for implementing independent policies and for transferring resources to particular member countries or activities. The EU budget is grossly

Figure 7.1. Long-Term Evolution of the EU Budget Adjusted for Enlargement, in Percent of GNP.
Source: EC (2013c, 2014d).

insufficient for any of these undertakings and limited in its competences. Moreover, no Eurozone budget is available. The resources managed under the common budget have been decreasing since the late 1990s as a share of the GDP (Figure 7.1). While the budget amounted to more than 1.2% of the European GDP for much of the 1990s, the revenue share to the Union GDP decreased to a bare 1% in 2013. However, the absolute level of revenue was more than €150 billion in that year. The amount of total commitments appropriations will increase to €168 billion by 2020, corresponding to 0.98% of the EU gross national income (GNI). The amount of total payment appropriations will be respectively at €156 billion and 0.91% (EC 2014d, p. 201). Thus, the level of the annual budgets in payment appropriations and actual implementation remained significantly below the ceilings since the end of the 1990s.

The budget revenue is made of three main groups of sources, which countries pay in the budget in rough proportion to their income level.

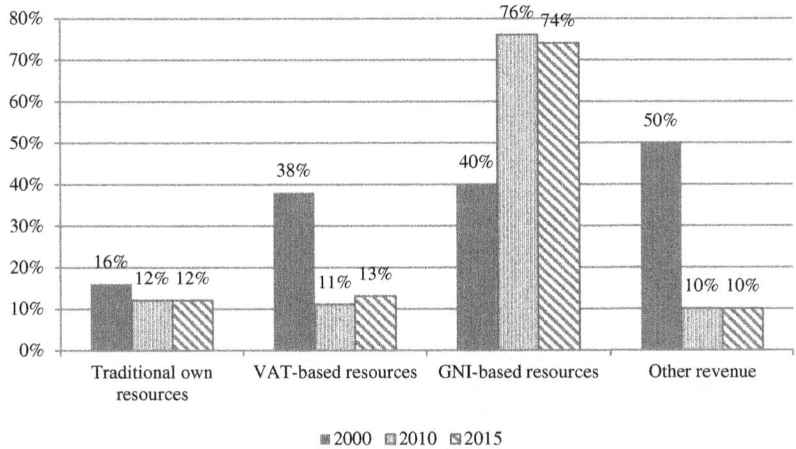

Figure 7.2. The Evolution of Budget Resources (in % of EU Funds).
Source: EC (2010b), EC (2015b).

The most important source is made of "own resources". These are sources that national authorities collect and transfer to the EU budget. The sources thus collected belong legally to the Union and make up nearly the entire revenue. The Union's has three types of its own resources. The most important source originates from a uniform rate applied to the GNI of each member state. Overall, these sources make up nearly three-quarters of the overall budget revenue. GNI-based sources are the only items that significantly increased as a share of the Union's overall budget during the last years. All other sources decreased (Figure 7.2). The Union's own sources also include those based on value added tax (VAT) through a uniform rate that is applied to each member country's harmonised VAT revenue. The third source is customs duties, levied on imports of products coming from non-EU countries. These two sources accounted respectively for 11% and 15% of the 2012 budget (see also EC 2014d).

The budget revenue also includes two other sources, whose quantitative importance is negligible. These are the contributions from non-EU countries to particular EU programmes and fines on companies that breach competition or other laws. Finally, other revenue sources include such items as taxes paid by EU staff on their salaries.

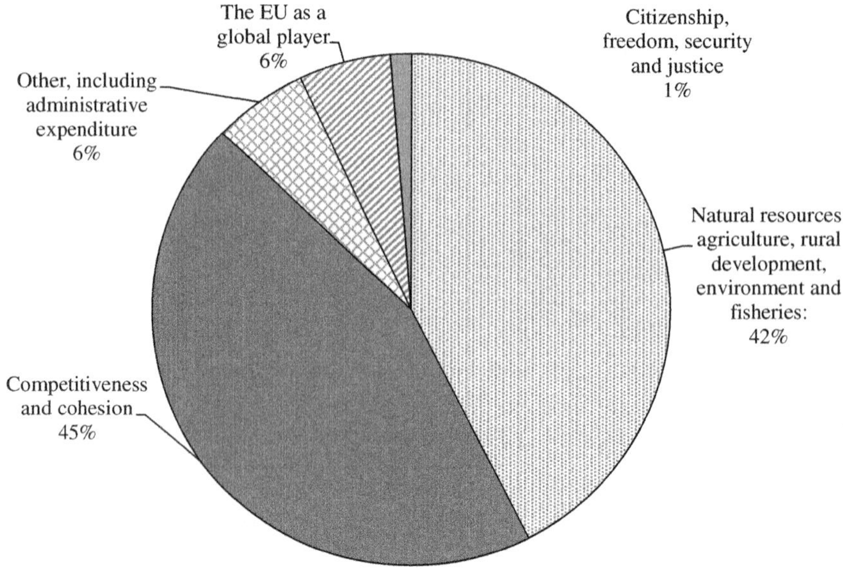

Figure 7.3. Budget Expenditure, 2007–2013.

Source: EC (2010b).

Most of the budget revenue is jointly managed by the European Commission and the member countries. This makes up more than three-quarters of the entire resources of the Union budget. The European Commission manages directly less than one quarter of the revenue (22% in 2010). The Commission manages around 1% of the revenue jointly with international partners, or this revenue goes to third countries.

The Union budget was also changing significantly on the expenditure side. Traditionally, the most important item was expenditures linked to the Common Agricultural Policy (CAP) (Baldwin and Wyplosz 2012). The share of the CAP, also including expenditures linked to the environment and fisheries, is presently well below half of the Union budget expenditure (Figure 7.3). Expenditures linked to competitiveness and cohesion constitute the item that expanded the most; they are presently more important than expenditures for agriculture and natural resources.[127] Less important

[127] The EU support to agriculture was subject to important reforms during the recent years, to avoid distortions that accumulated through the years. Traditionally, agriculture absorbed most of the common budget (Baldwin and Wyplosz 2012).

expenditure items include administrative expenditures linked to the working of the Union and its organs and expenditures linked to foreign policy of the Union and related activities. The smallest item finances the management of justice and security at the Union level.

In using its budget, the Union follows certain priorities. These are constrained by some fundamental principles and procedures and are limited by rules. While all member countries benefit from the EU budget, the principle of solidarity informing the EU programmes and the Union cohesion policy requires that less prosperous member countries receive a higher share of the budget expenditures. However and in spite of these sound principles, the practice may be different. For instance, it was shown that the CAP advantages disproportionately some rich member countries and, within these, the large and rich farms over the smaller and weaker ones (Baldwin and Wyplosz 2012).

The management of the Union budget is under several constraints and limits. The most important is the need to have fully balanced budgets, a principle that is stipulated in EU treaties. The Union budget is also under the "own resources ceiling". According to this principle, there is a maximum spending limit that national governments and parliaments agree on. This limit is currently set at 1.24% of the Union's GNI, which corresponds to €293 per EU citizen. The management of the Union budget is under the financial regulation adopted by the European Council and the EU Parliament. More important and severe is the fact that the Union budget is defined in a multiannual financial agreement that the European Parliament, the European Council and the European Commission have to reach. If some member countries such as Great Britain in the negotiations that led to the adoption of the 2014–2018 Union budget, intend to decrease the size and role of the EU budget, the outcome can only be restrictive.

The primary goals of the common budget are cohesion, structural objectives and development. These goals are important for the working of the Union and for its solidity. Yet no resources exist, nor would existing rules permit this, for pursuing countercyclical policies. This is a major contradiction of EU integration. A process that intends to contribute, among other things, to the growth and prosperity of its member countries is unable to agree on setting up proper instruments for managing anticyclical short-term policies. The problem with expenditures is that they are allocated and used following fixed, long-run parameters, such as the level of regional development compared to the EU average. Thus, budget expenditures are irrelevant for stability policy purposes.

The EU budget is also too small and its structure too rigid to serve for countercyclical purposes. It is insufficient to afford the growing dualism between vulnerable and resilient countries within the Eurozone. The EU budget purpose and action are limited to redistribute financial resources to areas or sectors which are less developed relative to the EU average and to politically and socially sensitive sectors, such as agriculture and research. The Union tried to set up a risk sharing system. This works as an automatic fiscal transfer mechanism to the advantage of areas or sectors that the own resources ceiling and the financial regulation affected adversely. Although theoretically accepted, this development is politically difficult to implement. The crisis accelerated the consideration of a risk sharing mechanism through fiscal transfers and centralised public spending or at least through fiscal equalisation mechanisms, a standard implementation in common currency areas and federations. Their implementation in the Eurozone would be important in order to avoid that large country-level shocks may become systemic for the area as a whole (Bluedorn *et al.* 2013; Furceri and Zdzienicka 2013).

The common budget has an implicit element of flexibility built in: some countries are net recipients of the EU budget and others are net contributors (Figure 7.4 and Table 7.5). In reality, it is not easy to calculate net contributions, since the outcome depends on which items are included and which items are excluded, considering that they are not country specific.[128] Data in Figure 7.4 are in euros per capita and are calculated starting from total expenditures net of administrative expenditures, since

[128] There are five common methods to calculate net contributions to the EU budget: a) simple balance between contributions made and disbursements received for each member state; b) excluding administrative expenditures related to hosting EU institutions; c) excluding traditional own resources belonging in the EU, and thus outside the member country's influence; d) simple net positions including traditional own resources, but excluding collection costs; and e) excluding administrative expenditures and traditional own resources, as done in the operating budget balances of the European Commission. For comparative calculations made using the five methods see Heinen (2011b). See also Pasimeni (2014).

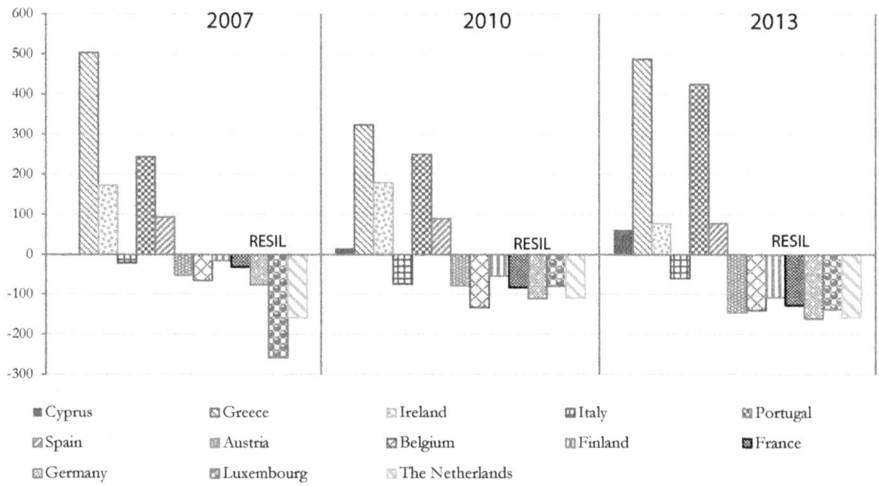

Figure 7.4. Net Receipts from the EU Budget Per Capita (€).
Note: Data are calculated by subtracting administrative expenditures from total expenditures.
Source: Author's own analysis of data from European Commission, Financial Programming and Budget (2 February 2015) (http://ec.europa.eu/budget/figures/interactive/index_en.cfm).

these are not country-specific. These data show that all resilient countries and one vulnerable country are net contributors.

The European Commission, when calculating net contributions, uses the individual countries' contributions in the form of own resources, such as VAT and GNI, as the basis (DP 2015). It excludes from the calculations agricultural levies and customs duties, since the Commission does not regard these as country-specific contributions. Similarly, administration costs are excluded from expenditures. These data give a picture similar to that presented in Figure 7.5 and Table 7.5, even though absolute figures are slightly different.

In general, net contributors are large and rich countries and net recipients are smaller and relatively poorer countries of Central Eastern and Southern Europe. Poland alone absorbs a quantity of budget resources comparable to Germany's contribution. This outcome is linked to long-term variables, such as regional development levels, and has no policy motivation. The result is that sometimes the countries' positions in the EU budget may be at odds with the countries' economic and financial

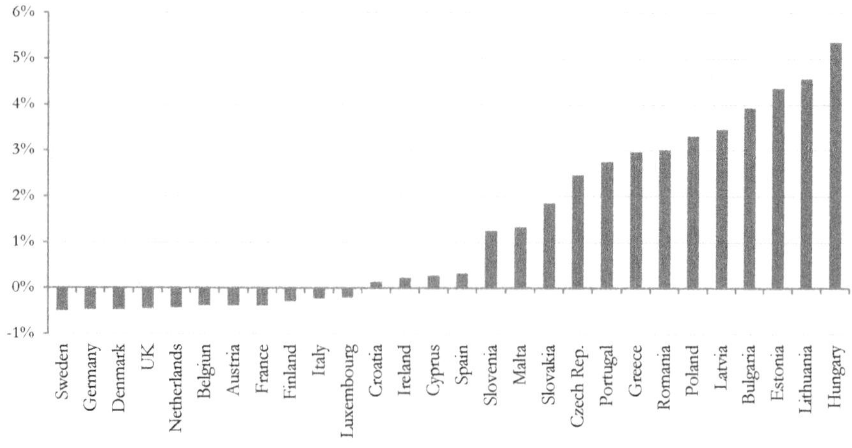

Figure 7.5. Net Receipts from the EU Budget in % of GNI, 2013.

Note: Data are calculated by subtracting administrative expenditures from total expenditures.
Source: Author's own figure based on data from European Commission, Financial Programming and Budget (2 February 2015) (http://ec.europa.eu/budget/figures/interactive/index_en.cfm).

situations. The most evident case in point is that of Italy, a country that has been in financial distress and economic difficulty for years. The same applies to Cyprus in 2007. It is also useful to consider that countries such as Belgium and Luxembourg are actually significant net recipients, when administrative expenditures are considered. Both countries, in fact, host important EU institutions and get an indirect economic advantage from this fact.

The EU budget allocation, then, does not really contrast the Eurozone dualism between vulnerable and resilient countries, and in some parts even strengthens it. However, it is fair to consider that, in relation to the economies' sizes, a degree of solidarity among countries is evident. The 11 net contributors make a relatively modest effort compared to the size of their economies, equal to 0.38% of their GNI in 2013. This corresponds to less than €150 per capita (Figure 7.5). Net contributors, in fact, include all the largest and richest economies of the EU, except Spain. At the same time, the 17 net recipients obtained a considerable support equal to 2.44% of their GNI, or nearly €279 per capita.

Table 7.5. Net Receipts from the EU Budget (2009, Negative Amounts Show Net Contributions).

	2007			2010			2013		
	1	2	3	1	2	3	1	2	3
EU27/28	5773.20	11.58	0.05%	735.93	1.46	0.01%	2677.39	5.32	0.02%
Austria	−438.54	−52.94	−0.16%	−659.45	−78.96	−0.23%	−1186.57	−145.72	−0.38%
Belgium	−702.16	−66.34	−0.21%	−1442.98	−133.12	−0.40%	−1456.50	−140.10	−0.38%
Bulgaria	349.30	46.13	1.22%	897.72	120.96	2.54%	1538.12	197.16	3.93%
Croatia							54.50	12.66	0.13%
Cyprus	−2.81	−3.71	−0.02%	11.75	14.35	0.07%	44.05	60.94	0.27%
Czech Rep.	717.78	70.00	0.59%	2088.56	199.63	1.50%	3432.24	336.65	2.46%
Denmark	−487.60	−89.52	−0.21%	−600.50	−108.50	−0.25%	−1221.01	−226.21	−0.47%
Estonia	234.47	174.60	1.56%	673.62	505.23	4.98%	775.50	567.61	4.35%
Finland	−80.11	−15.18	−0.04%	−288.97	−54.00	−0.16%	−560.23	−107.33	−0.29%
France	−2029.76	−31.89	−0.11%	−5405.46	−83.60	−0.27%	−7974.82	−128.02	−0.38%
Germany	−6266.76	−76.13	−0.25%	−9076.21	−110.95	−036%	-13262.38	−160.69	−0.47%
Greece	5609.62	503.39	2.59%	3612.30	323.00	1.67%	5379.28	487.35	2.96%
Hungary	1652.85	164.20	1.79%	2754.57	275.06	2.99%	4974.30	491.69	5.36%
Ireland	746.65	172.03	0.46%	812.52	178.60	0.62%	311.88	77.41	0.22%
Italy	−1251.02	−21.49	−0.08%	−4436.74	−74.96	−0.29%	−3450.90	−6002	−0.22%

(*Continued*)

Table 7.5. (*Continued*)

	2007			2010			2013		
Latvia	499.16	225.98	2.45%	675.37	318.50	3.67%	806.58	354.30	3.46%
Lithuania	807.14	248.35	2.92%	1360.06	432.87	5.03%	1522.00	447.79	4.56%
Luxembourg	−122.76	−257.79	−0.41%	−40.17	80.02	-0.15%	-62.70	−137.82	−0.20%
Malta	30.87	76.11	0.57%	53.29	128.72	0.90%	89.67	224.26	1.33%
The Netherlands	−2590.59	−158.37	−0.45%	−1805.61	−108.94	−0.31%	−2572.94	−158.26	−0.43%
Poland	5289.06	138.73	1.76%	8451.30	221.43	2.48%	12319.59	322.58	3.32%
Portugal	2556.20	242.69	1.56%	263479	249.19	1.58%	4452.86	425.17	2.75%
Romania	653.34	30.92	0.54%	1252.66	61.72	1.02%	4172.31	193.87	3.01%
Slovakia	644.30	119.91	1.21%	1353.49	251.09	2.08%	1302.75	242.51	1.85%
Slovenia	105.73	52.59	0.31%	426.36	208.29	1.22%	437.14	218.96	1.25%
Spain	4180.11	93.34	0.41%	4164.55	89.59	0.40%	3281.61	77.13	0.32%
Sweden	−841.77	−92.37	−0.24%	−1191.42	−127.55	−0.33%	−2139.61	−238.38	−0.50%
UK	−3489.54	−57.14	−0.17%	−5539.49	−88.62	−0.32%	−8329.32	−139.30	−0.44%

Notes: Data are calculated by subtracting administrative expenditures from total expenditures.

Column 1: Net receipts from the EU budget (€ million)

Column 2: Net receipts from the EU budget per capita (€)

Column 3: Net receipts from the EU budget in % of GNI

Source: Author's own table based on data from the European Commission, Financial Programming and Budget (2 February 2015) (http://ec.europa.eu/budget/figures/interactive/index_en.cfm).

Although the distinction of member countries between net contributors and net receivers depicts a certain degree of solidarity within the Union, such solidarity is linked to the structural and long-term features of member countries. This is important for the long-term internal convergence of the Union. It also responds to concerns of fairness and solidarity upon which European integration is based. These are also at the basis of the political and social sustainability of the integration process. Yet it is insignificant in cases of financial or economic distress.

This use of the budget is also important in that internal convergence is critical for the sustainability of integration in fully open economies. Support to poorer and relatively backward countries and regions is important, both directly and indirectly. Directly, the support increases the population's standard of living, increases investment and employment, and improves infrastructure and public administration. Indirectly, the EU support may be important for increasing the attractiveness of the country or region for both the local population and foreigners, avoiding both the outflow and inflow of resources. If EU support fosters real convergence of the most vulnerable economies, this outcome would contribute to attenuate an important reason for asymmetric outcomes of shocks in member countries.

Yet the economic role of EU contribution is modest, with the exception of the mostly small and relatively poor new member countries. After unification, the German government implemented massive transfers of resources to the advantage of former Eastern Germany.[129] This effort represented a heavy burden for the German economy, even if part of it was indirectly financed by the inflow of foreign capital, following the increase of interest rates that the Deutsche Bundesbank implemented.

7.8 Federalism vs Intergovernmental Agreements and Coordination

If one considers the common budget as the most important federalist achievement of the EU in the economic domain, together with the euro in

---

[129] "Over a period of 20 years, German reunification has cost €2 trillion, or an average of €100 billion a year" ("Interview with Former German Finance Minister", 2011).

the monetary field, one should conclude that the former achievement was modest indeed. It was also asymmetric in that the common budget remained at a much lower level than national budgets and the allocation of its resources is under long-term and rigid criteria. This leaves national governments as the sole responsible for fiscal policies, albeit based on stringent shared rules and under the control of the Union and the peer countries.

The federalist agenda often intertwined with the intergovernment approach. The two had mostly a positive cohabitation and often complementarity, perhaps at the cost of some excessive bureaucratisation of the integration process. Governments never gave up their prerogatives and were always careful to keep effective control over their assets. However, they were often ready to compromise and invest in the common good, also by transferring some of their sovereignty to the little common government that was set up.[130] Although they wanted their sacrifices to be compensated with advantages, sometimes they were willing to do so in the frame of a long-term perspective. The federalist agenda thus led to such fundamental achievements as the single market and the common currency, in a win-win situation.

Yet something went wrong and the crisis revealed the shaky structure of the Union. On one side, the management of federalist achievements was

[130] There is some debate within and around the EU on whether some provisions of the European agreements allow for an "invisible extension of competences", particularly of the European Commission. The potential Trojan horse would be in particular Article 352 of the TFEU. In fact, this article introduces a "flexibility clause", which enables the EU to act beyond the power of action conferred upon it by the Treaties in support of EU objectives when other Treaty articles do not suffice. However, this clause is framed by a strict procedure and by restrictions in terms of its application and cannot be used to extend EU competences. In fact, any proposal made in this sense must have the unanimous agreement of the Council and, following the entry into force of the Lisbon Treaty, the consent of the European Parliament. Moreover, some governments (e.g. the German government) need the prior approval from both houses of their national Parliament. At the end, it seems fair to say that Article 352 and other provisions cannot be used to extend the Union's competences, but can give some flexibility to its functioning, provided all countries agree. This flexibility, which may be important in pursuing to common good of the union, is apparently becoming a shared pragmatic way to a mild softening of austerity policies, which is apparently moving some steps after the third dramatic Greek crisis in summer 2015.

short of institutional aspirations. As a consequence, the common institutions and government (a European government of the economy) remained incomplete and were not in line with technical achievements (the common currency). On the other side, the crisis stopped the implementation of the federalist agenda and gave much power back to the intergovernmental management.

There is a degree of role play here. While the Commission is certainly eager to increase its competences and power, it is also true that, particularly in a period of crisis when austerity policies are imposed to implement unpopular decisions, national governments are just as eager to ascribe such decisions to the EU or to "Brussels". However, national constituencies of vulnerable countries are increasingly reading this attitude as bowing to the resilient countries and in particular to the German government. Again, the Greek drama in summer 2015 provides important teachings on the short-sightedness of this kind of national opportunism.

The danger went unrecognised before the crisis and the Union worked fairly well, albeit with growing conflicts and disagreements as the number of members increased. It is important to understand why things apparently changed with the crisis. There are two interlinked reasons: (a) the growing number of increasingly diverse member countries; (b) the untenable architecture and structure of the Union.

Looking at the first reason, it is important to appreciate the growing difficulty in coordinating an increasing number of diverse member countries with incomplete institutions and governance. In this sense, difficulties result from a classical problem of collective action in a complex context. Indeed, difficulties appeared already in early 2000s, well before the international crisis appeared. This was in particular on the occasions of the Treaty of Nice in 2001 and even more so of the Treaty establishing a constitution for Europe in 2004. The revival of national governments and the intergovernmental approach was an effective shortcut to the solution of this complexity.

According to the second reason, the crisis simply revealed the untenable architecture and structure of the Union, the incompleteness and asymmetry of common institutions, and lack of coordination among member countries. The crisis anticipated the appearance of problems that had to appear anyway. Before the crisis, the EU relied much upon well-established routines. However complicated and lengthy, these routines were reasonably well tested. The crisis required fast decisions, which were difficult to make given institutional incompleteness.

Resorting to the intergovernmental method raised conflicts. Under the effect of the crisis, decisions tended to have discrete effects and countries were afraid to be disadvantaged or missing any compensation within a politically feasible perspective. Only a well-established government of the economy could take credible commitments to the common solution of problems.[131] It could also give member countries credible guarantees that nobody would lose permanently and that everybody would be better off. The lack of a common government and the asymmetric economic and political weight of member countries made agreements difficult and shortened the time horizon. The unanimity principle also gave small countries a disproportional political weight and made solutions open to moral hazard. However, the growing problems and costs induced countries to agree on muddling through the crisis in a reasonably coordinated way, albeit through ineffective and counterproductive conservative policies and at significant costs for member countries, particularly so for vulnerable countries.

It is probably fair to say that both reasons contribute to explaining the difficulties. They interacted in making the Union ineffective in fighting the crisis and imposed important and unnecessary costs and difficulties to the economically most vulnerable among its members. The question is whether the Union became excessively unequal and therefore structurally ineffective through enlargements or whether the mistake was to enlarge before having created a common government.

It is also useful to consider the existence of an "implicit discrimination" within the EU (see Section 7.10) (Bertrand *et al.* 2005; Stiglitz 2012,

[131] An alternative is that one member country plays the role of the leader (Tamborini 2015). In the EU and the Eurozone, such country could only be Germany, for its economic and financial weight and for its traditionally orderly finances. However, this solution meets political problems deriving from history and also from some more recent international mistakes (e.g. in the case of former Yugoslavia or, recently, Ukraine). The traditional solution to this politically uneasy situation was the German-French "duopoly", which could have anyway only an informal, yet effective role in a union among equals.

p. 69). While formal European institutions are careful in avoiding any discrimination among member countries — so much so that, for example, in the voting system the citizens of small countries still have a disproportionate voting power today — the existing situation and the daily practice may be different. Implicit discrimination is "*unintentional* and outside of the discriminator's awareness" (Bertrand *et al.* 2005, p. 94).

Implicit discrimination within the EU may have different origins. Some are a consequence of established situations and routines. One form was briefly presented above: some countries in a difficult economic situation (such as Italy and also Cyprus) are or were net contributors to the common budget, while others in stronger position (such as Belgium, Luxembourg and the Czech Republic) are net recipients. This is formally correct, since the EU budget is managed along structural lines. Yet this fact contributes to unbalance further the economic situation of some countries. Some other forms derive from the geographical location: e.g. Southern European countries are the target of uncontrolled immigration from third countries and have to afford the costs for managing it, albeit with some support from the EU. Moreover, vulnerable countries even miss out on the advantages from immigration, since the most qualified immigrants move rapidly to Northern European countries or elsewhere.

However, the most important case of implicit discrimination descends from the institutional incompleteness of the Union. The asymmetric effect of external shocks is intensified by the common currency and cannot be accommodated either through sovereign national fiscal policies or through the common government of the economy. This situation discriminates against vulnerable countries. These countries have to pay a price that goes beyond their own existing demerits, without a clear advantage for resilient countries. When the Union has to choose how to react to an external shock, each national government is interested in having policies that do not disadvantage the own country. However, if situations differ through countries, unique policies advantage some countries and disadvantage others. Lacking compensating mechanisms, the outcome is implicit discrimination that unique policies impose upon some member countries. The lack of a common government prevents the possibility that disadvantaged countries are compensated, at least *ex post.* All these consequences and problems can be seen best in the case of the common currency.

7.9 Monetary Unification and Financial Integration

The adoption of the euro was the outcome of a long process of rule setting and monetary and financial convergence. It was carefully prepared and implemented, yet it was also a gamble. In fact, the common currency was introduced without political unification and without a common government of the economy and presented serious flaws (Nuti 2015a).

The first ideas and preparation of the Economic and Monetary Union dated back to the 1960s. However, a common currency was not foreseen in the first treaties. The need was also not urgent, since the Bretton Woods system of fixed, although adjustable exchange rates worked well and gave stability to the European economies. When, at the end of the decade, the international monetary system started to show growing strain, the idea of a common currency started to be considered. It became part of the 1969 Barre Plan of the European Commission.

The Barre Plan became the basis for the 1970 Werner Report. The Report foresaw the creation of the EMU in several successive stages. Unfortunately, the goal of a common currency became soon a victim of the economic instability caused by the disruption of the Bretton Woods monetary system and the oil crisis. Instability prompted European countries to adopt different national policies to react to the shocks. In order to give some solidity to the European monetary situation, the nine member countries of the EEC (the six funding member countries plus Denmark, Ireland, and the United Kingdom) established the European Monetary System (EMS) in 1979. The EMS was based on fixed but adjustable exchange rates among the nine currencies. The framework for the convergence of monetary and economic policies was thus created. The EMS succeeded in promoting greater monetary stability and put the basis for a progressive liberalisation of capital markets.

Following the Single European Act of 1986, a committee of monetary policy experts, including the governors of the EC central banks, was formed to work out a new strategy for the EMU. The result was the Delors Report, which foresaw three steps for implementing the EMU. It was on this basis that the European Currency Unit (ECU) became freely used and the member countries agreed on the Treaty on European Union (the Maastricht Treaty) in 1992. The Treaty established the EU, set the foundations of EMU and foresaw the approach and timetable for its implementation.

The EMU was implemented in three stages. First, all internal barriers to the free movement of goods, persons, services, and capital among member states were abolished on 1 July 1990. Second, the European Monetary Institute (EMI) was created on 1 January 1994 for managing monetary unification, as a predecessor of the ECB. The latter was established on 1 June 1998, thus replacing EMI. An important component of this stage was the enforcement of fiscal discipline and the convergence of the economic and monetary policies of member countries. The centrepiece of this were the adoption by the European Council of the SGP in Amsterdam on 16–17 June 1997 and the establishment of a new exchange rate mechanism (ERM II), both intended to provide the basis for monetary stability in the EU. Third, countries participating in the third stage were selected and the conversion rates of the currencies of the participating countries were irrevocably fixed on 1 January 1999. On the same date, the euro was introduced as the single currency, although it circulated physically only since 1 January 2002. At the same time, the SGP was implemented.[132] In the first round, 11 member countries were accepted. Other countries followed in the next few years, thus increasing to 19 the number of the Eurozone countries.[133]

---

[132] In order to strengthen the fiscal responsibility of the member countries, two major SGP reforms were introduced: the so-called Sixpack and the Fiscal Compact. The former entered into force on 13 December 2011. Its goal was to introduce greater surveillance over national public deficits and macroeconomic imbalances. The Fiscal Compact entered into force on 1 January 2013 as an intergovernmental treaty making the SGP rules stricter. With the exception of the Czech Republic and the United Kingdom, all EU member states signed and enforced the Fiscal Compact.

[133] Austria, Belgium, Cyprus, Estonia, Finland, France, Germany, Greece, Ireland, Italy, Latvia, Lithuania, Luxembourg, Malta, the Netherlands, Portugal, Slovakia, Slovenia, and Spain adhere presently (early 2015) to the Eurozone. Greece entered on 1 January 2001, Slovenia became the 13th member of the euro area in January 2007, Cyprus and Malta in 2008, Slovakia in 2009, Estonia in 2011, Latvia in 2014 and Lithuania in 2015. With the

Starting from 1999, the common monetary policy belongs in the competence of the Eurosystem, which is the monetary authority of the Eurozone. The Eurosystem includes the member states that have adopted the euro. It consists of the ECB and the central banks of the Eurozone, whose function is to implement the monetary policy decided by the ECB. The primary objective of the Eurosystem is to maintain price stability, defined as "a year-on-year increase in the Harmonised Index of Consumer Prices (HICP) for the euro area of below 2%".[134] The ECB Governing Council clarified that it aims to maintain inflation rates below, but close to, 2% over the medium term.

Without prejudicing its primary objective, the Eurosystem also supports the general economic policies in accordance with the principles of an open market economy. In this perspective, the Eurosystem contributes to functions that are in part or fully still under the competence of national authorities, including the supervision of credit institutions and the stability of the financial system. The ECB also has an advisory role both to the EU and national authorities on monetary matters, and, together with national central banks (NCBs), collects and publishes statistical information.

Since not all EU member countries are considered to be ready to join the euro or are unwilling to do so (the United Kingdom and Denmark chose to opt out), the Union also set up a European System of Central Banks (ESCB). The ESCB comprises the central banks of all EU member countries, including non-euro countries, and is coordinated by the ECB.[135] The ESCB primary objective is the same, although less severe, as the Eurosystem's: price stability. Moreover, the ESCB is called to strengthen

exception of the United Kingdom and Denmark, the other EU member countries are obliged to adopt the euro once they meet the relevant criteria.

[134] For a criticism of this definition see Svensson (2002). According to Svensson, the target is ambiguous and asymmetric. It is also less effective as an anchor for inflation expectations than a point inflation target.

[135] According to Article 127 of the Treaty on the Functioning of the European Union (Lisbon Treaty), the fundamental tasks of the ESCB are: a) to define and implement the monetary policy of the Union; b) to conduct foreign exchange operations; c) to hold and manage the official foreign reserves of the member states; and d) to promote the smooth operation of payment systems.

monetary and financial cooperation between the Eurosystem and the non-euro EU member countries.

Following the economic crisis and with the goal of creating a safer and sounder financial sector, the European Commission gathered in a single rulebook a set of legislative texts, that all financial actors in the member countries have to comply with. Rules include stronger prudential capital requirements for banks, improved depositor protection, and rules for preventing and managing bank failures. The single rulebook is the foundation of the banking union. In order to improve the resilience to the crisis in the Eurozone, a Single Supervisory Mechanism (SSM) and a Single Resolution Mechanism (SRM) for banks were set up. These are important steps for the creation of the Banking Union.

When planning the economic organisation of the EU, it was conceived that common currency and monetary policy were to protect the Eurozone from external symmetric shocks. The operative duty for this function was assigned to the Eurosystem, and more in general the ESCB. The flexibility for reacting to asymmetrical shocks was to rely on fiscal policies that were left to national governments (Buti and Sapir 1998).

It became evident soon that separating the two basic macro-policies was impossible, even more so when considering the substantial differences existing among the financial situations of the Eurozone countries. The Eurosystem was soon in charge of acting also as a leading financial authority, with the aim of safeguarding financial stability and promoting European financial integration. This role became preeminent when the international crisis put the euro under stress. This role also played a central part in forcing all member countries, in particular the Eurozone countries and the countries willing to adopt the euro, to make their economies converge to the commonly set benchmarks (convergence criteria). This was important in order to guarantee more similar financial conditions and a context of price stability. Unfortunately, this reasonable purpose fostered new problems.

Financial integration is fundamental in a common currency area for the implementation of monetary policy, the effective and balanced transmission of its effects throughout the euro area, and the smooth flow of payments. First, financial integration supports financial stability and economic growth by creating larger, more liquid and competitive markets. These generate additional possibilities for risk diversification and better exploitation of economies of scale and scope. This is important for both business and families, who can get access to a larger variety of financial products at lower cost and better conditions. Second, financial integration supports the Eurosystem by promoting the smooth operation of payment systems. The latter is important for the safe and efficient functioning of securities clearing and settlement systems. The new banking union gives the ECB new roles that should assure greater transparency, lower risk and greater stability of the European banks included in the banking union.

In view of the importance of financial integration for the common monetary system and monetary policy, the ECB has an important role in contributing to it vis-à-vis member countries and economic actors. This role consists fundamentally of two groups of activities: general support and technical contribution. General support includes advice on the legislative and regulatory framework serving the financial system and direct rule-making. It also includes monitoring the state of European financial integration and publishing a yearly report on financial integration in Europe. Technical contribution consists of two critical instruments: SEPA and TARGET2.[136] SEPA is the Single Euro Payments Area that European banks implement with the support of the ECB and the European Commission. It has the goal of making cashless payments across Europe fast, cheap and safe.

TARGET2 is an integrated and harmonised European payment system.[137] A further development, under way in 2015, is TARGET2-Securities (T2S). This system aims at setting up a single IT platform — built, owned and operated by the Eurosystem — for moving securities and money between buyers and sellers. The system intends to integrate and harmonise the currently fragmented securities settlement infrastructure in Europe. It also aims at reducing the costs of cross-border securities settlement within the euro area and participating non-euro countries, and at increasing com-

[136] It was initially set up as the TARGET (Trans-European Automated Real-time Gross Settlement Express Transfer) system by linking the 11 national large-value payment systems of the original Eurozone member countries in 1999. The system was developed in 2008 into a technically centralised and more efficient system called TARGET2.

[137] The number of banks directly participating in TARGET2 is 1,007 (August 2015) in 22 European countries. To these, 837 indirect participants and 5,037 correspondents should be added. Around 56,000 banks worldwide can send and receive payments via the system. See ECB (2015a).

petition and choice amongst providers of post-trading services. The ECB also operates the Correspondent Central Banking Model (CCBM), a framework set up in 1999 to enable banks in the Eurozone to submit all assets eligible for use as collateral for Eurosystem monetary policy operations or intra-day credit in TARGET2. The new CCBM2, under development, should be based on one single platform, thus allowing more standardisation.

TARGET2 allows for an estimate of the multilateral effects of sovereign debt. TARGET2-balances measure the share of NCBs credit to private banks that is used for international transactions. In this way and considering that countries are owners of NCB, TARGET2 turns a domestic credit of an NCB which is part of the Eurosystem into a multilateral loan of the country with respect to the Eurosystem (Steinkamp and Westermann 2014). This raises the risk that the remaining Eurosystem countries may run losses if these loans are not repaid. The striking difference between resilient and vulnerable countries during the crisis is evident and formed a mirror image (Figure 7.6).[138] The difference is striking particularly in

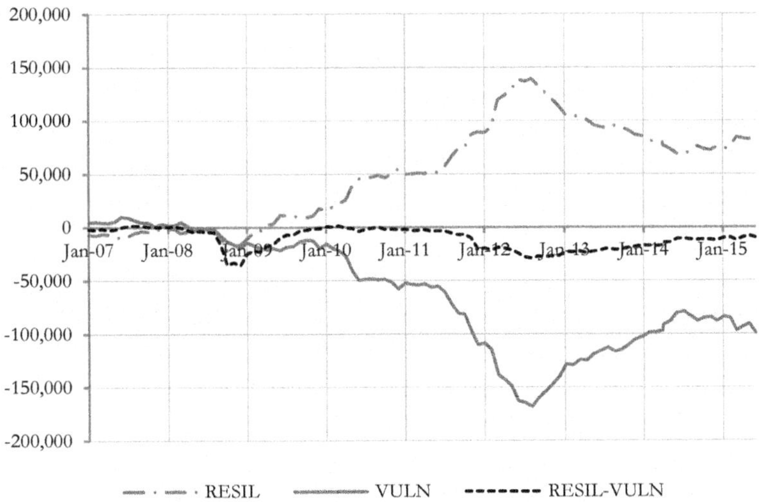

Figure 7.6. TARGET2-balances (Millions €).
Source: Author's own analysis of data from Steinkamp and Westermann (2014) (http://www.eurocrisismonitor.com/Data.htm).

[138] The positions of Austria, Belgium and France were mildly negative throughout the period, while that of Italy was positive until mid-2011.

summer 2012, when the negative position of Spain and Italy exploded nearly €435 billion and €290 billion, respectively), with a mirror positive position of Germany of more than €750 billion.

7.10 Monetary and Financial Integration as Sources of Implicit Discrimination

The construction of the EU was a careful, politically negotiated and technically sophisticated process of progressive integration of European economies. It required deep commitment, mutual understanding and political determination by all participants. Yet the outcome is visibly disappointing under many perspectives, excessively rigid and costly. It is to be seen whether it is flexible enough to change, following mounting internal and external pressure. The question is: who is to be blamed? Is it the inability of member countries and common institutions to effectively implement an impeccable blueprint? Is it the effect of excessive opportunism by some countries, typically vulnerable ones, which saw the Union as an excellent opportunity for free riding? Or is the excessive rigidity and short-terminism or resilient countries imposing ill-conceived austerity policies? Or did the blueprint and its implementation introduce unforeseen reasons for ineffectiveness and discrimination? This section concentrates on the third question. The first and the second questions were discussed in the previous sections of this chapter and are considered again in the next chapter.

Different critics highlighted dissimilar aspects. There are reasons to maintain that each of these explanations has some good reasons behind it. Among the mistakes in the integration agenda, the most serious one, that received the most attention, was the introduction of the common currency. Critics emphasised that a currency was always introduced after political unification was implemented. Doing it the other way round in the European Union was a gross mistake (Nuti 2015a). Yet it is clear that this was a conscious decision, one that was intended to put national governments and countries under pressure and push the integration agenda further. The set up of the euro created serious difficulties during the crisis. The real mistake of "Eurocrats" was not the introduction of the euro, but their inability to foresee proper devices that could be activated in case of a crisis. Yet it is too early to foresee the failure of euro implementation. It may still be true that "Eurocrats" were right after all and that the "mistakes" committed with the euro could accelerate political unification and institutional completion.

It is also undoubtedly true that some of the member countries were reluctant when it came to implement the agreements, treaties and common institutions. Perhaps the most blatant collective example is the fate of the Lisbon strategy of 2000. The strategy aimed at making the EU "the most competitive and dynamic knowledge-based economy in the world capable of sustainable economic growth with more and better jobs and greater social cohesion" by 2010. At the national level, most member countries have a long history of failure at fully complying with the EU standards and regulations of the single market. Various member countries are effectively resisting the European Court of Justice ruling, by prolonging the duration of their infringement cases and by lengthening the judgment implementation or the internal market provisions (EC 2015j).

There is also a genuinely political question: some member countries acted in an opportunistic or egoistic way. They did this either by excessively insisting on getting help and support from the EU well beyond their actual needs, even by not providing accurate information. Although various of these were vulnerable countries and new (post-2004) member countries, some of the old member countries also used this opportunity. The case of Thatcher's Great Britain is still well known and evident in the statistics.

There was a different form of opportunism that came to the fore during the crisis. This form had a particularly strong political impact on the integration process. This is the case of the countries that were under scrutiny or placed under the procedure for excess deficit, the so-called corrective arm of the SGP. The corrective arm ensures that member countries adopt appropriate policy responses to rectity excessive deficits or debts under the Excessive Deficit Procedure (EDP) (EC 2015k).

The EDP follows a step-by-step procedure that is outlined in Article 126 of the Lisbon Treaty. The procedure starts with a member country having violated either the deficit threshold or 3% of GDP, or threatening to do so, or the debt threshold of 60% of GDP, or when the excessive debt is not diminished at a satisfactory pace. Some additional factors are considered before starting a procedure. These include the worsening of the fiscal position due to exceptional events outside the control of the member country, such as in the case of natural disasters or a severe economic downturn. Even in these cases, the excessive deficit needs to be close to the reference value and be temporary.

When an EDP is launched, the country under procedure is required to take measures that promise to reinstate the country's compliance with European rules. This is usually done in the form of a letter of intent that the national government submits to the European Commission. Opportunism may manifest itself in one of two ways: cooking the budget (the case of Greece in 2004)[139] or not complying with the content of the letter of intent (the case of Italy in 2011).[140] Both cases put the common trust under stress and led to negative prejudice against non-performing countries.

However, there is a more general case to consider, a case that could answer the following question: did the blueprint and its implementation introduce unforeseen reasons for ineffectiveness and discrimination? The problem derives from three important features of European integration. First, countries in very different situations are included in the process, and no important equilibrating or compensating mechanism is foreseen. Thus, countries in different conditions are treated in the same way and must rely mostly (the limited European budget apart) upon their own resources to fix the problems deriving also from the undifferentiated treatment and rigid rules. Second, the above introduces an element of implicit discrimination. There is also a third element: the activation of multilateral support

[139] In 2004, Greece admitted that it published fudged budget figures to gain entry to the euro and that the true budget deficit was massively understated at least since 1999.

[140] On 5 August 2011, the outgoing ECB president, Jean-Claude Trichet and the incoming president, and ongoing governor of the Bank of Italy, Mario Draghi wrote a classified letter to the Italian government. This took place at the peak of a dramatic crisis of European stock exchanges and a strong increase of the spread between Italian and German long-term interest rates. The letter requested a set of stabilisation measures that the Italian government promised to implement, in exchange for a massive ECB support through the purchase of Italian bonds on the secondary market. The Italian government guaranteed the implementation of measures that it was not able or willing to implement in the following months.

foresees a *de facto* transfer of financial sovereignty to the lender and controller, the so-called "troika" (the EU, the ECB and the IMF). The troika has typical short-term financial objectives, that do not coincide with the beneficiary country's long-term development and even institutional and structural reforms are typically foreseen for their short-term stabilising effects.[141]

While conscious discrimination has well-known negative economic, social and psychological consequences, implicit discrimination influences behaviour in different ways. In particular, "... even theoretically controllable behaviours may operate with greater automaticity under certain situational conditions. ... Time pressure and stress are two situational influences likely to first generate an acceleration of the mental process, and then an attempt to reduce the amount of information needing processing. This type of "cognitive load", also occurs in the form of conflicting yet simultaneous task demands and excessive attentional demands:

> ... [M]any seemingly controllable behaviours may be prone to implicit attitudes under conditions of ambiguity, and ... implicit discrimination is more likely to occur in situations where multiple, non-racist explanations for the behaviour might exist. Thus, some conditions under which implicit attitudes may arise are threefold: inattentiveness to task, time pressure or other cognitive load, and ambiguity. (Bertrand *et al.* 2005, p. 95)

These conditions, which come from the work of psychologists applied to economic context, hold importance also for the European integration, particularly so within the Eurozone and during the crisis. It is clear that the crisis imposes, particularly in moments of greater dangers, "time pressure and stress" and thus generates "an acceleration of the mental process" in decision-makers. This is particularly true if one considers the resistance that countries in difficulty may oppose in trying to ease their situation

[141] In the July 2015 agreement on Greece, there apparently is a mild, mostly implicit — yet potentially important — step toward reforms aimed also at strengthening the country's long-term development.

vis-à-vis the EU. This situation easily results in "conflicting yet simultaneous task demands and excessive attentional demands".[142]

Implicit discrimination can exist when countries in very different conditions and situations share the same fundamental institutions (the common currency, the SGP), without effective compensation mechanisms (a common government of the economy, a common sizeable budget, a lender of last resort or at least fiscal equalisation mechanisms). Under these conditions, a more vulnerable and less efficient economy, sharing the same currency with more resilient and more efficient economies, meets an internal appreciation of the real exchange rate. In order to counteract this effect, that jeopardises its competitiveness, and being impossible to rely on common support, the vulnerable country can only use internal devaluation, i.e. decrease directly wages and other costs. Even leaving the distortive effects on incentives and political effects aside,[143] internal devaluation shrinks the domestic market, an outcome not compensated in alternative ways, either by domestic or external sources.

There is no need for conscious, open and purposeful discrimination. Discrimination is created by the differences in starting positions and conditions, national interest, the fear of resilient countries of having to foot the bill of monetary or financial instability, stable and undifferentiated common rules, as well as the incompleteness of institutions and policy instruments. The negative consequences of this situation are real enough to make the situation of vulnerable countries difficult and socially costly.

7.11 Conclusion: The Problematic Nature of the Euro

The exchange rate of the euro depends primarily upon the economic and financial strength of resilient countries and the reputation of the Union and the ECB. These factors generate strong and stable exchange rates, a fact that further discriminates implicitly vulnerable and unbalanced countries, which need weak exchange rates. The only opportunity for vulnerable countries is to reform their economies in order to make them

---

[142] Once again, the dramatic bargaining over Greece in summer 2015 offers plenty of examples and supports to this view.

[143] On these distortive effects, see Stiglitz (2012).

competitive with a fixed and strong exchange rate. Yet they have neither the resources nor the time to finance and make the necessary investment. Missing common support in exchange for credible commitments on their side, vulnerable countries are pushed to rely on internal devaluation as the only available option, which only worsens their situation.

The problematic nature and role of the euro descend from its ill-defined nature as a common currency and the multiple aims the euro was called to serve. These are the traditional efficiency gains of a common currency, including lower transaction costs, price transparency and more competition, removal of foreign exchange uncertainty and risk, and stronger resilience to external symmetric shocks. To these, the benefits of an international currency can be added, given the international importance of the euro. A second set of aims of the euro, which descends in part from efficiency gains, includes the support to economic growth and the convergence of economies (Baldwin and Wyplosz 2012; De Grauwe 2014).

The trickiest aim is the third one: the euro was intended to foster development and European integration. The efficiency gains that the common currency was expected to deliver were seen as fundamental to accelerating the process of catching up of the European economies and give Europe a central economic role in the world. Since catching-up processes are typically faster in less developed countries, which have most to gain from integration both economically and technically, the common currency was expected to foster internal convergence among member countries. Moreover, the common currency was expected to create common interest and will, and demand extensive and deep coordination among national governments, which would ease political unification.

The Eurozone was innovative in the way it was planned and implemented. It could be considered as an incomplete OCA forced by common political will and social support. Institutional theories highlight that informal institutions are sticky and change slowly. They may also be powerful and hamper the working and effect of formal institutions. The vicissitudes of the euro show that sticky national informal institutions were stronger than envisaged. This effect was particularly strong in countries under the stress of implementing formal convergence policies, especially when also fighting against the negative effects of an international financial and economic crisis.

Important questions in economic transformations are to assess how institutions were set up, why they were left incomplete, and in whose interest. These questions become important and tricky when sticky national institutions, particularly informal ones, fail to converge and incentives to convergence are ineffective. Formal institutions should be called to serve the common interest. However and since the latter is ill defined, national interests play an important role in defining institutions, in a double sense. First is the defence of national interests, making sure that common institutions avoid jeopardising national interests. Unfortunately, each country has its own goals and priorities. These are not always in harmony, and sometimes are in conflict with those of other countries. Public finances are a very important case of divergence of interests among nations.

Second is the goal of pursuing national gains as part of the gains from cooperation. Pursuing a whole that has a value superior to the sum of the parts is the economic and political rationale of European integration and the euro adoption. Any member country could thus obtain a net benefit. Institutions are important in defining the national distribution of the benefits from cooperation. Yet if national priorities and goals and the economic situation of the member countries are different, there are many different meanings, nature and definitions of the common interest and of benefits.

Moreover, common institutions are not impermeable to political and social pressures, to economic and political events and to interpretations. Under these conditions, it may be difficult for economic agents to form precise expectations about the present situation and the future course of events. Consequently, economic calculation becomes difficult and its outcome uncertain, making collective action costly, inefficient, perhaps ineffective. The outcome could also be unstable, particularly if some countries are asked to pay a price in the present in order to make the common benefit materialise, while other countries can gain a share of that benefit in the present. The construction of the euro offers plenty of examples in this sense.

The problem is that the Eurozone construction requires mutual trust among the member countries, to work smoothly and take advantage of growth. Unfortunately, events prove that this trust is largely missing and lately decreased further (Piattoni 2016). The consequences become acute in periods of financial distress and economic crisis. Lack of mutual trust means that time horizons of the Union policies are shortened and each country must be financially disciplined in the short run. As a consequence, adjustment is entirely left to countries in distress. The absence of trust makes avoiding intercountry distribution of income a rational behaviour.[144] However, the consequence is that additional severe costs are imposed upon vulnerable countries during periods of great vulnerability of their economy. This may easily increase their vulnerability to external shocks and prevent the possibility of recovery.

At the end, the Eurozone looks like an incomplete OCA forced by inconsistent political will and action, amidst sticky informal national institutions and incomplete formal common institutions. Due to the former, formal common institutions may lack credibility, are exposed to national opportunism, and are weakened by the waning mutual and common trust. This conclusion opens important criticalities for the management of the Eurozone and European economies during the crisis. It also requires that institutions are completed and proper policies are defined at the common and national levels. These are considered in the following chapters.

[144] This situation does not exclude the possibility to have separately negotiated intercountry support for countries in distress. Indeed, this remains the only flexible type of intervention.

Part III

Outcomes and Ways Out

A wretched soul bruised with adversity,
We bid be quiet when we hear it cry;
But were we burdened with like weight of pain,
As much, or more, we should ourselves complain.

— William Shakespeare, *The Comedy of Errors*, Act II, Scene 1

8

Policies and their Frames

Policies in the Eurozone are tailored to the implementation of the common rules as devised in the Stability and Growth Pact (SGP). The SGP was based on a short-run set of conduct rules and practices, motivated by the need to make all member countries converge to a financially sustainable situation in an institutionally incomplete context. The alternative possibility of proceeding through intercountry transfers was ruled out to avoid moral hazard and the fundamental lack of mutual trust and even fiscal equalisation seem to be far away. Unfortunately, a deep problem undermines the sustainability of the Eurozone: in a regional integration made of partially sovereign economies in different economic conditions and with diverse national institutions, there is an urgent need for institutional and structural, long-term reforms and policies to foster the convergence of the real economies and financial situations. It is only on the bases of these policies that short-term stabilisation policies can be sustainable and fruitful.

However, in the Eurozone the basic rules for national policymaking are to keep financial discipline, in order to safeguard the euro without imposing costs or difficulties on other countries. As a consequence, the existence and stability of the common currency had to be pursued by means of national efforts, but with little mutual coordination and adaptation through complementary policies. A partial exception comes from the bilateral or multilateral support in case of bailing out. There is not much room for truly common investment in this perspective, apart from the modest common budget. Fiscal adjustment is entirely left to the country in distress, albeit with some degree of flexibility in case of exceptional circumstances. Common instruments for sharing the burden of adjustment, such as instruments for debt mutualisation, were adamantly refused so far. Thus, the common currency had to work exclusively on the basis of self-discipline of each participant. Unfortunately, this means different things for countries in dissimilar conditions and situations. The concern for moral hazard and the lack of trust became the leading factors for the establishment of a particular financial and monetary system that created significant cost, risks and ineffectiveness for policymaking.

8.1 Strategies and Plans

There is a contradiction in the Eurozone buildup. While the goal of fostering a viable common currency area among so different countries is a long-term, perhaps secular endeavor, rules are to be met in the short term. In reality, the European Union (EU) tried to implement long-term strategies aiming at promoting growth, innovation and competitiveness. Such was the Lisbon strategy and such is the Europe 2020 strategy.

The Lisbon strategy was a development and innovation plan implemented between 2000 and 2010 aimed at solving the European difficulties in keeping pace with globalisation and the challenges of the knowledge-driven economy. The strategy set as a strategic goal for the decade to make the EU as "the most competitive and dynamic knowledge-based economy in the world, capable of sustainable economic growth with more and better jobs and greater social cohesion" (LEC 2000). The means devised to achieve this ambitious goal were the transition to a knowledge-based economy and society, the modernisation of the European social model, and the use of an appropriate macroeconomic policy mix. Most of the strategy objectives were not met and the strategy was considered to be "an ambitious program with mixed results" (Samardžija and Butković 2010), or a plain failure (Wyplosz 2010). However, others have observed that the strategy had important intangible effects, in particular "the awareness of the need to introduce reforms and to plan and report on their monitoring" (Rodriguez *et al.* 2010).

Upon the expiration of the Lisbon strategy, the EU launched its new Europe 2020 strategy (EC 2010a). Although the final goal is similar to the former strategies, the approach is different. In fact, it tries to start from a critical consideration of former mistakes by reducing the span of goals and concentrating on a more limited number of targets. Moreover, the new strategy sets the exit from the crisis and the start of a new "smart, sustainable and inclusive" growth as its fundamental goals. These goals are translated into five objectives, to be reached by 2020, related to employment, innovation, education, social inclusion, and climate and energy. Degrees of flexibility in the strategy come from the fact that each member country adopts a set of national targets in each of these areas, while the EU implements concrete actions to support the overall strategy.

A peculiarity of both these strategies is that they are defined upon the initiative of the European Commission, but concern areas where the Commission only has partial competence. Therefore, the success of the strategies requires that there is fundamental agreement between the Commission and member countries and that all member countries share the aims and the spirit of the strategy. To avoid risks of moral hazard, it is also necessary that the Commission is endowed with precise monitoring and effective enforcement. It is thus important that this approach may also offer the opportunity for a useful measurement and assessment of the implementation of targets by member countries (Pasimeni 2016).

At the end of 2014, the new president of the European Commission, Jean-Claude Juncker presented a new European plan for investment estimated at €315 billion over 3 years from 2015 to 2017 (EC 2014d). The motivation for this plan lies in the dramatic consequences of the crisis on the growth of the European economy and employment. As a consequence of the crisis, the level of investments in the EU has dropped by about 15%

compared to 2007 (see Section 5.2). However, the drop was definitely more significant in vulnerable countries, on average more than 40%.[145] The EU provides the European Fund for Strategic Investments (EFSI) a guarantee of €16 billion and the European Investment Bank (EIB) one of additional €5 billion. The remaining sources of around €294 billion should come from member states, public national promotional or development banks, regional authorities and private investors. The goal is to reach a multiplier of at least 15 of the common guarantee.

The plan works through a new EFSI set up within the EIB and targeting investment projects with high economic and social significance. The Fund resources are concentrated in two areas. The first area includes strategic investments of European significance in broadband, energy and transport infrastructure; education, research and innovation; and renewable energy and energy efficiency. The second area includes risk finance for small and medium-sized enterprises (SMEs) through direct equity and additional guarantees for high-quality securitisation of SME loans. The first area is foreseen to obtain overall €240 billion of investment, the second one approximately €75 billion.

There are three aspects to the EFSI that are worth stressing. First, projects are not linked to particular countries or fields and they are chosen on a competitive basis. This means that countries which contribute to the Fund have no guarantee that they get back a certain number of projects. Second, in order to foster countries' contribution, the Commission guarantees to take a "favourable position" towards capital paid in the Fund, when assessing the country's position within the SGP requirements. This could mean that such contribution is not accounted in the budget's deficit. Third, to be successful the plan should generate a high amount of investments, which would not have taken place without the intervention of the EU and the EIB.

These are the issues that have received most criticism (Claeys *et al.* 2014; Veugelers 2014). In fact, the foreseen multiplier effect is 15, i.e. one euro of EU-EIB guarantee should generate 15 euros of investment that would not happen without the Fund investments. The Commission con-

---

[145] The drop was 25% in Italy, 36% in Portugal, 38% in Spain, 39% in Ireland and 64% in Greece (EC 2014d).

siders this multiplier a "prudent average", based on past experience from EU and EIB programmes. However, it is to be seen whether this is a reliable prediction in a depressed EU economy. As noted for the strategies, it has to be considered that the Commission cannot go much beyond this. Indeed, it has no jurisdictional competence and the necessary resources for intervening directly. This leads back to the incomplete architecture of the EU and the Eurozone.

Strategies and the investment plan have as a target the revitalisation of the European economy in order to make it more innovative and competitive, with scant success so far. However, the bulk of European policies are managed primarily through short-term macroeconomic policies, particularly in the Eurozone. As a consequence, short-term macroeconomic policies deserve particular attention.

8.2 Traditional Policy Options for Financial Troubles

A sovereign country confronted with a crisis following from unbalanced finances, like the one the Eurozone countries are experiencing, could use a host of policies to re-establish its balance and prosperity. There are three groups of possible policies that can be used under these circumstances. First, monetary and fiscal policies can be used to fix the budget balance through fiscal and monetary management. Second, the depreciation of the currency, protectionism, and support to exports can help a country to regain competitiveness — at least in the short-medium run — and balance the budget. Third, microeconomic policies can be used to make markets and firms more efficient, stimulate competition and trigger liberalisation, improve the efficiency and effectiveness of the public administration and the fiscal system, and gain public revenue from privatisation. All these policies can help to balance the public budget via additional revenue and decreased expenditures.

However, not all these policies can actually be freely used in a country that wants to be part of the integrated world economy. In particular, protectionism can hardly be used on a massive scale. The same is true for depreciation and the management of the interest rate. These limits become insurmountable in a monetary union. In this case, national depreciation is ruled out, because the currency is unique. The first group of monetary and fiscal policies can only be used in part. Having a common currency and a unique central bank, the countries in a monetary union delegate monetary policies to the common central bank. Therefore, monetary policies can only be used to fix symmetric shocks and are unavailable to fine tuning intercountry differences. At the same time, national fiscal policies must be disciplined and coordinated in a monetary union, in order to avoid jeopardising the common currency and the area fiscal and economic stability. If member countries in a monetary union do not trust each other and unless they set up a common government of the economy capable of distributing assets among countries, the discipline must hold strictly in the short run. Discipline could be enforced in a longer time only if trust is strong, the countries and their citizens share a solid and shared view of their common future, mutual commitment is credible, and some kind of effective third party or peer enforcement is available.

Within the Eurozone, policy choice is strictly limited. While monetary policy belongs in the competence of the ECB, the SGP, the European Commission and the peer control of the Council strictly constrain national fiscal policies. At the same time, short-term common fiscal policies are inexistent. The only room for supporting countries in financial distress lies in the flexibility hosted in European treaties, particularly the SGP, and the interpretation that the Council and the Commission give of the situation of a particular country through the periodical evaluation of the financial situation of member countries. The third type of policies, microeconomic policies and including reforms, is fully available to national governments in a monetary union. These are indeed the core of national policymaking for regaining competitiveness by decreasing domestic prices. When the exchange rate cannot be managed by national governments and foreign prices cannot be influenced, e.g. through discriminatory customs duties, competitiveness can be improved by reducing domestic costs and prices and quality improvement. There are various ways of decreasing prices, including diminishing taxes, cutting wages, improving productivity, and reducing transaction costs. All these actions need reforms.

The problem is that member countries in a monetary union have to keep balanced budgets. In unbalanced economies and in the short run, this typically means implementing austerity policies. This opens a conflict between short-run stabilisation and medium- to long-run improvement of growth and competitiveness, i.e. through investments. Improving competitiveness in a monetary union can hardly be obtained in the short run, since the lack of depreciation and protectionism as policy instruments leave only time-consuming reforms as an option. This leads governments to use internal devaluation instead, or investment. Unfortunately, resources for investments are among the victims of austerity. A further problem is that internal devaluation nearly inevitably meets social and technical opposition, resistance and obstacles, which contribute to postponing its effect in time.

The essence of internal devaluation is that a country implementing macroeconomic stabilisation has two main options: raise taxes and decrease public expenditure. First, a government could raise taxes in order to increase public revenue. It is important that the tax increase affects activities with low effect on domestic demand and income, such as imported goods, rents and short-term financial activities. Increasing taxation of immobile activities (real estate) also offers a possibility, but may have negative consequences for the building industry and contribute to push the country towards deflation, due to the usually great importance of this industry in national income. Other forms of tax increase (particularly on mobile resources, such as labour and capital) have dubious or plainly negative aggregate consequences, including higher production costs, inflation, lower demand, weaker incentives, and flight of resources. Fighting tax evasion and more in general the underground economy offer better and more effective alternative sources of additional revenue for the state. Tax evasion is particularly impressive in vulnerable countries such as Italy, Spain, Portugal, and Greece (Barbone *et al.* 2013; Schneider and Buehn 2009). Fighting it and recovering substantial revenue for the public budget require political will and technical ability, which may entail reforms and upgrading the public administration and the fiscal system.

Another important source of public revenue is privatisation of state assets. However, privatisation glut needs to be avoided to keep up values of the assets to be privatised and competition should be a major concern of privatisation policies (Dallago 1994, 1999). Moreover, privatisation simply converts a future flow of revenue from the use of the public asset into a lump-sum from its sale. This means that today's public budget improves to the disadvantage of future budgets. The only net social gain comes from increased efficiency in the use of the privatised asset, which usually comes from greater competition.

Decreasing public expenditure, possibly through careful spending reviews, offers a second option for pursuing financial stabilisation. A necessary condition is that the decrease hits activities having low effect on the demand of domestic production, such as expenses on imported goods or public subsidies to rent-seeking or powerful pressure groups. By decreasing public expenditure, an additional positive effect may be curbing inflation and interest rates, thus fostering competitiveness. However, this type of policy is likely to have negative effects on domestic demand and increase unemployment.

A third option would be to decrease taxes on incomes and the tax wedge on labour, thus decreasing wage costs and improving price competitiveness of production. Other measures with a similar goal, but dubious stabilising consequences, include decreasing pension rights (either by diminishing replacement rates or postponing retirement age) and weakening welfare support without diminishing the employees' contribution to their financing. Negative effects include depression of demand and social tensions. A further effect is substitution of private demand: since employees have to use resources to finance pension plans and buy welfare services, they may have to reduce other types of consumption. The effect on labour incentives is probably negative, unless the policy is linked to a general and socially shared plan of national revival and intergenerational fairness. The weakening of the welfare system without reforming it would cause serious long-term social problems, including decreasing social mobility and worsening health of much of the population. However, as stressed in supply-side economics, decreasing the tax wedge could reinforce the incentive to enterprising and supplying labour.

National governments in the Eurozone can use the three aforementioned types of policies. There is a fourth instrument, namely inflationary policies. Inflation is a classical option for devaluating debts against national income, thus contributing to solving problems of public finances. In a common currency area, inflation in one country causes its real exchange rate to appreciate and is not sustainable. Inflation only works if it involves the entire currency area, leading to the depreciation of the overall debt and the weakening of the exchange rate of the common currency.

However, inflation in the Eurozone would conflict with the ECB mandate and the political commitment of various countries, particularly Germany, to price stability.

A fifth possibility for a country would be to leave the currency to regain full control over policies (Eichengreen 2007). This would allow the country to gain competitiveness through depreciation. It is not clear whether a member country of the Eurozone could exit the common currency, since the treaties are unclear and contradictory on this issue.[146] However, even if politically possible, this situation would be economically doubtful and very risky (Deo *et al.* 2011; UBS 2012). Public debts of the Eurozone countries are denominated in euros and would either remain so, at least in the case of foreign owners of the debt and depending on the legal system governing these debts, or would lead to expropriation of value of investors, if debt is converted in the new national currency. The latter, in fact, would be extremely weak against the euro in the case of vulnerable countries. Thus, the value of debts expressed in euros would increase strongly in real terms compared to GDP, which would be

[146] The presumed irreversibility of the adoption of the euro is still somehow subject to uncertainty, as the debate of Grexit clarified. Article 50(1) of the Lisbon Treaty stipulates that any member country may withdraw from the Union ("Any Member State may decide to withdraw from the Union in accordance with its own constitutional requirements."). Much more complex is the event of an exit from the euro. No explicit provision exists for this case. Moreover, references are contradictory. The Maastricht Treaty, in a protocol on transition to the third stage of Economic and Monetary Union, states "the irreversible character of the Community's movement to the third stage of Economic and Monetary Union", namely, the adoption of the euro. However, two further protocols annexed to the Maastricht Treaty grant the United Kingdom and Denmark the legal right not to move to the third stage of EMU. Article 140(3) of the Lisbon Treaty stipulates that the Council shall "irrevocably fix the rate at which the euro shall be substituted for the currency of the Member State concerned, and take the other measures necessary for the introduction of the euro as the single currency in the Member State concerned." However, this statement hardly is an impediment to a country exiting from the common currency. All in all, according to a study for the British House of Commons discussing the possibility for Greece to leave the euro (Miller 2012), "There appears to be a majority opinion that if Greece wanted to leave the Euro it would have to leave the EU first", according to Article 50(1) of the Lisbon Treaty. Even less clear is the case — and the mere possibility — of the expulsion of a country from the Eurozone.

devalued accordingly. Moreover, the financial reputation of the country abandoning the euro would be shaken and financing public debt and investment would become even harder, because of higher interest rates and credit rationing. This option entails true default, including freezing, rescheduling or consolidating the public debt.

An interesting alternative option foresees the split of the euro into two euros, one adopted by resilient countries and the other one being used by vulnerable countries, to the presumed advantage of both groups (Steinherr 2013).

8.3 Policies in the Eurozone: A Few SWOT Hints

The fact that Eurozone member countries have limited sovereignty in fiscal policies and the Eurozone is nearly sovereign in monetary policies creates policy void. In this policy architecture, the Eurozone stability in front of symmetric shocks can be dealt with through the common monetary policy, and through the common control of national fiscal situations and related policies. No policy really exists to fix the distress of vulnerable countries.

This void can be filled in two ways: balanced finances and convergent real economies. With balanced finances and convergent real economies, the internal effects of asymmetric shocks are avoided and common monetary and coordinated fiscal policies are effective and fit the needs of all countries. Unfortunately, this is a hypothetical situation that does not exist even within small countries. While a sovereign country can fix the problems through the national government and its policies, the Eurozone cannot.

Policymaking under the Eurozone conditions is particularly problematic. A draft SWOT analysis[147] can help clarifying the fundamental aspects of the issue. Major policy strengths include the clarity of objectives and the

[147] SWOT analysis is a structured analytic tool that identifies and evaluates the strengths, weaknesses, opportunities and threats involved in a project, a product, a business venture, a place, an industry, an organisation, a region or a country, a situation. The analysis usually requires the specification of the objective(s) pursued and the identification of the internal and external factors that may support or hinder the achievement of that objective.

predictable conduct of both common and national policymaking. This may have positive effects for the stabilisation of expectations, the fiscal discipline that is imposed upon member countries and their governments, the continuous monitoring of the economic situation of member countries by a specialised and neutral third party endowed with (mild) enforcement power (the European Commission, the peers), and the publicity given to the outcome of the monitoring.

Yet the situation also presents major weaknesses. These include the short-term perspective, the rigidity and the spillovers of macroeconomic policies — both monetary policies and the constraints over fiscal policies — which are tailored to a much larger area. Policies are consequently unable to deal properly with the asymmetric effect of economic events and to take into consideration the different features and needs of the economies and societies of member states. An implicit consequence of this setup of policies, one that is not openly wanted but nevertheless real, is that the attention to short-run economic fundamentals leads policies to concentrate on the short run to the disadvantage of growth and development.

Moreover, uncoordinated national policies of fiscal consolidation or expansion have effects for the other countries in a union, while benefits are not shared according to the policy effort. This may open important moral hazard effects in policymaking. For instance, fiscal consolidation in one member country improves the fiscal situation in only this country, but causes a contraction of the domestic economic activity which spills over to other countries in the form of reduced demand for imports. Other countries thus afford costs without sharing the benefit. This may induce countries to apply too much consolidation and, conversely, too little fiscal stimulus. In fact, in this latter case the costs of the stimulus are financed by one country, but other countries enjoy part of the gains through increased exports.

Common policies are incomplete in the fundamental sense that they do not include fiscal policies. Common fiscal affairs are limited to few, simplified and rigid rules included in the SGP. This very fact imposes limits upon national fiscal policies, with the consequence that these must be used in vulnerable countries to pursue a quasi-objective: a balanced budget. This goes inevitably to the detriment of the true objective of fiscal policies: full employment, macroeconomic equilibrium and growth. Unfortunately, common monetary policies also have problems. Indeed, the mandate of the European Central Bank (ECB) is incomplete and limited to price stability, although lately this mandate became broader through a pragmatic evolution (ECB 2015b).[148] True, the ECB can also take into consideration the general economic policies in the Union, but this can only do "without prejudice to the objective of price stability" (Article 127 of the Treaty on the Functioning of the European Union). In a time of interest rates approaching the zero bound and high risk of deflation, a central bank can no longer reduce the interest rate to encourage economic growth and the effectiveness of monetary policy is reduced as a macroeconomic tool (Bernanke *et al.* 2004; Cœuré 2015; Eggertsson and Woodford 2003; Gerlach and Lewis 2010; Yates 2002).

This limited mandate has negative effects, particularly for vulnerable countries. These, under the effect of their own demerit or their bad luck with external circumstances, are left without policy support to their revival. The lack of solidarity and a degree of opportunism by resilient countries make the situation even more difficult for vulnerable countries. Resilient countries have both advantages in adopting this stance: they may get advantages through additional market shares and capital inflow and they attempt to avoid the vulnerable countries' moral hazard. In a sense, as the previous chapter showed, policies in the Eurozone are based on implicit discrimination.

Policies in the Eurozone offer various opportunities for improvement. The most important opportunity for member countries lies in the strong incentive to implement internal reforms, which promise to make their economies more resilient and competitive. Indeed, given the common monetary policies and the limited domain for national fiscal policies, microeconomic and social reforms are the most important instrument at national level. Unfortunately, implementing reforms amidst short-term

[148] As mentioned in Section 7.9, the ECB's Governing Council announced that "Price stability is defined as a year-on-year increase in the Harmonised Index of Consumer Prices (HICP) for the euro area of below 2%." The rationale for this definition is that "Inflation rates of below, but close to, 2% are low enough for the economy to fully reap the benefits of price stability." Moreover, "the definition makes clear that not only inflation above 2% but also deflation (i.e. price level declines) is inconsistent with price stability."

and rigid austerity is all the more difficult. Austerity and reforms are preconditions for the vulnerable member countries to receive common support. Unfortunately, such support comes generally *ex post*, after the country paid a price that can weaken its economic and social fabric for years to come and jeopardise its political stability. On the plus side, going through a serious stabilisation and reform process offers the country the opportunity to strengthen its reputation and build stronger trust in other member countries.

Opportunities for improvement and completion also concern common institutions. Indeed, the crisis made the perils of the present situation clear. The limited sovereignty of member countries in fiscal policies should be complemented in some way at common level. For instance, there should be a larger common budget or some mutualisation of national debt. The common monetary policy should include lending of last resort in some way. The alternative, with the present institutional architecture of the Eurozone unchanged, would be the different national economies departing further away.

Unfortunately, the existing situation presents serious threats, which can have long-term negative consequences. The most serious and permanent threats come from the decrease of investments, the lack of growth and economic decline. In the short and medium term, unemployment represents a serious threat to standards of living and social cohesion, let alone political stability. There is a serious menace of growing populist movements and the diffusion of anti-European sentiments around the Eurozone and mounting militant social and political opposition.

The complexity of the situation requires careful examination of policies and policy options. Weaknesses and threats are serious and sizeable. Yet strengths are not negligible and opportunities are important. Clearly, the outcome of the present deadlock depends upon careful policymaking, but also upon the common determination to undertake bold and forward-looking steps.

8.4 Framing Policies

Policies should be placed in the frame of the factors that inspire, influence, constraint and support them (Keeney 2004). Frames define what is desirable and what is possible in policymaking. Frames also give reason of the probability of making mistakes, because of the influence of wrong or biased theories, powerful interests, incomplete recognition of the existing situation, and insufficient knowledge of the effectiveness and effects of policies.

Policy framing is a concept used in social sciences and public policy to analyse and explain the process by which actors, including policymakers, try to understand complex situations, take and implement decisions, and act. Framing is important, because different actors and decision makers may have different understanding and perceptions of the same situation. Framing includes devices that help to reduce the complexity and uncertainty that derive in such circumstances and to assign roles to different actors. In doing so, framing also allocates decision making power and the outcomes of decisions and actions.

The fundamental components of the frame are the prevailing policy theories, external context, structural features of the economy, existing institutions, and long-term internal and external processes. In the case of Eurozone policies, one should consider also the sharing of competences among national and common governments, and the interaction among the member countries. These factors, taken together, define which policies can be used, their effectiveness, and their consequences. Among the latter, the effect of common policies on the member states and their regions is particularly important for both the economic strength of the Eurozone and for its economic and political viability and stability. Since some of these factors were already treated in previous chapters, this chapter concentrates on the salient features of those factors that were not considered so far.

Standard economic theory presumes that economic actors have well-defined and independent preferences. However, behavioural psychology and behavioural economics have demonstrated that economic decision making and behaviour may be under the influence of systematic misperceptions (Kahneman and Tversky 1984, 2000; Kahneman *et al.* 1982; Tversky and Kahneman 1981). Such decision making and behaviour do not correspond to the standard principles of rationality, yet they may be predictable, since biases are consistent and systematic. Framing influences our perceptions, judgment and consequently decisions and behaviour. Individual or group components of the society can manipulate frames in order to pursue personal or group interests. Such manipulation of frames influences perceptions and thus decision making and behaviour, in a way that can be self-enforcing.

Another limitation of standard economic theories is that they consider the case of individual actors making choices repeatedly, as is typically the case in markets. However, many individual decisions are discrete — such as buying a durable good or taking decisions on savings for pensions. It is evident that, in the case of the Eurozone, the choice of policy rules and decisions are discrete and valid for the long term. Such rules constitute important frames, together with their prevailing interpretation. Rules are chosen typically after long and detailed bargaining and interaction among governments and remain in force for long periods of time. Frames of Eurozone policies also include the enforcement of policies, with limited room to manoeuver.

Framing may be defined as a social construction concerning thought and communication and with influence on actions. Thought frames consist of the simplified mental representations and interpretations of reality. Both thought and communication frames exercise a selective influence over perceptions that economic and political actors have of the meanings attributed to words, phrases, or situations. Through this, they influence decision making and activities.

In the case of the Eurozone, framing is made of concepts and theoretical perspectives on how common European organs, national governments, societies, individuals, and groups perceive, adapt, organise, and communicate about the process of European integration, the nature and the role of the common currency, and the relation among member countries. This construction is in part shaped by technical factors — in particular the prevailing "official" economic and political theories that have guided European integration and the implementation of the euro. However, framing is defined also by the effects of European history, political will, social support for integration, and intercountry relations of cooperation and trust or distrust.

Communication frames consist of the transmission of frames among different actors. Information that underlies thought and communication frames is under the influence of "confirmatory bias" (Rabin and Schrag 1999), leading to "equilibrium fictions" (Hoff and Stiglitz 2010). According to the confirmatory bias, individuals tend to better remember information that is consistent with their prior beliefs. In turn, beliefs are influenced by such factors as the organisation of society, technology, power relations and wealth. Information is consequently seen as relevant and reinforces the original beliefs. Inconsistent information is more likely to be ignored or forgotten. Confirmatory biases can generate equilibrium fictions, i.e. a strong and persistent set of beliefs which is consistent with the information and the evidence submitted to the confirmatory bias.

Eurozone policies offer strong evidence of the importance of frames and of confirmatory bias and equilibrium fictions, as shown in the next sections. Eurozone frames ("Euroframes") are primarily based on the European treaties and the SGP. Such frames encourage particular interpretations of the economic situation (the absolute priority of balanced public finances) and discourage other interpretations (the consequences for growth and employment), often well beyond economic rationality. Indeed, Eurozone information and communication are typically centred on the state of public finances and their equilibrium is presented as an absolutely necessary precondition for the prosperity of the Eurozone and for other objectives.

By framing policies, the Eurozone is effectively able to make member countries and common organs understand and act on complex and ill-defined situations. One important reason why situations are complex and ill-defined is the existence of potential opportunism and moral hazard by member countries. By contextualizing information in the fundamental Eurozone institutions and practices, Euroframes are important because they reduce the ambiguity of inter-European issues, give stability to the European construction, and make behaviour of European organs and national governments more predictable. As a consequence, uncertainty is decreased, and decision making may be simpler, less cumbersome and cheaper. Yet frames and equilibrium fictions in the Eurozone also explain the rigidity and the ineffectiveness of the EU approach. In spite of some flexibility built in the treaties and pacts, the EU approach is slow in reacting to external events and separates discipline, which has priority, from the consideration of support. This is so independently from the causes of the problems and the general economic conditions. An important effect is shortening of time horizon in adjustment processes and disregard for growth.

Thus, it is important to understand whether Eurozone analyses and policies are under the negative influence of systematic misperception and misjudgment due to framing, or whether there are alternative frames competing with formal ones. To understand this, it is necessary to keep into consideration the Eurozone features, as recalled in the previous chapters. It is also necessary to consider the broader context and long-term trends of the world economy and the Eurozone policy framework. This is done in the two following sections.

8.5 Policy Theories and Practices

Some of the important factors framing policies are external to the Eurozone. The most important of such factors are the prevailing economic and policy theories and practices; the international context, in particular the features and effects of globalisation, the financialisation of the economy and the enduring consequences of the international crisis; the general concept of European integration in relation to national preferences and priorities; and the consequences for institutional evolution and policy competence and decision-making, including the sharing of competences among national and common governments.

The economic and policy theories that prevailed during the first critical phase of the Eurozone crisis included the revised Washington Consensus and German orthodoxy in monetary policy. The latter characterised the construction of the euro and the common institutions and monetary policies, and also the subordination of fiscal policies to monetary policies. These theories and related policies prevailed until 2012, when the growing difficulties they caused became evident at both the international and European level. Since then, important changes were introduced, but so far this generated more coherent repositioning only at international level. Eurozone theories are still muddling through.

The revised Washington Consensus (RWC) was the dominant theoretical and policy basis of the activity of international organisations, particularly the International Monetary Fund (IMF), the World Bank and the US government.[149] The revision of the Consensus came out of

[149] On the original definition of the Washington Consensus that reflected originally the experience of stabilisation policies in Latin America, see Williamson (1990, 1993). Later

the Consensus failure, principally when applied to the transformation countries in Central and Eastern Europe. The revision tried, among other things, to better incorporate the institutional architecture of the relevant country into the theory and policies. It also provided better attention to the failure of markets in promoting development and to distributive consequences. In any case, the revision failed to consider the mounting tensions in the world economy and devise policies that could contribute to keep those tensions at bay, let alone solve them. Indeed, there are many reasons to believe that RWC policies contributed to further strengthen those tensions. This they did by further pushing the financialisation of the world economy and by giving priority to macroeconomic stabilisation over growth and employment. Another consequence of those policies was that inequalities increased significantly in most countries. The growing mass of financial means was thus meeting stagnant purchasing power.

The RWC failed to really grasp the deep and far reaching origins of the Eurozone institutional and policy incompleteness and national policy impotence. The priority given to macroeconomic stability and stabilisation, however theoretically sound in their meaning and practice, failed to consider that vulnerable Eurozone countries in critical real and financial situations were bound to see their situation worsen as a consequence of those policies within the given institutional architecture.

Internally to the Eurozone, the dominant theories and views were those typical of the German monetary orthodoxy as derived from ordoliberalism.[150] Ordoliberalism was developed at the Freiburg School by such economists as Walter Eucken and Franz Böhm, particularly in the 1930s

---

writings by John Williamson recognised some of the criticism received and the necessity to move to a better, revised Washington Consensus. However, he rebated that many of his critics misinterpreted his analysis and message, as much as international organisations and governments following his advice did (see Williamson 2000, 2004b). On the revised Washington Consensus, see the special issue edited by Gnos and Rochon (2004), and Stiglitz (1998, 2004). For a comparison of the two versions of the Consensus, see Marangos (2012).

[150] An important ordoliberal analysis of European monetary unification is Sinn (2014). Sinn maintains that the ECB has been too accommodating and that bailouts have created dangerous moral hazards. On ordoliberalism and related policies, their origin, content and

and 1940s. Ordoliberalism was the leading economic and social thought at the basis of the social market economy established in Germany after World War II.

Equally important were German policy preferences, as influenced by the German historical experience with hyperinflation and its social and political consequences. When the project of the euro started to take form, Germans were prudent and lacked enthusiasm. They understandably feared the loss of control over a sound national currency. The German mark had a strong reputation as sound and well-managed currency and German monetary authorities had a strong reputation for prudence and soundness. The new currency looked ill-defined to them, since it was shared with countries that were not considered as good examples of monetary stability and soundness.

In order to overcome the German lack of enthusiasm and considering that without Germany monetary unification had no meaning, it was agreed that the common monetary institutions and policies would follow the German model and practice. It was also agreed that the governance of the ECB would reflect this engagement, while recognizing a *de facto* veto power to Germany over the appointment of the ECB president.

It is important to clarify that the German position goes well beyond the political and psychological effects of the experience with hyperinflation. After all, German hyperinflation in 1921–1924 was in large part the deliberate effect of the German monetary policies aimed at avoiding the burden of war reparations.[151] However, this traumatic experience and the German historical and philosophical traditions were the basis upon which the ordoliberal view and theory of the modern economy and policymaking developed in the late 1920s. This approach reached maturation with the *Soziale Marktwirtschaft* (social market economy), that led post-war reconstruction and the German economic miracle.

approach to the crisis, see Bonefeld (2011, 2012, 2013), Dullien and Guerot (2012), Ptak (2009), Sally (1996), Schnyder and Siems (2013), and Young (2014).

[151] The total reparations imposed upon Germany at Versailles amounted to 132 billion gold marks, to be paid in hard currency. One way Germany used to soften the massive economic burden of reparations was to print banknotes on a massive scale, which were then used to buy the foreign currency needed to pay reparations. See Ferguson (1999). See also Keynes (1920).

Ordoliberalism can be considered a variant of neoliberalism in which, in contrast with laissez-faire liberalism, the conditions for a free market economy are guaranteed by the authority and action by a strong state. Ordoliberalism depicts a form of state-centric liberalism, in which the strong state is the political form of free markets, and competition and enterprising are political tasks. Economic freedom is a fundamental tenet of ordoliberalism, but economic freedom is ordered freedom. Along with law and order, among the necessary conditions are also social policies. These aim at including and captivating workers and making them participate in the economy also as depositors of property rights, both as private owners and through co-determination. This aim is addressed also to avoid the radicalisation of trade unions and workers' political movements (Bonefeld 2012, 2013; Schnyder and Siems 2013).

This German idiosyncrasy is at the basis of the position that Germany consistently held and successfully imposed on European institutions during the crisis (Dullien and Guerot 2012; Young 2014). Unfortunately, this approach is at odds with much of the rest of the Eurozone, which has a different, albeit variegated institutional and consequently policy stance. It is from this deep institutional and political difference that comes much of the conflict on policies within the Eurozone. While many countries need more relaxed stabilisation policies, also attentive to growth, Germany sees the rule-based ordoliberal approach as a panacea for the Eurozone countries that have to regain competitiveness.[152]

Ordoliberal principles are at the basis of the construction of the ECB and its policy stance in support to austerity and price stability, the centrepiece of the Eurozone policies, at the expense of economic growth (Blyth 2013). This construction held at least until the ECB under the presidency of Mario Draghi prudently and progressively changed position, under the pressure of mounting problems. Acting as the only really common

[152] "Through its dominance of the euro system, Germany is exporting ordoliberal ideology to the rest of the single currency bloc. It is hard to think of a doctrine that is more ill suited to a monetary union with such diverse legal traditions, political system and economic conditions than this one. And it is equally hard to see Germany ever giving up on this. As a result the economic costs of crisis resolution will be extremely large" (Münchau 2014). However, there may be an interesting albeit prudent change of the position of the German government going on, following the agreement over Greece in summer 2015.

institution, the ECB endeavored to pursue monetary policies which could be effective also for countries with non-ordoliberal institutional settings. Although the German policy position slowly evolved, as a consequence of the failure of the policies it imposed on the Eurozone, the way towards sustainable and effective policies is still a long one.

An interesting qualification of this framework leads back to German unification, and in particular to two aspects of the process. First, in spite of the spread of suspicion and fears of a future of German economic dominance and political hegemony over Europe, European countries accepted German unification. Second, European countries accepted *de facto* to co-finance German unification through higher interest rates and capital export to Germany. Both aspects revealed a strong manifestation of European confidence in the new unified Germany and politically and morally pushed Germany to accept the common currency.

These events are important in the present situation and for understanding the evolution of monetary integration. Germany was not an active promoter of the grand project of monetary integration, because it had not much to gain but had much to lose. The rational deal was therefore a simple one: Germany accepted being part of monetary unification, but it pretended that this would take place on the basis of German rules and practices. The other countries accepted the deal, since their common currency stood to gain from the German reputation and sound management, at the cost of giving up traditional soft monetary policies and the implementation of some reforms.

What was not clear was that the solution required the other countries to adopt German-type institutions. Hidden in this deal were two further dangers, whose effects became evident as soon as the international crisis put the common currency under stress. First, the new currency required consistent conduct by all countries. Apart from credible and consistent political engagement, this was difficult, since countries had so far followed different and even divergent monetary and fiscal policies. Some countries (first among these was Germany, with the transitory exception of the post-unification years) pursued monetary rigor and fiscal restraint with balanced public budgets, also thanks to low tax evasion. At the same time, other countries (such as Italy since the 1970s) made rather extensive use of depreciation policies to regain competitiveness and had unbalanced public budgets and high public debts, also because of high tax evasion.

Attempts at strengthening monetary and fiscal discipline in the late 1980s and early 1990s were unsuccessful in changing the conduct of policies and the behaviour of enterprises. The inability of some countries to maintain policy rigour led to the 1992 monetary crisis of the Italian lira and the British pound. Following this period of instability, the Maastricht criteria were enforced since 1993 to obligate countries to adopt monetary and fiscal conduct compatible with the common currency. These criteria were the basis for the final "examination" of the countries that intended to be part of the common currency. This took place in 1998 and was based on the 1997 macroeconomic implementation in each country.

The process was reasonable, yet it harboured a politically motivated contradiction: while the objective (the common currency) was a long-term and apparently irreversible one, the time over which the assessment for membership was taken was a short-term one. Thus the critical question that remained unanswered for some time was: to what extent did the short-term conduct reflect the long-term expected behaviour of member countries after they joined the common currency? Were all member countries credible in their commitment, or did they (or some of them) enter the process with hidden reservations? Was such commitment realistic, given the national economic and social features and situation? Could they renounce the commitment under internal economic, social and political pressures?

Some countries (Italy and Belgium in particular) did not fully respect the Maastricht criteria in the case of the ratio of public debt to GDP. Yet in 1996 and 1997, they implemented tremendous fiscal efforts and respected the other fundamental Maastricht criterion that is public deficit over GDP. Moreover, both countries were founding members of the European Coal and Steel Community in 1952 and the Treaty of Rome in 1957. It was politically difficult to keep them out of the common currency. As a consequence, the agreement included the clause that even if a country did not fully meet the Maastricht criteria it could still join the common currency, provided that the country showed clear signs of convergence to the criteria.

However politically sound this approach was, it clearly harboured uncertainty about future contingencies. What would happen if a country does not comply with commitments and obligations? What would happen in the instance where a country was unable to comply with the required conduct? In time, the SGP was implemented to deal with this danger. This eventuality is at the basis of the second danger behind the agreements for introducing the common currency: these agreements disregarded differences in economic structures of member countries.

Different policies that European countries adopted before joining the euro reflected in part political preferences. To a large degree, they reflected different economic structures. In particular, countries that used repeatedly depreciation to regain competitiveness were countries specialised in goods and services with high demand elasticity. Repeated depreciation pushed those countries to further deepen their specialisation. Countries with sound currencies were specialised in producing goods and services with inelastic demands, either because of fast technical progress or the high quality of production. In a prospective monetary union, the first group of countries should have pursued wage moderation in the short run to keep costs under control, free resources for investment, and attract capital for investment from resilient countries. Since these policies were socially and politically difficult, a solution was found in growing public debts.

The effect of different economic structures in an incomplete monetary union was disregarded for years, while tensions accumulated. The need to finance growing public debts offered high remuneration, low-risk opportunities to savers and capitalists. However, these resources were subtracted from the productive economy, since public expenditure went often to finance higher incomes and unproductive expenditures. An important reason was that there was social and political pressure in vulnerable countries to make incomes convergent with those of resilient countries. As a consequence, vulnerable countries were under multiple negative pressures: high labour costs, high interest rates, high taxes to finance growing deficits and public debts.

Why did this accumulation of tensions not lead to a structural crisis of the Eurozone? There were two interconnected elements in this: the private insurance mechanism and the hidden Eurozone umbrella. Under the private insurance mechanism, private capital flowed from resilient countries to vulnerable countries, in search for higher remuneration. Unfortunately, much of the inflow of capital went to create real estate and financial bubbles. This situation was risky, given the European agreements and rules. Yet markets did not account for this danger: interest rates progressively converged and remained unified all over the Eurozone, until the international crisis inverted the trend. As a matter of fact, markets were under the conviction that a sort of Eurozone umbrella existed, one that would help countries in difficulties. Markets did not really believe in the effectiveness of the "no-bailout" clause.

8.6 Inspiring Principles and Implementation Mechanisms

The origin of monetary integration inspires and explains the underlying institutional architecture. The idea at the basis of monetary unification, an idea very much in line with ordoliberal principles, was that each national economic situation had to be fully compatible with the common currency. This had to be done through rules that each country had to comply with, such as those defined in the Maastricht criteria and SGP. When a national economy was out of line compared to the convergence criteria or was hit by a shock, it had to adjust through three microeconomic mechanisms involving the quantity of factors, wages and prices, and productivity (Buti and Sapir 1998).

The implementation of rules and the control over the effectiveness of adjustment mechanisms had to be under the control of a strong government. Defining the latter, though, was more complicated. The strong government was duly replaced by an incomplete government, the European Commission, with a detailed and strong mandate of controlling member countries' economic achievements in the short run. This incomplete government was complemented by the peers' governments, through the Council, in which the largest economy possessed an overwhelming role and power. The outcome was a burdensome government powerful enough in pushing the brake, but powerless and uninterested in using the gas when needed.

The present system of relying on national adjustment mechanisms is costly and difficult for economies in stress and may require substantial amount of time to bring effect. An alternative would be the establishment of a fiscal union. There are various arguments in favour of a fiscal union and others against it (Allard *et al.* 2013; Bordo *et al.* 2011; Enderlein *et al.* 2012; Mody 2015).

Arguments in favour of a fiscal union include better fiscal coordination and stronger fiscal discipline, which would help to avoid moral hazard effects in policymaking (see Section 8.3) and fiscal competition among member countries; greater effectiveness of a properly combined monetary-fiscal policy mix that would help contrasting the asymmetric effect of shocks; countervailing the power of an independent ECB; greater confidence in the viability of the union that fiscal integration fosters, thus helping to curb speculative attacks against vulnerable countries. Finally, the centralised management of fiscal issues and resources would move the compensation of the effects of the crisis from *ex post*, as it is presently the case, through the provision of subsidised financial support to countries under stress, to an *ex ante* system of risk sharing. This would have the advantage of reducing the time needed to implement crisis management policies and would decrease the cost for countries under stress in terms of foregone output, lost employment and outflow of resources. These advantages would decrease the likelihood of future crises or decrease the severity when a crisis occurs and would diminish the risk of systemic spillovers.

There are also important arguments against a fiscal union. The standard one is the need to contrast asymmetric shocks, which requires nationally diversified budgets, taxation and spending. A fiscal union would require stronger control on national budgets and the transfer of (part of) the fiscal responsibility to the union, with the consequent loss of stabilisation capacity at the country level. This would also imply loss of national sovereignty over the budget and fiscal policies, which would face significant obstacles in national governments. A second counter-argument is political and has to do with two issues: the fiscal policy system to be adopted and applied (in particular, whether it is an ordoliberal system or a Keynesian system) and who decides which to adopt. The latter is a major issue, given the present democratic deficit of the Union. There is also a third, legal question: existing EU treaties provide only a limited legal basis for a fiscal union. This would require significant legal reforms, which would also need the approval of non-Eurozone countries. An alternative would be to proceed through intergovernmental agreements outside the EU framework (the Fiscal Compact is an example of such an agreement). This solution would avoid the risk of inefficiency in the common management of finances and of failures in implementing fiscal discipline, but would be institutionally a weaker solution and would involve extensive and continuous negotiations. Finally, there may also be serious moral hazards in a fiscal union, where less disciplined countries may have an implicit incentive to rely on the common safety net and soften their fiscal discipline. This would transform the fiscal union into a transfer union, to the disadvantage of fiscally disciplined countries. These are also the countries which have the lowest real level of taxation compared to the amount of services they offer their citizens. There would be the risk that the level of taxation in a fiscal union moves to the higher real level of less disciplined countries. Clearly a well-working fiscal union must rely on transparent and accountable rules and management to be sustainable.

The danger hidden in the present construction was automatic cross-subsidisation via monetary or fiscal processes. Expansionary monetary policy, a large common budget financing countries in difficulty, or national budgets running high deficits, all meant that the financially disciplined and economically resilient countries would have financed the less disciplined and vulnerable ones. This is fine, indeed even fundamental in a politically unified country. But the EU was not, is not, and would not likely be for long time to come a unified country of any sort. Under these conditions, the only politically sustainable way to stay together is to remain economically and financially separate, but with separate budgets subject to the same rules, whose compliance was duly controlled though the same mechanisms.

The best way of achieving this goal was to leave common monetary and economic institutions incomplete, the common budget close to irrelevance, national economies and finances clearly separated, and national institutions under strict surveillance. The Lisbon treaty translated this view in three basic principles: (a) no-monetisation: Article 123(1) prohibits monetary financing;[153] (b) no-socialisation: Article 124 prohibits the

[153] "Overdraft facilities or any other type of credit facility with the European Central Bank or with the central banks of the Member States (hereinafter referred to as 'national central banks') in favour of Union institutions, bodies, offices or agencies, central governments, regional, local or other public authorities, other bodies governed by public law, or public undertakings of Member States shall be prohibited, as shall the purchase directly from them by the European Central Bank or national central banks of debt instruments."

privileged access to financial institutions;[154] (c) no-bailout: Article 125(1) makes illegal for common or national organs to assume the debts of another country.[155] Added to these fundamental principles of conduct, there are the fiscal provisions to avoid excessive government deficits (Article 126)[156] and the SGP.

The SGP was initially proposed by German finance minister Theo Waigel in the mid-1990s with the aim of ensuring fiscal responsibility by all member countries in the monetary unification process. The SGP has the nature of a secondary legislation based on Articles 121 and 126 of the Lisbon Treaty and is defined by a resolution[157] and two Council regulations taken in July 1997. The latter define respectively the so-called "preventive arm"[158] and "dissuasive arm"[159] of the pact. The pact itself is a set of rules designed to ensure that member countries coordinate their fiscal policies and pursue sound public finances. To guarantee compliance, the

---

[154] "Any measure, not based on prudential considerations, establishing privileged access by Union institutions, bodies, offices or agencies, central governments, regional, local or other public authorities, other bodies governed by public law, or public undertakings of Member States to financial institutions, shall be prohibited."

[155] "The Union shall not be liable for or assume the commitments of central governments, regional, local or other public authorities, other bodies governed by public law, or public undertakings of any Member State, without prejudice to mutual financial guarantees for the joint execution of a specific project. A Member State shall not be liable for or assume the commitments of central governments, regional, local or other public authorities, other bodies governed by public law, or public undertakings of another Member State, without prejudice to mutual financial guarantees for the joint execution of a specific project."

[156] "Member States shall avoid excessive government deficits" (Article 126(1)). The article continues by giving details on the monitoring system and on the procedures in case of non-compliance by countries.

[157] "Resolution of the European Council on the Stability and Growth Pact" taken in Amsterdam on 17 June 1997, http://eur-lex.europa.eu/LexUriServ/LexUriServ.do?uri=CELEX:31997Y0802(01):EN:HTML.

[158] Council Regulation (EC) No 1466/97 of 7 July 1997 on the strengthening of the surveillance of budgetary positions and the surveillance and coordination of economic policies, http://eur-lex.europa.eu/LexUriServ/LexUriServ.do?uri=CONSLEG:1997R1466:20111213:EN:PDF.

[159] Council Regulation (EC) No 1467/97 of 7 July 1997 on speeding up and clarifying the implementation of the excessive deficit procedure, http://eur-lex.europa.eu/LexUriServ/LexUriServ.do?uri=CONSLEG:1997R1467:20111213:EN:PDF.

pact foresees that the European Commission and the Council implement the fiscal monitoring of the member countries and issue yearly recommendations for policies to be followed in case of non-compliance. The two arms define respectively the actions to be followed for assessing the compliance by member countries and the procedures to be implemented in case of excessive deficit.

The provisions of the SGP were further strengthened by means of the so-called "fiscal compact". The fiscal compact is part of the Treaty on Stability, Coordination and Governance in the Economic and Monetary Union (TSCG) signed in Brussels on 2 March 2012. This treaty makes the SGP more stringent. It oversees the implementation of a balanced budget rule at the national level, which various countries put in their constitutions, and a further strengthening of the excessive deficit procedure.

This is ordoliberalism at the European level, with strict rules and strong control over member countries replacing the strong government. This is apparently strictly binding over national governments, and this is the (com)pact's strength. Yet its weakness is as great: strict rules and strong control mean little without a credible third party to enforce them. This third party could only be a common, sovereign government, which is ruled out. Indeed, strict rules and strong control are justified by the refusal of a common government. The construction is based on the presumption of pure altruism and good will or at least direct interest by each member country and the great value of national reputation in the respect of the rules. However, this opens potentially the door to national opportunism and may find an unstable solution in the prevalence of a country — the *de facto* enforcer — over the others.

Much depends upon the effectiveness of control and the credibility of punishment for non-compliers. The fiscal compact oversees that member countries limit their structural deficit[160] to 0.5% of GDP. In case of non-compliance, the country is subject to a set of sanctions in the preventive

[160] Following the harsh effects of the crisis on public budgets of member countries, the EU adopted a fiscal framework computing first the cyclical component of the budget and then subtracting it from the actual budget balance. The cyclically-adjusted budget balance (CAB) corresponds to the deficit/surplus-to-GDP ratio that would prevail if the economy was running at potential (Mourre *et al.* 2014).

and corrective arms of the SGP which increase with the successive stages of non-compliance up to a fine of up to 0.2% of the country's GDP (Angerer 2015).[161] This is certainly not a particularly strong economic deterrent. However, more important may be its political meaning and the rule that the European Stability Mechanism (ESM) can provide support only to countries that ratify the fiscal compact and follow its provisions.[162]

The fiscal compact is not binding from a legal perspective either. In fact, it is an ordinary international treaty implying that the contracting countries accept binding constraints to constitutional matters, such as their national budget. However, these are as a rule of higher legal order than international treaties. For this reason, member countries were suggested to include the fiscal compact in their constitutions, as some

---

[161] Sanctions have the following intensification: a) in case of failure to adjust towards the medium-term objective (MTO) for the budgetary position or expenditure rule not respected (preventive arm), there is an interest-bearing deposit of 0.2% of GDP; b) opening of the excessive deficit procedure (EDP) (if the country was already sanctioned under the preventive arm or if the breach of the threshold was particularly serious) the sanction is a non-interest-bearing deposit of 0.2% of GDP; c) when a country fails to take effective action to correct the excessive deficit, the fine amounts to the 0.2% of GDP; d) after repeated failure to take effective action to correct the excessive deficit, there are a fine of 0.2% of GDP and a variable component. In the first three cases, the Commission proposes the sanction which is approved unless opposed by a qualified majority in the Council. The last sanction is decided on the basis of normal qualified majority voting. In this case, there may also be a so-called macro-economic conditionality (in force since end 2013 for all EU countries) which entails the possible suspension of up to five European structural and investment funds.

[162] "STRESSING the importance of the Treaty establishing the European Stability Mechanism as an element of the global strategy to strengthen the economic and monetary union and POINTING OUT that the granting of financial assistance in the framework of new programmes under the European Stability Mechanism will be conditional, as of 1 March 2013, on the ratification of this Treaty by the Contracting Party concerned and, as soon as the transposition period referred to in Article 3(2) of this Treaty has expired, on compliance with the requirements of that Article". The European Stability Mechanism (ESM) was established at the European Council meeting in December 2010, and implemented since 8 October 2012, as a permanent mechanism for crisis resolution in the Eurozone. The ESM issues debt instruments in order to finance loans and other forms of financial assistance to the Eurozone countries.

did.[163] This solution was considered as a device useful to the German government to justify politically the approval to rescue operations in front of a domestic constituency, who is anyway not contrary in its majority to such operations (Gros 2012). However, various countries prefer to rely on normal laws. Most countries have created the legal basis for setting up independent fiscal councils, but only few have appointed the members (Burret and Schnellenbach 2013).

The main difficulty with the fiscal compact is that there is no precise and irrefutable method to calculate structural deficits. Moreover, there is no precise way to adjust fiscal imbalances, since this involves different aspects of economies, societies and polities, including demand and supply elasticities and the output gap. The fiscal compact is also difficult to enforce. There are different reasons for weak enforcement. One is certainly the difficulty for countries in economic stress to continue with austerity measures, which would further reduce their output and increase their debt/GDP ratio. Another reason is that governments and international organisations tend to use over-optimistic official forecasts. Frankel and Schreger (2013) find that in the Eurozone this is true particularly for countries whose budget deficit is above the 3% of GDP level when forecasts are made. These considerations led some to observe that the fiscal compact is becoming ineffective (Frankel 2013; Gros and Alcidi 2014), which seems to be a fair conclusion.

8.7 The General Concept of European Integration

This institutional architecture of the Eurozone created a monetary system formally in line with the re-contextualisation of ordoliberal principles in a multi-country union, whereby tough rules, monitoring and enforcement replace the strong state. Yet this system is hardly effective and sustainable, in view of large intercountry differences and the consequences of the crisis. It is consequently costly and counterproductive in its economic effects.

Although one could read a punishing attitude in all this by resilient countries adverse to vulnerable countries, this explanation is unconvincing.

[163] Only Italy, Slovenia, and Spain provided for the introduction of the SGP provisions in their constitution.

Some media statements and attitudes apart (see also the Geithner files, footnote 3 in Chapter 11), there is no room as a rule for such attitudes in policymaking or official decisions and documents. The strong and deep integration of European economies, the success of monetary unification and the evident benefits for all countries involved up to the crisis are sufficient elements to reject an explanation based on conspiracy. Something deeper and more permanent is at play. The problem lies in the institutional, architecture of monetary unification, an architecture that was set up to guarantee Germany against the potential destabilising consequences of less balanced economies and softer policies, which vulnerable countries were supposedly used to and that allowed Germany and other resilient countries to transfer their monetary and financial reputation to vulnerable countries.

It is the very history and essence of Europe that make economic, monetary and financial integration absolutely important and desirable. Yet it is the same history and essence of Europe that make such integration difficult, when it goes beyond the rather loose frame of a common market. Full political integration establishing a unique government of the economy goes to the very heart of nation building, for which each European country fought hard for centuries. Behind political unification, there is typically a common culture, language, and history. These factors tend to divide Europe, not unify it. Why should economic and political rationality and will through formal institutions overcome simply and rapidly what centuries of history and deeply settled informal institutions have built up? The real question is therefore how to find a way forward under the existing circumstances, one that builds upon these conditions and is not held hostage by them.

The fathers of the EU were wise in choosing a process of integration based on unanimity and small progressive steps. It was slow and cumbersome, yet no better alternatives existed. To the merit of this construct was also the fact that all member countries were treated as equals, a brave decision in the post-war years, one that was based on and inspired trust. Indeed, two of the largest founding members — Germany and also Italy — were defeated during the war. The desire of countries, their citizens and leaders of eliminating the possibility of devastating wars strongly supported the integration process. The same effect had the countries' awareness that the alternative was political irrelevance and economic decline in a world that witnessed the irresistible surge of world superpowers outside the old core of Europe. The outcome was an increasing degree of mutual trust among governments and countries. One important aspect of the early years of European unification was that only six countries were involved and these countries shared many of the features of continental European capitalism. The importance of this relatively simple construction should not be dismissed, particularly in comparison with the high number and institutional and cultural variety of the present day EU.

Were the founding fathers wise also in inverting the standard implementation of monetary integration? As the Werner Report theorised and being impossible to follow the standard path from political unification to monetary unification, the only alternative to paralysis was consistency and endurance in economic and policy harmonisation and integration.[164] Substantial economic integration and political coordination were implemented since the first steps of European integration. This created powerful economic interests and political cooperation. Europeans were firmly in favour of European integration. The European economies were considered sound and strong and able to catch up to the US economy.

Thus the problem included four variables, each of which had a positive sign for the common currency: (a) European economies were growing and thus each economy could rely on open markets and inflow of capital that European integration guaranteed; (b) the effects of the growing and deeper economic and financial integration created powerful common interests in the further growth and depth of integration and its extension to new fields; (c) political and social support by governments and the society were strong and possibly growing around the project of a common

[164] "Having regard to the marked differences existing between the member countries in the realization of the objectives of growth and stability, there is a grave danger of disequilibria arising if economic policy cannot be harmonized effectively" (Werner Report, 1970, p. 8). "...on the plane of institutional reforms the realization of economic and monetary union demands the creation or the transformation of a certain number of Community organs to which powers until then exercised by the national authorities will have to be transferred. These transfers of responsibility represent a process of fundamental political significance which implies the progressive development of political cooperation. Economic and monetary union thus appears as a leaven for the development of political union, which in the long run it cannot do without" (Werner Report, 1970, p. 12).

currency; and (d) the confidence in the architecture and implementation of the integration process for consensus building and peer pressure were sound enough to keep trust and confidence up. The positive effect of these four variables was augmented by the confidence in the high value of the expected gains from the monetary union.

Economic integration requires simple rules and behaviour that do not impinge on the deep governance of national economies: common technical standards (e.g. on hazardous contents in products), fair trade practices (e.g. on competition), avoidance of discrimination (e.g. protectionism), and compatible monetary policies (e.g. avoidance of competitive depreciation). The outcome is a great economic advantage from integration at the modest cost of coordinating trade policies and technical standards. The common currency significantly changes the intimate economic sovereignty of countries, since a currency is perhaps the most fundamental and universal formal economic institution.

The adoption of the euro generated new powerful constraints for the conduct of governments and economic actors. With the common currency, any monetary decision by the common central bank had consequences for each member country. Consequences were asymmetric in an area with so many institutional and structural differences among countries. While the central bank had to take decisions looking at the overall situation of the Eurozone, this did not coincide with the situation of any of its member countries. There are two reasons why the German economy may have been implicitly favoured and other economies implicitly discriminated against. The disadvantaged economies were those whose situation was the most distant from the average one in the union.

The first reason is that the construction of monetary unification took place along the re-contextualised precepts of ordoliberalism and the German tradition. The second reason is that Germany is the largest economy in the Eurozone, even more so if one considers the strong economic attraction of the German economy over surrounding countries. The strength and stability of the common currency critically depend upon the situation of the strongest economy. Thus monetary decisions reflect primarily the needs of the latter, to the disadvantage of those countries, whose economic situation is most distinct. The latter see their situation become more difficult, not only because of their inability to adapt to the new institutions, but also for the implicitly unfavourable stance of monetary decisions. This is an important case of implicit discrimination.

8.8 The International Context

Some of the important factors that frame policies are external to the Eurozone. In these cases, Eurozone policies are either without direct competence or the Eurozone itself is one among many players, albeit an important one. Among these factors, the international context and the international crisis stand out for their importance.

The international context was and is important for the openness of markets, the role of finance, currencies, migration, and current accounts (Table 8.1). Under all these factors, the EU and Eurozone are important players in a broader context. Thus, they can influence the processes, but must also adapt. There is no doubt that globalisation influenced and continues to strongly influence the process of European integration. The EU, then, must play with the fundamental rules that make participation in globalisation compatible with economic and institutional integration and common and national policy goals. The Eurozone, in addition, must play as an integrated area in the currencies market. All this may be at odds with the different situations of its member countries. The Eurozone institutional incompleteness and slow governance prevent that these differences are smoothed away through policies and internal transfers.

Financialisation of the world economy and the impressive development of financial markets are perhaps the most important components of the international context. Financial activities and capital are the most mobile among economic resources, and in open economies the flight of these resources can easily put an economy in great difficulty. The situation of the Eurozone is rather unbalanced in this field. The Eurozone is a world power in financial and capital markets, yet none of the world dominating financial and capital markets is within the Eurozone. They are either in foreign countries (United States, China, Japan, Switzerland) or in European member countries which does not adopt the euro (Great Britain).

The Eurozone needs these markets, yet it must play within the rules established elsewhere and the use of foreign currencies, without the benefits that accrue from hosting a world financial and capital hub.

Table 8.1. The Eurozone and Globalisation.

		Internal Integration		Policy Goals	
Globalisation	External Adaptation	*Economic*	*Institutional*	*Common*	*National*
Financialisation and capital markets	Liberalisation and full participation in international organisations and agreements	Strong	Unique market	Institutional reforms, full active participation	Indirect management through micro-policies
Public finances	Overall balanced	Unstable because of divergent national economies	Rigid rules with no integration, adjustment left to countries	Convergent national situations	Adapt to common criteria and parameters
Economic performance	Weak and worsening (slowing performance)	Asymmetric among countries	National duty under common control	No common goal nor instrument	Bounded by common financial rules
The euro	Sound management to create trust	—	ECB mandate	Manage stability and (secondary) support the economy	Stable/lower real exchange rate, decrease interest rate spread
Mobility of resources	Partial and limited (labour, land property) or improving/full (capital, intellectual property, bank information)	Full (capital), partial and limited (labour, land property)	Institutionally full, actual limits (labour, institutions)	Improve mobility, with limits (e.g. recognition of degrees)	Some limits, attract resources, avoid unfavourable flows

(*Continued*)

Table 8.1. *(Continued)*

		Internal Integration		Policy Goals	
Globalisation	**External Adaptation**	***Economic***	***Institutional***	***Common***	***National***
Trade openness	Nearly full, limits due to technical and ethical standards, health safety, embargos, limits on sensitive technologies	Unique market	Common institutions, no barriers	International and multilateral agreements	Adaptation
Current account balance	Long-term balanced, occasionally strong surplus	Weak and internally asymmetric	Weak limits to imbalances	Adjustment left to deficit countries	National interest
Effects of the crisis	Avoid contagion	Lack of common adjustment mechanisms and institutional instruments	Common fiscal criteria and monitoring and enforcement (Fiscal compact)	Balanced budgets	Austerity

Table 8.2. Stock Exchanges.

	Market Capitalisation	Trade Value	Number of Listed Companies
		(2011, USD Billions)	
New York Stock Exchange (NYSE)	14,242	20,161	8,000
Deutsche Börse	1,185	1,758	765
London Stock Exchange	3,266	2,871	3,000
		In percent	
NYSE/DB	12.02	11.47	10.46
DB/NYSE	8.32	8.72	9.56
LSE/DB	2.76	1.63	3.92
DB/LSE	36.28	61.23	25.50

Source: Author's own table based on World Stock Exchanges (http://www.world-stock-exchanges.net/top10.html).

The difficulties in influencing the institutions and policies governing and managing these markets have been clearly highlighted through the repeated EU failures. These concerned the failed attempt at harmonising taxation of activities in these markets and the failure to set up a stock exchange capable of competing with the dominant stock exchanges on equal footing (Table 8.2).[165]

[165] The largest Eurozone stock exchange is Deutsche Börse. Deutsche Börse is the 10th largest stock exchange in the world with some 765 listed companies, market capitalisation of US$1,185 billion and trade value of US$1,758. For comparison, respective figures for New York Stock Exchange (NYSE) are more than 8,000, US$14,242 and US$20,161. Thus NYSE is more than 11 times larger than DB. The London Stock Exchange is the fourth in the world ranking of stock exchanges. It has around 3,000 listed companies, US$3,266 market capitalisation and US$1,758 trade value. Data refer to 2011 (World Stock Exchanges, http://www.world-stock-exchanges.net/top10.html). It is worth mentioning the existence of two pan-European stock exchanges: Euronext, headquartered in Amsterdam (formed from stock exchanges in Belgium, France, the Netherlands and Portugal) and OMX, composed of Scandinavian and Baltic stock exchanges. There also exists a transatlantic network of stock exchanges: NYSE Euronext.

Since the Eurozone needs these important markets, but is not hosting and controlling them, it has to play according to the rules and the conduct of those alien markets or has to enter alliances in subordinate positions. This gives the Eurozone an obvious disadvantage, which divergent interests and strategies among Eurozone member countries can only enlarge, making inter-European alliances complex.

The disadvantaged situation in the international financial and capital markets, dominated by Anglo-Saxon and emergent countries, requires that the Eurozone: (a) plays according to rules that are defined and managed elsewhere; (b) takes on credible commitments and follow reliable conduct and policies to convince highly mobile international investors to provide the Eurozone with abundant, stable and cheap financial resources and keep Eurozone investors based at home; and (c) has an institutional architecture that allows Eurozone governments to take the needed decisions and implement them in due time to give confidence to markets. These three requirements restrict institutional and policy freedom of the Eurozone in such a way, that some of its member countries are more disadvantaged than others.

First, existing rules of financial and capital markets favour capital and financial assets over other variables, such as labour incomes. When financial assets are highly mobile and the dominant countries do not agree among themselves on the rules, there may be a race to the bottom. The winner is the country which is able to implement the rules most favourable to financial activities and capital. This not only leads to increasing inequalities, but also curbs policy freedom to the disadvantage of countries which do not host the most important financial and capital markets. Consequences are particularly unfavourable in taxation: disadvantaged countries have to keep low taxation of financial activities and capital, without having the benefits of strong and sizeable financial markets. Conversely, they have to transfer taxation to labour, consumption and possibly real estate, which likely have negative consequences for the domestic market.

Second, Eurozone countries have to take on credible commitments and implement reliable policies to convince highly mobile international investors that it is worthwhile and safe to invest in the Eurozone. The most important components are sound public finances, macroeconomic stability and fair exchange rates. All guarantee against the danger of inflation, which would change the relative value of financial investments, and of potential policies that could restrict the freedom and advantages of investors, e.g. through an increase of taxation of financial activities or the danger of sovereign default. However, these conditions disadvantage vulnerable countries, which ironically need most the inflow of international financial resources. Moreover, the lack of inflation keeps the burden of public debt high, particularly in vulnerable countries.

Third, as a disadvantaged participant in financial globalisation, the Eurozone must have an institutional architecture that allows it to take and implement the necessary decisions to lend confidence to financial and capital markets. Since speed and timing is of fundamental importance, this situation requires that financial and monetary decisions have priority over decisions concerning more directly the real economy, including development, industrial, and labour policies. Once again, this has asymmetric consequences within the Eurozone, depending on the different features and situations of individual countries.

The perspective of the impossible trinity of policies highlights one important aspect of the Eurozone idiosyncratic situation (see also Section 6.8). The impossible trinity originates in the Mundell–Fleming framework of an open economy and is supported by empirical studies of government policies. According to this hypothesis, a country cannot implement simultaneously three policy goals: full capital mobility, fixed exchange rates and independent monetary policy.[166] A country can only pursue two of them.

The reason for this is explained by the uncovered interest rate parity condition: in a flexible exchange rate regime, arbitrage ensures that a difference in nominal interest rates between two countries, discounted for the risk premium, is equal to the expected change in exchange rates between the two countries' currencies. Hence, a country intending to keep fixed exchange rates cannot fix its nominal interest rate independently and cannot consequently follow an independent monetary policy, or has to give up capital mobility.

---

[166] Often quoted cases of financial crises, caused by the attempt to follow simultaneously the three policies, are the Mexican peso crisis (1994–1995), the 1997 Asian financial crisis (1997–1998), and the Argentinean financial collapse (2001–2002). For a historical analysis, see Obstfeld and Taylor (1997), and Obstfeld *et al.* (2004). For an application to developing and emerging economies, see Aizenman and Ito (2014).

The choice of the two policy goals depends upon the institutional framework of the country. We may have three different cases. The first possibility is to have full capital mobility and an independent monetary policy. In this case, a flexible exchange rate regime is necessary for policy sustainability. This is the case for various Western countries, including the United States, Great Britain and Japan. It is also the case for the Eurozone, which keeps a flexible exchange regime against other currencies, while guaranteeing capital mobility and pursuing an independent monetary policy. A second possibility is to have fixed exchange rates and an independent monetary policy. In this context, government authorities should choose to have capital control. This was the case of China until summer 2015, for example. The last case is when a country gives up an independent monetary policy, while keeping full capital mobility and fixed exchange rates. This is the situation for the member countries in the Eurozone.[167]

It is important to distinguish the short run from the long run when discussing the effects of the international context. In the short run, the Eurozone responded rationally to the requests deriving from its participation in the process of globalisation. Yet this swift and credible participation contributed to widening the differences among the Eurozone member countries. In the long run and in the lack of complete common institutions, widening differences led to a setback in the process of Eurozone integration.[168] This in turn jeopardised not only the common currency, but also the smooth Eurozone participation in the global financial and capital markets. In fact, capital outflow was and is a reality for vulnerable Eurozone countries. Therefore, the short-run success is not sustainable without solving the aggregation of long-run drawbacks. The latter requires bold internal reforms, particularly in vulnerable countries, and growth policies.

---

[167] Pisani-Ferry (2012) introduced a different version of the impossible trinity based on the peculiar features of the European monetary integration. The trilemma is among the lack of joint responsibility over public debts, the strict no-monetary financing rule, and the national character of banking systems. See also Beck and Prinz (2012).

[168] The latest ECB report on the international use of the euro clearly recognises this aspect: "The on-going adjustment and rebalancing process in the euro area and the moves towards a genuine Economic and Monetary Union, including the completion of the banking union, remain, therefore, of the essence" (ECB 2014b, p. 9).

One way of increasing the Eurozone's international economic standing and resilience is through increasing the international role of the common currency. The euro has gained some ground as an international currency, somewhat greater than the sum of the previous currencies of its member countries, primarily the German and French currencies. The euro is presently second only to the US dollar as a reserve currency in various countries. However, its role is much less important than that of the US dollar and is mainly limited to Eurozone financial assets (Eurozone securities) and trade (ECB 2014b). The most noticeable exception is the use of the euro as a parallel currency in central, eastern and south-eastern Europe. However, the confidence of markets in the common currency fostered sustained capital inflow to the Eurozone, which led to the appreciation of the currency.

Other important components of the international context that influence Eurozone policies include labour and trade. It was already noted earlier in Chapter 5 that labour mobility in the Eurozone is insufficient for an optimum currency area. Not only does immigration, although important and sizeable in the Eurozone, fail to compensate for the reduced labour mobility, it also attracts mostly unqualified workers, particularly in vulnerable countries, while highly qualified national workers expatriate, mainly to the United States and Great Britain (Arslan *et al.* 2014; Dallago 2014; Münz 2014).

Low labour mobility and weak contribution of immigration to upgrading the features of the Eurozone labour market, particularly in vulnerable countries, have two distinct effects. First, adjustment processes must go through other and more costly channels to regain competitiveness, such as through internal devaluation. Second, the low mobility of labour opens the possibility for policies to take an anti-labour stance, e.g. in the form of bad quality labour contracts. The intent is to create jobs through cheaper labour and not through investment. This may have negative consequences for the size of the domestic market and for the international specialisation of Eurozone countries. Also, in this case, asymmetric and divergent solutions and paths characterise different Eurozone countries, with most resilient countries taking a different approach.

Finally, trade openness creates important frames for policies belonging in the international context. The Eurozone is one of the most trade-intensive areas in the world and all its economies are open or very open. Some economies depend critically upon foreign trade, which represents more than 100% of GDP (e.g. the Netherlands). For other larger economies, trade is fundamental (e.g. Germany, France, Italy), while some important branches flourish only thanks to exports (e.g. tourism). It is therefore of the utmost importance that the EU and the Eurozone are part of international trade agreements and comply with international rules. This requires that the area pursues competitiveness in an open market. The particular situation of the Eurozone also makes difficult to manoeuvre the exchange rate as a policy device. Indeed, the exchange rate manoeuvre would have asymmetric consequences for the member countries, depending on their industrial and trade structures.

Two aspects of foreign trade are particularly delicate for the Eurozone. The first one concerns the situation of the current account balance. Until 2003, the Eurozone was balanced overall, both externally and internally. The situation changed in the years before the crisis. While the overall balance remained in substantial equilibrium between 2004 and 2008, a considerable internal divergence evolved (EC 2013a). Strong countries (including Germany, Finland, Austria, and the Netherlands) accumulated sizeable surpluses, while the situation of vulnerable countries was negative for a similar magnitude.[169] Such divergence happened primarily due to the resilient countries, which regained competitiveness by reforming their economies.[170]

During the crisis, successful adjustment took place, but the burden was placed almost exclusively upon vulnerable countries. By 2013, the current account deficit in vulnerable countries was converted into a surplus, mainly by decreasing imports. This achievement succeeded in balancing

[169] According to Eurostat (2015a), Germany's current account surplus was 7.4% of its GDP in 2007 and between 5.9% and 6.8% in each of the following years, up to and including 2011. In 2012, it was again at 7.4% and 7.5% in 2013. In the Netherlands, surpluses were even higher. Vulnerable countries — with the major exceptions of Italy and (except in 2008 and 2009) Ireland — had a continuous current account deficit since the mid-1990s. The deficit increased rapidly since 2004 and was more than 10% in 2008. After this year, the deficit decreased progressively and became a surplus (+1.3%) since 2013.

[170] The most relevant recent case was the Hartz reform of the labour market in Germany (Möller 2014, 2016).

current accounts within the Eurozone and led to halve Germany's surplus with other Eurozone countries as a share of GDP, compared to 2007. However, Germany and the Netherlands's overall current account surplus continued to be sizeable and above the limit of +6% foreseen by the EU. As a consequence, the Eurozone current account was close to balance in 2009–2011, but it increased again to a surplus of 2.3% of Eurozone GDP in the first half of 2013.

The second aspect of foreign trade had to do with international agreements. The EU was traditionally a strong supporter and an active partner in international economic agreements. The international crisis changed the traditional approach to trade agreements. Before the crisis, the standard approach was to conduct multilateral rounds under the aegis of international organisations, such as General Agreement on Tarrifs and Trade (GATT) or World Trade Organization (WTO). When the crisis started to cause difficulties that postponed solutions, a host of bilateral agreements of more modest impact were used. Following the crisis, the EU pursued — similar to other countries, such as the United States and Japan — the establishment of regional agreements among economic and trade blocs of comparable strength, outside of multilateral frameworks. Along with the EU–Japan free trade agreement, the most important regional agreement involving the EU is the Transatlantic Trade and Investment Partnership (TTIP).

TTIP is an ambitious bilateral agreement between the EU and the United States.[171] In a period of prolonged economic difficulties and prudent or restrictive fiscal policies, trade liberalisation offers alternatives to support economic activity, without worsening public finances. This may be particularly important for the Eurozone and even more so for vulnerable economies, provided that austerity policies do not compromise their competitiveness and financial equilibrium. A trade agreement of the importance and reach of TTIP could therefore support productivity and growth and, beyond these, various other variables that are more difficult to appreciate and estimate *ex ante*. These include scale and scope economies, technical progress, and resource allocation (BI 2014, pp. 30–31).

[171] On the position of the European Commission in the negotiations and related documents, see EC (2015l). On the European Parliament position, see EP (2015).

Negotiations for TTIP started in 2013, but soon faced serious difficulties. The main problems apparently concerned the liberalisation of tariffs, the modes of protecting foreign investors, consumers' health and safety, and non-discriminatory public procurement. Particularly complex are the negotiations on the harmonisation of regulation and technical standards for the production of goods and services. Both partners to the TTIP have powerful interests in defending their own standards and extending their influence over the rest of the world. This is also the case because regulation and standards strongly influence investment decisions, including foreign direct investments (FDIs).

8.9 The Frame of Long-Term Trends: Inter-European Dynamics and Interest Contrasts

The varying and diverging situations of member countries and the incompleteness of common institutions make policymaking particularly challlenging in the Eurozone. The former is the cause of divergent intercountry interests and needs in policy choices and making. The latter causes ineffectiveness in dealing with intertwined problems at the Eurozone level. Taken together, these two features restrict policy choice and policymaking in the Eurozone, making policies less effective, and imposing serious costs on all countries, in particular to the vulnerable ones.

Differences of national economic systems within the Eurozone are significant particularly in the case of financial and capital markets. Overall, banks have a greater role within the Eurozone than in the Anglo-Saxon world and stock exchanges have a lesser and weaker role.[172] Banks are generally more resilient to market panic, but are usually more prudent and less flexible in their attitude and operations. While these features may give Eurozone economies better management and greater resilience, they easily forego opportunities and slow down responsiveness.

When banks are under distress or foresee potential difficulties, such as an increase of the share of bad loans, they decrease credit to the economy, thus causing recovery to be slower and more delayed. Another feature of this system is the intertwining of banks with other financial organisations,

[172] See Dietl 1998 and the literature on the variety of capitalism mentioned in Chapter 4.

enterprises and governments. When banks go through distress, this strength becomes a weakness. The entire economy is at risk and when important economic actors (e.g. a large firm or a number of smaller ones) are in distress, banks are also at risk. Due to their critical role in the economy, the contestability of banks' ownership is seen with suspicion by governments and other constituencies.

In these circumstances, common policies tend to the minimal common denominator: avoid negative consequences for countries complying with common rules, namely resilient countries. Although this is sound in principle, it overlooks the most critical aspect: how can vulnerable countries move away from the present unbalanced and vulnerable situation to greater stability and respect of common parameters, if they do not have the necessary time to comply and the necessary resources? This is the fundamental and unsolved problem of the Eurozone, to be discussed further, particularly in Chapters 11 and 12.

The internal divergence of the Eurozone has various components (Table 8.3), but has one political commonality: the will of all member countries to continue to play together and afford sacrifices in order to converge to the commonly chosen standards. The real policy divergence is about the way to reach that situation and the sharing of costs.

The main components of internal divergence concern exchange rates, fiscal and monetary policies, the coordination of national policies, national and common reforms, and the relation between short- and long-term policies. In regards to the first component, exchange rates, the common interest would be to keep coincidence of national real exchange rates with the nominal exchange rate. Unfortunately national real exchange rates diverge and this makes impossible to have a nominal exchange rate of the common currency that is equally favourable to all countries.

The divergence among national real exchange rates and the latter divergence from the nominal exchange rate of the euro are due to different reasons. The common currency makes it difficult to adjust these divergences. In general, vulnerable countries see their real exchange rate appreciate, while resilient countries see their own depreciate. Among the causes is the weaker international specialisation of vulnerable countries in production whose terms of trade worsen. Other reasons include faster growth of wages and salaries compared to productivity; higher public deficit and

Table 8.3. Eurozone Internal Divergence.

Divergence	Common Interest	Strong Countries	Vulnerable Countries
Nominal exchange rate of the euro and national real exchange rates	Coincidence of national real exchange rates and favourable nominal exchange rate for balanced balance of payments	Strong nominal exchange rate (attract capital and get high rewards from inelastic exports outside the Eurozone) and competitive own real exchange rate (high competitiveness and Eurozone exports)	Weak nominal exchange rate (support inelastic exports outside the Eurozone and discourage capital export) and competitive own real exchange rate (high competitiveness and Eurozone exports)
Fiscal policies	Balanced finances, active automatic stabilisers and growth supporting policies	Balanced finances of vulnerable countries without burdening their own	Balanced finances also through common support mutualisation of debts, loose convergence criteria and commonly financed growth policies
Monetary policies	Price stability plus monetary policies in line with potential income. Favourable exchange rate with foreign currencies to support trade and attract capital.	Monetary policies favouring price stability and stable growth	Monetary policies favouring low inflation to ease the burden of debt and stimulate investments
Coordination of national policies	Coordinate national policies and pursue complementarities (e.g. in managing current accounts or supporting austerity in vulnerable countries through expansion in resilient countries)	Policies should be tailored to common parameters without intercountry coordination until vulnerable countries improve their financial position	Coordinate national policies in order to have resilient countries supporting their convergence and reform efforts (adjustment shared with resilient countries)

National reforms	Convergence of all countries to a compatible institutional setting and convergence of national productivity	Evolve national institutions along the lines of supposedly more effective and efficient own institutions	National reforms financed (also) by common resources and common support (including the golden rule on investments excluded from of convergence criteria)
Common reforms and completion of the Eurozone institutional architecture	Coherent institutional architecture tuned to common goals, effective and with low implementation and compliance costs	Convergence of vulnerable countries to their own stronger standards that become common	More flexible institutions taking the situation of vulnerable countries into due consideration (e.g. more flexibility in the SGP and parameters, allow common support through the ECB)
Short-term stabilisation versus growth	Short-term stabilisation should be reached mainly through automatic stabilisers financed during the years of expansion, so to free resources for supporting growth; establish a common co-financed fund for investment	Run surpluses due to their own merit (fiscal and trade) and finance growth	Soften short-term stabilisation (by common support, by postponing it in time, or by diluting it statistically through the golden rule) and finance growth (with own and common resources)

public debt compared to resilient countries; lack of investment and ailing productivity; inefficient public administration and in general higher transaction costs.

Vulnerable countries suffer from unfavourable developments in both costs and investment. While the cost of imported inputs is roughly the same as in resilient countries, thanks to the common currency, domestic costs diverge due to a set of nationally idiosyncratic factors: social and demographic dynamics in the case of wages and some services, various inefficiencies in the case of infrastructure and several inputs, and the greater spread of corruption and tax evasion.

An important social factor that puts vulnerable countries at a disadvantage is the existence of a demonstration effect at work in the EU. Wages, salaries and consumption tend to converge to that of the richer, resilient member countries, while productivity in vulnerable countries remains lower. This effect is significant, particularly in the non-competitive sector, but it exists also in the competitive sector. Also demographic dynamics have negative effects in vulnerable countries, and translate in pressure on public pension systems. While the former effect leads to decreasing export shares of vulnerable countries, the latter increases public deficits and public debt.

In vulnerable countries, gross hourly wages grew faster than in resilient ones, while labour productivity levels and trends and investment dynamics disadvantaged vulnerable countries,[173] some service sectors and manufacturing branches apart (Sondermann 2012). As a consequence, unit labour costs (ULC) diverged until 2009 (OECD database). In a monetary union

[173] Labour productivity in vulnerable countries does not show a consistent picture. In Italy, labour productivity was considerably higher than the EU average in 2000, but decreased to the EU average by 2010. Other vulnerable countries fared better. In Spain, labour productivity decreased to the EU average by 2000, but it returned to the original relative level that was well above the EU average by the end of the decade. Productivity in Greece was constantly about 20% below the EU average, and it only worsened with the onset of the economic crisis. Productivity in Germany and France was remarkably higher than in vulnerable countries, although still decreasing compared to the EU average. Therefore, in the second half of the last decade Spain's productivity converged to Germany and France's, while Italy's diverged (Eurostat database). See also Sections 3.3, 3.4, 3.6 and 4.2, Mamuneas and Ketteni (2014).

without common government of the economy, growing relative ULC in vulnerable countries cause price inflation. This happened in the Eurozone until 2012–2013 when internal deflation was effective, mainly through labour dismissals. Price inflation led to real exchange rate appreciation and loss of competitiveness by the vulnerable countries, thus worsening their position in international trade and discouraging the inflow of FDIs.[174] The negative effect for vulnerable countries was stronger in third markets than in the Eurozone markets, due to the strength of the euro in currency markets. The common currency was strong against most currencies, starting a few months after its physical introduction. This was due to the monetary policy tuned to resilient countries, the reputation that resilient countries have in the international financial markets, their current account surplus and the inflow of capital from third countries.

Along with the aforementioned problems, which impinge upon real national exchange rates, inefficiencies also constitute an unfavourable development for vulnerable countries, one that made their domestic costs diverge from that of the resilient countries. Inefficiencies differ between countries and result from different factors, including lack of investment, less developed infrastructure, excessively small size of enterprises, inefficient bureaucracy and high costs of doing business (see Chapter 10). Finally, corruption and tax evasion are generally more widespread in vulnerable than in resilient countries (Figure 8.1).

Austerity policies are a second major cause of internal divergence in the Eurozone. An incomplete monetary union is interested in long-term balanced finances, which avoid intercountry transfers and leave the option of activating automatic stabilisers when necessary and policies to support growth when possible. Long-term balanced finances guarantee the most ample and flexible policy freedom to a government.

In any monetary union, there are different situations between member countries or regions. These differences result from various factors, including

---

[174] According to the Organisation for Economic Cooperation and Development (OECD), real exchange rates based on ULC in manufacturing increased considerably since the beginning of the last decade in both Italy and Spain (respectively 135.1 and 128.8 in 2010, given 2001=100). During this same period, Germany had decreasing real exchange rates (91.1) and France slightly increasing ones (109.7). The average real exchange rate for the Eurozone was 121.0. See also Sheets and Sockin (2012).

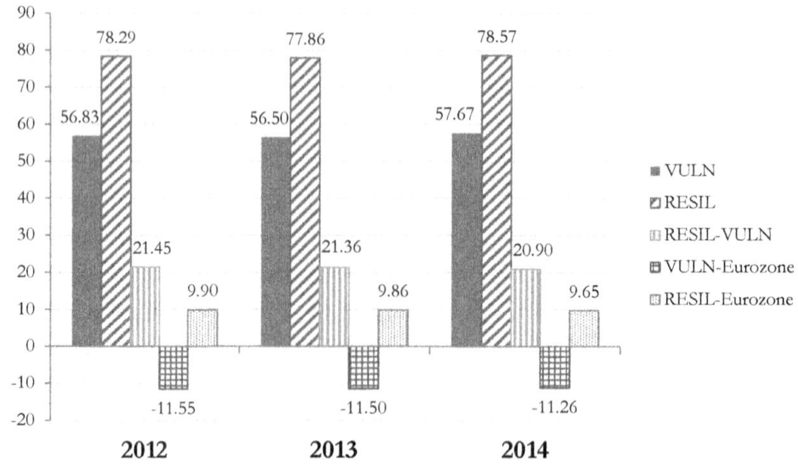

Figure 8.1. The Corruption Perceptions Index in the Eurozone.
Source: Author's own figure based on data by Transparency International (http://www.transparency.org/cpi2014/results).

inherited situations (such as high public debts inherited from the past), and different levels of development and geographical segmentation (such as the existence of a backward area in a country requiring special concern), and social problems (unfavourable demographic structure, widespread unemployment). However, the divergence may also derive from political opportunism (the attempt to solve a country's problems at the cost of the union), economic illusion (the hope that it is sufficient to join the common currency to solve problems, such as benefitting from decreased interest rates), and lack of political will and capacity (for instance, the political inability to decrease public debt). What distinguishes an incomplete monetary union is that there are no common instruments to bridge or compensate for those differences and national instruments also falter.

Monetary policy forms the third component of the Eurozone's internal divergence. This is a common policy, and in the domain of the Eurosystem it is directed by the ECB. The Eurosystem has one mandate: pursue the interest of the Eurozone. Yet the Eurosystem is also made up of the representatives of national central banks, who have to keep in consideration the interests of their own countries. Only the ECB is run by a directorate and a president who are, by their very mandate, above the particular interests of individual member countries. While the ECB directorate runs operational activities in the monetary domain, it is the Eurosystem governance that decides on strategic issues. It is easy to see that, under these conditions, resilient countries have the upper hand in exerting effective pressure upon a common decision. The mandate of monetary policy is to pursue price stability and, secondary to this goal, support the Eurozone economy in approaching its potential income. This is a recipe for a strong currency, in line with the interest of resilient countries. Only the severe pressure of real events can alter this institutionally defined outcome.

The fourth component of internal divergence derives from uncoordinated national policies. In an economic and monetary union, countries should coordinate national policies in order to pursue complementarities. During the crisis, the most important way of doing so is to manage the Eurozone current accounts so to support exports by vulnerable countries, thus overcoming the negative effect of the strong common currency. Expansionary fiscal policies in resilient countries would create additional demand, to the benefit of exports also from vulnerable countries and in compensation of the negative effects of austerity policies on domestic demand. At the same time, increasing demand in resilient countries would decrease their exports to both vulnerable and third countries, thus helping to keep a limit on the current account surplus of the Eurozone.

Divergence of interests and needs also concerns policy timing. For resilient countries, policy discipline means that vulnerable countries have to put their finances and economies in order through austerity policies and reforms. This is to avoid the danger of having to finance policies and interventions that would be to the advantage of vulnerable countries, but much to the cost of resilient countries. For vulnerable countries, policy discipline takes away important policy instruments (in particular, fiscal policy) and has negative long-term consequences by depressing investment and consumption. Therefore, vulnerable countries are interested in having resilient countries first supporting their convergence and reform efforts. This does not necessarily require direct support in the form of a transfer of financial resources. Political support could probably be sufficient in most cases to send a clear message to markets that vulnerable countries are not risky partners.

National reforms are the fifth component of the Eurozone's internal divergence. It is in the common interest of the Eurozone monetary management to have all countries converge to a compatible institutional architecture. A compatible institutional architecture would consist of effective common and national institutions and supportive national and local informal institutions. Compatible and effective institutional architecture would streamline interests, decision-making, and conduct of individual member countries.

Since fully compatible national institutional architectures were not the starting point, institutional reforms are needed. Such reforms leave informal institutions out of reach. These are more resilient to change, since they are linked to idiosyncratic economic, social and political features and long-term processes, but are also fundamental in defining preferences. Although reforms of formal institutions influence informal institutions, the process takes a long time. Since formal institutions are under the influence of informal institutions, institutional convergence is a long process. Institutional compatibility is a more reasonable perspective. Such compatibility involves not only the relations among national institutional architectures; it also concerns the compatibility between informal institutions and reformed formal institutions and the activation of compensating mechanisms in case of incompatibilities, including political will and social support to converge.

Important divergent interests also exist in the case of the reform of national institutions. According to resilient countries, economic and social institutions of all member countries should be molded along the lines of the supposedly more effective and efficient own institutions. The case of privatisation and the buildup of labour markets and financial sectors are important cases in point. In the view of resilient countries, vulnerable member countries would benefit from taking advantage of their experience and achievements. Vulnerable countries are not so much against this perspective; they also see reforming their institutions as an important opportunity to modernise and improve the working of their economy. Yet they have clear the difficulties in going from the existing institutional architecture to the promised one and the likely clash with their informal institutions. Therefore, they are interested in reforming their national institutions also by means of common resources and common support.[175]

The sixth component of internal Eurozone divergence includes completing the Eurozone institutional architecture. This is a shared goal in the Eurozone, yet its particular form and timing are considered differently by diverse countries. In fact, a particular institutional reform has different outcomes, depending on the situation and features of the member country. The institutional architecture chosen for the ECB, including its narrow mandate, is an important case in point. The kind of institutional architecture pursued is not the only thing of importance. What also matters is the path taken to complete the architecture. The path would make a great deal of difference in terms of adaptation and transformation costs, their allocation to individual countries, and the economic, political, and social sustainability of the process. In the case of the ECB, a better consideration of national idiosyncrasies would require a broader mandate, perhaps similar to that of the US Federal Reserve, and broader policy instruments to help countries in difficulty.

The final component of Eurozone internal divergence has to do with the conflict between short-term stabilisation and growth. It is in the common interest to pursue short-term stabilisation through automatic stabilisers as much as possible. According to the EU view, powerful automatic stabilisers should be financed in the years of economic growth through budget surpluses. This would create the resources necessary for supporting growth during the years of crisis. However appealing this perspective is, it is not in tune with the existing situation. Strong countries easily share this perspective, in particular if during years of crisis they can count on capital inflow from vulnerable countries. Vulnerable countries meet with greater

[175] Institutions are coordinated and feature complementarities, so to form a coherent system, together with the organisations where those institutions are embedded. This coherence makes the change of particular institutions a particularly delicate process, whose outcome is uncertain and ridden with unforeseen and unwanted consequences. Wisely enough, the Eurozone aims at streamlining outcomes (e.g. balanced budgets) more than the way and the institutions through which these are obtained. Unwisely enough, in the case of Greece in summer 2015, the "troika" (the EC, the ECB and the IMF) apparently entered the dangerous terrain of "advising" the Greek government the institutions to change and how to do so (e.g. concerning the pension system).

difficulties, both because they are typically less developed and economically vulnerable, because the demonstration effect in incomes and consumption work to their disadvantage, and because their public finances are weaker, but this is more important for economic growth. They need longer periods for stabilising their public finances and for restructuring their use in favour of expenditures with long-term economic returns. Fiscal equalisation would help to manage this divergence.

8.10 Conclusions

It is hard to see in the present Eurozone institutional architecture and practice anything that can be considered a truly common and institutionalised approach to smoothing out intercountry differences and diverging interests. These differences have indeed increased during the crisis. Smoothing is mostly done through political cooperation, formal and informal monetary and fiscal flexibility, and political and social commitment to the monetary union. Vulnerable countries have so far shown a remarkable degree of commitment to the common destiny and resilience in the face of extremely high costs and difficulties. Strong countries were perhaps more flexible and supportive in deeds than in words. However, they reacted more out of concern for the stabilisation in selected vulnerable countries than by a genuine conviction that a different approach is necessary.

The Eurozone may be facing a double framing of policies: that of resilient countries plus the formal Eurozone institutions and that of vulnerable countries. Only the ECB has consistently tried to mediate between these two frameworks in recent years. These frameworks influenced the perceptions that economic and political actors, and particularly national governments, have. Perceptions refer to the situations and the meanings attributed to statements and positions taken by Eurozone organs or national governments. Perceptions have in turn influenced decision-making and activities, particularly in adapting to common institutions and requirements.

Due to framing, different Eurozone member countries express varying positions and policy preferences. They also interpret existing evidence and information under the influence of confirmatory biases, leading to alternative equilibrium fictions in resilient and vulnerable countries. Yet political and social commitment of vulnerable countries, patience and some pragmatic flexibility on the side of resilient countries, and ingenuity by Eurozone institutions and in particular the ECB may have the effect of fostering the fading away of different and divergent confirmatory biases and consequently of equilibrium fictions. There may be convergence of framing under way in the direction of shared "Euroframes". But it is still a long way to coherence and effectiveness.

"When a country is well governed, poverty and a mean condition are things to be ashamed of. When a country is ill governed, riches and honor are things to be ashamed of."

— Confucius, *The Analects*, Chapter VIII:13.

9

The Crisis and the Incomplete Institutional Architecture

The peculiar framing, together with the incompleteness of the institutional construction put Eurozone policies into an uneasy situation. In vulnerable countries, policies had difficulties in pursuing their primary objective of balanced finances. Indeed, they worsened economic performance and caused problems for which there apparently are no policy remedies. Moreover, the shared competences of Eurozone organs and national governments are sources of economic and political conflict. Last but not least, political and social dangers are wandering in the skies of the Eurozone.

Policies within the Eurozone are incomplete and counter-productive as a consequence of incomplete institutions. Policymaking met an increasing lack of trust among countries and between the European Commission and selected Eurozone member countries, which further shortened the time horizon of policymaking. Policies have in many cases negative consequences for the entire area. The policy spectrum is also largely incomplete, since attention and policymaking are concentrated on financial issues, in particular on public finances. A new trilemma of policymaking appeared, due to the incomplete institutional architecture of the Eurozone. Financial policy activity is mostly concentrated on keeping national policies within the narrow limits of conservative parameters and apparently severe and rigid treaties and pacts. Common fiscal policies are without a common budget and monetary policies are institutionally constrained. These policies have negative consequences for the real economy in vulnerable countries and, through production and trade linkages, also in resilient countries. The ailing real economy jeopardises the fixing of finances and weakens social and political support for the Eurozone and more in general the European Union (EU).

The Eurozone risks being trapped in a non-cooperative game for managing what, after all, remains a common pool of resources, determining the present and the future of Europe. Since 2008, problems have mounted, following the inefficacy of the incomplete institutional architecture, policy framing, incompleteness and asymmetry of policymaking, and policy constraints. Most important, in vulnerable countries domestic markets and investment shrank; inequalities intensified and mobility slowed down; unemployment and poverty increased; problems with growth and development became serious. The Eurozone is at risk of splitting apart, at least in economic and financial terms. The little revival that the Eurozone witnessed in early 2015 is due to ECB action, the following depreciation of the euro and the low oil price, more than on its own merit. Institutional reforms, national and common alike, continue, but do so at a pace which falls short of the needs. The only really important novelty is the European Central Bank's (ECB) new stance in supporting the Eurozone viability.

There cannot be doubts that macroeconomic, monetary and financial stability within the Eurozone are a must, without which the entire construction would crumble. Yet pursuing stability under the formal Eurozone conditions is jeopardising the long-run outcome of the real economy, is putting the sustainability and effectiveness of policies at risk, and is polarising national conditions that may radicalise positions and make differences permanent.

Various observers and even important EU officers expressed criticism of Eurozone institutions.[176] It may be true that Eurozone institutions are deficient, but it is hard to conceive that this is the only or even the prevalent explanation of the design of these institutions and their continuous existence. Other, deeper and more resilient issues must be at stake. Aware of its shortcomings, the Eurozone is reacting to the problems and criticism with some pragmatism and flexibility in the interpretation and implementation of the common rules. This raises even more questions: is this enough? Does a flexible interpretation respond effectively to the problems? Or does it weaken the rules of the game, without making the game more effective and helping the players to fix their situation?

9.1 Contagion

In a highly integrated world economy, both positive and negative effects of an event in one part of that economy — be it a country, an industrial or financial firm, a natural event, or something else — would spread to other parts. Contagion is particularly effective in finances, both for the strict and deep linkages of financial activities throughout the world and because of the speed with which financial events take place and diffuse. The term "systemic risk" is used to denote a situation when contagion surges to general relevance, involving banking and financial markets as well as the related payment and settlement systems. Systemic risk usually includes simultaneous financial instability in most of the economic system (Constâncio 2011; De Bandt and Hartmann 2000; ECB 2009, 2010; Gerlach 2009; Pokutta *et al.* 2011).[177]

---

[176] Romano Prodi, the then president of the European Commission, released the following statement in an interview with the daily newspaper *Le Monde*, given on 18 October 2002: "I know very well that the Stability Pact is stupid, like all decisions that are too rigid.... The Stability Pact is imperfect, we need a more intelligent mechanism and more flexibility." Quoted in Apel (2002).

[177] ECB (2009, pp. 134–135) stresses that two perspectives of systemic risk exist. "One perspective is to describe it as the risk of experiencing a *strong* systemic event. Such an event adversely affects a number of systemically important intermediaries or markets (including potentially related infrastructures). The trigger of the event could be an *exogenous* shock (idiosyncratic, i.e. limited in scope, or systematic, i.e. widespread), which means

The term "contagion" was first used in economics with the emergence of the 1997 crisis in Asia, referring to the spread of financial market turmoil across countries (Claessens and Forbes 2001). Contagion is a rather elusive concept. Dornbush *et al.* (2000) review the meaning of the concept and how it is treated. They define financial contagion "...as a significant increase in cross-market linkages after a shock to an individual country (or group of countries), as measured by the degree to which asset prices or financial flows move together across markets relative to this comovement in tranquil times." These effects may be sometimes due to panic or other forms of irrational behaviour. Yet most of the time, contagion is the outcome of rational behaviour of economic and financial actors, who follow their interests or, in case they are agents of dispersed principals, their incentives. Also coordination and informational problems may play a role.

The elusiveness of the term lies in the fact that what may look as contagion may be the effect of simple linkages among economies and countries. Openness of the economies, in particular when coupled with relatively small size and specialised production and trade profile in few

---

from outside the financial system. Alternatively, the event could emerge *endogenously* from within the financial system or from within the economy at large. The systemic event is *strong* when the intermediaries concerned fail or when the markets concerned become dysfunctional (in theoretical terms this is often a non-linearity or a regime change). One can distinguish between a "horizontal" perspective of systemic risk, where attention is confined to the financial system, and a "vertical" perspective of systemic risk in which the two-sided interaction between the financial system and the economy at large is taken into account. Ideally, the severity of systemic risk and systemic events would be assessed by means of the effect that they have on consumption, investment and growth or economic welfare broadly speaking." See also GOT (2001). According to Gerlach (2009), there are three important characteristics of systemic risk: "First, it must impact on a 'substantial portion' of the financial system. Thus, it is risk to the financial system as a whole. ... Second, systemic risk involves spillovers of risk from one institution to many others. In turn, this implies that in measuring it, attention should presumably be focused on the ways in which adverse shocks affecting one or a few institutions can be transmitted to the financial system at large, that is, on the interlinkages between institutions. ... Third, episodes in which systemic risk materialised would typically be associated with highly adverse macro economy effects in the absence of rapid and strong policy responses. By this standard, it is clear that the current episode of financial instability reflects a systemic crisis. However, while this definition is clear, it is also rather abstract. In order to measure and to control systemic risk, it must be made operational."

products, exposes a country to shocks from negative events in their larger trade partners or the markets in which they are specialised (Briguglio *et al.* 2009). In general, financial integration and deep trade and production links make economies vulnerable, as much as regional patterns of specialisation or integration and business cycle coordination. Under these conditions, events in the international financial market or particular financial operators or events in the goods markets and production and trade can transmit shocks through countries and cause volatility in exchange rates, stock prices, sovereign spreads, and capital flows. Although the effect of institutional factors and microeconomic conditions is less studied and known, the Eurozone offers an important case for considering the great importance that these factors have in causing contagion within an institutionally integrated area.

It is useful to distinguish between real and financial contagion, depending on the nature of the variables that cause and spread contagion. Moreover, it is useful to distinguish between external and internal contagion. The former is contagion spreading from one economically sovereign country to another economically sovereign country, or groups of countries. Internal contagion takes place among countries which are part of an economic and monetary union, such as the Eurozone is. This intra-Eurozone contagion is discussed in the next chapter.

There are different types of external contagion (Dornbush *et al.* 2000; Eichengreen *et al.* 1996; Kaminsky and Reinhart 2000; Masson 1998). Each type has distinct causes, greatly different mechanisms by which it can spread, and different implications. Policy measures should carefully take these differences into account (Moser 2003). The first type is also called as "fundamental-based contagion" (Calvo and Reinhart 1996), in that changes in the normal interdependence among economies may transmit, during a period of crisis, adverse shocks through real currency and financial linkages. The features of this kind of contagion, the mechanisms and channels through which it works, and the degree of the adverse effects were the issues of much research, particularly since the 1997 Asian crisis (Baur 2012; Forbes and Rigobon 2001, 2002; Gross and Kok 2013; Kaminsky and Reinhart 2000; Kenourgios and Dimitriou 2015; Luchtenberg and Viet Vu 2015; Ozkan and Unsal 2012; Pritsker 2000; Rigobon 2002).

International banking integration, important for increasing economic efficiency and growth, proved to be a significant factor of countries' vulnerability to contagion (Mendoza and Quadrini 2009; OECD 2012b; Van Rijckeghem and Weder 1999). This may happen, for example, when banks respond to the deterioration of their balance sheet by reducing cross-border loans, and thus also spread shocks to initially immune countries. Particularly in situations of inadequate global liquidity and low capitalisation of banks, international banking integration led to unprecedented transmission of financial instability.

In the second type, contagion derives from the behaviour of economic and financial agents, even in case of a lack of tension in the fundamentals of an economy. This channel, termed as the "social learning channel", can generate contagion through panic (Trevino 2014). From a general point of view, this kind of contagion is caused by collective irrationality, such as in the event of financial panic caused by loss of confidence and spread of particular information, or increased risk aversion, leading to herd behaviour. In all these cases, collective irrationality may result from individually rational behaviour.

It is difficult to identify empirically the existence of contagion in pure forms. According to Constâncio (2011), at least four different criteria are used in the literature to identify contagion. These include: "(i) the transmission is in excess of what can be explained by economic fundamentals; (ii) the transmission is different from regular adjustments observed in tranquil times; (iii) the events constituting contagion are negative extremes; and (iv) the transmission is sequential, for example in a causal sense." However, there is no agreement as to which criteria are sufficient or necessary to qualify a contagion event.

The case of the Eurozone is in part distinct, in that it was under the influence of an external contagion imported from the United States, and of a contagion internal to the Eurozone which started thereafter. The transatlantic contagion was important both in its own effects, and as detonator of the European crisis. This was the case even if European countries and economic actors were overall more prudent than the United States in managing their economies and finances. Yet the Eurozone had a sufficient amount of home-grown problems, which justified worries about its sustainability and the effects on economic performance. Fighting contagion required swift and resolute policy action, as the US did. Home-grown problems and institutional incompleteness and asymmetry rendered the Eurozone largely powerless and even counterproductive in policymaking.

9.2 The Crisis: A Comparison

The crisis started, as shown in Chapter 2, in the United States following a prolonged period of excess credit, itself the outcome of accommodating monetary and fiscal policies (Mills 2010; Razin and Rosefielde 2011). The effects of the US crisis reached the Eurozone through financial, real, policy, political, and psychological linkages. The international transmission of the US financial and economic crisis is thus often understood as a contagion process. It is useful to distinguish the cross-country transmission of shocks from the more normal development of synchronised shocks in different countries. The latter are due less to the presence of a channel of contagion than to similar structural vulnerabilities. In the case of the cross-country transmission of shocks, it is also important to distinguish the pure negative effects of the imported contagion from the home-grown negative events that the imported contagion may possibly foster.

In order to clarify what is of a more general bearing and what is more idiosyncratic to the peculiar Eurozone situation, it is useful to single out the following three components of the crisis: (1) the common features and events which fuelled synchronised shocks in the US and in the EU; (2) the channels of transmission of external shocks to the Eurozone through the fundamental economic and financial linkages between the US and the EU; and (3) the Eurozone idiosyncratic factors that let a minor crisis like the Greek one to evolve into a systemic crisis. It is also important to understand how those three aspects interact. The third component is the topic of the next chapter.

Indeed, there were three domestic sources of fragility in the Eurozone countries: banks, sovereign debt, and financial bubbles. These put various Eurozone economies at risk in the event of a sudden financial arrest (Caballero 2010). Many Eurozone banks were in a fragile state (Ireland and Spain for example), owing to easy credit and massive adoption of financial innovations, high leverage ratios, circumvention of financial regulation and high risk investments. Various economies were under the effect of unbalanced budgets (Greece) and high debts (Italy). Real estate and financial bubbles were serious causes of financial stress (e.g. Ireland and Spain).

What made these features potentially threatening for the Eurozone stability were their asymmetric presence in different countries and their interconnection with national institutional idiosyncrasies and Eurozone institutional incompleteness. Domestic sources of structural and policy vulnerability (including accumulated public and private debt stocks, market rigidity, labour market features, unfavourable demography, inequalities, fiscal policies) caused the differential domestic effects of the common monetary policy. Together, these factors played an important role in explaining the differential vulnerability and resilience, and hence performance of individual European countries.

The first component of the Eurozone crisis included the long-run economic expansion since the 1980s, led by technical progress and the financialisation of the Western economies. As shown in Chapter 2, these features were more pronounced in the United States, yet they were relevant also in Western Europe. As a consequence, business cycles were overall synchronised on both sides of the Atlantic.

The economic and financial linkages between the US and EU formed the fundamental channels of transmission of external shocks to the Eurozone. While Eurozone banks were generally more prudent than their US counterparts, the situation of many Eurozone banks was still fragile. In fact, they held a large share of derivatives based on US subprime residential mortgage: when the US housing bubble burst they shared in the losses. The stock market collapse and the money market's sudden contraction also led to a halt of bank credit in the Eurozone. Real and monetary processes strengthened financial ones through trade and production linkages and the appreciation of the euro.

EU export to the US market accounted for 23.2% of total EU exports in 2006. Exports started to decrease in 2007 and by 2009 reached a cumulative fall of 26%. Their share of total EU exports decreased to 18.7% by 2009. EU imports from the United States decreased definitively less and the drop was concentrated in 2009 at 14.5%. As a consequence, imports from the US as a share of total EU imports remained more stable and even increased between 2008 and 2009, due to the strong contraction of EU imports during that year.

The unfavourable evolution of the trade balance with the United States was due to both the crisis, which decreased demand for imports, particularly in the United States, and the strong real appreciation of the euro before 2008. While the EU trade balance with the United States continued to be in surplus, the surplus decreased significantly: from nearly €94 billion in 2006 down to nearly €45 billion in 2009, according to DG Trade. The volatility of other currencies and of the price of commodities worsened the adverse impact on the European economy.

Synchronised shocks in the US and the EU were fuelled by the same factors, in particular the rapid financialisation of the economy and the considerable expansion of soft credit. Synchronised shocks appeared in the form of a housing bubble, massive circumvention of weak financial regulation, high financial leverage, risky financial innovation, and investments in high risk assets. However, the situation in European countries was varied and this created additional difficulties to policymaking in the Eurozone.

The housing bubble is a good example. The housing bubble was fundamental in causing the crisis in the United States (see Chapter 2). In the Eurozone, it was significant in fuelling the crisis in Spain: prices increased approximately threefold in 1985–1991 and again in 1996–2008. House prices between 2002 and 2008 doubled in Spain and increased by approximately 70% in both France and Ireland. In other countries, such as Italy, price increases were more moderate, while in Germany there was no housing bubble.[178]

Real house prices in the United States rose by roughly 50%, reaching a peak in 2006, according to OECD data (Glick and Lansing 2010). House prices in various countries increased more than in the US, measured at their peaks, including in Ireland (172%), United Kingdom (146%), Spain

---

[178] Sources on the housing market include ECB Statistical Data Warehouse *Residential Property Price Indicator* (https://sdw.ecb.europa.eu/browse.do?node=2120781), Eurostat house price index (http://appsso.eurostat.ec.europa.eu/nui/show.do?dataset=prc_hpi_q&lang=en), OECD *Focus on House Prices* (http://www.oecd.org/eco/outlook/focusonhouseprices.htm) and OECDiLibrary (http://www.oecd-ilibrary.org/economics/house-prices_2074384x-table17), IMF *Global Housing Watch* (http://www.imf.org/external/research/housing/), and The Economist's property prices indicators (http://www.economist.com/topics/property-prices).

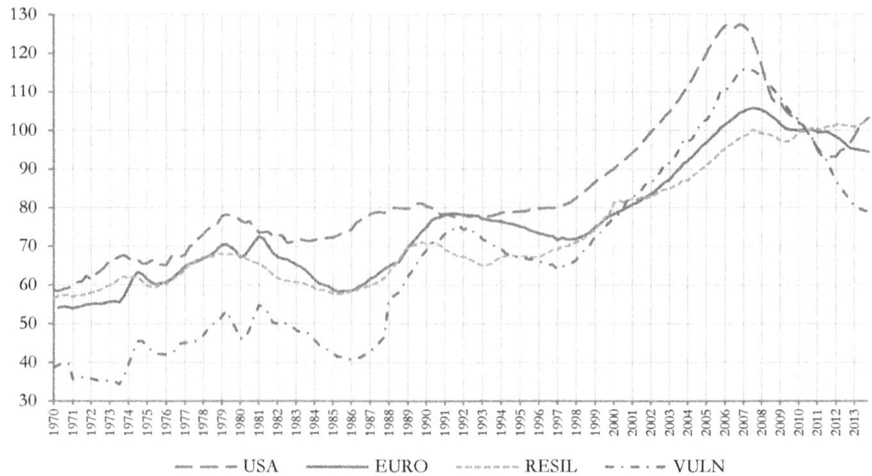

Figure 9.1. Real House Prices*.

Note: *Seasonally adjusted, index based in 2010, deflated using the private consumption deflator from the national account statistics.

Source: Author's own figure based on data from OECD Housing Prices database.

(118%), France and Sweden (108%), Denmark (89%), the Netherlands (75%), and Italy (61%). In all these countries, booming house prices far exceeded the growth in disposable incomes over the same period. Although real house prices fell in Germany and Japan over this period, house prices in both countries increased significantly during the late 1980s and early 1990s. It is fair to conclude that housing bubbles were widespread.

The data suggest that house prices moved in different ways in vulnerable and resilient countries. Figure 9.1 shows the changes in real house prices. This allows them to avoid the effect of inflation, which was significantly different within the Eurozone in many of the years considered (see in particular Table 4.2). On average, real house prices increased much more in the United States than in the Eurozone in the fifteen years preceding the crisis. When the housing bubble burst, which happened between 2006 and 2007, the fall of prices in the United States was faster and greater than in the Eurozone.

Some important differences existed between vulnerable and resilient countries in the Eurozone. The main difference was that deviations from the trend in the first group of countries were larger than in the latter group. The second difference was that the housing bubble, between the second part of the 1990s and 2007, was particularly evident in vulnerable countries: on average, real prices increased by more than 80% in vulnerable countries between the beginning of 1997 and the beginning of 2007.[179] This was a faster increase than in the United States, where real prices in the corresponding period (from the end of 1996 to the end of 2006) increased by nearly 60%. In the corresponding period (from early 1997 to the third quarter of 2007), real prices in resilient countries increased by only 45%, mainly thanks to the stability of prices in Germany.

Differences were even greater in the post-crisis depression in the housing market. While the housing bubble first burst in the United States in late 2006 and depressed prices to 73% level of the bubble's apex, this country was also the first to recover: prices already started to increase in early 2012 and by the end of 2014 they gained nearly 11%, thus returning to approximately 81% level of the real price apex. Overall, the movement of real, prices in the Eurozone was more moderate, but this was the result of two extreme movements. In resilient countries, real price movements were definitely moderate: real prices decreased by a mere 3% between the apex of the expansion in the third quarter of 2007 and the second quarter of 2009. After this modest decrease, real prices in resilient countries slowly recovered, returning to a level slightly higher than that before the crisis, of approximately 2%. Overall, prices at the end of 2013 were 5% higher than in the trough. Quite different was the situation in vulnerable countries: in these countries real housing prices continued to fall compared to early 2007. The fall was greater than in the United States, although the pace was somewhat more moderate, since it was spread over a longer period of time. Overall, real house prices in vulnerable countries at the end of 2013 decreased to 68% of prices at the beginning of 2007.

[179] The exact timing is different in the individual countries. In the period before the start of the bubble in the second half of the 1980s, real prices were slightly growing in both the United States and the resilient countries of the Eurozone. However, real prices in vulnerable countries decreased between the beginning of 1991 and the end of 1996 by approximately 16%. However, this period of decrease followed a period of rapid increase of real prices in vulnerable countries, between the beginning of 1986 and the end of 1991, when prices increased by 85% (based on OECD Housing Prices database).

Housing is an important component of the wealth of households and was the basis of the increasing indebtedness of households in the period before the crisis. Household debt, which includes mortgage loans and consumer debt, is defined as all liabilities of a household that require payments of interest or principal to the creditor. Household debt is an important economic indicator and its significant rise was observed to have historically coincided with many severe economic crises. This relation was strict in the crisis that started in 2007 in the United States. Household leverage ratios, which measure the indebtedness of a household relative to their income or wealth, increased considerably in nearly all Western countries. Their decrease is generally considered as a necessary condition for recovery. This event usually meant that the financial vulnerability of households increased and the financing cost, and possibly the access to new credit, worsened.

Household leverage ratio, measured as debt of households and non-profit institutions serving households (NPISHs) as a percentage of net disposable income (NDI), reveals some interesting information (Figure 9.2).[180] The debt of households was definitely high in Japan, at around 140% of NDI, compared to other Western economies until early 2000s, after which date it slightly decreased. Debt in the United Kingdom increased at an outstanding pace since 2000 and until 2007, when it was 182% of NDI, by far the highest level reached in Western countries. Also debt in the United States increased, albeit somewhat more slowly: it reached its peak in 2007 at 143% of NDI.

[180] Other sources confirm that household leverage ratio (debt to disposable income) in 2007 was higher in various European countries than in the United States, where it was around 130% (Glick and Lansing 2010). Countries with leverage ratios higher than in the US included Denmark (199%), Ireland (191%), and the Netherlands (185%). However, most European countries had lower ratios, including Italy (43%), France (60%), Belgium (64%), and Germany (82%). The ratio increased significantly by 42% in the US from 1997 to 2007. However, the growth was higher in various European countries, including Ireland (85%), the Netherlands (82%), Denmark (69%), Portugal (65%), Spain (52%), the United Kingdom (52%), and Norway (50%). The increase was more contained in Austria (13%), Belgium (14%), and France (15%), while in Germany (–2%) and Japan (–5%) the ratio decreased.

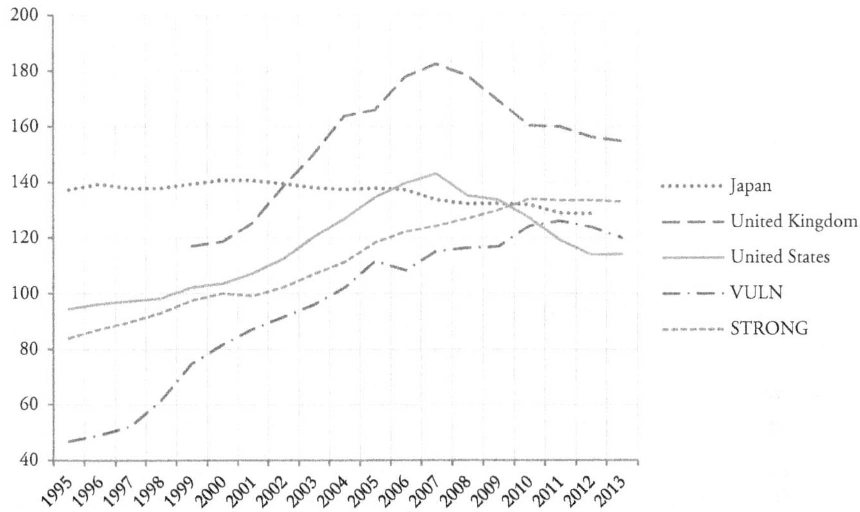

Figure 9.2. Debt of Households and NPISHs, as a Percentage of NDI, 1995–2013. *Source*: Author's own figure based on data from the OECD database.

The case of Eurozone countries is somehow different. The first observation is that debt in resilient countries was constantly higher than in vulnerable countries. However, the distance between the two groups of countries decreased rapidly up to the mid-2000s, after which it remained approximately stable at around 10% of NDI. Overall, Eurozone countries clearly had lower household indebtedness than the other countries until 2010. After this date, debt in resilient countries as a share of NDI was second only to the United Kingdom and started to decrease very slowly, from 134% of NDI to 133% in 2013.[181] Debt in vulnerable countries reached its peak in 2011 at 126% of NDI and decreased to 120% by 2013.

[181] The case of the Netherlands stands apart. Household debt to NDI reached the level of 290% in 2010 and slightly decreased to less than 282% in 2013. Overall, Italy was the most moderate country, with a debt to NDI at 38% in 1995, gradually rising to 90% by 2010 and staying virtually unchanged afterwards. Germany started from a higher level of 97% in 1995, reached 117% in 2000 and decreased afterwards to 94% by 2013. In France, the debt to NDI was 66% in 1995, more than 107% in 2010 and 104% in 2013.

Strictly linked to household debt is the case of subprime lending, which was issued on subprime mortgages in the United States. According to the US Department of Housing and Urban Development, subprime loans are for persons with blemished or limited credit histories, most typically members of minorities.[182] Since these borrowers have poorer quality collateral and increased credit risk, these loans carry a higher rate of interest and less favourable terms than prime loans. The problem with these loans was that, in order to spread risk, lending financial institutions packaged them into mortgage-backed securities (MBS). It was the ultimate default of these securities that critically contributed to the 2007 financial crisis. In fact, serious delinquencies started in 2006 and were substantially higher among subprime mortgages, particularly those with adjustable rates (FCIC 2011). In 2009, more than 40% of adjustable-rate subprime mortgages were delinquent, as against an average for all loans of 14%. The rate of troubled mortgages was around 20% of fixed-rate subprime and adjustable-rate prime mortgages and 5% of fixed-rate prime mortgages. Correspondent shares in European countries were substantially lower. It was after all the nature of social inequalities in the US, as reflected in economic and financial inequalities, which gave the critical push to the crisis.

Mian and Sufi (2009) found that there was an unprecedented relative growth in mortgage credit in those areas of the United States where there was a disproportionately large share of subprime borrowers as of 1996. The expansion of mortgage credit from 2002 to 2005 in these areas occurred despite their sharply declining relative (in some cases,

---

[182] Minorities were over-represented in the subprime lending market. According to a study by the US Department of Housing and Urban Development based on almost 1 million mortgages reported in 1998 under the Home Mortgage Disclosure Act (HMDA), the number of subprime refinance loans increased ten-fold from 1993 to 1998 and seven-fold in value (HUD 2009). The study found that in 1998 subprime loans were three times more likely in low-income neighborhoods (26% of total loans) than in high-income neighborhoods (11% of total loans in moderate-income neighborhoods and 7% in upper-income neighborhoods). Moreover, subprime loans in 1998 were five times more likely in black neighborhoods than in white neighborhoods and even homeowners in high-income black neighborhoods were twice as likely as homeowners in low-income white neighborhoods to have subprime loans.

absolute) income growth. Indeed, this was the only period in which income and mortgage credit growth were negatively correlated. The expansion in mortgage credit to subprime borrowers and its dissociation from income growth were closely correlated with the increase in securitisation of subprime mortgages. The sharp increase in mortgage defaults in 2007 was significantly amplified in the areas where subprime borrowers concentrated.

Household leverage was a powerful statistical predictor of the severity of the 2007–2009 recession across US counties (Mian and Sufi 2010). This observation also concerns credit card borrowing: US counties where people relied most on credit card borrowing reduced durable consumption significantly more following the financial crisis of the fall of 2008. Household leverage growth and dependence on credit card borrowing as of 2006 explain a large part of what happened during the crisis, including consumer default, house price decrease, unemployment, fall of residential investment, and worsening of durable consumption.

Subprime lending expanded significantly in the second part of the 1990s and the first part of the 2000s. The share of subprime lending was 10.6% of the entire mortgage market in 1997 and 7.4% in 2002 (FCIC 2011). This share increased rapidly to above 23.5% or US$600 billion by 2006, the largest increase being concentrated in 2004 (from 8.3% in 2003 to 20.9%). A dramatic collapse followed: the share was 9.2% in 2007 and a mere 1.7% in 2008. Most of these mortgages were securitised: in 2006 the share of securitised mortgages was three-quarters of the total and in 2007 was 100%. During this period, government-sponsored enterprises funded more than half of the mortgages.

Asset-backed securities started to grow at an outstanding rate in the 1990s (FCIC 2011). Their overall value was negligible in 1985, reached US$100 billion in 1991, US$200 billion in 1994 and US$900 billion in 1999. Only a part of these securities derived from home equity. In 1999, the most important source for asset-backed securities was credit card loans, at nearly US$300 billion; loans for car purchases were around US$100 billion. The overall value of asset-backed commercial paper outstanding was close to US$1.25 trillion in summer 2007, but plummeted close to US$750 billion by the end of the year and then to US$350 billion by the end of 2010.

Easy mortgage credit explains the rapid increase of the leverage ratio in certain countries. These are also the countries where house prices increased most over the same period. Countries where household leverage increased most before the crisis were also the countries that experienced the most severe recession, measured by the decline of real consumption. These findings confirm the role that unsustainable credit policies and borrowing attitudes had in causing and fueling the crisis.

9.3 The Transatlantic Transmission of the Crisis

Financial and economic events in the United States reached the EU and the Eurozone through different channels. Important among these were the following: financial meltdown that caused increasing interest rates and restrictive credit policies also in the EU; the decrease of exports to the United States, which fell by 18% in 2009 in the case of the EU-27; the competitive effect of a weaker dollar; financial contagion, in particular through subprime derivatives that European banks held in abundant quantities in their portfolio; the negative effect of consumer and business uncertainty that originated in the US; the effect of the US crisis on rating agencies, which became much more prudent particularly vis-à-vis sovereign debts.

The burst of the housing bubble in the United States triggered the crisis in that country. The transmission of the external shock of the US crisis to the EU and the Eurozone worked through the important economic and financial linkages between the US and the EU. The burst of the housing bubble caused the fall of the value of mortgage-backed securities. This, in turn, damaged financial institutions in the United States, but the effect spread abroad. In fact, subprime securities were internationally held. Many European banks had considerable amounts of these securities in their portfolio. Initially, the Eurozone appeared to remain relatively unharmed by the US contagion. The first European casualty of the crisis was Iceland. Iceland was victim of a heavy systemic bank crisis which started in October 2008 and continued through 2011. All three main privately owned commercial banks found impossible to refinance short-run debt and withstand a run on deposits and consequently collapsed.

The country had to request assistance from the International Monetary Fund (IMF), the first developed country to do so in 30 years. The country's GDP, after it increased significantly for years, fell by a combined 9.3% from 2008 through 2010 (Hart-Landsberg 2013) or by 65% when calculated in euros (Danielsson 2008). A host of negative effects followed: a currency crisis, stock market crisis, repayment crisis for businesses and households, and a housing crisis. The national currency, the krona, fell by more than 80% against the euro in 2008; the stock market lost 75% of its value. The unemployment rate increased from 1% in 2007 to 8% in 2009 and the number of hours that employees worked decreased significantly. Real wages fell by 4.2% in 2008 and 8% in 2009.

The crisis spread to some countries in the EU that retained the use of their national currencies. In Great Britain, the government had to intervene as soon as 2007 to rescue Northern Rock, the first large commercial bank to require emergency government funding as a result of the crisis. Great Britain entered into recession in the second quarter of 2008. In that year, the global credit crunch caused the decrease of house prices and diminished consumer spending. This made 2008 the worst year since the recession of the early 1990s. Other EU member countries in Central-Eastern Europe had structural and financial weaknesses of their own and entered into a deep crisis in 2008. The expansive fiscal policy and the accumulation of a large external debt in the years before 2008 turned Hungary into one of the most financially vulnerable countries in Europe (EEAG 2012; Valentinyi 2012). Due to the seriousness of the crisis, Hungary was the first EU country needing an IMF-administrated international bailout — with the contribution of the EU and the World Bank — as soon as 2008.

Other vulnerable countries in the region included the Baltic countries, at that time neither one a member of the Eurozone (Kattel and Raudla 2013; Macys 2012). The three countries, Estonia, Lithuania and Latvia, enjoyed high growth levels between 2004 and 2007. However, overheating in this period accumulated tensions in the economy: double-digit inflation, housing boom, real exchange rate appreciation, rapid wage growth, rapidly growing net foreign liabilities, and mounting current account deficits. In early 2008, when credit supply slowed down and credit conditions tightened, domestic bubbles burst. US events aggravated the domestic crisis, which rapidly spread to the real economy. Fall in domestic private and public demand and shrinking exports caused a dramatic fall of GDP by 14.3% in Estonia, 14.8% in Lithuania and 17.7% in Latvia. Unemployment reached the highest level in the EU by that time, around 18%.

The crisis soon spread to the Eurozone. In summer 2007 one of the largest Eurozone banks, BNP Paribas, froze redemptions for three investment funds, as a consequence of its heavy exposure to the US subprime contagion. Counterparty risk among banks increased dramatically and interbank interest rates soared (EC 2009). In the spring of 2008, three major failures involved Bear Stearns in the United States, Northern Rock in the United Kingdom and Landesbank Sachsen in Germany. These were followed by various other failures of major banks half a year later: Lehman Brothers, Fannie Mae and Freddie Mac, AIG, Washington Mutual, Wachovia, Fortis, the banks of Iceland, Bradford & Bingley, Dexia, ABN-AMRO and Hypo Real Estate. Under the threat of a systemic meltdown, governments started various rescue operations (see Chapter 11).

According to the European Commission, financial vulnerability depended on three main partially correlated factors: (a) the extent to which housing markets had been overvalued and construction industries oversized; (b) the export dependency of the economy and the current account position; and (c) the size of the financial sector and/or its exposure to risky assets (EC 2009). It was shown above that the first factor, housing markets, was important in explaining the crisis in the United Kingdom, France, Ireland, Spain and the Baltic countries. The second factor, strong export dependency and high current account surpluses, exposed Germany, the Netherlands, and Austria to the sharp contraction of world trade. Other countries which were running large current account deficits, most notably in Central and Eastern Europe, were exposed to the risk of reversals of capital flows. The third factor, the size of the financial sector and its exposure to risky assets, particularly US subprime assets, was particularly high in countries hosting important financial centres, particularly in the United Kingdom, Ireland and Luxembourg. Vulnerability also characterised countries hosting cross-border banking activities and those more exposed to emerging market risk in Central and Eastern Europe, notably Austria, Belgium and Sweden.

The transatlantic contagion was in part a cause of crisis in the EU and in part it revealed the financial and economic weaknesses of unbalanced European economies. The reaction to the crisis also exposed the ineffectiveness of the Eurozone policy construction. While non-Eurozone EU member countries were free to use all the policy instruments and measures they considered to be appropriate, Eurozone member countries found themselves strictly constrained and nearly powerless.

9.4 Home-Grown Problems

In sovereign countries, policies are used to combat the causes and the effects of the crisis and to create the conditions for economic revival. In an incomplete monetary union, which lacks a common government of the economy and a lender of last resort, policies have a different nature and meaning. Policies must avoid unwanted distribution of resources and costs among member countries. Under these conditions, a fundamental contradiction develops between the institutional architecture (which requires uniformity of conditions) and the differences among member countries. Under the push of the incomplete institutional architecture and related policies, those intercountry differences expand further and put the system sustainability at risk.

There were understandable and valid reasons for placing emphasis on stabilisation goals and to tailor policy objectives and their implementation to this end. In the EU parlance, this was sometimes defined as "homework" or "home-duties", meaning that austerity policies should first stabilise the national economy and balance finances. Austerity thus became a necessary condition for future growth. However, this also means that policies fundamentally had a short-run perspective.

Unfortunately, this approach overlooked the deep economic and financial differences that existed among the Eurozone member countries. Under these conditions, austerity policies had deeply asymmetric consequences for different countries. Economic and institutional performance in the Eurozone suffered as a consequence, and resilient and vulnerable countries increasingly diverged. Vulnerable countries were particularly disadvantaged, yet even resilient countries had to pay a price due to the economic, financial and institutional linkages and interlocking among member countries. Although there was some flexibility and common help within the Eurozone, internal discipline and austerity seen as necessary precondition became a serious liability for the Eurozone's performance and even jeopardised its existence.

The time elapsed since the crisis has witnessed significant consolidation and progress, together with dangerous breakdowns and failures. Consolidation and progress were of particular concerns for the relations among member countries. In spite of conflicts on what exactly was to be done with policies and reforms and what price vulnerable member countries had to pay before getting common support, all countries accepted that domestic macroeconomic and fiscal consolidation was a necessary condition, as much as reforms were as well. However, breakdowns and failures threatened the long-run economic and political sustainability of the Eurozone and the growth and development prospects of its member countries. There may be reasons for concern about the costs of the Eurozone in terms of foregone development and growth opportunities, and of unemployment and prospects, particularly for the younger generations. Moreover, it has to be seen whether the modest common help actually supported the vulnerable countries or their (often foreign-owned) financial institutions.

An assessment of policies implemented so far in terms of achievements and progress and of failures and costs is therefore necessary to devise the path to the future. Was monetary union a bad idea, was it premature, or does it need a longer-than-thought period of adaptation to bring about the desired fruits? Is monetary union a good idea that turned sour because of incomplete institutions and inadequate policies? Or is the lack of a true cooperative spirit, the egoism and opportunism of member countries the cause of troubles?

The EU is based primarily on shared rules and common control. In fact, even the main controller and enforcer, the European Commission, is still largely appointed by member countries based on national representation, even if the European Commission needs the approval of the European Parliament. The latter played a stronger role than in the past in the definition of the new European Commission in 2014. Also the Eurozone has a composite nature, and even the European Central Bank (ECB) is an incomplete government of the currency, although lately it evolved into a more complete and effective government in practical terms.

Intercountry trust and shared perspectives and goals are of the utmost importance. Common goals are partial and mostly passive, even within the Eurozone: price stability is the primary goal, of which financial stability is the precondition. As a consequence of these arrangements, the main responsibility for the stability and growth of national economies is left in the end to national governments. However, the common governance strongly restricts the freedom and consequently the effectiveness of national governments in the policy domain. Trust and commonality of intents are consequently put under stress, in particular in the short run.

The Eurozone common policymaking system is ill-defined, incomplete, insecure, vulnerable, unconfident, and unstable. Missing a direct competence over policymaking and an autonomous and discretionary common budget to support it, there is no true common policymaking.[183] The only partial exception is that of monetary policies, which are in any case submitted to serious institutional constraints. Indeed, what is common and supersedes the domain of national governments are a set of rules, parameters, and procedures and formal and often uncertain control and enforcement. Truly common initiative is extremely limited and the fundamental role of the Eurozone is to oversee that member countries comply with the agreed parameters. This system is inevitably subject to bureaucratisation and intergovernmental trading, pressure, and conflict, and in the end is ineffective and counterproductive. Unfortunately, this conclusion does not guarantee that there are better alternatives.

9.5 Financial Institutions and Financial Management

The buildup and evolution of the Economic and Monetary Union relied on national governments managing the financial system. In this system, the common monetary institutions and policies would deal with symmetric shocks, while decentralised national fiscal systems and policies would deal with asymmetric shocks, including those which would derive

[183] Mario Draghi, the ECB president, repeatedly warned about the insufficiency of the ECB action and called member countries to agree on the dramatically necessary fiscal actions for resolving the crisis.

to different member countries from the common monetary policy (Buti and Sapir 1998).

Although the fiscal system was bound to remain decentralised to the member states, it was clear that intercountry coordination was necessary. One important reason for this was that financial market integration in the EU went quite far, and fiscal policies in a monetary union had important spillovers. Moreover, coordination of fiscal policies featured important advantages for both the countries and the Eurozone. There are various types of fiscal policy spillovers. These include such positive spillovers as synchronised business cycles, which ease monetary policy and increase its effect, and a spillover of borrowing costs. However, there may also be negative spillovers, such as the deficit bias of some countries, which may lead to the danger of excessive deficit. Negative spillovers may pose different threats for the common currency, including debt monetisation, fiscal indiscipline, the risk of public debt default, and the risk of bailout obligations by partner countries.

The coordination of fiscal policies in a monetary union has important advantages. In particular, coordination can replace inter-state or EU transfers and the problematic political issues going with them. In a monetary union, a country loses the most important instruments to deal with idiosyncratic shocks: exchange rate adjustment and independent monetary policy. However, other instruments are available cross-country. Their activation in an economic and monetary union should be easier and more effective: price and wage adjustment, labour mobility, saving and borrowing, investment in other countries of the union, and direct insurance (Draghi 2014; Furceri 2013; Furceri and Zdzienicka 2013; Van Beers *et al.* 2014).[184]

The problem with the Eurozone is that these mechanisms for risk sharing are by far less effective than in a monetary union like the United States. Moreover, their effect falls sharply in severe downturns, i.e. when

[184] In the United States, the private risk-sharing mechanism is quite effective: around two-thirds of economic shocks are absorbed via integrated financial markets. Conversely, in the Eurozone the consequence of credit and capital markets in smoothing income is much less effective.

they are needed most (Furceri and Zdzienicka 2013).[185] Van Beers *et al.* (2014) find that the share of the GDP smoothing in the Eurozone is rather small, much lower than in the United States and decreasing over time. The authors consider three different channels through which smoothing of temporary shocks to GDP takes place: capital markets, fiscal transfers, and total savings. First, capital can move from one country to another, thus sharing risk via cross-ownership of productive assets. Second, income differences can be smoothed through fiscal transfers among regions or countries. Third, lending and borrowing on credit markets can smooth consumption differences.

Statistically, only the third channel is significantly different from zero over the entire time period in the Eurozone. The importance of this channel decreased over time, but increased during the crisis. In fact, during the crisis this channel absorbed around 39% of the shocks among the Eurozone member countries. Neither the capital market channel, nor fiscal transfers contributed significantly to the absorption of shocks, although their role increased. Moreover, the capital market channel had a negative smoothing effect since the crisis.[186] Overall, the unsmoothed share of the shocks to GDP increased significantly from 49% in the period 1972–2012 to 76% in 2008–2012, i.e. during the crisis.

The private risk-sharing mechanism (also called private insurance mechanism), thus, is not a particularly effective replacement for a risk-sharing union. In the Eurozone, the latter is ruled out through different rules and supposedly replaced by financial integration and the common

---

[185] According to the president of the ECB (Draghi 2014), since direct fiscal transfers are ruled out in the Eurozone and labour mobility is low, having effective additional mechanisms for cross-country risk-sharing is essential. This means in particular "deepening financial integration in ways that improve private risk-sharing — that is, through having more diversified financial portfolios that can spread risk and reward across regions, and more integrated credit markets that can smooth consumption patterns." These mechanisms should complement the ability of the Eurozone member countries to have economies "flexible enough to find and exploit their comparative advantages, so as to benefit from the Single Market. And they also have to be flexible enough to respond quickly to short-term shocks, including through adjustment of wages or reallocating resources across sectors."

[186] See Furceri (2013) and Furceri and Zdzienicka (2013) for similar results.

surveillance. In this construction, the common support to countries in difficulty and financial distress is not ruled out, but has to follow different channels and typically involves international organisations. As a matter of fact, common support is not a matter belonging in the Eurozone. In fact, the Lisbon treaty introduced a no-bailout clause, in order to avoid the situation in which partner countries have bailout obligations for other member countries. This prohibition was thought to guarantee the Eurozone, together with the prohibition to member countries to monetise their deficit, from dangerously softening fiscal discipline. Investors did not believe in the effectiveness of the no-bailout clause since this was not really applied in the crisis years.

Financial markets play important functions in the economy. They match lending and borrowing needs by transforming maturity, since they borrow typically short-term and lend mostly long-term. Financial markets also perform intermediation between savers and borrowers and match lending and borrowing needs in different forms, providing both risk and debt capital. Financial markets also deal with inherent risk against the promise of future repayment and thus provide risk diversification. The bigger and more liquid financial markets are, the more they can diversify risk.

The integration of financial markets, financial infrastructures and financial institutions results in important benefits. Financial markets are characterised by economies of scale that allow for a larger variety of financial products at a lower cost. Since they operate through networks of borrowers and lenders, financial markets are characterised by network externalities. Their integration may enhance the transmission of monetary policy impulses and contributes to safeguard financial stability and the smooth operation of payment systems. However, these important functions are neither necessarily easy nor are they free of risk. Indeed, financial markets are affected by pervasive asymmetric information to the advantage of borrowers.

The process of European integration had important consequences for capital markets, both through their integration and the effect of the common currency. The integration of capital markets and the elimination of exchange rates through the adoption of the euro diminished risk and promised to increase the profit rate adjusted to risk, other things being equal. It became easier and less risky for investors to diversify, which promised to increase investment.

Empirical verification of these assumptions is not easy. Beyond the difficulties in defining capital and rates of return, many other economic and social variables also intervened to complicate the picture. Yet having a fair picture of the profitability of an economy and what influences it is important for different reasons. Profits are useful indicators of the financial health of enterprises, their ability to use internal resources to finance investments and to attract external financing. Profits also reflect the structural rigidities of the economy and their variation through time. Profits may influence inflation through the price-setting behaviour of enterprises and reflect the effect of economic shocks. Furthermore, profits are important determinants of consumption, since they are a component of households' total income, e.g., in the form of distributed dividends.[187]

In order to assess the effect of monetary unification on profits and investment, it is important to have a clear picture of shocks that hit the economy during the relevant period. Maurin *et al.* (2011) analysed profits in the four largest Eurozone countries (Germany, France, Italy and Spain) and the Eurozone as a whole. They considered three main sectors (manufacturing, construction and services) in each economy over the period 1988–2010. Profit shares, the ratio of profits to nominal value added, behaved differently in the three sectors. In manufacturing, profit shares were highly synchronised across countries, while in the construction sector profit shares followed idiosyncratic dynamics and were highly volatile. The highest and least volatile profit share was in the services sector.

The authors also studied the sensitivity of profits to four distinctive structural shocks: demand shock, employment shock, wage shock and price mark-up shock. They found that the magnitude and extent of responses differed significantly across countries and sectors, presumably as a function of the different features of the economies. Predictably, the signs of the effects of shocks on profits were positive in the case of demand and negative in the case of wage shocks. Price mark-up shocks had a positive effect on

[187] Gross profits are used to many purposes. The largest part is used to pay taxes and remunerate capital by means of interest payment and dividends distributed to shareholders. The residue is the saving of non-financial corporations.

profits initially, but this was turned into a negative effect once increased prices caused demand to fall. In the four countries considered and the Eurozone, Maurin *et al.* (2011) found that the fluctuations in the growth rate of profits since the end of the 1990s were primarily driven by demand shocks. This was particularly clear in Germany and, to a lesser extent, in the Eurozone. This effect was especially evident during the crisis in all countries considered and the Eurozone. Other shocks tended to reciprocally offset and wage shocks appeared, which were of minor importance in general, except in Spain.

Chan-Lee and Sutch (1985) used different measures to get a detailed picture for OECD economies. They found a widespread declining trend in profit rates for the period 1960–1982, although with large differences in rates of return across countries and across branches.[188] These differences were associated with variations in depreciation rates. Low growth and depressed capacity utilisation accompanied these negative trends in profit rates during the 1970s. However, they also found some sign of recovery of for the profit rates in early 1980s.

Using a different time span, dataset and estimation methods, Oulton and Rincon-Aznar (2009) found that the real rate of return did not show a clear trend in most countries.[189] The trend, however, varied considerably across the 10 branches considered within each country.[190] Moreover, the real rate of return in the market sector was relatively similar across countries. Spain and Italy are notable exceptions, featuring exceptionally low and exceptionally high real rates of return respectively.

---

[188] The authors define profit rates as gross operating surplus over gross value added. Rate of return is gross operating surplus as a percentage of gross capital stock.

[189] The average nominal rate of return is defined as profit minus (true) depreciation costs and minus capital losses (or plus capital gains). Each of these variables is expressed as a percentage of the value of assets at the beginning of the year.

[190] The authors estimated the real rate of return to capital in 14 countries in 10 branches of the market sector plus the entire market economy in the years 1971–2005. Of the 14 countries, 11 are EU members — eight of them are in the Eurozone — and three are outside the EU. The measure of capital used by the authors is an aggregate over seven types of asset: three ICT assets (computers, communications equipment, and software) plus machinery and equipment, nonresidential structures, transport equipment, and other.

It is not easy to assess the true effect of monetary unification in these findings. An indirect hint can be obtained by comparing profit rates in the Eurozone with that of countries outside it, in particular the United States and non-euro EU member countries. According to the findings by Chan-Lee and Sutch (1985), profit rates in the United States were higher than in future Eurozone member countries, although the difference decreased in early 1980s.

Conversely and referring to 2007, Leythienne and Smokova (2009) found that non-financial companies in the Eurozone and the EU had higher profitability and higher investment in proportion to their value added than in the United States. However, they also found sizeable differences among countries (Figure 9.3). The share of profit (gross operating surplus in gross value added) increased as compared to the share of labour in most countries in the 2000–2007 period (Figure 9.4). This conclusion held for the Eurozone, the EU and the US.

Within the Eurozone, it appeared that vulnerable countries had both the highest gross investment rates and profit shares of non-financial corporations in the years 1995–1997. The trend of investment rates was

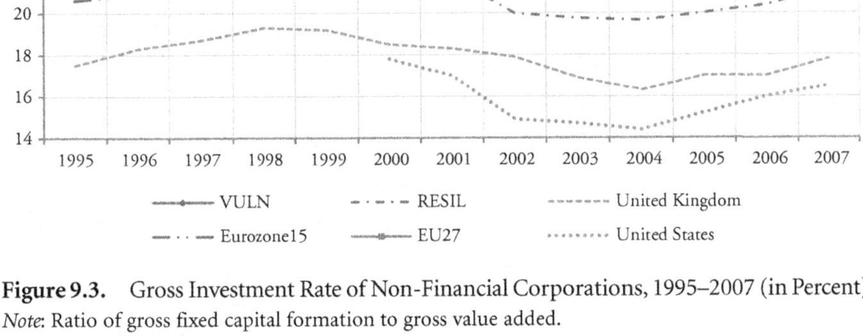

Figure 9.3. Gross Investment Rate of Non-Financial Corporations, 1995–2007 (in Percent).
Note: Ratio of gross fixed capital formation to gross value added.
Source: Author's own interpretation of data from Leythienne and Smokova (2009).

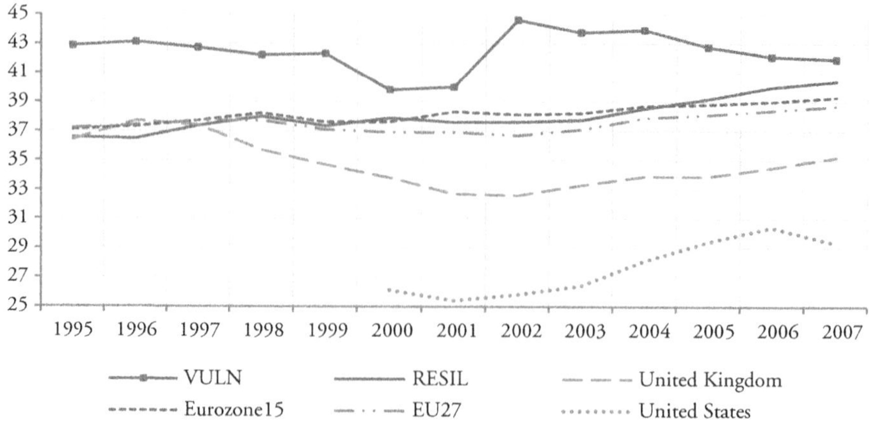

Figure 9.4. Profit Share of Non-Financial Corporations, 1995–2007 (in Percent).
Note: Share of gross operating surplus to gross value added.
Source: Author's own interpretation of data from Leythienne and Smokova (2009).

growing, while profit shares remained stable. Over the entire period, however, both variables fluctuated significantly from one year to the other. In the case of resilient countries, the trend of investment rates was slightly decreasing, while that of profit shares was increasing.

The cost of capital actually decreased in the EU up to the crisis. Using the harmonised long-term interest rates as a proxy for the cost of capital, the Eurozone success appears to be undeniable, particularly in vulnerable countries. The convergence of interest rates in the Eurozone countries to the lowest level was achieved by the late 1990s. Only Greece needed a few more years. The coincidence of interest rates in the Eurozone remained unchanged until 2008 when, under the effect of the crisis, divergence took over again, at a shocking pace (Figure 9.5).

Monetary unification also had important effects in financial markets. The common currency eliminated the currency risk within the Eurozone, leading to more competition and consequently to better performance, and provided the benefits obtained from a world currency. Greater competition weakened or removed dominating positions and the rents associated with them. By fostering the integration of financial markets, the common currency also allowed for better exploitation of economies of scale and supported greater diversification of financial investments.

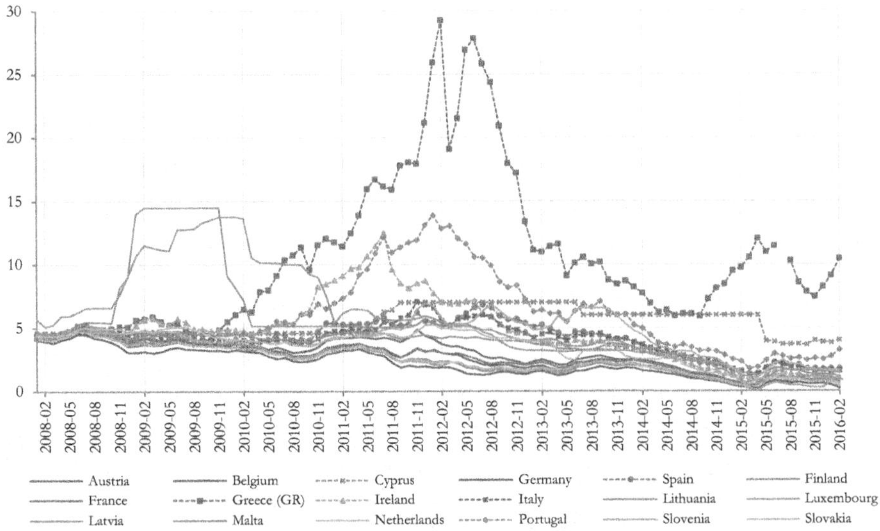

Figure 9.5. Harmonised Long-Term Interest Rates in the Eurozone.[191]
Notes: Long-term interest rate for convergence purposes, monthly data on debt security issued, 10 years' maturity.
Source: Statistical Data Warehouse, ECB.

Financial market integration, together with monetary unification, had important consequences for the evolution of the banking system and for bond and stock markets. In spite of expectations and European efforts, the restructuring of the banking system took place mostly at national level. This outcome was due to different reasons, including: differences among national regulations, repeated harmonisation efforts notwithstanding; the existence of several non-regulatory non-tariff barriers; different traditions and different financial and banking systems; national differences in the tax treatment of savings; and political efforts by national governments to keep large banks in the ownership of national owners.

[191] Harmonised long-term interest rates are interest rates for long-term government bonds. They are denominated in Euro for Eurozone member countries and in national currencies for other EU member countries. Proxies derived from private sector bond yields or interest rate indicators are used when no harmonised long-term government bond yields are available.

A somewhat similar evolution could be noticed in bond markets and stock markets, although a slight move towards European integration could be noticed. Bond markets were characterised by the convergence of interest rates up to the crisis, but bond ownership remained mostly national. Also stock markets presented a strong home bias for different reasons, including the existence of important information asymmetry and in spite of the disappearance of currency risk. However, increased cross-border holding of equity could be noticed.

Eurozone financial institutions continued to remain typically national, as much as financial management did. In consideration of their cross-benefits and cross-detriments, financial markets were coordinated at the Union level, particularly the Eurozone level. In order to ensure the stability of the common monetary institutions and policies, national financial institutions and management were progressively constrained by means of what can be considered a set of true EU financial institutions. Eurozone member countries also agreed to give up a fundamental part of their sovereignty in fiscal matters, for the sake of improving the efficacy of the entire system and the advantages derived by member countries. Therefore, countries agreed to set up common financial institutions, which coexisted with the nominal sovereignty of national governments in financial matters.

This solution probably avoided excessive internal contagion to the EU and the spread of related costs to other countries. However, this same solution prevented the possibility to fix distress in a particular country rapidly and effectively, at a reasonable cost for that country and the international community.

9.6 Financial Instruments of the Monetary Union

An instrument such as the EU budget is of no use for policymaking in a monetary union, although it may be important for solving structural problems. It is of the utmost importance for the stability of the common currency that finances in the Eurozone are under control and converging to mutually compatible values. This is important to avoid actions by individual member countries which could jeopardise the stability of prices and the exchange rate of the common currency. For this reason and as soon as the issue of the common currency was put on the agenda, the Union started to devise common instruments for managing national finances.

While in the monetary domain the plan was to fully transfer sovereignty from member countries to the Union, in the financial domain the blueprint was to condition and limit national sovereignty in such a way that would not conflict with or jeopardise the common currency. Given the EU and Eurozone's construction, the limitations to national financial sovereignty had to be voluntarily agreed upon by member countries. As a result, the Stability and Growth Pact (SGP) was adopted and the Eurogroup and the Economic and Financial Affairs Council (Ecofin) were formed. Given their binding nature, these can be considered as common financial institutions endowed with effective policy instruments. Such instruments can be used to manage common financial issues and discipline member countries. They effectively limit national financial sovereignty, whenever this enters in conflict with the common objectives and the stability of the EU economy and the common currency.

The common financial system presently includes three different components. It includes a multilateral pact, the SGP that the Eurozone member countries subscribed to as a necessary step in the adoption of the common currency. The second component is made of direct control and procedures by the European Commission and the Council of Ministers on the member countries' compliance with the Pact and other requirements. The most important direct control is the periodical reviews of member countries' economic and monetary accomplishments, such as those undertaken to prevent and correct macroeconomic imbalances and excess deficit.

The third component includes the pressure by the peers. This is the essence of the Eurogroup and Ecofin's role and responsibility. The Eurogroup is made of the finance ministers of the Eurozone, while Ecofin is an organ of the Council of the European Union made up of ministers voting on matters only affecting the Eurozone. Following the peer review of a country's economic and financial situation, the peers put pressure upon the country's government towards adopting particular measures. These are the measures that the peer governments consider necessary to defend and pursue the stability and prosperity of the Eurozone. Even if the country remains formally sovereign, the peer pressure is quite effective and can be occasionally reinforced by warnings and suggestions that the European Commission or the ECB release. Needless to say, the effectiveness of the pressure also depends upon the particular financial situation and the economic strength of the country under scrutiny.

The SGP was adopted in 1997 after the Maastricht Treaty introduced the "excessive deficit procedure". The intent behind the Pact was to give greater strength to the convergence criteria adopted at Maastricht and convert them into a permanent and binding regime. The Maastricht Treaty circumscribed the access to the euro to countries sharing compatible financial and monetary situations, based on a set of criteria. In turn, the SGP adopted a more active stance and imposed "virtuous" behaviour on each Eurozone country. Since fiscal policies are in the remit of sovereign nations, the final competence for the SGP was given to Ecofin, i.e. to the group of peers.

The SGP includes four important components. First, it defines what is meant by excessive deficit: following the Maastricht criteria, this was initially defined as a deficit above 3% of GDP. The limit was softened in 2005 in case of exceptional circumstances, such as a decrease of GDP. When the 3% limit is exceeded, the second component intervenes. This is the preventive arm: its role is to encourage the relevant member country's compliance through a national Stability Programme. If this second step fails, the third step is undertaken. This consists of a corrective arm and has two components: an early warning that the country is running an excess deficit, followed by the excessive deficit procedure. Finally, sanctions can be imposed on the non-complying country in the form of non-remunerated deposit at the Commission. Sanctions, never been imposed so far, can run from 0.2% to 0.5% of the country's GDP and may be transformed into an eventual fine after two years of non-compliance.

Its apparent formalism and rigidity notwithstanding, the Pact includes provisions for giving some flexibility to the management of finances of countries in difficulty. In this way, the Pact allows some room for countercyclical fiscal policies. The Pact considers that in the Eurozone a 1% decline of GDP growth worsens the budget deficit of a country by 0.5% of GDP on average.[192] Since this is considered to be a significant

[192] The fiscal multiplier was considered to be at 0.5. However, after the IMF revision, the supposition of the SGP seems out of order. See Section 11.2.

amount with potentially serious consequences on financial stability, the Pact includes a recommendation that in years of growth the budget is balanced or in surplus. This would create the financial resources for financing automatic stabilisers to become active in bad years.

In spite of the 2005 reform that made the Pact somewhat more flexible, during the crisis it appeared that the remaining rigidity of the Pact would cause additional difficulties for the countries in the most vulnerable situations. Thus, the Pact runs the risk of worsening financial fragility and imbalances. Therefore, a new version of the Pact was devised, that takes into consideration the economic and financial situation of the countries hit by the crisis. This is the Euro Plus Pact (E+P), whose provisions try to distinguish what results from a country's economic mismanagement from what results from the crisis. The country should not suffer further for the latter. The E+P is designed as a more stringent successor to the SGP, stipulating a set of quantitative targets meant to strengthen cost competitiveness of the member countries (Gabrisch and Staehr 2014). Moreover, some member states of the EU make concrete commitments to a list of political reforms, intended to improve their fiscal strength and competitiveness.

The E+P was adopted in March 2011, but so far it has not been implemented consistently. In spite of this, it played an important role in the management of the consequences of the crisis and of the situation of the vulnerable countries. The E+P includes three provisions. Perhaps the most important one is the adoption of the cyclically adjusted primary budget based on a zero output gap. This is the basic concept for evaluating the existence of excess deficit. This definition introduces two important novelties. First, the budget is cyclically adjusted in the sense that decreased revenue due to the gap between current GDP and potential GDP (zero output gap) is discarded from the calculation of the deficit. Second, the primary budget is considered, i.e. passive interests due to public debt are disregarded. The aim in this case is to concentrate on the current financial management, for which the incumbent government is responsible, to leave out of consideration the debt accumulated by previous governments and generations.

This provision on the primary budget is favourable to highly indebted countries and reasonable if the goal is to stabilise running finances during a serious crisis. Nevertheless, the provision could run the danger of dealing more favourably with high debt countries than with low debt countries, thus weakening the effort to bring debt under control. To avoid these pitfalls, the evolution of the debt is also used to evaluate policies. In this way, high debt countries are not punished for what they inherited from the past, but are evaluated on the basis of what they are doing for decreasing the weight of that legacy.

The E+P also intends to make decision procedures more certain and automatic, in order to avoid endless bargaining and conflict. To this end, a "fiscal compact" was introduced as part of the Treaty on Stability, Coordination and Governance in the Economic and Monetary Union of 2012. The fiscal compact oversees the implementation of balanced budget rule at the national level and further strengthening of the excessive deficit procedure within the SGP.

In Title III, the fiscal compact outlines a set of requirements and related actions that countries have to follow. The fundamental rule is that the general government budgets need to be balanced or in surplus. The fiscal compact introduces, as a novel element, a varying upper limit to the deficit of 3% of GDP, which depends on the level of debt of the relevant country. A very stringent rule is introduced for those countries having a debt-to-GDP ratio above 60%: they must reduce the part of the debt exceeding the ceiling at an average rate of at least one-twentieth per year.[193]

The fiscal compact also introduces an automatic correction mechanism, when it becomes clear that the country has failed to converge to the balanced budget rule. Although it is the member country that defines the exact implementation of the mechanism, this must comply with the directive published by the European Commission. The automatic correction mechanism is embedded, together with the balanced budget rule, in domestic law. A country under an Excessive Deficit Procedure must prepare an Economic Partnership Programme (EPP) and submit it to the Commission and the Council. The EPP details the reform programme that

---

[193] This provision may be mild for countries which are slightly above 60%, but may be prohibitive for countries substantially above that limit and still fighting with the effects of the crisis. For instance, Italy had a public debt in 2014 around 134% of GDP. This means that Italy is to find additional resources corresponding to approximately 3.7% of its GDP (approximately €67 billion) every year to decrease its excess public deficit by one twentieth.

the country undertakes to correct the excessive deficit in an effective and durable way. The fiscal compact also oversees a better coordination of the issuance of public debt by all member countries in the form of national plans. Plans are submitted in advance to the European Commission and the Council.

These rules look reasonable, although rigorous, for an incomplete monetary union made of countries close to fiscal balance. However, when countries are in significantly different economic and financial situations and possess varied institutional features, the severity and rigidity of the fiscal compact risks placing vulnerable countries in an unbearable situation. The fiscal compact is clearly based on a gross underestimation of the depth and duration of the crisis and its effects on finances. Predictably, the fiscal compact is implemented with a substantial amount of flexibility and postponement.

Unfortunately, however reasonable they may be under certain circumstances, the fundamental common financial institutions are characterised by a negative approach, i.e. made of limits, prohibitions and penalties. This may be necessary in an incomplete monetary union in order to ensure cooperation among member countries and help economic actors and decision-makers to foresee the probable course of economic events. This in turn is fundamental for easing economic calculation and forming reliable expectations, both of which are fundamental bases for decision-making. However, these institutions are geared to prevent and forbid, and lack a positive and constructive arm for promoting and supporting. The ordoliberal inspiration is clear. Unfortunately, these institutions are implemented in an area that misses, in most of its components, the necessary preconditions. This deficiency unbalances common institutions and policies and risks to lead the Eurozone to policy impotence and economic disruption.

9.7 Conclusion

The main steps to integration were under the fading influence of the original commitment: integrate in order to avoid future tensions and wars and help Europe regain an international economic and political role. Mutual trust, driven as much by fear as by love, was the centrepiece of the

European integration project and was the core of the original federalist project. The more the memory of wars faded away and the more integration proceeded, the more the technocratic management of the integration process replaced mutual trust. This is today the core of the intergovernmental approach to European integration.

Ironically the common currency, which represents the crown of the federalist project, was implemented in an inter-governmental and technocratic way. The price paid is existence of incomplete institutions. Negative experiences of some vulnerable countries in complying with commitments increased the discomfort of integration and led to increasing mutual distrust, particularly between resilient and vulnerable countries. The risk is that the integration process is entering a deadlock.

Christopher Clark (2012) describes the situation well, having in view the risk represented by the European situation immediately before World War I:

> It was notable that the actors in the Eurozone crisis, like those of 1914, were aware that there was a possible outcome that would be generally catastrophic (the failure of the euro). All the key protagonists hoped that this would not happen, but in addition to this shared interest, they also had special — and conflicting — interests of their own. Given the interrelationships across the system, the consequences of any one action depended on the responsive actions of others, which were hard to calculate in advance, because of the opacity of decision-making processes. And all the while, political actors in the Eurozone crisis exploited the *possibility* of the general catastrophe as leverage in securing their own specific advantages. (p. 555)

It is therefore important to understand why European institutions, and Eurozone institutions in particular, are left incomplete and in whose interests were they set up in such a way. Although institutions are called to serve the common interest, the latter is ill defined. As a consequence, national interests played an important role in defining institutions in two ways. First was the defence of national interest, at least in the minimal sense that common institutions should avoid jeopardising what is important for individual countries. Unfortunately, each country has its own goals and priorities, which are not always in harmony, and sometimes in conflict with those of the other countries. Public finances are a very important case of inter-national divergence of interests.

Second was the goal of pursuing direct national gains from common institutions in the form of special provisions or transfers, together with the collective gains from cooperation. If the whole had a value superior to the sum of the parts — this being the fundamental economic and political rationale of European integration and the adoption of the euro — any member country could obtain a net benefit. However, the allocation of the collective benefit to individual countries depended upon institutions. Thus, common institutions were placed at the crossroads of different trade-offs. The most important among the potential trade-offs in the Eurozone was the one existing between monetary and financial stability on one hand and easing financial constraints on the other. The latter aspect of the trade-off was sometimes interpreted as a precondition to economic growth, as much as other countries saw monetary and financial stability as necessary preconditions to the same goal.

Depending on which side of the trade-off prevailed and was embedded in institutions, consequences for individual countries were quite different also in an intertemporal sense. The outcome could be unstable, particularly if some countries were asked to pay a price in the present in order to make the common and their own benefit materialise in the future, while other countries gained a share of that benefit in the present. Under these conditions, collective action was costly, inefficient, perhaps ineffective and unstable. A further problem with incomplete institutions was that monetary policies under these conditions and in a time of crisis led to implicit discrimination, as seen in Section 7.10. The construction of the euro offered plenty of examples in these senses, as the following chapter would explain.

I leave the reader to imagine the condition of the unfortunate fowls swinging by the legs with their heads downwards in the hands of a man agitated by all the tumults of passion; and whose arm moved more in accordance with the violence of his feelings, than with sympathy for the unhappy animals whose heads became conscious of sundry terrific shocks, which they resented by pecking at one another, — a practice too frequent with companions in misfortune.

— Alessandro Manzoni, *The Betrothed*, Chapter III.

10

Internal Contagion and the Eurozone Economies

In the perspective of the monetary union, the European Union (EU) envisioned a common monetary policy that could deal with symmetric shocks, and national fiscal policies for taking care of asymmetric shocks and national idiosyncrasies. This approach was the only pragmatic solution available, given the incomplete institutional construction of the union and the nearly irrelevant and structural role of the common budget. Particularly limiting were the lack of a common government of the economy and of a lender of last resort, the provisions of no-monetisation and no-socialisation of the deficit and debt and the no-bailout clause. Even fiscal equalisation was actually rejected, except in the indirect, partial and mild form allowed through the common budget.

These rules prevented the effective mutual support among countries and sharply divided the fate of each country from that of the other countries in the monetary union. At the same time, rules took away much of the national policy freedom and effectiveness. Countries had mutual responsibility, but they lacked mutual support. Even worse was the lack of joint responsibility for public finances, which caused bank-sovereign interdependence at the national level, which in some countries reached dangerous levels. These two features could not coexist with the prohibition of monetary financing of the debt without causing a serious and potentially destabilising vulnerability of the Eurozone.

The situation that resulted from these rules created new problems: the coordination between monetary and fiscal policies belonging in different governments led to the difficulty of finding a balance between common stability and having the option to fix national problems. The former necessarily had priority for the sake of the monetary union and fiscal policies became subordinated to monetary policies via stringent criteria and quasi-rigid rules, as outlined in the Maastricht criteria and the Stability and Growth Part (SGP). This solution created serious problems for the effectiveness of monetary policies during the crisis and converted fiscal policies into a liability for vulnerable countries. The effects for resilient countries were mixed: it was a boon, thanks to the inflow of capital, low interest rates and greater competitiveness vis-à-vis vulnerable countries which had to struggle under these conditions. However, it was also a bane, in the form of decreased demand by vulnerable countries and the potential destabilisation of financial markets. The financing of dramatically needed reforms in vulnerable countries became all the more difficult. This could lead to the long-run decline of the Eurozone.

The present problem lies in the fact that individual Eurozone countries are in distinct situations under various perspectives. In spite of the initial examination through the convergence criteria and the common supervision before introducing the euro and in spite of the fact that the majority of Eurozone countries share continental capitalist institutions, there are important differences among Eurozone countries. Important institutional differences concern, e.g., the role of governments. Other differences involve policies, e.g. the effectiveness of national fiscal and monetary policies. Still other differences are in stocks and flows, in particular in public debts and deficits, and in the real economy (Table 10.1). Important examples of the latter are dissimilarities of international specialisation, size structure of enterprises, technical progress, labour relations and productivity. Such differences make institutional and policy incompleteness particularly damaging and unsustainable in the long run.

There are three possible solutions to such differences: the union, the market, and the intercountry solution. According to the union (federalist) solution, a common government of the economy should have been created to redistribute resources within the monetary union and a lender of last resort should have been created. According to the market solution, an effective private risk-sharing mechanism is sufficient. This solution requires completely open and integrated markets, guaranteeing the free flow of resources to the countries in greater need and therefore with higher risk and returns. Finally, the intercountry solution requires that each member country disciplines its finances by keeping balanced budgets and reforming its economy. In this way, each country converges to the same virtuous economic blueprint. A combination of the three solutions is also possible. For example, an intercountry solution is eased through the private risk-sharing mechanism typical of the market solution, while fiscal equalisation is between the intercountry and the union solution.

All appeared to be fine in the Eurozone, until the external environment was friendly and no major shock was around. Under these conditions, the three solutions were partially interchangeable and led to similar results, albeit in different ways. They could even lead to similar long-term outcomes, if resources were properly invested in growth-supporting activities. Each solution hides dangers, though. The union requires political unification sooner or later and runs the risk of a political stalemate. The market solution runs the risk of creating financial instability and bubbles, in particular if investors are under the illusion of the existence of a protective umbrella of a union. Finally, the intercountry solution is rigid and bureaucratic and puts vulnerable countries in a difficult situation.

In the Eurozone, precious time was wasted when the world economy was growing rapidly. The Eurozone failed to take the need for national and common institutional reforms seriously, and it was restrained by resilient countries, and vulnerable countries also postponed the necessary reform and policy discipline.

Table 10.1. The Deficit and Debt of General Government, Percentage of GDP.

	2007			2009			2011			2013			2014		
	1	**2**	**3**	***1***	**2**	**3**	***1***	**2**	**3**	***1***	**2**	**3**	***1***	**2**	**3**
EU-28							−4.5	2.9	80.9	−3.2	2.7	85.5	−2.9	2.5	86.8
Eurozone–18							−4.1	3.0	85.9	−2.9	2.8	91.1	−2.4	2.6	92.0
Austria	−1.3	3.1	64.8	−5.3	3.2	79.7	−2.6	2.8	82.1	−1.3	2.5	80.9	−2.4	2.4	84.5
Belgium	0.0	3.8	86.8	−5.5	3.6	99.2	−4.1	3.4	102.0	−2.9	3.1	104.4	−3.2	3.1	106.5
Finland	5.1	1.4	34.0	−2.5	1.3	41.7	−1.0	1.4	48.5	−2.5	1.3	55.8	−3.2	1.3	59.3
France	−2.5	2.6	64.4	−7.2	2.4	79.0	−5.1	2.6	85.2	−4.1	2.3	92.3	−4.0	2.2	95.0
Germany	0.3	2.7	63.7	−3.0	2.6	72.6	−0.9	2.5	77.9	0.1	2.0	77.1	0.7	1.7	74.7
Luxembourg	4.2	0.3	7.2	−0.5	0.4	15.5	0.4	0.5	19.1	0.9	0.4	24.0	0.6	0.4	23.6
The Netherlands	0.2	2.0	42.7	−5.5	2.0	56.5	−4.3	1.8	61.3	−2.3	1.5	68.6	−2.3	1.4	68.8
RESIL	**0.9**	**2.3**	**51.9**	**−4.2**	**2.2**	**63.5**	**−2.5**	**2.1**	**68.0**	**−1.7**	**1.9**	**71.9**	**−2.0**	**1.8**	**73.2**

Cyprus	3.3	2.8	54.1	−5.5	2.4	54.1	−5.8	2.2	66.0	−4.9	3.1	102.2	−8.8	2.8	107.5
Greece							−10.2	7.3	171.3	−12.3	4.0	175.0	−3.5	3.9	177.1
Ireland	0.3	1.0	24.0	−13.9	2.0	62.3	−12.7	3.4	111.2	−5.8	4.4	123.2	−4.1	4.0	109.7
Italy	−1.5	4.8	99.7	−5.3	4.4	112.5	−3.5	4.7	116.4	−2.9	4.8	128.5	−3.0	4.7	132.1
Portugal	−3.0	2.9	68.4	−9.8	3.0	83.6	−7.4	4.3	111.1	−4.8	4.9	129.7	−4.5	5.0	130.2
Spain	2.0	1.6	35.5	−11.0	1.7	52.7	−9.4	2.4	69.2	−6.8	3.3	92.1	−5.8	3.3	97.7
VULN	**0.2**	**2.6**	**56.3**	**−9.1**	**2.7**	**73.0**	**−8.2**	**4.1**	**107.5**	**−6.3**	**4.1**	**125.1**	**−5.0**	**4.0**	**125.7**

Note: 1 = Net lending (+)/net borrowing (−).
2 = Interest, payable.
3 = Government consolidated gross debt.
Source: Eurostat database and author's own interpretation of data.

This chapter considers the difficulties faced by the Eurozone resulting from the crisis and contemplates the solutions that the three perspectives offer.

10.1 Internal Contagion

The beginning of the crisis in the EU was in great part the outcome of external contagion from the United States. The previous chapter introduced the distinction between external and internal contagion and discussed the former. While external contagion spreads from one economically sovereign country to another one, internal contagion moves from one country to another one in an economic and monetary union.

In the case of external contagion, it was the United States that was the prime cause: what initiated in that country after 15 September 2008, the day when Lehman Brothers filed for bankruptcy, soon spread its influence to Europe. Initially the problem was the shortage of dollars in the world market. To ease the problem, on 26 September and again on 29 September the US Federal Reserve, the European Central Bank (ECB), the Bank of England and the Swiss National Bank moved to expand US dollar liquidity. The liquidity shortage was soon felt felt in the Eurozone. On the same day on 29 September, the ECB Governing Council decided in favour of a special term refinancing operation, with the aim of increasing the overall liquidity of the Eurozone banking system. In the following days, further measures were implemented repeatedly to increase liquidity, decrease the cost of money and ease the access to credit (ECB 2008b, Stark 2009).

These measures were initially driven by the fear of external contagion. Gradually, though, it was internal contagion that became more influential. Under the influence of US events and as explained in the previous chapter, some European countries entered financial distress. The first European victims were external to the EU, as in the case of Iceland, or among the new member countries of Central-Eastern Europe, as in the case of Hungary and the Baltic countries. These countries had an independent currency at the time of their crisis.[194]

---

[194] The three Baltic countries joined the euro in succession. Estonia joined on 1 January 2011, Latvia on 1 January 2014 and Lithuania on 1 January 2015.

While initially the Eurozone appeared to be relatively safe, the situation soon changed. The effect of external contagion reached the periphery of the Eurozone and from there it propagated to other countries through internal contagion. The outcome was a divided monetary union, in which one part was in financial distress and economic recession and the other part was under political and policy pressure to contribute to the solution and losing economically through trade, financial and production linkages. Financial and economic distress in the Eurozone led soon to policy and institutional distress.

The crisis reached deeply unbalanced Eurozone member countries first: Greece, Ireland and Portugal. Each of these countries mismanaged the economy in idiosyncratic ways, although for years some of these economies were growing fast. The mismanagement was made possible by the ineffective implementation of common rules, under the political pressure to enlarge the union and the Eurozone. Even more importantly, these countries were the targets of massive inflow of capital from other Eurozone member countries and the easy access to cheap credit.

In a sense, they were enjoying the benefits of the supposed existence of a Eurozone umbrella covering and protecting all member countries, in spite of the official no-bailout rule. As a consequence, the three countries overspent, albeit in different ways (see Section 9.2). The problem with the US crisis and the following financial meltdown was that liquidity dried up, central banks' efforts notwithstanding. The following credit crunch and interest rates hike made public and private deficits and debts rapidly unsustainable.

Greece was the first victim. The Greek public debt soared under the conservative governments headed by Kostas Karamanlis from €160 billion in 2004 to €300 billion by 2009.[195] The socialist government headed by

[195] Data are from an article by Vittorio Da Rold in *Il Sole 24 Ore* of 7 April 2011. According to Eleftheriadis (2014), the debt-to-GDP in 2003, just before Karamanlis took power, stood at roughly 97%. The figure had inflated to nearly 130% at the end of his tenure in 2009 (129.7% according to Sapir *et al.* (2014)). It should be noticed that Eurostat refused to validate the fiscal data transmitted by the Greek government and asked for a revision already in March 2004. In May 2004, the European Commission accused Greece of "imprudent" and "sloppy" fiscal policies. Eurostat does not publish presently data for the years before 2006 in the case of Greece. Data for those years are still under recalculation.

George Papandreou, elected on 4 October 2009, announced that in reality the public financial situation was much worse than the official account indicated, and that the previous government had grossly manipulated public balance sheets. The real deficit was at 15%, more than twice the official figure.

The European Commission, the ECB and the International Monetary Fund (IMF) (the "Troika") agreed in May 2010 to finance a Greek Loan Facility with €110 billion through bilateral loans (Sapir *et al.* 2014).[196] This was the first case of a Eurozone country receiving financial assistance from the EU and the IMF still on a bilateral basis. Ireland followed on 21 November of the same year, while Portugal was the third country to follow in April 2011. In March 2013, Cyprus also applied for financial assistance.

Greece engaged in a harsh austerity programme, in particular by cutting budget expenditures and increasing taxes. Greece needed a Second Economic Adjustment Programme, which the Eurozone finance ministers decided on 14 March 2012. The programme oversaw financial assistance of €164.5 billion in total until the end of 2014.[197] Most of this sum was

[196] See EC (2015c).

[197] The Greek public debt in 2015 amounts to €322 billion according to Bloomberg Brief (Sbaihi 2015). This debt is owned in large part (62% or €195 billion) by Eurozone governments through bilateral loans and the EFSF. The IMF owns another 10% and the ECB 8%. The private sector owns 17%. Considering all the four channels through which governments provide financing (bilateral loans, participation in the European Financial Stability Facility (EFSF), capital owners of the ECB and the IMF), the total exposure of each Eurozone government to Greek public debt is the highest in Germany at €65 billion, France at €49 billion, and Italy at €43 billion. However, compared to their 2013 GDP the highest exposures are those of Slovenia (3.06%), Malta (3.03%), Spain (2.78%) and Italy (2.74%). In France and Germany, this share is lower (respectively at 2.38% and 2.37%). The Greek debt increased to approximately €393 billion or €35,630 per inhabitant by 7 December 2015 (NDC 2015). According to the World Economic Forum, there was a dramatic shift in the ownership of the Greek debt since 2012, while the total debt remained at a similar level (Vanham 2015). Shortly before the first bailout, at the end of 2011, the debt was owned in similar parts of a third each by foreign and Greek banks (10% foreign European banks, 8% foreign non-European banks, 15% Greek banks), by shareholders, and by governments and international organisations (15% within Eurozone, 15% the ECB, 6% the IMF). The 2012 bailout forced private bond holders, including Greek banks, to accept

provided by the Eurozone through the newly established European Financial Stability Facility (EFSF)[198] and one-eighth by the IMF. It was the first time that the Eurozone intervened through a common instrument of crisis management. The plan included a 50% reduction of the Greek debt held by private holders. A new renegotiation of the Greek debt followed in October 2012, which included lower interest rates on Greek loans.[199]

Sovereign debt crises spread to Ireland and Portugal in 2010 (Glover and Richards-Shubik 2014; Sapir *et al.* 2014). By 2011, the EU and the IMF also had to implement bailout programmes in these countries. While the origin of the Greek crisis lay mainly in the mismanagement of the public budget and its use for unproductive goals, the origin of the crisis in Ireland was a banking crisis. The crisis was caused by the massive losses that banks suffered from the housing market collapse in 2008. The Irish government intervened to support banks; in November 2010 it was forced to request for a €85 billion rescue package from the EU, the IMF and individual European countries. One-fifth of the package was financed by the Irish Treasury and the National Pension Reserve Fund. To obtain assistance, the country had to adopt severe policy measures.

The case of Portugal was again different. The financial distress of Portugal was mainly caused by the withdrawal of foreign investors under the effect of the international financial crisis. Foreign investors had previously financed the significant budget deficit of the country (10% in 2009). Due to the withdrawal, the country needed a bailout package of €78 billion to

---

a so-called "haircut". This meant a loss of about half their nominal debt holding, thus transferring the majority of Greek debt (about three-quarters) in the hands of European governments and the ECB. In 2015, Eurozone member countries hold 60% of the Greek debt, with the ECB owning another 6% and the IMF 10%.

[198] The Eurozone member countries created the EFSF in June 2010. The EFSF was intended as a temporary crisis resolution mechanism and provided financial assistance to Ireland, Portugal and Greece. The EFSF financed such assistance by issuing bonds and other debt instruments on capital markets. See EFSF.

[199] At the time of writing (summer 2015), a new negotiation wave is being finalised between Greece, the EC, the ECB and the IMF. This time the negotiation includes also a strategy for the recovery of the Greek economy, with the new Greek government led by the Syriza left wing party asking for growth supporting policies and the EU and the ECB insisting for (milder) austerity policies. A package of €86 billion as part of a third economic adjustment programme for supporting the Greek economy is under definition.

finance its deficit. The amount was granted in May 2011 in exchange for austerity measures.

At that point, in the second half of 2011, the focus of the crisis moved to the large vulnerable countries of the Eurozone: Italy and Spain. Both countries' current financial management was overall sound. In spite of this, both countries were at the centre of the crisis, albeit for different reasons. In the case of Italy, the main problem was the sizeable public debt, which in 2011 was at 116.4% of GDP, up from 102.3% in 2008, 112.5% in 2009 and 115.3% in 2010.[200] However, that debt existed well before the crisis (it was 116.9% of GDP in 1995 and 99.7% in 2007), and even during the latter the country was overall capable to moderate the growth of the debt.[201] The absolute size of the debt made the possibility of a bailout unlikely for the country. The need for a bailout was anyway excluded through a self-imposed austerity programme implemented since the end of 2011 by the new government led by the former EU commissioner Mario Monti. In spite of these efforts, the country was also under financial distress in 2012. Considerable capital outflow took place at a pace typically associated with currency crises: in the 12 months leading up to June 2012 the country lost €235 billion or 15% of its GDP, primarily due to foreign investors retreating from the country's bond markets (IMF 2012a, p. 27).

The situation of Spain was similar to that of Ireland, in that the crisis was provoked by the burst of the housing-market bubble, which left the banking sector highly exposed. Unable to solve the crisis of its banking

---

[200] General government gross debt, according to Eurostat data. See Eurostat database at http://ec.europa.eu/eurostat/tgm/table.do?tab=table&init=1&language=en&pcode=teina225&plugin=1.

[201] Data from Eurostat refer to general government consolidated gross debt. The country had to pay a significant share of its GDP as interests on public debt (general government consolidated gross debt): more than 11% of GDP in mid-1990s, down to more than 6% in early 2000s and less than 5% in 2007 and 2008, a share that remained approximately unchanged up to the present (Eurostat data). The deficit was below or at 3% of GDP between 1997 and 2000, between 3.1% and 4.2% between 2001 and 2006, between 1.5% and 2.7% in 2007 and 2008, 5.3% in 2009, 4.2% in 2010 and 3.5% in 2011. Since 2012, the deficit was slightly below or equal to 3%. As a consequence, the primary balance was constantly in surplus for the entire period of the monetary union, with the exception of 2009, when the primary balance registered a deficit of 0.9% of GDP.

system, the Spanish government had to request the EU's support to recapitalise Spanish banks in 2012 (see Chapter 11). The support was granted in exchange for self-imposed austerity policies. Also Spain, as all other vulnerable countries in distress, was hit by broad-based capital outflows, a significant part of which were in corporate bonds. These reached the value of €296 billion or 27% of 2011 GDP in the 12 months up to June 2012 (IMF 2012a, p. 27).

Cyprus joined the group of Eurozone countries in distress in 2011. The immediate cause of the crisis was rooted in the banks. The deeply unbalanced banking sector collapsed when there was a massive outflow of foreign capital, which was particularly important in this sector. This caused the insolvency of a large part of the financial sector of the country. Cyprus was also a victim of contagion from Greece. When private holders of Greek debt accepted to give up part of their outstanding rights through a "haircut" in 2012, panic spread to Cyprus. In fact, many of the devalued Greek bonds were held by Cypriot banks. The management of the Cypriot bailout was particularly troubled (Sapir *et al.* 2014). An agreement was reached to grant Cyprus a €10 billion bailout in March 2013.

10.2 From Contagion to Economic Fragility

A common feature of the bailout programmes in vulnerable Eurozone countries — or the lack thereof in Italy — was the adoption of austerity policies, either imposed by the EU and the IMF or self-imposed. These policies were part of the adjustment programmes agreed upon between national governments and the Troika and involved three different sets of conditionalities. These were fiscal and financial measures and structural reforms. Fiscal measures were addressed to balance public finances by decreasing public deficits and debts. Financial measures were aimed at strengthening the financial sector. Structural reforms were intended to make the economy more efficient and consequently enhance its competitiveness.

These policies were imposed or adopted to assure financial markets and consequently guarantee the access of vulnerable countries to those markets. Also thanks to different kinds and waves of ECB interventions, this was successfully implemented. Financial markets continued to finance vulnerable countries and, after years of turmoil and long-term instability, they did so by decreasing interest rates (Figure 9.5). Also the spread between interest rates paid by vulnerable countries compared to rates on German long-term bonds returned to decrease. This contributed to decrease the weight of the service of public debts in the GDP. However, the economic and social price paid for this outcome was high. GDP decreased and unemployment soared. As a consequence, the debt to GDP ratio increased significantly in all vulnerable countries, although in different measure.

In all countries, recessions were considerably deeper and longer lasting than foreseen by international organisations, the EU and national governments. This led to question the effectiveness and sustainability of austerity policies. In coincidence with the crisis, there also was an abrupt stop of private capital flow into vulnerable countries (Sapir *et al.* 2014). In Ireland and Greece, and in to a lesser degree in Portugal, capital outflow replaced inflow from previously. Government funding was made possible through different sources, in particular official financial assistance and the ECB liquidity.[202] In relative terms, the former channel was particularly important in Greece and also in Portugal. The latter played the main (albeit decreasing) role in Ireland and Cyprus and in part also in Portugal.

Policymakers were confident that the austerity policies imposed or self-imposed upon vulnerable countries would cause a transitory, relatively mild slowdown or recession of economic activity (Sapir *et al.* 2014). Indeed, bailout plans for all vulnerable countries envisioned a recovery of economic activity within a few months. Although forecasts were overall

[202] Greece alone received approximately 45% of the ECB main and longer-term refinancing operations in the last months of 2011 and the early months of 2012. Portugal received more than 10% (Sapir *et al.* 2014). The Eurosystem also provided so-called emergency liquidity assistance (ELA). Ireland received €70 billion at the beginning of 2011 under this heading, and Greece received more than €120 billion in the central months of 2012. ELA is an instrument outside of the common monetary policy which can be used to provide funds to banks that exceptionally and temporarily could not access normal Eurosystem operations. ELA consists in the provision by a Eurosystem national central bank of central bank money to support a solvent financial institution that is facing temporary liquidity problems. This assistance was the only form of common support existing for Greece in early 2015.

appropriate before the implementation of the Greek programme, afterwards forecasts were grossly overestimated. They completely missed considering the possibility of the serious and prolonged recession that took place. Errors of underestimation were particularly sizeable in the case of unemployment. Forecasts of the IMF World Economic Outlook were even revised upwards in October 2010. A more sober and realistic update only took place at the beginning of 2014.[203] This was the outcome of the revision of the effects of austerity policies on public debts and growth that the IMF undertook since 2013 (see Section 11.2). Support measures proved consequently insufficient or in some cases ineffective.

The outcomes of stabilisation measures were disappointing. However, there were important differences among countries. Vulnerable countries that went through some form of bailout (thus we are not considering Italy here) completed the stabilisation programmes, with the exception of Greece and Cyprus (Sapir *et al.* 2014). The first to complete its programme was Ireland in December 2013. In the following year, 2014, both Spain and Portugal exited, respectively in January and May. The programme for Cyprus is expected to end in April 2016. In the case of Greece, the first bailout programme — originally intended to end in June 2013 — was replaced by a second programme in March 2012. This programme expired at the end of 2014. Dramatic negotiations for a third economic adjustment programme of €86 billion between 2015 and June 2018 ended successfully in summer 2015. In return, Greece committed to implement drastic stabilisation measures.[204]

Recession was generally severe and prolonged and public debts increased significantly. The differences in growth rates between vulnerable and resilient countries were in favour of vulnerable countries until 2006 (Figure 10.1). With the crisis, the situation was reversed, except in 2009. Between 2010 and 2013 included, the performance of vulnerable countries

[203] Upward errors were a constant feature also of national forecasts, so much so that these can be considered a policy instrument to ease the weight of adjustment. See Blanchard and Leigh (2013), Hong and Tan (2014).

[204] The European Commission committed to mobilize further resources (up to € 35 billion to fund investment and economic activity) and to use the Investment Plan for Europe to support growth and help the creation of jobs up to 2020.

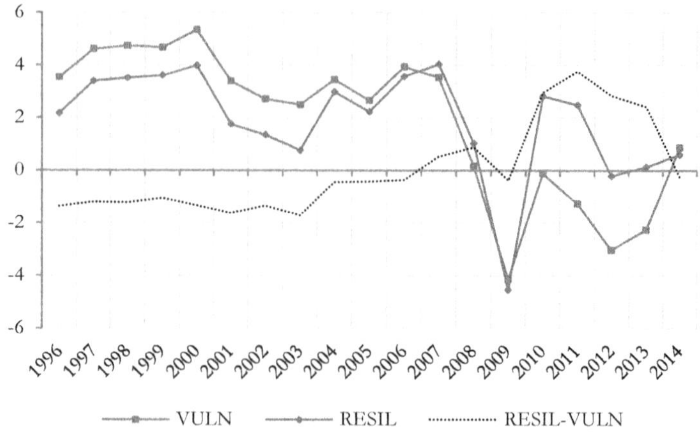

Figure 10.1. The Average Growth Rate in the Eurozone.
Source: Author's own analysis of Eurostat data.

was negative, while that of resilient countries was positive in 2010 and 2011 and stagnated afterwards. The difference of growth rates between the two groups of countries varied between 2.4% in 2013 and 3.7% in 2011. The situation was reversed again in 2014, to the slight advantage of vulnerable countries, entirely due to the dynamic growth in Ireland and, to a lesser extent, Spain. Performance of resilient countries was modest overall.

The group of vulnerable countries was uneven in growth rates and internally differentiated, more than in the case of resilient countries. The Irish economy was the first to enter a severe recession already in 2008. In 2009, Ireland had the worst performance in the Eurozone (Table 10.2).[205] Its output decreased cumulatively by 10%, while unemployment increased from 4.5% in 2006 to 14.7% in 2011. In 2014, unemployment rate decreased to 11.3%. The return to permanent growth started apparently in 2014, a year in which Ireland had the best performance among vulnerable countries (+4.8%).[206]

[205] The Baltic countries performed much worse in 2009. However, none of them was a member of the Eurozone at the time. Also Hungary, Romania and Slovenia had worse performances than Ireland in the EU, but none of them have adopted the euro so far. The only Eurozone country which in 2009 was worse than Ireland was Finland.

[206] Data quoted in this section are from Eurostat, unless otherwise specified.

Table 10.2. Yearly Growth Rates of GDP at Market Prices in Vulnerable and Resilient Countries (Chain Linked Volumes, Percentage Change over Previous Period).

		2007	2008	2009	2010	2011	2012	2013	2014
RESIL	Austria	3.6	1.5	−3.8	1.9	3.1	0.9	0.2	0.3
	Belgium	3.0	1.0	−2.6	2.5	1.6	0.1	0.3	1.1
	Finland	5.2	0.7	−8.3	3.0	2.6	−1.4	−1.3	−0.1
	France	2.4	0.2	−2.9	2.0	2.1	0.3	0.3	0.4
	Germany	3.3	1.1	−5.6	4.1	3.6	0.4	0.1	1.6
	Luxembourg	6.5	0.5	−5.3	5.1	2.6	−0.2	2.0	—
	The Netherlands	4.2	2.1	−3.3	1.1	1.7	−1.6	−0.7	0.9
VULN	Cyprus	4.9	3.6	−2.0	1.4	0.3	−2.4	−5.4	−2.3
	Greece	3.5	−0.4	−4.4	−5.4	−8.9	−6.6	−3.9	0.8
	Ireland	4.9	−2.6	−6.4	−0.3	2.8	−0.3	0.2	4.8
	Italy	1.5	−1.0	−5.5	1.7	0.6	−2.8	−1.7	−0.4
	Portugal	2.5	0.2	−3.0	1.9	−1.8	−4.0	−1.6	0.9
	Spain	3.8	1.1	−3.6	0.0	−0.6	−2.1	−1.2	1.4
RESIL		4.0	1.0	−4.5	2.8	2.5	−0.2	0.1	0.6
VULN		3.5	0.2	−4.2	−0.1	−1.3	−3.0	−2.3	0.9
RESIL−VULN		0.5	0.9	−0.4	2.9	3.7	2.8	2.4	−0.3

Note: — means no data.
Source: Author's own analysis of Eurostat data.

The recession in Portugal was severe and prolonged and similar to the situation in Cyprus. Portugal returned to a modest positive growth rate in 2014. In 2013 and 2014, Cyprus registered the worst performance among vulnerable countries. Spain returned to positive growth in 2014, the second highest among vulnerable countries after Ireland, after years of negative performance. Growth in Italy was still negative in 2014, for the third consecutive year.

The case of Greece is particularly daunting. The country has been in a severe depression and complex political situation since 2010. Austerity packages in this country were particularly severe and socially painful. They included strong wage cuts, layoffs of public employees, tax increases, dismantling of social security and public services. Although the country was able to achieve a budget surplus and to return to international financial markets by April 2014, economic conditions remained extremely weak. GDP contracted by more than 20% between 2009 and 2013 and domestic demand by nearly 28%. Unemployment was at 27% in 2013 and public debt was above 177% in 2014. According to the European Commission forecasts in spring 2015, unemployment should decrease to 25.6% in 2015 and gross public debt increase to 180.2% of GDP (EC 2015m). Growth is foreseen to be positive, but very modest (+0.5%) and inflation negative at −1.5%. The events followed in spring 2015 likely changed these perspectives in the short run, although in the medium and long run it may be different.

Some of the vulnerable economies started to grow again in 2014 and forecasts are mildly positive for 2015, particularly for Ireland and Spain (EC 2015h). The Spanish economy had a positive performance in 2013, albeit GDP growing at modest rates. Ireland was more successful and its economy expanded at around 5% in 2014. Forecasts are that Ireland should be the fastest growing Eurozone economy in 2015. Also the Portuguese economy should have a fair performance in 2015 and public debt should start to decrease over GDP. The Greek economy is now foreseen to go through negative growth in 2015, and its GDP is still at only 74% the level of 2007. The Italian economy had a particularly disappointing performance, with negative growth rates in both 2013 and 2014, although its perspectives are slightly better in 2015. Its GDP in 2014 was still at only 91% the level of 2007. Forecasts are negative for Cyprus, whose

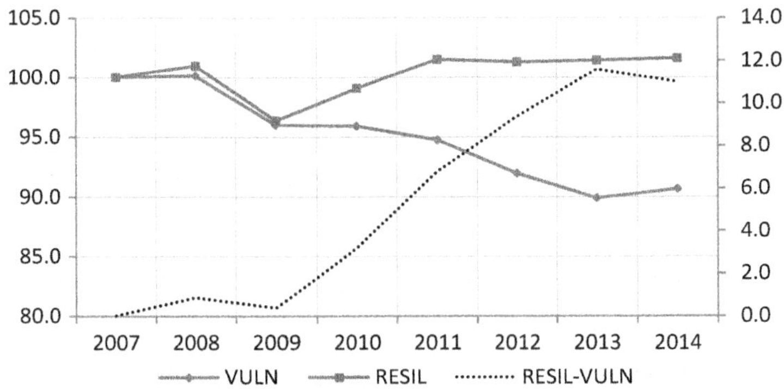

Figure 10.2. Cumulative Gain or Loss of GDP in the Eurozone, 2007 = 100.
Note: Right scale for RESIL-VULN.
Source: Author's own analysis of Eurostat data.

economy should continue to have a slightly negative performance in 2015 and return to positive growth only in 2016.

Although the recession seemed to be over in early 2015 in all vulnerable countries, except Cyprus and Greece, the situation continues to remain precarious. First, growth rates, albeit positive, are overall modest in most countries. Moreover, GDP is still lower than it was before the crisis in all vulnerable countries and the difference with resilient countries is dramatically large (Figure 10.2).[207] Second, the little revival of growth that vulnerable countries could achieve was due in large part to the expansive monetary policies that the ECB implemented, the depreciation of the euro and the low level of energy prices. Third and perhaps most important, growth continues to be fragile for various reasons.

The main reason why recovery was and is fragile is that under the pressure of austerity policies and due to a lack of national resolution, countries were generally slow in reforming their economies. At the same time, deep structural problems persisted, and that made it difficult for countries to concentrate on reforms. High unemployment is a particularly

[207] In resilient countries, by 2014 the GDP was above the 2007 GDP, except in Finland, where it was at 95% of the 2007 level, and the Netherlands, where it was at the same level (Eurostat database).

serious problem in all vulnerable countries and a dramatically difficult challenge in Greece and Spain. Even worse is the problem of youth unemployment, which in the case of Spain passed the level of 50% and across the entire Eurozone reached 23%. Along with depressed demand, one of the reasons is that in most vulnerable countries labour markets continue to be rigid, in particular in the management of working time and job mobility. Although some countries, e.g. Spain and Italy, started to reform their labour markets, most of the changes adopted so far have made easier to dismiss workers and decrease their rights. Reforms have hardly made easier to obtain employment. Austerity policies pursued adjustment through cheaper and insecure labour, not more qualified labour and workplace innovation.

Other structural problems include high public debts and weak banking sectors (Figure 10.3). Although public debts increased throughout the Eurozone, their growth was particularly daunting in vulnerable countries. One of the reasons was that bailout programmes paid particular attention

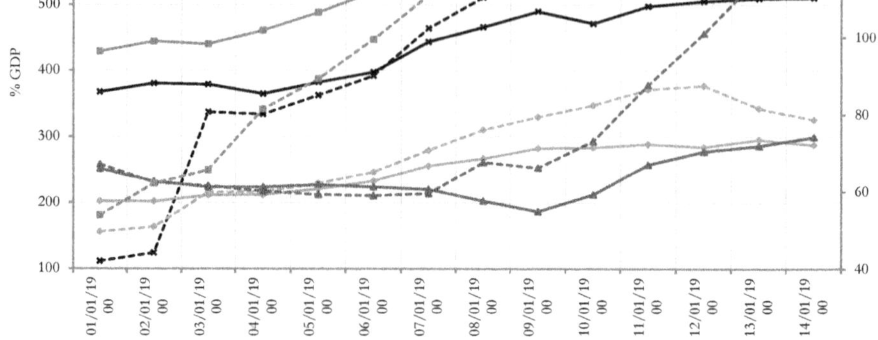

Figure 10.3 Liabilities in Resilient and Vulnerable Countries in Percentage of GDP.
Note: Total corporate financial assets/liabilities and Total corporate financial assets/liabilities of monetary financial institutions on the left axis, General government consolidated gross debt, and Gross debt-to-income ratio of households on the right axis.
Source: Eurostat.

to the situation of the banking sector, supporting governments in their effort to recapitalise banks. The outcome in most vulnerable countries — again with the partial exception of Italy — was that the private liabilities of banks were transformed into public debt, i.e. they were transferred to become the burden of taxpayers. Moreover, banks were pressed to buy public bonds, thus creating a potentially dangerous mixture of bank-sovereign interdependence.

The Eurozone adds policy fragility to the general economic and financial fragility (De Grauwe and Ji 2013, 2015a). During periods of distress, financial markets tend to be under the influence of panic and policymakers reacted by imposing austerity programmes on Eurozone member countries. The effect of austerity programmes was to diminish the strength of automatic stabilisers in government budgets. This generated, as a consequence, more intense economic downturns.

The insufficiency of the Eurozone institutional architecture in dealing with the crisis and taking the integration programme ahead was evident for years and generally shared in Brussels and Frankfurt. However, reforming the institutional architecture proved to be a daunting goal during the crisis and risked to become a massive case of failure of collective action. The ECB successfully extended its policy action well beyond the standard of the pre-crisis years, while remaining within the limits of its mandate. Important reforms, initiated since the fall of 2014 and still under way, include the creation of a fiscal union (see Chapter 11), strengthening the common control over national budgets, and establishing a Eurozone-wide banking union. These reforms of the common institutional architecture, however important, are insufficient to strengthen the Eurozone in the present crisis and to safeguard it from future crises (De Grauwe and Ji 2015a).

10.3 The Euro up to the Crisis: A Success Story?

In the first years of its existence, the euro can be considered a success story, with hidden dangers. Upon its introduction on 1 January 1999, the exchange rate to the dollar deteriorated rapidly. However, within few weeks after its introduction as a circulating currency on 1 January 2002, the euro started to appreciate (Figure 10.4). This was taken as evidence of the markets' confidence. The appreciation of the euro represented a serious problem for vulnerable countries, whose industrial and commercial

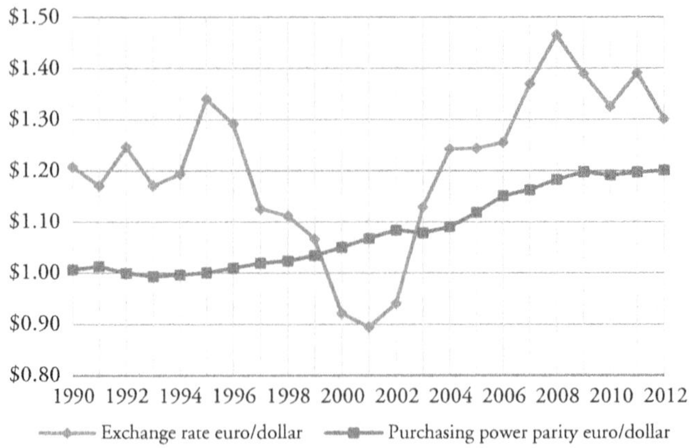

Figure 10.4. The Evolution of the Dollar to Euro Exchange Rate and Purchasing Power.
Source: Piketty (2014), *Capital in the 21st Century* (http://piketty.pse.ens.fr/en/capital21c2).

specialisation was in goods with relatively high price elasticity. However, the commercial disadvantage was compensated — and in most cases more than compensated — by other benefits of the common currency.

The effect of the common currency on inflation was important (Figure 10.5). Inflation decreased in all member countries, in some of them from around 20% in the 1970s and 1980s. In the following years, inflation remained stable at a low level of around 2%. This was in line with the ECB mandate (Figure 10.6) (EC 2013b). Price stability provided important advantages for consumers, business, and public finances and contributed to the descent of interest rates.

Low inflation led interest rates down in a stable way, until the crisis changed the situation. This positive result was due to the ECB policy and action and the end to competitive depreciations, thanks to the monetary union. Better management of public finances also played an important role, thanks to the clear benchmarks and the common control since the Maastricht Treaty. Falling long-term interest rates was the most sizeable among the advantages of the euro for highly indebted countries. Interest rates decreased rapidly and substantially since the mid-1990s and converged in all countries to a low level of around 3% on the eve of the crisis also in the case of households, thus easing their indebtedness (Figure 10.7).

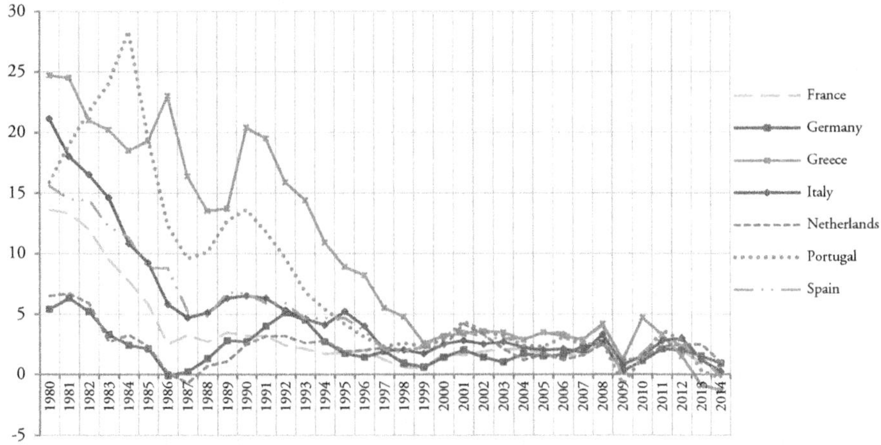

Figure 10.5. CPI Inflation, Annual Percentage Changes.

Source: OECD database.

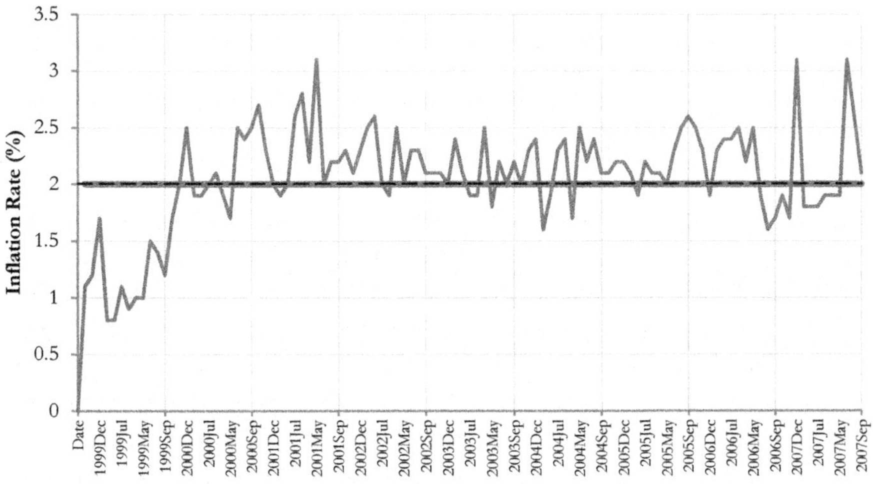

Figure 10.6. HICP Inflation Rate in the Eurozone, Yearly Change.

Source: ECB — Statistical Data Warehouse (http://sdw.ecb.europa.eu/home.do).

There were a number of important positive effects for Eurozone countries. The nature of the effect depended on the fiscal situation and the level of indebtedness of each country, and the policy priorities of the member states. Since government borrowing became less expensive, as

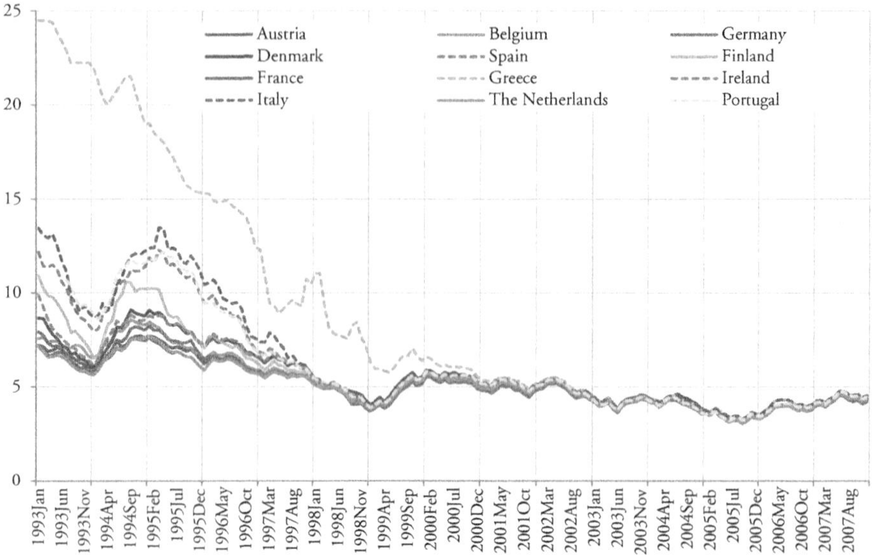

Figure 10.7. Retail Bank Interest Rates: Long-term Loans to Households.
Note: Long-Term Interest Rates for convergence purposes (10 years' maturity, monthly rate 1993–2014).
Source: ECB, Statistical Data Warehouse (http://sdw.ecb.europa.eu/browseTable.do?node=bbn4864&trans).

interest payments on national debt decreased, governments could use the saved resources for repaying public debt, financing investment, improving welfare and pension systems, increasing incomes of public employees, or reducing the tax burden. However, one should also consider that, in the case of debt largely owned by nationals — as was the typical case, at least in continental Europe — the substantial decrease of interest rates reduced a source of income for national investors. Unless the reduction of taxes compensated this decrease — which did not generally happen in vulnerable countries — investors (among which there were many families) felt they became poorer. They consequently diminished consumption or savings.

The positive effect was particularly important for countries which, due to the high level of public debt, had to pay high interest rates. For instance, the advantage for Italy, a highly indebted country with a public debt of 117% of GDP in 1995, was significant. Interest rates that Italy had to pay on the public debt were above 12% in 1995 and even higher in previous years. If we disregard the composite maturity of Italian public debt, a 12% yearly interest rate amounts to 14% of GDP. A decrease of the interest rate by 9% to 3% means that Italy saved around 10.5% of its GDP on a yearly basis.[208] The advantage for Greece in terms of decreasing interest rates was even greater and the percentage gain of Spain and Portugal was also slightly higher than Italy's. However, the advantage was important also for resilient countries, including Germany, France and the Netherlands which in the mid-1990s had to pay interest rates of between 7% and 8%.

The sound and prudent management of monetary unification and the euro brought about a general and significant fall of interest rates that benefited the entire Eurozone economy, but also created the danger of financial and real bubbles. A particularly important effect was the fall of mortgage rates, which decreased from around 8–14% in the early 1980s to an average of 5% on the eve of the crisis. A further important effect was that the volatility of interest rates declined substantially, thus decreasing the unpredictability of costs, easing forecasts and decision making by public and private operators, and supporting economic activity (EC 2013b).

The effect on transaction costs was also sizeable. It was calculated that, before the euro, persons travelling through all the EU countries and exchanging money at every border without making a single purchase would lose half their money in exchange costs. Being a world currency, the euro also meets no difficulty in being exchanged in third countries. It is estimated that up to 20% of euro banknotes are circulated outside the euro area (EC 2013b).

The effect on jobs was also positive. The common currency allowed companies doing business across European borders to avoid the risk of currency fluctuations and to pay exchange costs. These costs were estimated at around €20 to 25 billion annually within the EU, corresponding to some 0.3–0.4% of EU GDP. Since these costs disappeared within the Eurozone, enterprises could decrease correspondingly their prices or increase their income. This effect was expected to increase demand, investment and employment. The positive result in the Eurozone economies was

[208] Italian public debt (general government consolidated gross debt) decreased from 116.9% of GDP in 1995 to 100.0% in 2004. It then increased to 102.5% in 2006, decreased again to 99.7% in 2007, after which it increased up to 127.9% in 2013 (Eurostat).

important: since the adoption of the euro in 1999 and up to the crisis, more than 10 million new jobs were created, compared with only 1.5 million in the previous seven years (EC 2013b).

Cross-border trade within the Eurozone was expected to increase further, well beyond the effects of economic integration, thanks to the disappearance of exchange costs and currency risk. This positive effect acted on both the input and the output side of trade transactions: not only could enterprises sell into a much larger market without exchange costs and risk, but they could also find new supplies at lower costs. Thus costs decreased and supply increased: trade within the Eurozone was estimated to have increased between 4% and 10% since the introduction of the single currency (EC 2013b).

The enlarged domestic (Eurozone) market runs the risk of activating processes of trade diversion from the rest of the world to the Eurozone. As a matter of fact this risk did not materialise and, although trade within the Eurozone increased more, trade with the rest of the world also expanded. Since the Eurozone remained committed to trade liberalisation, an enlarged market with a common sound currency also became attractive for the rest of the world. The slightly growing international role of the common currency, which in many cases could be used as a means of payment to avoid exchange costs and risk, supported the attractiveness of trade to and from the Eurozone.[209] The international demand for euros also facilitated and made less expensive governments borrowing by Eurozone countries on international markets and gave the EU a stronger influence within international organisations.

The effect of the euro was less impressive in other fields. The common currency was expected to increase price transparency in a significant way and consequently to increase price convergence. However, this effect barely materialised. Indeed, large price differentials continued to exist among countries. Differences apparently had to do with transaction costs, lack of

[209] The share of the euro in global foreign exchange reserves rose from 18% in 1999 to over 26% in 2007 and nearly 28% in 2009, and down to 24.4% in 2013 and 22.2% in 2014. The most significant increase was in developing countries, where holdings increased from 18% held in 1999 to 30.2% in 2009. However, afterwards holding decreased to 24.1% by 2012 and 21.5% by 2014 (EC 2013d, IMF 2015c).

competition at the retail level and product differentiation. However, the common currency indirectly supported market integration in particular sectors, such as banking and insurance.

The positive effect of integrated private financial markets in an incomplete monetary union is vital, since the traditional public insurance system does not work. In a complete monetary and economic union, similarly to a country, the centralised budget allows for automatic transfers between the member countries. This role of the budget can offset asymmetric shocks. However, such a system is largely absent at European level, since the EU budget amounts to only 1% of GDP and is used for pursuing structural long-term objectives. The public insurance system exists in principle at national level, but European treaties and pacts significantly limit its role. Finally the public insurance system creates problems of moral hazard, which may jeopardise trust and cooperation among member countries.

However, the creation of the Economic and Monetary Union (EMU) activated the private market insurance mechanism, which assures that integrated capital markets allow for automatic insurance against shocks. The introduction of the euro provided major impetus to the integration of financial markets. The common currency made markets more efficient and competitive, and reduced the costs of cross-border money transfers in the Eurozone. This effect was expected to increase significantly the efficiency of financial markets and the allocation of capital. With more investment opportunities and competition being greater, and capital being free to move to alternative places and for various uses without exchange costs and risk, financial resources were expected to move to where they could be used most efficiently and spread risks more evenly. Indeed, the introduction of the euro offered the opportunity to create a much larger, more efficient single financial market, with a host of advantages for investors and savers. Advantages included more options for investing and borrowing, better return to investment, cheaper loans, more evenly spread risk, lower costs of financial intermediation encouraging more capital flows, and higher borrowing leading to more investment and consumption.

Although this effect existed in the Eurozone, it runs into serious problems, in particular because of ineffective national fiscal policies that made it difficult to calculate the effective risk. First, insurance primarily helped resilient countries. Second, differential risk hampered the working of the insurance system. This happened when markets realised that the no bailout clause was effective. Third, capital markets in the Eurozone kept a rather distinct national character, with many distinct rules and fiscal treatment.

The effects of the introduction of the euro were overall positive and resulted in the rapid expansion and integration of European bond and money markets, including the increase of cross-border bank deposits. As mentioned earlier, the yields on government bonds converged downwards, and the interest rates on retail loans also converged. However, many obstacles remained on the road to the full integration of financial markets in the Eurozone. Some of these were of a political nature and derived from the willingness of national governments and their constituencies to keep a degree of control, particularly over large banks. Some obstacles were of technical, regulatory, and administrative natures and regarded the work to be done for fully harmonising the structures and regulations of financial markets. These were necessary steps to remove remaining barriers, which prevented the full promotion of efficiency. Examples include the need to remove barriers arising from different ICT systems through common technical standards; the solution of legal issues for company mergers and takeovers; and the harmonisation of regulatory issues on how national markets operate. In spite of the European Commission's efforts, problems still remain.

A necessary component of integrated financial markets is the existence of a unified payment system. The Eurozone made important steps in this direction, although problems still remain. The cost for sending payments in euro from one country to another within the Eurozone was significantly decreased, including payment card transactions and withdrawals from ATMs, and credit transfers. Due to different types of transaction costs, costs were not fully coincident with those of transfers within the same country, as common rules required. An important step in the full integration of financial markets, a step that was initially planned for 2010, is the Single Euro Payments Area (SEPA).[210] SEPA is an initiative of

[210]The European Parliament and the Council of the EU adopted the SEPA Regulation ("Regulation (EU) No 260/2012 establishing technical and business requirements for credit

the European banking industry that the European Commission supports through a Directive on Payment Services. SEPA aims to facilitate bank transfers to make electronic payments across the Eurozone safer, as if they were done within the same country and subject to identical charges.

Overall, the euro had positive and important effects on economic stability and growth of the Eurozone. The EMU required that member countries closely coordinate their economic policies with the overall objective of maintaining economic stability, while the ECB monetary policy pursued low inflation. These actions created a policy mix favourable to create the conditions necessary for sustainable long-term growth. This indeed took place in most countries up to the crisis, with particular advantages for vulnerable and relatively backward countries (Figure 10.8).

Perhaps the most problematic and puzzling consequence of the euro was with regard to public finances. The expectation was that, given EMU and SGP, public finances of all member countries would move in the direction of sound and sustainable finances. This was undoubtedly the kind of convergence that the EU in general and the Eurozone in particular valued most and paid most attention and effort to. Indeed, the Union considered sound public finances as a necessary condition for growth, job creation, and sustainable welfare: "The commitment to sound and sustainable public finances is a commitment to ensuring economic growth and employment over the longer term. It also helps ensure that both today's and tomorrow's citizens are provided for fairly — for example, through adequate healthcare provision and pensions" (EC 2014b).

The euro was also expected to contribute to generate more resistance to external shocks. Greater resistance was to follow from the economic stability that the euro was expected to bring and the size and economic strength of the Eurozone. The latter was expected to make the Eurozone better able to absorb external shocks without job losses and lower growth.

---

transfers and direct debits in euro and amending Regulation (EC) No 924/2009") in February 2012. The Regulation established that Eurozone countries had to comply with the core provisions by 1 February 2014. SEPA became fully operational in all Eurozone countries on 1 August 2014 (EC 2015n). For non-Eurozone member countries, the deadline is 31 October 2016. Within those dates, SEPA Credit Transfer (SCT) and SEPA Direct Debit (SDD) should replace national euro credit transfer and direct debit schemes.

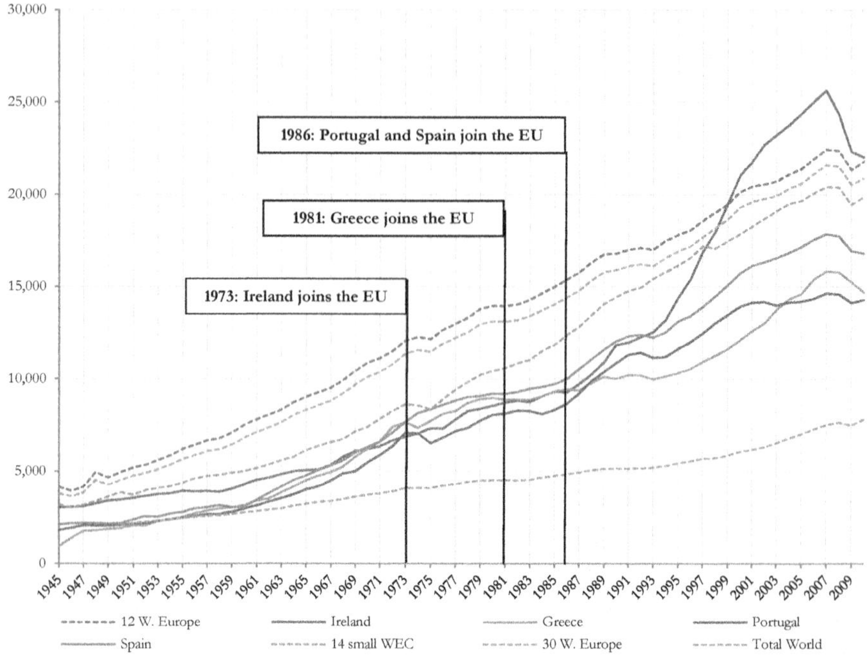

Figure 10.8. Growth in Europe (GDP Per Capita at 1990 International Geary–Khamis Dollars, 1945–2010).

Source: The Maddison-Project, 2013 version (http://www.ggdc.net/maddison/maddison-project/home.htm).

During the 1980s and the 1990s, the EU was under the influence of the major crises that originated in different parts of the world (Dallago and McGowan 2015a). However, the Union was itself the site of only one major crisis, the crisis of the European Exchange Rate Mechanism (ERM) in 1992–1993.[211] German reunification, which caused rapidly growing inter-

[211] The ERM was introduced in 1979 in preparation for the EMU and the introduction of the euro. It was the currency system of the member countries of the European Community, which aimed at reducing exchange rate variability and creating monetary stability. The ERM consisted of a semi-pegged monetary system expressed in ECU (European Currency Unit) and based on a parity grid of bilateral exchange rates among national currencies. Each currency was free to oscillate within a band of ±2.25% to the central parity, while four currencies (the Italian lira, the Spanish peseta, the Portuguese escudo, and the British pound) were allowed an oscillation band of ±6%.

est rates, and the twin deficits and higher inflation in Great Britain and Italy put the ERM under serious strain in 1992. Although Great Britain and Italy left the Mechanism and strongly depreciated their currencies,[212] the crisis remained isolated and the European monetary system recovered relatively quickly. So it is fair to say that this crisis was rather unconventional in that it derived primarily from the "virtuous" attempt of European countries to keep stable exchange rates among themselves. Given this remarkable record of domestic financial stability and resilience to external crises, it is even more impressive to witness what happened following the 2008 crisis.

The effect of the common currency on inequalities is also puzzling. In principle, the economic and financial stability that characterised monetary unification should have helped the less well-off, citizens and regions alike, to be better protected against the erosion of their incomes, wealth, savings and purchasing power. However, in most countries, disparities in both interpersonal distribution of income and wealth increased, particularly after the crisis. The lower and middle classes were relatively impoverished and the labour share remained unchanged or decreased in most countries since the 1980s, in spite of increased employment. This happened both within and outside the Eurozone and went in parallel with a noticeable process of intercountry convergence in the level of development and consumption until the crisis. The crisis, and in particular austerity policies in vulnerable countries and the regression of the welfare state dramatically changed also this kind of convergence and led to divergence both within and among member countries (Andor 2014; Dauderstädt and Keltek 2012).

Assessing the role of the euro for the European integration and for Eurozone economies is both difficult and uncertain, yet its construction was defective (Pisani-Ferry 2014). Many other factors intervened and interacted in determining the outcome. Moreover, not all proceeded in the desirable direction and at the hoped speed. National priorities remained partly disconnected, in particular in the case of such a sensitive issue as the nature of and control over major financial players. Financial organisations found new ways to restrict competition and reap benefits in the form of

[212] While Great Britain opted to remain outside ERM, Italy returned to the system at the end of 1997, with broadened bands and with adjusted central parity.

newly created transaction costs, to the disadvantage of savers and smaller borrowers and investors. Perhaps more important, governments found new ways to weaken the financial discipline that they were subject to, while investment and technical progress were hardly important issues in the process of integration.

All this is not due to the euro, but to bad economic and political actors. Not the euro, but the weak governance and management of the economic and monetary union made this possible. Were "eurocrats", the political and technical leaders and managers of the EU and the Eurozone, failed "masters of illusion" (Rosefielde and Mills 2007)? In part, this was possibly the case, since they acted in the belief that formal institutions were sufficient to change the behaviour of economic actors and the working of economies. Yet Eurocrats were and are largely denied real power, which continue to reside in national governments, and have a hard time in actually determining the European agenda. As a consequence, prominent politicians are unwilling to enter European institutions, and this in turn contributes to keep the latter weak. Yet various factors, prominently among which is the common currency, put national governments in a new position. Even if weak common organs are unable to constrain national governments and countries, peer pressure might be able to do so, particularly if their own countries' situations depend on the coordinated and disciplined behaviour of other national governments and countries.

What we see nowadays is something like the "Eurozone of the peers". In it, strong common institutions and organs (the SGP, the decision making process, the Eurogroup, Economic and Financial Affairs Council (Ecofin)) oblige governments to cooperate and adapt, whatever the economic and social cost is for doing so. Even if the advantages of the common currency may seem presently uncertain, the alternative of leaving the euro is such an economic and political threat, that no decision-maker risked putting it seriously on the decision making desk, not even in the case of Greece ("Greek exit", 2015). Indeed, the euro created such powerful intermingled interests and such a credible threat — both at common and national level — that muddling through looks better than the clear-cut decision to exit. Within this uneasy situation, voice can be of some use (Hirschman 1970), particularly for resilient countries, but not a decisive one. Only loyalty actually remains: stay within, cooperate, and keep a long time horizon, hopefully with the help of the peers. This recalls a peculiar European way of muddling through towards a cooperative outcome as inevitable as Axelrod (1984) previews.

If this perspective really works, national and common reforms are the right answer to convert muddling through into stronger and more cohesive Eurozone. If vulnerable countries are willing and able to endure the present difficulties, if resilient countries have a cooperative spirit and if common support is available for sustaining reform efforts, then all countries would find convenient to invest in reforming their own country and the Eurozone. Both perspectives play apparently an important role in giving some stability and positive perspectives to the present, difficult situation.

The strong common institution, the ECB, is gaining time through bold and resolute policies. Under these circumstances and the pressure of the crisis, the concerted will and action of national governments could revive and strengthen the euro project, together with the common institutions. If this succeeds, the federalist, supranational agenda can return sooner or later to design the future of Europe.

10.4 The Real Economic Effects of the Crisis

The introduction of the euro was meant to bring different benefits to the Eurozone economies and in particular to assure important efficiency gains (Baldwin and Wyplosz 2012; De Grauwe 2014); efficiency gains derived from larger and more integrated markets; disappearance of costs and risks for exchanging currencies one into another; price transparency and more competition; lower inflation; more efficient allocation of resources; the attraction of trade and investments; and stronger resilience to external shocks. When markets work smoothly in a stable external context, these advantages should be sufficient to guarantee the Eurozone countries sizeable gains in terms of more dynamic economic growth and job creation.

These advantages should offset, in normal conditions, the presence of macroeconomic market failures (Acocella 2011). However, during a crisis, institutional and macroeconomic market failures become prominent and bring significant costs. Indeed, in a monetary union its member countries lack sovereign policies to control adjustment processes according to the country's features, needs, and preferences. In a full monetary union, common policies are available, including the possibility to transfer resources to where they are needed. In an incomplete monetary union, as the Eurozone is, policy asymmetry and policy ineffectiveness dominate: monetary policies are common and fiscal policies are left to national governments in order to accommodate the asymmetric effects of shocks. Both policies are unusually restricted, due to the need of avoiding excessive advantages for individual countries or disadvantages and intercountry transfer of resources. To avoid this effect, hard financial discipline at the country level is necessary, with the consequence of depriving countries in greater need of the necessary instruments for fixing their situation. As a result, policies are potentially ineffective.

The incompleteness of institutions, policy asymmetry and ineffectiveness interacted with the lack of political integration, and the divergence of national economies in drawing the Eurozone deeply into a largely self-made crisis. National governments, particularly those of vulnerable countries, were under domestic pressure to soften their commitment to fiscal convergence, both because of the slower adaptation to integration of domestic economies and polities and to finance unproductive expenditures or wage increases not linked to productivity. This pressure was also strong because institutionalised common mechanisms for supporting countries in distress were virtually inexistent.

Within the Eurozone, the adjustment of unbalances — be they in public and private finances or in current accounts — was left to countries in distress, a form of moral hazard (Section 8.3). While the Eurozone does not have a common budget, the EU budget as an adjustment device is negligible and usually devoted to long-run goals: only 0.4% of the European GDP is devoted to competitiveness and convergence through the common budget. Common structural policies are virtually limited to co-investment into European networks and the support to convergence actions at the regional level.

Understanding the evolution of the real economy in the Eurozone is important for explaining the causes and the effects of the crisis, in a double sense. First, the real economy was an important channel for the transmission of the US crisis to the Eurozone. Second, the real economy was and continues to be a fundamental cause of Eurozone fragility. The EU economies experienced difficulties in keeping the growth pace with the United States and even more so with emerging economies since the 1990s

(Chapter 3). It was also during the last two decades that a new trend emerged in the European economy, one that was particularly deleterious for European integration and the sustainability of the common currency: growing divergence among the Eurozone economies. Divergence appeared in many variables, the most important being the external economy (foreign trade and capital flows), productivity and competitiveness (technical progress and labour markets), asymmetries and inefficiencies, inequalities, and the internal demand (including consumption and savings, investment, public expenditures).

1. *The external economy: foreign trade and capital flows.* Current accounts in the Eurozone were overall balanced up to 2008 (Figure 10.9). However, while until 2003 all countries had or were close to balanced current accounts, between 2004 and 2008 the positions of Germany and other resilient countries (Finland, Austria, the Netherlands) and that of vulnerable countries diverged considerably (EC 2013a). The current account surplus in Germany was 7.5% of GDP in 2007, more than 6% in each of the following years until 2011 included, and again 7% in 2012, 6.9% in 2013 and 7.6% in 2014. However, Germany's surplus with other Eurozone countries halved as a share of GDP since 2007.

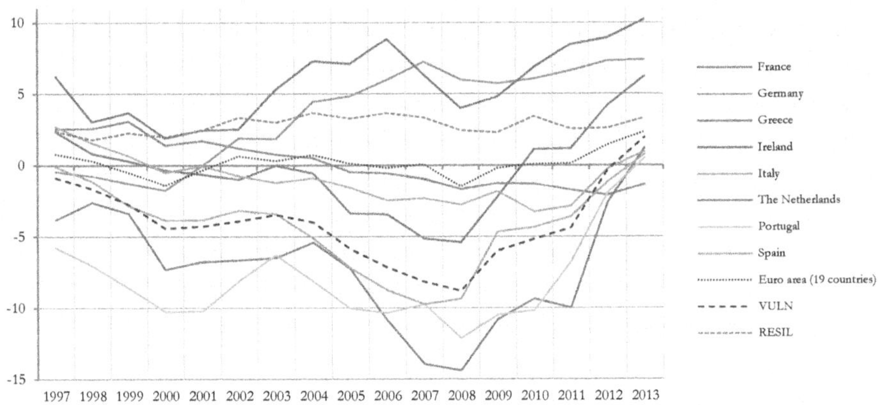

Figure 10.9. Current Account Balances (in Percentage of GDP).
Source: Author's own figure based on data from the OECD database.

The situation of vulnerable countries was negative for a similar magnitude compared to the Eurozone GDP, between 2% and 1.5% overall. Current account balance in vulnerable countries improved during the crisis, due to the adjustment processes they introduced. By 2013, the improvement was converted into a surplus, mainly by decreasing imports. Overall, the current account of the Eurozone was close to balance in 2009–2011. It then increased to a surplus of 2.4% of GDP in 2013 (Eurostat 2015a). However, external balance and surplus were the result of deep internal unbalances, made of robust exports of resilient countries and downward adjustment in vulnerable countries. This resulted into deeply unbalanced inter-EU trade (Table 10.3).

The divergence among Eurozone countries led to their deviating world market shares. Compared to 1999, in 2008 the world market share of Germany, a country which is specialised in research-intensive goods (Eurostat 2011), remained unchanged (8.73% and 8.72% respectively). In the same period, Italy's market share of goods and services decreased from 4.07% to 3.35% and that of Spain decreased from 2.28% to 2.14% (OECD database).

Resilient Eurozone countries with trade surplus kept balance of payment equilibrium by exporting capital to vulnerable countries (Table 10.4). Capital inflow from resilient Eurozone countries was particularly important in sustaining growth rates in Ireland and Spain. Vulnerable member countries offered excellent investment opportunities in the private sector (particularly in non-tradable activities such as construction and real estate) and in the public sector (state bonds). Unfortunately, the benefit for vulnerable countries was illusory, since much capital flow went to create bubbles or supported public debt. The benefit was also transitory, since capital flows inverted direction as soon as the crisis broke out.

2. *Productivity and competitiveness: technical progress and labour market, human capital.* Productivity and competitiveness in vulnerable countries developed unfavourably, until the crisis. There were many reasons for this: some were microeconomic reasons, others were systemic in nature. Unit labour costs (ULCs) in vulnerable and resilient countries continued to diverge until 2009, when the effect of austerity policies in vulnerable countries brought results (Table 10.5). Divergence was due to two reasons: first, gross hourly wages grew

Table 10.3. Intra-EU 27 Trade Balance by Member State (Millions €).

	2005		2007		2009		2011		2013	
	Intra EU-27	**Extra EU-27**	**Intra EU-27**	**Extra EU-27**	**Intra EU-27**	**Extra EU-27**	**Intra EU-27**	**Extra EU-27**	**Intra EU-27**	**Extra EU-27**
Austria	−10092	7696	−7709	7316	−9504	4557	−15885	5373	−13407	7279
Belgium	21539	−9110	27345	−13392	22173	−10694	18890	−12760	22464	−8498
Denmark	5227	2356	664	2986	3839	3859	4014	7532	1539	8502
Germany	98946	55260	126577	65668	71799	65411	55998	99937	43419	154014
Ireland	19479	13531	13479	14010	21403	16726	18900	23552	14215	22523
Greece	−18627	−12875	−22682	−18151	−19846	−14566	−12356	−11725	−9257	−9947
Spain	−36898	−40535	−48212	−51265	−17251	−30123	−7249	−43235	9205	−26212
France	−37210	4174	−52381	75	−63325	7067	−87277	−1600	−88849	12341
Italy	−186	−10200	6721	−16726	−2804	−3964	−5062	−21214	9622	19997
The Netherlands	116108	−82259	133624	−91646	120389	−81588	169833	−121356	176678	−115215
Portugal	−14858	−5387	−16362	−5281	−16484	−3203	−11738	−4669	−7608	−1647
Finland	−1600	6994	−855	6893	−3340	4712	−5563	1830	−7585	5346
VULN	−10218	−11093.2	−13411.2	−15482.6	−6996.4	−7026	−3501	−11458.2	3235.4	942.8
RESIL	27559.71	−2127	32466,43	−3157.14	20290.14	−953.71	20001.43	−3006.3	19179.86	9109.86

Source: OECD database and author's own calculations.

Table 10.4. International Investment Position* (Percentage of GDP, End-Of-Year Stocks).

	2006	2007	2008	2009	2010	2011	2012	2013
Austria	−12.9	−9.8	−10.1	−5.1	−5.2	−1.9	−3.1	−0.2
Belgium			46.7	54.8	59.8	56.5	48.4	48.8
Denmark	−0.3	−5.8	−5.1	0.9	12.9	28.0	36.8	38.5
Germany	25.2	24.1	23.2	30.0	30.8	28.7	34.7	42.9
Ireland	−5.1	−18.8	−72.9	−89.2	−84.3	−106.6	−109.6	−102.1
Greece			−74.1	−86.4	−98.3	−85.2	−109.2	−121.1
Spain							−90.0	−92.6
France			−13.3	−14.1	−8.5	−7.5	−11.3	−15.6
Italy	−22.8	−24.1	−24.7	−26.1	−24.7	−23.4	−28.6	−30.7
The Netherlands			−7.8	0.8	9.2	17.4	25.7	31.2
Portugal	−79.3	−88.8	−95.1	−107.9	−104.3	−101.0	−113.8	−116.2
Finland	−12.4	−25.9	−2.5	6.4	19.7	18.1	14.7	6.3
VULN	−35.7	−43.9	−66.7	−77.4	−77.9	−79.1	−90.2	−92.5
RESIL	−0.1	−4.4	4.4	10.5	17.0	19.9	20.8	21.7

Note: * Difference between the stock of financial assets and liabilities (all institutional sectors).
Source: OECD database and author's own calculations.

faster in vulnerable countries than in resilient ones (Table 10.6); and second, investment in the vulnerable countries slowed down.

There is evidence that also technical progress has slowed down, at least in part due to the abundant availability of cheap short-term and insecure jobs. Particularly serious appears to be the delay of some countries in the adoption of information and communications technology (ICT).[213] More in general, the weak economic system and the lack of reforms appear to be at the base of the negative performance.[214] As a consequence and apart

[213] Hassan and Ottaviano (2013) show that the relative fall of productivity in Italy is due to capital and labour misallocation, due primarily to limited ICT investment and penetration, and not to labour rigidity. Non-meritocratic and rigid management practices can greatly affect ICT exploitation, with negative effects on overall productivity growth.

[214] Looking for the roots of the Italian stagnation, Manasse (2013) argues that this is due primarily to the legacy of more than a decade of lack of reforms in credit, product and labour markets. OECD (2012c) concludes that it is important to act quickly in a wide range

Table 10.5. Unit Labour Costs (2005 = 100).

	2000	2001	2002	2003	2004	2005	2006	2007	2008	2009	2010	2011	2012
Belgium	81.95	84.97	87.06	87.81	87.71	88.94	90.71	92.70	96.20	100.06	100.00	102.37	106.61
Denmark	75.35	78.50	81.48	83.17	83.92	86.01	88.01	91.26	95.59	101.55	100.00	101.13	102.69
Finland	79.60	82.40	83.36	84.71	84.74	86.72	87.14	86.99	92.80	101.76	100.00	102.67	107.35
France	81.49	83.40	85.89	87.76	88.44	90.16	91.75	93.05	95.72	99.12	100.00	100.87	102.84
Germany	98.28	98.26	98.50	99.24	98.41	97.35	94.97	93.51	95.48	101.91	100.00	100.88	103.65
Greece	76.36*	76.31*	83.32*	84.32*	85.38	88.38	88.07	90.14	89.73	99.30	100.00	97.16	91.00
Ireland	81.06	85.26	86.95	92.21	96.09	101.47	105.46	109.52	115.29	107.94	100.00	97.13	97.67
Italy	77.14	79.42	82.15	85.71	86.95	89.23	90.64	92.28	95.88	100.09	100.00	100.64	102.70
The Netherlands	81.92	85.77	89.59	91.61	91.92	91.63	92.30	93.78	95.98	100.74	100.00	100.92	103.90
Portugal	82.03	84.89	87.51	90.60	91.33	94.69	95.29	96.06	98.99	101.40	100.00	98.47	94.53
Spain	76.48	78.77	81.10	83.64	85.83	88.90	91.65	95.20	100.47	101.73	100.00	98.50	95.34
VULN	77.76	79.94	83.38	86.47	88.56	91.99	93.96	96.79	100.34	102.26	100.00	98.36	96.68
RESIL	83.10	85.55	87.65	89.05	89.19	90.13	90.81	91.88	95.29	100.86	100.00	101.47	104.51

Note: * *Estimated values.*

Source: OECD database and author's own calculations.

Table 10.6. Hourly Earnings, 2010 = 100 (Yearly Growth Rates).

	2000	2001	2002	2003	2004	2005	2006	2007	2008	2009	2010	2011	2012	2013	2014
Austria	78.7	81.2	83	85	87	89.5	92.3	95	97.9	97.3	100	103.6	106.9	109.9	
Belgium	75.0	77.6	80.4	82.0	84.1	86.3	88.4	90.3	93.3	96.8	100.0	102.8	105.8	107.8	—
Denmark	70.8	73.8	76.7	79.5	82.0	84.9	87.5	90.8	94.9	97.8	100.0	101.9	103.4	104.7	106.1
Finland	69.1	72.4	75.0	78.1	80.9	84.0	86.4	89.2	94.0	97.8	100.0	102.5	105.5	107.9	109.6
France	75.5	78.2	80.6	82.3	84.8	87.6	90.6	93.7	96.4	97.3	100.0	102.8	105.0	107.0	—
Germany	82.0	84.3	86.4	88.5	89.4	90.9	92.6	94.6	97.5	99.3	100.0	103.1	106.8	108.2	—
Italy	73.0	75.9	78.4	80.3	82.8	85.4	87.6	89.5	93.0	97.4	100.0	102.2	104.3	106.4	—
Portugal	75.4	78.1	80.3	81.2	84.2	86.2	87.0	91.4	95.4	98.0	100.0	100.4	96.1	95.2	93.9
Spain	68.3	71.0	74.4	78.1	81.2	83.6	86.2	89.9	94.6	98.7	100.0	102.6	103.7	103.6	—
Eurozone-19	76	78.7	81.3	83.6	85.6	87.6	89.9	92.7	95.9	98.5	100	102.5	105	106.5	—
VULN	72.2	75.0	77.7	79.9	82.7	85.1	86.9	90.3	94.3	98.0	100.0	101.7	101.4	101.7	93.9
RESIL	75.2	77.9	80.4	82.6	84.7	87.2	89.6	92.3	95.7	97.7	100.0	102.8	105.6	107.6	107.9

Source: OECD database and author's own calculations.

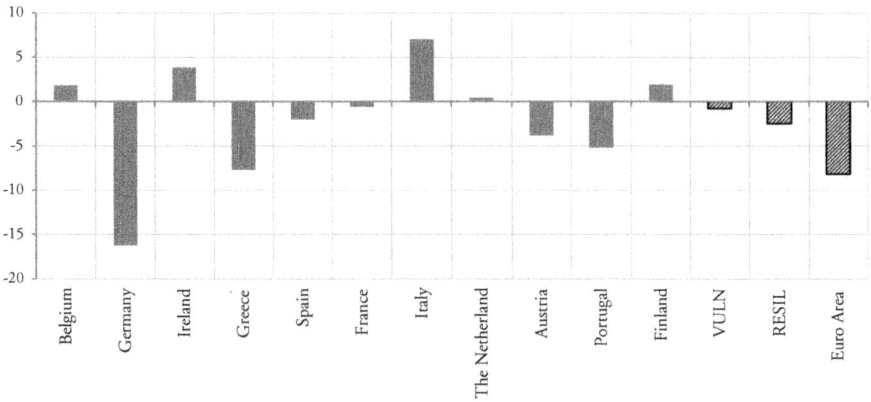

Figure 10.10. Harmonised Competitiveness Indicators for the Total Economy (Based on Unit Labour Costs Indices. Percentage Change since 1998 Q4).[215]

Source: European Central Bank (https://www.ecb.europa.eu/stats/exchange/hci/html/hci_ulct_A.en.html).

from selected service sectors and manufacturing branches (Sondermann 2012), labour productivity levels and trends revealed significant differences among the various countries and between resilient and vulnerable countries, to the disadvantage of the latter (Figures 4.1 and 10.10).

of policy areas. Tiffin (2014) offers a comprehensive assessment of Italian competitiveness, focusing on the role of innovation and the evolution of Italy's export market share. While Italy maintains a high-quality export mix, and the adaptability of small-scale specialised firms is still a source of strength, the country's future competitiveness needs the implementation of a comprehensive structural-reform agenda.

[215] For the euro area, the real effective exchange rate of the euro vis-à-vis 19 trading partners is displayed. For euro area countries, the chart shows the Harmonised Competitiveness Indicators (HCIs) calculated vis-à-vis the same 19 trading partners plus the other euro area countries. A positive change points to a decrease in cost competitiveness. HCIs intend to provide consistent and comparable measures of Euro area countries' price and cost competitiveness. HCIs are constructed using the same methodology and data sources that are used for the REERs of the Euro and are consistent with the Euro EERs. While the HCI of a specific country takes into account both intra and extra-Euro area trade (considering the most important trade partners), the Euro EERs are based on extra-Euro area trade only. The HCIs are calculated on the basis of weighted averages of bilateral exchange rates vis-à-vis the currencies of the trading partners of each euro area country and are deflated by appropriate cost or price indices (EBA 2015).

The deep differences among Eurozone countries were clearly revealed in interesting research by BofAML Global Research on the factors contributing to growth in the years up to the crisis and during the crisis (Boone *et al.* 2013a, 2013b) (Table 10.7). It appears that in resilient countries (France and Germany), growth came primarily (France) or exclusively (Germany) from capital and productivity growth, with little contribution from labour growth. The opposite happened in vulnerable countries (Italy and Spain), where the increase of employment and the number of worked hours were the main source of growth, the amount of capital coming on pair (Italy) or second (Spain). Factors linked to productivity (labour quality and total factor productivity (TFP)) contributed little or had a negative contribution.

For the period of the crisis, the study finds that the large output gap that appeared during the crisis was projected to persist over the period 2008–2014, generating rapid deflation. It is concluded that trend growth was badly damaged and the consequences will be felt in the long run, even in resilient countries. The collapse of productivity is a common feature of all economies, to which a sharp labour contraction in Spain and Italy is added.

Data on the number of hours actually worked in the Eurozone countries confirm that vulnerable countries have a constantly higher number of hours worked, although differences also exist among different countries within the same group (Figure 3.4). The difference was between 200–300 hours per year more in vulnerable countries than in resilient countries, a difference that remained rather constant through the entire period (Figure 10.11).[216] During the crisis, the inter-group difference decreased slightly, roughly between 10–25 hours per year.

The modest contribution of labour quality to growth in vulnerable countries recalls important differences in human capital between resilient and vulnerable countries (Table 10.8). The inability of vulnerable countries to invest (Table 10.9; see also Eurostat 2011) led vulnerable countries to decrease wages and use lower-skilled human capital (OECD 2011a, country notes; Eurostat 2011). This was done also by making increasing use of short-term and insecure jobs, with the further negative consequence

[216] A part of this difference is due to the particularly high number of hours worked in Greece, higher than the average of the other vulnerable countries by 50–90 hours during most of the period considered.

Table 10.7. Trend Growth Breakdown (1995–2007 and 2008–2014).

	France		Spain		Italy		Germany		UK	
	1995–2007	**2008–2014**	**1995–2007**	**2008–2014**	**1995–2007**	**2008–2014**	**1995–2007**	**2008–2014**	**1995–2007**	**2008–2014**
Labour quantity	0.3	0.0	2.1	−1.3	0.6	−0.6	−0.1	0.3	0.5	0.1
Labour quality	0.3	0.2	0.4	0.3	0.2	0.1	0.0	0.1	0.5	0.1
Capital	0.8	0.6	1.5	0.6	0.7	0.2	0.5	0.4	0.8	0.4
TFP	0.7	−0.5	−0.3	−0.2	0.0	−0.6	1.1	0.2	1.3	−0.6
Trend growth	**2.2**	**0.3**	**3.7**	**−0.7**	**1.5**	**−0.9**	**1.6**	**1.0**	**3.1**	**0.0**

Note: For the period 2008–2014 it is assumed that the crisis will last until 2014, and that the output gap (the cumulative gap between trend and observed output) will close only then.

Source: Author's own analysis of data from Boone *et al.* (2013a).

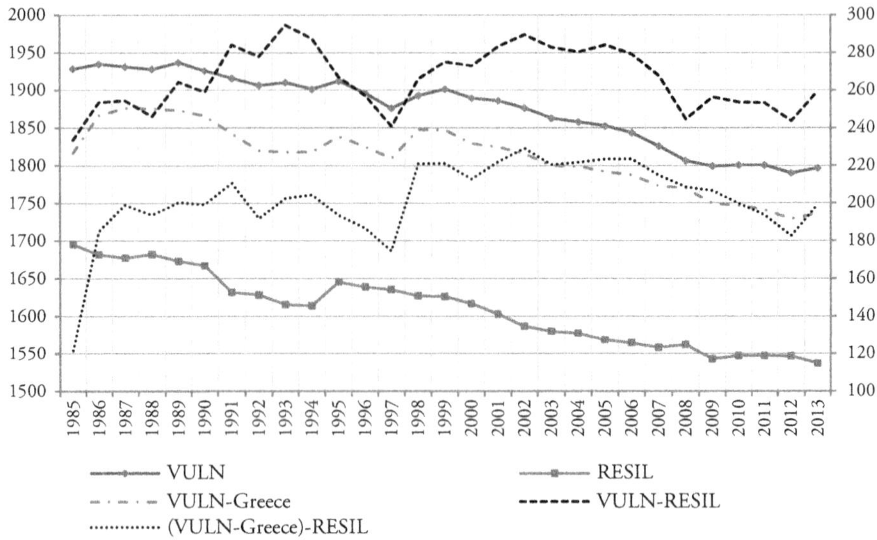

Figure 10.11. Number of Hours Actually Worked Annually Per Worker Per Group of Countries (Left Axis) and Difference between Groups (Right Axis).

Note: VULN: 1986–1997: includes Spain, Italy, Greece and Portugal; 1998–2013: Spain, Italy, Greece, Portugal and Ireland.

RESIL: 1985–1990 includes Belgium, Finland, France, the Netherlands and Luxembourg; 1991–1994: Belgium, Finland, France, the Netherlands, Luxembourg and Germany; 1995–2013: Belgium, Finland, France, the Netherlands, Germany, Luxembourg and Austria.

Source: Author's own figure based on data from the OECD database.

Table 10.8. R&D and Human Capital.

	Gross Domestic Expenditure on R&D (GERD) in % GDP, 2012	Early School Leavers, 2013	Total Public Expenditure on Education as % of GDP (For All Levels of Education Combined), 2011	Patents Applications (Per Million Inhabitants), 2010
Belgium	2.24	11.2	6.55	138.31
Denmark	3.02	11.4	8.75	228.79
EU-28	1.92	12.9	—	111.42
Finland	3.43	10.0	6.76	256.64

(*Continued*)

Table 10.8. (*Continued*)

	Gross Domestic Expenditure on R&D (GERD) in % GDP, 2012	Early School Leavers, 2013	Total Public Expenditure on Education as % of GDP (For All Levels of Education Combined), 2011	Patents Applications (Per Million Inhabitants), 2010
France	2.23	11.2	5.68	130.37
Germany	2.88	10.0	4.98	283.61
Greece	0.69	10.3	—	5.84
Ireland	1.58	8.5	6.15	68.79
Italy	1.26	17.4	4.29	75.25
The Netherlands	1.97	10.3	5.93	182.3
Portugal	1.37	20.3	5.27	8.9
Spain	1.27	26.0	4.82	32.1
VULN	1.23	16.50	5.13	38.18
RESIL	2.63	10.68	6.44	203.34

Source: OECD and Eurostat databases (http://ec.europa.eu/eurostat/web/science-technology-innovation/data/database).

of segmenting the labour market, typically along generational lines. Having chosen this weak route to competitiveness, vulnerable countries further specialised in labour-intensive branches (Memedovic 2009; Yilmaz 2008), thus entering into competition with emerging countries.

In a monetary union, growing ULC in one country or region are likely to cause price inflation in that country or region, unless higher costs are compensated by other changes through policies or reforms. This is the case of vulnerable countries in the Eurozone: vulnerable countries had higher inflation rates than resilient countries until the end of 2008. When internal deflation became effective, their inflation rate was constantly lower than in resilient countries. This happened since the second half of 2012 (Figure 10.12). Differential inflation is in turn the source of further asymmetries. Inflation differences, combined with the same nominal interest rate in the Eurozone, create large differences in real interest rates (Table 4.2, Figures 10.13 and 10.14).

Table 10.9. Gross Fixed Capital Formation (Chain Linked Volumes, Percentage Change over Previous Period).

		2005	2006	2007	2008	2009	2010	2011	2012	2013	2014
	EU-28	2.9	5.6	5.9	−0.5	−11.9	0.2	2.0	−2.8	−1.5	2.3
	Eurozone, var. comp.	2.5	5.2	4.9	−0.5	−11.0	−0.4	1.6	−3.7	−2.5	1.0
	RESIL average	1.8	3.7	6.5	3.1	−9.6	0.0	6.3	−0.8	−2.7	1.0
	VULN average	2.9	8.7	6.2	−2.3	−13.7	−8.4	−8.3	−13.0	−7.6	−0.4
	OTHER average	14.4	13.3	13.6	−4.5	−26.9	−0.2	11.1	0.7	1.0	5.2
RESIL	Belgium	6.5	3.5	6.3	2.9	−7.3	−0.1	4.1	0.0	−2.1	5.1
	Germany	0.3	7.0	4.4	1.2	−9.9	5.1	7.3	−0.7	−0.6	3.4
	France	2.9	3.6	5.5	0.9	−9.1	2.1	2.1	0.3	−1.0	−1.5
	Luxembourg	−3.1	2.1	8.4	9.9	−12.2	−0.2	14.4	2.4	−4.5	n.a.
	The Netherlands	2.9	7.2	6.5	4.8	−9.2	−5.6	5.6	−6.0	−4.0	3.4
	Austria	0.2	1.1	4.6	1.4	−7.3	−2.4	6.8	0.5	−1.5	0.5
	Finland	3.2	1.3	10.0	0.3	−12.5	1.1	4.1	−2.2	−5.3	−5.1

VULN	Ireland	14.4	4.0	2.7	−9.6	−20.6	−18.1	−2.6	5.2	−2.8	11.3
	Greece	−12.9	17.4	17.8	−6.6	−13.2	−20.9	−16.8	−28.7	−9.5	2.7
	Spain	7.5	7.4	4.4	−3.9	−16.9	−4.9	−6.3	−8.1	−3.8	3.4
	Italy	1.7	3.2	1.6	−3.1	−9.9	−0.5	−1.9	−9.3	−5.8	−3.3
	Cyprus	6.8	21.1	7.8	9.0	−13.9	−5.1	−9.4	−20.7	−17.1	−18.8
	Portugal	0.1	−0.8	3.1	0.4	−7.6	−0.9	−12.5	−16.6	−6.7	2.5
OTHER	Estonia	15.3	22.9	10.3	−13.1	−36.7	−2.6	32.7	10.9	2.3	−2.8
	Latvia	20.5	15.1	22.5	−9.2	−33.3	−20.0	24.2	14.5	−5.2	1.3
	Lithuania	n.a.	19.7	22.4	−4.2	−38.7	1.4	19.4	−1.6	7.0	8.0
	Malta	16.1	2.6	5.6	−9.2	−11.8	26.4	−17.8	−1.1	2.7	14.0
	Slovenia	3.5	10.2	12.0	7.0	−22.0	−13.7	−4.6	−8.9	1.9	4.8
	Slovakia	16.5	9.1	8.9	1.6	−18.7	7.2	12.7	−9.3	−2.7	5.7
	United Kingdom	1.6	3.3	5.3	−4.7	−14.4	5.9	2.3	0.7	3.4	7.8
	United States	5.5	2.2	−1.2	−4.8	−13.0	1.1	3.7	5.4	2.8	3.9

Source: Eurostat (http://ec.europa.eu/eurostat/tgm/table.do?tab=table&init=1&language=en&pcode=tec00011&plugin=1).

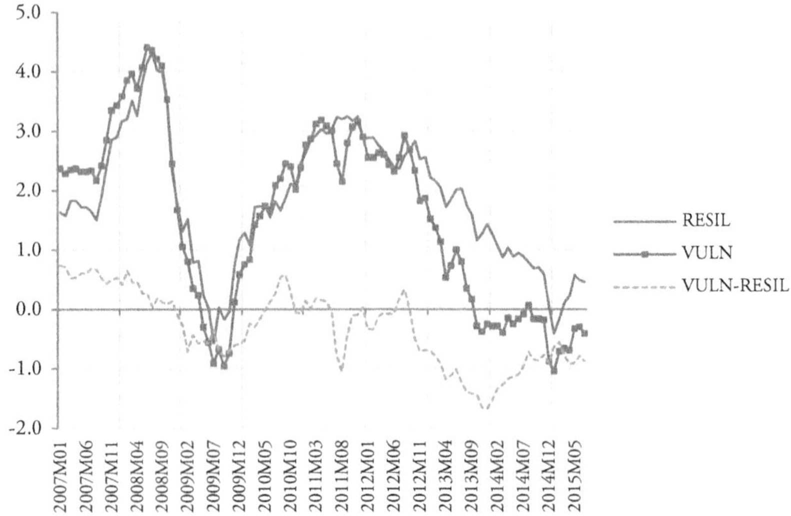

Figure 10.12. Harmonised Indices of Consumer Prices (2005 = 100) — Monthly Data (Annual Rate of Change).
Source: Author's own figure based on data from the Eurostat database.

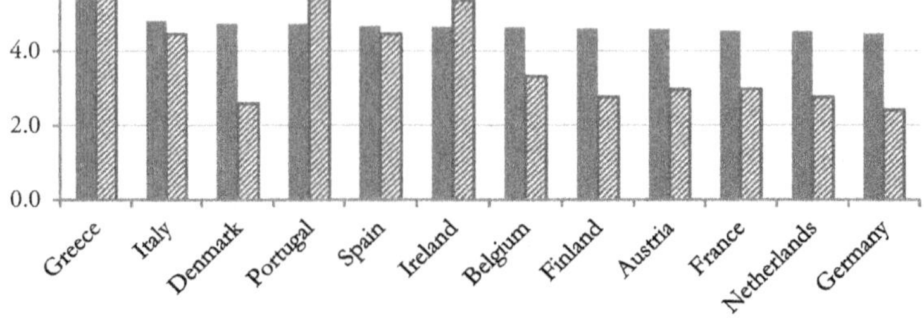

Figure 10.13. Average Real Interest Rates in Eurozone Countries (1997–2004) — EMU Convergence Criterion Series (Long-Term Interest Rates).
Source: Eurostat.

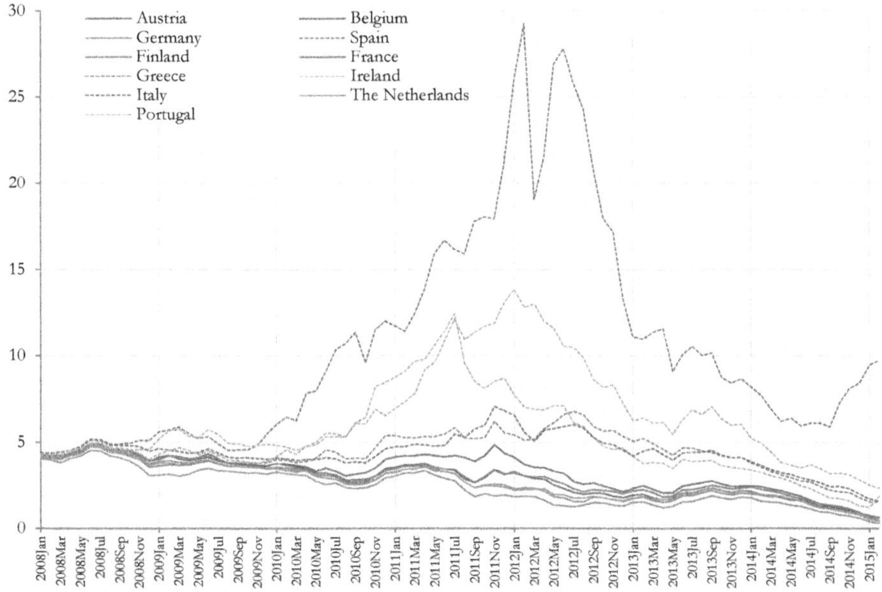

Figure 10.14. Retail Bank Interest Rates: Long-Term Loans to Households.

Note: Long-Term Interest Rates for convergence purposes (10 years' maturity, monthly rate 1993–2014).

Source: ECB, Statistical Data Warehouse (http://sdw.ecb.europa.eu/browseTable.do?node=bbn4864&trans).

Differential price inflation in vulnerable countries caused real exchange rate appreciation, to their disadvantage. This in turn caused loss of competitiveness, which worsened the position of vulnerable countries in international trade and discouraged the inflow of foreign direct investments. Since the nominal exchange rate of the common currency remained strong, the negative effect for vulnerable countries may be even greater in third markets. Factors supporting the strength of the exchange rate included the reputation that the Eurozone borrowed from resilient countries in the international financial markets, their current account surplus and the inflow of capital from riskier vulnerable countries.

3. *Asymmetries and inefficiencies.* Divergence among Eurozone countries also has its origins in different forms of institutional asymmetry and

economic inefficiency. Institutional asymmetries are important: they may be the outcome of different economic systems, historical developments and interests. They may also reveal different institutional and organisational answers to similar or different problems, such as the organisation of the production process or financing of economic activity. There are different sources of institutional asymmetries. Financial markets may vary in distinct countries in response to a range of market inefficiencies or idiosyncrasies. Examples include risk aversion by investors, who may prefer to deposit their money in banks; or the preference of firms for debt capital that allows owners to keep the control of the firm. Similar observations hold true for corporate governance systems of organisations (Dietl 1998; Ostrom 1990).

Labour market institutions present great variety among countries (Crouch 2012; Freeman 2008). Particularly important for economic performance is the nature and organisation of trade unions and differences between centralised and decentralised wage bargaining. Institutional variety of labour markets across countries also influences how shocks (e.g. price increases, or oil shocks) are transmitted. Different legal systems lead to different behaviour of economic actors, different types and features of contracts among parties, as well as different ways and intensity of the transmission of shocks (e.g. interest rate change) (La Porta *et al.* 2008; Ménard and Marais 2006). Welfare systems are typically important in Europe, but they have different features and organisations, different dimension and costs, and different incentive effect, even if convergence processes are clearly under way (Bouget 2003; Sapir 2006). As a consequence, they have different consequences for economic activity.

Some types of economic inefficiency are the outcome of failures of markets and the state as "imperfect alternatives" (Wolf 1988), at both the micro and macroeconomic levels. These inefficiencies are typically solved through different institutional and organisational responses (Dietl 1998). However, other inefficiencies are caused by the inability or the unwillingness of economic actors to coordinate their activity and find proper institutional and organisational solutions to inefficiencies, perhaps due to clashing interests or unsolved moral hazards. Important cases include the structural differences and the different quantitative importance of the irregular economy in different countries (Alessandrini and Dallago 1987; Dallago 1990; Schneider 2013; Schneider and Ernste 2000) or systemic inefficiencies, such as the lack of coordination between governments, financial organisations and companies of the same country in foreign markets.

An important group of inefficiencies has microeconomic nature and concerns the conditions under which economic activity takes place. These inefficiencies relate to various aspects of the life of enterprises: such as setting up and winding down, contracting, managing labour and capital, managing and solving contractual disputes, and pursuing technical progress. Inefficiencies also include the effective working of courts, simplification of practices for founding a business, and vocational training. There are various dissimilarities among countries, which explain inter-group differences (WB 2015a). However, these differences do not form a consistent pattern.

Overall, resilient countries are closer to the Doing Business frontier than vulnerable countries are, but the difference between the two groups of countries is not particularly large (Figure 10.15). Differences are contained in the case of several variables, such as starting a business, paying taxes, getting credit, and trading across borders. More significant differences exist in resolving insolvency, dealing with construction permits and getting electricity, to the advantage of resilient countries. There are two cases, registering property and protecting minority investors, in which vulnerable countries perform significantly better than resilient countries. In the case of enforcing contracts, the performance of resilient countries is much better than that of vulnerable countries.

Compared to the years before the crisis, resilient countries improved or maintained their standing in relation to the frontier, except in the case of getting credit, and which worsened significantly. The most noteworthy improvement was in paying taxes and protecting minority investors. The situation of vulnerable countries is more variegated. There were significant improvements in starting a business, registering property, paying taxes, and protecting minority investors. Contained was the progress in dealing with construction permits and trading across borders, while a modest worsening took place in enforcing contracts. In getting credit and resolving insolvency, vulnerable countries are clearly farther away from the frontier than they were before the crisis, which proves the worsening of

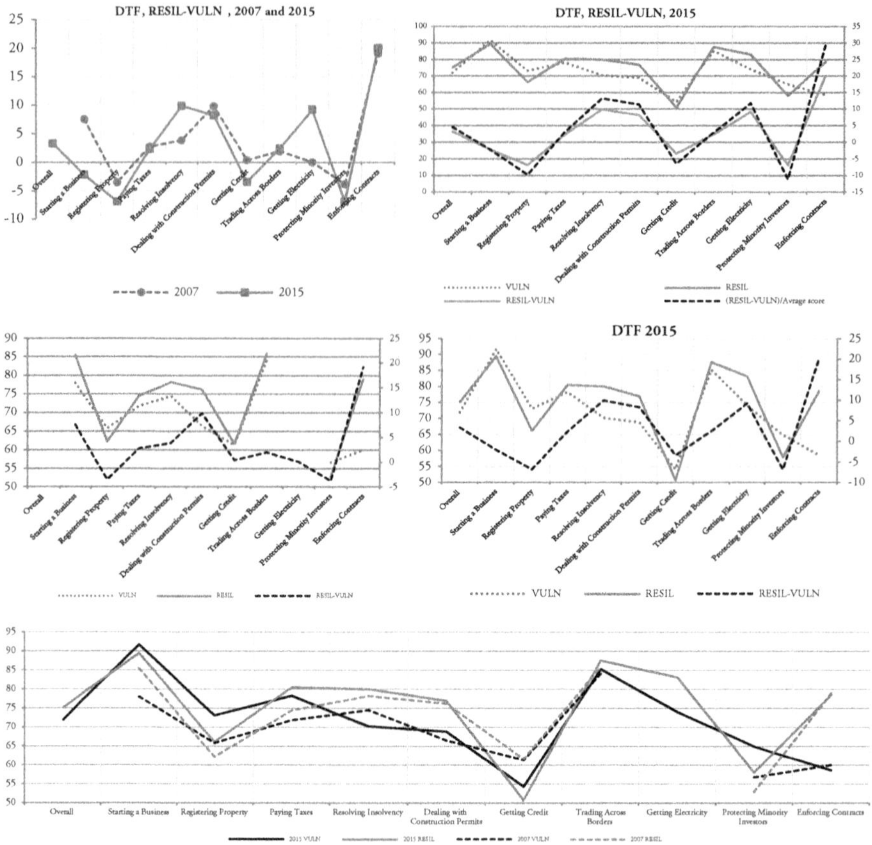

Figure 10.15. Distance to Frontier Score (DTF): Difference between Resilient and Vulnerable Countries, 2007 and 2015.[217]

Source: Author's own analysis of data from the Doing Business database (http://www.doingbusiness.org).

their relative performance. Getting credit is clearly the Achilles heel of vulnerable countries.

[217] The distance to frontier score captures the gap between an economy's performance and a measure of best practice across the entire sample of 31 indicators for 10 *Doing Business* topics (the labour market regulation indicators are excluded). An economy's distance to frontier score is indicated on a scale from 0 to 100, where 0 represents the worst performance and 100 the frontier. In any given year, the score measures how far an economy is from the best performance at that time. The difference between an economy's distance to

4. *Inequalities.* The increase of inequalities in a large number of countries, including within the Eurozone, in recent decades had serious negative economic consequences, together with social and political ones (Stiglitz 2012). Inequalities have negative consequences for incentives, including incentives to invest in human capital; for efficiency; for long-term economic stability and sustainability. Inequalities put the public budget under strain to mitigate social and political problems and avoid negative economic consequences and distort public investment and regulation. Since lower income earners have higher propensity to consumption than higher income earners, growing inequality depresses domestic demand and consequently incentives to investment. If the demonstration effect is active and if, consequently, lower income earners are striving for "keeping up with the Joneses", the effect may be negative savings and over-indebtedness. Real bubbles likely appear, typically in the form of housing bubbles. In the EU, this effect was important in Anglo-Saxon countries such as Great Britain and Ireland, but also in vulnerable Eurozone countries, such as Greece. Resilient countries were in general relatively immune from these phenomena.

Inequalities were on the rise throughout most European countries at least since the mid-1980s (OECD 2011a; OECD 2015b; OECD 2015c; OECD 2015d; OECD 2015e; OECD 2015f; Piketty 2014). This outcome was the consequence in particular of the deregulation of markets and of policies favouring capital and highly specialised professionals and disfavouring labour, but also of changes in the tax system.[218] Also the decline in unionisation was found to be strongly associated with the rise of income shares at the top (Jaumotte and Buitron 2015).[219] These effects

frontier score in any previous year and its score in 2014 illustrates the extent to which the economy has closed the gap to the regulatory frontier over time (WB 2015b).

[218] The increase of capital share was particularly significant in France, where it doubled since the mid-1980s. It was also important in Germany, a country where the contribution of capital income to total income inequality has increased from 8% to 15.5% in the past decade (OECD 2011b).

[219] In an IMF study, Jaumotte and Buitron (2015) find that the decline in unionisation is a key contributor to the rise of top income shares. On average, the decline in unionisation explains about half of the 5 percentage point rise in the top 10% income share. This finding

were significantly larger in vulnerable countries than in resilient countries. In Germany, the Hartz labour market reform of 2003–2005 led, among other things, to a significant decrease of wages for millions of employees, in the attempt to increase the competitiveness of the economy and create jobs.[220] This policy was successful in keeping employment at high levels also during the crisis and in leading German exports to success. However, this same policy kept domestic demand low, which contributed to the creation of additional problems for other European countries.[221] In vulnerable countries, growing fiscal wedges caused stagnating net wages, while the expansion of relatively cheap and insecure labour is credited for being a major explanation for stagnating productivity, since enterprises used labour as a substitute for investment.[222]

---

holds even after accounting for shifts in political power, changes in social norms regarding inequality, sectorial employment shifts (such as deindustrialisation and the growing role of the financial sector), and increases in education levels. Deunionisation is also associated with less redistribution of income, while reductions in minimum wages increase overall inequality considerably.

[220] The German labour market reform was successful in decreasing substantially long-term unemployment and reversing the trend of continuously increasing systemic unemployment. The reform can be credited for the increase of employment also during the crisis and for job stability, with several regions close to full employment and low youth unemployment. At the same time, wage inequality rose substantially and the size of the low-pay sector in Germany was higher than in almost all other European countries (Möller 2014, 2016).

[221] According to the US Treasury, "Germany's anaemic pace of domestic demand growth and dependence on exports have hampered rebalancing at a time when many other euro-area countries have been under severe pressure to curb demand and compress imports in order to promote adjustment. The net result has been a deflationary bias for the euro area, as well as for the world economy" (US Treasury 2013, p. 3). "Thus, the burden of adjustment is being disproportionately placed on peripheral European countries, exacerbating extremely high unemployment, especially among youth in these countries, while Europe's overall adjustment is essentially premised on demand emanating from outside of Europe rather than addressing the shortfalls in demand that exist within Europe" (US Treasury 2013, p. 10).

[222] In vulnerable countries, increasing distributive disparities were generally the effect of policies meant to deliver price competitiveness (Balducci and Staffolani 2002; Tronti 2008). During the crisis, the same effect was due to austerity policies and internal devaluation, which aimed to decrease wages.

Resilient and vulnerable countries are clearly worlds apart in income distribution (Figure 10.16). The difference between the two groups of countries is clear and rather constant at 3–6 points for most of the years. Another important difference appeared during the crisis: while the Gini coefficient slightly improved in resilient countries, in the case of vulnerable countries it worsened by around 1.3 points between 2007 and 2013. It is interesting to note that, among resilient countries, the Gini coefficient worsened by more than 3 points in both Germany and France. Among vulnerable countries, Gini coefficient in Portugal improved by 3.5 points during the crisis, although initially Portugal had the highest index among Eurozone countries. The coefficient improved also in Ireland, by nearly 2 points.

5. *Internal demand.* Increased inequalities together with the deepening of the crisis caused consumption and savings stress. This effect was clear in vulnerable countries, where inequalities were higher, the crisis effects

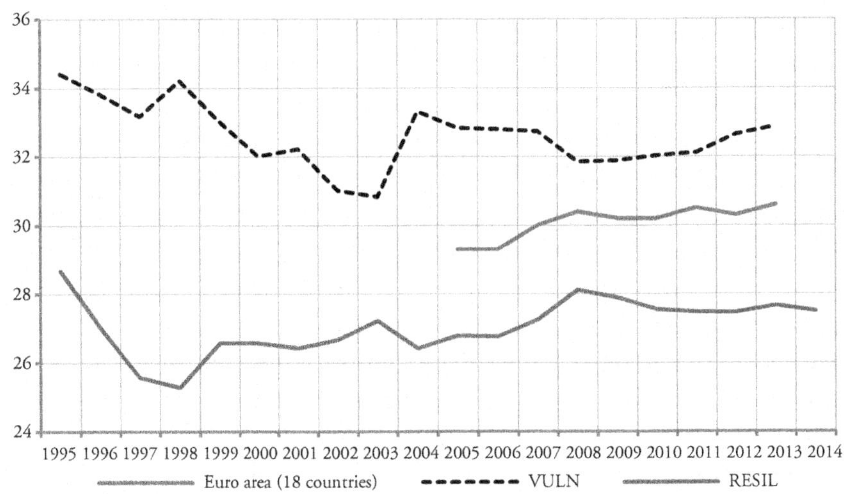

Figure 10.16. Gini Coefficient of Equivalised Disposable Income in Vulnerable and Resilient Countries.

Source: Author's own figure based on Eurostat data (http://ec.europa.eu/eurostat/tgm/table.do?tab=table&language=en&pcode=tessi190).

stronger, stabilisation policies harsher, and the drive to consumption in order to keep up with resilient and richer countries was greater. Consumption is usually more resilient to economic downturns than is income. Consumers tend to smooth out income shocks by using savings and borrowing. However, this holds until shocks are perceived to be temporary. When shocks look permanent and cause negative wealth effects, so that income recipients consider themselves to be permanently poorer, they adjust their consumption by decreasing it permanently (Jappelli and Pistaferri 2009; Krueger and Perri 2012).

According to the findings by Reinhart and Rogoff (2010), over two centuries and for more than 70 countries, the typical antecedent to domestic banking crises is private debt increase, which precedes or accompanies sovereign debt crisis. Private debt is fueled by both domestic banking credit growth and external borrowing. The behaviour of consumers and savers before and during the crisis show a consistent picture along these lines. What is peculiar within the Eurozone system is the unfolding of these trends.

Within the monetary union and given the uniform interest rate policy, and in spite of the economic union, the uneven inflation rates which have characterised Eurozone member countries caused different real interest rates. Different real interest rates, even after discounting for risk, together with different households psychologies and inter-Eurozone demonstration effects fueled different households' consumption, savings and investment behaviour. As a consequence, a substantial surge in private and foreign debts was experienced in vulnerable countries before the crisis. Resilient countries showed a different trend. In all these cases, the difference between vulnerable and resilient countries came out clearly, although national idiosyncrasies were important in explaining variations within each group.

Resilient countries had ratios to GDP of household saving rates constantly higher and consumption ratios constantly lower than vulnerable countries (Figures 10.17 and 10.18). While this difference may seem normal, with resilient countries being richer than vulnerable countries on average, what is unusual is the change of both variables through time. Economic growth should have brought about an increase of saving rates

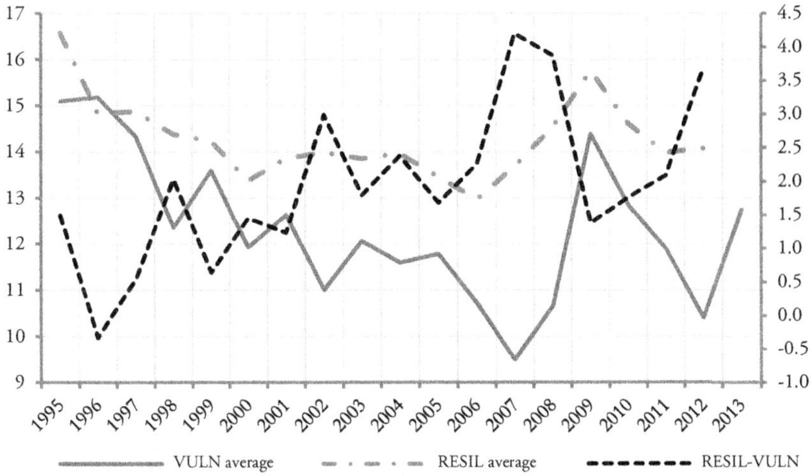

Figure 10.17. Gross Household Saving Rate in Vulnerable and Resilient Countries (Difference Resilient-Vulnerable on Right Scale).
Source: Author's own figure based on Eurostat data.

and a decrease of consumption rates in expanding vulnerable economies. However, in vulnerable countries, saving rates constantly decreased until the beginning of the crisis, increasing abruptly in 2008 and 2009, decreasing again in the following three years and increasing in 2013. The strongest variations were in Ireland and Spain. In Cyprus, changes were delayed by one year, while Italy had a rather smooth, yet constant decrease of the savings rates. Households' net saving rate in Greece was negative for the past decade and, following the crisis and stabilisation policies, private consumption decreased substantially. In Italy, a traditionally high savings country, and Spain, household net saving rates were already decreasing before the crisis. In Italy, the decline continued during the crisis.

In resilient countries, saving rates decreased until 2000, then remained stable until the beginning of the crisis. Their growth in 2008 and 2009 was significant, yet lower than in vulnerable countries. In the following years, saving rates decreased, at a somewhat milder pace than in vulnerable countries. In resilient countries, the pattern of saving rates was overall stable, with the exception of a surge in 2009 in Finland, Luxembourg and Belgium and a decrease in 2010 in Austria and the Netherlands. As a consequence,

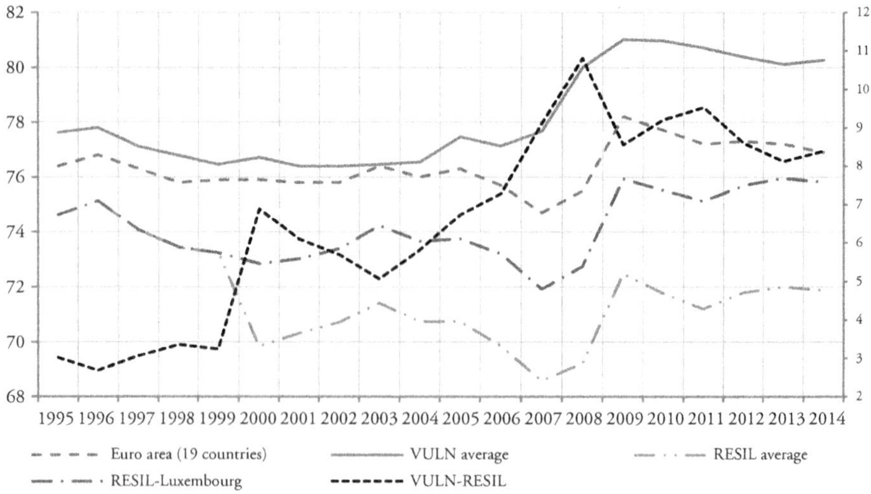

(a)

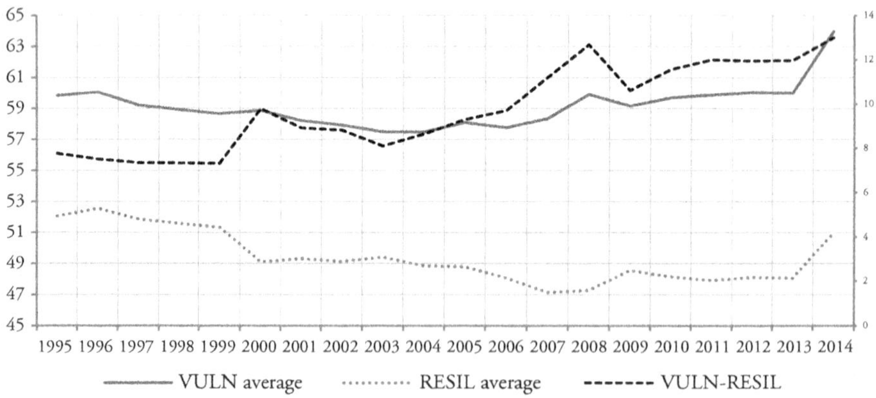

(b)

Figure 10.18. Final Consumption Expenditure (Figure a) and Final Consumption Expenditure of Households (Figure b) in Vulnerable and Resilient Countries as Percentage of GDP in Vulnerable and Resilient Countries (Differences on Right Scale).
Source: Author's own figures based on Eurostat data.

the difference of saving rates between resilient and vulnerable countries increased constantly until the crisis: in 2006 it was around 2%. Then it doubled to 4% in 2007 and 2008, falling abruptly to 1.5% in 2009 and returning to nearly 4% by 2012.

Final consumption expenditure of households as a share of GDP remained stable in vulnerable countries until 2007, increased by nearly 4%

in 2008 and 2009, then remained relatively stable (Figure 10.18). The share of final consumption expenditure in GDP was some 3% higher during the crisis than it was in 1996. This trend characterised all countries, although Italy and Spain showed more moderate variations. The behaviour of resilient countries was different in that the share decreased until the crisis, overall by some 6%. Similarly to vulnerable countries, there was a surge in 2009, then relatively stable until 2014. In 2014, final consumption expenditures in resilient countries as a share of GDP was some 3% lower than in 1996. However, much of the absolute difference in consumption expenditure is due to the particularly low share that the latter has in Luxembourg.

The difference between resilient and vulnerable countries in final consumption expenditure increased rapidly until 2008, overall by nearly 8 points, reflecting the moderation in resilient countries and the drive to consumption in vulnerable countries. However, this trend was reversed during the crisis, when the difference between the shares decreased by 2.5 points overall. The increasing divergence between the two groups of countries was continuous in the case of the final consumption expenditure of households (Figure 10.18b). Obviously, these trends are strongly influenced by the decreasing GDP value in vulnerable countries.

Investment activity in the Eurozone revealed a moderate divergence between resilient and vulnerable countries until the crisis and an inverse and rapidly growing divergence afterwards. The main reason for this crossed trend is the investment performance in vulnerable countries (Figure 10.19). Divergence was largely the result of austerity policies in vulnerable countries, but had its roots in the years preceding the crisis. In the mid-1990s, resilient and vulnerable countries invested approximately the same share of the GDP. Afterwards, up to 2008, the share remained roughly stable in resilient countries, but increased by approximately 4 points in vulnerable countries. With the crisis, investment rates in vulnerable countries decreased rapidly and in 2012 were approximately 10 points less than in 2007. Although all countries decreased investment shares, the decrease was overall moderate only in Italy. In resilient countries, investment rates started to decrease one year later, in 2009 and by 2012 they were less than 2 points lower. The trend was rather similar in all countries.

One important reason for the abrupt fall of investments in vulnerable countries during the crisis is that in previous years, investment growth

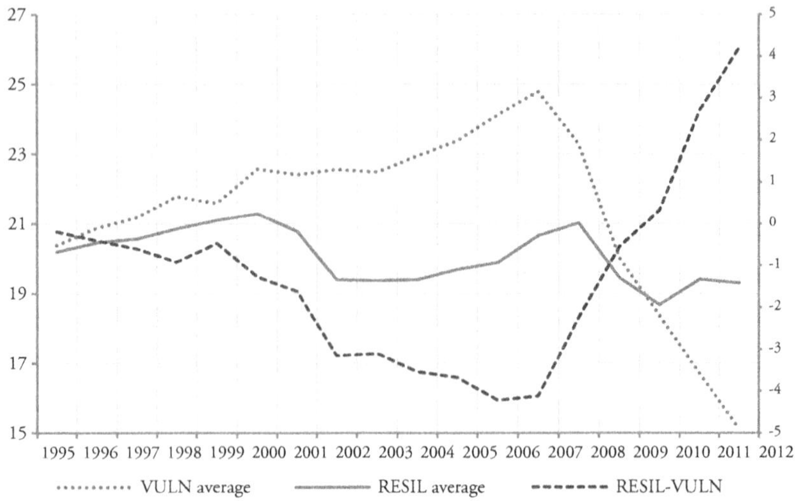

Figure 10.19. Total Investment to GDP Ratio in Vulnerable and Resilient Countries (Difference on Right Scale).
Source: Author's own figure based on Eurostat data.

often had the nature of a bubble build-up. The latter was financed by both domestic investment and foreign investment. Since 2008, investment activity continued to be depressed, particularly in vulnerable countries in both real estate and industrial equipment. This situation is not so much explained by low profitability and high indebtedness of firms. It is better explained by factors external to enterprises, in particular the depressed demand, tight credit supply by financial organisations and indebtedness. In fact and although profitability remains low in absolute terms, the profitability of firms in tradable sectors of vulnerable countries was recently restored relative to those in non-tradable sectors (EC 2013a). However, tradable sector firms did not respond to this improved profitability by investing more and firms in the tradable sectors of vulnerable countries invest less than what these firms' currently weak fundamentals would suggest. They also invest significantly less than similar firms operating in resilient countries.

One serious problem in vulnerable countries is the accumulation of debt by firms and households (Figure 10.20). In the years before the crisis, firms accumulated considerable debt, although large disparities existed

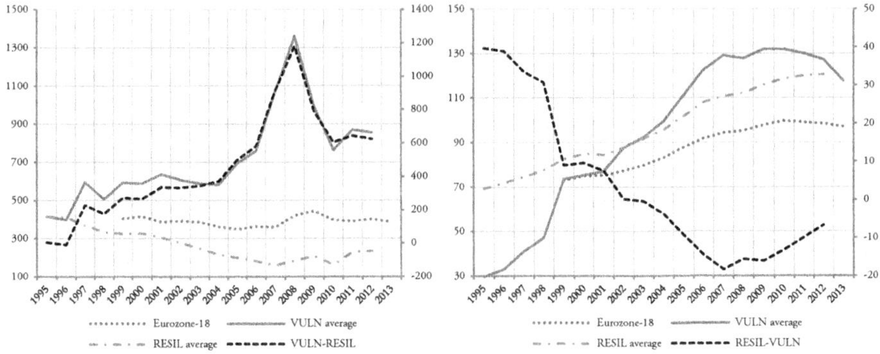

(a) (b)

Figure 10.20. Net Debt-To-Income Ratio, after Taxes, of Non-Financial Corporations (Left Chart) and Gross Debt-To-Income Ratio of Households to GDP (Right Chart) in Vulnerable and Resilient Countries (Differences on the Right Scale).
Source: Author's own figures based on Eurostat data.

among countries and among sectors (ECB 2013a). It was mainly in Spain and Portugal and, to a lesser extent, Ireland that loose financing conditions stimulated excessive borrowing by the corporate sector and overinvestment, noticeably in the construction sector. During the crisis, the high leverage of firms compelled them to decrease investments and this led the economy into a severe and persistent downturn. Indebtedness increased slightly in 2011, due to its growth in Italy and Portugal. In resilient countries, the indebtedness of firms decreased until 2007 and increased slightly during the crisis. As a consequence, the indebtedness of firms in vulnerable and resilient countries departed rapidly up to 2008. Afterwards, the rapid decrease of debt in vulnerable countries led to the narrowing of the gap between the two groups of countries until 2010.

Differences between the two groups of countries were less prominent in the case of household debt (Figure 10.18b). In the Eurozone (18 countries), household debt increased from 73% to nearly 100% of GDP from 1999 to 2010, after which it decreased very slightly. Household debt was much lower in vulnerable countries than in resilient countries until the end of the 1990s. However, interest rates decreased particularly rapidly in vulnerable countries during the period of monetary unification. Households responded by rapidly increasing their indebtedness, that matched a more stable, although growing, debt of the resilient countries in 2002. These trends continued until 2007, after which household debt in vulnerable countries stagnated and started to decrease in 2010, approaching again the level in resilient countries. Among vulnerable countries, the debt increased strongly in Ireland, Spain and Portugal. It increased also in Italy, but remained at much lower levels and Italy continues to be the Eurozone country where household debt is the lowest among the countries considered in the charts.[223]

10.5 Banks

An important reason for the difficulty of Eurozone economies was the state of the banks. Banks were most directly affected by the crisis in the United States, both through the direct relations that they had with banks in that country, their operation in international markets, and the holding in their portfolio of bonds which originated in US banks, including subprime derivatives. All this made the situation of Eurozone banks delicate. During the unfolding of the crisis, a new, serious domestic problem increased the precariousness of the banks' position: their entanglement with national sovereign debt.

There were two important driving forces affecting the state of the banks during the crisis (Caruana and Van Rixtel 2012). First, an important change took place in the perception and management of risk by financial actors. With the crisis, counterparty and liquidity risk became a prominent market concern and the risk resulting from the bad performance of the real economy had to be internalised. Second, imbalances in the form of excessive leverage and excessive maturity and liquidity transformation in the balance sheets of financial institutions needed to be fixed. However, adjustment through deleveraging led to the falling prices of assets and credit contraction and the contraction of cross-border and inter-bank lending. Adjustment and policies for limiting contagion caused market fragmentation and the segmentation of financial flows along national borders. This increased as a consequence the dependence of banks on ECB liquidity. Rapidly increasing risk aversion and volatility led to growing

[223] Within the Eurozone, household debt is lower in Latvia, Lithuania, Slovenia and Slovakia.

recourse to funding secured by collateral and spread further contagion within the Eurozone and outside it. Confronted with rapidly increasing risk, important external investors, such as US institutional investors, withdrew large sums of short-term funding from Eurozone banks.

One important aspect of the banking crisis in the Eurozone was the exposure of the large countries' banks to vulnerable countries (Tables 10.10, 10.11 and 10.12). Large German current account surpluses vis-à-vis current account deficits of vulnerable countries and the latter's low interest rates following the monetary unification led to a massive interconnectedness in the Eurozone (Baldwin and Gros 2010). This, in turn, increased the vulnerability of the Eurozone banking system. Such interconnectedness was a fundamental reason why the refinancing crisis in Greece was of such great importance to other Eurozone countries. While Greece counts for less than 2% of the Eurozone GDP, its crisis opened the way to a systemic crisis of the euro. The threat to the stability of resilient countries' banks was solved by transferring the distress to public budgets (see footnote 197 in this chapter).

Moreover, Eurozone banks also lent assertively outside the Eurozone and overleveraged. Particularly risky was the high exposure of European banks in Eastern European markets. When some of those economies went into default or risked to do so, lending banks risked to see their capital erode.[224] In the decade preceding the crisis, bank lending expanded massively.[225] This policy made banks particularly vulnerable to external shocks, such as the default in the US derivatives market. This shock faced tremendously exposed and highly leveraged banks, which financed governments and private operators in economically weak countries. Many Eurozone banks, when confronted with the danger of default caused by an external shock, put their domestic debtors under pressure, thus spreading further the shock within the Eurozone. In 2009–2010, the

---

[224] Important Eurozone banks such as Unicredit, Raiffeisen group, Erste Group and OTP started to report alarming increases in loan losses, both to corporate and household borrowers. This was linked in particular to the significant amount of bad loans, when local borrowers met with great difficulties in honouring debts in foreign currencies, after their currencies were depreciated.

[225] In Ireland total bank assets as a percentage of GDP rose from 360% in 2001 to 705% in 2007; in France from 229% to 373%; in Italy from 148% to 220%; and in Spain from 177% to 280% (Baldwin and Gros 2010).

Table 10.10. Eurozone International Claims of Domestically Owned Banks, Consolidated (Millions of US $).

		Reporting Country														
		Germany			France			Italy			Spain			Other EZ		
		2014–Q3	2012–Q4	2010–Q4	2014–Q3	2012–Q4	2010–Q4	2014–Q3	2012–Q4	2010–Q4	2014–Q3	2012–Q4	2010–Q4	2014–Q3	2012–Q4	2010–Q4
Counterparty location	**Cyprus**	4.432	7.819	9.058			3.166	1.112	1.378	1.615	85	51	83	13.036	14.242	13.881
	Greece	24.646	7.734	40.198	5.134	7.683	75.504	2.524	2.961	7.664	1.119	2.184	1.820	1.823	10.283	21.618
	Ireland	90.521	153.421	227.480	92.663	86.827	90.536	24.982	30.182	37.529	12.149	15.592	18.210	36.225	42.343	54.667
	Italy	259.910	260.841	319.820	516.094	534.501	593.901				86.056	65.036	66.060	65.420	71.026	120.649
	Portugal	30.874	41.743	79.646	24.150	30.074	43.448	8.461	6.378	12.696	109.632	113.152	130.754	5.838	7.943	15.862
	Spain	213.915	226.037	341.557	227.244	183.256	249.208	54.309	50.341	63.853				85.993	99.456	160.094

Source: Bank for International Settlements, consolidated banking statistics.

Table 10.11. Intra-Eurozone Banking Exposure: Eurozone Core Banks' Holding of Debt of Vulnerable Countries' Banks (Million US$).

	1999 — 4th Quarter	2014 — 3th Quarter	% Change
Greece	28,925	33,824	16.9
Ireland	68,723	153,001	122.6
Italy	283,554	546,171	92.6
Portugal	42,821	114,208	166.7
Spain	104,043	339,527	226.3
Total	528,066	1,186,731	124.7

Source: Bank for International Settlements, consolidated banking statistics.

Table 10.12. Eurozone Banking Exposure, Eurozone Core Bank's Holding of Vulnerable Countries, UK and USA Debts (Million US$), 2014 Q3.

	Exposure to						
Bank's Nationality	**Spain**	**United Kingdom**	**Greece**	**Ireland**	**Italy**	**Portugal**	**United States**
Austria	3,715	15,063	189	1,260	7,621	544	10,426
Belgium	8,762	21,032	29	16,817	10,716	360	16,233
Germany	106,387	422,993	29,532	56,434	110,862	19,113	499,138
Finland	185	3,024	—	—	192	64	390
France	129,062	239,027	2,092	43,290	326,928	12,798	569,488
The Netherlands	48,968	121,497	1,181	15,368	33,444	4,324	193,166

Source: Bank for International Settlements, consolidated banking statistics.

difficult financial situation that these events created in the Eurozone, particularly in its vulnerable countries, jeopardised the euro's credibility and stability.

One further problem was the failure of financial and banking regulation in the Eurozone. This failure opened the way to the high fragility of the financial system. One important reason was that Basel II favoured the undercapitalisation of the banking system. The system also contributed to the unfolding of the financial crisis through low capital coefficients, admission of hybrid capital, lax criteria for risk evaluation, and ample possibilities for circumventing the rules (Spaventa 2010).

These events led Eurozone banks to be overleveraged[226] at levels well above regulatory ratios (Gros and Micossi 2008). Again, there are important intercountry differences. While French and German (and British) banks were highly exposed, Italian and Spanish banks were subject to a more prudential domestic regulation and were less leveraged. One problem in managing imbalances and dealing with toxic assets was the lack of intra-Eurozone coordinated banking policy and the mild intervention by governments of some important countries, particularly France and Italy (Table 10.13). These deficiencies, whereby national governments responded in different ways, contributed to financial vulnerability of the largest Eurozone economies (Baldwin and Gros 2010).

10.6 Conclusion: Looking at Policies

The years elapsed since 2008 witnessed contradictory changes in Eurozone economies. Most important among them was the growing divergence between resilient and vulnerable economies. This divergence is evident in most indicators and may become permanent. While the indebtedness of firms and households decreased, sovereign debts continued to increase, particularly in vulnerable countries. Most worrying was that real indicators — from investment to consumption, from savings to microeconomic variables, from income to production — were all either worsening or stagnating in vulnerable countries.

In 2014, vulnerable economies still showed persistent and diffused weakness. At the same time, even resilient Eurozone economies were unable to grow at a safe rate, a rate that created employment at home and external demand sufficient to support vulnerable economies. In spite of some signs of recovery, the economic situation of the Eurozone did not show convincing signs of revival. According to the IMF (2014c), activity and investment in the Eurozone were still ailing. They continued to be weak and had yet to reach pre-crisis levels, primarily in vulnerable countries.

---

[226] The 13 largest European banks' average leverage ratios (shareholder equity to total assets) was 35, versus an average of 20 in the US.

Table 10.13. Interventions (Governments and Central Banks) in Favour of the Banking System in Europe during the Current Crisis (Billion Euros, 2008 to 30 September 2014).

		Recapitalisation Measures		Guarantees		Asset Relief Interventions		Liquidity Measures Other Than Guarantees		Total Recapitalisation and Asset Relief		Total Guarantees and Liquidity Measures	
		In € billion	As % of 2013 GDP	In € billion	As % of 2013 GDP	In € billion	As % of 2013 GDP	In € billion	As % of 2013 GDP	In € billion	As % of 2013 GDP	In € billion	As % of 2013 GDP
RESIL	Austria	40.13	12.80%	84.14	27.00%	0.60	0.20%	26.88	4.50%	40.73	13.01%	111.01	35.46%
	Belgium	23.32	6.10%	325.42	85.00%	28.22	7.40%	20.50	5.40%	51.54	13.47%	345.92	90.39%
	Finland	4.00	2.10%	50.00	26.00%	0.00	0.00%	0.00	0.00%	4.00	2.07%	50.00	25.85%
	France	29.24	1.40%	382.68	19.00%	4.70	0.20%	8.65	0.00%	33.94	1.65%	391.33	19.00%
	Germany	114.61	4.20%	455.85	17.00%	82.78	3.00%	9.50	0.00%	197.38	7.21%	465.35	17.00%
	Luxembourg	2.50	5.50%	7.05	16.00%	0.00	0.00%	0.32	0.00%	2.50	5.50%	7.37	16.21%
	The Netherlands	39.84	6.60%	200.00	33.00%	30.61	5.10%	54.00	0.20%	70.45	11.69%	254.00	42.15%
RESIL		**253.64**	**5.53%**	**1505.14**	**31.86%**	**146.91**	**2.27%**	**119.85**	**1.44%**	**400.54**	**7.80%**	**1624.98**	**35.15%**

(*Continued*)

Table 10.13. *(Continued)*

		Recapitalisation Measures		Guarantees		Asset Relief Interventions		Liquidity Measures Other Than Guarantees		Total Recapitalisation and Asset Relief		Total Guarantees and Liquidity Measures	
		In € billion	As % of 2013 GDP	In € billion	As % of 2013 GDP	In € billion	As % of 2013 GDP	In € billion	As % of 2013 GDP	In € billion	As % of 2013 GDP	In € billion	As % of 2013 GDP
VULN	Cyprus	1.80	10.90%	9.00	55.00%	0.00	0.00%	0.00	0.00%	1.80	10.91%	9.00	54.53%
	Greece	48.97	26.90%	85.00	47.00%	0.00	0.00%	15.74	4.00%	48.97	26.90%	100.74	55.34%
	Ireland	111.39	67.90%	554.18	338.00%	122.26	74.50%	40.73	0.00%	233.64	142.42%	594.91	362.64%
	Italy	22.00	1.40%	110.00	7.00%	0.00	0.00%	0.00	0.00%	22.00	1.41%	110.00	7.05%
	Portugal	32.25	19.50%	44.27	27.00%	4.00	2.40%	6.06	0.00%	36.25	21.88%	50.33	30.38%
	Spain	174.52	17.10%	321.05	31.00%	139.92	13.70%	32.65	0.08%	314.44	30.74%	353.70	34.58%
VULN		**390.93**	**23.95%**	**1123.50**	**84.17%**	**266.18**	**15.10%**	**95.18**	**0.68%**	**657.10**	**39.04%**	**1218.68**	**90.75%**
OTHER EURO	Estonia	0.00	0.00%	0.00	0.00%	0.00	0.00%	0.00	0.00%	0.00	0.00%	0.00	0.00%
	Latvia	0.83	2.50%	5.20	16.00%	0.54	1.60%	2.70	0.00%	1.36	4.11%	7.90	23.78%
	Lithuania	0.81	2.30%	0.29	1.00%	0.58	1.70%	0.07	0.00%	1.39	4.02%	0.36	1.05%
	Malta	0.00	0.00%	0.00	0.00%	0.00	0.00%	0.00	0.00%	0.00	0.00%	0.00	0.00%
	Slovakia	0.66	0.90%	2.80	4.00%	0.00	0.00%	0.00	0.00%	0.66	0.92%	2.80	3.88%
	Slovenia	4.27	12.10%	13.76	39.00%	4.54	12.90%	0.00	0.00%	8.81	24.97%	13.76	38.99%
OTHER EURO		**6.57**	**2.97%**	**22.05**	**10.00%**	**5.66**	**2.70%**	**2.77**	**0.00%**	**12.22**	**5.67%**	**24.82**	**11.28%**

NO EURO	Bulgaria	0.00	0.00%	0.00	0.00%	0.00	0.00%	0.00	0.00%	0.00	0.00%	0.00	0.00%
	Croatia	0.00	0.00%	0.00	0.00%	0.00	0.00%	0.00	0.00%	0.00	0.00%	0.00	0.00%
	Czech Rep.	0.00	0.00%	0.00	0.00%	0.00	0.00%	0.00	0.00%	0.00	0.00%	0.00	0.00%
	Denmark	14.55	5.80%	587.90	236.00%	2.30	1.00%	105.78	0.00%	16.85	6.77%	693.68	278.61%
	Hungary	1.07	1.10%	5.35	5.00%	0.04	0.00%	3.87	0.00%	1.11	1.13%	9.22	9.42%
	Poland	34.72	8.90%	33.89	9.00%	0.00	0.00%	0.00	0.00%	34.72	8.91%	33.89	8.70%
	Romania	0.00	0.00%	0.00	0.00%	0.00	0.00%	0.00	0.00%	0.00	0.00%	0.00	0.00%
	Sweden	5.03	1.20%	156.00	37.00%	0.00	0.00%	0.52	0.00%	5.03	1.20%	156.52	37.19%
	UK	114.62	6.00%	458.75	24.00%	248.05	13.10%	51.93	0.00%	362.67	19.10%	510.68	26.89%
NO EURO		**169.99**	**2.56%**	**1241.89**	**34.56%**	**250.39**	**1.57%**	**162.10**	**0.00%**	**420.38**	**4.12%**	**1403.99**	**40.09%**
TOTAL EU-27		**821.13**	**6.30%**	**3892.57**	**29.80%**	**669.13**	**5.12%**	**379.91**	**0.20%**	**1490.26**	**11.40%**	**4272.48**	**32.70%**

Source: European Commission (2015) — Competition — State Aid (http://ec.europa.eu/competition/state_aid/scoreboard/financial_economic_crisis_aid_en.html).

Presently, corporate and household sectors in most Eurozone countries are still subject to the influx of debt overhangs, which curb demand. Financial institutions, banks in particular, are still in an uneasy situation. Banks have weak budgets, which hinder the transformation of the abundant liquidity existing in the system into a flow of credit to the economy. Low inflation, and continuing deflation in some countries, although keeping nominal interest rates low, generate high real interest rates, which in turn burden real debts. All this translates into low demand and anemic or negative growth and leads to high and persistent unemployment.

The Eurozone economies are trapped into a negative feedback loop, from which they are unable to exit. As time elapses, the fault between resilient and vulnerable countries remains and widens in many aspects. This creates further economic problems that raise keen political questions and that markets are apparently unable to solve. It is therefore necessary to examine the policies.

Countries, therefore, when lawmaking falls exclusively to the lot of the poor cannot hope for much economy in public expenditure; expenses will always be considerable, either because taxes cannot touch those who vote for them or because they are assessed in a way to prevent that.

— Alexis de Tocqueville, *Democracy in America.*

11

Policies under the Blow of the Crisis

The incomplete monetary unification created a new situation, which governments and economic operators could only comprehend with time. This was particularly the case in those countries that had previously used depreciation as a means of solving problems of competitiveness. In non-competitive sectors, the transition to the new common currency created favourable conditions for businesses for adjusting prices upwards in the new currency. In the economically favourable conditions of the first years of monetary unification, wages and salaries could be adjusted upwards in countries that had lower levels, often independently of productivity. A kind of convergence to the highest and most expensive was led by a Eurozone demonstration effect that the common currency could carry on.

The most active in this sense were primarily economic operators in vulnerable countries.

The new situation provided national governments with no easy alternative of effective policy instruments. Worse still, governments lost monetary policy competences. Also, their control over fiscal policies was strongly constrained by Eurozone agreements and pacts, in particular the Stability and Growth Pact (SGP). At the same time, the Eurozone government — the European Commission and the European Central Bank (ECB) — were incomplete in their competences and largely powerless. Added to these far-reaching changes, the forceful progress of globalisation further circumscribed the policy competence and effectiveness of both the Eurozone and national governments.

The peculiar situation of the Eurozone in the policy domain is clearly highlighted in the so-called Eurozone "impossibility trinity". The traditional version of the impossibility trinity or "trilemma" is a fundamental tenet of international economics in open and integrated economies (see Section 8.8). According to the trilemma, it is impossible to have at the same time: (a) a stable foreign exchange rate, (b) free international capital mobility without capital controls, and (c) an independent monetary policy oriented toward domestic goals. The impossibility is both a hypothesis that stems from the interest rate parity condition and an empirical finding based on the failed attempts by governments to simultaneously pursue all three goals.[227]

According to the trilemma, monetary authorities can only choose and pursue simultaneously a combination of two of the above policy goals. They can choose among: (a) stable foreign exchange rate and free international capital mobility; (b) independent monetary policy and free international capital mobility, or (c) stable foreign exchange rate and independent monetary policy. The Eurozone implemented the unification of national currencies, thus creating a unique permanent exchange rate within the Eurozone. Since the Eurozone is also part of international integration,

[227] Obstfeld *et al.* (2004) study the coherence of international interest rates over more than 130 years in different monetary regimes. They conclude that the lessons borne out over a long span of modern economic history support the view of the trilemma as an effective guiding policy framework.

Eurozone countries are thus in condition (a), i.e. of having stable foreign exchange rates and being committed to free international capital mobility. As a consequence, they have to give up independent monetary policies oriented toward domestic goals.

The peculiar construction of the Eurozone highlights the existence also of a different type of impossibility trinity or new trilemma (Pisani-Ferry 2012). Considering the fundamental Eurozone institutions established by the Lisbon Treaty, the new trilemma appears involving: (a) the lack of joint responsibility over public debts, (b) the strict no-monetary financing rule, and (c) the national character of banking systems and bank-sovereign interdependence.[228]

The new trilemma highlights the difficult circumstances in which the Eurozone and its member countries have to operate in when making and implementing policy decisions. The limits to policies derive particularly from the incompleteness of the monetary integration, which lacks a common government of the economy and a complete mandate for its central bank. In the present crisis and given the inability of markets to self-adjust, the ineffectiveness of policies is a major problem and possibly a threat to the viability of the monetary union. The need for reforms is increasingly evident and in theory largely shared.

Three options for Eurozone reform descend from the new trilemma. These are: (a) a broader ECB mandate, (b) the building of a banking federation, and (c) a fiscal union with common bonds. The three options meet different problems and difficulties. According to Pisani-Ferry (2012), changing the ECB's mandate is the least feasible option. In fact, this option would require the ECB to credibly commit overwhelming forces in order to change market perceptions and behaviour. Given the limited mandate of the ECB, this would require that founding member countries agree on extending the mandate. The varying sensibilities of countries and national governments on the issue make this perspective unlikely in the present situation, at least at an institutional level. Yet major

[228] Beck and Prinz (2012) present the new trilemma in a somewhat different form and involving: (a) a no-bailout clause, (b) independent monetary policy, and (c) national fiscal sovereignty.

pragmatic steps were taken under the impact of the crisis, in particular since 2011.

The second option, building a banking federation, involves difficult and complex reforms and the need to weaken the national control over banks to be progressively transferred to the ECB. Implementing this option is not easy, yet the process of building a European banking union was started in 2012 and is moving ahead. Presently, it includes the buildup of a Single Supervisory Mechanism (SSM) and a Single Resolution Mechanism (SRM). However, a real breakthrough is still missing.

The third option, moving to a fiscal union, would signal the determination to pursue a structural solution for the present incompleteness of the Eurozone. Presently, the fiscal setting of the Eurozone consists primarily of fixed rules and related fiscal prohibitions, which limit the possibility for national governments to run fiscal policies, particularly in vulnerable countries. Rules and prohibitions are included in the SGP and the Fiscal Compact. Moving towards a more flexible fiscal union would require showing greater commitment to a stronger Economic and Monetary Union. A fundamental precondition is to rebuild trust among governments. In spite of the difficulties, this seems to be the most reasonable option. A reasonable perspective could be to proceed toward fiscal equilibrium.

The above considerations and proposals come out from the awareness that the present situation of the Eurozone is untenable and risky. It is also based on the evidence that policy ineffectiveness is a serious drawback in the present and can have permanent, negative consequences in the long run. The nature and evolution of policies are a fundamental aspect of the problem and of its solution. The present chapter considers the features and limits of the common policies and their evolution under the shadow of the crisis.

11.1 Danger Zone: Internal Deflation Policies

The effects of the financial crisis already became evident in the Eurozone in 2008. Together with acute financial distress, the crisis revealed important real consequences. Under the double blow of financial distress and real debility, a group of Eurozone countries, namely the vulnerable countries, started to drift apart because of their institutional and structural fragility and weak policies. Policies that were implemented to keep the crisis under control worsened the situation for those countries and could put resilient countries at an advantage (Dany *et al.* 2015). Concentrating Eurozone policies nearly exclusively on short-term financial issues for years led to overlook the deep real and institutional causes behind financial distress and made the solution more difficult.

The standard answer to the crisis was to implement austerity policies, based on the simple, indeed simplistic, idea that vulnerable countries were fragile because their finances were out of order. Implicitly, this meant that these countries were caught in a difficult situation because they mismanaged their finances. Countries in a sound financial positions and the European Commission considered with suspicion the request for different policy approaches that the vulnerable countries were advancing. On the one hand, some vulnerable countries, Greece in particular, but also Italy, were considered to be insufficiently committed to fix their unbalanced financial situation.[229] On the other hand, some resilient countries, notably Germany, were greatly exposed to the distress of vulnerable countries and

[229] The transcripts of interviews that Timothy Geithner, then US treasury secretary, gave to assistants preparing his book (Geithner 2014) provide important hints on what happened behind the scenes. They are also an interesting source of information on the political mood among governments during the Eurozone crisis. During a G7 finance ministers' meeting in Iqaluit in February 2010, at the time of the panic caused by Greece's restating of its accounts, European ministers were reported to state (Spiegel 2014): "We're going to teach the Greeks a lesson. They are really terrible. They lied to us. They suck and they were profligate and took advantage of the whole basic thing and we're going to crush them". On another occasion, Geithner reports that EU leaders approached President Barack Obama ahead of the November 2011 G20 summit in Cannes, France. They proposed him a plan to deny financial aid to Italy unless then Italian Prime Minister Silvio Berlusconi resigned. "They wanted us to basically say that we wouldn't support IMF money or any further escalation for Italy if they needed it if Berlusconi was prime minister." Geithner continues: "[T]o be sympathetic to them, the Germans' experience has been every time they buy a little bit of calm [on the] markets and the Italian spreads start to come down, Berlusconi reneges on anything he committed to do." It was perhaps to avoid further leaks that the US administration was not invited to take part in the meetings on the Greek crisis in 2015. Nevertheless, the prevailing mood was apparently no better, including unpolitical personal offences among European and international officials.

were risking a large share of their GDP in the event of the latter's default. The vulnerable countries' commitment to austerity policies was perhaps an inevitable step towards rebuilding and consolidating intergovernmental confidence. However, it was a unilateral step that lacked the more important constructive part, namely support to the reforms.

The real economy played no serious role in the analysis. But even worse was to disregard that, under the shadow of austerity policies, it was difficult, perhaps even impossible for vulnerable countries to fix their situation, even if they were determined to do so. Not only did the real economy suffer and the overall economic and social conditions of vulnerable countries worsen. The decline of output and the increase of unemployment became direct causes of growing financial distress and worsening public finances. The supposed cure created the conditions for serious default risks of vulnerable countries and greater risk for the Eurozone itself.

Before looking at alternative policies, it is important to understand why austerity policies created conditions that were worse than the ones they intended to fix. In fact, and while monetary and financial variables improved towards the end of 2012 compared to 2011 and most of 2012, the overall economic situation remained fragile and new dangers appeared. Stagnation or recession in vulnerable countries replaced the danger of financial and monetary melt-down. Growth rates were negative or irrelevant, unemployment high and growing, consumption and investment low and decreasing, and inter-Eurozone trade and world export shares declining. Prices decelerated well below the 2% target of the ECB and the risk of deflation appeared.

An important step towards a new policy stance came in 2012. In that year, the International Monetary Fund (IMF) proceeded to revise the estimates of the value that the fiscal multiplier had during the crisis (Blanchard and Leigh 2013). The revision was considerable and the IMF proceeded to change its policy stance in 2013 (IMF 2013a). The United States in turn gave a further push to change the Eurozone policy attitude, which the US administration considered to be problematic. Initially, the US attitude was mostly informal and indirect,[230] but since 2013 the pressure for more balanced and

[230] Geithner's transcripts mentioned in an earlier footnote provide interesting hints on the prudent attitude of the US administration. According to the transcripts, the US

overall expansive policies became open (US Treasury 2013). At the same time, the ECB became increasingly bold in the use of standard and unconventional instruments and policies. Growing signs of a somewhat bolder and more realistic and effective European approach to the management of the crisis took hold in 2014 and accelerated in 2015 (see next chapter). These changes proceeded prudently, yet they were important in moving the first, albeit timid step forward for modifying the standard Eurozone approach to the crisis and its counterproductive effects.

The standard approach in the vulnerable countries of the Eurozone was internal devaluation, a policy that dates back to the 1990s.[231] Policies of internal devaluation aim to reduce production costs and increase productivity to balance public budgets, regain competitiveness and balance current accounts, when currency depreciation is impossible or undesirable. If successful, internal devaluation should support shifting investments from non-tradable to tradable activities.

Devaluation can be obtained in different ways and can be accompanied by structural reforms supporting higher productivity. Governments can decrease wages of public sector employees to decrease the costs of the public sector. Governments can also invite and support the private sector to reduce wages to decrease labour costs and can make the labour market more flexible and institutionally less costly. This may have economic benefits if wage cuts are transferred into lower prices for consumers and in decreased costs for investors. The benefit may be particularly important if the purchasing power of consumers is not reduced and if lower costs increase investment in the tradeable sector. However, wage cuts have important drawbacks in terms of decreasing domestic demand, increasing inequalities and decreasing tax revenue. These drawbacks are significant if

---

administration attempted to reduce European panic and excessively passionate opinions and bring back European ministers to a more sober attitude in the case of Greece. In the case of the Italian prime minister, the US administration refused to cooperate in his ouster (Spiegel 2014).

[231] The concept of internal devaluation was first used during the economic crisis of Sweden during the 1990s and when Finland prepared to join the European Union in 1995. With the 2008 crisis, the concept and related policies became a standard in Eurozone countries with the aim of restoring competitiveness and balancing national budgets (Piton and Bara 2012).

lack of competition or other obstacles prevent or slow down the transfer of lower costs to prices.

Governments can also decrease payroll taxes in order to reduce the cost of labour. This is a useful solution if it is expected that lower taxes translate to greater economic activity, which in turn would increase tax revenues. However, vulnerable countries tend to have significant public debts and this solution may be difficult to implement, unless it is offset by the increase of other taxes, such as value added taxes on consumption or the taxation of real estate. The final effect depends upon the consequences of the different types of taxation on consumption, investments, exports and incentives.

Finally, governments can also decrease public expenditures and reach positive budgets without increasing taxation. These cuts may decrease red tape and unproductive expenditures, but may also decrease welfare, including pension provisions. Indeed, internal devaluation in vulnerable countries typically included reducing pension rights, either by diminishing replacement rates or postponing retirement age. It also included weakening welfare support without reducing the employees' social security payments.

Lower public demand, including lower welfare, inevitably decreases aggregate demand. However, if done in order to increase the efficiency of the public sector, this policy has general economic benefits. In this case, the public sector provides the same amount of services at a lower cost and this should increase both private demand and exports. However, if the effect of a decrease in costs in the public sector is not translated to other sectors (e.g. lower wages in the public sector or lower employment are not translated into lower prices and higher employment in the private sector), the overall output and employment decrease.

It is important to stress that internal devaluation is not an effective substitute for the standard external devaluation. First, external devaluation has immediate effects on all prices vis-à-vis the rest of the world. This increases immediately competitiveness, even if the effect on internal prices is delayed (J-curve effect of devaluation). Conversely, internal devaluation requires purposeful and active intervention, which may take a long time to be implemented and even longer to be effective (Bara and Piton 2012).

Moreover, it is likely to meet strong social opposition, particularly in the case of cuts in wages or welfare.

Second, internal devaluation is likely to increase inequalities more than external devaluation and create social problems (Petry 2014). In fact, it usually hits particular and numerous groups of people, in particular employees. Since powerful social groups may be successful in avoiding or stopping unfavourable measures or in offsetting unfavourable effects, a sense of unfairness may spread among those who are unfavourably hit. This may have negative political consequences and perhaps lead to more prudent consumption behaviour.

Third, cutting public expenditure and wages or increasing taxes has negative consequences on demand and may decrease inflation and possibly cause deflation, with negative consequences for economic growth and employment. If this happens, the debt/GDP ratio increases and the real value of public debt rises. Fourth, internal devaluation usually is implemented in countries having current account deficits. Using internal devaluation to fix external deficits is very costly in terms of lost output (Stockhammer and Sotiropoulos 2014). Fifth, the decrease of wages and unit labour costs may not translate into lower prices. This happens when higher profit margins and the nominal appreciation of the currency compensate for lower costs. In these cases, real effective exchange rates (REERs) may not improve when calculated using production prices or export prices (Uxó *et al.* 2014).

When all these factors are considered, it should not be a surprise to see that internal devaluation policies had contradictory and generally problematic outcomes (Piton and Bara 2012). The effect on private sector wages and prices was generally moderate and productivity recovery was limited. As a consequence, REERs depreciated to some extent. Current account surplus, when attained, was usually short-lived, since it relied more on the fall of domestic demand and much less on the improvement of competitiveness. The consequence of internal devaluation was generally a recession much longer and deeper than envisaged by its proponents, a recession that led businesses to increase their indebtedness. The consequent fall of tax revenues and the increase of budget expenditures to support the ailing market sector — banks in the first place — and the unemployed caused the increase of the public debt. Thus internal devaluation can actually have pro-cyclical effects. Negative economic and social consequences may be long-lasting, unless better alternatives are implemented, particularly a better coordination and stronger complementarity of Eurozone national policies (Peón and Rey 2013).

11.2 Detrimental Effects: Fiscal Policies and the Fiscal Multiplier

Following the crisis, the situation of vulnerable countries became problematic and was considered to be a threat to the soundness of the common currency and the stability of the economic and monetary union. As a consequence, vulnerable countries were pressed to implement internal devaluation and particularly its core, fiscal consolidation (higher taxation and government expenditure cuts). The first issue to clarify in order to get a sound overall picture of the situation and possible alternatives is to assess who is responsible for the difficult starting position of vulnerable countries. Once this is clear, it is necessary to explain why these policies did not work and why the Eurozone government and the governments of resilient countries insist on fiscal consolidation. Once this is clarified, it would be possible to consider the evolution of policies and look for a way out of the present difficulties of the Eurozone. The rest of the present chapter deals with the reasons for the fundamental failure of fiscal consolidation policies and the evolution of policies. The search for alternative solutions is the focus of the next chapter.

Vulnerable countries are both the cause and the victim of their difficult situation and that of the Eurozone. A degree of soft fiscal discipline was typical of the first decade of the Euro (Schuknecht *et al.*, 2011). This observation refers also to Germany and France in the first part of the last decade. At the same time, fiscal discipline of vulnerable countries such as Ireland and Spain was remarkable. Italy also pursued generally prudent fiscal policies after the euro was introduced, albeit in this case there were swings, depending on the government in charge. Greece proved to be a different case, as a country in which initially the government not only followed soft finances, but also forged budgets to hide what was actually happening. Yet all vulnerable countries shared responsibilities for the difficult situation, albeit in different forms (see Section 10.1).

These situations became problematic for the countries in questions and the entire Eurozone, because of the incomplete common institutions of the Eurozone. A number of observers, including the IMF and the US administration (IMF 2013b; Stiglitz 2014a; Tamborini 2015; US Treasury 2013; Wolf 2012), criticised resilient countries and particularly Germany for their egoism and short-sightedness in managing Eurozone policies and warned of the dangers that could result from this.[232] The problem is that adjustment and growth can only come in a complementary way, if both vulnerable and resilient countries play fair and cooperate. Each vulnerable country must give credible guarantees to other countries, while claiming with good reasons the EU's support. Resilient countries should understand that the common advantage and future are at stake. Unfortunately, for too many years and too often, vulnerable and resilient countries gave priority to their own short run and opportunistic interests and objectives and were in opposition to one another.

An incomplete monetary union can be sustainable only if a degree of trust exists among its member countries. Automatic rules can help, but cannot replace the willingness to cooperate and play fair. Monetary integration was built on the rule of financial discipline, in order to avoid the tricky question of deficit and debt mutualisation. The economic and monetary union was based on a set of ordoliberal clauses[233] reflecting the idea that market discipline, through higher interest rates to compensate for higher perceived default risk and credit rationing, is insufficient to restrain the financial behaviour of member countries.

[232] "If Germany and others are not willing to do what it takes — if there is not enough solidarity to make the politics work — then the euro may have to be abandoned for the sake of salvaging the European project" (Stiglitz 2013).

[233] It is useful to remind that the "no bailout" clause (Art. 125 TFEU) foresees that the Union or any member country is not liable or can assume the debts of another country or its institutions. The "non-monetisation" of public debt (Art. 123, 124 TFEU) foresees that the ECB or the national central banks cannot finance national debts. Other important rules concern national budget balancing (Art. 126 TFEU) and price stability (Art. 127 TFEU).

In an incomplete monetary union like the Eurozone, financial discipline is economically and politically fundamental, though one-sided. The EU clearly expressed its concern for financial discipline in various fundamental institutions: the Maastricht Agreement, the SGP, and the Fiscal Compact. An important problem with fiscal discipline in an incomplete monetary union is that member countries do not have full control over the currency in which their debt is denominated. It follows that these countries are more vulnerable to the loss of confidence of financial markets (De Grauwe 2011b). To avoid the risk of their financial stability and of liquidity crises transforming into solvency crises, countries must behave in ways that give confidence to markets. The more vulnerable an economy is, the more important is financial discipline.

Unfortunately, a country's compliance with the rules of the SGP proved not to be a reliable predictor of the economy's difficulties (Pisani-Ferry 2012). Indeed, vulnerable Eurozone countries, such as Ireland or Spain, had public finances that were sounder than non-euro countries like the UK, US or Japan. Nevertheless, they were faced with a dangerous situation (Table 11.1, De Grauwe 2011b).[234]

There were two additional problems with the construction and working of the Eurozone. The first problem was that markets did not really believe in the effectiveness of the TFEU clauses, in particular the no-bail-out clause. Once the crisis reached vulnerable countries, markets trusted that member countries in need would receive common support. This confidence maintained the trust in the common currency, confidence that

[234] According to IMF (2011) simulations, Greece and Ireland had to implement adjustments exceeding 10% of GDP to reach a 60% debt/GDP ratio by 2030. The adjustment was 5–10% of GDP in France, Spain and Portugal. Only in Italy, Belgium and Germany was the adjustment between 2% and 4%. For comparison, the adjustment was close to 14% in Japan and around 10% in the US and UK. According to IMF (2015a), some countries have a total financing need (maturing debt plus budget deficit) around 20% of GDP during each of the next three years (2015 to 2017). These countries are Spain (21.1% of its GDP on average during each of the three years), Italy (20.0%), Belgium (18.8%), Portugal (18.1%), and France (17.4%). The lowest need is for Germany (5.0%). On average, resilient countries have a total financing need equal to 11.2% of their GDP and vulnerable countries to 16.9%. The remaining Eurozone countries have the lowest need: 8.5%. Japan's total financing need is much higher (48.9%) and the US's is also high (19.4%).

Table 11.1. Gross Financing Need, 2015–2017, as a Percentage of GDP.

	2015			2016			2017		
	Maturing Debt	**Budget Deficit**	**Total Financing Need**	**Maturing Debt**	**Budget Deficit**	**Total Financing Need**	**Maturing Debt**	**Budget Deficit**	**Total Financing Need**
RESIL average	9.5	2.5	11.5	9.6	1.9	11.1	10.0	1.4	11.1
VULN average	15.2	3.1	18.3	14.7	2.2	16.9	13.7	1.7	15.4
OTHER average	5.2	2.5	7.6	7.4	2.2	9.6	6.1	2.1	8.2
Austria	5.8	1.7	7.5	5.7	1.7	7.4	6.8	1.5	8.3
Belgium	16.8	2.9	19.7	16.5	2.1	18.6	16.9	1.3	18.2
Finland	5.7	2.4	8.1	6.6	1.8	8.4	8.4	1.2	9.5
France	13.3	3.9	17.3	14.7	3.5	18.2	13.8	2.8	16.6
Germany	6.1	−0.3	5.8	6.2	−0.4	5.8	3.7	−0.4	3.4
The Netherlands	9.4	1.4	10.8	7.8	0.5	8.3	10.2	0.3	10.5
Ireland	7.8	2.4	10.2	6.7	1.5	8.2	5.6	0.6	6.2
Italy	18.8	2.6	21.4	18.2	1.7	19.8	17.8	1.1	18.9

(Continued)

Table 11.1. *(Continued)*

	2015			2016			2017		
	Maturing Debt	Budget Deficit	Total Financing Need	Maturing Debt	Budget Deficit	Total Financing Need	Maturing Debt	Budget Deficit	Total Financing Need
Portugal	17	3.2	20.1	14.7	2.8	17.5	14.2	2.5	16.7
Spain	17.2	4.3	21.5	19	2.9	21.9	17.3	2.5	19.8
Lithuania	7.1	1.4	8.4	5.9	1.6	7.5	4.5	1.6	6.1
Malta	4.4	1.8	6.3	6.4	1.6	8	5.7	1.5	7.2
Slovakia	4	2.6	6.6	6.4	2.3	8.7	6.7	1.8	8.5
Slovenia	5.3	4	9.2	10.7	3.4	14.2	7.4	3.4	10.8
United Kingdom	7.4	4.8	12.2	7.1	3.1	10.2	7.4	1.5	8.9
United States	15.8	4.2	20	16.4	3.9	20.3	14.4	3.4	17.8
Japan	46.5	6.2	52.7	46	5	50.9	38.7	4.3	43

Source: IMF (2015a).

continued until it became clear that this was not necessarily true. The second problem was that governments of resilient countries lost confidence in the ability of the European Commission to keep the opportunistic behaviour of some member countries at bay.

Both effects made it clear that the only realistic, yet inadequate answer was to put domestic finances in order before common support was to be provided. Unfortunately, lack of cooperation between member countries in different conditions created negative spillovers to the disadvantage of vulnerable countries. These effects were in the form of capital flight from vulnerable countries, higher interest rates and real exchange rate appreciation. This segmentation of the Eurozone led to the worsening of the Eurozone's domestic imbalances and weaknesses by an external symmetric shock like the US crisis. Jointly, these generated a set of asymmetric shocks that created the risk of multiple bad equilibria in an incomplete monetary union.[235]

Under the evidence of the negative effects of stabilisation policies, a remarkable convergence of opinions and analyses was reached among scholars and organisations known for having different theoretical and policy approaches. Stiglitz (2013) stated that "[t]he crisis caused the deficits and high debt, not the other way around, and the fiscal constraints that Europe has agreed will neither facilitate rapid recovery from this crisis nor prevent the next one."

The IMF published a series of important studies that highlighted an important reason for the negative outcome of stabilisation policies. The IMF called the attention to the underestimation of the value of fiscal multipliers in causing wrong policies and negative outcomes (Blanchard and Leigh 2013). In fact, "the multipliers used in generating growth forecasts have been systematically too low since the start of the Great Recession... [T]he multipliers implicitly used to generate these forecasts are about 0.5. So actual multipliers may be higher, in the range of 0.9 to 1.7" (IMF 2012b,

[235] "Events during the crisis suggest that currency union members ... are prone to multiple equilibria risks... The commitment of the ECB to intervene, if necessary and conditional upon fiscal adjustment, appears to have reduced the risk of 'bad equilibria' in the euro area (...). However, in practice intervention could require large purchases and there are likely to be limits on how much a central bank can do" (IMF 2013a, p. 12).

pp. 41–43). The analysis of data for 28 economies corroborated these results.

If the fiscal multiplier is much higher than envisaged when conceiving and implementing fiscal consolidation policies, output loss is much higher than previously believed. Consequently, the public debt/GDP ratio increases. Nuti (2013) showed that fiscal consolidation "will always necessarily result in an increase instead of a decrease of the Public Debt/GDP ratio, with respect to what that ratio would have been in the absence of fiscal consolidation, as long as the fiscal multiplier — or more precisely the weighted average of fiscal multipliers applicable to the composition of the fiscal package — is greater than the inverse of the country's Public Debt/GDP ratio."

According to the IMF (2013a), the crisis fundamentally changed our theoretical and policy knowledge: "The prevailing consensus before the crisis was that discretionary fiscal policy had a limited role to play in fighting recessions. ... For the management of business cycle fluctuations, monetary policy was seen as the central macroeconomic policy tool" (p. 16). After the crisis and "[w]hile debate continues, the evidence seems stronger than before the crisis that fiscal policy can, under today's special circumstances, have powerful effects on the economy in the short run" (p. 18). This is due to different reasons, including the "even stronger evidence than before that fiscal multipliers are larger when monetary policy is constrained by the zero lower bound (ZLB) on nominal interest rates, the financial sector is weak, or the economy is in a slump" (p. 18). Moreover, "it is worth recognizing the sizeable role that automatic fiscal stabilizers, the size of which varied across countries, played during the crisis. ... it appears that countries with smaller automatic stabilizers provided larger discretionary stimulus" (p. 25).

11.3 A Technical Support?

An easing of the Eurozone struggle with formal constraints came from the implementation of the new European System of National and Regional Accounts (ESA 2013). ESA 2010, the latest internationally compatible EU accounting framework, replaced ESA 95 and was fully implemented at the EU level, including compulsorily in all EU member countries, starting from September 2014. The new system serves as the central framework of reference for the social and economic statistics of the EU and its member countries. The structure of ESA 2010 follows from and is consistent with the System of National Accounts 2008 (2008 SNA), a set of worldwide guidelines on national accounting under implementation all around the world, produced under the joint responsibility of the United Nations, the IMF, Eurostat, the Organisation for Economic Cooperation and Development (OECD), and the World Bank.

The role of ESA 2010 is more delicate and demanding than in the case of 2008 SNA. In general, national accounting is important in that it provides the necessary information to policy decision-makers. ESA 2010 has this role, but goes well beyond it. In fact, national accounts in the EU, and in particular the Eurozone, are the source of the most important indicators that play a fundamental role in economic governance as defined in the SGP and the treaties, and obviously in monetary policy. Accounts based on ESA 2010 are important for calculating the fundamental fiscal parameters (the ratios of public deficit and debt to GDP) used in the Excessive Deficit Procedure (EDP) and the Macroeconomic Imbalances Procedure (MIP), while regional GDPs are used to distribute structural funds.

ESA 2010 both defines a method common to the entire EU and its member countries and a programme that each member country has to follow in transmitting data to Eurostat, according to specific deadlines. The method includes common standards, definitions, classifications and accounting rules that have to be used for compiling accounts and tables on a comparable basis (Eurostat 2014a).

ESA 2010 introduced various changes in national accounting. The most important changes are the following (Eurostat 2014a):

(a) Capitalisation of research and development (R&D) expenditures, replacing their treatment as intermediate consumption that has been followed thus far. While treating them as intermediate consumption leads the deduction of their amount from the global output and from operating profits, their capitalisation means that they are treated as other fixed assets, thus increasing the level of GDP of all countries proportional to their investment in R&D. The weighted average for the EU is an estimated increase of 1.9% of the EU GDP, as opposed to 2.5% in the United States.
(b) Military expenditures for the acquisition of durable weapon systems, including weapon carriers such as military aircrafts or vessels,

are treated in a similar way, in consideration of the fact that they can be used over many years. While so far they were computed as intermediate consumption, ESA 2010 treats them as gross fixed capital formation, regardless of the nature of the expenditure or the purpose intended for it. As a consequence of this change in accounting, the weighted average increase of EU GDP is around 0.1%, equal to the yearly consumption of this type of fixed capital.

(c) Goods sent abroad for processing are treated as exports according to ESA 95. The same goods, after being processed abroad and reimported in the first country, are treated as imports. ESA 2010 considers that many goods cross borders without changing ownership and consequently without entailing a consequential payment from the recipient to the sending country. In these cases, ESA 2010 considers that the recipient country does not export goods, but imports or exports processing services. As a consequence, in the new system these goods are not registered as gross exports and imports of goods, but the value of processing is registered as the export or import of services. Thus, the level of exports and imports of goods is slightly reduced in the national accounts and the balance of payments, while the level of exports and imports of services increases. The consequence of this is a change in the composition of trade, since exports and imports of goods diminish, while those of services increase by a corresponding amount. This change does not affect the amount of GDP, since the overall amount of foreign trade remains virtually unaffected and only its structure changes.

(d) ESA 95 registered only pension obligations for funded schemes. In ESA 2010, employment-related pension entitlements are registered, irrespective of whether the schemes are funded or not, and all accrued-to-date pension entitlements in social insurance are presented in a supplementary table. Lump sum payments that sometimes public corporations pay to governments in exchange for their taking over pension liabilities of these employers is not considered as revenue of the government, as was under ESA 1995, since this revenue is compensated by an increase in the pension obligations of the government. This change has some negative consequence for public deficits of countries that recently made such transactions (Portugal and Hungary).

(e) ESA 2010 introduces changes in the treatment of the contribution of non-life insurance services to GDP, previously based on the difference between premiums and claims, in order to smooth the level of a typically volatile output.
(f) Some other changes by ESA 2010 could moderately affect GDP or other variables, such as public deficit and debt. This effect is expected, for instance, from some reclassification of units.

The changes introduced by ESA 2010 have a small or negligible impact on annual GDP growth. Over the years from 1997–2013, the effect was around +/–0.1% for the 28 EU member countries. However the effect on the level of GDP is sizeable and, as a consequence, debt and deficit ratios to GDP decrease. This effect may be particularly important for some countries whose public finances are in a critical situation, since they could be freed from procedures of excess deficit.

Given the importance of the issue for the European Union (EU), and in particular the Eurozone, Eurostat asked member countries to estimate the effect of ESA 2010's methodological changes on their GDP. This issue is different from statistical changes, such as the improvement of data sources or the availability of new ones. These changes were introduced while implementing ESA 2010, and became available only after the actual implementation of ESA 2010 in September 2014.

Following the implementation of ESA 2010 and the introduction of other statistical improvements, the level of the 28 EU member countries' GDP rose by €59 billion or 3.7% in 2010 (Eurostat 2014b). Of this, 2.3% was due to the methodological changes and 1.4% to the statistical improvements. The bulk of the increase due to methodological changes, about 80% or +1.9%, is due to the capitalisation of R&D, while capitalisation of military expenditure contributes +0.2%. Since individual items, and particularly R&D and military expenses, differ sensibly among member countries, also the effect of the methodological changes differs among member countries (Table 11.2).[236]

[236] The introduction of 2008 SNA in the United States led to an increase of 3.5% of GDP for the years between 2010 and 2012. The capitalisation of R&D accounted for 2.5%. However, some of the changes that the United States implemented on that occasion

Table 11.2. Estimated Effect of ESA 2010 on GDP.[237]

Percentage of GDP Increase	Vulnerable Countries	Resilient Countries
0–1	—	—
1–2	IE, ES, IT, PT	LU
2–3		BE, DK, DE, FR
3–4		AT, NL
4–5		FI
+2.4	EU average	
+3.0		USA

Source: Author's own analysis based on EC (2014h). Reference year: mainly 2011.

These estimates offer the possibility of assessing the effect of accounting changes on vulnerable and resilient countries and to see whether these changes ease the Eurozone's situation relative to convergence criteria. The data in Table 11.2 show clearly that the expected positive effect is the greatest in resilient countries and the weakest in vulnerable countries (except Luxembourg). While the implementation of ESA 2010 improves the statistical situation of all EU countries, the relative effect is to further increase the gap between vulnerable and resilient countries.

However, it is important to consider another effect. Production, according to ESA 2010, includes the production of goods and services that are supplied to units other than their producers, and the own-account production of goods that are retained by their producers for their own final consumption or gross fixed capital formation (ESA 2013). These activities are considered as production, irrespective of being illegal or not-registered at tax, social security, statistical and other public authorities. In practical terms, since many own-account productions are economically unimportant in relation to the total supply of that good in a country, only

(capitalisation of entertainment, literary and artistic originals) and that generated a growth of GDP of +0.5% were already foreseen in ESA 1995 and already included in EU GDP. Therefore, a fair comparison with the +2.4 effect in the EU would be +3% in the United States.

[237] Estimates exist for 24 member countries, representing 97.7% of the EU GDP. Estimates refer in general to 2011. Estimates for Bulgaria, Croatia, Cyprus, Greece and Malta are missing. Two of these countries are Eurozone vulnerable countries.

the construction of dwellings, and the production, storage and processing of agricultural products are registered. The concept of production does not include the production of domestic and personal services that are generated and consumed within the same household, such as domestic services, when supplied by the same household.

An important indirect effect of ESA 2010, thus, is the registration of underground and illegal and criminal activities. The fundamental consideration is that all transactions should be fully registered in statistics. A transaction is any interaction between institutional units by mutual agreement. This consideration extends to illegal economic activities, provided that all parties involved enter the activities by mutual agreement. This definition includes, for example, purchases, sales or trade of illegal drugs or stolen property.

In principle, underground activities were also fully included in national accounting so far, although countries continued to differ in the extent they were doing so. In ESA 2010, registration should be full in all countries and adjustments should be taken into account when calculating ratios and other statistics referring to incomes and employment. Illegal activities, such as theft or the uncompensated seizure of assets imposed by law, in which one of the parties is an unwilling participant, are not included in production, as they cannot be considered as economic transactions (ESA 2013).

Since independent estimates of the relevance of illegal activities in European countries show that this is higher in vulnerable countries than in resilient countries (Figure 11.1), the likely effect is more positive for vulnerable countries than for resilient countries (Schneider 2012).[238] It is not clear yet the extent to which the two effects offset each other. Overall, ESA 2010 eased the situation of Eurozone member countries vis-á-vis convergence criteria. However, the relative position of vulnerable countries worsened slightly compared to resilient countries, except for the effect of the irregular and illegal economies.

---

[238] The inclusion of illegal activities contributed to the revision of GDP by 1.0% or €15.5 billion. Of these, €10.5 billion derived from the marketing of illegal drugs, €3.5 billion were from prostitution, and €0.3 billion from tobacco smuggling. With ESA 2010, the irregular economy was estimated at 11.5% of GDP in 2011. When illegal activities are included, the overall estimate is 12.4% of GDP (ISTAT 2014).

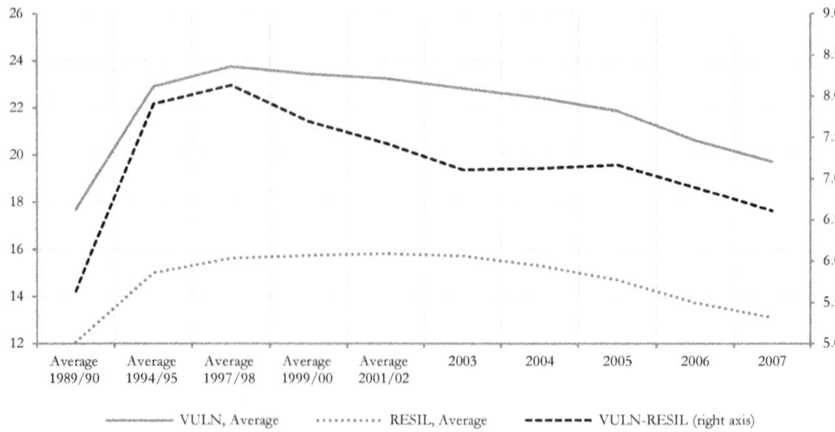

Figure 11.1. The Size of the Underground Economy (in % of Official GDP).
Source: Author's own figure based on data by Schneider (2012).

The new system has problems, though. Although the new national accounts better register economic activity, this is at the cost of growing contradictions in national accounts and their further departure from the original concept of welfare measurement. The new system also includes an important element of double counting: if parts of illegal transactions are accounted as income, expenses afforded to combat them — from police to burglary devices — should be considered as expenses for the production of income and subtracted from the income produced by illegal activities. This is not incorporated in ESA 2010. The same should happen with durable military assets, when used: if a missile is launched or a bomb is dropped to destroy a building, the value of the reconstruction work of that building should be subtracted from the value of the used durable military asset, although these actions usually take place in different countries. There apparently is a case of trade-off here between a better registration of individual activities and the heuristic value of national accounts.

11.4 A New Shock

In a critical moment of the Eurozone crisis, when it appeared that Europeans were finding better answers to their problems and a more pragmatic approach to the common rules, an external event opened up a new source of economic and political tensions and difficulties. This event, the international political conflict with Russia, created new sources of uncertainty and opened new fronts of risk, both economic and political. The crisis started in November 2013, went through a referendum and the annexation of Crimea by Russia in March 2014, and continued with civil war and an uneasy international settlement (Brunat 2016; Dallago and Rosefielde 2016). The crisis had an important economic component, caused by the disruption of the Ukrainian economy, the West imposing economic sanctions upon Russia and the latter economic retaliation, and tensions over gas supplies to the EU. The actual and potential consequences of the Ukrainian instability and the related political and economic conflict between the West and Russia appear as a new negative external shock.

The crisis over Ukraine has economic consequences that may turn out to be sizeable, although lately (as of spring 2015), they appear to be possibly declining. There are five such consequences, which are or may be mutually reinforcing: (a) consequences over trade; (b) instability and crisis of the Russian economy and the cost of economic support to Ukraine; (c) financial consequences; (d) spread of a general climate of political and economic uncertainty, that would negatively impact upon business and investment; and (e) potential effect over military expenditures, that could further strain public budgets. To these direct costs, other indirect costs should be added. In particular, the costs and problems of intra-European political instability relative to economic and political relations with Russia should be taken into consideration. European countries have different attitudes in this regard and a conflict of interests among EU member countries over foreign policy may arise.

Consequences over trade include: (a) the intra-European effect of the partial embargo over EU exports to Russia; (b) the intra-European effect of the counter-restrictions by Russia over imports from the EU; and (c) the potential voluntary restriction by Russia over strategic exports to the EU, primarily of energy sources.

Although the Russian economy is smaller than the French economy in terms of size, Russia is an important economic partner of the EU. It is particularly so for a number of EU member countries (the Baltic states, Finland, Poland, Slovenia, Slovakia, Bulgaria and the Czech Republic, in particular, but also Germany and Austria), and for some industries (textiles, pharmaceuticals, electrical equipment, machinery and transport equipment) and strategic goods (energy in particular), both on the import and the export side. The most strategic issue for the EU is the impact that the conflict over Ukraine has for the German economy, due to the importance that this economy has for the other EU member countries.

According to a Deutsche Bank report (DBR 2014), nearly one-third (31%) of Russian imports comes from the Eurozone and another 6% comes from the Eastern EU member countries outside of the monetary union (Poland, Czech Republic, Hungary, Bulgaria, Romania) (see also Havlik 2014). Other important exporters to Russia include China (16% of total Russian imports) and CIS countries (13%), of which Ukraine represents 6%. On the other hand, the United States has a rather marginal role as an exporter to Russia (5% of Russian imports), similarly to Japan.

Quite different is the picture when looked at from the perspective of Russian exports (Table 11.3). Due to the much larger size of the Eurozone economy compared to the Russian economy, only 4.7% of Eurozone exports go to Russia. This share is not negligible, but what makes it particularly critical is that, among the major Eurozone economies, Germany is the most exposed country to the trade risk.

Table 11.3. The Share of Russia in the EU-27 Total Exports of Goods.

	Vulnerable		**Resilient**		**Other-Euro**		**Non-Euro**	
	Cyprus	0.7	Austria	2.5	Estonia	10.7	Bulgaria	2.7
	Greece	1.7	Belgium	1.6	Latvia	11.5	Czech Republic	3.1
	Ireland	0.7	Finland	9.9	Lithuania	18.9	Denmark	1.9
	Italy	2.6	France	2.1	Malta	0.7	Hungary	3.0
	Portugal	0.7	Germany	3.1	Slovakia	4.2	Poland	5.5
	Spain	1.3	Luxembourg	1.1	Slovenia	3.5	Romania	2.3
			The Netherlands	1.3			Sweden	2.0
							UK	1.8
Average		**1.3**		**3.1**		**8.3**		**2.4**
EU27		**3.7**						

Source: DBR (2014) (original from National Customs, UNCTAD, Deutsche Bank).

Some 3.1% of total German exports go to Russia[239] and 1.5% of German GDP depends upon economic relations with Russia. Corresponding shares are lower in the other large Eurozone economies: 2.6% of exports for Italy, 2.1% for France, and 1.3% for Spain. The effect on GDP is also smaller, in view of the lower degree of openness of these economies compared to the German economy. Yet Russia is also a rather important partner for these countries. Even more significant are the exports to Russia by some small and open economies, both within the Eurozone and outside it. Among the former, particularly exposed are Lithuania, Latvia, Estonia and Finland. These countries are also extremely dependent upon Russian energy sources.

To evaluate the risk for the EU economy, it is important to assess which fall of Russian imports — and of Russian GDP — would have significant negative consequences on the Eurozone GDP, and in particular on that of Germany. According to Deutsche Bank (DBR 2014), the elasticity of overall imports to GDP growth in Russia is high (3.1), and even higher (3.5) is the elasticity in the case of Russian imports from Germany. With such high elasticity, a contraction of Russian GDP of 8.6% would be needed to cause a fall of German exports to Russia by 30%. This would directly cause a 0.5% decrease in the German GDP.[240]

Along with the effect of Western trade sanctions against Russia, negative consequences may derive through Russian counter-restrictions over imports from the EU. Even worse would be the consequences of a hypothetic voluntary restraint by Russia over strategic exports to the EU, primarily of energy sources. Russia is an important supplier of energy sources to the EU countries, but the dependence upon Russian sources is highly differentiated. The most heavily dependent are the Eastern member countries, including Finland and, as far as gas is concerned, Austria and Greece (Table 11.4). Germany's import of Russian energy is significant, but is not overwhelming. France, Italy, Spain, and the UK depend less. Overall, there

---

[239] The share of Russia in German exports looks low relative to the Eurozone figure because Eurozone export figures do not comprise intra-Eurozone trade, whereas national exports do.

[240] A 30% drop of German exports to Russia corresponds to 1% drop of total German exports — one third of 3.1% of total German exports that go to Russia (Table 11.3). This causes a drop of 0.5% of German GDP, given trade elasticity of 2.

Table 11.4. Imports of Energy from Russia as a Percentage of Total Imports: 2012.

	Coal	Oil	Gas
Vulnerable Countries			
Greece	4.8	29.4	79.3
Ireland	0.6	N.A	N.A
Italy	11.8	16.3	20.4
Spain	13.4	14.2	N.A
Strong Countries			
Austria	2.8	7.0	61.8
Belgium	21.9	9.1	23.8
Finland	41.5	68.5	100.0
France	12.6	15.1	16.1
Germany	19.3	28.6	34.6
The Netherlands	11.7	29.7	14.5
Non-Eurozone Countries			
Czech Republic	2.0	35.0	66.0
Hungary	1.9	78.6	81.4
Poland	51.3	83.7	82.6
UK	34.8	10.1	N.A
EU27	**19.2**	**24.5**	**29.4**

Note: 1. Natural gas data is from BP statistical review, as UNCTAD data was underestimating gas imports.
2. Natural gas data is for Europe (continent) and not EU27.
Source: DBR (2014) (original data from UNCTAD, BP Statistical Review, Deutsche Bank).

is no clear difference between vulnerable and resilient countries as far as energy dependence is concerned. Thus the conflict with Russia does not contribute to widen the spread between vulnerable and resilient countries.

At the same time, it is worth emphasising that any restriction of Russian exports of energy is a double-edged sword: indeed, exports of energy to the EU amount to 38% of total Russian exports by value. This consideration may open up diverse scenarios with regard to the economic consequences of energy export restrictions (DBR 2014). In a "mild scenario", only the gas supply transiting through Ukraine would be affected. This would have negative consequences only for south-eastern member countries, but not for Germany. It could be in part offset by some reverse flows from western member countries and the import of liquefied gas.

In a "peak scenario", Russia would reduce its supply to the EU across the board, including the gas flowing through the Nord Stream pipeline. Although this scenario would be very costly to Russia, the EU member countries would be placed in a very difficult situation. In this case, Germany would lack approximately 20% of its annual consumption. In this situation, it would be extremely difficult to supply eastern member countries. This event would trigger a deep recession in those countries. The recession, in turn, would spill over to Germany and other western member countries through the trade and production integration of these economies. The negative consequences for the Russian economy would be an additional blow to the EU economy.

Another critically important channel of economic spillover of the Ukrainian crisis is finance. Selective restrictions over Russian financial assets are in place and more important ones could follow, such as freezing Russian assets held in the US and the EU.[241] This move would have negative consequences for Russia and could induce Russia to retaliate by freezing US and EU assets in Russia. Moreover, the creditworthiness of Russian assets could decline. Retaliation by Russia or the deterioration of the creditworthiness of Russian assets could have serious consequences for the European banking sector, much more so than for American and Japanese banking sectors. On an absolute level, French banks are by far the most exposed among EU member countries, followed by Italian and German banks. However and relative to total bank assets, Austria is the worst off, followed by the Netherlands and Sweden, and then France and Italy (Table 11.5). In a period of tensions in capital markets and when the new European banking union is taking its first steps, 0.5% of total bank assets, as in France and Italy, may be considered a significant exposure to systemic

[241] In addition to this risk, a broader ban on trading with Russian financial institutions could be introduced, which could have implications for liquidity and profits and introduce a disruption of the international financial system.

Table 11.5. Banks' Claims over Russia in 2012/2013.

	Claims (US$ billion)	% of Total Bank Assets	Other Potential Claims (US$ billion)	% of Total Bank Assets
Vulnerable Countries				
Italy	28.6	0.5	5.7	0.1
Spain	1.0	0.0	0.2	0.0
Resilient Countries				
France	50.9	0.5	12.5	0.1
Germany	23.7	0.2	3.9	0.0
The Netherlands	17.6	0.6	n.d.	n.d.
Austria*	16.9	1.4	n.d.	n.d.
Non-Eurozone				
Sweden	14.0	0.6	2.0	0.1
UK	19.1	0.2	42.1	0.3
Non-EU				
US	36.7	0.2	92.9	0.6
Japan	16.3	0.1	2.3	0.0

Note: * 2012 data.

Source: DBR (2014) (original data from BIS, Deutsche Bank. The data pertain to Q3 2013 for "ordinary assets" (except for Austria) and to Q3 2012 for "other potential claims").

risk. Since risk is probably concentrated in a small number of banks, the possibility of systemic risk is further aggravated. Exposure of German and Spanish banks is very limited.

Although the exposure of the American banking sector to Russian risk is low, it has to be considered that "other potential claims" in BIS classification are particularly high in the case of US banks and also UK banks. This risk is low or negligible in the case of Eurozone and Japanese banks. These claims include derivative contracts, guarantees and trade credit. However, this contingent liability is of little significance for the banking sector as long as Russia does not default on its securities. In fact, a large part of these other claims comes in the form of guarantees, probably reflecting CDS contracts underwritten by large international banks located in the US and in the UK.[242]

Finally, it is useful to take into consideration that political and economic tensions and uncertainty had negative consequences for Russia through triggering capital outflows and depreciating the ruble. Consequences were declining equity prices and increasing bond yields. The Russian central bank reacted to these events by increasing its policy rate to 7% above the inflation rate. However, since February 2015 the rate decreased and the real rate became negative. Other effects include the slowdown of GDP growth rate and negative growth rate of investment. These events had a negative effect on the EU through the trade channel.

The Ukrainian scenario is unwelcome and dangerous for the Eurozone, even for its resilient member countries. Worse than commercial and financial risks and consequences, is the widespread sense of uncertainty and the distrust that a prolonged conflict would create in Europe. A general climate of political and economic uncertainty would have a negative impact on EU business and investment. This effect would be amplified by conflicting interests among EU member countries relative to economic and political relations with Russia and between the EU and the United States. The situation appears more worrying if Ukraine were to be added to the picture. Fortunately in summer 2015, it appears that the common EU-Russia economic interests are once again gaining momentum.

11.5 Policy Responses to the Crisis

During the early stages of the crisis, a consensus emerged at the international level about the fiscal and monetary policies deemed necessary to solve the Eurozone crisis. The EU, the ECB and the IMF alike agreed on a set of measures, including financial stabilisation, liberalisation, efficiency of the labour market, and sustainability of social security. The background

[242] A Credit Default Swap or CDS is an insurance against non-payment. It is a credit derivative contract, designed to transfer the risk of default of fixed income products from the purchaser of the CDS to the seller. The purchaser of the swap makes payments up until the maturity date of a contract to the seller of the swap. The latter agrees to pay off a third party debt if this party defaults on the loan.

interpretation of the causes and the current situation was along the lines identified by the revised Washington Consensus, as much as the cure also was. In the EU the influence of the ordoliberal view, that public discipline needed priority, was strong in Germany and other resilient countries, both in terms of their domestic position on policies and also with regard to their requests to the EU and vulnerable countries.

The policy measures that were suggested or forced via conditionality had two goals: first, decrease wages and social security in such a way so as to decrease production costs without having to invest and improve competitiveness in this manner. Moreover, make use of dismissals in the public sector so as to further decrease costs and improve productivity. The reduction of the public sector costs was identified as a fundamental adjustment mechanism, both directly and via the spillover effect this had on the behaviour of the private sector. This prescription was pretty much in line with the tenets of mainstream economics and not alien to ordoliberalism. Yet it also addressed an important practical problem of modern economies, burdened with an overgrown and often inefficient public sector. This was certainly the case of most vulnerable economies.

However, this prescription failed to take into consideration the fact that the public sector had a fundamental role in supporting demand and employment, let alone furnishing public services. This demand and employment role could be offset by growing exports only in small and very open economies. Downsizing the public sector, cutting wages, pension rights and employment, and decreasing public investments did not improve the effectiveness of the public sector and could have further disorganised it. Structural reforms as part of stabilisation policies thus failed to realise the most important goal: improve the quality and effectiveness of public services and the efficiency of the public sector. Stabilisation policies jeopardised institutional reforms.[243]

---

[243] In a challenging comparative analysis of pension reforms in Central and Eastern Europe, Müller (1999) shows that the outcomes in terms of reform and fiscal effect sustainability are quite different, depending on the particular ministry managing the reform. Outcomes were clearly less sustainable and effective when the responsible was the finance ministry which pursued fiscal goals.

The problem of inefficient markets and firms was addressed in the second type of policy measures. Liberalisation and privatisation, in particular that of public services and also of non-competitive markets, and labour market reforms were considered as fundamental for enhancing growth potential. Labour market structural reforms involved greater wage flexibility and the introduction or consolidation of firm-level bargaining systems.[244] This bargaining system is considered to better take into account the highly differentiated production and working conditions that may exist in different sectors, organisations and regions. Being more flexible and closer to local circumstances, firm-level bargaining was considered better in line with economic efficiency, capable of easing the hiring and dismissal of employees and cutting the labour tax wedge.

Another important piece of the approach is the reform of the pension system, usually in the form of postponing retirement age, reducing pension rights and linking pensions to social contributions and life expectancy in a better way. Although labour market reforms improved the fiscal sustainability of public sectors, they contributed to the weakening of trade unions and to the increase of inequalities (Jaumotte and Osorio Buitron 2015). In the depressed situation caused by the crisis, these reforms became important causes of decreasing consumption and therefore of recession.

These reforms became important components of austerity and particularly internal devaluation policies. They were endorsed by the ECB long before the onset of the crisis and were explicitly stated and advanced on several occasions. They constituted the backbones of the structural conditionality imposed by the "Troika" (EU, ECB and IMF) to Greece, Portugal and Ireland in exchange for the bailout packages. These reforms

---

[244] There is considerable heterogeneity in the levels at which bargaining takes place in the EU. In most Eurozone countries, the sectoral level of wage bargaining is dominant, with company-level agreements common as the second (or third) stage of bargaining. In Finland, Ireland and Slovenia, the national level of wage bargaining is dominant, although decentralised negotiations also take place as a second step. In France and Luxembourg, similarly to the UK and US, the company level is dominant and wage bargaining systems are highly decentralised (Du Caju *et al.* 2008). See also Soskice and Iversen (2001).

were also the core of the letter that the ECB sent to the Italian government on 5 August 2011, when Italian finances were under international speculative attacks.

The austerity policies that common fiscal rules imposed and reform programmes that European authorities and the IMF requested in exchange for support created a difficult economic and financial situation. Consequences were particularly negative for vulnerable countries, i.e. the countries that most needed reform and support. This situation created an uneasy game between national goals and opportunism on one side and common distrust and fragility to the risk of national default on the other side. The outcome was loss of time and excessive economic and social costs, with possible long-term damage. An important cost of the crisis management was the disregard for real economies, in particular their structural and institutional problems and technical progress. The slow progress of common governance and institutions, which in spite of difficulties went on mostly through pragmatic accommodation to emergency situations, was a meagre reward so far.

Institutional rigidity and the waning inter-government trust created a strange mix of apparently irrational situations: vulnerable countries were requested to cut public expenditures and wages, while resilient countries were requested to keep their public and private economy under strict control. Under normal circumstances, policies to combat the crisis would consist in expansionary monetary policies to increase liquidity and growing public deficits to support demand. This was done, with success, in the United States and also in Great Britain and other European countries outside the Eurozone. Alternatively, in a monetary union, surplus and resilient countries should run deficits in order to support adjustment in vulnerable countries through external demand. This is what the US administration asked the Eurozone since 2012. Also the IMF came to share this position, although somewhat later, in 2013.

Under the influence of incomplete institutions and the lack of intergovernmental trust, the Eurozone goal was to stabilise the economy by means of balanced budgets and wage moderation in the resilient countries and austerity cum internal devaluation in vulnerable countries. Under those conditions, the only hope was that external demand through exports supported Eurozone economies. This happened, but was quantitatively insufficient. It was also partial, since it advantaged more competitive resilient economies than less competitive vulnerable economies. It was thus insufficient to create sufficient demand and full capacity utilisation in vulnerable countries (Figure 11.2).

From 1990 and up to the end of 2007, the difference in capacity utilisation in manufacturing was rather stable at around 6% to the advantage of resilient countries, but the situation has changed dramatically with the crisis. In 2008 and 2009 the difference decreased to around 2%, since capacity utilisation in resilient countries decreased by 16%, while in vulnerable countries the fall was 13%, although in Italy, Greece and especially Cyprus the fall was well above the average.

However, resilient countries recovered much of the loss by mid-2011, although the utilisation fell again by 7% by the end of 2012 and remained approximately at that level afterwards. In vulnerable countries, the recovery during 2010 was less pronounced and the second dip started sooner, in the second quarter of 2011, followed by another dip. These data were

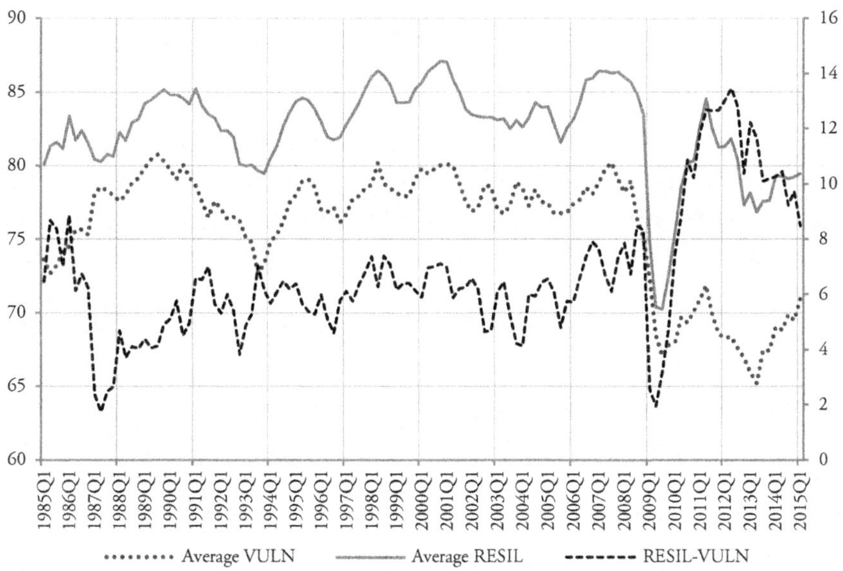

Figure 11.2. Current Level of Capacity Utilisation in Manufacturing Industry, in Percent, Seasonally Adjusted Data (Difference on the Right Scale).

Source: Author's own figure based on data from Eurostat database.

under the effects of the dramatic fall in Cyprus and Greece. On average, the degree of utilisation in the years after the crisis was some 10% below the pre-crisis average. As a consequence, the difference between the two groups of countries increased dramatically and reached 13.5% in the second quarter of 2012. Afterwards the difference decreased, but in early 2015 it is still at 8.5%. Clearly, this is further evidence of how dramatically necessary is a more flexible approach in the incomplete monetary and economic union, an approach that is tailored to the particular situation of individual countries.

Eurozone policies were called to limit the risk of contagion and re-establish the conditions for a proficient monetary integration of member countries. They were also called, as a precondition, to fix the potentially destabilising imbalances typical of vulnerable countries. Yet the rigidity of common fiscal rules and the initial passivity of the ECB had one potentially dangerous outcome: they increased the segmentation of the Eurozone. Irrespective of the original cause of their problems — be it public finances as in Greece and Italy, or private finances and bubbles such as in Cyprus, Ireland, Portugal and Spain — vulnerable countries were pushed further in a debt-recession vicious cycle until they were on the brink of deflation. At the same time, resilient countries had gains from this situation (Dany *et al.* 2015) but also higher risks, since they risked being destabilised through the unsustainable situation of vulnerable countries. The latter, under the cloud of rigid rules and very restrictive policies, were unable to afford the much needed modernisation of their economies and risked taking a step back in the international specialisation of their economies.

The problem in a monetary union in recession and in liquidity trap with interest rates at the zero bound is that only fiscal policies are effective in fixing localised problems. Indeed, this was the consideration that led the EU to leave fiscal policies in the hands of national governments. Unfortunately, the crisis made more stringent the need to place those policies under common control, which in the case of vulnerable countries means that fiscal policies are largely impracticable for fixing the problems. The EU is aware of this problem and strongly suggests that countries should run budget surpluses in years of expansion, so as to be able to run deficits in years of crisis. The suggestion is appealing, in particular for vulnerable countries, but fails to grasp the critical issue that it refers only to a future of growing economies, but is of no help in the present.

During the crisis, it would have been advantageous for vulnerable countries to follow an expansionary fiscal policy. However, this was difficult since these countries had high deficits and some of them also had high debts. A possible solution was to expand fiscal policies in resilient, balanced countries. In fact, these countries had debts in line with or below the level envisioned in the SGP. Such a solution required asymmetric business cycles within the Eurozone. Asymmetric business cycles in an incomplete monetary union are problematic, because they jeopardise the possibility of running monetary policies. In fact, under these conditions any active monetary policy would advantage some member countries and disadvantage others. These effects cannot be managed, since the monetary union lacks a common government of the economy.

Monetary authorities have to choose between passive monetary policies that advantage resilient countries, and active policies that help vulnerable countries. There are two problems with passive monetary policies. First, such policies tend to follow the median of the Eurozone, which falls within the domain of the economically larger and more powerful countries. Clearly, Germany has a natural disproportional influence in this. Passive monetary policies are easy to follow in an incomplete monetary union, since they are in line with the strict rules of the union and the limited mandate of the ECB. They are also supported by international markets, which see balanced and economically powerful countries as a guarantee for the soundness and reputation of the common currency. This belief was held until the evidence proved that it was misplaced. Second, the crisis introduced partially asymmetric business cycles between resilient and vulnerable countries. If passive monetary policies are under the disproportionately influenced by resilient countries, they further disadvantage vulnerable countries by keeping a strong exchange rate and high real interest rates.

Active monetary policies, in particular if they are tuned to the needs of vulnerable countries, could also run into difficulties. They are rational in an incomplete monetary union, at least in the long run, since they have effects similar to creating a pool of resources for supporting the revival of vulnerable countries. Yet the very essence of an incomplete monetary union, the lack of a common government with its enforcement power, is at odds with this solution. Resilient countries may assume correctly that the proposed solution would reward moral hazard and fail to discipline vulnerable countries. In the Eurozone, this point is supported by the behaviour of various countries, including both vulnerable and resilient ones, since the establishment of the convergence criteria. Curbing moral hazard is fundamental in an incomplete monetary union and resilient countries see this as a precondition to rebuild trust within the Eurozone. But this very reasonable aim is at odds with the goal of bailing vulnerable countries out in a permanent way. Clearly, only a political compromise may result in a reasonable solution.

Another Eurozone puzzle is that rigidity extended to monetary policies. The Eurozone was confronted with a double problem, based on the conflicting interests of resilient and vulnerable countries. Externally, the Eurozone is part of a monetary system based on floating exchange rates and high mobility of capital. Under these conditions, the traditional trilemma predicts that the Eurozone can have an independent monetary policy oriented toward domestic goals. The Eurozone as such had much to gain from an active expansionary monetary policy and the depreciation of its currency, as the United States did to combat the crisis. This policy in a monetary union could have different effects in different countries and would advantage vulnerable countries.[245]

In terms of the new trilemma, an active monetary policy would correspond to a partial softening of the strict no-monetary financing rule. However, such policy would allow the monetary union to keep the lack of joint responsibility over public debts as a device against moral hazard.

---

[245] Comunale (2015) provides an empirical study of the asymmetrical spillovers of the euro-US dollar exchange rate on the inflation in the euro zone. She divides the sample in two groups of countries: core and periphery, which correspond to the division between vulnerable and resilient countries used in this book. The paper tests the intra-euro area differences in exchange rate pass-through (ERPT), to assess whether the euro-US dollar exchange rate has a different impact on the country groups' performance. The findings show that the euro-US dollar is an important factor, although not the only key factor, in determining the asymmetry in HICP inflation between core and periphery.

However, the depreciation of the euro conflicted with the resilient countries' rigid fears of inflation and moral hazard. It also clashed with US policies and was in any case made even more difficult by the resilient countries' current account surplus. At the same time, resilient countries, with inelastic exports, stood to gain from a strong euro, while vulnerable countries with elastic exports were suffering.

The Eurozone was clearly in trouble and the euro in danger. In order to consolidate the common currency the financial situation had to be stabilised. However, incomplete and rigid policies worsened the economic situation in vulnerable countries to such a point that the financial situation deteriorated further, with high deficits and growing debts. The Eurozone was apparently caught in a trap, locked in a non-cooperative game for managing what after all remains a common pool of resources. Only the ECB, the only common institution with effective autonomy, could try to rescue the Eurozone and its member countries. Yet also this attempt met with difficulties and went through a long process of trial and some errors, as the next sections seek to explain.

11.6 The ECB: The View, Monetary Policy Instruments and Transmission Mechanism

According to Article 127 of the Treaty on the Functioning of the European Union (TFEU), in pursuing its objectives the Eurosystem "shall act in accordance with the principle of an open market economy with free competition, favouring an efficient allocation of resources". This article provides the basis of the operative framework of the Eurosystem. The Eurosystem is the monetary authority of the Eurozone, which includes the ECB and the national central banks (NCBs) of the Eurozone. The latter's function is to implement the monetary policy decisions taken by the ECB.[246]

[246] The Eurosystem is distinct from the European System of Central Banks (ESCB). The latter includes the ECB and the central banks of all EU member countries, comprising those not included in the Eurozone. The ESCB's primary objective is price stability throughout the EU. The ESCB has the further goal of improving monetary and financial cooperation between the Eurosystem and the member countries outside the Eurozone.

The ECB is the monopoly supplier of the monetary base in the Eurozone and as such it sets the conditions at which banks can borrow from the central bank and influences the conditions at which banks trade with each other in the money market. According to the ECB view,[247] in the short-run monetary policy decisions activate the monetary policy transmission mechanism. This defines the effects of policies upon economic variables, in the first place on prices and output. However, the ECB considers that in the long-run money is neutral. As a consequence, a change in the quantity of money in the economy can only influence the general level of prices, but not output or employment. Real variables are, in the long term, essentially determined by real factors.

In this view, inflation is ultimately a monetary phenomenon. A change in monetary policy can offset over time the short-run effect that other factors, such as variations in aggregate demand or technical change, have on prices. Therefore, in the long run a central bank should maintain stable prices in order to contribute to the growth potential of the economy. Indeed, maintaining price stability and safeguarding the value of the euro is the primary objective of the Eurosystem and the ECB. The objective of the stability of the general level of prices implies avoiding both prolonged inflation and deflation. Both are considered to be harmful to the economy and society and seen as preventing the achievement of high levels of economic activity and employment. Both events are actually the gates through which the ECB needs occasionally to deal actively with the real economy.

In its monetarist stance, the ECB monetary policy strategy relies on the consideration that monetary growth and inflation are closely related in the medium to long run. Given the uncertainty about the nature of economic shocks, the reliability of economic indicators, and the efficacy of the transmission mechanism, the monetary policy according to the ECB should be broadly based and take into account all relevant information influencing the economy. The fundamental policy aggregate is M3[248] over

---

[247] Whenever not specified, the sources of information are the publications and the website of the ECB. See also ECB (2011), Papademos and Stark (2010).

[248] The ECB defines M1 as currency in circulation plus overnight deposits. M2 comprises M1 plus deposits with an agreed maturity of up to and including two years and deposits redeemable at notice of up to and including three months. M3 comprises M2 plus

the medium- to long-term perspective. This choice is based on the conviction that, over sufficiently extended time horizons, the rate of money growth must be consistent with the price stability objective. It also derives from the consideration that there is no direct link between short-term monetary developments and monetary policy decisions.

In order to keep price stability, the ECB works out a coherent and structured monetary policy strategy, to pursue internal and external tasks. The aim of the former is to give the ECB's Governing Council the information and the analysis necessary to make decisions. The aim of the latter is to explain monetary policy decisions to the public and market actors. Both tasks serve, from the ECB's perspective, to support the effectiveness of monetary policy and enhance the credibility of the ECB in the financial markets.

The ECB uses a "two-pillar approach" to assess the nature and the extent of risks to price stability and define the intervention needed to correct them. The first pillar, economic analysis, is meant to assess the short- to medium-term determinants of price developments. These are considered to be influenced largely by the interplay of supply and demand in the goods, services and factor markets. Monetary analysis is the second pillar: considering the long-run link between money and prices, monetary analysis focuses on a longer-term horizon, primarily in order to cross-check the short- to medium-term indications coming from the economic analysis.

The ECB uses three sets of monetary policy instruments: open market operations, standing facilities, and reserve requirements (Acocella 2005). Open market operations are the most important instrument for monetary policy and can be conducted using reverse transactions, outright operations or the issuance of ECB debt certificates. Their role is to direct interest rates, manage the liquidity situation in the money market, and signal the monetary policy stance. These operations are of four kinds: (a) main refinancing operations (MRO), regular liquidity-providing reverse transactions with weekly frequency and one-week maturity; (b) longer-term refinancing operations (LTRO), liquidity-providing reverse transactions having a monthly frequency and three-month maturity; (c) fine-tuning

---

repurchase agreements, money market fund shares and units as well as debt securities with a maturity of up to two years.

operations, executed on an ad hoc basis in order to manage the liquidity situation in the money market and interest rates, particularly in the case of unexpected market liquidity fluctuations; and (d) structural operations, executed whenever the ECB wishes to adjust the structural liquidity position of the Eurosystem vis-à-vis the financial sector.

Standing facilities serve to provide and absorb overnight liquidity and influence interest rates. There are two types of standing facilities: (a) marginal lending facility, allowing financial institutions to obtain overnight liquidity from the NCBs against eligible assets at rates usually higher than market rates, and (b) deposit facility, used by financial institutions to make overnight deposits with the NCBs at rates generally lower than market rates. The third monetary policy instrument is minimum reserves, which financial institutions must keep on accounts with the NCBs. Reserve requirements include the definition of the reserve base, the reserve ratio,[249] and the remuneration.

A successful policy depends upon the transmission mechanism that links the ECB monetary policies with their effects on output and prices. Along with the influence of structural variables and institutional features, this effect depends upon the willingness of banks to contribute to the effective working of interbank markets. The reputation and credibility of the central bank are fundamental components of effective policies. To this end, the ECB aims at being forward-looking and specifying the goals, being consistent and systematic, and communicating clearly and openly in order to firmly anchor inflation expectations. According to the ECB, monetary policy should also escape excessive activism and have a medium-term orientation, in order to avoid contributing to the volatility of the real economy.

The ECB reads the working of the transmission mechanism in the following way. The central bank defines the official interest rate at which it provides funds to the banking system. Through this, it affects directly

---

[249] The reserve base includes deposits, debt securities, and money market paper. The reserve ratio was decreased from 2% to 1% starting from 18 January 2012 (ECB 2015c). Reserve holdings are remunerated at the Eurosystem's rate on its main refinancing operations.

money-market interest rates and, indirectly, lending and deposit rates that banks set for their customers. Changes in the official interest rates also affect the supply of credit, since it affects the probability that borrowers pay back their loans. Banks adapt accordingly the amount of credit lent to households and firms. Market interest rates influence expectations of future changes of the official interest rate, which in turn affect medium- and long-term interest rates and price developments. By influencing financing conditions and market expectations, monetary policy actions may trigger adjustments in asset prices, the exchange rate and, through the latter, the price of imported goods and hence inflation.

A change in interest rates and credit conditions also affects the behaviour of households and firms in their saving and investment decisions. This effect may be strengthened through the influence that movements in asset prices may have on consumption and investment, via wealth effects and effects on the value of collateral. A change in consumption and investment affects the level of domestic demand for goods and services relative to domestic supply, with consequences for the price level and the conditions in labour and intermediate product markets. Finally, a change in official interest rates affects the marginal cost that banks have to afford for obtaining external finance, depending on the level of the banks' capitalisation. This effect is important, particularly during a financial crisis, due to the uneven working of money markets.

The working of the transmission mechanism is particularly complex and its working arduous, due to the composite nature of the Eurozone and the incompleteness of its institutions. In particular, different structures of European economies and national institutions and idiosyncrasies segment the Eurozone economy and markets and make economic actors behave and react differently under the same circumstances.[250] As a consequence, economic actors in different countries afford different

[250] The ECB defines this situation as "financial fragmentation". Cœuré (2013) defines financial fragmentation as "... a type of financial disruption characterised by fault lines shaped by national borders, with ramifications within national borders, capital repatriation and sharp increases in the home bias in all market segments. Financial fragmentation results in renationalisation of savings, which in turn prevents euro area households and companies from reaping the full benefits of the single market for goods and services."

conditions and different consequences of the same increase of official interest rates.[251] The restricted mandate of the ECB and the limits this fact imposes upon its policy instruments circumscribe the ECB's policy action, and could potentially delay intervention and limit its capacity. The lack of unified fiscal policies and the SGP constraints may lead national governments to adopt fiscal policies that in fact counteract monetary policies. For instance, national austerity policies may render moderately soft common monetary policies ineffective. Thus, an active transmission mechanism of the monetary policy may be particularly difficult to obtain in the Eurozone.

11.7 Ineffective Monetary Policies: From Standard Measures to Extraordinary Measures

From a strictly monetary point of view, the ECB action was successful. The primary objective of the Eurosystem, i.e. price stability, was fulfilled. Since the adoption of the euro in 1999, the average inflation rate in the Eurozone was close to, but not higher than 2%, i.e. within the mandate of the ECB (Figure 11.3).

However, a successful implementation of the ECB mandate does not necessarily imply that the Eurozone economy was successful. Since the beginning of the crisis, it became evident that monetary policy was ineffective and fiscal policies were causing a prolonged recession. Later on the danger of deflation became evident, particularly in vulnerable countries. The real economy was not taking advantage of price stability. Consequences were at odds with the secondary goal of the Eurosystem, i.e. financial stability and financial integration. A prolonged recession in the Eurozone was jeopardising financial stability, splitting financial integration and, in the end, jeopardising price stability as defined in the ECB mandate. Indeed and particularly in 2009 and since 2012, prices decreased to levels compatible with the danger of deflation.

The Eurozone encountered an unusual problem, deriving from its institutional incompleteness. Lacking a common government of the economy, with the fiscal situation of the Eurozone split between resilient

[251] For example, ECB (2013b) estimates that the average cost of borrowing for non-financial corporations in Germany in the first quarter of 2013 was slightly more than 2.5% per year, while it was about 4% in Italy.

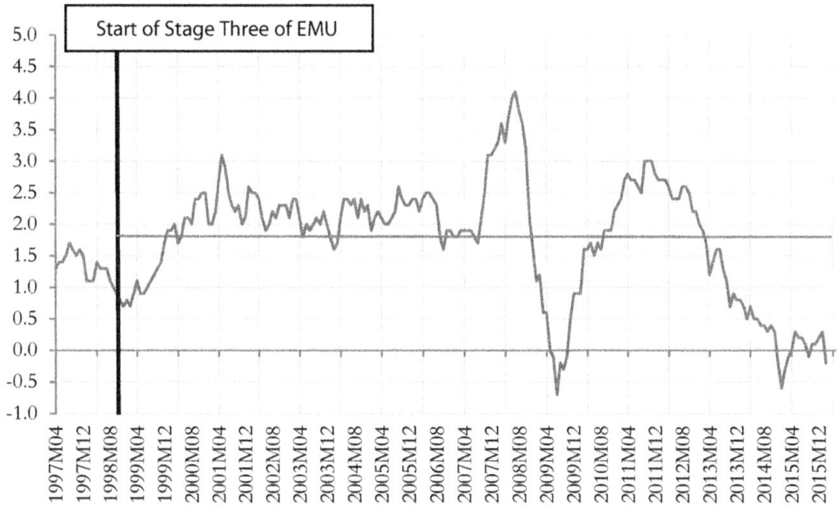

Figure 11.3. Overall Inflation in the Euro Area (HICP, Variable Composition) (Percentage Change).
Source: Eurostat database.

and vulnerable countries and with the Eurozone being based on the refusal of cross-financing among countries, fiscal policies were powerless. At the same time, the ECB mandate placed the emphasis on price stability and did not include a more active role in supporting the economy, as in the case of the US Federal Reserve. Since this situation jeopardised the working of the transmission mechanism of the monetary policy, the ECB started unconventional operations in as early as 2011, when financial distress in vulnerable countries reached a level dangerous for the very sustainability of the common currency.

These operations were started in an attempt to cope with the unusual problems that the crisis caused to an incomplete monetary union (Merler 2013; Sapir *et al.* 2014). The ECB implemented numerous policy measures to activate the transmission mechanism and enhance the banking system's access to liquidity. The most important among these measures were the progressive decrease of the ECB interest rate to historical minima;[252] liquidity allocated with a full allotment procedure whereby demand determines supply; collateral requirements eased in several waves; reserve

[252] At 0.05% since 10 September 2014 on fixed rate tenders in main refinancing operations.

requirement ratio eased to 1% since 18 January 2012; and finally a series of unconventional measures, starting with extraordinarily long-term refinancing operations with maturity of three years, that were initiated in late 2011 and early 2012.

Initially, the ECB adopted a standard and prudent approach to monetary policies. In summer 2007, due to the sub-prime crisis in the United States, financial market volatility increased considerably and investors started to sell risky equities. In August 2007, it became evident that various European banks were directly and indirectly exposed to the US sub-prime mortgage risk. They were also exposed to potential severe losses for their exposure to mortgage-backed securities. This led to the collapse of the interbank borrowing and lending market and to the jeopardising of the functioning of the euro money market. The ECB started to use its standard instruments and financed interbank money markets with overnight liquidity through fine-tuning operations, thus providing extra liquidity.

The international contagion caused dollar liquidity shortages worldwide at the end of 2007. A swap agreement with the US Federal Reserve System in December of that year allowed the ECB to provide dollars to euro area banks. In the summer and fall of the following year, the US crisis had a dramatic acceleration, with the collapse of Lehman Brothers and the start of the global financial crisis. The latter led to the collapse of activities in many financial markets, to the abrupt increase of short-term interest rates and to widespread uncertainty. Banks reacted by building up large liquidity reserves and tightening loan conditions. This spread the crisis to the real economy. Economic conditions deteriorated in most Western economies and international trade fell dramatically.

The ECB acted with substantial cuts of interest rates and extraordinary liquidity measures in October 2008. These measures were addressed to provide euro area banks with unlimited liquidity at an unusually low main refinancing rate. Banks had to offer adequate collateral, whose composition was widened. The main measure was weekly refinancing operations with a fixed-rate tender procedure and full allotment. The maturities of loans to banks were also lengthened.

Since international and Eurozone tensions did not decrease, the ECB announced a purchase programme for covered bonds in June 2009. This operation consisted in the outright purchase of assets that were important for the refinancing of banks, since they were eligible as collateral. These operations helped stabilise private financial markets, albeit at a low level of activity. However, sovereign debt, particularly that of vulnerable countries, was under severe pressure. Various Eurozone countries were faced with increasing difficulties and costs for refinancing their debt. Negative consequences were serious also for financial institutions, since these had governments bonds in their portfolio. While the former problem was no concern for the ECB, the latter was. In fact, the effectiveness of the transmission mechanism of monetary policy was impaired. Moreover, the government bond market was crucial for the economy in different ways: e.g. interest rates on government bonds had a direct influence on the interest rates of corporate bonds.

In order to help counteracting these unfavourable developments, in May 2010 the ECB introduced the Securities Markets Programme (SMP), on a temporary basis and with limited interventions.[253] The ECB and the Eurozone NCBs could purchase, in accordance with the Treaty on the Functioning of the European Union (TFEU), debt securities, mostly government bonds, only in the secondary market at market prices. The ECB proceeded to fully sterilise the amount purchased. The ECB absorbed the total amount of purchased bonds not yet matured from the market, in order to leave overall liquidity conditions unaffected. The programme was successful in preventing panic and the default of vulnerable countries, but could not give definite stability to public finances and even less contribute to economic revival. Afterwards, Eurozone member countries established a European Financial Stability Facility (EFSF) as a temporary crisis resolution mechanism in June 2010 (see Section 11.9).

11.8 Unconventional Monetary Policy Instruments and Programmes

Problems met with standard policies led the ECB to consider non-standard monetary policies. The decision was not without controversy,

[253] Eser and Schwaab (2015) assess the yield impact of asset purchases within the European Central Bank's Securities Markets Programme in five euro area sovereign bond markets from 2010–11. The authors find that, in addition to large announcement effects, there was an impact of approximately −3 basis points at the five-year maturity for purchases of 1/1000 of the outstanding debt. Purchases improved liquidity conditions and reduced default-risk premia, while the signalling of future low interest rates did not play a role.

particularly within the Governing Council. The main conflict was between the Executive Board of the ECB plus the majority of the representatives of NCBs and the representatives of NCBs of resilient countries, in particular the representative of the Deutsche Bundesbank.[254]

The recourse to non-standard, unconventional monetary policies finds its legal basis in their compatibility with the TFEU, although the latter does not specifically mention these policies. In this interpretation and in times of extraordinary financial market tensions, the ECB considers that the Eurosystem can make use, on an exceptional and temporary basis, of any instrument that is compatible with the Treaty and that is needed for achieving its objective to make the monetary policy transmission mechanism work. Since companies in the Eurozone rely much on bank financing, these measures are usually aimed at the banking sector.

Unconventional (or non-standard) monetary policies make use of various instruments. These include:

(a) Full-allotment liquidity provision through competitive tenders at fixed or variable interest rates. In normal circumstances and in the framework of open market operations, the Eurosystem assesses and allots the total liquidity that the banking sector needs through competitive tenders and at variable rate. In exceptional circumstances, the ECB may decide in advance to allot the full amount of liquidity that banks request, at a fixed interest rate. Exceptional circumstances include the financial crisis and the sovereign debt crisis;
(b) Expansion of the list of assets eligible as collateral. In order to improve the banks access to liquidity-providing operations, the Eurosystem can decide to modify the minimum requirements for collateral that banks have to provide when borrowing money from the Eurosystem;
(c) Targeted longer-term refinancing operation (TLTRO), that the ECB announced in June 2014. The Eurosystem can increase the frequency and the maturity of longer-term liquidity provision, above the standard one per month frequency and with a maturity of three months. These operations are aimed at improving bank lending to the euro area non-financial private sector over a window of two years;

---

[254] See Chapter 3, footnote 48.

(d) Liquidity provision in foreign currencies. In cooperation with other central banks, the Eurosystem can provide liquidity in foreign currencies, if banks access to such liquidity is insufficient;
(e) Outright purchase of specific debt securities. Several programmes of this kind have been implemented since 2009.[255] When the transmission mechanism does not function properly, the Eurosystem can purchase assets outright instead of merely accepting them as collateral, including public and private debt securities. The objective of these purchases is to sustain growth across the Eurozone compatible with price stability.

Although the option of making use of outright purchases has existed since 1999, the ECB started to employ them selectively only since June 2009, when the ECB started its first covered bond purchase programme. This programme can therefore be considered a transitory stage to a broader and more consistent use of unconventional policy instruments to fight the effects of the crisis. A broader and more consistent step in the use of unconventional policy instruments took place in May 2010, when the ECB decided to start the SMP. In both cases, the move played an important role

---

[255] Asset purchase programmes (APPs) include two private sector asset purchase programmes, used in case of risks of protracted period of low inflation, and the public sector purchase programme (PSPP). Programmes for the private sector include the third covered bond purchase programme (CBPP3) and the asset-backed securities purchase programme (ABSPP). Monthly purchases in public and private sector securities under these programmes will amount to €60 billion until the end of September 2016. Under CBPP3, the Eurosystem started to buy covered bonds on 20 October 2014 and will continue to do so for at least two years. ABSPP was started on 21 November 2014 and will last for at least two years. Its objective is to help banks to diversify funding sources and stimulate the issuance of new securities in order to help banks to provide credit to the real economy. CBPP3 and ABSPP are expected to have significant impact on the ECB's balance sheet. Under PSPP, initiated on 9 March 2015, the Eurosystem started to buy nominal and inflation-linked central government bonds and bonds issued by recognised agencies, international organisations and multilateral development banks located in the Eurozone. Purchased securities are made available for securities lending to support market liquidity and collateral availability in the market. Other programmes were terminated. These include the securities markets programme (SMP), covered bond purchase programme (CBPP1) and a second covered bond purchase programme (CBPP2).

in stopping the threat of disruption of financial markets, but was insufficient to invert the situation, and re-activating the transmission mechanism.

Although financial market organisations were not under the threat of distress and bankruptcy any more, thanks to unconventional measures, one important problem remained unresolved: these organisations did not provide credit to the economy or did so at excessively high interest rates, including a high risk premium. The ECB then moved to implement measures intended to support bank lending and money market activity. The Governing Council decided to implement two longer-term refinancing operations, on 21 December 2011 and on 29 February 2012, with a maturity of 36 months and at a fixed interest rate. It also decided to increase the availability of collateral by reducing the rating threshold for certain asset-backed securities and by allowing NCBs to accept as collateral additional credit claims, as a temporary solution and under their responsibility.

The two longer-term refinancing operations were successful in stabilising the situation of financial organisations. Yet the problem of sovereign debt of vulnerable countries remained open and worsened under the pressure of growing debts and falling GDP. Since economies were in recession or depression, the revenue of the public budgets was decreasing and economic and social expenditures were increasing. Since the GDP was decreasing, the ratio of debt to GDP was increasing.

One particular problem came from the successful outcome of unconventional operations by the ECB. National authorities and the ECB itself made it clear, albeit informally, that they expected that the cheap money that banks obtained through unconventional operations would be used in part to buy public bonds of the country of residence of the banks. This was not difficult for banks, since there were few good options to lend to private organisations. Moreover, interest rates on public bonds of vulnerable countries — that had an implicit political and economic European support — were more than appealing. The outcome was bank-sovereign interdependence, with large stocks of undiversified national public debt securities held by national banks.[256] Negative shocks to sovereign solvency

[256] Domestic banks held about one-fourth of the bonds issued by the state in Germany, Italy, Spain and Portugal in 2007. The proportion was less, but still significant, in France, the Netherlands and Greece. Only in Ireland were banks negligible holders of government

could interact with adverse shocks to bank solvency, thus increasing the exposure of vulnerable countries.

To ease the situation, the ECB initiated Outright Monetary Transactions (OMT), whereby the ECB purchases bonds issued by Eurozone member-states in secondary, sovereign bond markets. The Governing Council of the ECB announced the programme on 2 August 2012; the technical framework was formulated on 6 September 2012. In parallel, the SMP was terminated, having lost its significance after the new programme. OMT is activated when a Eurozone government asks for financial assistance and is aimed at safeguarding an appropriate monetary policy transmission and the singleness of the monetary policy. In particular, the programme aims at lowering borrowing costs by decreasing long-term bond yields. The programme requires policy conditionality to bond issuing countries, which have to engage in taking pre-agreed domestic economic measures. OMT does not inject directly liquidity in the economy, an important difference compared to Quantitative Easing (QE) operations. In fact, the former works through full sterilisation.

Along with important new forms of financial assistance to countries in difficulty, the ECB also proceeded to implement important institutional changes. One important step towards a more complete institutional architecture of the European monetary union was the beginning of the European banking union. Along with completing the economic and monetary union, the banking union is meant to apply common rules for banks in the Eurozone.[257] Started in June 2012, the banking union includes a SSM and a SRM.

---

securities. Public debt held by domestic banks increased after 2007, as banks replaced non-residents as holders of public debt in vulnerable countries, notably in Greece, Portugal and Ireland, and to a lesser extent in Spain and Italy. European institutions worked out a new set of rules for solving banks distress and bailout and pursued their restructuring, while avoiding that the cost was entirely paid by taxpayers.

[257] Common rules are meant to prevent bank crises (Capital Requirements Directive and Regulation MEMO/13/690) and define a common framework to bail out or wind down banks in distress (Directive on Bank Recovery and Resolution (BRRD) MEMO/14/297). Moreover, common rules are defined to ensure the full protection of deposits up to €100,000 (per depositor/per bank) in the entire EU (Directive on Deposit Guarantee Scheme–DGS MEMO/14/296).

According to the SSM and since November 2014, the ECB is the central prudential supervisor of financial institutions in the Eurozone. This system includes approximately 6,000 banks (MEMO/13/780). Also non-euro EU countries can join the SSM. In the new situation, there is a division of labour and strict cooperation between the ECB and NCBs. The former supervises directly the largest banks, while the latters continue to monitor the remaining banks.

The European Banking Authority[258] implemented a comprehensive EU-wide stress test of 123 banks during 2014, to assess the banks' financial health and resilience to adverse economic developments and reach a clear comparative view of their situation (EBA 2014). Results were published on 26 October 2014 and contributed to give more transparency into EU banks' balance sheets, with the aim of enhancing market discipline. EU banks under test strengthened their capital positions during 2014, before the EBA reviewed asset quality. As a result of the stress test, EU banks' common equity ratio (CET1) appeared to drop on average by 260 basis points, from 11.1% in 2013 to 8.5% in 2016. Data were published both in an aggregate form, and for each bank.

The second component of the banking union is the SRM (MEMO/14/295), which applies to banks covered by the SSM. Through this mechanism and in the cases when banks fail, bank resolution is managed through a Single Resolution Board (SRB) and a Single Resolution Fund (SRF). Both the Board and the Fund are financed by the banking sector.

After the dangerous financial and monetary tensions in the summer of 2011, the ECB interventions were effective in avoiding further speculative attacks to the common currency and in stabilising the money market. However, austerity continued to dominate fiscal policies. As a

---

[258] The European Banking Authority (EBA) was established on 1 January 2011 as part of the European System of Financial Supervision (ESFS), thus replacing the Committee of European Banking Supervisors. EBA is an independent EU Authority, whose goal is to ensure effective and consistent prudential regulation and supervision across the European banking sector. Its main task is to contribute to working out a single set of harmonised prudential rules for financial institutions throughout the EU, to be assembled into the European Single Rulebook. Moreover, EBA promotes convergence of supervisory practices and assesses risks and vulnerabilities in the EU banking sector.

consequence, the economies of vulnerable countries were stagnating or in recession, while their public debt continued to grow. Economies in recession witnessed decreasing revenues from taxation and growing expenditures, particularly for unemployment benefits and social programmes to combat poverty, and were unable to accumulate sufficient resources to repay the debt.

These conditions created a mix of events that pushed vulnerable economies to the brink of deflation. Austerity programmes required that public expenditures be decreased, including employment and the salaries of public employees. This also decreased demand for the private sector, which was already under negatively affected by the international crisis.

To avoid that, budget deficits grew beyond the limit set by the convergence criteria (3% deficit over GDP), benefits and pensions were cut. This further depressed demand. Worse still, it created deep and widespread uncertainty among employees and consumers: the continuing warnings issued by Eurozone authorities that vulnerable countries were not adequately adjusting their situation and that further austerity measures were necessary made employees and consumers expect their situation to worsen. They became increasingly pessimistic and prudent: consumption fell further and precautionary savings increased, in spite of falling incomes. Falling demand and negative economic perspectives led firms to moderate price increases at first, and subsequently to cut prices. Through the strict economic and financial relations among Eurozone countries, resilient countries were also negatively affected.

In spite of the clearly worsening economic situation, the European Commission and the European Council continued to privilege financial stability along the convergence parameters. Although political authorities tried to use the little flexibility that existed in the European treaties to ease the situation of the countries in difficulty, this flexibility was grossly insufficient to improve the conditions. Taken between ailing real economies and the markets' decreasing confidence in the common currency also during 2012, the Eurozone continued to risk collapse. It is at this point that the president of the ECB, Mario Draghi, made his famous "whatever it takes" statement. This statement was important to cool markets down and reestablish their confidence in the common currency. This statement may be seen as the starting point of an increasingly determined action by the ECB (ECB 2012).[259]

Confronted with the growing danger of deflation and the impotence of political authorities in reviving production and employment, the ECB decided at last to act along two lines. First, in summer 2013 the president of the ECB announced the ECB intention to act to depreciate the excessively strong euro. The intention was clear: if internal demand does not exist, a weaker euro should create the much needed external demand. Indeed, and in spite of the strong euro, exports of some Eurozone countries were high. However, these were resilient countries, Germany and the Netherlands in particular, which were running current account surpluses above what is usually considered in line with the convergence criteria (at 6% of GDP). In spite of that statement, the euro continued to remain strong.

The strong euro particularly disfavoured vulnerable countries, which suffered the double blow of failing domestic demand, and lack of demand by other Eurozone countries because of austerity, and lack of external demand because of the strong euro. Some of these countries were able to reach a surplus in their current accounts by decreasing imports, an effect of ailing production. A weaker euro was expected to increase their exports and thus translate into higher investment and production. However, the effect is rather complex, since the cost of imports also increases and the effect on the export depends upon various factors.

Simulations with the Commission's QUEST model suggest that a 5% depreciation of the euro's nominal effective exchange rate (NEER) may

[259] The full statement is: "Within our mandate, the ECB is ready to do whatever it takes to preserve the euro. And believe me, it will be enough." Timothy Geithner, who was US treasury secretary at the time, is credited for having stated: "[T]hings deteriorated again dramatically in the summer which ultimately led to him [Mario Draghi] saying in August, these things I would never write, but he off-the-cuff — he was in London at a meeting with a bunch of hedge funds and bankers. He was troubled by how direct they were in Europe, because at that point all the hedge fund community thought that Europe was coming to an end. I remember him telling me [about] this afterwards, he was just, he was alarmed by that and decided to add to his remarks, and off-the-cuff basically made a bunch of statements like 'we'll do whatever it takes'. Ridiculous." Geithner's statement is included in the 100 pages of transcripts of interviews Geithner gave to assistants preparing his book, *Stress Test: Reflections on Financial Crises* (Spiegel 2014).

increase real GDP in the euro area by around 0.3% in the first year and another 0.2% in the second year (EC 2015e). However, the effect of depreciation is likely to differ widely across member countries in function of the countries' NEER and their openness to trade. An important factor in explaining the effects of depreciation are the countries varying export price elasticities. Since elasticity is higher particularly in Italy and Spain — but also in Portugal, Austria and France — than in Germany, the euro's depreciation may actually support intra-Eurozone rebalancing. Moreover, the effect depends upon external demand. One advantage is that the euro is depreciating against the US dollar and US demand is strong. This should benefit open economies that export more to the US, such as Ireland. However, demand in emerging economies is getting weaker, while the euro appreciated for a while against the Russian ruble, a fact that particularly disadvantaged the Baltic countries. The overall impact on economic activity is unclear, since differences in export elasticity are in part offset by differences in trade openness and in integration in global value chains (EC 2014e).

The second line of intervention became officially known on 22 January 2015, when the ECB announced a massive expanded asset purchase programme. This decision aims at reviving Eurozone economies both directly and through the depreciation of the common currency. Asset purchases are expected to provide a much needed monetary stimulus to a stagnating Eurozone economy, in which most indicators of actual and expected inflation are at a historical low and with the risk that second-round effects on wage and price-setting further adversely affect medium-term price developments. In fact, key ECB interest rates are at a low 0.1%. It is expected that asset purchase, which provides the selling institutions with resources that they hopefully use to buy other assets and extend credit to the real economy, makes access to finance cheaper for firms and households. This effect should in turn support investment and consumption. This should push inflation rates towards 2%, the ultimate target of the ECB.

The programme consists of a series of open-ended massive asset purchases in the secondary market against central bank money. Purchases include bonds — typically long-term bonds — issued by euro area central governments, agencies and European institutions. The programme also includes asset purchase programmes launched in October 2014, which proved insufficient to move prices and output. The latter programmes include the asset-backed securities purchase programme (ABSPP) and the third covered bond purchase programme (CBPP3). Combined purchases amount to €60 billion per month, starting from March 2015. Purchases are foreseen to continue at least until September 2016 and in any case until the inflation rate is close to 2% over the medium term. The overall amount foreseen is €1.1 trillion, corresponding to €720 billion euros per year.

Much of the debate around the programme concern the effects of a possible default by some of the Eurozone countries. Critics are afraid that the programme introduces *de facto* a mutualisation of national debt. To avoid this danger, the ECB decided that only purchases of securities of European institutions by NCBs are subject to loss sharing. These securities amount to only 12% of the additional asset purchases. The ECB itself bought a further 8%. Therefore, only 20% of the additional asset purchases are subject to Eurozone risk sharing. The remaining 80% is allocated to NCBs, according to each state's share in the ECB's capital, roughly equivalent to the country's share in the Eurozone's GDP. This part is not subject to loss sharing.

A further guarantee against national default, though, lies in the conditions attached to sovereign bonds purchases. Purchases are limited to investment-grade issuers. As a condition for having their sovereign bonds purchased, countries which are rated below investment-grade (Greece and Cyprus) must comply with the terms of economic reform programmes negotiated with the "troika" (the IMF, the European Commission, and the ECB). Financial institutions in these countries, when facing liquidity problems, can be supported through Emergency Liquidity Assistance (ELA) (ECB 2015e).[260]

[260] ELA consists of the provision by a Eurosystem NCB of central bank money and/or any other assistance that may lead to an increase in central bank money to a solvent financial institution, or group of solvent financial institutions facing temporary liquidity problems. Such operation is not part of the common monetary policy, but needs the ECB authorisation. Responsibility and any costs and risk for the provision of ELA lie with the NCB concerned.

The new programme of asset purchases has therefore a double guarantee against potential mutualisation of national debts in case of national default: the pre-emptive conditionality of national reforms and the ex-post guarantee that most of the purchases remain on the budget sheet of NCBs. The former guarantee ensures that assets of countries in a particularly risky situation are not bought. The latter guarantees that countries themselves bear most of the risk. Both conditions should also give powerful incentives to countries to honour the commitment and comply with obligations.

In reality, these guarantees are more hypothetical than real. It is hard to imagine that in the Eurozone it is possible to safely isolate a country that defaults on its obligations. The negative consequences of one default would radiate to other countries indirectly and directly. Indirectly, Eurozone economies and financial systems are closely intertwined also through non-ownership relations and the default of one country would seriously affect the economies of others. Directly, it is normal for Eurozone NCBs to extend loans to other NCBs. For instance, Germany's central bank had net claims with the Eurosystem of €528 billion in January 2015, equivalent to 78% of its net external position (DBB 2015b).[261] The Deutsche Bundesbank was a net lender of more than €490.7 billion to banks in other Eurozone countries in December 2014 (DBB 2015a). This means that a default in one country would create serious losses in other member countries. This would probably make the loss-sharing limits ineffective. Experience shows that nevertheless the Eurozone has powerful tools for disciplining its member countries in difficulty and pushing them

[261] Of these, €513 billion were the Bundesbank's TARGET2 claims on 28 February 2015 (€515 billion at the end of January 2015). TARGET2 is a payment system that enables the speedy and final settlement of national and cross-border payments in central bank money. According to Buiter and Rahbari (2012), the Bundesbank's exposure to the monetary-policy-related items on the Eurosystem balance sheet was around €423bn or 16% of estimated 2012 GDP in September 2012. This compares to 37% of the Bundesbank's total balance sheet and its capital share in the ECB of 27.1%. Most of the exposure is with Spain (€119 billion or 4.5% of the GDP), Italy (€101 billion or 3.8%), France (€48 billion or 1.8%), Greece (€45 billion or 1.7%) and Ireland (€37 billion or 1.4%). See also Dor (2011).

to fix their finances and reform their economies. These are in particular the continuous surveillance and the peers' pressure upon its members.

The increasing determination of the ECB in stabilising financial markets and reactivating the normal working of Eurozone economies was important and met with significant success. Without the ECB's determination, the Eurozone would be definitely be worse off and the euro at risk. These measures helped the Eurozone to gain some time to find structural solutions to the Eurozone crisis, solutions that only governments could find and implement in a permanent and structural way. The inability of governments to do so is imposing a harsh price upon Eurozone economies: depression in some countries and stagnation in many others are prolonged beyond any reasonable limit. In spite of the strenuous fight of the ECB, the spectre of deflation did not disappear. It is now time to examine why governments have so far failed to contribute to coming up with a structural solution for the Eurozone's problems.

11.9 Mechanisms for European Bailouts

The no-bailout clause notwithstanding, some Eurozone member countries had to be bailed out. Yet this took place in peculiar ways. The EU established a set of special funds for bailing out countries in difficulty. These funds usually worked together with the ECB, for purchases of sovereign debt on secondary markets, and the IMF, for additional funding.[262] As explained in the previous section, a stabilisation mechanism was set up in May 2010 to safeguard financial stability against severe tensions in euro-area sovereign debt markets. The mechanism had two components: the European Financial Stabilisation Mechanism (EFSM) and the EFSF. The two mechanisms could be activated after a member state in need requests for financial assistance. The latter was given against a macroeconomic adjustment programme incorporating strict conditionality, agreed upon with the Commission and the ECB.

[262] In case an EU member country outside the Eurozone is in difficulty with its balance of payments, the EU can provide mutual assistance through Balance-of-Payments (BoP) assistance in the form of medium-term financial assistance.

The EFSM was set up as a temporary crisis resolution mechanism in May 2010 to provide funds for the purchase programme of covered bonds to Ireland, Portugal and Greece. The mechanism operated through the European Commission, which intermediated between the member country in need and financial markets. The European Commission could issue bonds and other debt instruments up to €60 billion in total in financial markets, acting on behalf of the EU and under an implicit EU budget guarantee. The advantage of this system was to take advantage of the EU AAA credit rating from the major rating agencies. The amount was lent to the member country in need, which had to repay all interests and loan principal via the Commission, with no debt-servicing cost for the Union.

The amounts activated were €22.5 billion for Ireland and €24.3 billion for Portugal over three years (2011–2014), for a total amount of up to €46.8 billion (EC 2015o). These amounts were disbursed over three years, between 2011 and 2014. Loan disbursements to both countries were concluded in 2014.

Financial assistance for Ireland amounted to €85 billion between December 2010 and the end of 2013 (EC 2015f). This programme was financed with an equal amount (€22.5 billion each) by the IMF, the EFSF (this part included €4.8 billion from pooled bilateral sources) and the EFSM. The rest came from the Irish Treasury and National Pension Reserve Fund (€17.5 billion). Financial assistance to Portugal amounted to €78 billion, financed in equal parts (€26 billion each) by the IMF, the EFSF and the EFSM (EC 2015g).

Greece obtained financial assistance of €164.5 billion in total under the second Economic Adjustment Programme for Greece (EAPG) between March 2012 and August 2014, then and extended to end of June 2015.[263] Of this amount, €144.7 billion were given by the European Commission; the IMF provided the remaining €19.8 billion. This second programme came after the first programme, active between May 2010 and June 2013, was concluded. The IMF financed the first programme with €30 billion; the additional €80 billion were financed in the form of a pool of bilateral support by Eurozone countries. The overall financial support to Greece in

[263] See EC (2015c).

the two programmes amounted to more than 100% of its GDP. In July 2015, EFSM was used to provide short-term assistance in the form of a bridge loan of €7.16 billion to Greece.

The EFSF was discontinued after 1 July 2013 as a mechanism for providing assistance to the three countries. However, its financial assistance to Greece was extended to 30 June 2015. Nevertheless, the Facility continues to operate in the activities related to its outstanding operations, in order to comply with the obligations of the three countries in repaying the loans and as an intermediary between the borrowers and the market lenders. These include loan repayments from beneficiary countries, interest and principal payments to holders of EFSF bonds, and roll over outstanding EFSF bonds.[264]After this is over, the EFSF will cease to exist.

On 8 October 2012 the European Stability Mechanism (ESM) started its operations and replaced the EFSF (ESM 2015a). ESM is a permanent crisis resolution mechanism and is currently the sole mechanism for financial assistance to Eurozone countries and responsible for reinforced economic surveillance. Its focus is on more effective enforcement measures for preventing the emergence of crises through conditionality. It has the nature of an intergovernmental institution under public international law, which cooperates very closely with the IMF. ESM has a paid-in capital of €80.5 billion, in accordance with the contribution key by Eurozone member countries, which is invested in high quality liquid assets. The overall authorised capital stock is €704.8 billion, with paid-in capital (€80.5 billion) and maximum lending capacity of €500 billion.

ESM has a diversified funding strategy which pools funds raised through bills, bonds and other funding instruments with maturities up to 30 years. Issuance may be made in different ways, via syndications, auctions, private placements or taps of existing lines of credit. The amount of assistance disbursed so far, out of the maximum lending capacity of €500 billion, was €47 billion provided to Spain, for the recapitalisation of its financial sector, and Cyprus. The remaining ESM's forward commitment capacity as of 30 September 2015 is €369.31 billion (ESM 2015b). ESM

[264] In fact, the maturity of loans provided to Ireland, Portugal and Greece is longer than the maturity of bonds issued by the EFSF.

financial assistance instruments include loans to Eurozone countries meeting severe financing problems; the purchase of bonds in primary and secondary debt markets; precautionary financial assistance in the form of credit lines; loans to countries for the recapitalisation of financial institutions; and direct recapitalisation of financial institutions.

The ESM's first intervention was in Spain (ESM 2015c). Following the alarm towards a capital shortfall identified in a number of Spanish banks, the Eurogroup approved a package of financial assistance for Spain of up to €100 billion in July 2012. The Spanish government requested a smaller amount and the ESM disbursed €39.5 billion in December 2012 and €1.8 billion in February 2013, for a total amount of €41.3 billion. The ESM financial assistance programme for Spain expired on 31 December 2013. Policy conditionality focused on the banking sector, including in-depth bank restructuring plans, accompanied ESM financial assistance.

Cyprus obtained loans in financial assistance following the March 2013 agreement with the Eurogroup and was subject to its macroeconomic adjustment program. This included downsizing of the country's financial sector, fiscal consolidation, pension and health care reform, structural reforms and privatisation. The ESM committed approximately €9 billion and the IMF another €1 billion (ESM 2015d). Of these, €5.8 billion were disbursed in eight disbursements between May 2013 and July 2015. The financial assistance facility covered the country's financing needs, including budgetary financing, the redemption of medium- and long-term debt, and the recapitalisation of financial institutions, except the country's two largest banks, which were subject to restructuring and resolution measures.

Greece came to be at the centre of the ESM's activities in summer 2015 (EC 2015c). The EC signed a Memorandum of Understanding (MoU) with Greece on 19 August in order to provide the country with stability support accompanied by a third economic adjustment program. The agreement includes the disbursement of financial assistance to Greece over three years (2015–2018) for up to €86 billion, linked to a set of conditionality. A first disbursement of €13 billion in August 2015 plus an additional €10 billion disbursement earmarked for bank recapitalisation and resolution address the country's needs against overdue payments, financial sector needs in the hope this will support production and the repayment of the €7.16 billion short-term bridge loan obtained in July 2015 under EFSM.

11.10 Currency Area: A Cage or a Trap? A Conclusion

Incomplete and asymmetric common institutions, differences in national institutions, ineffective and counterproductive policies, the lack of policy coordination, fading trust among Eurozone countries, and the working of markets, led the Eurozone in a difficult, perhaps untenable situation. Is the Eurozone in a cage or is it caught in a trap? In the words of Sinn (2014, p. 1): "As great as the beneficial effect of the European Union is, just as destructive has been the impact of the common currency on the cohesion of Europe."

In his seminal article, Robert Mundell (1961) highlighted the problem that an optimum currency area would meet in adjusting to external shocks. If each country keeps its own currency, a shift of demand from country B to country A causes unemployment in B and inflationary pressure in A. If prices in A increase, the worsening of A's terms of trade will somehow re-establish employment in B. However, if A adopts restrictive policies to cool inflation down and therefore prices and terms of trade do not change, all the burden of adjustment falls upon country B, that must reduce real income through recession, i.e. a decline in output and employment.

In a single currency including many countries, the condition for avoiding recession in deficit regions relies on the willingness of national authorities to shift the burden of international adjustment onto surplus countries. These would then inflate until unemployment in deficit countries is eliminated. Thus a currency area cannot prevent both unemployment and inflation among its members. And here lies the problem. In a common currency area with a single currency and many countries, similarly to the gold standard system, depression in one country would be transmitted to other countries through the foreign trade multiplier.

This chain of events poses the critical question of the divergent interests among individual member countries. Let us suppose that a labour market reform successfully decreasing labour cost in country A shifts demand to the advantage of that country and away from country B which did not undergo any reform. The reform was socially and politically painful, but now country A gets to reap the rewards, although the group of citizens of country B who gets most of the reward is probably different from the group of those who accepted lower wages for more jobs. Now country B, which did not reform and therefore lost demand and increased unemployment, pretends that country A undergoes inflation until unemployment in country B is eliminated. Namely, country B asks that the costs of reform be fully paid by country A, and yet shares all benefits with country B. It is not difficult to expect political and social opposition in country A to such a perspective.

Moreover, when the currency area is an open economy, if country A undergoes inflation the advantages would partly go outside the area; as a consequence, the benefit for B would be reduced. Political and social contrast would remain entirely between country A and country B, but the economic effects would be shared with the rest of the world. However, if the two countries have integrated economies, as is the case in an economic and monetary union, this mechanism would be helpful, at least as a complement to deeper action.

If there is full common governance in the currency area, a different possibility would exist: a common government could transfer resources from country A to country B, taking away in full or in part the advantage from reforms in country A and transfer it to country B. In an incomplete monetary union this could still be a sustainable solution, depending upon political institutions, their willingness to pursue redistribution, social acceptance, the danger of moral hazard, and trust among governments.

One advantage of this solution is that, if country B is asked to reform in exchange for the transfer of resources, economic cycles in the currency area would be synchronised again. This would re-establish the conditions for common policies with symmetric effects, a necessary condition for the long-run sustainability of a currency area with an open economy. The only truly efficient and politically sustainable solution is that country B must also reform. This scenario meets with two problems. First, reforms are costly and may momentarily disrupt production before improving conditions. Second, part of the formal and informal institutions and the economic and social features and conditions of the two countries may differ and the same reform in two different contexts could have vastly differing results. Apparently a mix of (substantial) reform and (some) redistribution could provide a sustainable and efficient solution. Moving towards solving this conundrum is the crux of the next chapter.

"... if something be not done, something will do itself one day, and in a fashion that will please nobody. This time is verily come for acting in it; how much more for consultation about acting in it, for speech and articulate inquiry about it!"

— Thomas Carlyle, *Condition of England Question*, 1839.

12

Conclusions: An Uneasy Match

During the crisis, the Eurozone tested and proved its resilience, yet the monetary union is at a crossroads. Access to larger and more liquid financial markets and larger and more competitive goods markets at lower interests and prices are sizeable advantages for the Eurozone member countries, their governments, firms and financial organisations, and their consumers. Yet these advantages are overshadowed by sizeable disadvantages and costs in terms of lost output and unemployment. Monetary integration has demonstrated itself to be backed by remarkable popular and political support, along with the more obvious support of the business community. Yet recurrent crises still loom.

The prolonged economic difficulties of the Eurozone and the lack of institutional and political breakthrough show that time may not work necessarily in favour of the monetary union. It is difficult to see how the monetary union can stay together in the long run by imposing unreasonable costs to a significant part of its citizens and if some of its member countries are unable or unwilling to implement the necessary reforms. If the performance of vulnerable economies does not converge to that of resilient countries or if substantial and credible progress in the direction of a complete union and growth policies is missing, the common currency imposes growing costs and stagnation or decline on vulnerable countries. A common currency leading to secular economic decline is neither desirable nor sustainable. In these circumstances, it may also be difficult to keep negative political consequences under control. An unfavourable external context may make this outcome more likely and serious.[265]

12.1 Towards a New Awareness

The crisis in the United States had major indirect effects in the Eurozone. In particular, it revealed the significant deep economic and financial differences among member countries. What was equally important was that these effects exposed the weak institutional foundations of the euro, the lack of intercountry solidarity and the rigidity of the Stability and Growth Pact (SGP). These weaknesses existed before the crisis and were fully Eurozone-made. Another negative effect of the external shock was that individual member countries tried to follow their own short-run interest, thus jeopardising the common purpose and mutual trust. The dominant financial austerity was in a sense a device for avoiding worse consequences in an uncooperative club of countries. In this situation, the common currency actually made economic and financial convergence more difficult.

However, reading the situation in this way risks confusing cause and effect. The international crisis raised doubts over the effective governance of the Eurozone economy and the euro, in spite of the European Central

[265] In its latest report, the IMF (2015b) foresees secular stagnation to remain as long as demand is weak and inflation is expected to stay below target for an extended period, amid constraints on monetary policy at the zero lower bound. This situation causes an increasing likelihood of damage to potential output. See also IMF (2014a). According to Lawrence Summers (2014), since the start of the crisis, policy concern was focused on avoiding secular stagnation. This concern arose primarily from the long-run effects of short-run developments and the inability of monetary policy to accomplish more when interest rates already reached their lower bound.

Bank's (ECB) increasingly resolute intervention and its interest rates being constantly lower than that in the US. One problem was that external financial and monetary events contributed to the instability of the Eurozone economy and had internally asymmetric consequences for vulnerable and resilient countries. Perhaps more important in the long run was that the international crisis exposed the weak institutional and policy base of the euro and the entire European project and highlighted the need to intervene at the root of the problems. Although the imperative to proceed with institutional completion and perhaps political integration is clearly felt and is apparently shared by governments, the road ahead is long and bumpy. Agreeing on general goals does not translate necessarily into clearly defined common objectives and even less concrete targets. Even if common objectives are defined and shared, there is no guarantee that their implementation would be timely and actually pursued the aim of strengthening of the union and improving the situation of its member countries.

Recognising that austerity policies were based on a wrong interpretation of the working of economies in a time of crisis, in particular concerning the value of the fiscal multiplier, is important for avoiding similar mistakes in the future. Yet this recognition is not sufficient for economies to emerge from the crisis. The present wider, pragmatic and mostly tacit use of flexibility built in Eurozone institutions and treaties and the important ECB action are useful to gain some time. However, only institutional and structural reforms and policies which are more in line with the real situation can fix the problems of the Eurozone.

Lack of national determination may delay the implementation of reforms. Unfortunately, the common currency itself makes more difficult and costlier for vulnerable countries to finance those reforms. There is a danger that the increase of debt to GDP ratio in vulnerable economies, which the debate on the fiscal multiplier in recession highlighted, may cause the retreat of vulnerable economies into a low level equilibrium. Negative consequences may extend to resilient Eurozone countries both via the integration among economies and tensions on the euro (EC 2014g).

The ECB's determination to do "whatever it takes" to support the euro helped ease financial and monetary distress (Pisani-Ferry and Wolff, 2012). However, these measures could not address the fundamental reasons for instability, nor could they complete the institutional setup of the Eurozone.

Mario Draghi, the president of the ECB, expressed this perspective very clearly. After having stated that monetary policy cannot create growth, since it cannot correct intercountry divergences descending from low growth potential and high structural unemployment, he stressed that:

> … we cannot expect those divergences to be addressed through means such as permanent transfers from economically resilient countries. The euro area was not created to be a union with permanent creditors and debtors. It is an area where each country, by exploiting its comparative advantages and the opportunities afforded by the Single Market, and by converging to the highest standards in terms of competitiveness and income, must be able to stand on its own two feet. (Draghi 2015)

The Eurozone conundrum is sufficiently clear in its elements, although perhaps not in its timing, composition and responsibilities. While a monetary union cannot survive if it is too far from being an optimum currency area, the Eurozone replaces its incompleteness in good part by means of political and social support. However, this support alone cannot offset major shortcomings: intercountry divergences (segmentation) and institutional incompleteness. To better manage these shortcomings, at least higher intercountry labour mobility is necessary. This is not foreseeable in the near future, for institutional, political and social reasons.

In the absence of a solution to these strategic problems, the Eurozone has turned to austerity policies. They guarantee that the problematic financial situation of vulnerable countries does not jeopardise the monetary union, nor does it require financial support by resilient countries. It is in a sense a least common denominator for cohabitation. However, this takes place at the price of limited and less effective policy instruments and restrictive policies to the disadvantage of the real economy and in particular employment and wages. Austerity as a policy mantra is wrong and dangerous, yet not much else is at hand in the present Eurozone.

The evidence of past policy failures and the commitment of vulnerable countries to the formal rules of the monetary union, even at significant or very high economic and social costs, are perhaps changing the scene.

A slow and bumpy policy consensus is developing for addressing the apparently intractable Eurozone problems. Yet new dangers have emerged. Financial distress, incomplete institutions with no bailout, non-monetary financing, and hard budget constraints have deprived the Eurozone of powerful countercyclical policies and led to bank-sovereign interdependence. Large stocks of undiversified national public debt securities are held by national banks even after the euro fostered some cross-border financing. The vulnerability of Eurozone countries increased, because adverse shocks to sovereign solvency could interact with adverse shocks to bank solvency. The ECB quantitative easing programme started in March 2015 aims to address this problem by transferring public debt bonds from private banks to national central banks. At the same time, the ongoing construction of a European banking union aims to strengthen large, systemic banks.

What the Eurozone finds particularly difficult is to identify a new, long-run strategy capable of incorporating the dramatic changes that the international crisis brought about in the international financial and economic system, the new perception that markets have of the common currency, and the fundamentally altered intercountry relations within the Eurozone. During the international crisis and the Eurozone crisis, the time horizons of governments and people dramatically shortened. It is therefore fundamental that a long-term institutional, economic and political strategic perspective is worked out, however difficult this may be. This is necessary to induce the Eurozone member countries to cooperate for the sake of the common good.

Such perspective should include policies supporting growth, institutional reforms for completing the Eurozone architecture, and institutional and structural reforms to make the Eurozone economies more competitive. Completing the institutional architecture of the Eurozone is the most daunting goal, since it impinges upon the national sovereignty of member countries and the stance and priorities of policymaking. The most important institutional reform areas include: (a) broader ECB mandate, (b) creation of a Eurozone banking federation, and (c) stronger EU budget and fiscal union with common bonds.

These reforms should constitute the building block of a deeper and stronger political union. The crisis made evident that reforms, both at the

Eurozone level and at national level, are extremely important and urgent. Member countries are clear that the present monetary union is not working properly and that it is the source of recurrent crises. They are also aware that the present economic stagnation is economically, politically and socially dangerous, if prolonged. There is also a certain degree of mutual understanding on where solutions could be found. Yet disagreement is still deep on the structure, quality and measure of these solutions. The recent debates on the ECB mandate and its interpretation, the features of the banking federation and the banks to be included in it, the features and financing of a fiscal union and the size and features of the EU budget, all provide clear evidence of the problems.

There is also disagreement on the meaning and content of structural reforms (EC 2015p).[266] Generally, what the EU means by this term are the changes that lead to or are preconditions of internal devaluation. The perspective is mostly macroeconomic and consists primarily of changes to the labour market or the pension system that decrease production costs, ease dismissals and decrease public expenditures. There is no clear evidence that these changes improve the microeconomic efficiency and effectiveness of European economies, in particular in the case of vulnerable countries. Moreover, these changes contribute to decrease the size of the domestic market and worsen the economic, social, and political mood of most consumers.

Better reforms, in particular decreasing transaction costs (e.g. administrative costs and costs of contract enforcement) and decreasing the tax wedge over economic activity (e.g. broaden the tax base through fighting tax evasion) are mentioned, but are rarely the focus of policymaking. Other important reforms are improving productivity by more and better investment, liberalisation and more competition, research and development (R&D), improving the quality of human capital, strengthening innovation,

[266] According to the European Commission, structural reforms address impediments to the fundamental drivers of growth by unshackling labour, product and service markets to foster job creation, investment, and productivity. These reforms aim to enhance an economy's competitiveness, growth potential and adjustment capacity. See also Canton *et al.* (2014). As a matter of facts, in vulnerable countries the policy accent is mostly, sometimes nearly exclusively on labour and often on decreasing the remuneration and rights of employees.

including social innovation. These were important components of the Lisbon strategy and play an important role in the Europe 2020 strategy.

It is perhaps the fundamental failure of the former and the uneasy life of the latter that contributed to shift the accent to what appears technically and politically easier: making labour cheaper and more flexible in the short-medium run, with scant concern for long-run consequences. To be sure, these policies may appear easier to implement thanks to the weakness of trade unions and social opposition in vulnerable countries and to bear fruits faster than other policies. Unfortunately, structural reforms imposed upon vulnerable countries as part of austerity policies made these countries stepping back in the quality of their international specialisation. This effect enlarged further the divergence between strong and vulnerable countries, particularly in technology intensive sectors (Palan 2013; Palan and Schmiedeberg 2008, 2010).

Europeans are clearly aware that something needs to be done. Yet the precise features of this something have far-reaching consequences and may change deeply the future of European countries. Preferences of European governments and, up to a point, countries are still different and perhaps apart. The precondition for an important change may be building up, though. The crisis changed the attitudes of Europeans (Eurobarometer 2014e; Stokes 2015), particularly in vulnerable countries.[267] The endurance of vulnerable countries in implementing austerity policies and the continuing popular support for the euro (Eurobarometer 2014f) are apparently re-establishing some degree of intercountry confidence and trust. The long and dramatic dispute between Greece and Eurozone institutions and other countries' governments in the first part of 2015, which

[267] Guiso *et al.* (2014) analyse the cross sectional and time series variation in pro-European sentiment in the EU-15 countries, based on Eurobarometer surveys. They find that the major steps forward undertaken in the integration process (the 1992 Maastricht Treaty and the 2004 enlargement) and the economic crisis seem to have reduced the pro-Europe sentiment, but not the support for the common currency within the Eurozone. This seems to create an untenable situation, one in which there is no desire to go backward, no interest in going forward, but it is economically unsustainable to stay still. The analysis of Eurobarometer surveys shows that the effect is negative in Southern European countries, where people seem to have lost confidence toward the EU. At the same time, though, Central and North Europeans seem to have gained a bit more confidence.

led the common currency to the brink of disruption, may perhaps sign the turning point towards a more sober and realistic management of the common currency. Europhobic parties, although stronger than in the past, appear to be unable to break through.

A window of opportunity may be opening for implementing sounder and longer-perspective policies and structural reforms. Time is also ripe for engaging in far reaching common and national institutional reforms. The Eurozone institutional architecture could be under transformation. These conclusions aim to identify the main dynamics in the Eurozone.

12.2 The Problem and the Consequences

The external shock coming from the United States was transmitted to the Eurozone through different channels. It fostered serious financial and real consequences and ultimately institutional effects, with different effects in diverse member countries. Financial distress was at its peak in 2010–2011. In 2010 Greece and Ireland needed urgent rescuing, followed in 2011 by Portugal and Cyprus, while Italy was in a critical situation with its public finances, although it could go on without any bailout. Spain followed in 2012, due to the financial distress of its private banks. Yet real distress, the fall of GDP to levels that in 2015 are still lower than before the crisis in several Eurozone countries, is still a worrying reality.

It may appear strange that the crisis hit countries (Cyprus, Ireland, and Spain) that were growing at high rates.[268] Moreover, their financial situation was not particularly problematic (De Grauwe 2011a). Public debt over GDP in 2009 was above 60% in Germany and France, but not in Spain and Cyprus, which also had lower budget deficit to GDP ratios than the EU average.

---

[268] Growth rates in the period 2005–2012 were good in Cyprus (+14.7%), Ireland (+10.2%) and Spain (+7.0%). This was roughly comparable to the performance of Germany (+11.6%), Finland (+10.0 %) and France (+7.2%), the average of the Eurozone (+6.7%) and the European Union (+8.0%). The performance of three vulnerable countries during the same period was definitely negative: Italy (−1.3%), Portugal (−1.4%), and Greece (−9.6%) (http://epp.eurostat.ec.europa.eu/tgm/refreshTableAction.do?tab=table&plugin=1&pcode=tec00115&language=en).

Vulnerability came from the economies' unbalanced and uncompetitive real economy, including low and stagnating productivity, high unemployment, and outdated international specialisation. Vulnerability also came from unbalanced public finances and high public debt. Growth came mostly from the external inflow of resources and public expenditure. Germany exported substantial amounts of capital, in particular to Ireland and Spain. Exposure in all vulnerable countries came also from their dependence on short-term foreign investors. When financial turmoil took over, capital inflow to vulnerable countries was reversed (IMF 2012a).

To stabilise a dangerous situation, the Eurozone ruled that countries in distress had to stabilise their public finances by means of restrictive financial policies and internal devaluation. The European Union (EU) and the ECB, usually with the support of the International Monetary Fund (IMF), guaranteed rescue packages to be extended to each country, after the positive assessment of progress in implementing policies. This was merely treating the symptoms, while overlooking the causes of unbalanced public finances.

International financial markets came to distrust the Eurozone project and manifested lack of confidence for vulnerable countries and skepticism towards the euro. The situation was particularly serious in 2011, on the occasion of Greece's and Cyprus' financial crises. The markets' attitude jeopardised the stabilisation policies and public debts increased significantly compared to GDP.

The dominant policy approach had problematic consequences in vulnerable countries. There was a timing mismatch between financial stabilisation, which received top priority, reforms of institutions and upgrading the real economy.[269] A firm and rapid financial stabilisation was a must under the cloud of international financial market uncertainty. Yet its

[269] Gechert *et al.* (2015) and Gechert and Rannenberg (2015) reexamine the effects of the Greek austerity programme on its economy via a counterfactual analysis that apply fiscal multipliers to fiscal consolidation measures that were implemented in Greece between 2010 and 2014. According to their findings, austerity explains almost the entire collapse of Greek GDP after 2009. In the absence of austerity, the Greek economy would have entered a prolonged period of stagnation, rather than a depression, and government debt-to-GDP ratio would have been somewhat lower, all other conditions remaining equal. If the consolidation was postponed until after the recovery of the Greek economy and implemented gradually, almost two thirds of the cost in terms of lost output could have been avoided.

implementation, including the choice of the particular stabilisation measures, needed to allow for the long-run sustainability of vulnerable economies. This required that the causes of vulnerability were dealt with, not only its effects. The previous chapter showed that vulnerability derived from ineffective economic structures and institutions and the lack of investment, along with financial disequilibrium and distress. Stabilisation policies grounded in austerity created a situation in vulnerable countries that was counterproductive even to their very financial stability.

One problem with the necessary cohabitation of stabilisation policies with institutional and structural policies and reforms is timing mismatch. Stabilisation must be decided and implemented rapidly under the pressure of financial markets, while institutional and structural policies and reform require a lengthy period of preparation. They are also slow to be implemented and have an effect. Timing mismatch may lead vulnerable countries — and resilient countries through economic and financial links — to a permanent low activity equilibrium.

Timing mismatch is also likely to create the conditions whereby stabilisation policies have a depressive effect through the financial multiplier. Namely, they are more effective in depressing GDP than in decreasing public debts. Following the fall of public revenues and the increase of social expenditures during a recession, public debts may even grow. Deficit and debt to GDP ratios worsen consequently, leaving vulnerable countries worse off. Economic and financial linkages also jeopardise the economic situation of resilient countries.

A third problem with a timing mismatch is internal to countries. Employees and pensioners paid most of the costs of stabilisation through higher unemployment and lower real incomes, through wage cuts and/or increased taxation. Since these are a group relatively disadvantaged in income and wealth distribution, inequalities increased. Indeed much of the stabilisation was in the form of labour market, social security and welfare devaluation. The governments of vulnerable countries cut wages of public employees, typically as part of the conditionality of bailout packages and also decreased employment in the public sector. Concerns for the efficiency of the public sector were secondary or disregarded altogether. Wages in the private sector were an important part of cost cutting measures that enterprises implemented to attempt to recover competitiveness.

The main victims of stabilisation, however, were the younger generations, who too often could not get jobs or had unskilled jobs with unsecure contracts. Their capacity to consume and invest in their own future was impaired as a consequence.

Internal devaluation through the cut of wages and welfare benefits has a host of negative consequences: decrease workers' present and future incomes with depressive consequences for demand; attenuate workers' rights and have dubious effects on labour incentives; diminish incentives to invest in human capital; foster emigration, including of the educated and the skilled and particularly the young ones; and discourage the inflow of foreign capital since the domestic market is unattractive and production costs remain higher than in emerging economies. This policy could still have positive effects on exports, but this effect could surpass the negative effect in the domestic market only in small and open economies.

The negative effects of internal devaluation were concentrated in vulnerable countries, which increased the vulnerable/resilient divide. While resilient countries, both before and after the crisis and in particular in Northern Europe, relied in great part on innovation, vulnerable countries went through the weak road to recover competitiveness. The outcome was recovery of competitiveness through lower wages and welfare and lower quality international specialisation. As a consequence, the Eurozone had a weaker output than any other major Western economy, including the EU average and is apparently losing the innovation race, with the exception of the resilient countries of Northern Europe. In 2014, the Eurozone GDP was still below the level it had at the beginning of the crisis (Figure 12.1).

The internal segmentation of the Eurozone between resilient and vulnerable countries finds a match in the divergent performance within the Eurozone (Figure 12.2). Output growth in any vulnerable country was below that of resilient countries. Such countries as Italy and Portugal, let alone Greece and Cyprus, are still below the GDP level they had before the crisis. Only Spain is slightly above that level and obviously Ireland as well.

The short-run economic and social effect of the timing mismatch is therefore negative. Yet a J-curve effect could exist, whereby the depressive and decreasing effect of stabilisation policies prepares the ground for the expansion and increase to follow. Unfortunately the recessive phase, in

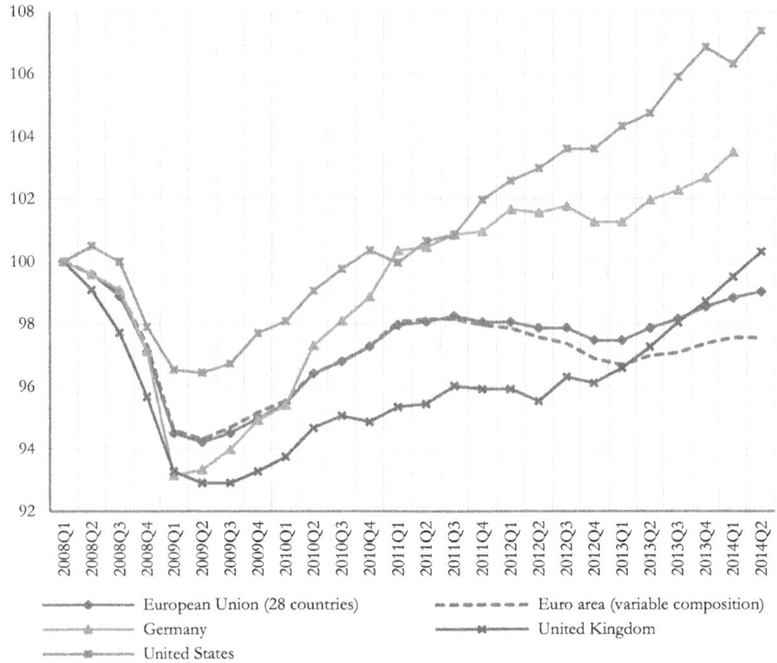

Figure 12.1. Real GDP, 2008Q1 = 100.
Source: Author's own figure based on the Eurostat database.

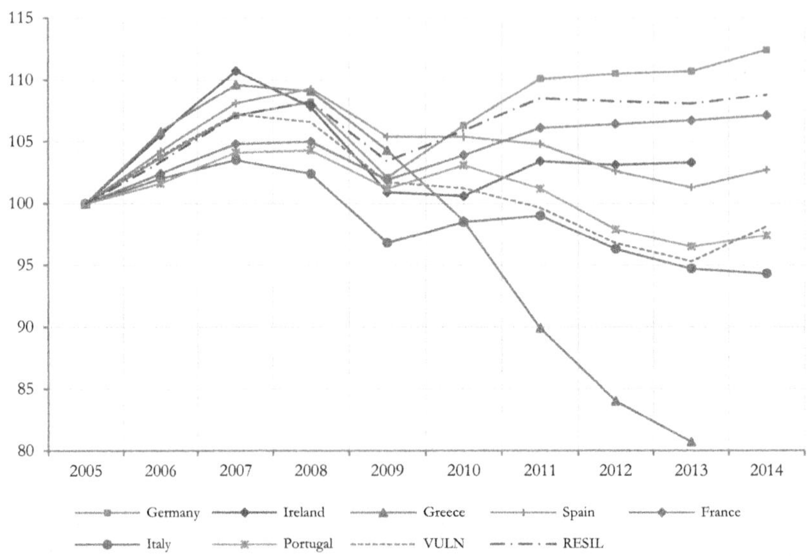

Figure 12.2. Real GDP, Eurozone, 2005 Q1 = 100.
Source: Author's own figure based on the Eurostat database.

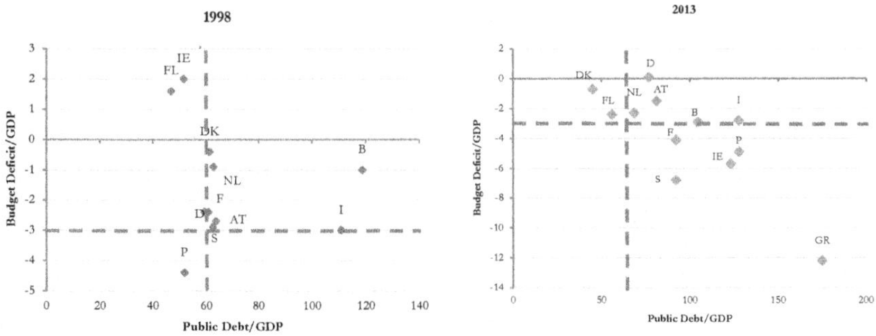

Figure 12.3. Compliance with Maastricht Criteria in 1998 and in 2013.
Source: Author's own figures based on the Eurostat database.

particular if coupled with rigid budget constraint, is more likely to worsen the conditions and the resources necessary for revival, including the implementation of institutional and structural reforms.

As the IMF calculation of the value of the fiscal multiplier during the crisis proves, the depressive effect of stabilisation policies decreases the denominator more than the nominator in the deficit/GDP and debt/GDP share. Both shares increased in all vulnerable countries, and also the resilient countries, although the increase was less than in vulnerable countries (Figure 12.3). The importance of these shares for policies and investors is such, which their growing value puts in motion further policy and market actions, such as further austerity and capital flight from vulnerable countries, which intensify financial distress and economic recession.

12.3. The Euro and Governance

The existence of important policy timing mismatch highlights that the way followed so far was unbalanced, incomplete, and self-defeating. To understand the nature of the problems and the potential solutions, it is necessary to return to considering the fundamental features of the common currency.

The establishment and introduction of the euro was an unprecedented undertaking. No group of sovereign countries had ever adopted a common currency without first implementing political unification. The introduction of the euro was a bet on the future through a multilateral contract among sovereign countries. However, future contingencies are impossible to foresee with a high degree of probability and in sufficient detail. Added to this, parties in the dealing had incomplete information on each other, the fundamental intentions of individual countries for entering the contract, their reaction to unforeseen contingencies and their inter-temporal distribution. As a consequence, the contract could only be incomplete and its evolution adaptive.

An incomplete contract leaves a broad discretionary area and creates as a consequence a great deal of uncertainty (Hart and Moore 1988). Uncertainty creates the danger of free riding and conflict in the relations between the parties to the contract and the evolution of the contract. To avoid this danger, complete governance is needed. Complete governance requires proper institutions and the allocation of discretionary power, to deal with unforeseen and unspecified contingencies. It also requires the existence of a third party having the power to enforce the contract whenever it is necessary. Discretionary power means having a government capable of taking and enforcing decisions. A third party means having an institution with credible power and reputation to intervene in an impartial way, when conflict arises.

The euro can be considered the outcome of an incomplete contract among quasi-sovereign countries. Complete governance in the case of a currency means having one monetary governance institution with full power in unforeseen contingencies. The most important governance institution is certainly a central bank, with full competences in monetary matters, including the ability to act as a lender of last resort if needed, and a government of financial issues with the discretionary power to transfer resources among the different parts of the union. The Eurozone has neither. The void is only partially filled by supportive collective and political will and the ECB's determination and effectiveness.

The Eurozone governance is incomplete and asymmetric. Governance is incomplete because there is no fiscal governance, except coordination based on shared treaties and pacts, and the role of the Council and the Commission. Also monetary governance lacks important requisites, such as a fully developed role as lender of last resort and common bank supervision. Governance is asymmetric because there are important differences between the monetary and the fiscal sides of governance.

Under these conditions and particularly when confronted with unforeseen contingencies, contract incompleteness and asymmetry are sources of moral hazard and conflicts. Although important exogenous factors support the Eurozone, including mutual economic interest, political will, and social support, the outcome is undetermined, transaction costs are high, and implementation of governance is time consuming and ineffective.

Asymmetric and incomplete governance yields ineffective policies. Policies are asymmetric in the sense that only monetary policies are in common and a rather powerful and effective governance system, the Eurosystem, runs them. Financial policies are not in the common domain: only financial rules are common through the SGP. However, these are constraints, not policies. Policies are incomplete, because no active financial policy can be used in countries that are under procedural constraints, such as in the case of a country under the procedure for excessive deficit. Unfortunately, this limitation covers virtually all of the Eurozone. Only financially balanced countries are free to use their financial policies and even this freedom is restricted by convergence criteria. It is evident that progress with financial adjustment was overall economically negative, although it was important for avoiding a financial meltdown and, more importantly, negative political consequences and conflicts among Eurozone member countries.

Also, there are problems with enforcement in the Eurozone. Enforcement belongs basically in peers (Eurogroup, Eurosystem), is based on formal rules defined in a pact (SGP), and works through predefined procedures, to be activated in the event of one particular short-run parameter, albeit one that is most important: excessive deficit. This system is financially effective, although cumbersome and one-sided. Its main drawback is to be tailored to formal and rigid rules with the goal of keeping or recovering internal financial equilibrium in the Eurozone. The latter is meant as the sum of national financial virtues, with little role for common constructive action. It does not pay attention to the consequences of financial stabilisation for economic growth and development, let alone social consequences. Even the growing pressure for implementing structural reforms is motivated more by balancing finances, and less by promoting growth and development. Governance, then, is effective, but incomplete. It is skewed to short-term perspectives and does not give proper relevance to the long-run conditions of sustainability of the common currency through growth and development.

If governance and policies are short of what is necessary, it is useful to see whether mutual economic interest can lead to more symmetric and complete institutions, to effective governance and policies. Since the most important source of differences of national interests is the diverging performance of national economies, it is helpful to consider whether converging situations and performance of national economies can be reached and how.

It is useful to remember that the common currency has a unique external exchange rate, equal for all member countries. If the performance of national economies is different, in particular if productivity diverges among member countries, there will be problematic domestic and external consequences. In particular, domestic prices in different countries do not converge or tend to diverge as much as real exchange rates do. The cumulative effect of these events makes national incomes and foreign trade performance to diverge. It is hard to see how an incomplete monetary union can survive under these conditions, unless member countries — resilient and vulnerable alike — are ready to continue to lend impressive amounts of resources to countries in distress, lending that may have dubious degrees of reimbursement. This amounts to converting taxpayers into lenders of last resort. Hence either the incomplete monetary union becomes complete as soon as possible, thus creating full and complete common policy competences and instruments, or the performance of national economies converges, so as to make policies less needed.

These questions lead to contemplate further, in the next section, the alternatives the Eurozone is confronted with, and to consider the issues of restructuring and reforms in the following section.

12.4 Alternatives

A consensus is developing among policymakers and scholars that policies and actions which were followed and implemented so far did not work. Those policies may have helped to avoid the worst consequences, including open default of some member countries or even the break-up of the

Eurozone. However, such policies failed to bring vulnerable economies back to growth and are not sustainable in the medium or long run.

However, scholars and policymakers disagree on what exactly should be done at this point to restore the sustainability of the Eurozone and promote the growth of vulnerable economies.[270] The main alternatives that are considered are the following. The first alternative consists of retaining austerity policies and softening them by using the flexibility that exists in European agreements (EC 2015a) or through more expansionary monetary policies. This is the present broad agreement in the Eurozone, albeit one that is not fully defined and still in part implicit. It includes the slowing down of the implementation of the budget adjustment envisisioned in the fiscal compact, in particular for countries with lower debts; the definition of the budget deficit in structural terms; and expansionary monetary policies within the present mandate of the ECB.

A second alternative, not in contrast with the former but preferably complementary to it, is the setting up of a European plan for investments. This is one of the important aims of the new European Commission appointed at the end of 2014 and headed by Jean-Claude Juncker.[271] The so-called Juncker plan foresees an overall investment of €315 billion over three years (2015–2017). Of these, €21 billion is financed and guaranteed by the newly established European Fund for Strategic Investments set up by the EU and the European Investment Bank. The rest should be financed by public and private contributions, with a leverage of 15.

A third alternative, again complementary to the preceding one, consists of solving the incompleteness of Eurozone institutions. A first, yet important step was moved in 2014 with the foundation of the European banking union.[272] The banking union mainly consists of the Single Supervisory Mechanism and Single Resolution Mechanism. These mechanisms are based upon a common financial regulatory framework ("single rulebook"). Bolder interpretations in the monetary fields consider

---

[270] The present conflict between the EU and the governments of its resilient countries and the new Greek government is actually on this issue.

[271] Claeys *et al.* (2014), Veugelers (2014). See also EC (2015q) and EIB (2015).

[272] Pisani-Ferry *et al.* (2012), EC (2015r).

transforming the ECB in a true lender of last resort. There are two versions of this view: lender of last resort only for private banks (Winkler 2014)[273] or also for governments (De Grauwe 2014; Goodhart and Schoenmaker 2014).[274] In any case many economists, particularly in Germany, oppose such views (Illing and König 2014).[275]

Mutualisation of sovereign debt was an important issue at stake, particularly in 2011 and 2012, when vulnerable countries were in serious distress and interest rates on their sovereign debt were rapidly and significantly increasing. Various scholars and policymakers advanced the idea of introducing bonds, defined in different ways, in order to pool the sovereign debt of Eurozone countries under joint liability, typically up to 60% of GDP foreseen in convergence criteria (Beetsma and Mavromatis 2012; Claessens *et al.* 2013). In this way, member countries become jointly responsible for anyone's debt, in full or above a certain threshold. Predictably, this solution encountered strong opposition, particularly by the governments of resilient countries. In fact, they were afraid to soften excessively the budget constraint of vulnerable countries[276] and of being called to pay the bulk of the cost.

---

[273] Winkler (2014) addresses four arguments that are used to explain why it is acceptable to have the ECB as a lender of last resort for banks, while this role for governments should be rejected.

[274] According to De Grauwe (2013), the ECB should also be the lender of last resort in the government bond markets of the monetary union, in order to prevent countries from being pushed into bad equilibria by self-fulfilling fears of liquidity crises in a monetary union. Goodhart and Schoenmaker (2014) maintain that, after the introduction of the euro, the national central banks continued to act as lenders of last resort because bank supervision remained at the national level. Since supervision moved to the ECB through the new banking union, so should the lender of last resort function for the larger, cross-border banks.

[275] Illing and König (2014) argue that it is questionable whether the purchase of government bonds of distressed countries is included in the ECB's mandate. They also suggest that the European Stability Mechanism (ESM) would be better suited to act as a lender of last resort for governments and it should be given access to ECB credit facilities in order to fully perform this function.

[276] Wyplosz *et al.* (2011) stress that eurobonds would reduce the odds of a sovereign crisis at the cost of creating a very serious moral hazard and softening discipline promotion. This refers in particular to the Juncker/Tremonti proposal of December 2010, a proposal

The preceding proposals are under discussion and seem to be in some way under implementation. The most critical one are Eurobonds, which so far were never formally accepted. Yet some partial forms of debt mutualisation are used: the most recent ECB programme of expanded asset purchase actually includes a share of indirect debt mutualisation (see Section 11.8). Other proposals are sometimes debated. These include the idea of a political union, although a first step, the plan for a European constitution, failed in 2004. Another radical proposal is to abandon convergence criteria, either as an extraordinary measure during the crisis or as a permanent reform. Proposals like the latter seem too radical to be seriously considered, since they would *de facto* mean to abandon the common currency, or at least go to the full mutualisation of public debts.

A fourth alternative, perhaps the most controversial one, would be to set up a common economic government. It is not always clear what this means and what would be needed, particularly in legal and institutional terms, provided that member countries agree on this perspective. While a real unique government (a European economic and finance ministry with full sovereignty) would be the strongest version, it is not the most realistic one for the time being. Such an accomplishment would give a compelling institutional and policy solution to the management of the economy and finances, but would open new questions. The keenest ones would be the intercountry distributive consequences of fiscal policies and perhaps also their inflationary effects. While the latter could be rather easily manageable, given the independence of the ECB, the former would require compensatory agreements among countries. Simplification on the side of policymaking would consequently be compensated by much increased complexity in the management of consequences. A European minister with limited sovereignty, acting as a pivot and coordinator of national ministers, together with a form of partial debt mutualisation (e.g. up to

privileging crisis solution at the cost of encouraging fiscal indiscipline. Other proposals, such as the one advanced by Delpla and von Weizsäcker, use the idea of Eurobonds to promote fiscal discipline, while overlooking the need to reduce the odds of a sovereign crisis. Wyplosz *et al.* (2011) support an intermediate proposal that would both alleviate the threat of crises and enhance discipline, although they admit that no idea of this sort has been put forward so far. See also Claessens *et al.* (2013).

the 60% of GDP) seem more realistic achievements. When they show their positive effects, government building could proceed to more ambitious forms.

A good starting point for proceeding towards a more effective monetary union would be to reach a consensus on past accomplishments and on the problems ahead. Unfortunately, there is no such consensus and there is still a fundamental disagreement on how policies should be changed and institutions completed. Disagreement also concerns the future of the common currency and the fate of some of its member countries.

Radical options for some country to leave the euro or to break up the monetary union are sometimes proposed also by serious scholars.[277] The debate on the option for one country to leave the common currency came recurrently back, particularly in the case of Greece (Nuti 2015b). The neologism "Grexit" was coined to refer to this event. Calculations were prepared to estimate the probable cost to both Greece and the other Eurozone countries (Mchugh 2014). The conditions for a country to leave the euro and for the others to adapt were enquired (Bootle 2011).

There are both institutional and economic problems to this event. Institutionally, European treaties do not foresee this possibility. It was suggested that before leaving the euro a country should leave first the EU. Economically, the event would be a massive blow to that country in both financial and political terms. Financially, the probable strong depreciation of the new national currency to the euro would decrease real incomes and savings, while national public and private debt, at least the external one, would remain in euros. Added to this, there is the intractable problem of loans that a country like Greece obtained from European institutions and member countries and from the IMF as a bailout attempt. All these loans are denominated in euros: an exit would dramatically increase their real

[277] In a presentation on "The Future of Europe" at UBS International Center of Economics in Society, University of Zurich, Basel, January 27, 2014, Joseph Stiglitz said that "...leaving the euro will be painful but staying in the euro will be more painful." "The argument that there are significant advantages to sharing a common currency is at best questionable. If you look at the overall benefits Europe, the Eurozone has enjoyed from having a common currency, looking at it from 2000 to say 2014, I think net, you would say, it has probably been a negative" (Stiglitz 2014b).

value and oblige the country to default or else lenders would suffer massive losses. The country would be closed off from international markets for years and would find extremely difficult and costly to obtain finance. Politically, the country could remain isolated for a long time, with severed financial and trade relations. These consequences would more than compensate the economic advantage that the country would obtain from a much weaker currency.

A different, less dramatic option would be for Germany or other resilient countries to leave the euro (Steinherr 2013). This would not be costly for these countries, since their currency would appreciate, thus making their debts denominated in euros less expensive. Yet appreciation would be disadvantageous in trade relations.

Apparently less problematic is the event of an orderly exit to two or more currencies, each one common to a more homogeneous group of countries. There are two variants to this event. According to one, the euro should split into two: one for resilient countries and one for vulnerable countries (Steinherr 2013). This event would probably run lower economic costs than the cases discussed above. However, in political terms it would probably be worse and destroy the very ideal reasons for which the continental integration was set up in the post-war period. A second variant foresees an orderly dismantling of the Eurozone, starting with the exit of the most competitive countries (Kawalec and Pytlarczyk 2013). The euro should remain for a while the common currency of less competitive countries and the ECB should be preserved as the central bank for all Eurozone member countries, even after some of those countries replaced the euro with new currencies. A proper management would limit the economic and financial risks and costs throughout the process. It is doubtful that this solution would contribute to rebuilding confidence in the future of Europe.

Three alternative positions in the recent analytical and political scenario of the common currency appear worthy of consideration. They have in common deep criticism of how the monetary integration was implemented and share keen concern for not losing the value of past efforts and present sacrifices. However, they diverge on the solutions. According to the first position, the mistake was introducing the euro too soon and in an incomplete way (Nuti 2015a). The euro was introduced before political and fiscal integration, and integration of defence and foreign policy. The ECB lacks independence and is forbidden to purchase government bonds in primary markets. The member countries have increasing divergence of the monetary, fiscal and real parameters, which EU austerity aggravated. Under these conditions, there is a very high risk that the Eurozone will face low growth and prolonged slump over at least the next decade (Guerrieri 2015). To avoid this danger, common institutions should be completed and policies changed through the creative evolution of the ECB and the relaxation of EU austerity. Growth should be also promoted through symmetric macroeconomic adjustment, an effective joint-liability banking union, and a mix of Keynesian and Schumpeterian policies based on long-term investments.

Improper fiscal management is not the fundamental cause of the Euro crisis for the second position (Steinherr 2015). External imbalances, lack of governance, lack of clarity on the no-bailout clause, and disregard for how to cope with any crisis are at least equally important. Since the focus on reinforced fiscal rules neither deals with the causes of the crisis nor with the magnitude of the institutional problems, other measures are needed: ad hoc and once-and-for-all measures to get out of the crisis, and treaty changes to strengthen the monetary union and to better define responsibilities for each member.

The question of asymmetric power and roles within the Eurozone, the core issue of the third position, is the fundamental question to be disentangled for solving the crisis (Tamborini 2015). It is the unwillingness of the dominant economic power, Germany, to take on the responsibility that goes with economic power that prevents the Eurozone from moving forward. As a leader, Germany would represent the common good, a role that would require different policy priorities and new policies in exchange for the possibility to exert greater control. This would require an ambitious programme of institutional reforms to create a new economic and monetary union.

These three positions share the goal of revitalising the Eurozone by upgrading institutions, investing in the real economy and changing policies. These are fundamental parts of the definitive and sustainable answers to the present problems.

12.5 An Uneasy Match

The fundamental problem that the Eurozone is affording concerns the necessity to pursue fiscal stabilisation, institutional reforms and economic growth and development at the same time. The inability to manage the crisis was due to the lack of complete and effective institutions, and of coordination and trust among the member countries. From these factors, there came the dominance of rigid short-term objectives and policies, at both the common and national levels. These factors also explain the weakening of the transmission mechanism of the common monetary policy, its asymmetric effects in different countries and the poor response of national economies to policies. The final consequences are poor performance, loss of international competitiveness, and permanent damages to the European economic potential and the life of European citizens, particularly in the vulnerable countries.

So far the Eurozone governance and national governments concentrated almost exclusively on financial stability. However, as discussed in previous chapters, many of the roots of the Eurozone crisis are microeconomic and real in nature. Under these circumstances, the prevailing approach in Brussels and the capital cities of some of the resilient countries was generating solutions leading to counterproductive and depressive outcomes. Although these first concern vulnerable countries, their unfavourable effects spread to resilient countries through financial and real linkages. A major detrimental effect in the long term is that the negative consequences are spread unevenly and typically and disproportionately affect the population living with fixed incomes. Particularly damaging are the consequences for a very high number of young people, without recourse to steady employment, stable social protection or protective regulations (Cappellari and Staffolani 2008; Standing 2011). This risks leading to a permanent decrease of the potential GDP, thus causing a structural worsening of the debt-GDP ratio. The consequences could be the downfall of stabilisation policies and the disruption of social cohesion.

There is growing awareness in the Eurozone that institutional reforms are necessary for deepening integration, but this awareness is still short of what is required. There is an urgent need for a comprehensive strategy for Eurozone stabilisation, institutional completion and consolidation, and economic recovery and development. This comprehensive strategy should place the necessary short-term stabilisation measures into the long-term perspective of institutional and economic development. It should also include a more flexible and differentiated approach to stabilisation policies.[278]

Clearly, it would mean the greatest effort from vulnerable countries. Resilient countries should support this effort with complementary policies and with their contribution to the reform of common institutions. Time matters and vulnerable countries should get a longer-term and more flexible framework in exchange for greater effort and more credible commitment. To do so, it seems inevitable that third party enforcement by common organs and institutions should be strengthened, with a longer time perspective in mind and a more balanced mandate between financial stability and economic growth and development.

There is a growing awareness within the Eurozone that a common currency cannot continue without a common governance of the economy. The Eurozone is not a sovereign country and cannot easily implement large-scale intercountry redistributive policies without meeting with political and social opposition from the resilient countries. What is still missing in the Eurozone is the political and institutional awareness that financial stabilisation measures and even the reform of the institutional architecture lead nowhere if not coupled with measures and reforms aimed at improving the efficiency and effectiveness of the microeconomic structure of the economy, in particular in vulnerable countries, and promoting growth. All these individual measures and reforms should be coordinated at both the common level and intercountry level.

The question of reforms is particularly important and complex. There is an international agreement, strongly supported by the EU and international organisations such as the IMF, the World Bank and the Organisation for Economic Cooperation and Development (OECD), that the revival of

---

[278] Buti and Carnot (2015) propose a rule of thumb governing fiscal expansion that is consistent for a group of countries, and for each country individually. Different governments should apply different levels of consolidation or stimulus depending on their country's situation. Positive spillovers to other member countries would strengthen the effectiveness of policies. De Grauwe and Ji (2015b) show that a programme of quantitative easing successfully targeting deflation can be structured so that it does not mix fiscal and monetary policy. It would thus not impose a risk on taxpayers of resilient countries.

vulnerable countries needs structural reforms. According to the European Commission, structural reforms are fundamental, since they address obstacles to the fundamental drivers of growth.[279] Reforms, in this view, coincide with the liberalisation of labour, product and service markets, in the belief that this would strengthen competition, encourage an economy's job creation and investment, improve productivity and in the end enhance competitiveness, growth potential and adjustment capacity.

These reforms are essential, in particular for vulnerable countries. The ineffective and inefficient working of markets is in fact a fundamental reason for vulnerability. The problem with these reforms, however, is not in their nature or importance, but in the way they are proposed and implemented. As a matter of fact, they are urged more as a precondition for internal devaluation than for their intrinsic importance. While this pressure, and their being part of conditionality packages in exchange for financial support, may be important to overcome a national stalemate and foot dragging, requests for structural reform tend to overlook other important aspects. These have to do with the partial nature of these reforms and the intertemporal features of reform implementation.

The situation of national markets is usually as much the result of deep seated habits and privileges as of the lack of alternatives. A typical case is given in the labour market: liberalisation means, among other things, professional and spatial mobility. Lack of mobility may be the outcome of unjustified privileges, but may also be the outcome of quality control, particularly in continental Europe, and job specific investments, the lack of a dynamic and affordable housing market, or the policy attempt to support a less developed region or social group. These are important aspects that should be considered and managed, not to stop structural reforms, but to master these reforms together with other important aspects of life in a country. These aspects have usually to do with formal or informal institutions and for this reason this book stresses the need to manage simultaneously both institutional and structural reforms. This is the only way to ensure sustainability and effectiveness of reforms and, in the end, their economic benefits.

---

[279] EC (2015p), Canton *et al.* (2014). A similar definition is used by Alesina *et al.* (2008). See also OECD's *Going for Growth*, which also explicitly considers reform of taxation, public administration and civil justice.

The intertemporal side of structural reforms is important and generally forgotten. Activating competition in the services or product markets is difficult, both politically and technically. The opposition of strong and well-organised privileged groups gaining from inefficient markets (enterprises, self-employed professionals), perhaps with effective political connections in government parties, can be very strong and effective. It is also difficult because liberalisation processes are typically long and complex and often require going through various levels of courts.

Conversely, labour market reforms may be easier, at least in times of crisis and where there is a serious threat of unemployment. The likely outcome is that labour market reforms are implemented, while the others lag behind. If so, the danger is that labour market reforms decrease wages (both directly and indirectly, as costs, such as those of mobility, are transferred to employees) and social security. This would decrease the purchasing power of employees and create uncertainty about their future, effects which are not compensated for by the decrease of prices, due to delayed reforms of other markets. Thus, even putting aside such issues as the likely negative effect on incentives and the social conflict these reforms may cause, the consequence would be decreased internal demand, a fact that certainly does not spur growth.

The need to consider and manage also the institutional side of competitiveness and growth and the intertemporal aspects of reforms should lead governments to embed structural reforms in the broader framework of institutions and time and also consider alternatives and solutions to foster support to reforms. An alternative would be a progressive global tax on capital, as proposed in Piketty (2014). Another possibility would be to compensate employees who, due to structural reforms and not only in vulnerable countries, have lost income, rights and perspectives in a way that does not worsen costs or productivity. This could be done, e.g. by compensating employees with property rights or by giving them decision-making and participation rights in their workplace (EC 2015s).[280]

---

[280] This latter perspective is actively supported by the European Commission under its support to workplace innovation, including the reinforced 2012 EU Industrial Policy Communication and the European Workplace Innovation Network (EUWIN). The latter is a Europe-wide learning network launched in 2013 to support this priority by improving the performance of organisations and the quality of jobs in a sustainable way.

The issue of reforms is particularly daunting. An important aim of reforms in the Eurozone is to pursue the institutional convergence of Eurozone economies and lay the groundwork for structural convergence as necessary conditions for the viability of the common currency. There is a need to reform the Eurozone institutional architecture through common reforms, and there is a need to reform the institutional architecture of member countries and strengthen institutional convergence. Reforms could be pursued and implemented both through a federalist agenda or through an intergovernmental agenda. The process would be different in the two cases and would lead to different outcomes.

A federalist agenda would start from a common vision of the nature and the future of the Eurozone, would implement a consistent reform of the common institutional architecture, and would require each member country to reform in order to support the federalist implementation. The outcome would be strong, but coordination and implementation costs would be high. One critical problem of this approach is that a common agenda cannot reflect all national priorities with the same importance. This opens inevitably the issues of compromise and compensation. Delegation of more decision-making power to the European Parliament and to the European Commission, possibly appointed by the elected Parliament, would ease this process. Commitment of individual countries needs to be full and credible, and moral hazards need to be replaced by trust among member countries, with credible enforcement by the common and accountable organs. Common support and action and coordination of reforms are also important, so as to overcome the blocking of reforms by interest groups. The construction and evolution of the ECB may provide some interesting hints as to how this process could unfold.

The intergovernmental agenda avoids these problems, but falls short of true integration. Yet this is perhaps the only viable perspective in the present. The main difference with the present situation is that the organs of the Eurozone governance and national governments agree on a long-term agenda of comprehensive and coordinated measures and reforms, supported by a stronger common budget than the present one. The European Commission and the ECB took a bolder position than in the past and national governments of resilient countries appear to be aware of the dangers and the need to change their standing. However, a true coordination among the different organs, a genuine commonality of vision and intent and a long-run comprehensive strategy for reform and revival are still missing.

One advantage of proceeding in a coordinated way to reform is the possibility of avoiding the race to the bottom in the efforts to reform. If the latter happens, the solution of the problems of one country in the short run creates problems for other countries. A case in point is the Hartz reform in Germany. Germany took the first move at the right time and implemented important reforms in the early 2000s. These reforms bore important fruit by improving the German economy's competitiveness, at some cost to employees. Other countries, such as Italy, that postponed the needed reforms for years, are paying the price of having ineffective and inefficient institutions and markets and low competitiveness. Yet Germany used the reforms to the exclusive advantage of its economy and refused to reflate, being in the position to do so, in order to support vulnerable countries.

Reform in one part of the monetary union and lack of reform in another part causes diverging competitiveness within the Eurozone. Such dissimilarity bears significant responsibility for the national crises in weak economies. In fact, the unwillingness or inability of vulnerable countries to reform in time and the very success of resilient countries to reform made any subsequent effort by non-reforming countries more difficult and costlier, unless reformed countries take a more cooperative approach. Although this outcome largely affects non-reforming countries, the consequent debacle of their economy in turn affects reformed countries through trade and financial linkages.[281]

[281] Examples of national reforms needed particularly in vulnerable countries are various and are influenced by the particular situation of each country. Particularly important are fostering and supporting entrepreneurship and enterprise foundation and growth, job creation, labour management, flexicurity and workplace innovation, simplification of administrative rules, promoting the effectiveness of bureaucracy, restructuring economic specialisation, promoting innovation, fostering the formation of human capital and research, and promoting growth and development.

12.6 Muddling Through a *Terra Incognita:* Towards A New Pragmatism?

The Eurozone is confronted with the consequences of past mistakes. Some were common, others were a result of national opportunism with consequent moral hazards, others from the ordoliberal lack of cooperation by resilient countries. There is perhaps truth in the accusation that introducing the euro too early, before the necessary accomplishments of political and fiscal integration and amidst incomplete institutions was wrong (Nuti 2015a; Pisani-Ferry 2012; Rosefielde and Razin 2012). However, it should be noted that the euro was conceived also as a device for fostering European economic and political integration as earlier as in 1970, particularly in the Werner Report. In the same vein, it was also considered an important expedient to urge member countries to reform their economies.

The Werner Report (1970) had a progressive and bold view of the European integration. The report was not particularly concerned with imposing hard rules of financial behaviour upon the members of the monetary union and saw intercountry transfers, including transfers of sovereignty, and political coordination and integration as necessary complements to the monetary union.[282]

With such an approach, the Werner Report's view is that "only the global balance of payments of the Community vis-à-vis the outside world is of any importance. Equilibrium within the Community would be realised at this stage in the same way as within a nation's frontiers, thanks to the mobility of the factors of production and financial transfers by the public and private sectors" (Werner Report, 1970, p. 10). With hindsight, this statement refers more to a model economic and monetary integration than to the European reality.

---

[282]"To ensure the cohesion of economic and monetary union, transfers of responsibility from the national to the Community plane will be essential. These transfers will be kept within the limits necessary for the effective operation of the Community and will concern essentially the whole body of policies determining the realization of general equilibrium. In addition, it will be necessary for the instruments of economic policy to be harmonized in the various sectors" (Werner Report, 1970, p. 10).

The other fundamental report on the future of European integration is the Delors Report (1989), named after the chairman of the committee assigned to come up with a plan for European integration.[283] This report envisaged a greater role for national governments and consequently a softer role and nature of the European Community. However, it anticipated the necessity for countries to be bound in their financial freedom, in order not to destabilise the monetary union. In this sense, the Delors Report correctly predicated the path of European integration and highlighted its essential character and, finally, problem: if countries, which are different from many perspectives, not only economic ones, want to integrate also monetarily, they need to place "a wide range of decisions… [that] remain the preserve of national and regional authorities" and these decisions "would have to be placed within an agreed macroeconomic framework and be subject to binding procedures and rules." The need to coordinate and check national policymaking derives from the potential impact that these decisions have "on the overall domestic and external economic situation of the Community and their implications for the conduct of a common monetary policy". This approach "would permit the determination of an overall policy stance for the Community as a whole, avoid unsustainable differences between individual member countries in public-sector borrowing requirements and place binding constraints on the size and the financing of budget deficits" (Delors Report 1989, p. 14).

The Werner Report's trust in private resource mobility, in particular labour, was never particularly high in Europe and continues to be problematic. This approach implicitly expects not only geographical and sectorial mobility, but also high price flexibility, which is hardly a feature of continental European economies. The approach also overlooks the fact that there may be structural features that put particular countries or regions at a permanent disadvantage. These are consequently unable to offer convenient conditions for investment. The approach also presupposes that there are transfers of public resources, thus overlooking the

[283] Jacques Lucien Jean Delors was a minister in France before being appointed for three terms as President of the European Commission between January 1985 and December 1994. The Werner Report was prepared by a working group chaired by Pierre Werner, Luxembourg's Prime Minister and Minister for Finances.

long-term coexistence within the economic and monetary union of countries with overall disciplined and balanced public finances and other countries which, for various reasons, were unable or politically unwilling to do so. Here lies much of the problem of the Eurozone: insufficient resource mobility and structural problems that prevent resource mobility, unbalanced public finances which make potential support by financially sound countries problematic.

The Delors Report is more realistic in this sense, which is understandable also in view of the nearly two decades that have elapsed since the Werner Report. The Delors Report anticipates and mirrors rather well the situation that had evolved and the solutions that were implemented. In the Eurozone, exchange rate adjustments are no longer available to correct economic imbalances. "Such *imbalances might arise* because the process of adjustment and restructuring set in motion by the removal of physical, technical and fiscal barriers is unlikely to have an even impact on different regions or always produce satisfactory results within reasonable periods of time. Imbalances might also emanate from labour and other cost developments, external shocks with differing repercussions on individual economies, or divergent economic policies pursued at national level... None the less, such imbalances, if left uncorrected, would manifest themselves as regional disequilibria. Measures designed to strengthen the mobility of factors of production and the flexibility of prices would help to deal with such imbalances" (Delors Report 1989, p. 15) ("emphasis in the original").

This statement in the Delors Report leads us to consider the fundamental role of reforms. Reforms are essential yet they always meet a crucial timing problem: reforms are costly in the short term and promise advantages in the long run. This is the usual problem of the inter-temporal (and perhaps inter-generational) allocation of costs and advantages. Yet in the Eurozone, there is the additional problem of the intercountry allocation of costs and disadvantages. Countries that have to reform the most, i.e. that have to bear the greatest costs and face the most difficulties, are the countries that suffered most at the institutional level, in particular the loss of the exchange rate adjustment.

These countries are requested to follow the lead of resilient countries and reform boldly. However, they may once again encounter an inter-temporal problem: by the time they had reformed, resilient countries may well continue to be ahead. If so, vulnerable countries may be required to afford the costs of reforms without being able to resolve once and for all their relative disadvantage compared to resilient countries. This clearly poses a political and social problem of how to guarantee vulnerable countries that — if they proceed with the costly reforms as they are required — they would not be at a permanent disadvantage. The danger is that vulnerable countries are unable to invest due to the lack of their own resources and inability to attract external resources, since they offer unattractive rewards or greater risk. At the same time, resilient countries become stronger through investment and technical progress, also financed with the resources that leave the vulnerable countries.

These issues lead back to the Werner Report. They raise the fundamental question of whether it is possible that the Eurozone, under pressure stemming from its inability to find convenient common solutions to its daunting problems, returns to the central question of political unification. Are the euro and the problems that threaten its sustainability pushing the Eurozone to comply with what it should have started with? If so, the euro could be seen in the future as the lever by means of which Europeans succeeded in freeing themselves of their nationalistic stance for good. The euro would in this case help Europeans replace historically dangerous nationalisms with sounder national sentiments. These would contribute to make European integration more varied and lively, yet sound. A failure of the process could instead invert the outcome and strengthen nationalistic contrasts.

To avoid the unpleasant choice between the nation and the common, the process of European integration was progressively transformed — from its political start based on a common vision based on the tragedy of World War II and idealism — into a technical, nearly mechanical process. It worked reasonably well for decades and produced wellbeing and political stability for Europeans. The crisis interrupted the illusion and recalled Europeans back to the hard reality of the economy and to the necessity to remind that economic integration is (also) a fundamental political and social question.

12.7 Conclusions

A rather consistent and considerable split between two groups of countries, vulnerable and resilient ones, is perhaps the most distinctive feature of the Eurozone. The split existed before the crisis, but it was the management of the crisis that made it evident and potentially dangerous for the monetary union. Large and persistent dissimilarities between different regions or countries are not unusual. What makes the Eurozone distinct is that it lacks a common government of the economy and a lender of last resort. Although, under the impact of the crisis, important steps were implemented towards surrogate solutions (the peers' governance and ECB activism), the Eurozone is still deeply unbalanced and incomplete in terms of policymaking. There is a serious problem for vulnerable countries due to their lack of effective policy instruments. This fact makes the situation of vulnerable countries potentially hazardous for other vulnerable countries and even for resilient countries.

Often economies come out stronger from a crisis, after having learned from their previous mistakes and implementing proper institutional and policy solutions. The question is, in the case of the Eurozone, whether the long-term common goals dominate over shorter-run goals. Apparently the time is ripe for bolder steps forward towards a deeper and more complete monetary, economic and perhaps political integration. Europeans may start to be convinced that the only way forward is to build *ex post* what the others have implemented *ex ante*. This refers to a common government of the economy managing fiscal policy, a lender of last resort fully managing the common currency, and a common political government.

Thanks to the crisis and in spite of all the difficulties and shortcomings, the Eurozone member countries may start to become aware that a common currency requires a cooperative interaction even in times of severe crisis, needs a longer perspective, and requires better defined and shared economic and political priorities. In short, mutual trust is fundamental, particularly when institutions are incomplete.

Vulnerable countries proved themselves to have remarkable endurance during the crisis and withstood the economic and social costs and difficulties of onerous and detrimental austerity policies. They also continued to support their participation in the common currency, with notable fortitude. This perseverance may play a fundamental role in a new Eurozone, since it shows that all Eurozone member countries consider the common currency as their top priority, to which the present welfare can be sacrificed. It may give reliable guarantees to resilient countries on the commitment of vulnerable countries in playing a cooperative game. If so, it is now (also) up to resilient countries to demonstrate that they share the same belief and determination. It should also be up to them to show that they did not forget the common support they enjoyed on different occasions in the past, be it German unification or past crises. What is certain is that the Eurozone cannot continue as it did in the years since the crisis started.

Chapter 8 introduced the issue of policy frames as an important reason for Eurozone's misunderstanding and contrasts. If the crisis was effective in changing the attitude and the perspective of member countries, then one can expect that economic, political and social commitment of vulnerable countries, patience and some pragmatic flexibility on the side of resilient countries, and ingenuity by Eurozone institutions and in particular the ECB may foster the gradual fading away of confirmatory biases and consequently of equilibrium fictions. If this is correct, there may be some convergence of framing in the direction of shared "Euroframes", a necessary precondition for the success of reforms.

Yet the present Eurozone landscape is still patchy and much work must be done. The positive outcomes of the crisis mentioned above appear to be under way, yet it is difficult to believe that they have already reached the critical mass necessary to break through and structurally change the Eurozone. Various signs of a new spirit can be seen: the determination of the ECB; the determination of vulnerable countries to reform; some increasing flexibility of the new European Commission established in 2014 and its greater determination to support growth; and some pragmatism by resilient countries. Could these signs be the start of a new implicit agreement, trading internal reforms in exchange for more flexible convergence criteria, and hopefully of long-term criteria in place of short-term constraints? There is a reasonable hope that the agreement over Greece in the summer of 2015 goes in this direction.

If so, a danger still exists: that vulnerable countries push ahead in the illusion that the old austerity game is over soon. The critical issue would then be: is the vulnerable countries' commitment to reform their economies solid and long-lasting and beyond any danger of opportunistic reversal? Is the time of austerity endured so far sufficient to convince the European Commission and resilient countries that vulnerable countries are credible in their commitment and that insisting on the ways of the past is negative for everybody and destructive for some of the vulnerable countries? Or is the pressure from vulnerable countries to ease austerity policies proof that after all, they did not change and were simply waiting opportunistically, in the hope that resilient countries would give up? Does the present economic situation of the Eurozone allow for such a change of tactics, if not strategy?

Positive signs are perhaps slowly overtaking the negative elements. It is to be seen whether Eurozone change is fast enough, while also considering external circumstances, to take advantage of the new mood. But there is a further possibility: implicitly concerted and coordinated muddling through, perhaps the outcome of tensions like the one that saw Greece in conflict with resilient Eurozone countries and European institutions.

Muddling through could perhaps be a useful tactic, if short lived. It could ease the situation by maximising the use of flexibility that exists in the treaties and pacts and couple it with a supportive ECB attitude and action and the take-off of the EC's investment plan. This approach would gain some time for the implementation of reforms and maintaining pressure. It would also contribute to consolidating intergovernmental trust, and open some possibilities for slow economic revival.

However, this would be insufficient to solve the problems of vulnerable countries. Yet, it could be effective in overcoming the residual difficulties on the road to reforming vulnerable economies and towards a more collaborative and institutionally more complete Eurozone. After all, this method should be congenial to European countries and rather similar to the approach used to build up the EU and the Eurozone: step by step, through a predefined and preannounced trajectory mixed with much intergovernmental bargaining. If this period of transition brings the hoped stability and policy progress, then conditions would be ripe to proceed with more demanding goals: political unification, including a Eurozone government of the economy.

These measures, together with a complete central bank, would progressively dilute the clauses — no bailout, no-mutualisation and no-monetisation — that are hindering the takeoff of an effective and complete monetary unification. The long-run interest of Europeans pushes in this direction. Yet the short-run political and economic interest of European nations may push in other directions. Above all, it is imperative to note that there is a dangerous democratic deficit in the management of Europe and that time may not be on the side of building a more effective union. Only a bolder and more forward looking European governance based on credible commitment and enforcement can allow common interest to take over, with the support of mutual trust and forward looking national governance.

Bibliography

Acemoglu, David and James A. Robinson (2012), *Why Nations Fail: the Origins of Power, Prosperity and Poverty*, New York: Crown Publishers.

Acocella, Nicola (2005), *Economic Policy in the Age of Globalisation*, Cambridge: Cambridge University Press.

Adrian, Tobias and Hyun Song Shin (2009), 'The Shadow Banking System: Implications for Financial Regulation', *Staff Report No. 382*, July, Federal Reserve Bank of New York (https://www.newyorkfed.org/medialibrary/media/research/staff_reports/sr382.pdf).

Afonso, António and Ana Sequeira (2010), 'Revisiting Business Cycle Synchronization in the European Union', School of Economics and Management, Technical University of Lisbon, *Working Papers*, WP 22/2010/DE/UECE.

Aggarwal, Raj and John W. Goodell (2014), 'Cross-national differences in access to finance: Influence of culture and institutional environments', *Research in International Business and Finance*, Vol. 31, pp. 193–211.

Ahmad, Nadim, François Lequiller, Pascal Marianna, Dirk Pilat, Paul Schreyer and Anita Wölfl (2003), 'Comparing Labour Productivity Growth in the OECD Area: The Role of Measurement', *OECD Statistics Working Paper 2003/5.*

Aiello, Francesco, Valeria Pupo and Fernanda Ricotta (2010), 'Un'analisi territoriale della produttività totale dei fattori in Italia', *Working Paper 07/2010*, Dipartimento di Economia e Statistica, Università della Calabria, April.

Aiginger, Karl and Wolfgang Leitner (2002), 'Regional concentration in the United States and Europe: Who follows whom?', *Weltwirtschaftliches Archiv*, Vol. 138, No. 4, pp. 652–679.

Aizenman, Joshua and Hiro Ito (2014), 'Living with the trilemma constraint: Relative trilemma policy divergence, crises, and output losses for developing countries', *Journal of International Money and Finance*, Vol. 49, Part A, pp. 28–51.

Alesina, Alberto, Silvia Ardagna and Vincenzo Galasso (2008), 'The Euro and Structural Reforms', *NBER Working Paper 14479*, November (http://www.nber.org/papers/w14479).

Alessandrini, Sergio and Bruno Dallago (1987), eds., *The Unofficial Economy. Consequences and Perspectives in Different Economic Systems*, Aldershot: Gower.

Allard, Céline, Petya Koeva Brooks, John C. Bluedorn, Fabian Bornhorst, Katharine Christopherson, Franziska Ohnsorge, Tigran Poghosyan, and an IMF Staff Team (2013), 'Toward a Fiscal Union for the Euro Area', *IMF Staff Discussion Note SDN/13/09*, September, Washington DC: International Monetary Fund.

Alvaredo, Facundo, Anthony B. Atkinson, Thomas Piketty, and Emmanuel Saez (2013), 'The Top 1 Percent in International and Historical Perspective', *Journal of Economic Perspectives*, Vol. 27, No. 3, pp. 3–20.

Amable, Bruno (2003), *The Diversity of Modern Capitalism*, Oxford: Oxford University Press.

Andor, László (2014), *Imbalances & Inequalities in the EU: Challenges to the Europe 2020 Strategy*, Lecture at Université Libre de Bruxelles, Brussels: 10 October (http://europa.eu/rapid/press-release_SPEECH-14-684_en.htm).

Angerer, Jost (2015), *Stability and Growth Pact — An Overview of the Rules*, Briefing of the Directorate-General for Internal Policies and the Economic Governance Support Unit of the European Parliament, 6 May 2015 (http://www.europarl.europa.eu/RegData/etudes/note/join/2014/528745/IPOL-ECON_NT(2014)528745_EN.pdf).

Antonczyk, Christian and Astrid Juliane Salzmann (2014), 'Overconfidence and optimism: The effect of national culture on capital structure', *Research in International Business and Finance*, Vol. 31, May, pp. 132–151.

Aoki, Masahiko (2001), *Toward a Comparative Institutional Analysis*, Cambridge, MA. and London, MIT Press.

Aoki, Masahiko, Timur Kuran and Gérard Roland (2012), eds., *Institutions and Comparative Economic Development*, Palgrave Macmillan.

Apel, Rainer (2002), 'Maastricht Stability Pact is dead, awaits official burial', *Executive Intelligence Review*, 1 November 2002.

Aquino, Antonio, Lidia Mannarino, Valeria Pupo, Fernanda Ricotta and Marianna Succurro (2012), 'La dinamica della produttività in Italia: aspetti teorici ed empirici', *Economia italiana*, No. 3, pp. 677–705.

Arcand, Jean-Louis, Enrico Berkes and Ugo Panizza (2012), 'Too Much Finance?', *IMF Working Paper WP/12/161.*

Arslan, Cansin, Jean-Christophe Dumont, Zovanga Kone, Yasser Moullan, Caglar Ozden, Christopher Parsons and Theodora Xenogiani (2014), 'A New Profile of Migrants in the Aftermath of the Recent Economic Crisis', *OECD Social, Employment and Migration Working Papers*, No. 160, Paris: OECD.

Ash, Ken (2015), 'The emergence of global value chains: Implications for trade policy and trade agreements', in Bruno Dallago and John McGowan (eds.), *Crises in Europe in the Transatlantic Context: Economic and Political Appraisals*, Abingdon, Oxfordshire: Routledge, pp. 21–34.

Asher, Martin A., Robert H. Defina, and Kishor Thanawala (1993), 'The misery index: Only part of the story', *Challenge*, Vol. 36, No. 2, March-April, pp. 58–62.

Atkinson, Anthony B., Thomas Piketty and Emmanuel Saez (2011), 'Top incomes in the long run of history', *Journal of Economic Literature*, Vol. 49, No. 1, pp. 3–71.

Atkinson, Tyler, David Luttrell, and Harvey Rosenblum (2013), 'How Bad Was It? The Costs and Consequences of the 2007–09 Financial Crisis', *Staff PAPERS Federal Reserve Bank of Dallas*, No. 20, July.

Axelrod, Robert (1984), *The Evolution of Cooperation*, New York: Basic Books.

Baird, Katherine (2014), 'US Social Policy in an Era of Middle Class Decline: Is It Drifting from the Poor?', *LIS Working Paper Series No. 617*, Luxembourg Income Study (LIS), October, (http://www.lisdatacenter.org/wps/liswps/617.pdf).

Balczerowicz, Leszek, Andrzej Rzońca, Lech Kalina, and Aleksander Łaszek (2013), *Economic Growth in the European Union*, Brussels: The Lisbon Council.

Balducci, Renato and Stefano Staffolani (2002), 'Efficient Bargaining, Labour Share and Employment', in Renato Balducci and Stefano Staffolani (eds.), *Income Distribution, Growth and Employment*, Napoli: ESI, Vol. 1, pp. 27–53.

Baldwin, Richard and Daniel Gros (2010) 'Introduction: The euro in crisis — What to do?' in Richard Baldwin, David Gros and Luc Laeven (2010), *Completing the Eurozone Rescue: What More Needs to Be Done?*, London: VoxEU.org (http://www.voxeu.org/sites/default/files/file/Eurozone_Rescue.pdf).

Baldwin, Richard and Charles Wyplosz (2012), *The Economics of European Integration*, 4th ed., New York: McGraw Hill.

Bara, Yves-Emmanuel and Sophie Piton (2012), 'Internal vs. External devaluation', *La Lettre du CEPII*, No. 324, 1 August (http://www.cepii.fr/PDF_PUB/lettre/2012/let324ang.pdf).

Barbone, Luca, Misha V. Belkindas, Leon Bettendorff, Richard Bird, Mikhail Bonch-Osmolovskiy and Michael Smart (2013), *Study to Quantify and Analyse the VAT Gap in the EU-27 Member States. Final Report*, Warsaw: Center for Social and Economic Research (CASE), Warsaw and Central Planning Bureau (CPB), The Hague on behalf of the European Commission, July.

Barsky, Robert B. and Lutz Kilian (2000), 'A Monetary Explanation of the Great Stagflation of the 1970s', *NBER Working Paper Series*, Working Paper 7547, February (http://www.nber.org/papers/w7547).

Baumol, William J., Robert E. Litan, and Carl J. Schramm (2007), *Good Capitalism, Bad Capitalism, and the Economics of Growth and Prosperity*, New Haven & London: Yale University Press.

Baur, Dirk G. (2012), 'Financial contagion and the real economy', *Journal of Banking and Finance*, Volume 36, Issue 10, October 2012, pp. 2680–2692.

Bayoumi, Tamim and Hali Edison (2002), 'Is Wealth Increasingly Driving Consumption?', October (http://www.dnb.nl/en/binaries/con5_bayoumi_tcm47-152784.pdf).

Bayoumi, Tamim, Mika Saito and Jarkko Turunen (2013), 'Measuring Competitiveness: Trade in Goods or Tasks?', *IMF Working Paper WP/13/100*, International Monetary Fund.

BEA (US Department of Commerce, Bureau of Economic Analysis) (2008), A *Guide to the National Income and Product Accounts of the United States (NIPA)* (http://www.bea.gov/national/pdf/nipaguid.pdf).

BEA (2014), 'U.S. International Transactions', International Transactions, International Services, and International Investment Position Tables (Retrieved 1 December 2014 from http://www.bea.gov/iTable/iTable.cfm?ReqID=62&step=1#reqid=62&step=6&isuri=1&6221=0&6220=0&6210=1&6200=1&6224=&6223=&6222=0&6230=1).

Beck, Hanno and Aloys Prinz (2012), 'The trilemma of a monetary union: Another impossible trinity', *Intereconomics*, Volume 47, No. 1, January/February, pp. 39–43 (http://www.econstor.eu/bitstream/10419/98237/1/734509405.pdf).

Beck, Thorsten, Berrak Buyukkarabacak, Felix Rioja, and Neven Valev (2008), 'Who gets the credit? and does it matter? Household vs. firm lending across countries', *Policy Research Working Paper Series No. 4661*, The World Bank.

Beetsma, Roel and Konstantinos Mavromatis (2012), 'An Analysis of Eurobonds', *CEPR Discussion Paper Series No. 9244* (http://www.cepr.org/active/publications/discussion_papers/dp.php?dpno=9244).

Beine, Michel, Pauline Bourgeon and Jean-Charles Bricongne (2013), 'Aggregate Fluctuations and International Migration', *CESifo Working Paper No. 4379*, August.

Bélyácz, Iván and Erzsébet Szász (2015), 'The deeper roots of the financial system's propensity to crisis: The role of financialization in the global crisis', in Bruno Dallago and John McGowan (eds.), *Crises in Europe in the Transatlantic Context: Economic and Political Appraisals*, Abingdon, Oxfordshire: Routledge, pp. 35–50.

Bena, Jan and Kai Li (2014), 'Corporate Innovations and Mergers and Acquisitions', *The Journal of Finance*, Vol. 69, No. 5, pp. 1923–1960.

Bentivogli, Chiara and Patrizio Pagano (1999), 'Regional disparities and labour mobility: The Euro-11 versus the USA'; *Labour*, 13, pp. 737–760.

Bernanke, Ben S. (1983), 'Nonmonetary effects of the financial crisis in the propagation of the Great Depression', *American Economic Review*, Vol. 73, No. 3, pp. 257–276.

Bernanke, Ben S. (2004), *Essays on the Great Depression*, Princeton: Princeton University Press.

Bernanke, Ben S. (2012), 'Some Reflections on the Crisis and the Policy Response', Remarks presented to the conference on "*Rethinking Finance: Perspectives on the Crisis*", New York: Russell Sage Foundation and The Century Foundation, 13 April (http://www.federalreserve.gov/newsevents/speech/bernanke20120413a.pdf).

Bernanke, Ben S., Vincent R. Reinhart and Brian P. Sack (2004), 'Monetary Policy Alternatives at the Zero Bound: An Empirical Assessment', *Finance and Economics Discussion Series*, No. 48, Divisions of Research & Statistics and Monetary Affairs, Washington, DC: Federal Reserve Board (http://core.ac.uk/download/pdf/6893868.pdf).

Bernstein, Michael A. (2006), 'The American economic policy environment of the 1990s: Origins, consequences, and legacies', in Rhode and Toniolo (2006a), pp. 263–279.

Bertoli, Simone, Herbert Brücker and Jesús Fernández-Huertas Moraga (2013), 'The European Crisis and Migration to Germany. Expectations and the Diversion of Migration Flows', *IZA Discussion Paper No. 7170.*

Bertrand, Marianne, Matilde Bombardini, and Francesco Trebbi (2014), 'Is it whom you know or what you know? An empirical assessment of the lobbying process', *American Economic Review*, Vol. 104, No. 12, pp. 3885–3920.

Bertrand, Marianne, Dolly Chugh, and Sendhil Mullainathan (2005), 'Implicit Discrimination', *American Economic Review Papers and Proceedings*, Vol. 95, No. 2, pp. 94–98.

BI (2011a), *Annual Report*. Abridged version. Ordinary Meeting of Shareholders, Rome, 31 May 2011.

BI (2011b), 'The Governor's Concluding Remarks', Ordinary Meeting of Shareholders, Rome, 31 May 2011.

BI (2014), *Relazione Annuale Presentata all'Assemblea Ordinaria dei Partecipanti anno 2013 (Annual Report 2013)*, Rome: Bank of Italy, 30 May 2014.

Bivens, Josh and Lawrence Mishel (2015), 'Understanding the Historic Divergence between Productivity and a Typical Worker's Pay: Why It Matters and Why It's Real; *EPI Briefing Paper*, Washington D.C.: Economic Policy Institute, September 2 (http://www.epi.org/publiation/understanding-the-historic-divergence-between-productivity-and-a-typical-workers-pay-why-its-matters-and-why-it's-real/)

Blanchard, Olivier and Daniel Leigh (2013), 'Growth Forecast Errors and Fiscal Multipliers', *IMF Working Paper WP/13/1*, January.

Blinder, Alan S. (1979), *Economic Policy and the Great Stagflation*, New York: Academic Press.

Blinder, Alan S. (2013), 'The macroeconomic policy paradox: Failing by succeeding', *The ANNALS of the American Academy of Political and Social Science*, Vol. 650, No. 1, pp. 26–46.

Blinder, Alan S. and Jeremy B. Rudd (2008), 'The Supply-Shock Explanation of the Great Stagflation Revisited', *NBER Working Paper Series*, Working Paper 14563, December (http://www.nber.org/papers/w14563).

Blöchliger, Hansjörg (2013), 'Fiscal Equalisation — A Cross-Country Perspective', in Hansjörg Blöchliger, *Fiscal Federalism 2014: Making Decentralisation Work*, Paris: OECD, pp. 99–116.

Blöchliger, Hansjörg and Claire Charbit (2008), 'Fiscal Equalisation', *OECD Economic Studies*, No. 44, 2008/1.

Bluedorn, John, Davide Furceri, Florence Jaumotte, Franziska Ohnsorge, Tigran Poghosyan and Aleksandra Zdzienicka (2013), *Toward A Fiscal Union For The Euro Area: Technical Background Notes*, Washington, DC: International Monetary Fund, September (http://www.imf.org/external/pubs/ft/sdn/2013/sdn1309tn.pdf).

Blyth, Mark (2013), *Austerity. The History of a Dangerous Idea*, Oxford: Oxford University Press.

Bonefeld, Werner (2011), 'Social Market Economy and Big Society: German Neoliberalism and the Politics of Austerity', Paper Presented at the meeting of the Northern IPE Network Meeting, Sheffield University, 4 November.

Bonefeld, Werner (2012), 'Freedom and the strong state: On German ordoliberalism', *New Political Economy*, Vol. 17, No. 5, pp. 633–656.

Bonefeld, Werner (2013), 'German neoliberalism and the idea of a social market economy', Journal of Social Sciences, Pre-print, Phitsanulok, Thailand.

Bonin, Holger, Werner Eichhorst, Christer Florman, Mette Okkels Hansen, Lena Skiöld, Jan Stuhler, Konstantinos Tatsiramos, Henrik Thomasen and Klaus F. Zimmermann (2008), 'Geographic Mobility in the European Union: Optimising its Economic and Social Benefits', *IZA Research Report No. 19*, July.

Boone, Laurence, Céline Renucci, and Ruben Segura-Cayuela (2013b), 'Eurozone: Looking for growth', *VOX, CEPR's Policy Portal*, 25 March.

Boone, Laurence, Ruben Segura-Cayuela and Nick Bate (2013a), 'Europe: When will growth return?', *European Economic Viewpoint*, Bank of America Merril Lynch, 15 February (http://www.merrilledge.com/publish/content/application/pdf/gwmol/EuropeanEconomicsViewpoint.pdf).

Bootle, Roger (2011), *Leaving the euro: A practical guide,* A submission for the Wolfson Economics Prize MMXII by Capital Economics, London: Capital Economics (http://www.policyexchange.org.uk/images/WolfsonPrize/wep%20shortlist%20essay%20-%20roger%20bootle.pdf).

Bordo, Michael D., Agnieszka Markiewicz and Lars Jonung (2011), 'A Fiscal Union for the Euro: Some Lessons from History', *NBER Working Paper No. 17380*, September (http://www.nber.org/papers/w17380).

Bordo Michael D. and Christopher M. Meissner (2012), 'Does Inequality Lead to a Financial Crisis?', *NBER Working Paper Series* 17896, March (http://www.nber.org/papers/w17896.pdf).

Bornhorst, Fabian, Esther Perez-Ruiz, John C. Bluedorn, Davide Furceri, Florence Jaumotte, Franziska Ohnsorge, Tigran Poghosyan, and Aleksandra Zdzienicka (2013), *Toward a Fiscal Union for the Euro Area: Technical Background Notes*, Washington DC: International Monetary Fund, September.

Boschma, Ron and Gianluca Capone (2014), 'Relatedness and Diversification in the EU-27 and ENP Countries', *Papers in Evolutionary Economic Geography* No. 14.07, Utrecht University, Urban & Regional Research Centre Utrecht.

Bouget, Denis (2003), 'Convergence in the social welfare systems in Europe: From goal to reality', *Social Policy & Administration*, Vol. 37, No. 6, December pp. 674–693.

Bouis, Romain, Ane Kathrine Christensen and Boris Cournède (2013), 'Deleveraging: Challenges, Progress and Policies', *Economics Department Working Papers No. 1077*, Paris: OECD.

Bräuninger, Dieter and Christine Majowski (2011), 'Labour Mobility in the Euro Area'. Deutsche Bank Research, *Reports on European integration EU Monitor 85*.

Briguglio, Lino, Gordon Cordina, Nadia Farrugia and Stephanie Vella (2009), 'Economic Vulnerability and Resilience: Concepts and Measurements', *Oxford Development Studies*, Vol. 37, No. 3, pp. 229–247.

Bronfenbrenner, Martin (1969) ed., *Is the Business Cycle Obsolete?*, New York and London: Wiley.

Brueckner, Markus and Daniel Lederman (2015), 'Effects of Income Inequality on Aggregate Output', *Policy Research Working Paper 7317*, June, Washington, DC: The World Bank.

Brülhart, Marius and Rolf Traeger (2003), 'An Account of Geographic Concentration Patterns in Europe', *HWWA Discussion Paper*, No. 226.

Brunat, Eric (2016), 'Where goes Russia? The risks of a new continental divide', in Bruno Dallago, Gert Guri and John McGowan (eds.), *A Global Perspective on the European Economic Crisis*, Abingdon, Oxfordshire: Routledge.

BS (2014), *Harnessing European Labour Mobility: Scenario Analysis and Policy Recommendations*, Gütersloh: Bertelsmann Stiftung.

Buch, Claudia M. (2000), 'Capital Market Integration in Euroland: The Role of Banks', *German Economic Review*, Vol. 1, No. 4, pp. 443–464.

Bugamelli, Matteo, Luigi Cannari, Francesca Lotti and Silvia Magri (2012), 'Il gap innovativo del sistema produttivo italiano: radici e possibili rimedi', *Questioni di Economia e Finanza (Occasional Papers 121/2012)*, Bank of Italy, April.

Buiter, Willem H., Giancarlo M. Corsetti and Paolo A. Pesenti (1998), 'Interpreting the ERM crisis: Country-specific and systemic issues', *Princeton Studies in International Finance*, No. 84, March.

Buiter, Willem H. and Ebrahim Rahbari (2012), 'TARGET2 Redux: The Simple Accountancy and Slightly More Complex Economics of Bundesbank Loss Exposure through the Eurosystem', *Discussion Paper No. 9211*, Centre for Economic Policy Research, November.

Burret, Heiko T. and Jan Schnellenbach (2013), 'Implementation of the Fiscal Compact in the Euro Area Member States', *Working Paper* 08/2013, November (partly updated in January 2014).

Buti, Marco and Nicolas Carnot (2015), 'What is a 'responsible' fiscal policy today for Europe?', *VOX, CEPR's Policy Portal*, 24 February (http://www.voxeu.org/article/defining-responsible-fiscal-policy-europe).

Buti, Marco and André Sapir (1998), eds., *Economic Policy in EMU: A Study by the European Commission Services*, Oxford: Clarendon Press.

Caballero, Ricardo J. (2010), 'Sudden financial arrest', *IMF Economic Review*, Vol. 58, No. 1, pp. 6–36.

Calvo, Guillermo A., Alejandro Izquierdo and Luis-Fernando Mejía (2004) 'On the Empirics of Sudden Stops: the Relevance of Balance-Sheet Effects',

Working Paper 10520, NBER Working Paper Series (http://www.nber.org/papers/w10520.pdf).

Calvo, Sara, and Carmen Reinhart (1996), 'Capital flows to Latin America: Is there evidence of contagion effect?', in Guillermo Calvo, Morris Goldstein, and Eduard Hochreiter, eds., *Private Capital Flows to Emerging Markets after the Mexican Crisis.* Washington, DC: Institute for International Economics.

Canton, Erik, Isabel Grilo, Josefina Monteagudo, Fabiana Pierini and Alessandro Turrini (2014), 'The Role of Structural Reform for Adjustment and Growth', *ECFIN Economic Brief*, No. 34, June (http://ec.europa.eu/economy_finance/publications/economic_briefs/2014/pdf/eb34_en.pdf).

Cappellari, Lorenzo and Stefano Staffolani (2008), 'The evolution of labour market inequalities: An introduction', *Labour*, Vol. 22, June, pp. 1–5.

Cariolle, Joël (2011), 'The Economic Vulnerability Index. 2010 Update', *Working Paper 9 — Development Indicators*, Fondation pour les études et recherches sur le développement international, March (http://www.ferdi.fr/sites/www.ferdi.fr/files/publication/fichiers/I9-Cariolle-Eng_web.pdf).

Caroleo, Floro Ernesto and Francesco Pastore (2010), 'Structural Change and Labour Reallocation Across Regions: A Review of the Literature', in F.E. Caroleo, and F. Pastore (eds.), *The Labour Market Impact of EU Enlargement, A New Regional Geography of Europe?*, Heidelberg: Physica/Springer, pp. 17–47.

Caruana, Jaime and Adrian Van Rixtel (2012), 'International financial markets and bank funding in the euro area: Dynamics and participants', *Bank for International Settlements* (http://www.bis.org/publ/othp18.pdf).

Castro, Vitor (2011), 'The impact of the European Union fiscal rules on economic growth', *Journal of Macroeconomics*, Vol. 33, pp. 313–326.

Caudal, Nicolas, Nathalie Georges, Vincent Grossmann-Wirth, Jean Guillaume, Thomas Lellouch and Arthur Sode (2013), 'A budget for the euro area', *Trésor-Economics*, No. 120, October.

CB (2013), *International Comparisons of Manufacturing Productivity & Unit Labor Costs Trends 2012*, The Conference Board (https://www.conference-board.org/ilcprogram/index.cfm?id=20992).

CBO (2011), *Trends in the Distribution of Household Income between 1979 and 2007*, Washington DC: Congress of the United States, Congressional Budget Office, October.

Cecchetti, Stephen G. and Enisse Kharroubi (2012), 'Reassessing the Impact of Finance on Growth', *BIS Working Papers No. 381.*

Chan-Lee, James and Helen Sutch (1985), 'Profits and Rates of Return in OECD Countries', *OECD Economics Department Working Papers*, No. 20, OECD Publishing (http://dx.doi.org/10.1787/468348310348).

Charron, Nicholas, Carl Dahlström and Victor Lapuente (2012), 'No law without a state', *Journal of Comparative Economics*, Vol. 40, pp. 176–193.

Chen, Vivian, Abhay Gupta, Andre Therrien, Gad Levanon and Bart van Ark (2010), 'Recent productivity developments in the world economy: An overview from the Conference Board Total Economy Database', *International Productivity Monitor*, No. 19, Spring, pp. 3–19.

Chen, Wen-Hao, Michael Förster and Ana Llena-Nozal (2013), 'Globalisation, Technological Progress and Changes in Regulations and Institutions — Which Impact on the Rise of Earnings Inequality in OECD Countries?', *LIS Working Paper Series No. 597*, Luxembourg Income Study (LIS) (http://www.lisdatacenter.org/wps/liswps/597.pdf).

Cingolani, Isabella, Giulia Felice and Lucia Tajoli (2015), 'External Imbalances in the European Union and International Fragmentation of Production: Is There a Link?' *Centro Studi Luca D'agliano Development Studies Working Papers* No. 386, April.

CJEU (2015), 'Advocate General's Opinion in Case C-62/14. Peter Gauweiler and Others v Deutscher Bundestag', Luxembourg: Court of Justice of the European Union, *Press Release No. 2/15*, 14 January (http://curia.europa.eu/jcms/upload/docs/application/pdf/2015-01/cp150002en.pdf).

Claessens, Stijn and Kristin Forbes (2001), 'International financial contagion: An overview of the issues and the book', *in* Stijn Claessens and Kristin J. Forbes (eds.), *International Financial Contagion*, New York: Springer US, pp. 3–17.

Claessens, Stijn, Ashoka Mody and Shahin Vallée (2013), 'Paths to Eurobonds', *IMF Working Paper WP/12/172*, July (https://www.imf.org/external/pubs/ft/wp/2012/wp12172.pdf).

Claeys, Grégory, André Sapir and Guntram B. Wolff (2014), 'Juncker's investment plan: No risk — no return', *Bruegel*, 28 November (http://www.bruegel.org/nc/blog/detail/article/1491-junckers-investment-plan-no-risk-no-return/).

Clark, Christopher (2012), *The Sleepwalkers: How Europe went to war in 1914*, London: Allen Lane (quotation from the 2014 edition by Harper Perennial, New York).

Cœuré, Benoît (2013), 'The Economic Consequences of Low Interest Rates', public lecture at the International Center for Monetary and Banking Studies, Geneva, 9 October (https://www.ecb.europa.eu/press/key/date/2013/html/sp131009.en.html).

Cœuré, Benoît (2015), 'How Binding is the Zero Lower Bound?', Speech at the conference *Removing the zero lower bound on interest rates*, London: Imperial College Business School/Brevan Howard Centre for Financial Analysis, CEPR and the Swiss National Bank, 18 May (https://www.ecb.europa.eu/press/key/date/2015/html/sp150519.en.html).

Cohan, Peter (2010), 'Big Risk: $1.2 Quadrillion Derivatives Market Dwarfs World GDP', *Daily Finance blog*, 9 June (http://www.dailyfinance.com/2010/06/09/risk-quadrillion-derivatives-market-gdp/).

Cohen, Ivan K., Fabrizio Ferretti and Bryan McIntosh (2014), 'Decomposing the misery index: A dynamic approach', *Cogent Economics & Finance*, Vol. 22, No. 991089 (http://www.tandfonline.com/doi/pdf/10.1080/23322039.2014.991089).

Collignon, Stefan and Piero Esposito (2013), eds., *Competitiveness in the European Economy*, London: Routledge.

Comunale, Mariarosaria (2015), 'Euro-Dollar Polarization and Heterogeneity in Exchange Rate Pass-Throughs within the Euro Zone', *CEIS Working Paper No. 333*, 13 March.

Constâncio, Vítor (2011), 'Contagion and the European Debt Crisis', ECB Keynote Lecture, Bocconi University/Intesa Sanpaolo conference on "*Bank Competitiveness in the Post-crisis World*", Milan, 10 October (http://www.ecb.europa.eu/press/key/date/2011/html/sp111010.en.html).

Corak, Miles (2013), 'Income inequality, equality of opportunity, and intergenerational mobility', *Journal of Economic Perspectives*, Vol. 27, No. 3, pp. 79–102.

Cordina, Gordon (2004), 'Economic vulnerability and economic growth: Some results from a neo-classical growth modelling approach', *Journal of Economic Development*, Vol. 29, No. 2, December, pp. 21–39.

Crafts, Nicholas (2003), 'Prospects for European economic growth: An historical perspective', in Oesterreichische Nationalbank, *Fostering Economic Growth in Europe*, Vienna, pp. 69–82.

Crafts, Nicholas (2006), 'The world economy in the 1990s: A long-run perspective', in Rhode and Toniolo (2006a), pp. 21–42.

Crafts, Nicholas (2012), 'Western Europe's growth prospects: An historical perspective', *CAGE Online Working Paper Series*, Coventry: Department of Economics, University of Warwick (http://wrap.warwick.ac.uk/57767).

Crafts, Nicholas and Gianni Toniolo (1996), eds., *Economic Growth in Europe since 1945*, Cambridge, UK: Cambridge University Press.

Crew, Michael A. and Paul R. Kleindorfer (2002), 'Regulatory economics: Twenty years of progress?', *Journal of Regulatory Economics*, Vol. 21, No. 1, pp. 5–22.

Crouch, Colin (2012), 'National varieties of labour market exposure', in Glenn Morgan and Richard Whitley (eds.), *Capitalisms and Capitalism in the Twenty-First Century*, Oxford: Oxford University Press, pp. 90–115.

Dabla-Norris, Era and Paul Wade (2001), 'Rent Seeking and Endogenous Income Inequality', *IMF Working Paper* WP/01/15, February.

Dallago, Bruno (1990), *The Irregular Economy. The 'Underground' Economy and the 'Black' Labour Market*, Aldershot: Dartmouth.

Dallago, Bruno (1994), 'Some reflections on privatization as a means to transform the economic system: The Western experience', in Hans-Jürgen Wagener (ed.), *The Political Economy of Transformation*, Heidelberg: Physica-Verlag, pp. 113–143.

Dallago, Bruno (1999), 'Privatization: The teaching of Western experiences', in Iván Major (ed.), *Privatization and Economic Performance in Central and Eastern Europe: Lessons to be Learnt from Western Europe*, Cheltenham: Edward Elgar, pp. 1–42.

Dallago, Bruno (2004), 'Comparative economic systems and the new comparative economics', *The European Journal of Comparative Economics*, Vol. 1, No. 1, pp. 59–86.

Dallago, Bruno (2014): 'The Crisis, the Monetary Union, and Migration', *SEEMIG Working Papers*, No. 6, November, Budapest: Hungarian Demographic Research Institute.

Dallago, Bruno and Chiara Guglielmetti (2012), 'Eurozone and global financial imbalances', in Steven Rosefielde, Masaaki Kuboniwa, and Satoshi Mizobata (eds.), *Two Asias: The Emerging Postcrisis Divide*, Singapore: World Scientific, pp. 379–417.

Dallago, Bruno and John McGowan (2015a), eds., *Crises in Europe in the Transatlantic Context: Economic and Political Appraisal*, London and New York: Routledge.

Dallago, Bruno and John McGowan (2015b), 'Introduction: The European crisis in the transatlantic context', in Bruno Dallago and John McGowan (eds.), *Crises in Europe in the Transatlantic Context: Economic and Political Appraisals*, Abingdon, Oxfordshire and New York, NY: Routledge, pp. 1–18.

Dallago, Bruno and Steven Rosefielde (2016), *Transformation and Crisis in Central and Eastern Europe: Challenges and Prospects*, Abingdon, Oxfordshire: Routledge.

Danielsson, Jon (2008), 'The first casualty of the crisis: Iceland', *VOX, CEPR's Policy Portal*, 12 November (http://www.voxeu.org/article/how-bad-could-crisis-get-lessons-iceland).

Dany, Geraldine, Reint E. Gropp and Gregor von Schweinitz (2015), 'Germany's Benefit from the Greek Crisis', *IWH Online 7/2015*, Halle: Leibniz-Institut Für Wirtschaftsforschung Halle — IWH (http://www.leibniz-gemeinschaft.de/

en/media/news/news-single/article/deutschland_profitiert_von_eurokrise_100002049/).

Dao, Mai, Davide Furceri and Prakash Loungani (2013), 'Moving closer? Changing patterns of labour mobility in Europe and the US', *VOX, CEPR's Policy Portal*, 1 December (http://www.voxeu.org/article/labour-mobility-europe-and-us).

Dao, Mai, Davide Furceri and Prakash Loungani (2014), 'Regional labour market adjustments in the US and Europe', *IMF Working Paper Working Paper No. 14/26*, February.

Darvas, Zsolt, Pia Hüttl, Silvia Merler, Carlos de Sousa and Thomas Walsh (2014), *Analysis of Developments in EU Capital Flows in the Global Context*, Final Report, No. MARKT/2013/50/F, Brussels: Bruegel, November.

Dauderstädt, Michael and Cem Keltek (2012), 'Eurocrisis: Inequality is growing again in Europe', *Perspective*, September, Berlin: Friedrich-Ebert-Stiftung (http://library.fes.de/pdf-files/id/ipa/09331.pdf).

Davis, Steven J. and John Haltiwanger (2014), 'Labor Market Fluidity and Economic Performance', *NBER Working Paper No. 20479*, September.

DB (2012), *Doing Business in a More Transparent World*, Washington, DC: The World Bank.

DBB (2015a), *Monthly Report*, Deutsche Bundesbank, Vol. 67, No 2, February.

DBB (2015b), 'Time series BBK01.EU8148B: MEMO ITEM: External position of the Bundesbank since the beginning of EMU/Claims within the Eurosystem/TARGET 2 (net)', Macro-economic time series, (http://www.bundesbank.de/Navigation/EN/Statistics/Time_series_databases/Macro_economic_time_series/its_details_value_node.html?tsId=BBK01.EU8148B).

DBR (2014), *Who is Exposed to Russia?*, Deutsche Bank Research, 20 March, report written by Gilles Moec and Marco Stringa.

De Bandt, Olivier and Philipp Hartmann (2000), 'Systemic Risk: A Survey', European Central Bank, *Working Paper Series*, Working Paper No. 35, November.

De Grauwe, Paul (2010) 'Fighting the wrong enemy', *VOX, CEPR's Policy Portal*, 19 May (http://www.voxeu.org/article/europe-s-private-versus-public-debt-problem-fighting-wrong-enemy).

De Grauwe, Paul (2011a), 'The Governance of a Fragile Eurozone', *CEPS Working Documents*, 4 May (http://ceps.eu/book/governance-fragile-eurozone).

De Grauwe, Paul (2011b), 'Managing a fragile Eurozone', *CESifo Forum*, Vol. 12, No. 2, pp. 40–45.

De Grauwe, Paul (2013), 'The European Central Bank as lender of last resort in the government bond markets', *CESifo Economic Studies*, Vol. 59, No. 3, pp. 520–535.

De Grauwe, Paul (2014), *Economics of Monetary Union*, 10th ed., Oxford: Oxford University Press.

De Grauwe, Paul and Yuemei Ji (2012), 'Self-Fulfilling Crises in the Eurozone: An Empirical Test', *CEPS Working Document No. 366*, June and *Journal of International Money and Finance*, Vol. 34, April 2013, pp. 15–36.

De Grauwe, Paul and Yuemei Ji (2013), 'Panic-driven austerity and its implication for the Eurozone', *VOX, CEPR's Policy Portal*, 21 February (http://www.voxeu.org/article/panic-driven-austerity-eurozone---and-its-implications).

De Grauwe, Paul and Yuemei Ji (2015a), 'Has the Eurozone Become Less Fragile? Some Empirical Tests', *CESifo Working Paper No. 5163*, January.

De Grauwe, Paul and Yuemei Ji (2015b), 'Quantitative easing in the Eurozone: It's possible without fiscal transfers', *VOX, CEPR's Policy Portal*, 15 January, (http://www.voxeu.org/article/quantitative-easing-eurozone-its-possible-without-fiscal-transfers).

Decressin, Jörg and Antonio Fatás (1995), 'Regional labor market dynamics in Europe', *European Economic Review*, 39, pp. 1627–1655.

Deininger, Klaus and Lyn Squire (1996), 'A New Data Set Measuring Income Inequality', *The World Bank Economic Review*, Vol. 10, No. 3, September, pp. 565–591.

Delanty, Gerard (1995), *Inventing Europe: Idea, Identity, Reality*, Basingstoke: Palgrave Macmillan.

Delgado, Mercedes, Christian Ketels, Michael E. Porter and Scott Stern (2012), 'The Determinants of National Competitiveness', *NBER Working Paper 18249*, National Bureau of Economic Research.

Delors Report (1989), *Report on Economic and Monetary Union in the European Community*, Committee for the Study of Economic and Monetary Union, 17 April (http://ec.europa.eu/economy_finance/publications/publication6161_en.pdf).

Deo, Stephane, Paul Donovan and Larry Hatheway (2011), 'Breaking up the Euro', *Global Economic Perspectives*, UBS Investment Research, 6 September (https://wikileaks.org/gifiles/attach/12/12089_euro%20break%20up%20by%20ubs.pdf).

Deutsche Börse (2008), *The Global Derivatives Market. An Introduction*, April, Frankfurt am Main: Deutsche Börse AG.

Dhyne, Emmanuel, Jerzy Konieczny, Fabio Rumler and Patrick Sevestre (2009), 'Price Rigidity in the Euro Area: An Assessment'. Final Report, *European Economy*, Economic Papers 380, May.

Dietl, Helmut M. (1998), *Capital Markets and Corporate Governance in Japan, Germany and the United States: Organizational Response to Market Inefficiencies*, Abingdon, Oxfordshire: Routledge.

Dinan, Desmond (2004), *Europe Recast: A History of European Union*, Palgrave Macmillan.

Dor, Eric (2011), 'The Enormous Loans of the Deutsche Bundesbank to Distressed European Countries' Central Banks', Working Paper Series 2011-ECO-08, *IESEG Working Paper Series 2011-ECO*-08, School of Management (LEM-CNRS), Catholic University of Lille, November (http://ssrn.com/abstract=1964658).

Dornbush, Rudiger, Yung Chul Park, and Stijn Claessens (2000), 'Contagion: Understanding how it spreads', *The World Bank Research Observer*, Vol. 15, No. 2, August, pp. 177–197.

DP (2015), 'Which countries are net contributors to the EU budget?', Copenhagen: The Danish Parliament, EU Information Centre (http://english.eu.dk/faq/faq/net_contribution).

Draghi, Mario (2010), 'Trade, competitiveness and Europe', *EFIGE (European Firms in the Global Economy) Scientific Workshop and Policy Conference*, Rome, 18 June 2010.

Draghi, Mario (2014), 'Stability and prosperity in Monetary Union', Speech delievered at the University of Helsinki, Helsinki, 27 November (http://www.bis.org/review/r141127i.pdf).

Draghi, Mario (2015), 'Introductory statement at the Italian Parliament', *Speech by Mario Draghi, President of the ECB, at the Italian Parliament*, Rome, 26 March 2015 (http://www.ecb.europa.eu/press/key/date/2015/html/sp150326.en.html).

Du Caju, Philip, Erwan Gautier, Daphne Momferatou and Melanie Ward-Warmedinger (2008), 'Institutional Features of Wage Bargaining in 23 European Countries, the US and Japan', *Working Paper Series No. 974*, European Central Bank, December.

Duesenberry, James S. (1949), *Income, Saving and the Theory of Consumer Behavior*, Cambridge, MA: Harvard University Press.

Dullien Sebastian, and Ulrike Guerot (2012), 'The long shadow of ordoliberalism: Germany's approach to the euro crisis', European Council on Foreign Relations, *Policy Brief*, ECFR/49, February.

Dumenil, Gerard and Dominique Levy (2011), *The Crisis of Neoliberalism*, Cambridge, MA and London: Harvard University Press.

Durand, Mattine and Claude Giorno (1987), 'Indicators of international competitiveness: Conceptual aspects and evaluation', *OECD Journal: Economic Studies*, Paris: OECD, Vol. 9, pp. 147–182 (https://www1.oecd.org/eco/outlook/33841783.pdf).

Dustmann, Christian, Bernd Fitzenberger, Uta Schönberg and Alexandra Spitz-Oener (2014), 'From sick man of Europe to economic superstar: Germany's resurgent economy', *Journal of Economic Perspectives*, Vol. 28, No. 1, pp. 167–188.

Dynan, Karen E., Jonathan Skinner and Stephen P. Zeldes (2004), 'Do the rich save more?', *Journal of Political Economy*, Vol. 112, No. 2, pp. 397–444.

EBA (2014), *Results of 2014 EU-Wide Stress Test: Aggregate Results*, Report, European Banking Authority, 26 October.

EBA (2015), 'Harmonised Competitiveness Indicators'. (http://www.ecb.europa.eu/stats/exchange/hci/html/index.en.html).

EC (1988), Council Directive of 24 June 1988 for the implementation of Article 67 of the Treaty, *Official Journal of the European Communities*, 8 July, No L 178/5 (88/361/EEC), Brussels: European Commission (http://eur-lex.europa.eu/legal-content/EN/TXT/PDF/?uri=CELEX:31988L0361&rid=2).

EC (1990), 'One market, one money: An evaluation of the potential benefits and costs of forming an economic and monetary union', Brussels: European Commission, *European Economy — Economic Papers*, No. 44, October.

EC (2008a), 'EMU@10: Successes and challenges after 10 years of Economic and Monetary Union', *European Economy*, No. 2, June, Brussels: European Commission.

EC (2008b), *European Union. Public Finance*, 4th ed., Brussels: European Commission (http://ec.europa.eu/budget/library/biblio/publications/public_fin/EU_pub_fin_en.pdf).

EC (2009), 'Economic Crisis in Europe: Causes, Consequences and Responses', *European Economy*, No. 7/2009, Brussels: European Commission.

EC (2010a), *Europe 2020: A European Strategy for Smart, Sustainable, and Inclusive Growth*, COM (2010) 2020, Brussels: European Commission.

EC (2010b), *The European Union Budget at a Glance*, Brussels: European Commission (http://ec.europa.eu/budget/library/biblio/publications/glance/budget_glance_en.pdf).

EC (2012), *Green Paper. Shadow Banking*, 19 March, COM(2012) 102 final, Brussels: European Commission (http://ec.europa.eu/internal_market/bank/docs/shadow/green-paper_en.pdf).

EC (2013a), *Quarterly Report on the Euro Area*, Brussels: European Commission, Vol. 12, No. 4.

EC (2013b), 'Consumer Benefits', Economic and Financial Affairs, Brussels: European Commission (http://ec.europa.eu/economy_finance/euro/why/consumer/index_en.htm).

EC (2013c), Multiannual financial framework 2014–2020 and EU budget 2014. The figures, Brussels: European Commission, Luxembourg: Publications Office of the European Union (http://bookshop.europa.eu/en/multiannual-financial-framework-2014-2020-and-eu-budget-2014-pbKV0413055/?CatalogCategory ID=mpgKABstFogAAAEjbIUY4e5K).

EC (2013d), 'An international currency', The euro, Why the euro?, Brussels: European Commission, Economic and Financial Affairs (http://ec.europa.eu/economy_finance/euro/why/international/index_en.htm) (last update: 4 September 2013).

EC (2014a), 'An Investment Plan for Europe', Brussels: European Commission, *Communication from the Commission to the European Parliament, the Council, the European Central Bank, the European Economic and Social Committee, the Committee of the Regions and the European Investment Bank*, 26 November, COM(2014) 903 final.

EC (2014b), 'Economic stability and growth', Economic and Financial Affairs, Brussels: European Commission (http://ec.europa.eu/economy_finance/euro/why/stability_growth/index_en.htm).

EC (2014c), *Convergence Report 2014*, European Economy 4/2014, Brussels: European Commission.

EC (2014d), *European Union. Public Finance*, 5th Edition, Brussels: European Commission.

EC (2014e), 'Member state vulnerability to changes in the euro exchange rate', *Quarterly Report on the Euro Area*, Brussels: European Commission, Vol. 13, No. 3, October, pp. 27–33.

EC (2014f), *Price and Cost Competitiveness: Quarterly Data on Price and Cost Competitiveness of the European Union and its Member States*, Brussels: European Commission, Directorate-General For Economic And Financial Affairs, ECFIN/E-4, First quarter.

EC (2014g), *Results of In-Depth Reviews under Regulation (EU) No 1176/2011 on the Prevention and Correction of Macroeconomic Imbalances*, Brussels: European Commission, Communication from the Commission to the European Parliament, The Council and the Eurogroup, COM(2014) 150 final, 5 March.

EC (2014h), 'Questions and Answers: European System of Accounts 2010', Brussels: European Commission, Press releases database, Press Release details, 16 January 2014 (http://europa.eu/rapid/press-release_MEMO-14-21_en.htm) (last update: 22 October 2015).

EC (2015a), 'Making the Best Use of the Flexibility within the Existing Rules of the Stability and Growth Pact', Brussels: European Commission, *Communication from the Commission to the European Parliament, the Council, the European Central Bank, the Economic and Social Committee, the Committee of the Regions and the European Investment Bank*, Strasbourg, 13 January (http://ec.europa.eu/economy_finance/economic_governance/sgp/pdf/2015-01-13_communication_sgp_flexibility_guidelines_en.pdf).

EC (2015b), *EU Budget at a Glance*, Luxembourg: European Commission (http://ec.europa.eu/budget/biblio/publications/publications_en.cfm#BAG2015).

EC (2015c), 'Financial assistance to Greece', Brussels: European Commission, Economic and Financial Affairs (http://ec.europa.eu/economy_finance/assistance_eu_ms/greek_loan_facility/index_en.htm).

EC (2015d), *European Union Trade in the World: Index*, Brussels: European Commission (http://trade.ec.europa.eu/doclib/docs/2006/september/tradoc_122532.pdf).

EC (2015e), 'European Economic Forecast', *European Economy*, Winter 2015, 1/2015, Brussels: European Commission, Directorate-General for Economic and Financial Affairs.

EC (2015f), 'Post-Programme Surveillance for Ireland', Brussels: European Commission (http://ec.europa.eu/economy_finance/assistance_eu_ms/ireland/index_en.htm) (Last updated 14 September 2015).

EC (2015g), 'Post-Programme Surveillance of Portugal', Brussels: European Commission (http://ec.europa.eu/economy_finance/assistance_eu_ms/portugal/index_en.htm) (Last updated 17 July 2015).

EC (2015h), 'Spring 2015 Economic Forecast: Tailwinds Support the Recovery,' Brussels: European Commission (http://ec.europa.eu/economy_finance/eu/forecasts/2015_spring_forecast_en.htm).

EC (2015i), *Trade. Export Helpdesk*, Brussels: European Commission (http://exporthelp.europa.eu/thdapp/display.htm?page=st%2fst_Statistics.html&docType=main&languageId=en) (last update: 36 November 2015).

EC (2015j), 'Performance per governance tool', Brussels: European Commission, The EU Single Market, Single Market Scoreboard, Brussels: European Commission (http://ec.europa.eu/internal_market/scoreboard/performance_by_governance_tool/index_en.htm) (last update: 6 October 2015).

EC (2015k), 'The Corrective Arm', Brussels: European Commission, Economic and Financial Affairs, Brussels: European Commission (http://ec.europa.eu/economy_finance/economic_governance/sgp/corrective_arm/index_en.htm) (last update: 17 November 2015).

EC (2015l), Trade, Transatlantic Trade and Investment Partnership (TTIP), Brussels: European Commission (http://ec.europa.eu/trade/policy/in-focus/ttip/) (last update: 18 November 2015).

EC (2015m), 'Greece', Economic and Financial Affairs, EU economic situation, Economies of the Member States, Brussels: European Commission, (http://

ec.europa.eu/economy_finance/eu/countries/greece_en.htm) (last update: 27 May 2015).

EC (2015n), 'Commission's role in SEPA', Banking and Finance, Payment Services, Single Euro Payments Area (SEPA), Brussels: European Commission (http://ec.europa.eu/finance/payments/sepa/role/index_en.htm) (last update: 27 November 2015).

EC (2015o), 'European Financial Stabilisation Mechanism (EFSM)', Economic and Financial Affairs, Brussels: European Commission (http://ec.europa.eu/economy_finance/eu_borrower/efsm/index_en.htm) (last update: 9 September 2015).

EC (2015p), 'Structural reforms', Economic and Financial Affairs, Brussels: European Commission (http://ec.europa.eu/economy_finance/structural_reforms/index_en.htm) (Last update: 30 July 2015).

EC (2015q), 'Investment Plan', Jobs, growth, investment', Brussels: European Commission (http://ec.europa.eu/priorities/jobs-growth-investment/plan/index_en.htm).

EC (2015r), 'Banking union', Banking and finance, Brussels: European Commission (http://ec.europa.eu/finance/general-policy/banking-union/index_en.htm) (Last update: 24 November 2015).

EC (2015s), 'Workplace innovation', Internal Market, Industry, Entrepreneurship and SMEs, Brussels: European Commission (http://ec.europa.eu/growth/industry/innovation/policy/workplace/index_en.htm) (Last update: 2 December 2015).

ECB (2004), *Report on EU Banking Structure*, Frankfurt am Main: European Central Bank, November (https://www.ecb.europa.eu/pub/pdf/other/eubankingstructure2004en.pdf).

ECB (2008a), 'Globalization and the Competitiveness of the Euro Area', *Occasional Paper Series No. 97*, Frankfurt am Main: European Central Bank.

ECB (2008b), 'Press conferences in 2008', Frankfurt: European Central Bank (https://www.ecb.europa.eu/press/pressconf/2008/html/index.en.html).

ECB (2009), 'The Concept of Systemic Risk', *Financial Stability Review*, December, Frankfurt am Main: European Central Bank, pp. 134–142.

ECB (2010), 'New Quantitative Measures of Systemic Risk', *Financial Stability Review*, December, Frankfurt am Main: European Central Bank, pp. 147–153.

ECB (2011), 'The Monetary Policy of the ECB 2011', European Central Bank (http://www.ecb.europa.eu/pub/pdf/other/monetarypolicy2011en.pdf).

ECB (2012), 'Verbatim of the remarks made by Mario Draghi', Speech by Mario Draghi, President of the European Central Bank at the Global Investment

Conference in London, 26 July 2012 (https://www.ecb.europa.eu/press/key/date/2012/html/sp120726.en.html)

ECB (2013a), *Corporate Finance and Economic Activity in the Euro Area. Structural Issues Report 2013*, Task Force of the Monetary Policy Committee of the European System of Central Banks, Occasional Paper Series, No. 151, August.

ECB (2013b), 'Assessing the retail bank interest rate pass-through in the euro area at times of financial fragmentation', *Monthly Bulletin*, August, pp. 75–91.

ECB (2014a), 'Guide to Banking Supervision', Frankfurt am Main: European Central Bank, November (https://www.bankingsupervision.europa.eu/ecb/pub/pdf/ssmguidebankingsupervision201411.en.pdf?404fd6cb61dbde0095c8722d5aff29cd).

ECB (2014b), *The International Role of The Euro*, Frankfurt am Main: European Central Bank, July.

ECB (2015a), 'Target2' (Retrieved 2 December from https://www.ecb.europa.eu/paym/t2/html/index.en.html).

ECB (2015b), 'The definition of price stability', Frankfurt: European Central Bank (https://www.ecb.europa.eu/mopo/strategy/pricestab/html/index.en.html).

ECB (2015c), 'How to calculate the minimum reserve requirements', Monetary Policy, Instruments, Minimum reserves, Frankfurt am Mein: European Central Bank (https://www.ecb.europa.eu/mopo/implement/mr/html/calc.en.html).

ECB (2015d), 'Monetary policy' (https://www.ecb.europa.eu/mopo/html/index.en.html).

ECB (2015e), 'Emergency liquidity assistance (ELA) and monetary policy', onetary Policy, Frankfurt am Mein: European Central Bank (https://www.ecb.europa.eu/mopo/ela/html/index.en.html).

ECo (2012), *Treaty on Stability, Coordination and Governance in the Economic and Monetary Union*, Brussels: European Council (http://www.consilium.europa.eu/european-council/pdf/Treaty-on-Stability-Coordination-and-Governance-TSCG).

ECORYS (2011), *Study on the cost competitiveness of European industry in the globalisation era — Empirical evidence on the basis of relative unit labour costs (ULC) at sectoral level*, Framework Contract Sector Competitiveness (ENTR06/054), Final Report, ECORYS Nederland BV, Study Lead Partner: Cambridge Econometrics, Cambridge, 28 September.

ECR (2014), *European Competitiveness Report 2014. Helping Firms Grow*, Commission Staff Working Document SWD(2014)277 final, Brussels: European Commission.

EEAG (2012), 'The Hungarian Crisis', *The EEAG Report on the European Economy*, Munich: CESifo, pp. 115–130.

Eggertsson, Gauti B. and Michael Woodford (2003), 'The Zero Bound on Interest Rates and Optimal Monetary Policy', *Brookings Papers on Economic Activity*, No. 1 (http://www.brookings.edu/~/media/Projects/BPEA/Spring-2003/2003a_bpea_eggertsson.PDF).

EIB (2015), 'Investment Plan for Europe', Luxembourg: European Investment Bank (http://www.eib.org/about/invest-eu/index.htm).

Eichengreen, Barry (1991), 'Is Europe an Optimum Currency Area?', *NBER Working Paper* No. 3579, January (http://www.nber.org/papers/w3579.pdf).

Eichengreen, Barry (2006), 'Managing the World Economy in the 1990s', in Rhode and Toniolo (2006a), pp. 43–68.

Eichengreen, Barry (2007), 'The Breakup of the Euro Area', *NBER Working Paper* No. 13393, September (http://www.nber.org/papers/w13393).

Eichengreen, Barry (2011), 'Europe's Inevitable Haircut', *Project Syndicate* (http://www.project-syndicate.org/commentary/europe-s-inevitable-haircut).

Eichengreen, Barry, Maurice Obstfeld and Luigi Spaventa (1990), 'One Money for Europe? Lessons from the US Currency Union', *Economic Policy*, Vol. 5, No. 10, pp. 117–187.

Eichengreen, Barry, Andrew K. Rose and Charles Wyplosz (1996), 'Contagious Currency Crises', *NBER Working Paper 5681* (http://www.nber.org/papers/w5681).

Eichengreen, Barry and Peter Temin (2010) 'Fetters of Gold and Paper', *NBER Working Paper No. 16202*, July (http://www.nber.org/papers/w16202).

Eleftheriadis, Pavlos (2014), 'Misrule of the few: How the oligarchs ruined Greece', *Foreign Affairs*, November/December.

Elsner, Benjamin and Klaus F. Zimmermann (2013), '10 Years After: EU Enlargement, Closed Borders, and Migration to Germany', *IZA Discussion Paper No. 7130*, January (http:// http://ftp.iza.org/dp7130.pdf).

Enderlein, Henrik (coordinator), Peter Bofinger, Laurence Boone, Paul de Grauwe, Jean-Claude Piris, Jean Pisani-Ferry, Maria João Rodrigues, André Sapir and António Vitorino (2012), *Completing the Euro. A road map towards fiscal union in Europe. Report of the "Tommaso Padoa-Schioppa Group"*, Berlin and Paris: Notre Europe (http://www.institutdelors.eu/media/completingtheeuroreportpadoa-schioppagroupnejune2012.pdf?pdf=ok).

EP (2015), TTIP: Transatlantic Trade and Investment Partnership, Washington, D.C.: European Parliament, Liaison Office with U.S. Congress (http://www.europarl.europa.eu/us/en/parliamentary_relations/ttip.html).

Epstein, Gerald A. (2005) ed., *Financialization and the World Economy*, Cheltenham: Edward Elgar.

ERP (2013), *Economic Report of the President*, Washington: United States Government Printing Office.

ERP (2014), *Economic Report of the President*, Washington: United States Government Printing Office.

ESA (2013), *European System of Accounts ESA 2010*, Brussels: Eurostat, 2013.

Eser, Fabian and Bernd Schwaab (2015), 'Evaluating the impact of unconventional monetary policy measures: Empirical evidence from the ECB's Securities Markets Programme', *Journal of Financial Economics* (forthcoming) (https://www.aeaweb.org/aea/2015conference/program/retrieve.php?pdfid=669).

Eurobarometer (2014a), *The Euro Area. Report*, Flash Eurobarometer 405, European Commission, October.

Eurobarometer (2014b), *Public Opinion in the European Union. First Results*, Standard Eurobarometer 82, European Commission, December.

Eurobarometer (2014c), *Tables of Results. Public Opinion in the European Union*, Standard Eurobarometer 82, European Commission, November.

Eurobarometer (2014d), *Europeans in 2014. Report*, Special Eurobarometer 415, European Commission, July.

Eurobarometer (2014e), 'Coping with the Crisis. Aggregate Report', European Commission, *Eurobarometer Qualitative Study*, November.

Eurobarometer (2014f), 'Public Opinion in the European Union. First Results', European Commission, *Standard Eurobarometer 82*, Autumn, Fieldwork: November.

European Financial Stability Facility (EFSF) (n.d.), 'About EFSF' (http://www.efsf.europa.eu/about/index.htm).

European Stability Mechanism (ESM) (2015a), 'About us' (http://www.esm.europa.eu/about/index.htm).

European Stability Mechanism (ESM) (2015b), 'Lending capacity (Forward Commitment Capacity)' (http://www.esm.europa.eu/assistance/FCC/index.htm).

European Stability Mechanism (ESM) (2015c), 'Spain (concluded)', Financial Assistance, (http://www.esm.europa.eu/assistance/spain/)

European Stability Mechanism (ESM) (2015d), 'ESM financial assistance for Cyprus', Financial Assistance, (http://www.esm.europa.eu/assistance/cyprus/index.htm).

Eurostat (2011), *External and Intra-EU Trade. A Statistical Yearbook. Data 1958–2010*, Brussels: European Commission.

Eurostat (2012) 'Population and social conditions. 23% of EU citizens were at risk of poverty or social exclusion in 2010', Eurostat Statistics in focus, 9/2012.

Eurostat (2014a), *Why a New ESA?*, Technical Press Briefing, Brussels: Eurostat, 16 January.

Eurostat (2014b), 'European system of national and regional accounts — ESA 2010' (http://ec.europa.eu/eurostat/statistics-explained/index.php/European_system_of_national_and_regional_accounts_-_ESA_2010) (last modified on 8 December 2014).

Eurostat (2015a), 'Balance of the Current Account', 2 March (http://ec.europa.eu/eurostat/tgm/table.do?tab=table&language=en&pcode=tec00043).

Eurostat (2015b), 'Labour cost levels (lc_lci_lev), Reference Metadata in Euro SDMX Metadata Structure (ESMS)' (Last updated 26 March 2015 http://ec.europa.eu/eurostat/cache/metadata/en/lc_lci_lev_esms.htm).

Eurostat (2015c), 'People at risk of poverty or social exclusion' (Last updated January 2015 http://ec.europa.eu/eurostat/statistics-explained/index.php/People_at_risk_of_poverty_or_social_exclusion).

Ezcurra, Roberto, Pedro Pascual and Manuel Rapún (2006), 'Regional specialization in the European Union', *Regional Studies*, Vol. 40, No. 6, pp. 601–616.

Fagerberg, Jan, Martin Srholec and Mark Knell (2007), 'The competitiveness of nations: Why some countries prosper while others fall behind', *World Development*, Vol. 35, No. 10, pp. 1595–1620.

Faini, Riccardo (2006), 'Europe: A continent in decline?', in Rhode and Toniolo (2006a), pp. 69–88.

Fama, Eugene F. (1970), 'Efficient capital markets: A review of theory and empirical work', *Journal of Finance*, Vol. 25, No. 2, pp. 383–417.

Fama, Eugene F. (1991), 'Efficient Capital Markets: II', *Journal of Finance*, Vol. 46, No. 5, pp. 1575–1617.

FCIC (2011), *The Financial Crisis Inquiry Report*, Final Report of the National Commission on the Causes of the Financial and Economic Crisis in the United States, Submitted by the Financial Crisis Inquiry Commission, Washington, DC: Official Government Edition, January (http://www.gpo.gov/fdsys/pkg/GPO-FCIC/pdf/GPO-FCIC.pdf).

Feldstein, Martin (1991), 'Does one market require one money?: Policy Implications of Trade and Currency Zones', 1991 Annual Conference of the Federal Reserve Bank of Kansas City.

Ferguson, Niall (1999), *The Pity of War*, New York: Basic Books.

Field, Alexander (2006), 'Technical Change and US Economic Growth: The Interwar Period and the 1990s', in Rhode and Toniolo (2006a), pp. 89–117.

Fischer, Joschka (2015), 'The Return of the Ugly German', *Project Syndicate*, 23 July (https://www.project-syndicate.org/commentary/return-of-the-ugly-german-by-joschka-fischer-2015-07).

Forbes, Kristin and Roberto Rigobon (2001), 'Measuring Contagion: Conceptual and Empirical Issues', in Stijn Claessens and Kristin J. Forbes (eds.), *International Financial Contagion*, New York: Springer US, pp. 43–66.

Forbes, Kristin J. and Roberto Rigobon (2002), 'No Contagion, Only Interdependence: Measuring Stock Market Comovements', *The Journal of Finance*, Vol. 57, No. 5, October, pp. 2223–2261.

Förster, Michael, Ana Llena-Nozal and Vahé Nafilyan (2014), 'Trends in Top Incomes and their Taxation in OECD Countries', *OECD Social, Employment and Migration Working Papers*, No. 159, Paris: OECD (http://dx.doi.org/10.1787/5jz43jhlz87f-en).

Foster, John Bellamy and Robert W. McChesney (2013), *The Endless Crisis: How Monopoly-Finance Capital Produces Stagnation and Upheaval from the USA to China*, New York: Monthly Review Press.

Fox, Justine (2009), *The Myth of the Rational Market. A History of Risk, Reward, and Delusion on Wall Street*, New York: Harper Collins.

Frank, Robert H. (1985), *Choosing the Right Pond: Human Behavior and the Quest for Status*, New York: Oxford University Press.

Frank, Robert H. (1997), 'The frame of reference as a public good', *Economic Journal*, Vol. 107, November, pp. 1832–1847.

Frank, Robert H. (2007), *Falling Behind: How Rising Inequality Harms the Middle Class*, Berkeley: University of California Press.

Frankel, Jeffrey (2006), 'Could the twin deficits jeopardize US hegemony?', *Journal of Policy Modeling*, Vol. 28, pp. 653–663.

Frankel, Jeffrey (2013), 'The Future of the Currency Union', *Faculty Research Working Paper Series* RWP13-015, Harvard Kennedy School, May.

Frankel, Jeffrey A. and Andrew K. Rose (1998), 'The endogeneity of the optimum currency area criteria', *Economic Journal*, Vol. 108, No. 449, pp. 1009–1025.

Frankel, Jeffrey and Jesse Schreger (2013), 'Over-optimistic official forecasts and fiscal rules in the eurozone', *Review of World Economics*, Vol. 149, No. 2, pp. 247–272.

Franz, Wolfgang, Clement Fuest, Martin Hellwig and Hans-Werner Sinn (2010) 'A euro rescue plan', *CESifo* Forum, Vol. 11, No. 2, pp. 101–104.

Freeman, Richard B. (2008), 'Labor Market Institutions around the World', *CEP Discussion Paper No. 844*, London: Centre for Economic Performance, London School of Economics and Political Science, January (http://eprints.lse.ac.uk/19647/1/Labor_Market_Institutions_Around_the_World.pdf).

Freeman, Richard B. (2013), 'Failing the test? The flexible U.S. job market in the Great Recession', *The ANNALS of the American Academy of Political and Social Science November*, Vol. 650, No. 1, pp. 78–97.

Friedman, Milton (1997). 'The Euro: Monetary Unity To Political Disunity?' Project Syndicate, 28 August (http://www.project-syndicate.org/commentary/the-euro--monetary-unity-to-political-disunity).

FSB (2011), *Shadow Banking: Strengthening Oversight and Regulation. Recommendations of the Financial Stability Board*, Basel: Financial Stability Board, 27 October (http://www.financialstabilityboard.org/wp-content/uploads/r_111027a.pdf?page_moved=1).

Furceri, Davide (2013), *Toward a Fiscal Union for the Euro Area: Technical Background Notes*, Washington, DC: International Monetary Fund, September.

Furceri, Davide and Georgios Karras (2008), Business-cycle synchronization in the EMU, *Applied Economics*, Vol. 40, No. 12, pp. 1491–1501.

Furceri, Davide and Aleksandra Zdzienicka (2013), 'The Euro Area Crisis: Need for a Supranational Fiscal Risk Sharing Mechanism?', *IMF Working Paper* WP/13/198, September.

Furman, Jeffrey L., Michael E. Porter, and Scott Stern (2002), 'The determinants of national innovative capacity', *Research Policy*, Vol. 31, pp. 899–933.

Gabrisch, Hubert and Karsten Staehr (2014), 'The Euro Plus Pact: Cost Competitiveness and External Capital Flows in the EU Countries', *Working Paper Series* No. 1650, March (published in *JCMS Journal of Common Market Studies*, pp. 1–19).

Gáková, Zuzana and Lewis Dijkstra (2008), 'Labour mobility between the regions of the EU-27 and a comparison with the USA', EPC, *European Union Regional Policy* No. 02/2008.

Gáková, Zuzana and Lewis Dijkstra (2010), 'Labour Mobility between the Regions of the EU-27 and a Comparison with the USA', *Princeton Working Paper* 100976, (http://epc2010.princeton.edu/papers/100976).

Galbraith, John Kenneth (1954), *The Great Crash 1929*, London: Penguin, 1961; Boston: Houghton Mifflin, 1954.

Galbraith, John Kenneth (1990), *A Short History of Financial Euphoria*, New York: Viking Penguin; Knoxville: Whittle Direct Books.

GAO (2013), *Financial Regulatory Reform: Financial Crisis Losses and Potential Impacts of the Dodd-Frank Act*, GAO-13-180, US Government Accountability Office, January.

Gechert, Sebastian and Ansgar Rannenberg (2015), 'The costs of Greece's fiscal consolidation', *Policy Brief*, Macroeconomic Policy Institute (IMK), March (http://www.boeckler.de/pdf/p_imk_pb_1_2015.pdf).

Gechert, Sebastian, Andrew Hughes Hallett and Ansgar Rannenberg (2015), 'Fiscal multipliers in downturns and the effects of Eurozone consolidation', *CEPR Policy Insight No. 79*, February.

Geithner, Timothy F. (2014), *Stress Test. Reflections on Financial Crises*, New York: Crown.

Gerlach, Stefan (2009), 'Defining and Measuring Systemic Risk', Brussels: European Parliament, Committee on Economic and Monetary Affairs, November (http://www.europarl.europa.eu/activities/committees/studies.do?language=EN).

Gerlach, Stefan and John Lewis (2010), 'The Zero Lower Bound, ECB Interest Rate Policy and the Financial Crisis', *Working Paper No. 254/2010*, July, Amsterdam: De Nederlandsche Bank NV.

GII (2014), *The Global Innovation Index 2014: The Human Factor in Innovation*, second printing. Fontainebleau, Ithaca, and Geneva: Cornell University, INSEAD, and World Intellectual Property Organization (WIPO), Soumitra Dutta, Bruno Lanvin, and Sacha Wunsch-Vincent (eds.).

Giuliodori, Massimo and Roel Beetsma (2008), 'On the relationship between fiscal plans in the European Union: An empirical analysis based on real-time data', *Journal of Comparative Economics*, Vol. 36, pp. 221–242.

Glăvan, Bogdan (2004), 'The Failure of OCA Analysis', *Austrian Economics*, Vol. 7, No. 2 (Summer) pp. 29–46.

Glick, Reuven and Kevin J. Lansing (2010), 'Global household leverage, house prices, and consumption', *FRBSF Economic Letter* 2010-01, 11 January (http://www.frbsf.org/economic-research/publications/economic-letter/2010/january/global-household-leverage-house-prices-consumption/).

Glover, Brent and Seth Richards-Shubik (2014), 'Contagion in the European sovereign debt crisis', *VOX, CEPR's Policy Portal*, 12 November (http://www.voxeu.org/article/contagion-european-sovereign-debt-crisis).

Gnos, Claude and Louis-Philippe Rochon (2004), 'What is next for the Washington consensus? The fifteenth anniversary, 1989–2004', *Journal of Post Keynesian Economics*, Vol. 27, No. 2, pp. 187–193.

Goetzmann, William N., Liang Peng, and Jacqueline Yen (2009), 'The Subprime Crisis and House Price Appreciation', *NBER Working Paper No. 15334*, September.

Goodhart, Charles A.E. (1988), 'The two concepts of money: Implications for the analysis of optimal currency areas', *European Journal of Political Economy*, Vol. 14, pp. 407–432.

Goodhart, Charles A.E. and Dirk Schoenmaker (2014), 'The ECB as lender of last resort?', *VOX, CEPR's Policy Portal*, 23 October (http://www.voxeu.org/article/ecb-lender-last-resort).

GOT (2001), 'Report on Consolidation in the Financial Sector', Group Of Ten, January (http://www.bis.org/publ/gten05.pdf).

Granovetter, Mark (1985), 'Economic action and social structure: The problem of embeddedness', *American Journal of Sociology*, Vol. 91, No. 3, pp. 481–510.

'Greek exit from the euro is not a risk worth taking'. (2015). *Financial Times*, 17 March (http://www.ft.com/cms/s/0/4d952142-cc9d-11e4-b5a5-00144feab7de.html#axzz3oi38cRTX).

Greenwood, Robin and David Scharfstein (2013), 'The growth of finance', *Journal of Economic Perspectives*, Vol. 27, No. 2, pp. 3–28.

Gros, Daniel (2012), 'The Treaty on Stability, Coordination and Governance in the Economic and Monetary Union (aka Fiscal Compact)', *CEPS Commentary*, 8 March (https://www.ceps.eu/publications/treaty-stability-coordination-and-governance-economic-and-monetary-union-aka-fiscal).

Gros, Daniel and Cinzia Alcidi (2011), 'Adjustment Difficulties and Debt Overhangs in the Eurozone Periphery', *CEPS Working Document*, 347, May (http://aei.pitt.edu/31785/4/WD_347_Gros_&_Alcidi_GIPSY_update.pdf).

Gros, Daniel and Cinzia Alcidi (2014), 'The Case of the Disappearing Fiscal Compact', *CEPS Commentary*, 5 November (https://www.ceps.eu/publications/case-disappearing-fiscal-compact).

Gros, Daniel and Stefano Micossi (2008), 'The beginning of the end game', *VOX, CEPR's Policy Portal*, 20 September (http://aei.pitt.edu/11581/1/1712[1].pdf).

Gross, Marco and Christoffer Kok (2013), 'Measuring contagion potential among sovereigns and banks using a mixed-cross-section GVAR', European Central Bank, *Working Paper Series* No. 1570/August.

Guerrieri, Paolo (2015), 'The risk of a prolonged stagnation in the Eurozone and policy challenges', in Bruno Dallago and John McGowan (eds.), *Crises in Europe in the Transatlantic Context: Economic and Political Appraisals*, London and New York: Routledge, pp. 180–188.

Guillaumont, Patrick (1999), 'On the Economic Vulnerability of Low Income Countries', CERDI-CNRS, Université d'Auvergne (http://siteresources.worldbank.org/INTPOVERTY/Resources/WDR/stiglitz/Guillau2.pdf).

Guillaumont, Patrick (2011), 'The Concept of Structural Economic Vulnerability and Its Relevance for the Identification of the Least Developed Countries and Other Purposes (Nature, Measurement, and Evolution)', *CDP Background*

Paper No. 12, September (http://www.un.org/en/development/desa/policy/cdp/cdp_background_papers/bp2011_12.pdf).

Guiso, Luigi, Paola Sapienza and Luigi Zingales (2014), 'Monnet's Error?', *Brookings Panel on Economic Activity*, September (http://www.brookings.edu/about/projects/bpea/papers/2014/monnets-error).

Hall, Peter A. and David W. Soskice (2001) eds., *Varieties of Capitalism. The Institutional Foundations of Comparative Advantage*, Oxford: Oxford University Press.

Hall, Peter A. and Kathleen Thelen (2009), 'Institutional change in varieties of capitalism', *Socio-Economic Review*, Vol. 7, pp. 7–34.

Hall, Robert E. and Charles I. Jones (1999), 'Why Do Some Countries Produce So Much More Output Per Worker Than Others?', *Quarterly Journal of Economics*, Vol. 114, No. 1, pp. 83–116.

Hallet, Martin (2000), 'Regional Specialisation and Concentration in the EU', European Commissions, *Economic Papers*, No. 141, March.

Hamilton, Daniel S. (2014), 'TTIP's Geostrategic Implications', Paper presented at the international conference on (A Global Perspective on the European Crisis), University of North Carolina at Chapel Hill, 18–20 September.

Hanke, Steve H. (2014), 'Measuring misery around the world', *Globe Asia*, May, pp. 22–25.

Hanusch, Marek (2012), 'The Doing Business Indicators, Economic Growth and Regulatory Reform', *Policy Research Working Paper 6176*, The World Bank, August.

Hart, Oliver and John Moore (1988), 'Incomplete Contracts and Renegotiation', *Econometrica*, Vol. 56, No. 4, pp. 755–785.

Hart-Landsberg, Martin (2013), 'Capitalism, Crisis, and Resistance. Lessons from Iceland', *Monthly Review*, Vol. 65, No. 5, October (http://monthlyreview.org/2013/10/01/lessons-iceland/).

Haskel, Jonathan, Robert Z. Lawrence, Edward E. Leamer, and Matthew J. Slaughter (2012), 'Globalization and U.S. Wages: Modifying Classic Theory to Explain Recent Facts', *Journal of Economic Perspectives*, Vol. 26, No. 2, pp. 119–140.

Hassan, Fadi and Gianmarco I. P. Ottaviano (2013), 'Productivity in Italy: The great unlearning', *VOX, CEPR's Policy Portal*, 30 November (http://www.voxeu.org/article/productivity-italy-great-unlearning).

Hassel, Anke (2014), 'Adjustments in the Eurozone: Varieties of Capitalism and the Crisis in Southern Europe', *LSE 'Europe in Question' Discussion Paper Series*, LEQS Paper No. 76/2014, May.

Havlik, Peter (2014), 'Economic Consequences of the Ukraine Conflict', *Policy Notes and Reports 14*, The Vienna Institute for International Economic Studies (wiiw), November (http://wiiw.ac.at/economic-consequences-of-the-ukraine-conflict-p-3427.html).

Hayek, Friedrich A. von (1990), *Denationalisation of Money: The Argument Refined. An Analysis of the Theory and Practice of Concurrent Currencies*, Third Edition, London: The Institute of Economic Affairs.

Heinen, Nicolaus (2011a), 'A European Transfer Union. How large, how powerful, how expensive?', *EU Monitor 81*, Frankfurt am Main: Deutsche Bank Research, 2 August.

Heinen, Nicolaus (2011b), 'EU net contributor or net recipient. Just a matter of your standpoint?', *Deutsche Bank Research*, 11 May (https://www.dbresearch.com/PROD/DBR_INTERNET_EN-PROD/PROD0000000000273546.pdf).

Heinz, Frigyes Ferdinand and Melanie Ward-Warmedinger (2006), 'Cross-Border Labour Mobility within an Enlarged EU', *Occasional Paper Series No. 52*, European Central Bank.

Hellman, Joel, Geraint Jones, and Daniel Kaufmann (2000), 'Seize the State, Seize the Day: State Capture, Corruption, and Influence in Transition Economies', *World Bank Policy Research Working Paper No. 2444*, Washington, DC: The World Bank (http://siteresources.worldbank.org/INTWBIGOVANTCOR/Resources/seize.pdf).

Higgins, Bryon (1993), 'Was the ERM crisis inevitable?', *Economic Review*, Fourth Quarter, pp. 27–40.

Hill, Steven (2014), 'Ready or not, Transfer Union here we come', *Social Europe*, 21 February (http://www.socialeurope.eu/2012/02/ready-or-not-transfer-union-here-we-come/).

Hirschman, Albert O. (1970), *Exit, Voice, and Loyalty: Responses to Decline in Firms, Organizations, and States*, Cambridge, MA: Harvard University Press.

HLG (2013), *Innovation Policy Management: Report and Recommendations*, June, Brussels: High Level Group.

HLG (2014), *Inspiring and Completing European Innovation Ecosystems. Blueprint*, August, Brussels: High Level Group.

Hoff, Karla and Joseph E. Stiglitz (2010), 'Equilibrium fictions: A cognitive approach to societal rigidity', *American Economic Review: Papers & Proceedings*, Vol. 100 (May), pp. 141–146.

Hoffmann, Jürgen (2004), *Co-ordinated continental European market economies under pressure from globalisation. Case study: Germany's "Rhineland capitalism"*, Toronto: The Canadian Centre for German and European Studies (http://ccges.apps01.yorku.ca/wp/wp-content/uploads/2008/12/hoffmann-co-ordinated-continental-european-market-economies-under-pressure-from-globalisation-case-study-germanys-rhineland-capitalism.pdf).

Holden, Steinar and Fredrik Wulfsberg (2008), 'Downward nominal wage rigidity in the OECD', *The B.E. Journal of Macroeconomics*, Vol. 8, No. 1, Article 15, pp. 48.

Holmstrom, Bengt and Steven N. Kaplan (2001), 'Corporate governance and merger activity in the United States: Making sense of the 1980s and 1990s', *Journal of Economic Perspectives*, Vol. 15, No. 2, pp. 121–144.

Hong, Pingfan and Zhibo Tan (2014), 'A Comparative Study of the Forecasting Performance of Three International Organizations', United Nations, Department of Economic and Social Affairs, *DESA Working Paper No. 133*, ST/ESA/2014/DWP/133.

Hout, Michael (2015), 'A summary of what we know about social mobility', *The ANNALS of the American Academy of Political and Social Science*, January 2015, Vol. 657, No. 1, pp. 27–36.

Huber, Peter (2007), 'Regional labour market developments in transition: A survey of the empirical literature', *European Journal of Comparative Economics*, Vol. 4, pp. 263–298.

Huber, Peter (2009), 'Regional Labour Market Disparities in an Enlarged European Union', in Bruno Dallago and Paul Blokker (eds.), *Regional Diversity and Local Development in the New Member States*, Houndmills, Basingstoke: Palgrave Macmillan, pp. 122–165.

HUD (2009), 'Subprime Lending Report. Unequal Burden: Income and Racial Disparities in Subprime Lending', Archives, Washington, D.C.: U.S. Department of Housing and Urban Development (http://archives.hud.gov/reports/subprime/subprime.cfm) (content archived: January 20, 2009).

Husted, Steven and Shuichiro Nishioka (2013), 'China's fare share? The growth of Chinese exports in world trade', *Review of World Economy*, Vol. 149, No. 3, pp. 565–585.

ICC (2013), *Open Markets Index*, Paris: ICC Research Foundation, International Chamber of Commerce, April.

Illing, Gerhard and Philipp König (2014), 'The European Central Bank as lender of last resort', *DIW Economic Bulletin 9. 2014* (http://www.diw.de/documents/publikationen/73/diw_01.c.488640.de/diw_econ_bull_2014-09-3.pdf).

IMF (2008), *World Economic Outlook*, Washington, DC: International Monetary Fund, April.

IMF (2011), *Fiscal Monitor*, Washington, DC: International Monetary Fund, September.

IMF (2012a), *Global Financial Stability Report. Restoring Confidence and Progressing on Reforms*, Washington, DC: International Monetary Fund, October (http://www.imf.org/external/pubs/ft/gfsr/2012/02/pdf/text.pdf).

IMF (2012b), *World Economic Outlook: Coping with High Debt and Sluggish Growth*, Washington DC: International Monetary Fund.

IMF (2013a), *Reassessing the Role and Modalities of Fiscal Policy in Advanced Economies*, IMF Policy Paper, Washington, DC: International Monetary Fund, 21 June (http://www.imf.org/external/np/pp/eng/2013/072113.pdf).

IMF (2013b), 'Germany, 2013 Article IV Consultation', *IMF Country Report No. 13/255*, August.

IMF (2014a), *World Economic Outlook: Legacies, Clouds, Uncertainties*, Washington, DC: International Monetary Fund, October.

IMF (2014b), *Global Financial Stability Report. Risk Taking, Liquidity, and Shadow Banking: Curbing Excess While Promoting Growth*, Washington, DC: International Monetary Fund, October (http://www.imf.org/external/pubs/ft/gfsr/2014/02/pdf/text.pdf).

IMF (2014c), *2014 Article IV Consultation with the Euro Area Concluding Statement of the IMF Mission*, 19 June (http://www.imf.org/external/np/ms/2014/061914.htm).

IMF (2015a), *Fiscal Monitor. Now Is the Time Fiscal Policies for Sustainable Growth*, Washington, DC: International Monetary Fund, April.

IMF (2015b), *World Economic Outlook: Uneven Growth. Short- and Long-Term Factors*, Washington, DC: International Monetary Fund, April.

IMF (2015c), 'International reserves', IMF Annual Report 2015 (http://www.imf.org/external/pubs/ft/ar/2015/eng/pdf/AR15_AppI.pdf)

'Interview with Former German Finance Minister Peer Steinbrück: "Germans Will Have to Pay"', *Spiegel Online International*, 12 September 2011 (Retrieved 12 October 2015 from http://www.spiegel.de/international/europe/interview-with-former-german-finance-minister-germans-will-have-to-pay-a-785704-3.html).

Isaksson, Anders (2007), 'Determinants of Total Factor Productivity: A Literature Review', *Staff Working Paper 02/2007*, Vienna: United Nations Industrial Development Organization, Research and Statistics Branch, July.

ISTAT (2014), 'European System of Accounts — Esa 2010: Questions and Answers', 14 March (http://www.istat.it/en/archive/115500).

Ito, Takatoshi and Tokuo Iwaisako (1995), 'Explaining Asset Bubbles in Japan', *NBER Working Paper* No. 5358, November.

Jansen, W. Jos and Ad C. J. Stokman (2014), 'International business cycle co-movement: The role of FDI', *Applied Economics*, Vol. 46, No. 4, pp. 383–393, DOI: 10.1080/00036846.2013.844327.

Jappelli, Tullio and Luigi Pistaferri (2009), 'Does Consumption Inequality Track Income Inequality in Italy?', *CSEF Working Paper*, 229, May.

Jappelli, Tullio and Luigi Pistaferri (2010), 'Does Consumption Inequality Track Income Inequality in Italy?', *Review of Economic Dynamics*, Vol. 13, No. 1, January, pp. 133–153.

Jappelli, Tullio and Luigi Pistaferri (2013), 'Fiscal policy and MPC heterogeneity', *CFS Working Paper*, No. 2013/14 (http://www.econstor.eu/bitstream/10419/87681/1/771574223.pdf).

Jarand, Michael (2015), 'The Effects of a Wage Increase by Large Corporations on the Macroeconomy', Washington DC.: The Peterson Institute for International Economics, 17 January (http://blogs.piie.com/realtime/?p=4734).

Jauer, Julia, Thomas Liebig, John P. Martin and Patrick Puhani (2014), 'Migration as an Adjustment Mechanism in the Crisis? A Comparison of Europe and the United States', OECD Social, Employment and Migration Working Papers No. 155, January, Paris: OECD.

Jaumotte, Florence and Carolina Osorio Buitron (2015), 'Power from the People', *Finance & Development*, IMF, March.

Kahanec, Martin (2012), 'Labor Mobility in an Enlarged European Union', *IZA Discussion Paper No. 6485*, April.

Kahneman, Daniel, Jack L. Knecht and Richard H. Thaler (1991), 'Anomalies: The endowment effect, loss aversion, and status quo bias', *Journal of Economic Perspectives*, Vol. 5, No. 1, pp. 193–206.

Kahneman, Daniel, Paul Slovic, and Amos Tversky (1982), eds., *Judgment under Uncertainty: Heuristics and Biases*, Cambridge: Cambridge University Press.

Kahneman, Daniel and Amos Tversky (1984), 'Choices, values, and frames', *American Psychologist*, Vol. 39, No. 4, pp. 341–350.

Kahneman, Daniel, and Amos Tversky (2000), eds., *Choices, Values and Frames*, Cambridge: Cambridge University Press.

Kaiser, Wolfram, Brigitte Leucht and Morten Rasmussen (2008) (eds.), *The History of the European Union. Origins of a Trans- and Supranational Polity 1950–72*, Abingdon: Routledge.

Kaletsky, Anatole (2015), 'Why the Greek Deal Will Work', *Project Syndicate*, 22 July (https://www.project-syndicate.org/print/why-the-greek-deal-will-work-by-anatole-kaletsky-2015-07).

Kaminsky, Graciela L. and Carmen M. Reinhart (2000) 'On crises, contagion, and confusion', *Journal of International Economics*, Vol. 51, No. 1, pp. 145–168.

Kattel, Rainer and Ringa Raudla (2013), 'The Baltic Republics and the crisis of 2008–2011', *Europe-Asia Studies*, Vol. 65, No. 3, pp. 426–449.

Kawalec, Stefan and Ernest Pytlarczyk (2013), 'Controlled Dismantlement of the Eurozone: A Proposal for a New European Monetary System and a New Role for the European Central Bank', *Working Paper No. 155*, Warsaw: National Bank of Poland (http://www.nbp.pl/publikacje/materialy_i_studia/155_en.pdf).

Keeney, Ralph L. (2004), 'Framing public policy decisions', *International Journal of Technology, Policy and Management*, Vol. 4, No. 2, pp. 95–115.

Kenen, Peter (1969), 'The theory of optimum currency areas: An eclectic view', in Robert Mundell and Alexander K. Swoboda (eds.), *Monetary Problems in the International Economy*, Chicago: University of Chicago Press, pp. 41–60.

Kenourgios, Dimitris and Dimitrios Dimitriou (2015), 'Contagion of the Global Financial Crisis and the real economy: A regional analysis', *Economic Modelling*, Vol. 44, pp. 283–293.

Keynes, John Maynard (1920), *The Economic Consequences of the Peace*, New York: Harcourt, Brace and Howe.

Kim, Teakdong, Bonwoo Koo and Minsoo Park (2013), 'Role of financial regulation and innovation in the financial crisis', *Journal of Financial Stability*, Vol. 9, No. 4, pp. 662–672.

Kindleberger, Charles P. (1978), *Manias, Panics, and Crashes: A History of Financial Crises*, New York: Basic Books.

Kočenda, Evžen, Ali M. Kutan and Taner M. Yigit (2008), 'Fiscal convergence in the European Union', *North American Journal of Economics and Finance*, Vol. 19, pp. 319–330.

Kolasa, Marcin (2010), 'Real Convergence and Its Illusions', *Working Paper Series No. 1231*, August, Frankfurt am Main: European Central Bank.

Konstantakopoulou, Ioanna and Efthymios Tsionas (2011), 'The business cycle in Eurozone economies (1960 to 2009)', *Applied Financial Economics*, Vol. 21, No. 20, pp. 1495–1513, DOI: 10.1080/09603107.2011.579060.

Korinek, Anton and Jonathan Kreamer (2014), 'The Redistributive Effects of Financial Deregulation: Wall Street Versus Main Street', *BIS Working Papers* No 468, Bank for International Settlements, September.

Kouparitsas, Michael A. (2001), 'Is the United States an Optimum Currency Area? An Empirical Analysis of Regional Business Cycles', *WP 2001–22*, Federal Reserve Bank of Chicago.

Krueger, Anne (1974), 'The political economy of the rent-seeking society', *American Economic Review*, Vol. 64, No. 3, pp. 291–303.

Krueger, Dirk and Fabrizio Perri (2012), 'How Do Households Respond to Income Shocks?', Rome: Bank of Italy (https://www.bancaditalia.it/pubblicazioni/altri-atti-convegni/2012-macroec-after-flood/PERRI-paper-hholds_response_oct2012.pdf).

Krugman, Paul (1991), *Geography and Trade*, Cambridge, MA: The MIT Press.
Krugman, Paul (2009), *The Conscience of a Liberal: Reclaiming America from the Right*, London: Penguin Books.
Krugman, Paul (2011), 'Can Europe be saved?', *The New York Times*, January 12.
Kumhof M., and Rancière R. (2010), 'Inequality, Leverage and Crises', *IMF Working Paper* WP/10/268, November.
La Porta, Rafael, Florencio Lopez-de-Silanes and Andrei Shleifer (2008), 'The economic consequences of legal origin', *Journal of Economic Literature*, Vol. 46, No. 2, pp. 285–332.
Lane, Philip R. (2013), 'Capital Flows in the Euro Area', *European Economy*, Economic Papers No. 497, April (http://ec.europa.eu/economy_finance/publications/economic_paper/2013/pdf/ecp497_en.pdf).
Lapavitsas, Costas (2009), 'Financialised capitalism: Crisis and financial expropriation', *Historical Materialism*, Vol. 17, No. 2, pp. 114–148.
Lapavitsas, Costas, Annina Kaltenbrunner, Duncan Lindo, J. Michell, Juan Pablo Painceira, Eugenia Pires, Jeff Powell, Alexis Stenfors and Nuno Teles (2010), 'Eurozone crisis: Beggar thyself and thy neighbour', *Journal of Balkan and Near Eastern Studies*, Vol. 12, No. 4, pp. 321–373.
Lazonick, William and Mary O'Sullivan (2000), 'Maximizing shareholder value: A new ideology for corporate governance', *Economy and Society*, Vol. 29, No. 1, pp. 13–35.
LEC (2000), *Presidency Conclusions*, Lisbon European Council, 23 and 24 March, (http://www.consilium.europa.eu/en/uedocs/cms_data/docs/pressdata/en/ec/00100-r1.en0.htm).
Lechman, Ewa (2009), 'Okun's and Barro's Misery Index as an Alternative Poverty Assessment Tool. Recent estimations for European countries', MPRA Paper No. 37493, Munich (Published in: Growth and innovation — selected issues. Monograph. Gdańsk, 2009) (http://mpra.ub.uni-muenchen.de/37493/).
Lemieux, Thomas (2008), 'The changing nature of wage inequality', *Journal of Population Economics*, Vol. 21, No. 1, pp. 21–48.
Levi-Faur, David (2005), 'The global diffusion of regulatory capitalism', *The ANNALS of the American Academy of Political and Social Science*, Vol. 598, No. 1, pp. 12–32.
Levi-Faur, David and Jacint Jordana (2005), eds., 'Globalizing Regulatory Capitalism', special issue of *The ANNALS of the American Academy of Political and Social Science*, Vol. 598, No. 1, pp. 6–9.
Levine, Ross (2005), 'Finance and Growth: Theory and Evidence', in Philippe Aghion and Steven N. Durlauf (eds.), *Handbook of Economic Growth*, Volume

1A, Amsterdam: Elsevier, pp. 865–934 (also in http://thannaletchimy.webs.com/Topic%201.pdf).

Leythienne, Denis and Tatjana Smokova (2009), 'Business profit share and investment rate higher in the EU than in the USA. Profits and investment of non-financial corporations, 1995–2007', Eurostat: *Statistics in Focus* 28/2009.

Loayza, Norman V. and Luis Serven (2010), eds., *Business Regulation and Economic Performance*, 2010, Washington, DC: World Bank.

Luchtenberg, Kimberly F. and Quang Viet Vu (2015), 'The 2008 financial crisis: Stock market contagion and its determinants', *Research in International Business and Finance*, Vol. 33, pp. 178–203.

Macys, Gediminas (2012), 'The crisis and economic recovery in Baltic Countries', *International Journal of Humanities and Social Science*, Vol. 2, No. 19, October, pp. 202–209.

Maddison, Angus (1995), *Monitoring the World Economy, 1820–1992*, Development Centre Studies, Paris: OECD.

Malkin, Israel and Fernanda Nechio (2012), 'U.S. and Euro-Area Monetary Policy by Regions', *FRSBSF Economic Letter*, 2012–6 (February 27) (http://www.frbsf.org/economic-research/publications/economic-letter/2012/february/us-europe-monetary-policy/).

Mallaby, Sebastian (2011), 'Germany is the real winner in a transfer union', *Financial Times*, 24 November.

Mamolo, Marija and Sergei Scherbov (2009), 'Population Projections for Forty-Four European Countries: The Ongoing Population Ageing', *European Demographic Research Papers* 2/2009, Vienna: Vienna Institute of Demography of the Austrian Academy of Sciences (http://www.oeaw.ac.at/vid/download/edrp_2_09.pdf).

Mamuneas, Theofanis and Elena Ketteni (2014), 'Multilateral Comparisons of Productivity among European Countries', *Economic Analysis Papers No. 10–14*, Economics Research Centre, University of Cyprus, December.

Manasse, Paolo (2010), 'Stability and Growth Pact: Counterproductive proposals', *VOX, CEPR's Policy Portal*, 7 October (http://www.voxeu.org/article/stability-and-growth-pact-counterproductive-proposals).

Manasse, Paolo (2013), 'The roots of the Italian stagnation', *VOX, CEPR's Policy Portal*, 19 June (http://www.voxeu.org/article/roots-italian-stagnation).

Manasse, Paolo and Nouriel Roubini (2009), 'Rules of thumb for sovereign debt crises', *Journal of International Economics*, Vol. 78, No. 2, pp. 192–205.

Manchin, Miriam (2004), 'Determinants of European cross-border mergers and acquisitions', *European Economy, Economic Papers*, Brussels: European Commission.

Mandel, Benjamin R. (2012), 'Why Is the U.S. Share of World Merchandise Exports Shrinking?', *Current Issues in Economics and Finance*, Vol. 18, No. 1 (www.newyorkfed.org/research/current_issues).

Manyika, James, Jacques Bughin, Susan Lund, Olivia Nottebohm, David Poulter, Sebastian Jauch, and Sree Ramaswamy (2014), *Global Flows in a Digital Age: How Trade, Finance, People, and Data Connect the World Economy*, McKinsey Global Institute.

Marangos, John (2012), 'The post-Keynesian retort to "After the Washington Consensus"', *Journal of Post Keynesian Economics*, Vol. 34, No. 4, pp. 583–610.

Marer, Paul (2016), 'The euro and East Europe: Six insiders, six outsiders. Why so?', in Bruno Dallago, Gert Guri and John McGowan (eds.), *A Global Perspective on the European Economic Crisis*, Abingdon, Oxfordshire: Routledge.

Marshall, Alfred (1890), *Principles of Economics*, Houndmills, Basingstoke: Palgrave Macmillan, 2013.

Martini, Maíra (2014), 'State Capture: An Overview', *Anti-Corruption Help Desk*, 11 March, Transparency International (http://www.transparency.org/files/content/corruptionqas/State_capture_an_overview_2014.pdf).

Masson, Paul (1998), 'Contagion: Monsoonal Effects, Spillovers, and Jumps between Multiple Equilibria', *IMF Working Paper WP/98/142*. Washington, DC: International Monetary Fund.

Matthijs, Herman (2010), 'The Budget of the European Union', *IES Working Paper* 4/2010, Brussels: Institute for European Studies (IES).

Maurin, Laurent, Moreno Roma and Igor Vetlov (2011), 'Profit Dynamics across the Largest Euro Area Countries and Sectors', European Central Bank, *Working Paper Series* No. 1410, December.

Mazower, Mark (1998), *Dark Continent: Europe's Twentieth Century*, New York: Vintage Books.

McAllister, Richard (2009), *European Union. An Historical and Political Survey, 2nd Edition*, Abingdon: Routledge.

Mchugh, David (2014), 'Here's what it would cost for Greece to leave the euro', *Business Insider UK* (http://uk.businessinsider.com/heres-what-it-would-cost-for-greece-to-leave-the-euro-2015-2?r=US).

McKinnon, Ronald (1963), 'Optimum currency areas', *American Economic Review*, Vol. 53, September, pp. 717–724.

Meade, James E. (1957), 'The balance of payments problems of a free trade area', *The Economic Journal*, Vol. 67, No. 267, September, pp. 379–96.

Memedovic, Olga (2009) 'Industrial Development and the Dynamics of International Specialization Patterns', *Research and Statistics Branch Working Paper 23/2009*, Unido.

Memedovic, Olga and Lelio Iapadre (2009), 'Industrial Development and the Dynamics of International Specialization Patterns', *Research and Statistics Branch Working Paper* 23/2009, Unido.

Ménard, Claude and Bertrand du Marais (2006), 'Can we rank legal systems according to their economic efficiency?', in Peter Nobel (ed.), *New Frontiers of Law and Economics*, Zürich: Schulthess Verlag, pp. 7–28.

Mendoza, Enrique G. and Vincenzo Quadrini (2009), 'Financial Globalization, Financial Crises and Contagion', *NBER Working Paper Series*, Working Paper 15432 (http://www.nber.org/papers/w15432).

Merler, Silvia (2013), 'The liquidity quandary: On the risk connected to normalisation of the Eurozone liquidity condition, *Bruegel* (http://www.bruegel.org/nc/blog/detail/article/1177-the-liquidity-quandary/).

Merler, Silvia and Jean Pisani-Ferry (2012a), 'Sudden Stops in the Euro Area', *Bruegel Policy Contribution*, No. 2012/06, March.

Merler, Silvia and Jean Pisani-Ferry (2012b), 'Sudden stops in the Euro area', *Review of Economics and Institutions*, Vol. 3, No. 3, Article 5.

Meyer, Bruce D. and James X. Sullivan (2013), 'Consumption and Income Inequality and the Great Recession', *American Economic Review: Papers & Proceedings*, Vol. 103, No. 3, pp. 178–183.

Mian, Atif R. and Amir Sufi (2009), 'The Consequences of Mortgage Credit Expansion: Evidence from the U.S. Mortgage Default Crisis', *Quarterly Journal of Economics*, Vol. 124, No. 4, pp. 1449–1496.

Mian, Atif R. and Amir Sufi (2010), 'Household Leverage and the Recession of 2007–09', *IMF Economic Review*, Vol. 58, No. 1, pp. 74–117.

Miller, Vaughne (2012), 'Can Greece legally withdraw from the euro?', *Standard Note* SN/IA/6342, London: House of Commons Library.

Mills, Daniel Quinn (2009), *The World Financial Crisis 2008–2010: What Happened, Who Is To Blame, And How To Protect Your Money*, Lexington, KY: CreateSpace.

Mills, Daniel Quinn (2010), *The World Financial Crisis 2008–2010*, Lexington, KY.

Minsky, Hyman P. (1974), 'The modeling of financial instability: An introduction', in *Modelling and Simulation*, Vol. 5, Proceedings of the Fifth Annual Pittsburgh Conference, Instruments Society of America, pp. 267–272.

Minsky, Hyman P. (1982), *Can "It" Happen Again?: Essays on Instability and Finance*, Armonk, NY: M. E. Sharpe.

Minsky, Hyman P. (1992), 'The Financial Instability Hypothesis', *Working Paper No. 74*, The Jerome Levy Economics Institute of Bard College (http://www.levyinstitute.org/pubs/wp74.pdf) and in Philip Arestis and Malcom Sawyer (eds.), *Handbook of Radical Political Economy*, Aldershot: Edward Elgar, 1993.

Mody, Ashoka (2015), 'Living (Dangerously) Without a Fiscal Union', *Bruegel Working Paper 2015/03*, March (http://bruegel.org/wp-content/uploads/imported/publications/WP_2015_03.pdf).

Molina, Óscar and Martin Rhodes (2007), 'The political economy of adjustment in mixed market economies: A study of Spain and Italy', in Bob Hancké, Martin Rhodes and Mark Thatcher (eds.), *Beyond Varieties of Capitalism: Conflict, Contradictions and Complementarities in the European Economy*, Oxford: Oxford University Press, pp. 223–251.

Möller, Joachim (2014), 'In the Aftermath of the German Labor Market Reforms — Is there a Qualitative-Quantitative Trade-off?', Nuremberg: Institute for Employment Research, The Research Institute of the Federal Employment Agency (IAB), 31 January.

Möller, Joachim (2016), 'Did the German Model Survive the Labor Market Reforms?', in Bruno Dallago, Gert Guri and John McGowan (eds.), *A Global Perspective on the European Economic Crisis*, Abingdon, Oxfordshire: Routledge.

Molloy, Raven, Christopher L. Smith and Abigail K. Wozniak (2011), 'Internal Migration in the United States', *NBER Working Paper Series* No. 17307.

Moravcsik, Andrew (1998), *The Choice for Europe: Social Purpose and State Power From Messina to Maastricht*, Ithaca, NY: Cornell University Press.

Morgan, Glenn and Richard Whitley (2012) eds., *Capitalisms and Capitalism in the Twenty-First Century*, Oxford: Oxford University Press.

Moser, Thomas (2003), 'What is international financial contagion?', *International Finance*, Vol. 6, No. 2, pp. 157–178.

Mourre, Gilles, Caterina Astarita and Savina Princen (2014), 'Adjusting the budget balance for the business cycle: The EU methodology', *European Economy*, Economic Papers 536, November (http://ec.europa.eu/economy_finance/publications/economic_paper/2014/pdf/ecp536_en.pdf).

Müller, Katharina (1999), *The Political Economy of Pension Reform in Central-Eastern Europe*, Cheltenham: Edward Elgar.

Münchau, Wolfgang (2014), 'The wacky economics of Germany's parallel universe', Financial Times online, 16 November (http://www.ft.com/intl/cms/s/0/e257ed96-6b2c-11e4-be68-00144feabdc0.html#axzz4390yuNIL).

Mundell, Robert (1961), 'A theory of optimum currency areas', *American Economic Review*, Vol. 51, No. 4, pp. 657–665.

Mundell, Robert (1969), 'A Plan for a European Currency', paper prepared for discussion at the American Management Association Conference on Future of the International Monetary System, New York, 10–12 December 1969 (http://www.knopers.net/webspace/marketupdate/A_Plan_For_a_European_Currency.pdf).

Mundell, Robert (1973), 'Uncommon Arguments for Common Currencies', in Harry G. Johnson and Alexander K. Swoboda (eds.), *The Economics of Common Currencies*, London: Routledge, pp. 114–132.

Münz, Rainer (2014), 'The Global Race for Talent: Europe's Migration Challenge', *Bruegel Policy Brief*, No. 2014/02, March (http://bruegel.org/2014/03/the-global-race-for-talent-europes-migration-challenge/).

NDC (2015), National Debt of Greece, National Debt Clocks.org (http://www.nationaldebtclocks.org/debtclock/greece).

Nechio, Fernanda (2011), 'Monetary Policy When One Size Does Not Fit All', *FRBSF Economic Letter* 2011–18 (13 June) (http://www.frbsf.org/publications/economics/letter/2011/el2011-18.html).

North, Douglass C. (1981), *Structure and Change in Economic History*, New York and London: Norton.

North, Douglass C. (1989), 'Institutions and economic growth: An historical introduction', *World Development*, Vol. 17, No. 9, pp. 1319–1332.

North, Douglass C. (1990), *Institutions, Institutional Change and Economic Performance*, Cambridge: Cambridge University Press.

Nuti, Domenico Mario (2013), *Perverse Fiscal Consolidation*, paper presented at the international conference on Economic and Political Crises in Europe and the United States: Prospects for Policy Cooperation, Trento, 7–9 November.

Nuti, Domenico Mario (2015a), 'The euro area: Premature, diminished, divergent', in Bruno Dallago and John McGowan (eds.), *Crises in Europe in the Transatlantic Context: Economic and Political Appraisals*, London and New York: Routledge, pp. 171–179.

Nuti, Domenico Mario (2015b), 'Grecia, la misura è colma' (Greece, enough is enough), *Sbilanciamoci*, Newsletter No. 414, 7 May (http://www.sbilanciamoci.info/Sezioni/capitali/Grecia-la-misura-e-colma-29641).

Obstfeld, Maurice (1997), Discussants: Alberto Alesina and Richard N. Cooper, 'Europe's Gamble', *Brookings Papers on Economic Activity*, No. 2, pp. 241–317.

Obstfeld, Maurice, Jay C. Shambaugh, and Alan M. Taylor (2004), 'The Trilemma in History: Tradeoffs among Exchange Rates, Monetary Policies, and Capital Mobility', *NBER Working Paper Series 10396*, March (http://www.nber.org/papers/w10396).

Obstfeld, Maurice and Alan M. Taylor (1997), 'The Great Depression as a Watershed: International Capital Mobility over the Long Run', *NBER Working Paper* No. 5960, March.

OECD (2005a), International Comparisons of Labour Productivity Levels — Estimates for 2004, September 2005, Paris: OECD (http://www.oecd.org/std/productivity-stats/29880166.pdf downloaded on 20 February 2014).

OECD (2005b), *Economic Policy Reforms 2005: Going for Growth*, Paris: OECD.

OECD (2008), Annex 2: OECD Estimates Of Labour Productivity Levels, Paris: OECD (http://www.oecd.org/std/productivity-stats/40526489.pdf).

OECD (2011a), *Divided We Stand: Why Inequality Keeps Rising*, December, Paris: OECD (http://www.oecd.org/els/soc/dividedwestandwhyinequalitykeepsrising.htm).

OECD (2011b) *Divided We Stand: Why Inequality Keeps Rising. Country Note: France*, December 2011, Paris: OECD (http://www.oecd.org/fr/els/soc/49177803.pdf).

OECD (2011c) *Divided We Stand: Why Inequality Keeps Rising. Country Note: Germany*, December 2011, Paris: OECD (http://www.oecd.org/els/soc/49177659.pdf).

OECD (2011d) *Divided We Stand: Why Inequality Keeps Rising. Country Note: Spain*, December 2011, Paris: OECD (http://www.oecd.org/els/soc/49177772.pdf).

OECD (2011e) *Divided We Stand: Why Inequality Keeps Rising. Country Note: Italy*, December 2011, Paris: OECD (http://www.oecd.org/els/soc/49177743.pdf).

OECD (2012a), *Addressing the Competitiveness Challenges in Germany and the Euro Area*, "Better Policies" series, October.

OECD (2012b), 'Financial Contagion in the Era of Globalised Banking?', *OECD Economics Department Policy Notes*, No. 14, June.

OECD (2012c), *Italy: Reviving Growth and Productivity*, Paris: OECD, September.

OECD (2014a), *OECD International Direct Investment Statistics 2014*, Paris: OECD Publishing (http://dx.doi.org/10.1787/idis-2014-en).

OECD (2014b), 'Focus on Top Incomes and Taxation in OECD Countries: Was the Crisis a Game Changer?', Paris: OECD, Directorate for Employment, Labour and Social Affairs, May (www.oecd.org/social/inequality-and-poverty.htm).

OECD (2014c), 'Focus on Inequality and Growth — December 2014', Paris: OECD, Directorate for Employment, Labour and Social Affairs, December (http://www.oecd.org/els/soc/Focus-Inequality-and-Growth-2014.pdf).

OECD (2014d), *OECD Economic Outlook*, 96, November, Paris: OECD.

OECD (2014e), *Economic Policy Reforms 2014: Going for Growth*, Paris: OECD.

OECD (2014f), *OECD Economic Surveys. European Union. Overview*, April, Paris: OECD.

OECD (2014g), *OECD Employment Outlook 2014*, OECD Publishing (http://dx.doi.org/10.1787/empl_outlook-2014-en).

OECD (2014h), 'Table I.7. Top statutory personal income tax rate and top marginal tax rates for employees', *OECD.Stat* (http://stats.oecd.org/index.aspx?DataSetCode=TABLE_I7#).

OECD (2015a), Growth in GDP Per Capita, Productivity and ULC, Paris: OECD (http://stats.oecd.org/Index.aspx?QueryId=54566).

OECD (2015b), *In It Together: Why Less Inequality Benefits All*, Paris: OECD Publishing (DOI: http://dx.doi.org/10.1787/9789264235120-en).

OECD (2015c), *In It Together: Why Less Inequality Benefits All: France*, 21 May, Paris: OECD (http://www.oecd.org/fr/france/OCDE2015-Tous-Concernes-Inégalite-FRANCE.pdf).

OECD (2015d), *In It Together: Why Less Inequality Benefits All: Germany*, 21 May, Paris: OECD (http://www.oecd.org/germany/OECD2015-In-It-Together-Highlights-Germany.pdf).

OECD (2015e), *In It Together: Why Less Inequality Benefits All: Italy*, 21 May, Paris: OECD (Italy: http://www.oecd.org/italy/OECD2015-In-It-Together-Highlights-Italy.pdf).

OECD (2015f), *In It Together: Why Less Inequality Benefits All: Spain*, 21 May, Paris: OECD (http://www.oecd.org/spain/OECD2015-In-It-Together-Highlights-Spain.pdf).

O'Rourke, Kevin H. and Alan M. Taylor (2013), 'Cross of euros', *Journal of Economic Perspectives*, Vol. 27, No. 3, pp. 167–192.

Orszag, Peter (2007), 'Estimated Costs of U.S. Operations in Iraq and Afghanistan and of Other Activities Related to the War on Terrorism', *CBO Testimony before the Committee on the Budget*, U.S. House of Representatives, 24 October.

Orszaghova, Lucia, Li Savelin and Willem Schudel (2013), 'External Competitiveness of EU Candidate Countries', *Occasional Paper Series No. 141*, European Central Bank, January.

Ostrom, Elinor (1990), *Governing the Commons: The Evolution of Institutions for Collective Action*, Cambridge: Cambridge University Press.

Oulton, Nicholas and Ana Rincon-Aznar (2009), 'Rates of Return and Alternative Measures of Capital Input: 14 Countries and 10 Branches, 1971–2005', Centre for Economic Performance, LSE, *CEP Discussion Papers No. 957*, November.

Ozkan, F. Gulcin and D. Filiz Unsal (2012), 'Global Financial Crisis, Financial Contagion and Emerging Markets', *IMF Working Paper* WP/12/293, December.

Pagden, Anthony (2002) ed., *The Idea of Europe: From Antiquity to the European Union*, Cambridge: Cambridge University Press.

Palan, Nicole (2013), *Structural Change and Convergence: An Empirical Analysis of Production Structures in Europe*, Frankfurt am Main [u.a.]: PL Acad. Research, European university studies/Series V, Economics and management.

Palan, Nicole and Claudia Schmiedeberg (2008), 'Specialization Patterns of European Countries' (http://www.fiw.ac.at/fileadmin/Documents/Veranstaltungen/Forschungskonferenz/4._foko/Einreichungen_und_Praesentationen/43.Palanetal.Specialization%20of%20Countries.pdf).

Palan, Nicole and Claudia Schmiedeberg (2010), 'Structural convergence of European countries', *Structural Change and Economic Dynamics*, Vol. 21, pp. 85–100.

Palley, Thomas I. (2007), 'Financialization: What it is and why it matters', *PERI Working Paper Series No. 153*, Amherst: University of Massachussets, November.

Palley, Thomas I. (2013), *Financialization. The Economics of Finance Capital Domination*, Houndmills, Basingstoke: Palgrave Macmillan.

Papademos, Lucas D. and Jürgen Stark (2010) eds., 'Enhancing monetary analysis', European Central Bank (http://www.ecb.europa.eu/pub/pdf/other/enhancingmonetaryanalysis2010en.pdf?9b2f67ca8f678ab8168c947b3dc7bd76).

Parker, David (2002), 'Economic regulation: A review of issues', *Annals of Public and Cooperative Economics*, Vol. 73, No. 4, pp. 493–519.

Parker, David and Colin Kirkpatrick (2012), 'The Economic Impact of Regulatory Policy: A Literature Review of Quantitative Evidence', *Expert Paper* No. 3, August, Paris: OECD.

Parsons, Craig (2003), *A Certain Idea of Europe*, Ithaca, NY: Cornell University Press.

Pasimeni, Paolo (2014), 'An optimum currency area', *The European Journal of Comparative Economics*, Vol. 11, No. 2, pp. 173–204.

Pasimeni, Paolo (2016), 'Assessing the Europe 2020 Strategy', in Bruno Dallago, Gert Guri and John McGowan (eds.), *A Global Perspective on the European Economic Crisis*, Abingdon, Oxfordshire: Routledge.

Pejovich, Svetozar (1995), *Economic Analysis of Institutions and Systems*, Springer.

Pentecôte, Jean-Sébastien, Jean-Christophe Poutineau and Fabien Rondeau (2015), 'Trade integration and business cycle synchronization in the EMU: The negative effect of new trade flows', *Open Economies Review*, Vol. 26, No. 1, pp 61–79.

Peón, David and Fernando Rey (2013), 'Playing with fire: Internal devaluation for the GIPSI countries', *ISRN Economics*, Vol. 2013 (2013), Article ID 891795, 20 pages (http://dx.doi.org/10.1155/2013/891795).

Petry, Johannes (2014), 'Assessing the Effects of Internal Devaluation Strategy in the Wake of the Eurozone Crisis: An Analysis of Labour Market Flexibilisation and the Working Poor in Europe', ECPR Standing Group on the European Union, 7th Pan-European Conference on the European Union, 5–7 June 2014, The Hague, the Netherlands (http://ssrn.com/abstract=2450641 or http://dx.doi.org/10.2139/ssrn.2450641).

Pfeffer, Fabian T., Sheldon Danziger, and Robert F. Schoeni (2013), 'Wealth disparities before and after the Great Recession', *The ANNALS of the American Academy of Political and Social Science November*, Vol. 650, No. 1, pp. 98–123.

Philippon, Thomas and Ariell Reshef (2013), 'An international look at the growth of modern finance', *Journal of Economic Perspectives*, Vol. 27, No. 2, pp. 73–96.

Piattoni, Simona (2016), 'The european crisis: Testing the trust foundations of an economic and monetary union', in Bruno Dallago, Gert Guri and John McGowan (eds.), *A Global Perspective on the European Economic Crisis*, Abingdon, Oxfordshire: Routledge.

Pignal, Stanley (2010), 'EU workers aid fund failing to pay out', *Financial Times*, 6 September (http://www.ft.com/intl/cms/s/0/8cd8016c-b9d3-11df-8804-00144feabdc0.html).

Piketty, Thomas (2014), *Capital in the Twenty-First Century*, Cambridge, MA and London: The Belknap Press of Harvard University Press.

Piketty, Thomas and Emmanuel Saez (2003), 'Income inequality in the United States, 1919–1998', *The Quarterly Journal of Economics*, Vol. 118, No. 1, pp. 1–39.

Piketty, Thomas and Emmanuel Saez (2006), 'The evolution of top incomes: A historical and international perspective', *The American Economic Review Papers and Proceedings*, Vol. 96, No. 2, pp. 200–205.

Piketty, Thomas and Gabriel Zucman (2013), 'Capital is Back: Wealth-Income Ratios in Rich Countries 1700–2010', mimeo., 16 December (http://piketty.pse.ens.fr/files/PikettyZucman2013RevQJE.pdf).

Pinder, John (2001), *The European Union: A Very Short Introduction*, Oxford: Oxford University Press.

Pisani-Ferry, Jean (2012), 'The Euro Crisis and the New Impossible Trinity', *Bruegel Policy Contribution, No. 2012/01*, January (http://bruegel.org/wp-content/uploads/imported/publications/pc_2012_01_.pdf).

Pisani-Ferry, Jean (2014), *The Euro Crisis and its Aftermath*, Oxford: Oxford University Press.

Pisani-Ferry, Jean and Silvia Merler (2012), 'Sudden stops in the Eurozone', *VOX CEPR's Policy Portal*, 2 April (http://www.voxeu.org/article/public-capital-flows-replacing-private-flows-eurozone-what-it-means-policy).

Pisani-Ferry, Jean, Andre Sapir, Nicolas Veron and Guntram B. Wolff (2012), 'What Kind of European Banking Union?', *Bruegel Policy Contribution No. 2012/12*, June.

Pisani-Ferry, Jean and Guntram B. Wolff (2012), 'Is LTRO QE in disguise?', *VOX, CEPR's Policy Portal*, 3 May (http://www.voxeu.org/article/ltro-quantitative-easing-disguise).

Piton, Sophie and Yves-Emmanuel Bara (2012), 'Internal devaluation: Nothing but sweat and tears?', *le blog du CEPII*, 7 August (http://www.cepii.fr/blog/bi/post.asp?IDcommunique=121).

Pokutta, Sebastian, Christian Schmaltz, and Sebastian Stiller (2011), 'Measuring Systemic Risk and Contagion in Financial Networks', 26 February (http://ssrn.com/abstract=1773089).

Polasek, Wolfgang and Christian Amplatz (2003), 'The Maastricht criteria and the euro: Has the convergence continued?', *Journal of Economic Integration*, December 2003, Vol. 18, No. 4, pp. 661–688.

Porter, Michael E. (1990), *The Competitive Advantage of Nations*, New York: The Free Press.

Pritsker, Matt (2000), 'The Channels for Financial Contagion', 11 August, Washington, DC: The Federal Reserve Board (http://siteresources.worldbank.org/INTMACRO/Resources/Pritsker.pdf).

Ptak, Ralf (2009), 'Neoliberalism in Germany: Revisiting the ordoliberal foundations of the social market economy', in Philip Mirowski and Dieter Plehwe (eds.), *The Road From Mont Pèlerin: The Making of The Neoliberal Thought Collective*, Cambridge, MA: Harvard University Press, pp. 124–125.

Rabin, Matthew and Joel L. Schrag (1999), 'First impressions matter: A model of confirmatory bias', *Quarterly Journal of Economics*, Vol. 114, No. 1, pp. 37–82.

Rajan, Raghuram G. (2005), 'Has Financial Development Made the World Riskier?', *NBER Working Paper Series*, Working Paper 11728 (http://www.nber.org/papers/w11728).

Rajan, Raghuram G. (2010), *Fault Lines: How Hidden Fractures Still Threaten the World Economy*, Princeton, NJ: Princeton University Press.

Rajan, Raghuram G., and Luigi Zingales (2001a), 'Financial systems, industrial structure, and growth', *Oxford Review of Economic Policy*, Vol. 17, No. 4, pp. 467–482.

Rajan, Raghuram G., and Luigi Zingales (2001b), 'The influence of the financial revolution on the nature of firms', *American Economic Review*, Vol. 91, No. 2, pp. 206–211.

Razin, Assaf and Steven Rosefielde (2011), 'The Currency and Financial Crises of the 1990s and 2000s', *NBER Working Paper No. 16754*, February (http://www.nber.org/papers/w16754).

Reich, Robert (2007), *Supercapitalism. The Battle for Democracy in an Age of Big Business*, New York: Alfred A. Knopf.

Reich, Robert (2010), *Aftershock: The Next Economy and America's Future*, New York: Vintage.

Reiff, Ádám and Fabio Rumler (2014), 'Within- and Cross-Country Price Dispersion in the Euro Area', *European Central Bank Working Paper Series* No. 1742, November.

Reinhart, Carmen M. (2012), 'A Series of Unfortunate Events: Common Sequencing Patterns in Financial Crises', Centre for Economic Policy Research, *Discussion Paper Series No. 8742*, January.

Reinhart, Carmen M. and Sara Calvo (1996), 'Capital flows to Latin America: Is there evidence of contagion effects?', in Guillermo A. Calvo, Morris Goldstein and Eduard Hochreiter (eds.), *Private Capital Flows to Emerging Markets After the Mexican Crisis*, Washington DC: Peterson Institute for International Economics, pp. 151–171.

Reinhart, Carmen M. and Kenneth S. Rogoff (2009), *This Time Is Different: Eight Centuries of Financial Folly*, Princeton: Princeton University Press.

Reinhart, Carmen M. and Kenneth S. Rogoff (2010), 'Debt and Growth Revisited', *VOX, CEPR's Policy Portal*, 11 August (http://www.voxeu.org/article/debt-and-growth-revisited).

Reinhart, Carmen M. and Kenneth S. Rogoff (2011), 'From financial crash to debt crisis', *American Economic Review*, Vol. 101, August, pp. 1676–1706.

Reinstaller, Andreas, Werner Hölzl, Johannes Kutsam, and Christian Schmid (2012), 'The development of productive structures of EU Member States and their international competitiveness', European Commission, DG Enterprise and Industry, Vienna: WIFO (Austrian Institute of Economic Research), November.

Rhode, Paul W. and Gianni Toniolo (2006a) eds., *The Global Economy in the 1990s. A Long-run Perspective*, Cambridge: Cambridge University Press.

Rhode, Paul W. and Gianni Toniolo (2006b), 'Understanding the 1990s: A long-run perspective', in Rhode and Toniolo (2006a), pp. 1–20.

Rigobon, Roberto (2002), 'Contagion: How to measure it?', in Sebastian Edwards and Jeffrey A. Frankel (eds.), *Preventing Currency Crises in Emerging Markets*,

National Bureau of Economic Research, Chicago: University of Chicago Press, pp. 269–334 (http://www.nber.org/chapters/c10638).

Rodriguez, Ricardo, John Warmerdam and Claude Emmanuel Triomphe (2010), *The Lisbon Strategy 2000–2010. An Analysis and Evaluation of the Methods Used and Results Achieved. Final Report*, Brussels: European Parliament, Directorate General for Internal Policies, Policy Department A: Economic and Scientific Policy, Employment and Social Affairs.

Rodrik, Dani (1996), 'Understanding economic policy reform', *Journal of Economic Literature*, Vol. 34, No. 1, pp. 9–41.

Rodrik, Dani (2009), *One Economics, Many Recipes: Globalization, Institutions, and Economic Growth*, Princeton: Princeton University Press.

Rodrik, Dani (2010), 'Thinking the Unthinkable in Europe', *Project Syndicate*, 10 December (http://www.project-syndicate.org/commentary/thinking-the-unthinkable-in-europe).

Rodrik, Dani (2011), *The Globalization Paradox: Democracy and the Future of the World Economy*, New York and London: W. W. Norton.

Rogoff, Kenneth (2011), 'The Second Great Contraction', *Project Syndicate*, 2 August (http://www.project-syndicate.org/print/the-second-great-contraction).

Rose, Andrew K. (2000), 'One money, one market: the effect of common currencies on trade'. Economic Policy, Vol. 15, pp. 7–46.

Rosefielde, Steven and Assaf Razin (2012), 'A tale of politically-failing single-currency area', *Israel Economic Review*, Vol. 10, No. 1, pp. 125–138.

Rosefielde, Steven and D. Quinn Mills (2007), *Masters of Illusion: American Leadership in the Media Age*, Cambridge: Cambridge University Press.

Rostow, Walter W. (1960), *The Stages of Economic Growth, a Non-Communist Manifesto*, Cambridge: Cambridge University Press.

Roubini, Nouriel and Stephen Mihm (2010), *Crisis Economics: A Crash Course in the Future of Finance*, London: The Penguin Press.

Rousseau, Peter L. and Richard Sylla (2003), 'Financial systems, economic growth, and globalization', in Michael D. Bordo, Alan M. Taylor, and Jeffrey G. Williamson (eds.), *Globalization in Historical Perspective*, Chicago: University of Chicago Press, pp. 373–416 (also in http://www.nber.org/chapters/c9594.pdf).

Saez, Emmanuel and Gabriel Zucman (2014), 'Wealth Inequality in the United States Since 1913: Evidence from Capitalized Income Tax Data', *NBER Working Paper* 20625, National Bureau of Economic Research, October (http://www.nber.org/papers/w20625).

Saiki, Ayako and Sunghyun Henry Kim (2014), 'Business Cycle Synchronization and Vertical Trade Integration: A Case Study of the Eurozone and East Asia', *Working Paper No. 407*, Amsterdam: De Nederlandsche Bank NV, January.

Sala-i-Martin, Xavier and Jeffrey Sachs (1991), 'Fiscal Federalism And Optimum Currency Areas: Evidence for Europe from the United States', *NBER Working Papers Series* No. 3855, NBER.

Sally, Razeen (1996), 'Ordoliberalism and the social market: Classical political economy from Germany', *New Political Economy*, Vol. 1, No. 2, pp. 233–257.

Samardžija, Višnja and Hrvoje Butković (2010) eds., *From the Lisbon Strategy to Europe 2020*, Zagreb: Institute for International Relations (IMO).

Sapir, André (2006), 'Globalization and the reform of European social models', *Journal of Common Market Studies*, Vol. 44, No. 2, pp. 369–390.

Sapir, André, Guntram B. Wolff, Carlos de Sousa and Alessio Terzi (2014), *The Troika and Financial Assistance in the Euro Area: Successes and Failures*, Study on the request of the Economic and Monetary Affairs Committee, Brussels: European Parliament, February.

Sbaihi, Maxime (2015), 'Who Hurts Most If Greece Defaults?', Bloomberg Brief. Economics Europe (http://www.bloombergbriefs.com/content/uploads/sites/2/2015/01/MS_Greece_WhoHurts.pdf).

Scatigna, Michela, Robert Szemere, and Kostas Tsatsaronis (2014), 'Residential property price statistics across the globe', *BIS Quarterly Review*, September, pp. 61–76.

Schäuble, Wolfgang (2015), 'There Is No German Dominance', Spiegel Interview with Wolfgang Schäuble conducted by Klaus Brinkbäumer, Michael Sauga and Christian Reiermann, *Spiegel Online International*, 17 July (http://www.spiegel.de/international/germany/interview-with-german-finance-minister-wolfgang-schaeuble-a-1044233.html).

Schmidt, Torsten and Lina Zwick (2013), 'Uncertainty and Episodes of Extreme Capital Flows in the Euro Area', *Ruhr Economic Papers #461*, October (http://en.rwi-essen.de/media/content/pages/publikationen/ruhr-economic-papers/REP_13_461.pdf).

Schneider, Friedrich (2005), 'Shadow economies around the world: What do we really know?', *European Journal of Political Economy*, Vol. 21, pp. 598–642.

Schneider, Friedrich (2012), 'The Shadow Economy and Work in the Shadow: What Do We (Not) Know?', *IZA Discussion Paper No. 6423*, March.

Schneider, Friedrich (2013), *The Shadow Economy in Europe*, ATKearney (http://ec.europa.eu/digital-agenda/futurium/sites/futurium/files/futurium/library/Schneider%20-%202013%20-%20The%20Shadow%20Economy%20in%20Europe%20%2C%202013.pdf).

Schneider, Friedrich and Andreas Buehn (2009), 'Shadow economies and corruption all over the world: Revised estimates for 120 countries', *Economics: The Open Access, Open Assessment E-Journal*, Vol. 1, Version 2, 27 October 2009 (http://www.economics-ejournal.org/economics/journalarticles/2007-9/version-2/at_download/file).

Schneider, Friedrich, Andreas Buehn and Claudio E. Montenegro (2010), 'Shadow Economies All over the World. New Estimates for 162 Countries from 1999 to 2007', The World Bank, *Policy Research Working Paper 5356.*

Schneider, Friedrich and Dominik H. Enste (2000), 'Shadow Economies: Size, Causes, and Consequences', *The Journal of Economic Literature*, Vol. 38, No. 1, pp. 77–114.

Schneider, Friedrich and Dominik H. Enste (2002), *The Shadow Economy: An International Survey*, Cambridge: Cambridge University Press.

Schnyder, Gerhard and Mathias Siems (2013), 'The ordoliberal variety of neoliberalism', in Suzanne J. Konzelmann and Marc Fovargue-Davies (eds.), *Banking Systems in the Crisis: The Faces of Liberal Capitalism*, Abingdon: Routledge, pp. 250–268 (http://papers.ssrn.com/sol3/papers.cfm?abstract_id=2142529).

Schreft, Stacey L., Aarti Singh, and Ashley Hodgson (2005), 'Jobless recoveries and the wait-and-see hypothesis', *Economic Review*, Fourth Quarter, pp. 81–99.

Schuknecht, Ludger, Philippe Moutot, Philipp Rother and Jürgen Stark (2011), 'The Stability Pact: Growth and Reform', *Occasional Paper No. 129*, European Central Bank.

Schulmeister S., Schratzenstaller M. and Picek O. (2008), 'A General Financial Transaction Tax Motives, Revenues, Feasibility and Effects', mimeo., Österreichisches Institut für Wirtschaftsforschung (WIFO).

Scitovsky, Tibor (1958), *Economic Theory and Western European Integration*, Stanford: Stanford University Press.

Sheets, Nathan and Robert A. Sockin (2012), 'Germany's "Windfall" from Euro-Area Membership and European Imbalances', *Empirical and Thematic Perspectives*, 27 January, Citigroup Global Markets (https://ir.citi.com/DkHnljPA17OJBCgYbBozk5GXsbpJTG9K2O7tG8tU2LUrX%2BP7wkUYWw%3D%3D).

Shiller, Robert J. (2000), *Irrational Exuberance*, Princeton: Princeton University Press.

Shiratsuka, Shigenori (2003), 'The Asset Price Bubble in Japan in the 1980s: Lessons for Financial and Macroeconomic Stability', *BIS Paper No. 21, Real Estate Indicators and Financial Stability*, Proceedings of a joint conference organised by the BIS and the IMF in Washington DC, 27–28 October 2003, Bank for International Settlements and International Monetary Fund, April 2005, pp. 42–62.

Shleifer, Andrei, and Robert W. Vishny (1997), 'A survey of corporate governance', *Journal of Finance*, Vol. 52, No. 2, pp, 737–783.

Sinn, Hans-Werner (2000), 'Germany's Economic Unification: An Assessment after Ten Years, *NBER Working Paper Series*, Working Paper 7586.

Sinn, Hans-Werner (2010), 'Rescuing Europe', *CESifo* Forum, 11, Special Issue, pp. 1–22.

Sinn, Hans-Werner (2014), *The Euro Trap. On Bursting Bubbles, Budgets, and Beliefs*, Oxford: Oxford University Press.

Smets, Frank and Raf Wouters (2005), 'Comparing shocks and frictions in US and Euro Area business cycles: A Bayesian DSGE approach', *Journal of Applied Econometrics*, Vol. 20, pp. 161–183.

Smith, Roy C. (2014), 'Six years after the crisis', *Journal of Financial Perspectives*, Vol. 2, No. 2, pp. 75–86.

Sondermann, David (2012), 'Productivity in the Euro Area. Any Evidence of Convergence?', *Working Paper Series 1431/2012*, Frankfurt am Main: European Central Bank, April.

Soskice, David and Torben Iversen (2001), 'Multiple wage bargaining systems in the single European currency area', *Empirica*, Vol. 28, No. 4, pp. 435–456.

Spaventa, Luigi (2010) 'How to Prevent Excessive Current Account Imbalances', *Eurointelligence* (https://www.eurointelligence.com/).

Spiegel, Peter (2014), 'Draghi's ECB management: the leaked Geithner files', Brussels Blog, *Financial Times*, 11 November 2014 (http://blogs.ft.com/brusselsblog/2014/11/11/draghis-ecb-management-the-leaked-geithner-files/).

Spinelli, Altiero and Ernesto Rossi (1941), *The Ventotene Manifesto*, Ventotene: The Altiero Spinelli Institute for Federalist Studies, pp. 75–96 (http://www.cvce.eu/content/publication/1997/10/13/316aa96c-e7ff-4b9e-b43a-958e96afbecc/publishable_en.pdf).

Standing, Guy (2011), *The Precariat: The New Dangerous Class*, London and New York: Bloomsbury Academic.

Stark, Jürgen (2009), 'Monetary Policy before, during and after the financial crisis', Speech at the University of Tübingen, Tübingen, 9 November 2009 (https://www.ecb.europa.eu/press/key/date/2009/html/sp091109.en.html).

Steinherr, Alfred (2013), 'Why Germany Should Leave the Euro', Paper presented at the international conference on Economic and Political Crises in Europe and the United States. Prospects for Policy Cooperation, University of Trento, 7–9 November (http://web.unitn.it/files/download/31972/steinherr_the_euro_at_bay.pdf).

Steinherr, Alfred (2015), 'Some policy proposals for the euro malaise', in Bruno Dallago and John McGowan (eds.), *Crisis in Europe in the Transatlantic Context. Economic and Political Appraisals*, Abingdon, Oxfordshire: Routledge, pp. 189–193.

Steinkamp, Sven and Frank Westermann (2014), 'The role of creditor seniority in Europe's sovereign debt crisis', *Economic Policy*, Vol. 29, No. 79, pp. 495–552.

Stiglitz, Joseph E. (1998), 'More Instruments and Broader Goals: Moving Toward the Post-Washington Consensus', *1998 WIDER Annual Lecture*, Helsinki, January.

Stiglitz, Joseph E. (2002), *Globalization and Its Discontents*, New York: W.W. Norton.

Stiglitz, Joseph E. (2004), 'The Post Washington Consensus Consensus', *The Initiative for Policy Dialogue* (http://policydialogue.org/files/events/Stiglitz_Post_Washington_Consensus_Paper.pdf).

Stiglitz, Joseph E. (2006), *Making Globalization Work*, New York: W. W. Norton & Company.

Stiglitz, Joseph E. (2010), *Freefall: America, Free Markets, and the Sinking of the World Economy*, New York: W. W. Norton & Company.

Stiglitz, Joseph E. (2012), *The Price of Inequality*, New York: W.W. Norton & Company.

Stiglitz, Joseph E. (2013), 'An agenda to save the euro', *Social Europe Journal*, 5 December (http://www.social-europe.eu/2013/12/agenda-to-save-the-euro/).

Stiglitz, Joseph E. (2014a), 'Europe's Austerity Zombies', *Project Syndicate*, 26 September (http://www.project-syndicate.org/print/joseph-e--stiglitz-wonders-why-eu-leaders-are-nursing-a-dead-theory).

Stiglitz, Joseph E. (2014b), 'Stiglitz: Leaving the euro painful but staying in more painful' (https://www.youtube.com/watch?v=6FzI-5baKsI) (published on 22 February 2014).

Stiglitz, Joseph E. and Linda J. Bilmes (2008), *The Three Trillion Dollar War: The True Cost of the Iraq Conflict*, New York: W. W. Norton & Company.

Stockhammer, Engelbert and Dimitris P. Sotiropoulos (2014), 'Rebalancing the euro area: The costs of internal devaluation', *Review of Political Economy*, Vol. 26, No. 2, pp. 210–233.

Stokes, Bruce (2015), *Faith in European Project Reviving. But Most Say Rise of Eurosceptic Parties Is a Good Thing*, Washington, DC: Pew Research Center, 2 June (http://www.pewglobal.org/files/2015/06/Pew-Research-Center-European-Union-Report-FINAL-June-2-20151.pdf).

Summers, Lawrence H. (2014), 'U.S. economic prospects: Secular stagnation, hysteresis, and the zero lower bound', *Business Economics*, Vol. 49, No. 2, pp. 65–73.

Svensson, Lars E.O. (2002), 'A Good Thing Could Happen at the ECB: An Improvement of the Eurosystem's Definition of Price Stability', Briefing paper for the Committee on Economic and Monetary Affairs (ECON) of the European Parliament for the quarterly dialogue with the President of the European Central Bank, September (http://citeseerx.ist.psu.edu/viewdoc/download?doi=10.1.1.15.2375&rep=rep1&type=pdf).

Syverson, Chad (2010), 'What determines productivity?', *VOX, CEPR's Policy Portal*, 25 June (http://www.voxeu.org/article/what-determines-productivity).

Syverson, Chad (2011), 'What determines productivity?', *Journal of Economic Literature*, Vol. 49, No. 2, pp. 326–365.

Tachibanaki, Toshiaki (2005), *Confronting Income Inequality in Japan: A Comparative Analysis of Causes, Consequences, and Reform*, Cambridge, MA and London: The MIT Press.

Taleb, Nassim Nicholas (2007), *The Black Swan: The Impact of the Highly Improbable*, London: Penguin Books.

Tamborini, Roberto (2015), 'EMU 2.0 and the German problem', in Bruno Dallago and John McGowan (eds.), *Crises in Europe in the Transatlantic Context: Economic and Political Appraisals*, Abingdon, Oxfordshire: Routledge, pp. 194–200.

Tanzi, Vito (1999), 'Uses and abuses of estimates of the underground economy', *The Economic Journal*, Vol. 109, No. 456, pp. F338–F347.

Task Force (2010), *Strengthening Economic Governance in the EU: Report of the Task Force to the European Council*, Brussels, 21 October 2010 (http://www.consilium.europa.eu).

Taylor, A. J. P. (1961), *The Origins of the Second World War*, New York: Simon and Schuster, 2005 reprint.

Taylor, John B. (1993), *Macroeconomic Policy in a World Economy: From Econometric Design to Practical Operation*, New York: W.W. Norton.

TF (2015), Thomson Financial, Institute of Mergers, Acquisitions and Alliances (IMAA) analysis, Vienna (http://www.imaa-institute.org/statistics-mergers-acquisitions.html).

Ticktin, Hillel (2011) ed., *Marxism and the Global Financial Crisis*, Abingdon, Oxfordshire: Routledge.

Tiffin, Andrew (2014), 'European Productivity, Innovation and Competitiveness: The Case of Italy', *IMF Working Paper No. 14/79*, May.

de Tocqueville, Alexis (1969), *Democracy in America*, ed. J. P. Mayer, trans. George Lawrence, vol. 1. Originally published in 1835–1840.

Toporowski, Jan (2013), 'International credit, financial integration, and the euro', *Cambridge Journal of Economics*, Vol. 37, No. 3, pp. 571–584.

ToR (1957), The Treaty of Rome, 25 March 1957 (http://ec.europa.eu/archives/emu_history/documents/treaties/rometreaty2.pdf).

Transparency International (2009), *The Anti-Corruption Plain Language Guide* (http://www.transparency.org/whatwedo/publication/the_anti_corruption_plain_language_guide).

Trevino, Isabel (2014), 'Channels of Financial Contagion: Theory and Experiments', New York: New York University, 18 January (https://files.nyu.edu/it384/public/Isabel_Trevino_jmp.pdf).

Trichet, Jean-Claude (2007), 'Governance and Convergence: the State of Play in the Euro Area', Speech at the Conference "Euro zone — Converging or Drifting Apart?", organised by the European Parliament (Committee of Economic and Monetary Affairs), Open Debate with National Parliaments, Brussels, 28 February.

Trichet, Jean-Claude (2011), 'The Euro Area and Its Role in the Global Economy', Remarks by Jean-Claude Trichet upon reception of the 2011 Global Economy Prize, Kiel, 19 June, (https://www.ecb.europa.eu/press/key/date/2011/html/sp110619.en.html).

Tridico, Pasquale (2011), 'Varieties of Capitalism and Responses to the Financial Crisis: The European Social Model versus the US Model', *Working Paper No. 129*, Rome: Department of Economics, University of Roma Tre.

Tronti, Leonello (2008), 'Wage Distribution, Labour Productivity and Growth: The Role of the Bargaining Model' (http://www.aiel.it/Old/bacheca/SASSARI/papers/tronti.pdf).

Tsiapa, Maria (2013), 'New aspects on the industrial concentration patterns of the European Union', *Discussion Paper Series*, Vol. 19, No. 2, pp. 35–62, Department of Planning and Regional Development University of Thessaly.

Tsuru, Kotaro (2000), 'Finance and Growth: Some Theoretical Considerations, and a Review of the Empirical Literature', *Economics Department Working Papers No. 228*, Paris: OECD.

Tullock, Gordon (1967), 'The Welfare costs of tariffs, monopolies, and theft', *Western Economic Journal*, Vol. 5, No. 3, pp. 224–232.

Tullock, Gordon (1993), *Rent Seeking*, Aldershot: Edward Elgar.

Tversky, Amos and Daniel Kahneman (1981), 'The framing of decisions and the psychology of choice', *Science*, Vol. 211, No. 4481, pp. 453–458.

UBS (2012), 'Greek exit: Potential asset class impact', UBS Chief Investment Office, *Global Risk Watch*, 24 May (https://www.ubs.com/global/en/bank_for_banks/news/topical_stories/edition_56.html).

UNCTAD (2014), *World Investment Report 2014*, Geneva: United Nations Conference on Trade and Development.

UN DESA (2014), 'LDC criteria' (http://www.un.org/en/development/desa/policy/cdp/ldc/ldc_criteria.shtml).

USCB (2013), *Income and Poverty in the United States*, U.S. Census Bureau (https://www.census.gov/hhes/www/income/data/historical/inequality/table_IE-1A2.pdf).

US Treasury (2013), *Report to Congress on International Economic and Exchange Rate Polices*, Washington, DC: US Department of the Treasury, Office of International Affairs, 30 October.

Uxó, Jorge, Jesús Paúl and Eladio Febrero (2014), 'Internal Devaluation in the European Periphery: The Story of a Failure', Department of Economics and Finance, University of de Castilla — La Mancha, *Working Papers DT 2014/2.*

Valentinyi, Akos (2012), 'The Hungarian crisis', *VOX, CEPR's Policy Portal*, 19 March (http://www.voxeu.org/article/hungarian-crisis).

van Ark, Bart, Mary O'Mahony, and Marcel P. Timmer (2008), 'The productivity gap between Europe and the United States: Trends and Causes', *Journal of Economic Perspectives*, Vol. 22, No. 1, pp. 25–44.

van Beers, Nancy, Michiel Bijlsma and Gijsbert Zwart (2014), 'Cross-Country Insurance Mechanisms in Currency Unions: An Empirical Assessment', *Bruegel Working Paper* 2014/04, March.

van der Zwan, Natascha (2014) 'Making sense of financialization', *Socio-economic Review*, Vol. 12, No. 1, pp. 99–129.

Vanham, Peter (2015), 'How Greece's debt has shifted since the last bailout', Agenda, Geneva: World Economic Forum. 30 June (https://agenda.weforum.org/2015/06/how-greeces-debt-has-shifted-since-the-last-bailout/).

Van Rijckeghem and Beatrice Weder (1999), 'Sources of Contagion: Finance or Trade?', International Monetary Fund, *IMF Working Paper WP/99/146*, October.

van Treeck, Till (2009a), 'The political economy debate on "financialization": A macroeconomic perspective', *Review of International Political Economy*, Vol. 16, No. 5, pp. 907–944.

van Treeck, Till (2009b), 'The Macroeconomics of "Financialisation" and the Deeper Origins of the World Economic Crisis', IMK Working Paper 9-2009,

IMK at the Hans Boeckler Foundation, Macroeconomic Policy Institute (http://www.boeckler.de/pdf/p_imk_wp_9_2009.pdf).

van Treeck, Till and Simon Sturn (2012), 'Income Inequality as a Cause of the Great Recession? A Survey of Current Debates,' *ILO Working Papers 470934*, Geneva: International Labour Organization (http://www.ilo.org/public/libdoc/ilo/2012/112B09_175_engl.pdf).

Varela, Gonzalo J. (2013), 'Export Diversification in Twelve European and Central Asian Countries and the Role of the Commodity Boom', *Policy Research Working Paper 6472*, June, Washington DC: The World Bank.

Veblen, Thorstein (1899a), *Conspicuous Consumption*, London: Penguin Books.

Veblen, Thorstein (1899b), *The Theory of the Leisure Class*, New York: Macmillan.

Veblen, Thorstein (1909), 'The limitations of marginal utility', *Journal of Political Economy*, Vol. 17, November, pp. 151–175.

Veugelers, Reinhilde (2014), 'The Achilles' Heel of Juncker's Investment Plan', *Bruegel*, 8 December (http://www.bruegel.org/nc/blog/detail/article/1498-the-achilles-heel-of-junckers-investment-plan/).

Von Weizsäcker, J. (2008), 'Divisions of Labour: Rethinking Europe's Migration Policy', *Bruegel Blueprint Series*, No. 6, Brussels.

WB (2005), *Economic Growth in the 1990s: Learning from a Decade of Reform*, Washington, DC: The World Bank.

WB (2014), *Doing Business 2015. Going beyond Efficiency: Regional Profile 2015, European Union (EU)*, Washington DC: The World Bank.

WB (2015a), *Doing Business 2015: Going beyond Efficiency*, Washington, DC: The World Bank.

WB (2015b), 'Distance to frontier and ease of doing business ranking', *World Bank, Doing Business 2015: Going beyond Efficiency* (http://www.doingbusiness.org/~/media/GIAWB/Doing%20Business/Documents/Annual-Reports/English/DB15-Chapters/DB15-DTF-and-DBRanking.pdf).

WEF (2014), *The Global Competitiveness Report 2014–2015*, Klaus Schwab (ed.), Geneva: World Economic Forum (http://www3.weforum.org/docs/WEF_GlobalCompetitivenessReport_2014-15.pdf).

WEF-EU (2014), *The Europe 2020 Competitiveness Report: Building a More Competitive Europe*, Geneva: World Economic Forum.

Werner Report (1970), 'Report to the Council and the Commission on the realisation by stages of Economic and Monetary Union in the Community', *Bulletin of the European Communities*, Supplement 11/1970 (http://aei.pitt.edu/1002/1/monetary_werner_final.pdf).

Weyerstraß, Klaus (2003), 'Explaining Investment Trends in European Union Countries', *Discussion Paper No. 174*, Halle: Halle Institute for Economic Research (IWH), June.

Wilkinson, Richard and Kate Pickett (2009), *The Spirit Level: Why Equality Is Better for Everyone*, London: Penguin Books.

Williamson, John (1990), 'What Washington means by policy reform', Chapter 2 in *Latin American Adjustment: How Much Has Happened?*, John Williamson (ed.), Washington: Institute for International Economics.

Williamson, John (1993), 'Democracy and the "Washington consensus"', *World Development*, Vol. 21, No. 8, pp. 1329–1336.

Williamson, John (1999), 'What Should the Bank Think About the Washington Consensus', *Background Paper to the World Bank's World Development Report 2000*, July.

Williamson, John (2000), 'What should the World Bank think about the Washington Consensus?', *World Bank Research Observer*, Vol. 15, No. 2, pp. 251–264.

Williamson, John (2004a), 'A Short History of the Washington Consensus', Paper presented at Foundation CIDOB conference on "From the Washington Consensus towards a new Global Governance", Barcelona, 24–25 September 2004.

Williamson, John (2004b), 'The strange history of the Washington consensus', *Journal of Post Keynesian Economics*, Vol. 27, No. 2, pp. 195–206.

Winkler, Adalbert (2014), 'The ECB as Lender of Last Resort: Banks versus Governments', *Special Paper 228*, LSE Financial Markets Group Special Paper Series, February (http://www.frankfurt-school.de/clicnetclm/fileDownload.do?goid=000000575799AB4).

Wolf, Charles Jr. (1988), *Markets or Governments: Choosing between Imperfect Alternatives*, Cambridge, MA and London: The MIT Press.

Wolf, Martin (2010), 'Germans are wrong: The Eurozone is good for them', *Financial Times*, 7 September (http://www.ft.com/intl/cms/s/0/195dfa18-bab2-11df-b73d-00144feab49a.html).

Wolf, Martin (2012), 'The riddle of German self-interest', *Financial Times*, 29 May (http://www.ft.com/intl/cms/s/0/4fe89d8c-a8df-11e1-b085-00144feabdc0.html).

Wolfers, Justin and Jan Zilinsky (2015), 'Higher wages for low-income workers lead to higher productivity', Washington DC: Peterson Institute for International Economics, 13 January (http://blogs.piie.com/realtime/?p=4700).

Wolff, Edward N. (2014), 'Household wealth trends in the United States, 1983–2010', *Oxford Review of Economic Policy*, Vol. 30, No. 1, pp. 21–43.

Wray, L. Randall (2000), 'The Neo-Chartalist Approach to Money', *CFEPS Working Paper No. 10*, Center for Full Employment and Price Stability, July.

WTO (1996), 'Trade and foreign direct investment', *WTO News: 1996 Press Releases*, PRESS/57, 9 October (http://www.wto.org/english/news_e/pres96_e/pr057_e.htm).

WTO (2015), 'Regional trade agreements', (http://www.wto.org/english/tratop_e/region_e/region_e.htm).

Wynne, Mark A. and Janet Koech (2012), 'One-size-fits-all monetary policy: Europe and the U.S.', *Economic Letter*, Vol. 7, No. 9, Federal Reserve Bank of Dallas, September.

Wyplosz, Charles (2010), 'The failure of the Lisbon strategy', *VOX, CEPR's Policy Portal*, 12 January (http://www.voxeu.org/article/failure-lisbon-strategy).

Wyplosz, Charles, Stefan Collignon, Guillermo De La Dehesa, Jacques Delpla, Jakob Von Weizsäcker, and Sylvester C.W. Eijffinger (2011), *Eurobonds: Concepts and Implications. Compilation of Notes for the Monetary Dialogue of March 2011*, European Parliament, Directorate General for Internal Policies (http://www.europarl.europa.eu/document/activities/cont/201201/20120130ATT36516/20120130ATT36516EN.pdf).

Yates, Tony (2002), 'Monetary Policy and the Zero Bound to Interest Rates: A Review', *Working Paper Series*, Working Paper No. 190, October, Frankfurt am Main: European Central Bank.

Yilmaz, Bahri (2008), 'Foreign Trade Specialization and International Competitiveness of Greece, Portugal, Spain, Turkey and the EU 12', *Center for European Studies Working Paper Series #166.*

Young, Brigitte (2014), 'German ordoliberalism as agenda setter for the euro crisis: Myth trumps reality', *Journal of Contemporary European Studies*, Vol. 22, No. 3, pp. 276–287.

Zhu, Feifei (2014), 'Corporate governance and the cost of capital: An international study', *International Review of Finance*, Vol. 14, No. 3, pp. 393–429.

Zimmermann, Klaus F. (2009), 'Labor Mobility and the Integration of European Labor Markets', *Discussion Papers 862*, Berlin: DIW, March.

Zingales, Luigi (2008), 'Corporate governance', in Steven N. Durlauf and Lawrence E. Blume (eds.), *The New Palgrave Dictionary of Economics*, 2nd ed., Palgrave Macmillan.

Index

CPSIA information can be obtained at www.ICGtesting.com
Printed in the USA
BVOW06*1400260516

449370BV00003B/3/P

9 789814 759014